D0964069

Webster's International Atlas

THIRD EDITION

Created in Cooperation with the Editors of
ENCYCLOPÆDIA BRITANNICA

FEDERAL STREET PRESS

A Division of Merriam-Webster, Incorporated
Springfield, Massachusetts

Copyright © 2013 by Merriam-Webster, Incorporated

Federal Street Press is a trademark of Federal Street Press,
a division of Merriam-Webster, Incorporated.

All rights reserved. No part of this book covered by the copyrights hereon may be reproduced or copied in any form or by any means—graphic, electronic, or mechanical, including photocopying, taping, or information storage and retrieval systems—without written permission of the publisher.

This edition published by
Federal Street Press
a Division of Merriam-Webster, Incorporated
P.O. Box 281
Springfield, MA 01102

Federal Street Press books are available for bulk purchase for sales promotion and premium use. For details write the manager of special sales, Federal Street Press, P.O. Box 281, Springfield, MA 01102

ISBN 978-1-59695-137-2

Printed in Malaysia

2nd printing Imago 3/2013 Jouve

Contents

Preface

This atlas provides basic information about each of the 195 countries of the world, the fifty states, the District of Columbia, and the five territories of the United States. It has been completely revised and updated to incorporate the most current information available.

A full page is provided for each country, two for each state, and one for each territory with information including a full-color map showing both populated places and major natural features, a locator map, and a fact box containing important information about the country, state, or territory. There is also a representation of the country, state, or territory flag with a brief flag history.

Additional information appears in tables at the back of the book that show islands and regions that are dependencies of other countries, country capitals with their populations, and major world cities with their geographical coordinates, as well as the world's longest rivers, tallest mountains, and largest lakes.

This colorful, compact book was created by the editors of Encyclopædia Britannica in association with the editors of Merriam-Webster. It has been designed as a handy, affordable resource to help readers better understand our changing world.

Map Abbreviations

Ala.	Alabama
Ark.	Arkansas
Arm.	Armenia
ASEAN	Association of Southeast Asian Nations
Azer.	Azerbaijan
Belg.	Belgium
Calif.	California
C.A.R.	Central African Republic
Caricom	Caribbean Community
CFA	Communauté Financière Africaine (African Financial Community)
Conn.	Connecticut
D.C.	District of Columbia
Del.	Delaware
Dem.	Democratic
Den.	Denmark
E	east(ern)
Fla.	Florida
Fr.	France
ft.	foot (feet)
GNP	gross national product
I.	Island
Ill.	Illinois
Ind.	Indiana
Indon.	Indonesia
Is.	Islands
km.	kilometer(s)
La.	Louisiana
Mass.	Massachusetts
Md.	Maryland
mi.	mile(s)
Mich.	Michigan
Minn.	Minnesota
Miss.	Mississippi
Mt.	Mount
Mtn.	Mountain
Mts.	Mountains
N	north(ern)
Nat'l	National
N.C.	North Carolina
NE	northeast(ern)
N.H.	New Hampshire
N.J.	New Jersey
N.P.	National Park
NW	northwest(ern)
N.Y.	New York
N.Z.	New Zealand
Okla.	Oklahoma
Penin.	Peninsula
Penn.	Pennsylvania
Pk.	Peak
Port.	Portugal
Pt.	Point
Rep.	Republic
R.I.	Rhode Island
S	south(ern)
S.C.	South Carolina
SE	southeast(ern)
sq.	square
St.	Saint
SW	southwest(ern)
Switz.	Switzerland
Tenn.	Tennessee
Turkmen.	Turkmenistan
U.A.E.	United Arab Emirates
U.K.	United Kingdom
U.S.	United States
Va.	Virginia
Vt.	Vermont
W	west(ern)
Wash.	Washington
Wis.	Wisconsin
W.Va.	West Virginia

Guide to Map Projections

Technically, the earth is not round but is flattened at the poles and takes a shape most accurately described as an ellipsoid. The deviation from a perfect sphere is relatively minor, and although the distinction is of critical importance in surveying and geodesy, for most purposes it can be assumed that the earth is spherical.

A globe is the only true means of representing the surface of the earth and maintaining accurate relationships of location, direction, and distance, but it is often more desirable to have a flat map for reference. However, in order for a round globe to be portrayed as a flat map, various parts of the globe's surface must stretch or shrink, thereby altering the geometric qualities associated with it. To control this distortion, a systematic transformation of the sphere's surface must be made. The transformation and resultant new surface is usually derived mathematically and is referred to as the map projection.

An infinite number of map projections can be conceived, but the only ones which are effective are those projections which ensure that the spatial relationships between true (known) locations on the three-dimensional sphere are preserved on the two-dimensional flat map.

The four basic spatial properties of location are area, angle, distance, and direction. No map projection can preserve all four of these basic properties simultaneously. In fact, every map will possess some level of distortion in one or more of these dimensions. The map surface can be developed such that individual properties are preserved to a certain extent, or that certain combinations of properties are preserved to some extent, but every projection is, in some way, a compromise and must distort some properties in order to portray others accurately.

Choosing a Map Projection

The question of which map projection is best might be better stated as which map projection is most appropriate for the intended purpose of the map. For example, navigation demands correct direction, while road atlases will be concerned with preserving distance. Another important consideration is the extent and area of the region to be mapped. Some common guidelines include the use of cylindrical projections for low latitudes, conic projections for middle latitudes, and azimuthal projections for polar views. World maps are rather special cases and are commonly shown on a class of projection that may be neither equal-area nor conformal, referred to as compromise projections, typically on an oval grid.

Common Map Projections

Name	Class	Attribute	Common Uses
Mercator	Cylindrical	Conformal	Best suited for navigation uses, but often used inappropriately for world maps.
Sinusoidal	(Pseudo-cylindrical)	Equal-area	Used occasionally for world maps and in combination with Mollweide to derive other projections.
Mollweide	(Pseudo-cylindrical)	Equal-area	Used for world maps, especially for showing thematic content.
Lambert Conformal Conic	Conic	Conformal	Used extensively for mapping areas of extensive east-west extent in the mid-latitudes (such as the U.S.).
Albers Equal-area	Conic	Equal-area	Similar to Lambert Conformal Conic in use.
Polyconic	Polyconic	Neither Equal-area nor Conformal	Used by U.S. Geological Survey in mapping topographic quadrangles and was used for early coastal charts and some military mapping.
Bonne	(Pseudo-conic)	Equal-Area	Frequently used in atlases for showing continents.
Gnomonic	Azimuthal	Equal-Area	Used most frequently in navigation.
Stereographic	Azimuthal	Conformal	Most often used for topographic maps of polar regions and for navigation.
Orthographic	Azimuthal	Neither Equal-area nor Conformal	Most popular use is for pictorial views of earth, especially as seen from space.

Map Legend

Cities and Towns

Ottawa ⊛ National Capital

Edinburgh ◉ Second level political capital

São Paulo • City symbol

■ Other administrative center

Boundaries

International

Disputed

Defacto

Line of control

Political subdivisions

Other Features

SERENGETI NATIONAL PARK ■ National park

Mount Everest 29,028 ft. ▲ Mountain Peak

Dam

Falls

Rapids

River

Intermittent river

Canal

Aqueduct

Reef

Countries of the World

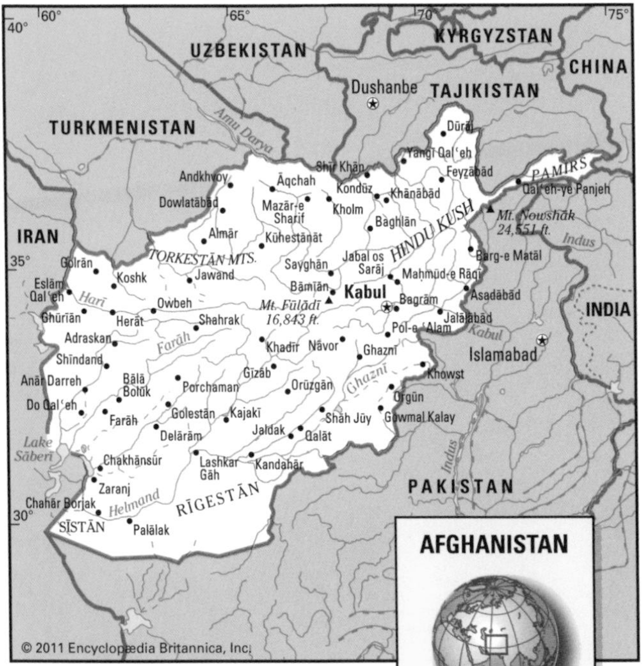

Official name: Islamic Republic of Afghanistan
Head of state and government: President
Official languages: Dari (Persian); Pashto
Monetary unit: afghani
Area: 257,072 sq. mi. (652,864 sq. km.)
Population (2010): 26,290,000
GNI per capita (2008): U.S.$466
Principal exports (2008–09): dried fruits/nuts 45.1%, carpets 27.5%, fresh fruits 7.6% *to:* Pakistan 48.4%; India; 25.0%; Russia 6.8%

Ethnolinguistic Composition

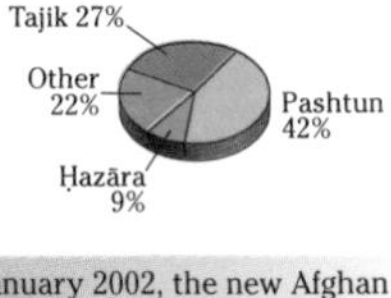

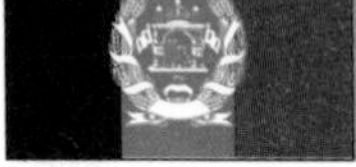

After the fall of the Taliban in January 2002, the new Afghan Interim Authority brought back the 1928 tricolor (black for the past, red for blood shed for independence, and green for hope), adding: the Arabic "Afghanistan" and "There is no deity but God; Muhammad is the messenger of God." It keeps the mosque, two flags, and wheat.

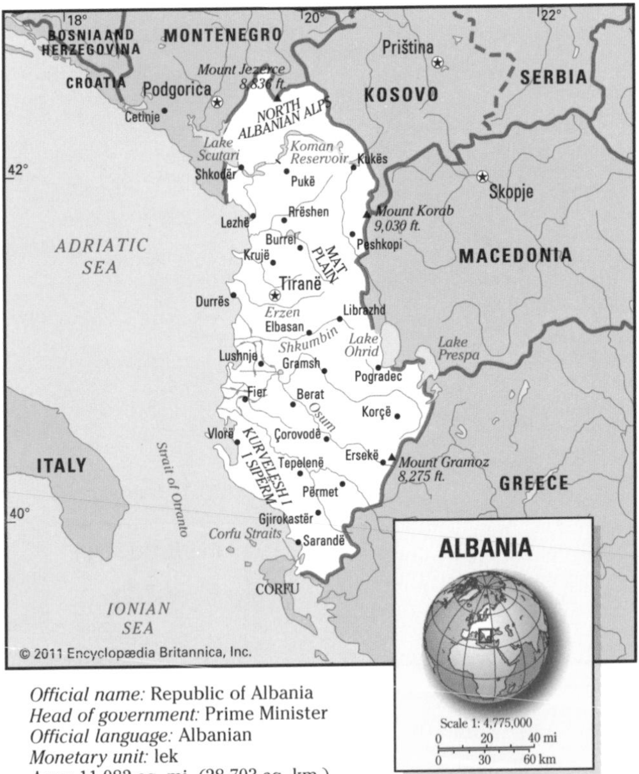

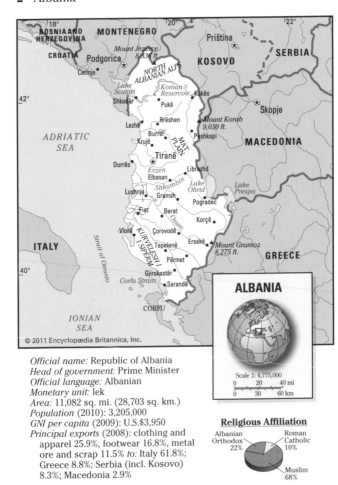

Official name: Republic of Albania
Head of government: Prime Minister
Official language: Albanian
Monetary unit: lek
Area: 11,082 sq. mi. (28,703 sq. km.)
Population (2010): 3,205,000
GNI per capita (2009): U.S.$3,950
Principal exports (2008): clothing and apparel 25.9%, footwear 16.8%, metal ore and scrap 11.5% *to:* Italy 61.8%; Greece 8.8%; Serbia (incl. Kosovo) 8.3%; Macedonia 2.9%

Religious Affiliation

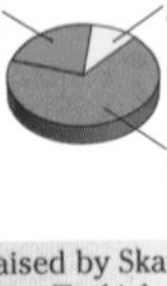

On Nov. 28, 1443, the flag was first raised by Skanderbeg, the national hero. After independence from Turkish rule was proclaimed on Nov. 28, 1912, the flag was flown by various regimes, each of which identified itself by adding a symbol above the double-headed eagle. The current flag, which features only the eagle, was adopted on May 22, 1993.

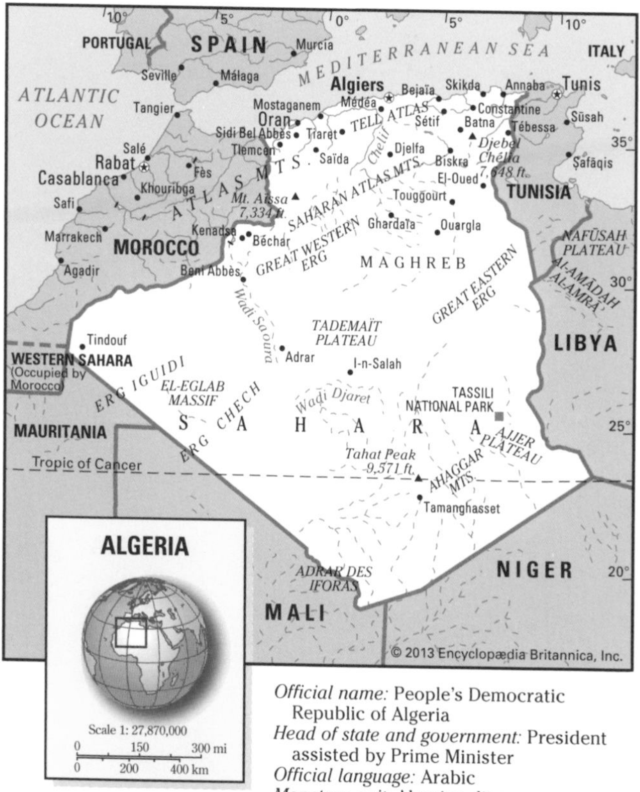

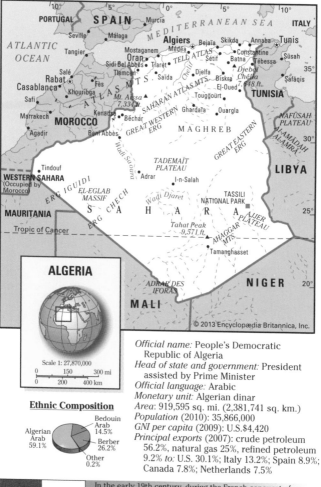

Official name: People's Democratic Republic of Algeria
Head of state and government: President assisted by Prime Minister
Official language: Arabic
Monetary unit: Algerian dinar
Area: 919,595 sq. mi. (2,381,741 sq. km.)
Population (2010): 35,866,000
GNI per capita (2009): U.S.$4,420
Principal exports (2007): crude petroleum 56.2%, natural gas 25%, refined petroleum 9.2% *to:* U.S. 30.1%; Italy 13.2%; Spain 8.9%; Canada 7.8%; Netherlands 7.5%

Ethnic Composition

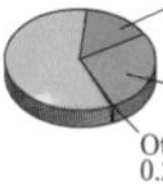

In the early 19th century, during the French conquest of North Africa, Algerian resistance fighters led by Emir Abdelkader supposedly raised the current flag. Its colors and symbols are associated with Islam and the Arab dynasties of the region. The flag was raised over an independent Algeria on July 2, 1962.

© 2011 Encyclopædia Britannica, Inc.

Official name: Principality of Andorra
Head of government: Head of Government
Official language: Catalan
Monetary unit: euro
Area: 179 sq. mi. (464 sq. km.)
Population (2010): 83,900
GNI per capita (2008): U.S.$43,975
Principal exports (2007): electrical machinery 25.0%, motor vehicles 18.5%, optical and photo equipment 10.9% *to* (2008): Spain 69.5%; France 15.5%; Germany 4.6%

Ethnic Composition

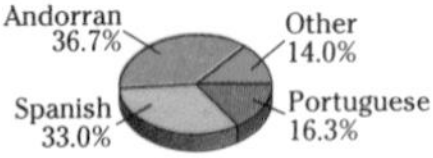

The flag may date to 1866, but the first legal authority for it is unknown. The design was standardized in July 1993. Possible sources for its colors are the flags of neighboring Spain (red-yellow-red) and France (blue-white-red). The coat of arms incorporates both French and Spanish elements dating to the 13th century or earlier.

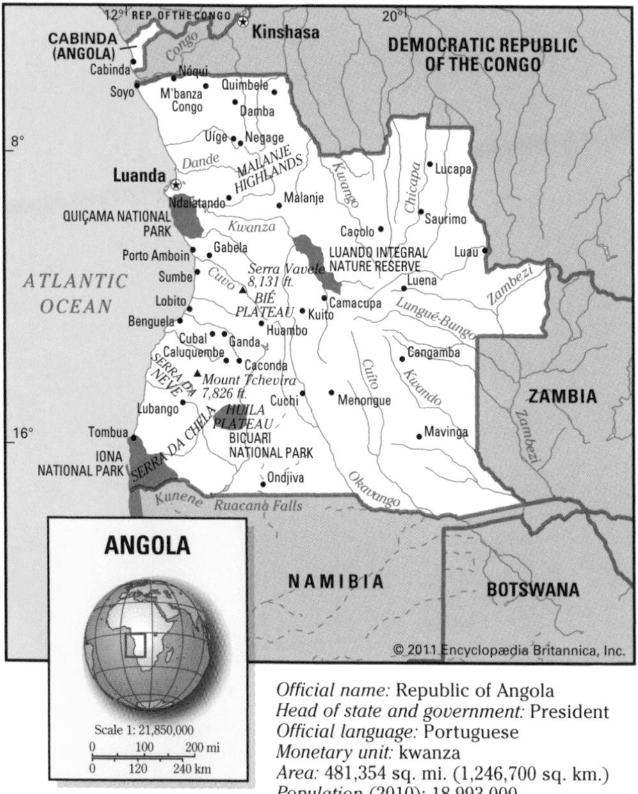

Official name: Republic of Angola
Head of state and government: President
Official language: Portuguese
Monetary unit: kwanza
Area: 481,354 sq. mi. (1,246,700 sq. km.)
Population (2010): 18,993,000
GNI per capita (2009): U.S.$3,490
Principal exports (2006): crude petroleum 94.2%, diamonds 3.6%, refined petroleum 0.9% *to* (2008): China 32.9%; U.S. 28.7%; France 6.0%; South Africa 4.5%

Ethnic Composition

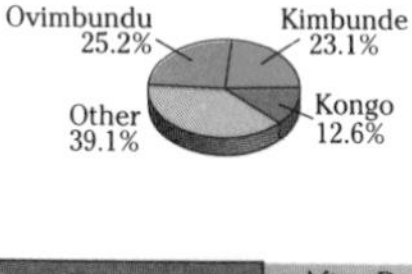

After Portugal withdrew from Angola on Nov. 11, 1975, the flag of the leading rebel group gained recognition. Inspired by designs of the Viet Cong and the former Soviet Union, it includes a star for internationalism and progress, a cogwheel for industrial workers, and a machete for agricultural workers. The black stripe is for the African people.

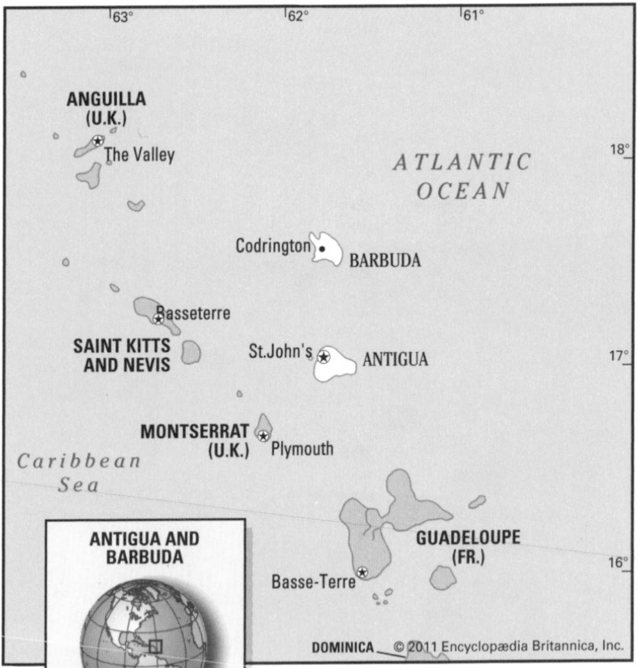

Official name: Antigua and Barbuda
Head of government: Prime Minister
Official language: English
Monetary unit: Eastern Caribbean dollar
Area: 170.5 sq. mi. (441.6 sq. km.)
Population (2010): 90,300
GNI per capita (2009): U.S.$12,130
Principal exports (2007): refined petroleum 57.6%, telecommunication equipment 6.6%, generators 3.0% *to* U.S. 23.5%; Barbados 8.2%; Dominica 6.1%; U.K. 4.2%

Religious Affiliation

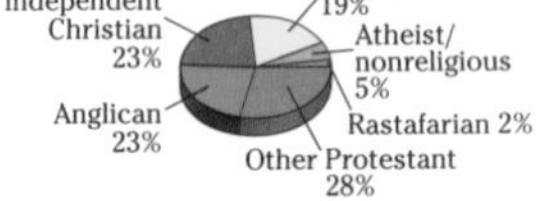

When "associated statehood" was granted by Britain on Feb. 27, 1967, the flag was introduced, and it remained after independence (Nov. 1, 1981). Red is for the dynamism of the people, the V-shape is for victory, and the sun is for the climate. Black is for the majority population and the soil, blue is for the sea, and white is for the beaches.

Official name: Argentine Republic
Head of state and government: President
Official language: Spanish
Monetary unit: peso
Area: 1,073,520 sq. mi. (2,780,403 sq. km.)
Population (2010): 40,666,000
GNI per capita (2009): U.S.$7,600
Principal exports (2008): cereals 10.8%, soybean animal foodstuffs 10.2%, road vehicles/parts 9.2%, petroleum 7.2% *to:* Brazil 18.9%; China 9.1%; U.S. 7.9%; Chile 6.7%

Ethnic Composition

The uniforms worn by Argentines when the British attacked Buenos Aires (1806) and the blue ribbons worn by patriots in 1810 may have been the origin of the celeste-white-celeste flag hoisted on Feb. 12,1812. The flag's golden "sun of May" was added on Feb. 25,1818, to commemorate the yielding of the Spanish viceroy in 1810.

Official name: Republic of Armenia
Head of government: Prime Minister
Official language: Armenian
Monetary unit: dram
Area: 11,484 sq. mi. (29,743 sq. km.)
Population (2010): 3,090,000
GNI per capita (2009): U.S.$3,100
Principal exports (2008): ferro alloys 19.8%, cut diamonds 13.8%, wine and brandy 13.4%, nonferrous metals 11.4%, aluminum foil 3.5% *to:* Russia 20.3%; Germany 17.4%; Netherlands 12.4%; Belguim 8.6%

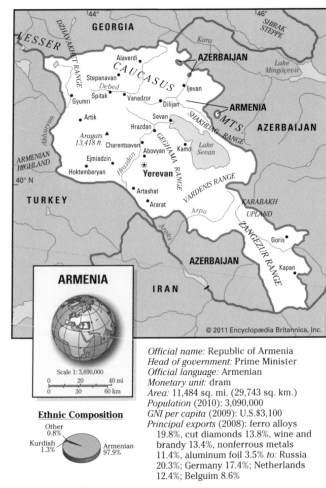

Ethnic Composition

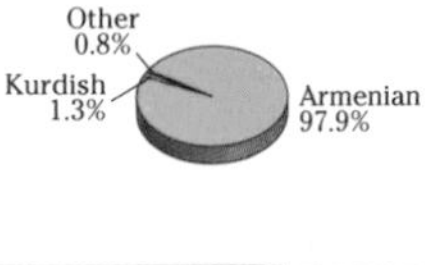

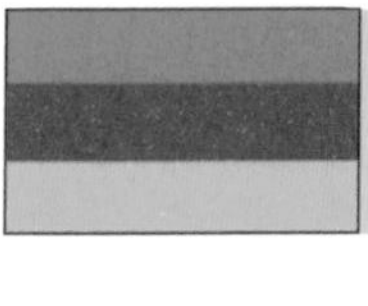

In 1885 an Armenian priest proposed adopting the "rainbow flag given to the Armenians when Noah's Ark came to rest on Mt. Ararat." On Aug. 1, 1918, a flag was sanctioned with stripes of red (possibly symbolizing blood), blue (for homeland), and orange (for courage and work). Replaced during Soviet rule, it was readopted on Aug. 24, 1990.

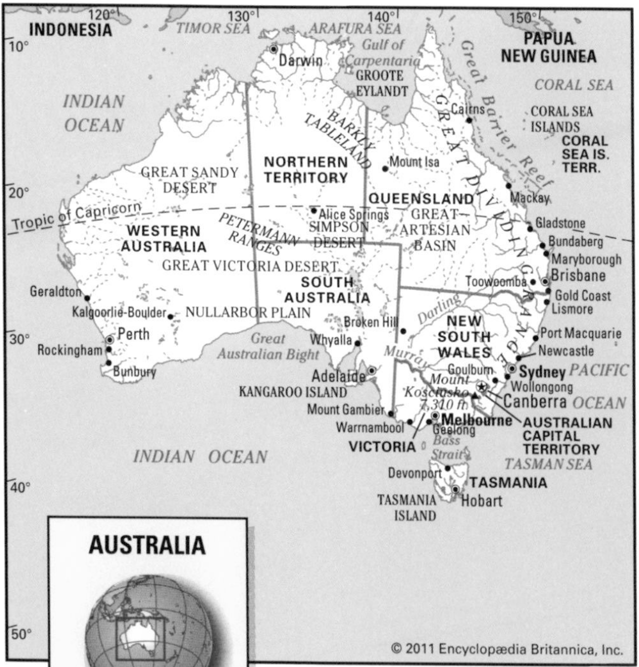

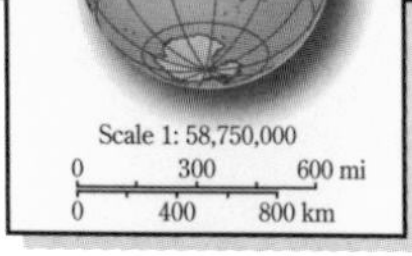

Age Breakdown

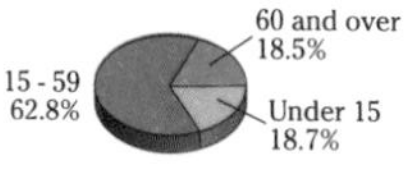

Official name: Commonwealth of Australia
Head of government: Prime Minister
Official language: English
Monetary unit: Australian dollar
Area: 2,973,952 sq. mi. (7,702,501 sq. km.)
Population (2010): 22,403,000
GNI per capita (2009): U.S.$43,770
Principal exports (2008): mineral fuels 32%, crude petroleum 4.7%, metal ore and scrap 22.6%, food and beverages 9.8%, cereals 2.7% *to:* Japan 22.9%; China 14.6%; South Korea 8.3%; India 6.1%; U.S. 5.5%

After Australian confederation was achieved on Jan. 1, 1901, the flag was chosen in a competition. Like the blue flags of British colonies, it displays the Union Jack in the canton. Also shown are the Southern Cross and a "Commonwealth Star." The design became official on May 22, 1909, and it was recognized as the national flag on Feb. 14, 1954.

Official name: Republic of Austria
Head of government: Chancellor
Official language: German
Monetary unit: euro
Area: 32,386 sq. mi. (83,879 sq. km.)
Population (2010): 8,382,000
GNI per capita: U.S.$38,550
Principal exports (2008): machinery and apparatus 28.7%, road vehicles/ parts 9.6%, chemical products 9.6%, iron and steel 6.6% *to:* Germany 29.7%; Italy 8.6%; United States 4.4%; Switzerland 4.2%

Religious Affiliation

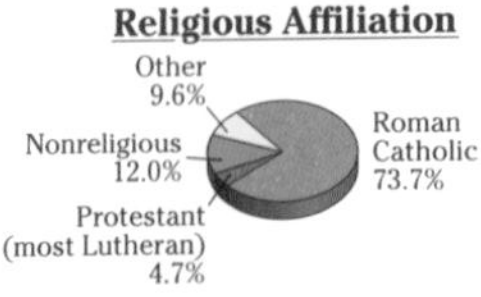

The colors of the Austrian coat of arms date from the seal of Duke Frederick II in 1230. With the fall of the Austro-Hungarian Empire in 1918, the new Austrian republic adopted the red-white-red flag. The white is sometimes said to represent the Danube River. The imperial eagle, with one or two heads, has been an Austrian symbol for centuries.

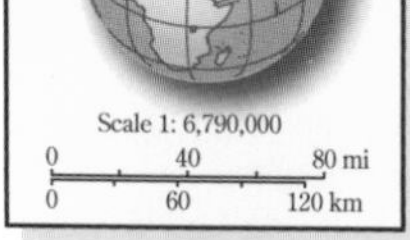

Official name: Republic of Azerbaijan
Head of state and government: President assisted by Prime Minister
Official language: Azerbaijanian
Monetary unit: manat
Area: 33,400 sq. mi. (86,600 sq. km.)
Population (2010): 9,062,000
GNI per capita (2010): U.S.$4,840
Principal exports (2008): crude petroleum 92.5%, refined petroleum 4.3% *to:* Italy 40.2%; U.S.$12.6%; Israel 7.6%; India 5.0%; France 4.9%

Ethnic Composition

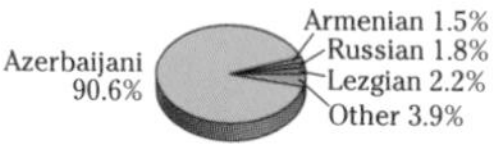

In the early 20th century anti-Russian nationalists exhorted the Azerbaijanis to "Turkify, Islamicize, and Europeanize," and the 1917 flag was associated with Turkey and Islam. In 1918 the crescent and star (also symbols of Turkic peoples) were introduced. Suppressed under Soviet rule, the flag was re-adopted on Feb. 5, 1991.

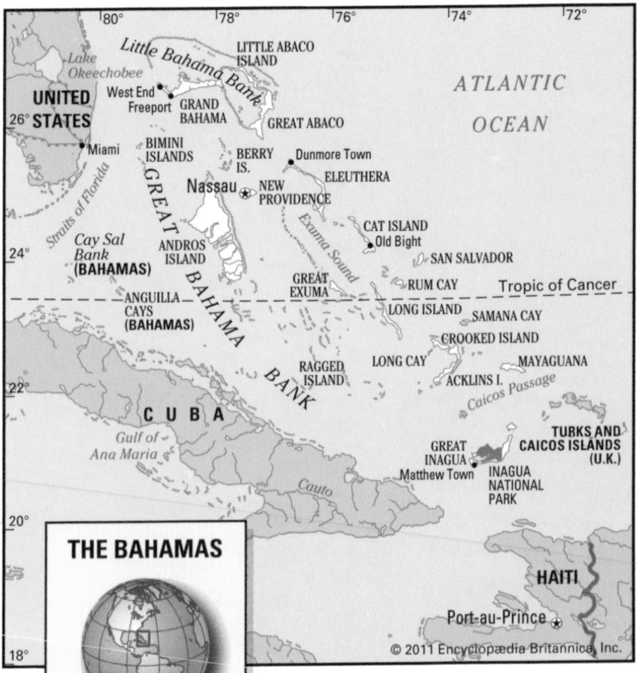

Official name: Commonwealth of The Bahamas
Head of government: Prime Minister
Official language: English
Monetary unit: Bahamian dollar
Area: 5,382 sq. mi. (13,939 sq. km.)
Population (2010): 347,000
GNI per capita (2007): U.S.$21,021
Principal exports (2008): polystyrene 21.6%, refined petroleum 20.2%, organic chemicals 10.8%, crayfish 9.5% *to:* U.S. 69.9%; Canada 5.2%; Germany 4.4%; France 3.6%; Netherlands 3.0%

Ethnic Composition

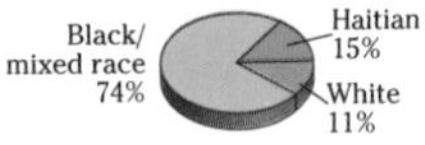

The flag of The Bahamas was adopted on July 10, 1973, the date of independence from Britain. Several entries from a competition were combined to create the design. The two aquamarine stripes are for the surrounding waters, the gold stripe is for the sand and other rich land resources, and the black triangle is for the people and their strength.

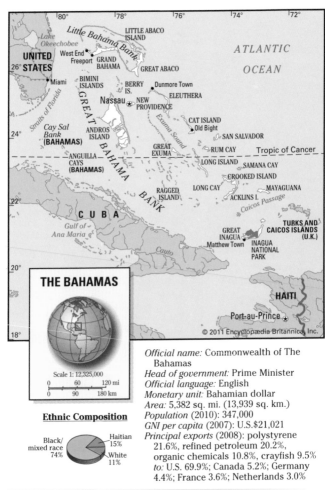

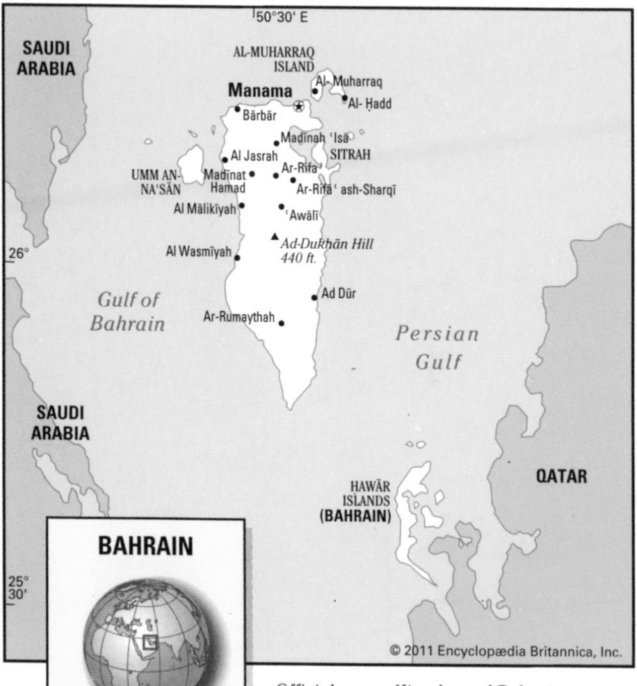

Official name: Kingdom of Bahrain
Head of government: Prime Minister
Official language: Arabic
Monetary unit: Bahrain dinar
Area: 292.5 sq. mi. (757.5 sq. km.)
Population (2010): 1,216,000
GNI per capita (2008): U.S.$25,420
Principal exports (2007): refined petroleum, 79.1%, aluminum 9.0%, urea 2.4%, iron agglomerates 1.4% *to:* (2006); Saudi Arabia 20.9%; United States 9.3%; India 6.8%; Singapore 6.5%

Religious Affiliation

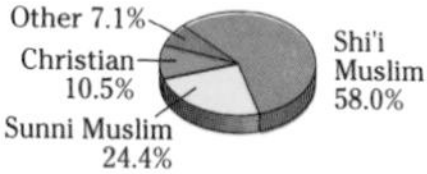

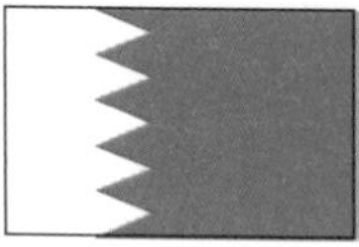

Red in this flag represents the Kharijite sect of Islam, dominant about 1820, and white stands for amity with the British, who brought peace to the strife-torn Persian Gulf then. After many versions of the design had been used by Bahrain, on February 14, 2002 it adopted the current flag, specifying that the dividing line must be serrated into five white triangles.

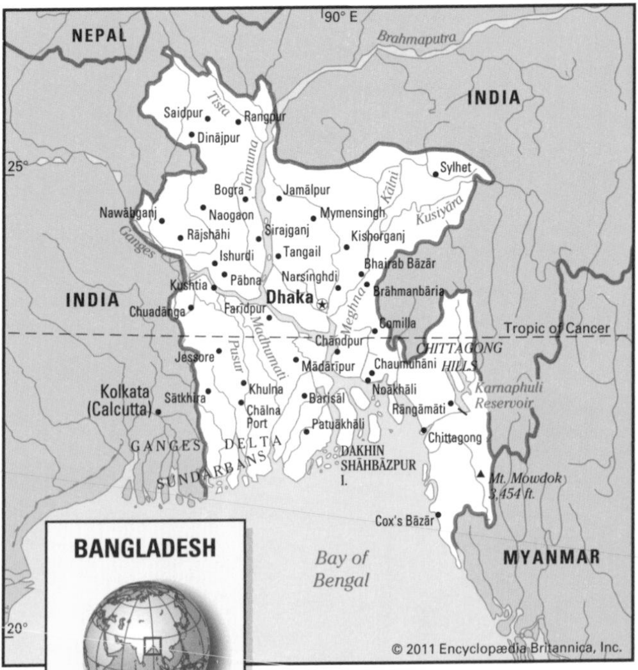

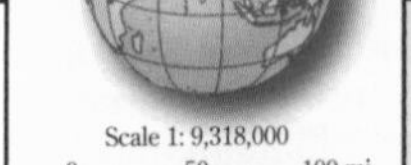

Official name: People's Republic of Bangladesh
Head of government: Prime Minister
Official language: Bengali (Bangla)
Monetary unit: Bangladesh taka
Area: 56,977 sq. mi. (147,570 sq. km.)
Population (2010): 158,066,000
GNI per capita (2009): U.S.$590
Principal exports (2003–04): knitted or woven clothing or accessories 71.5%, shrimp 4.6%, leather 2.2% *to:* U.S. 25.7%; Germany 15.2%; U.K. 9.5%; France 6.5%

Religious Affiliation

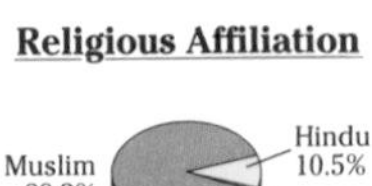

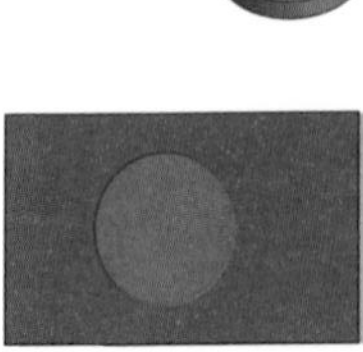

The flag is dark green to symbolize Islam, plant life, and the hope placed in Bengali youth. Its original design included a red disk and a silhouette of the country. On Jan. 13, 1972, the silhouette was removed and the disk shifted off-center. The disk is the "rising sun of a new country" colored by the blood of those who fought for independence.

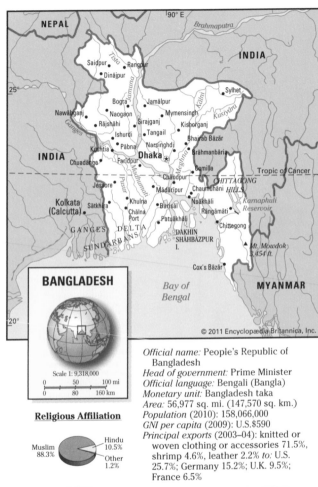

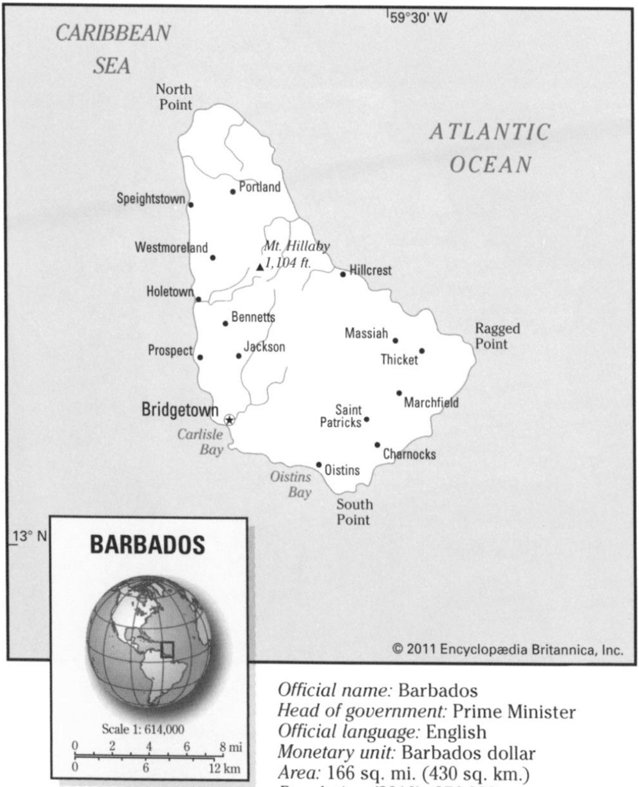

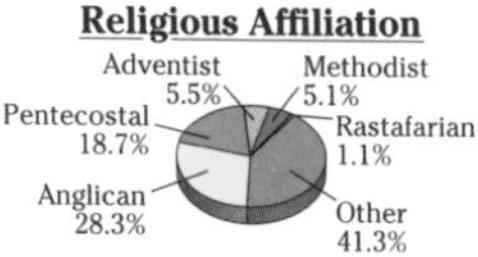

Official name: Barbados
Head of government: Prime Minister
Official language: English
Monetary unit: Barbados dollar
Area: 166 sq. mi. (430 sq. km.)
Population (2010): 276,000
GNI per capita (2008): U.S.$13,829
Principal exports (2008): refined petroleum 20.2%, food 12.6%, medicines 8.3%, rum 7.3% *to:* United States 21.0%; Trinidad and Tobago 9.5%; United Kingdom 9.1%; St. Lucia 5.4%

The flag was designed by Grantley Prescod, a Barbadian art teacher. Its stripes of blue-yellow-blue are for sea, sand, and sky. The black trident head was inspired by the colonial flag of Barbados, which featured a trident-wielding Poseidon, or Neptune, figure. The flag was first hoisted on Nov. 30, 1966, the date of independence from Britain.

Official name: Republic of Belarus
Head of state and government: President assisted by Prime Minister
Official languages: Belarusian; Russian
Monetary unit: Belarusian ruble
Area: 80,200 sq. mi. (207,600 sq. km.)
Population (2010): 9,457,000
GNI per capita (2009): U.S.$12,380
Principal exports (2008): refined petroleum 33.0%, potassium chloride 10.3%, food 6.5%, road vehicles/parts 6.4% *to:* Russia 32.2%; Netherlands 16.9%; Ukraine 8.5%; Latvia 6.6%; Poland 5.5%

Ethnic Composition

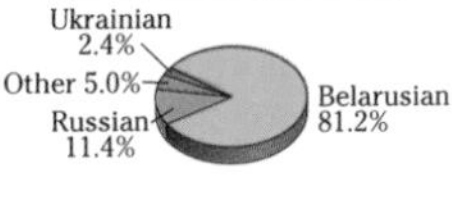

In 1951 the former Soviet republic created a striped flag in red (for communism) and green (for fields and forests), with the hammer, sickle, and star of communism. In 1991–95 an older design was used, but the Soviet-era flag was then altered and readopted without communist symbols. The vertical stripe is typical of embroidery on peasant clothing.

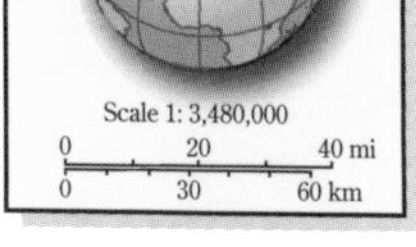

Official name: Kingdom of Belgium
Head of government: Prime Minister
Official languages: Dutch; French; German
Monetary unit: euro
Area: 11,787 sq. mi. (30,528 sq. km.)
Population (2010): 10,868,000
GNI per capita (2009): U.S.$36,520
Principal exports (2008): machinery and apparatus 12.2%, road vehicles/parts 10.5%, pharmaceuticals 8.6%, food 7.3%, iron and steel 5.9%, refined petroleum 5.8% *to:* Germany 19.9%; France 17.4%; Netherlands 12.3%

National Composition

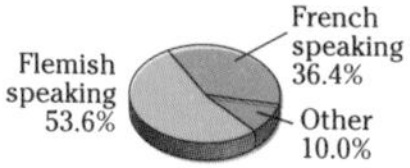

A gold shield and a black lion appeared in the seal of Count Philip of Flanders as early as 1162, and in 1787 cockades of black-yellow-red were used in a Brussels revolt against Austria. After a war for independence, the flag was recognized on Jan. 23, 1831. By 1838 the design, which was influenced by the French tricolor, became standard.

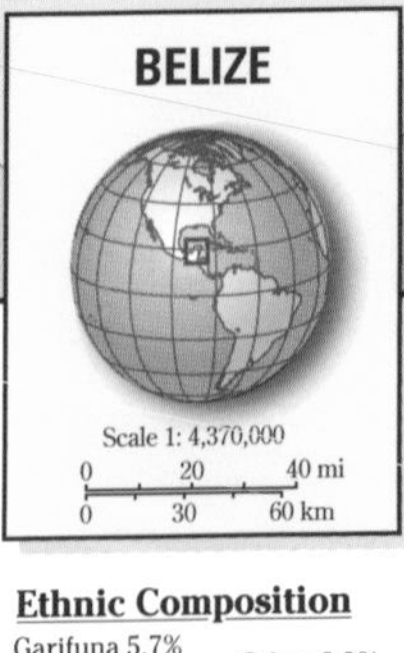

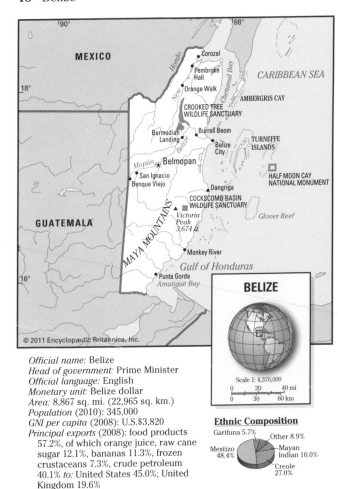

Official name: Belize
Head of government: Prime Minister
Official language: English
Monetary unit: Belize dollar
Area: 8,867 sq. mi. (22,965 sq. km.)
Population (2010): 345,000
GNI per capita (2008): U.S.$3,820
Principal exports (2008): food products 57.2%, of which orange juice, raw cane sugar 12.1%, bananas 11.3%, frozen crustaceans 7.3%, crude petroleum 40.1% *to:* United States 45.0%; United Kingdom 19.6%

Ethnic Composition

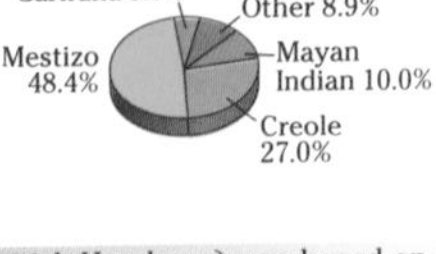

The flag of Belize (former British Honduras) was based on the flag of the nationalist People's United Party. Its coat of arms shows a mahogany tree, a shield, and a Creole and a Mestizo. The red stripes, symbolic of the United Democratic Party, were added on independence day (Sept. 21, 1981), when the flag was first officially hoisted.

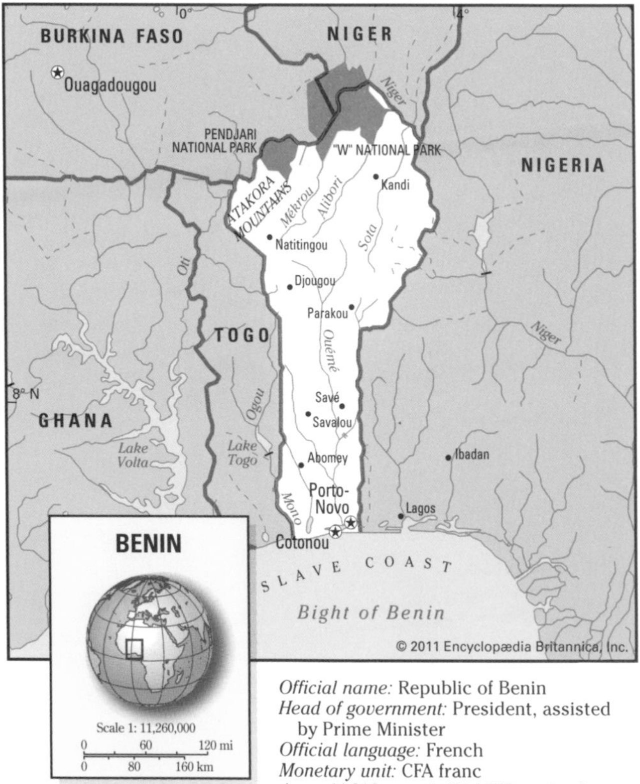

Ethnic Composition

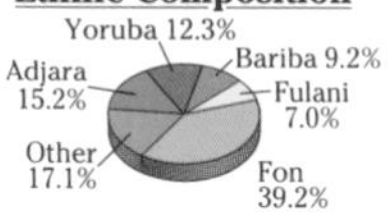

Official name: Republic of Benin
Head of government: President, assisted by Prime Minister
Official language: French
Monetary unit: CFA franc
Area: 44,310 sq. mi. (114,763 sq. km.)
Population (2010): 9,056,000
GNI per capita (2009): U.S.$1,510
Principal exports (2006): raw cotton 40.4%; cigarettes 15.6%; food products 13.6% *to:* China 24.0%; Nigeria 8.7%; India 8.6%; Niger 7.2%

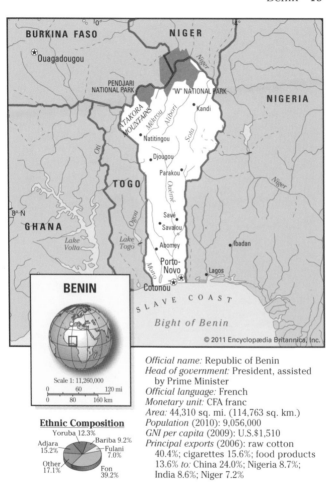

Adopted on Nov. 16, 1959, the flag of the former French colony used the Pan-African colors. Yellow was for the savannas in the north and green was for the palm groves in the south. Red stood for the blood of patriots. In 1975 a Marxist-oriented government replaced the flag, but after the demise of Communism it was restored on Aug. 1, 1990.

Official name: Kingdom of Bhutan
Head of government: Prime Minister
Official language: Dzongkha (a Tibetan dialect)
Monetary unit: ngultrum
Area: 14,824 sq. mi. (38,394 sq. km.)
Population (2010): 700,000
GNI per capita: U.S.$5,300
Principal exports (2008): electricity 48.8%, ginger 45.3%, iron and steel 1.3%, oranges 1.1% *to:* India 95.1%; Bangladesh 2.8%

Ethnic Composition

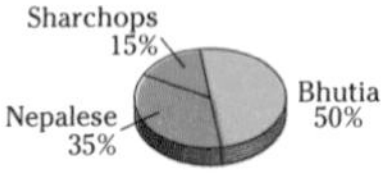

The flag of Bhutan ("Land of the Dragon") features a dragon grasping jewels; this represents natural wealth and perfection. The white color is for purity and loyalty, the gold is for regal power, and the orange-red is for Buddhist sects and religious commitment. The flag may have been introduced as recently as 1971.

Official name: Plurinational State of Bolivia
Head of state and government: President
Official languages: Spanish and 36 indigenous languages
Monetary unit: boliviano
Area: 424,164 sq. mi. (1,098,581 sq. km.)
Population (2010): 9,947,000
GNI per capita (2009): U.S.$1,630
Principal exports (2009): natural gas 40.6%, minerals 38.1%, soybeans 9.6% *to:* Brazil 36.7%; Argentina 8.7%; U.S. 8.6%; Japan 8.5%; Venezuela 5.0%

Ethnic Composition

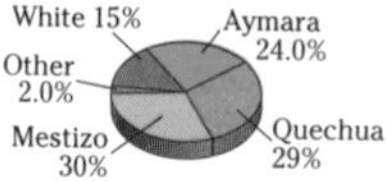

A version of the flag was first adopted on July 25, 1826, but on Nov. 5, 1851, the order of the stripes was changed to red-yellow-green. The colors were often used by the Aymara and Quechua peoples; in addition, red is for the valor of the army, yellow for mineral resources, and green for the land. The current flag law dates from July 14, 1888.

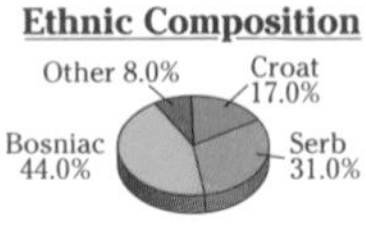

Official name: Bosnia and Herzegovina
Head of government: Prime Minister
Official languages: Bosnian; Croatian; Serbian
Monetary unit: convertible marka
Area: 19,772 sq. mi. (51,209 sq. km.)
Population (2010): 3,839,000
GNI per capita (2009): U.S.$4,700
Principal exports (2008): aluminum 8.8%, metal manufactures 8.4%, iron and steel 7.4% *to:* Croatia 19.2%; Serbia 15.1%; Germany 13.5%; Italy 12.6%; Slovenia 9.2%

Under communist Yugoslavia (1946 to 1992), the Socialist Republic of Bosnia and Herzegovina flew a red banner with a small Yugoslav national flag in the canton. At independence, March 3, 1992, there was no flag acceptable to Bosnians, Serbs, and Croats. So, the UN established a flag (February 4, 1998) not symbolic of any ethnic, religious, or political group.

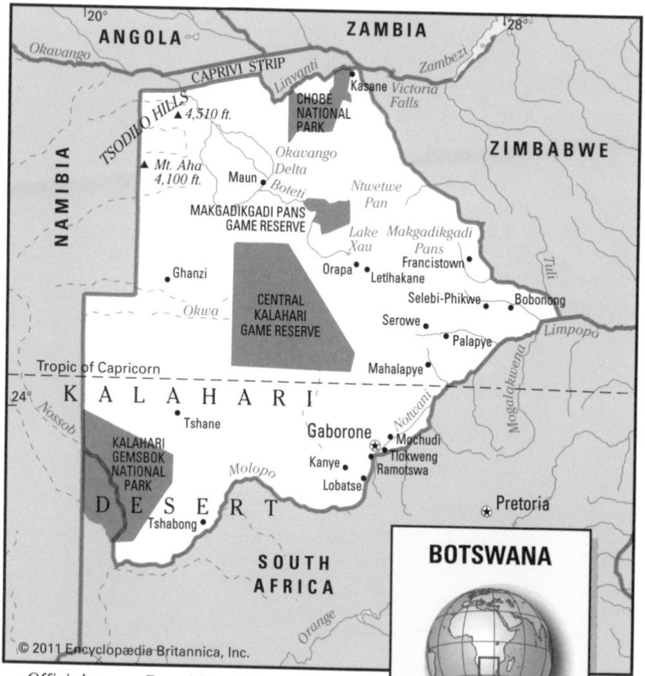

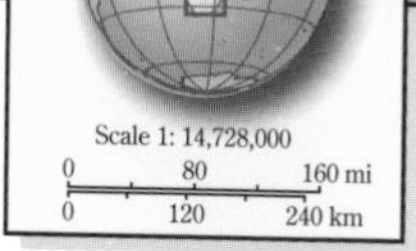

Official name: Republic of Botswana
Head of state and government: President
Official language: English
Monetary unit: pula
Area: 224,848 sq. mi. (582,356 sq. km.)
Population (2010): 2,029,000
GNI per capita (2009): U.S.$6,260
Principal exports (2008): diamonds 64.5%, nickel matte 14.0%, apparel and clothing accessories 5.4% *to:* U.K. 56.8%; South Africa 20.3%; China 4.9%; Zimbabwe 4.5%

Ethnic Composition

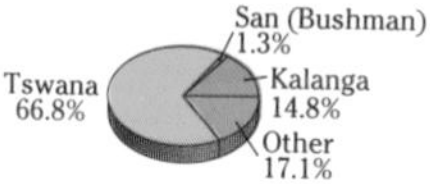

Adopted in 1966, the flag was designed to contrast symbolically with that of neighboring South Africa, where apartheid was then in effect. The black and white stripes in Botswana's flag are for racial cooperation and equality. The background symbolizes water, a scarce resource in the expansive Kalahari Desert.

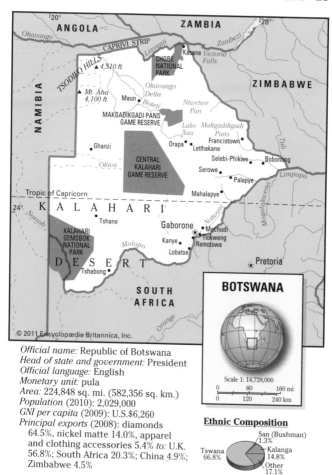

Official name: Federative Republic of Brazil
Head of state and government: President
Official language: Portuguese
Monetary unit: real
Area: 3,287,612 sq. mi. (8,514,877 sq. km.)
Population (2010): 193,253,000
GNI per capita (2009): U.S.$8,070
Principal exports (2001): food products 18.9%, machinery and apparatus 10.2%, iron ore and concentrates 8.4% *to:* U.S. 14.0%; Argentina 8.9%; China 8.3%; Netherlands 5.3%

Ethnic Composition

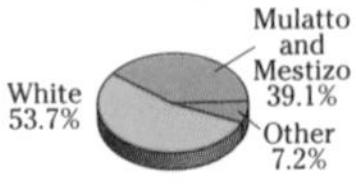

The original flag was introduced on Sept. 7, 1822, when Dom Pedro declared independence from Portugal. In 1889 the blue disk and the motto Ordem e Progresso ("Order and Progress") were added. The Brazilian states and territories are symbolized by the constellations of stars. Green is for the land, while yellow is for gold and other mineral wealth.

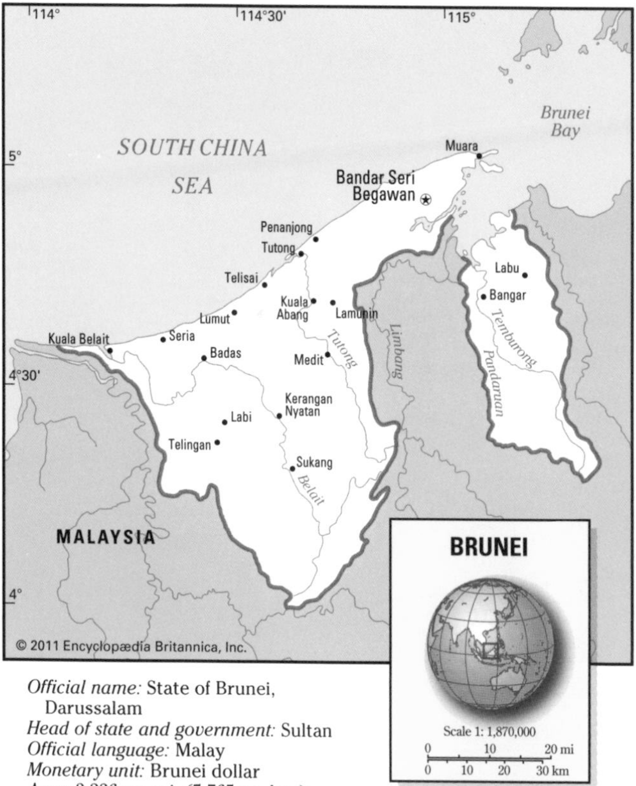

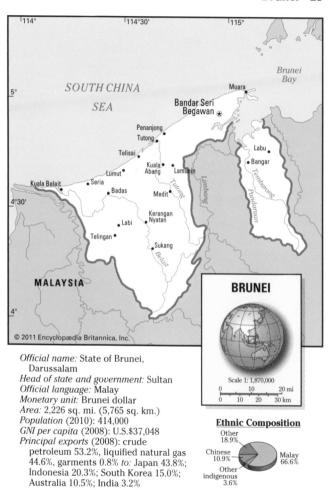

Official name: State of Brunei, Darussalam
Head of state and government: Sultan
Official language: Malay
Monetary unit: Brunei dollar
Area: 2,226 sq. mi. (5,765 sq. km.)
Population (2010): 414,000
GNI per capita (2008): U.S.$37,048
Principal exports (2008): crude petroleum 53.2%, liquified natural gas 44.6%, garments 0.8% *to:* Japan 43.8%; Indonesia 20.3%; South Korea 15.0%; Australia 10.5%; India 3.2%

Ethnic Composition

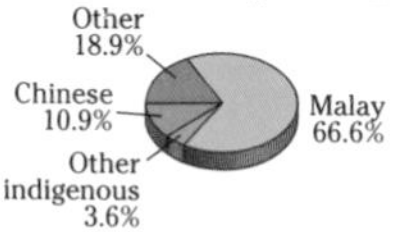

On becoming independent from Britain, January 1, 1984, Brunei adopted this flag. The colors stand for the sultan (yellow) and his two ministers (white and black), while red is for the national coat of arms in the center. Its crescent is for Islam, the state religion, and reads, "Always render service by the guidance of God." The ribbon below says, "Brunei, abode of peace."

Official name: Republic of Bulgaria
Head of government: Prime Minister
Official language: Bulgarian
Monetary unit: lev
Area: 42,858 sq. mi. (111,002 sq. km.)
Population (2010): 7,562,000
GNI per capita (2009): U.S.$5,770
Principal exports (2008): base and fabricated metals 20.7%, machinery and apparatus 13.4%, refined petroleum 13.4% *to:* Germany 11.2%; Greece 9.4%; Italy 9.3%; Romania 8.6%

Ethnic Composition

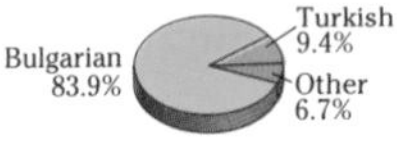

The flag was based on the Russian flag of 1699, but with green substituted for blue. Under communist rule, a red star and other symbols were added, but the old tricolor was reestablished on Nov. 27, 1990. The white is for peace, love, and freedom; green is for agriculture; and red is for the independence struggle and military courage.

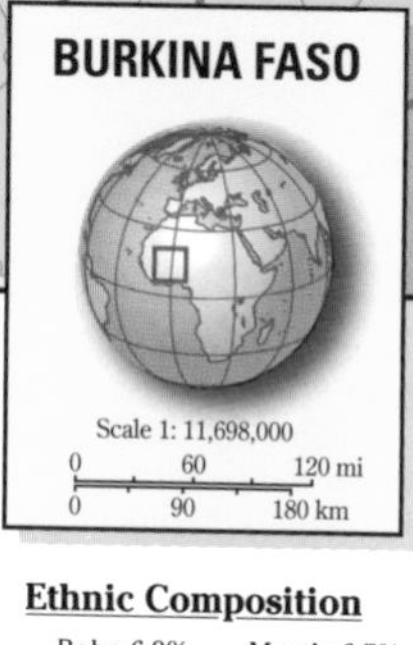

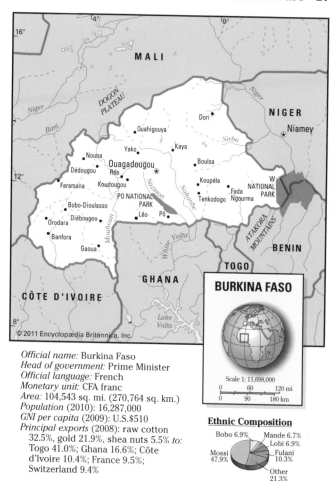

Official name: Burkina Faso
Head of government: Prime Minister
Official language: French
Monetary unit: CFA franc
Area: 104,543 sq. mi. (270,764 sq. km.)
Population (2010): 16,287,000
GNI per capita (2009): U.S.$510
Principal exports (2008): raw cotton 32.5%, gold 21.9%, shea nuts 5.5% *to:* Togo 41.0%; Ghana 16.6%; Côte d'lvoire 10.4%; France 9.5%; Switzerland 9.4%

Ethnic Composition

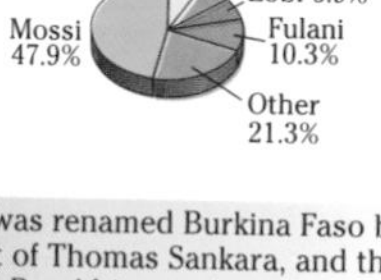

On Aug. 4, 1984, Upper Volta was renamed Burkina Faso by the revolutionary government of Thomas Sankara, and the current flag was adopted with Pan-African colors. The yellow star symbolizes leadership and revolutionary principles. The red stripe is said to stand for the revolutionary struggle, while the green stripe represents hope and abundance.

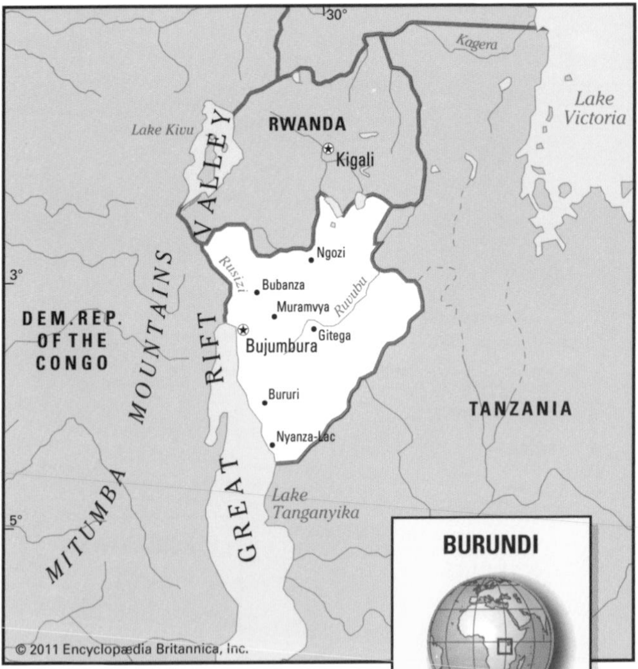

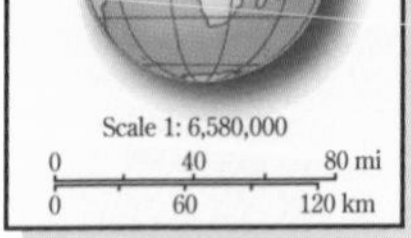

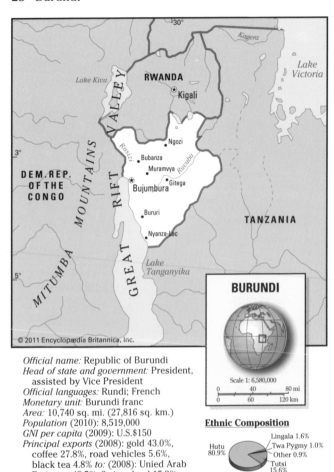

Official name: Republic of Burundi
Head of state and government: President, assisted by Vice President
Official languages: Rundi; French
Monetary unit: Burundi franc
Area: 10,740 sq. mi. (27,816 sq. km.)
Population (2010): 8,519,000
GNI per capita (2009): U.S.$150
Principal exports (2008): gold 43.0%, coffee 27.8%, road vehicles 5.6%, black tea 4.8% *to:* (2008): Unied Arab Emirates 43.5%; Switzerland 15.3%; Belgium 6.1%; Kenya 5.4%

Ethnic Composition

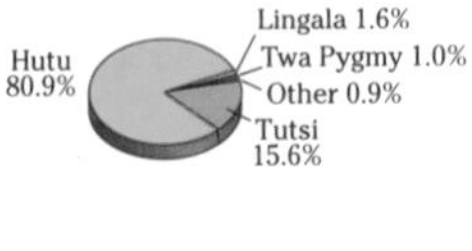

The flag became official on June 28, 1967. Its white saltire (diagonal cross) and central disk symbolize peace. The red color is for the independence struggle, and green is for hope. The stars correspond to the national motto, "Unity, Work, Progress." They also recall the Tutsi, Hutu, and Twa peoples and the pledge to God, king, and country.

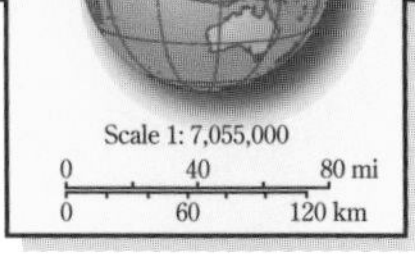

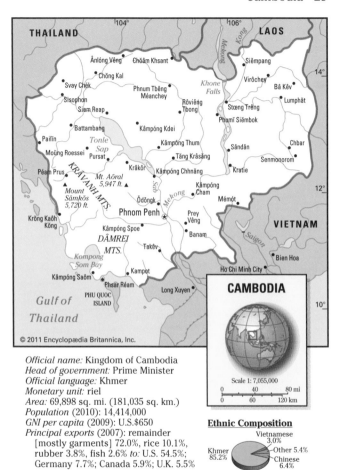

Official name: Kingdom of Cambodia
Head of government: Prime Minister
Official language: Khmer
Monetary unit: riel
Area: 69,898 sq. mi. (181,035 sq. km.)
Population (2010): 14,414,000
GNI per capita (2009): U.S.$650
Principal exports (2007): remainder [mostly garments] 72.0%, rice 10.1%, rubber 3.8%, fish 2.6% *to:* U.S. 54.5%; Germany 7.7%; Canada 5.9%; U.K. 5.5%

Ethnic Composition

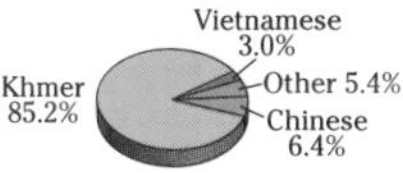

Artistic representations of the central ruined temple of Angkor Wat, a 12th-century temple complex, have appeared on Khmer flags since the 19th century. The current flag design dates to 1948. It was replaced in 1970 under the Khmer Republic and in 1976 under communist leadership, but it was again hoisted on June 29, 1993.

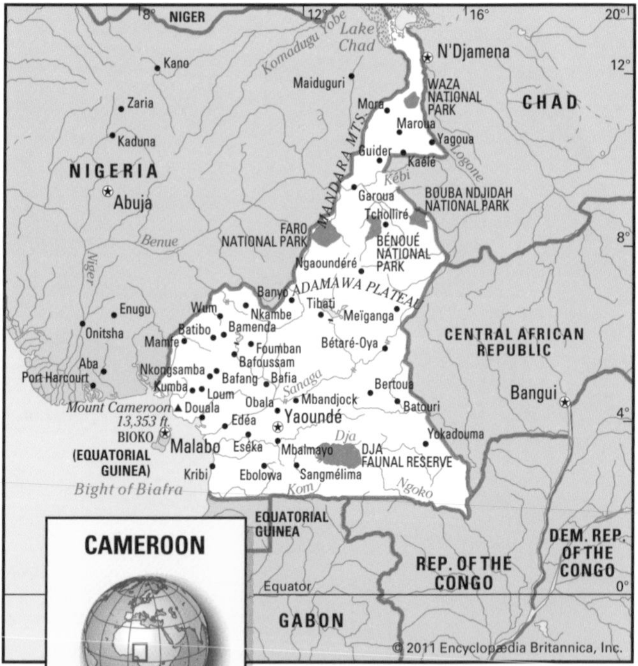

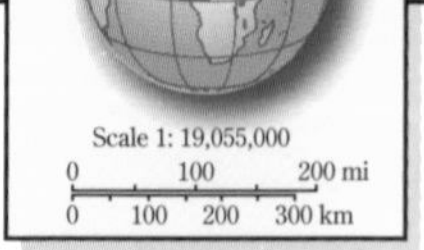

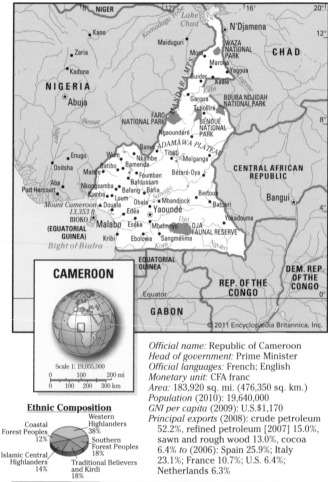

Official name: Republic of Cameroon
Head of government: Prime Minister
Official languages: French; English
Monetary unit: CFA franc
Area: 183,920 sq. mi. (476,350 sq. km.)
Population (2010): 19,640,000
GNI per capita (2009): U.S.$1,170
Principal exports (2008): crude petroleum 52.2%, refined petroleum [2007] 15.0%, sawn and rough wood 13.0%, cocoa 6.4% *to* (2006): Spain 25.9%; Italy 23.1%; France 10.7%; U.S. 6.4%; Netherlands 6.3%

Ethnic Composition

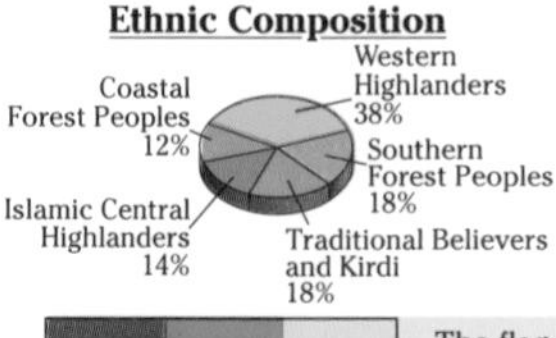

The flag was officially hoisted on Oct. 29, 1957, prior to independence (Jan. 1, 1960). Green is for the vegetation of the south, yellow for the savannas of the north, and red for union and sovereignty. Two yellow stars were added (for the British Cameroons) in 1961, but these were replaced in 1975 by a single star symbolizing national unity.

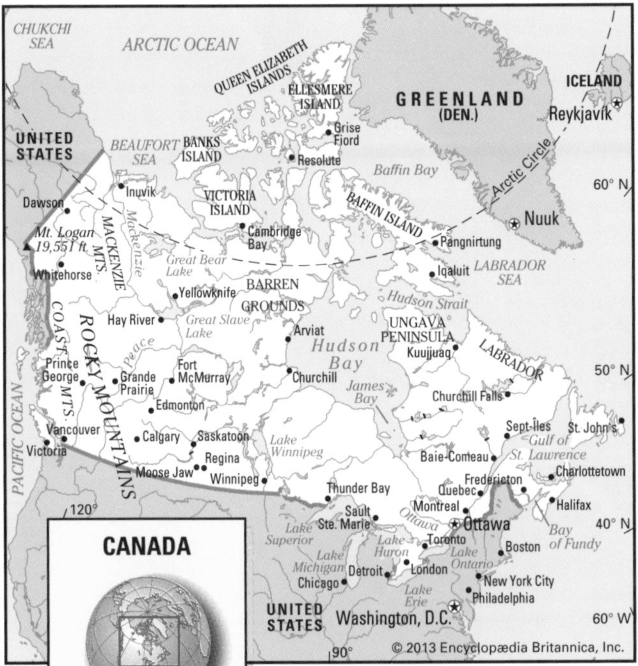

Official name: Canada
Head of government: Prime Minister
Official languages: English; French
Monetary unit: Canadian dollar
Area: 3,855,103 sq. mi. (9,984,670 sq. km.)
Population (2010): 34,132,000
GNI per capita (2009): U.S.$42,170
Principal exports (2008): mineral fuels 26.9%, equipment, machinery and apparatus 11.6%, road vehicles 10.7%, chemicals and chemical products 8.3%, food products 6.6% *to:* U.S. 76.9%; U.K. 2.9%; China 2.4%; Japan 2.3%; Mexico 1.2%

Population By Mother Tongue

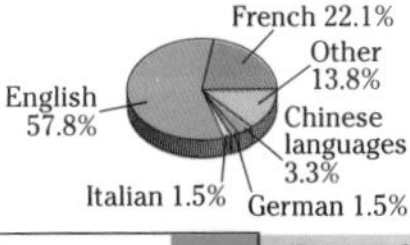

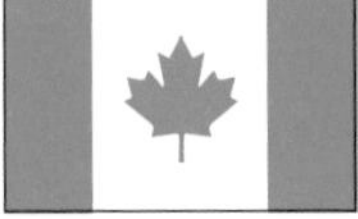

During Canada's first century of independence the Union Jack was still flown, but with a Canadian coat of arms. The maple leaf design, with the national colors, became official on Feb. 15, 1965. Since 1868 the maple leaf has been a national symbol, and in 1921 a red leaf in the coat of arms stood for Canadian sacrifice during World War I.

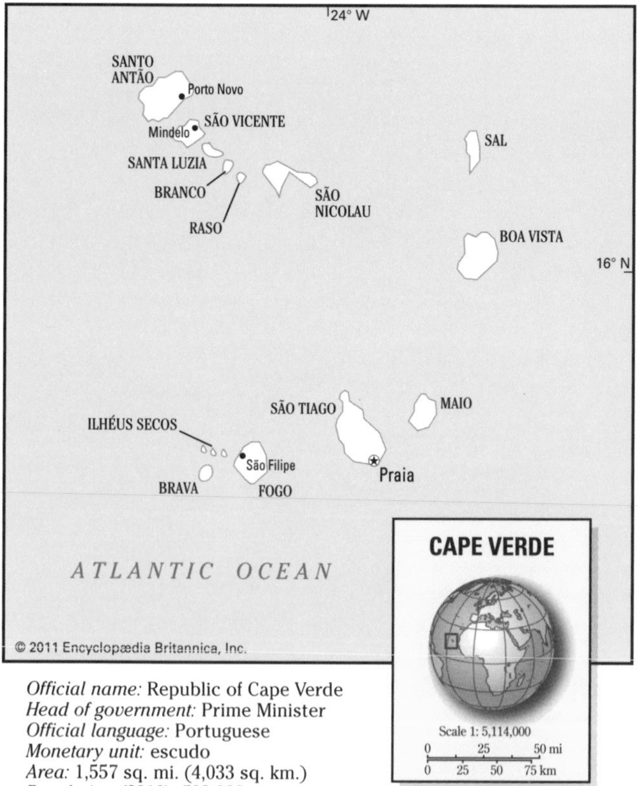

Official name: Republic of Cape Verde
Head of government: Prime Minister
Official language: Portuguese
Monetary unit: escudo
Area: 1,557 sq. mi. (4,033 sq. km.)
Population (2010): 509,000
GNI per capita (2009): U.S.$3,010
Principal exports (2007): refined petroleum 49.8%, transport containers 15.8%, fresh fish 8.3%, clothing 5.7% *to:* Côte d'Ivoire 30.7%; Portugal 21.6%; Netherlands 15.2%; Spain 9.1%

Religious Affiliation

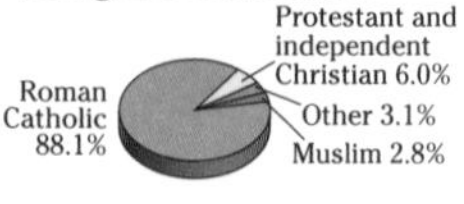

After the elections of 1991, the flag was established with a blue field bearing a ring of 10 yellow stars to symbolize the 10 main islands of Cape Verde. The stripes of white-red-white suggest peace and national resolve. Red, white, and blue also are a symbolic link to Portugal and the United States. The new flag became official on Sept. 25, 1992.

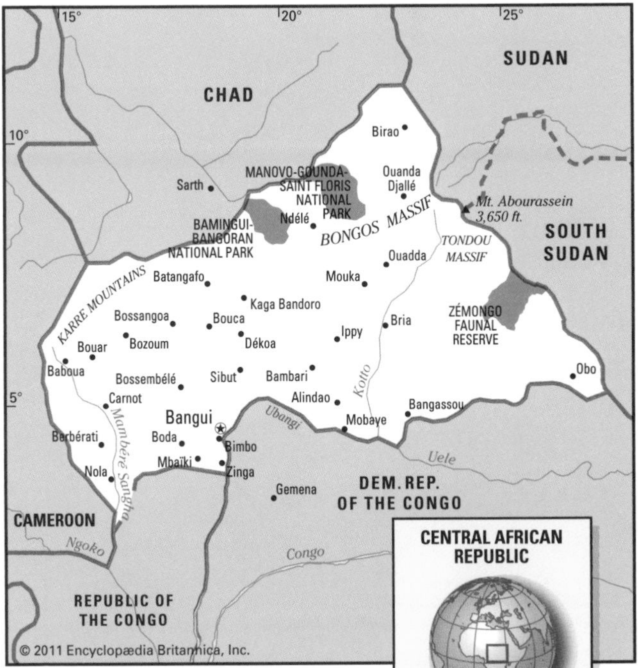

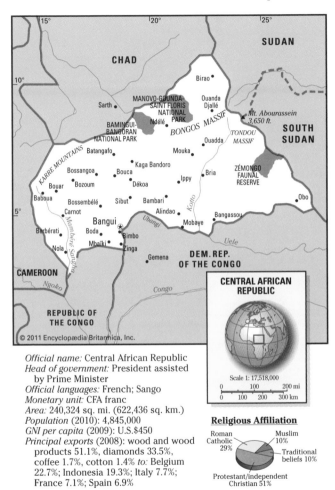

Official name: Central African Republic
Head of government: President assisted by Prime Minister
Official languages: French; Sango
Monetary unit: CFA franc
Area: 240,324 sq. mi. (622,436 sq. km.)
Population (2010): 4,845,000
GNI per capita (2009): U.S.$450
Principal exports (2008): wood and wood products 51.1%, diamonds 33.5%, coffee 1.7%, cotton 1.4% *to:* Belgium 22.7%; Indonesia 19.3%; Italy 7.7%; France 7.1%; Spain 6.9%

Religious Affiliation

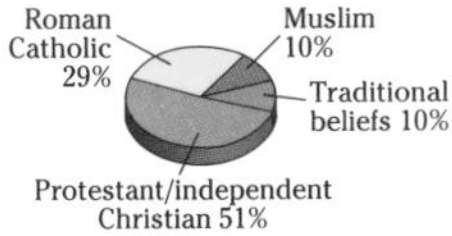

Barthélemy Boganda designed the flag in 1958. It combines French and Pan-African colors. The star is a guide for progress and an emblem of unity. The blue stripe is for liberty, grandeur, and the sky; the white is for purity, equality, and candor; the green and yellow are for forests and savannas; and the red is for the blood of humankind.

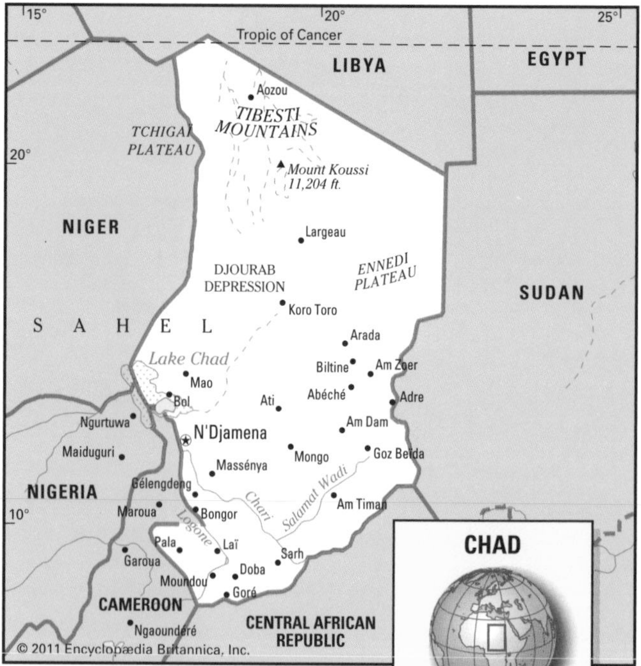

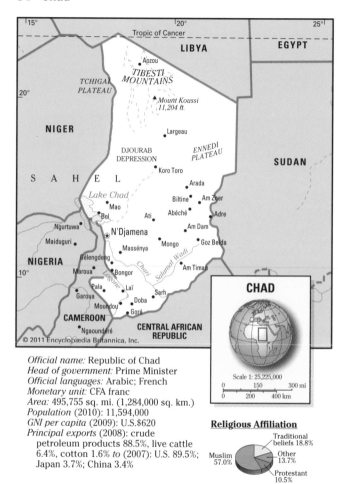

Official name: Republic of Chad
Head of government: Prime Minister
Official languages: Arabic; French
Monetary unit: CFA franc
Area: 495,755 sq. mi. (1,284,000 sq. km.)
Population (2010): 11,594,000
GNI per capita (2009): U.S.$620
Principal exports (2008): crude petroleum products 88.5%, live cattle 6.4%, cotton 1.6% *to* (2007): U.S. 89.5%; Japan 3.7%; China 3.4%

Religious Affiliation

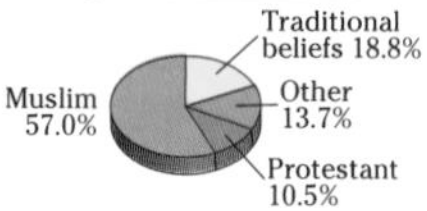

In 1958 a tricolor of green-yellow-red (the Pan-African colors) was proposed, but that design was already used by the Mali-Senegal federation, another former French colony. Approved on Nov. 6, 1959, the current flag substitutes blue for the original green stripe. Blue is for hope and sky, yellow for the sun, and red for the unity of the nation.

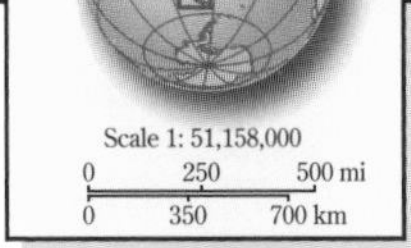

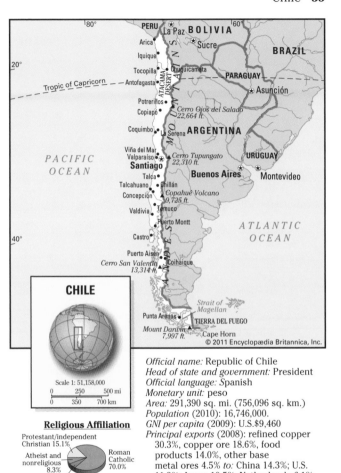

Official name: Republic of Chile
Head of state and government: President
Official language: Spanish
Monetary unit: peso
Area: 291,390 sq. mi. (756,096 sq. km.)
Population (2010): 16,746,000.
GNI per capita (2009): U.S.$9,460
Principal exports (2008): refined copper 30.3%, copper ore 18.6%, food products 14.0%, other base metal ores 4.5% *to:* China 14.3%; U.S. 11.3%; Japan 10.5%; Netherlands 6.1%; Brazil 6.0%

Religious Affiliation

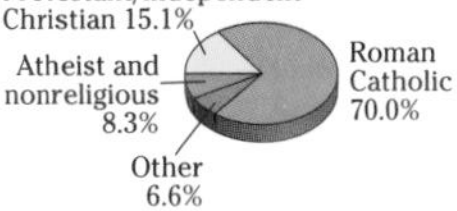

On Oct. 18, 1817, the flag was established for the new republic. The blue is for the sky, and the star is "a guide on the path of progress and honor." The white is for the snow of the Andes Mountains while the red recalls the blood of patriots. In the 15th century the Araucanian Indians gave red-white-blue sashes to their warriors.

Age Breakdown

The flag was hoisted on Oct. 1, 1949. The red is for communism and the Han Chinese. The large star was originally for the Communist Party, and the smaller stars were for the proletariat, the peasants, the petty bourgeoisie, and the "patriotic capitalists." The large star was later said to stand for China, the smaller stars for minorities.

Official name: People's Republic of China
Head of government: Premier
Official language: Mandarin Chinese
Monetary unit: Renminbi (yuan)
Area: 3,696,100 sq. mi. (9,572,900 sq. km.)
Population (2010): 1,338,085,000
GNI per capita (2009): U.S.$3,620
Principal exports (2008): machinery and apparatus 42.3%, of which computers 12.4%; garments 8.4%; chemicals and chemical products 5.5%; iron and steel 5.0% *to:* U.S. 17.7%; Hong Kong 13.3%; Japan 8.1%; South Korea 5.2%; Germany 4.2%

Official name: Republic of Colombia
Head of state and government: President
Official language: Spanish
Monetary unit: peso
Area: 440,831 sq. mi. (1,141,748 sq. km.)
Population (2010): 44,205,000
GNI per capita (2009): U.S.$4,950
Principal exports (2008): crude petroleum 24.7%, food 13.1%, coal 12.2%, chemicals 7.8%, refined petroleum 7.3%, iron and steel 3.3% *to:* U.S. 38.0%; Venezuela 16.2%; Ecuador 4.0%; Switzerland 2.5%; Peru 2.3%

Ethnic Composition

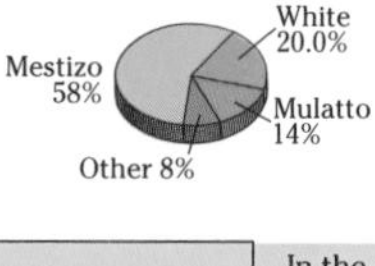

In the early 19th century "the Liberator" Simon Bolivar created a yellow-blue-red flag for New Granada (which included Colombia, Venezuela, Panama, and Ecuador). The flag symbolized the yellow gold of the New World separated by the blue ocean from the red of "bloody Spain." The present Colombian flag was established on Nov. 26, 1861.

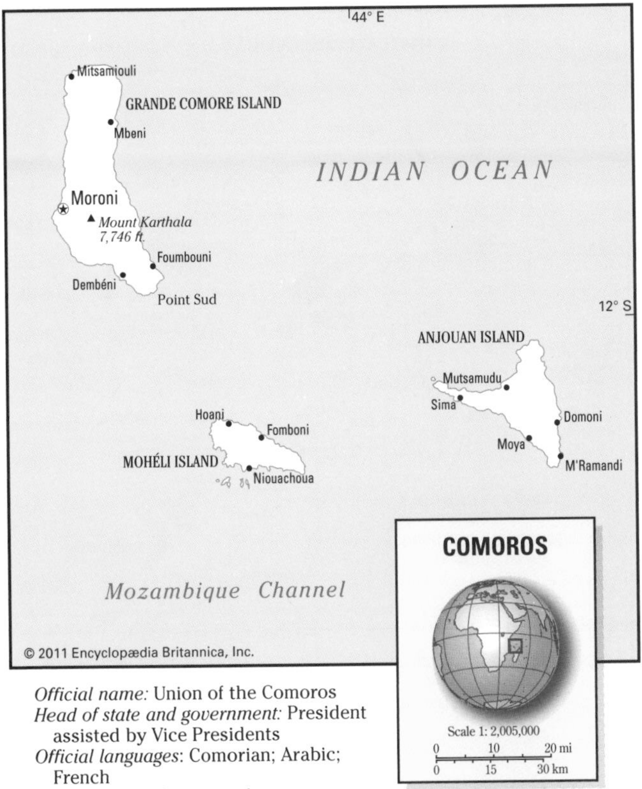

Official name: Union of the Comoros
Head of state and government: President assisted by Vice Presidents
Official languages: Comorian; Arabic; French
Monetary unit: Comorian franc
Area: 719 sq. mi. (1,862 sq. km.)
Population (2010): 691,000
GNI per capita (2009): U.S.$870
Principal exports (2008): ylang-ylang 26.6%, vanilla 21.3%, cloves 20.1% *to:* France *c.* 29%; Turkey *c.* 16%; Greece *c.* 12%; Brazil *c.* 10%

Age Breakdown

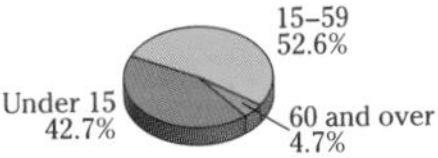

After more than 76 years of independence from France, and many different flags, on December 23, 2001, Comoros raised the current flag, in conjunction with a new constitution meant to ensure national unity. A variation of a design from 1963, its green background and its crescent reflect Islam, and its four white stars represent the islands in the Comoros archipelago.

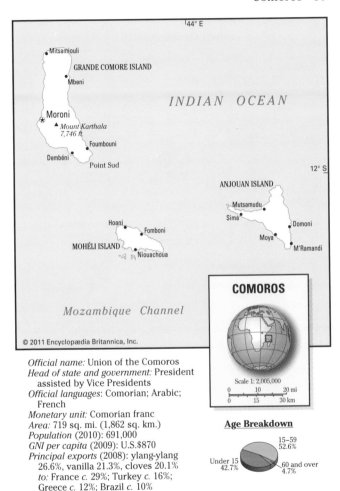

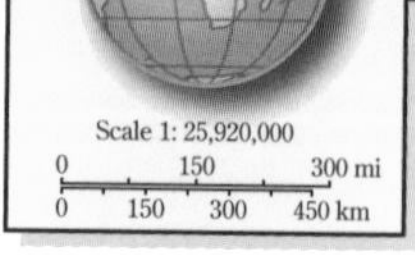

Ethnic Composition

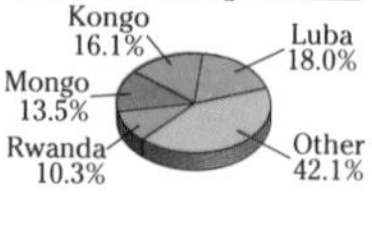

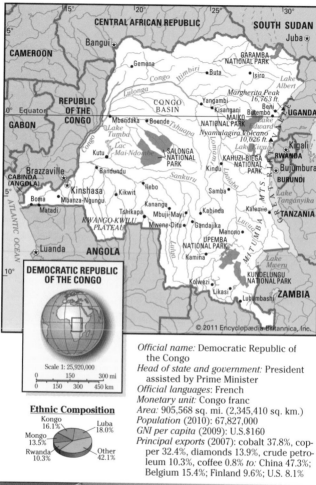

Official name: Democratic Republic of the Congo
Head of state and government: President assisted by Prime Minister
Official languages: French
Monetary unit: Congo franc
Area: 905,568 sq. mi. (2,345,410 sq. km.)
Population (2010): 67,827,000
GNI per capita (2009): U.S.$160
Principal exports (2007): cobalt 37.8%, copper 32.4%, diamonds 13.9%, crude petroleum 10.3%, coffee 0.8% *to:* China 47.3%; Belgium 15.4%; Finland 9.6%; U.S. 8.1%

Also called the flag of Congo-Kinshasa, the 1877 blue flag, with a star for light in the "Dark Continent," was returned February 18, 2006. Independent from Belgium in 1960, in 1971 Congo's name changed to Zaire, and there was a new flag. The revolution under the leadership of Laurent Kabila brought back the name of Congo in 1997.

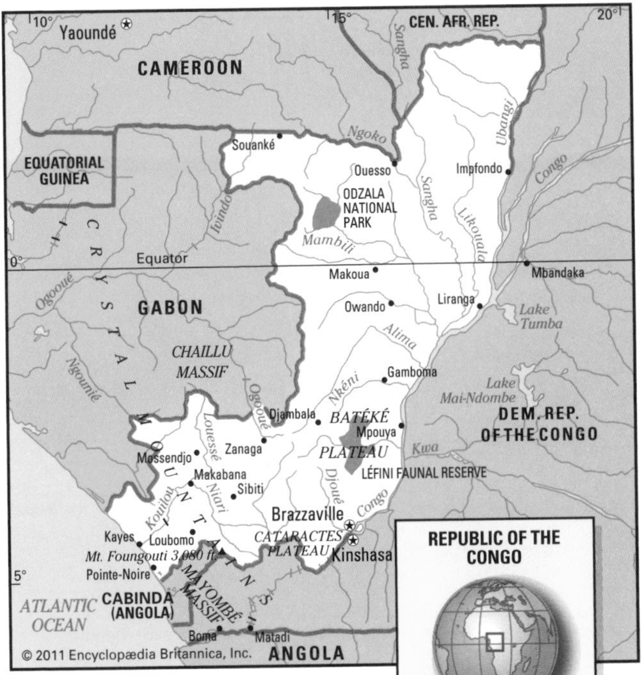

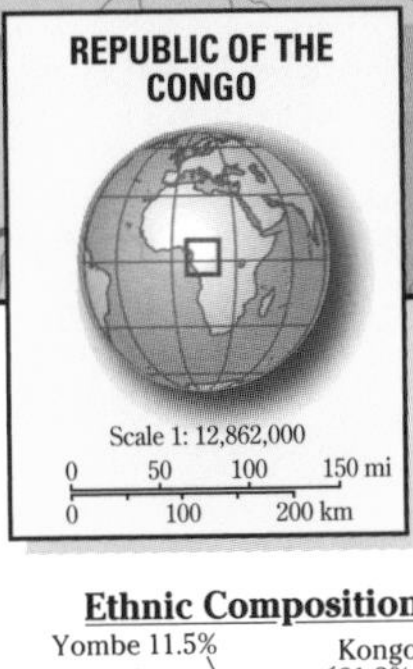

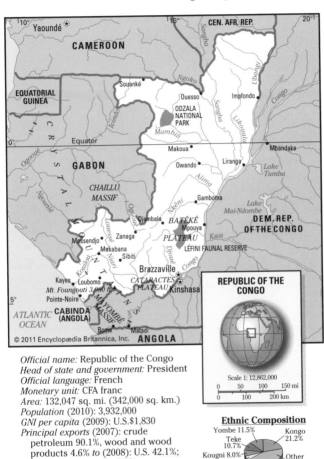

Official name: Republic of the Congo
Head of state and government: President
Official language: French
Monetary unit: CFA franc
Area: 132,047 sq. mi. (342,000 sq. km.)
Population (2010): 3,932,000
GNI per capita (2009): U.S.$1,830
Principal exports (2007): crude petroleum 90.1%, wood and wood products 4.6% *to* (2008): U.S. 42.1%; China 30.1%; France 5.6%

Ethnic Composition

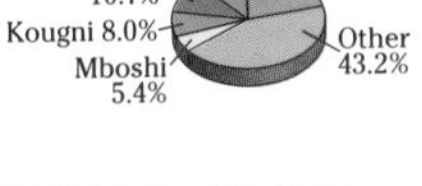

First adopted on Sept. 15, 1959, the flag uses the Pan-African colors. Green was originally said to stand for Congo's agriculture and forests, and yellow for friendship and the nobility of the people, but the red was unexplained. Altered in 1969 by a Marxist government, the flag was restored to its initial form on June 10, 1991.

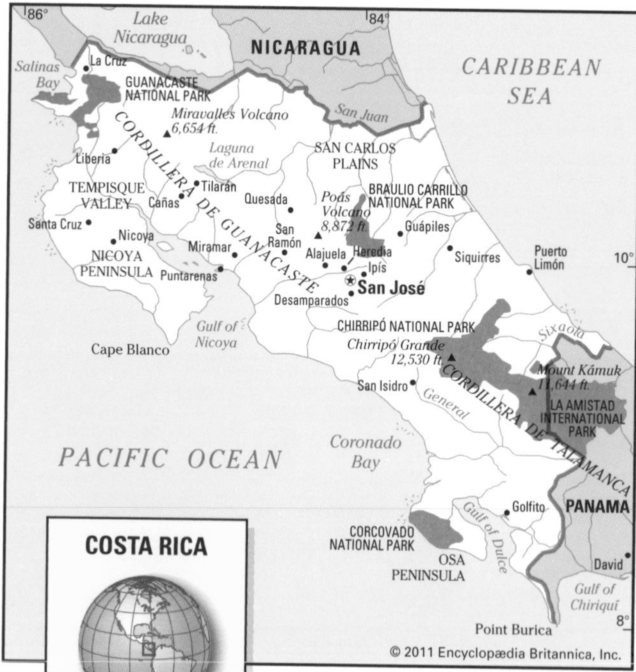

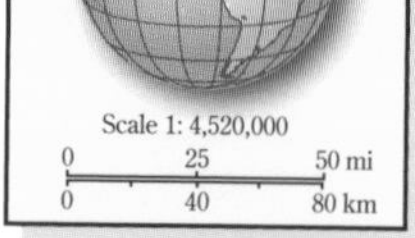

Official name: Republic of Costa Rica
Head of state and government: President
Official language: Spanish
Monetary unit: Costa Rican colón
Area: 19,730 sq. mi. (51,100 sq. km.)
Population (2010): 4,516,000
GNI per capita (2009): U.S.$6,260
Principal exports (2008): food 29.4%; office machines and computer parts 10.8%; electronic integrated circuits/micro-assemblies 10.7% *to:* United States 38.2%; China 6.3%; Netherlands 5.1%; Nicaragua 4.1%; Hong Kong 4.0%

Ethnic Composition

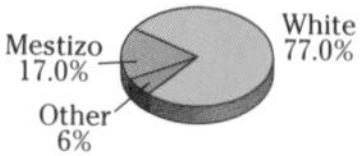

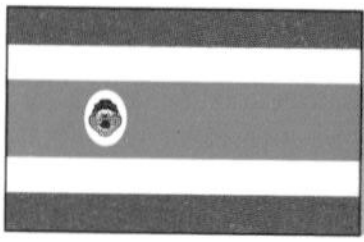

The blue and white stripes originated in the flag colors of the United Provinces of Central America (1823–40). On Sept. 29, 1848, the red stripe was added to symbolize sunlight, civilization, and "true independence." The current design of the coat of arms, which is included on government flags, was established in 1964.

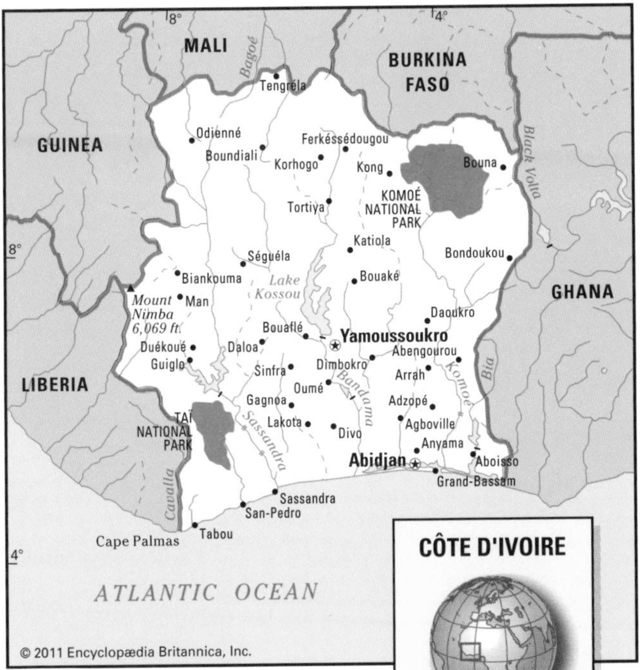

Official name: Republic of Côte d'Ivoire [Ivory Coast]
Head of state and government: President assisted by Prime Minister
Official language: French
Monetary unit: CFA franc
Area: 123,863 sq. mi. (320,803 sq. km.)
Population (2010): 21,059,000
GNI per capita (2009): U.S.$1,060
Principal exports (2008): cocoa [all forms] 27.0%, crude petroleum 15.6%, natural rubber 5.1% *to:* France 13.9%; Netherlands 11.3%; U.S. 9.7%; Germany 7.1%

Religious Affiliation

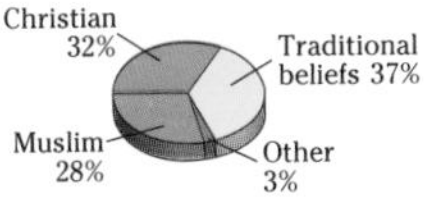

Adopted on Aug. 7, 1959, the flag of the former French colony has three stripes corresponding to the national motto (Unity, Discipline, Labor). The orange is for growth, the white is for peace emerging from purity and unity, and the green is for hope and the future. Unofficially the green is for forests and the orange is for savannas.

Official name: Republic of Croatia
Head of government: Prime Minister
Official language: Croatian
Monetary unit: kuna
Area: 21,831 sq. mi. (56,542 sq. km.)
Population (2010): 4,426,000
GNI per capita (2009): U.S.$13,810
Principal exports (2008): machinery and apparatus 18.2%, mineral fuels 12.9%, ships and boats 11.5%, chemical products 9.9%, food 7.4% *to:* Italy 19.1%; Bosnia and Herzegovina 15.4%; Germany 10.7%; Slovenia 7.8%; Austria 5.8%

Ethnic Composition

During the European uprisings of 1848, Croatians designed a flag based on that of Russia. In April 1941 the fascistic Ustasa used this flag, adding the checkered shield of Croatia. A communist star soon replaced the shield, but the current flag was adopted on Dec. 22, 1990. Atop the shield is a "crown" inlaid with historic coats of arms.

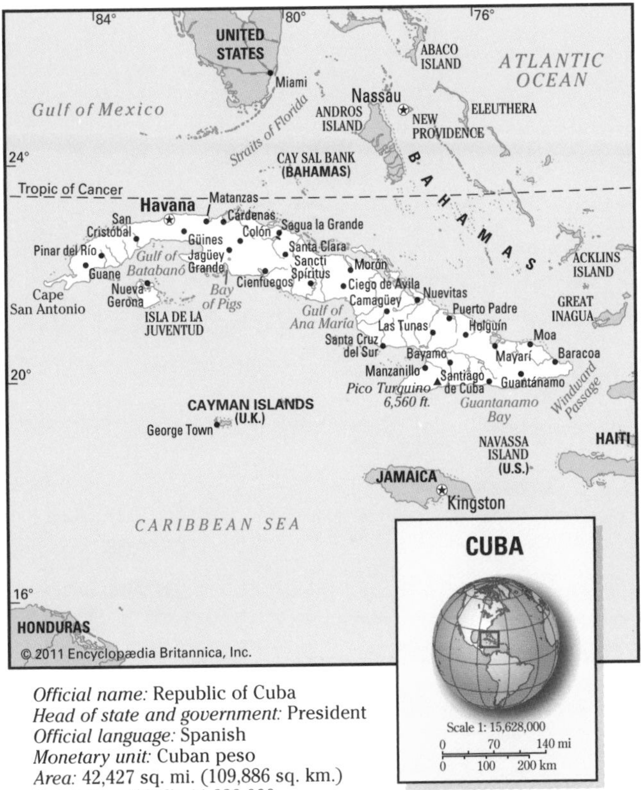

Official name: Republic of Cuba
Head of state and government: President
Official language: Spanish
Monetary unit: Cuban peso
Area: 42,427 sq. mi. (109,886 sq. km.)
Population (2010): 11,239,000
GNI per capita (2008): U.S.$5,512
Principal exports (2005): nickel oxide 46.3%, raw sugar 7.1%; cigars/cheroots/cigarillos 9.8%, medicine 9.1%; *to* (2008): Canada 20.9%; China 18.4%; Venezuela 11.3%; Netherlands 7.8%; Spain 5.4%

Religious Affiliation

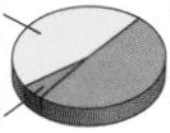

In the mid-19th century Cuban exiles designed the flag, which was later carried into battle against Spanish forces. It was adopted on May 20, 1902. The stripes were for the three military districts of Cuba and the purity of the patriotic cause. The red triangle was for strength, constancy, and equality, and the white star symbolized independence.

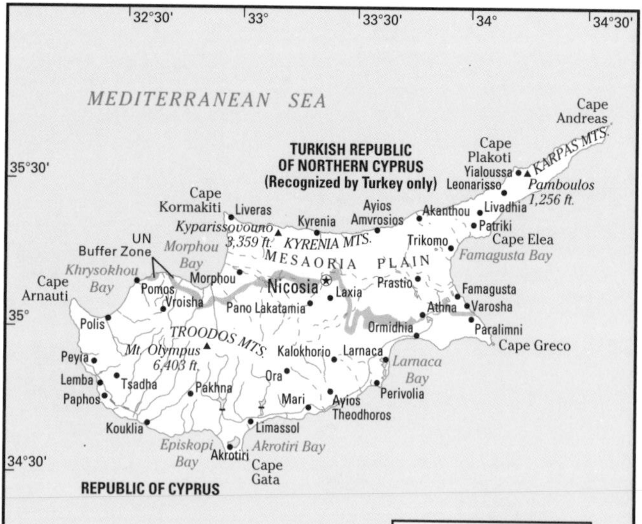

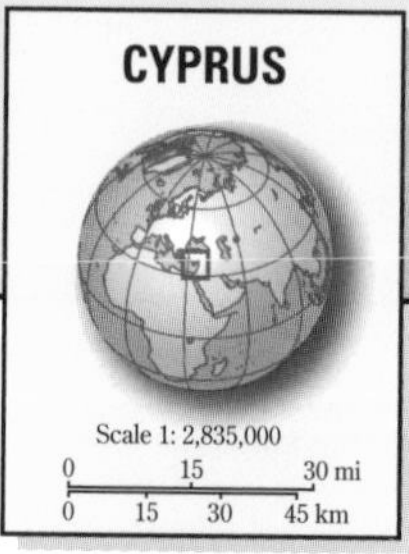

Official name: Republic of Cyprus
Head of state and government: President
Official languages: Greek; Turkish
Monetary unit: euro
Area: 2,276 sq. mi. (5,896 sq. km.)
Population (2010): 805,000
GNI per capita (2008): U.S.$29,100
Principal exports (2008): refined petroleum 19.8%, food 16.9%, medicine 9.2%, prostheses/body implants 6.1% *to:* Greece 18.8%; U.K. 10.2%; Germany 5.3%

Age Breakdown

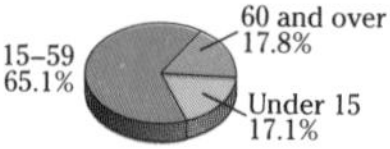

On Aug. 7, 1960, the Republic of Cyprus was proclaimed with a national flag of a neutral design. It bears the island in silhouette and a green olive wreath, for peace. In 1974 there was a Turkish invasion of the island. A puppet government, which adopted a flag based on the Turkish model, was set up on the northern third of Cyprus.

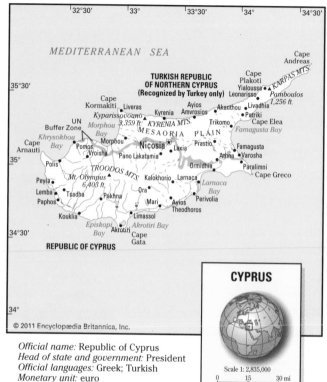

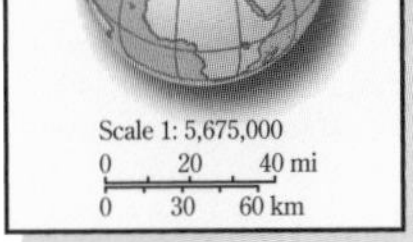

Official name: Czech Republic
Head of government: Prime Minister
Official language: Czech
Monetary unit: koruna
Area: 30,450 sq. mi. (78,865 sq. km.)
Population (2010): 10,526,000
GNI per capita (2009): U.S.$17,310
Principal exports (2008): machinery and apparatus 36.0%, motor vehicles 15.6%, base/manufactured metals 10.9%, chemicals 5.7% *to:* Germany 30.7%; Slovakia 9.2%; Poland 6.5%; France 5.3%; U.K. 4.8%

Ethnic Composition

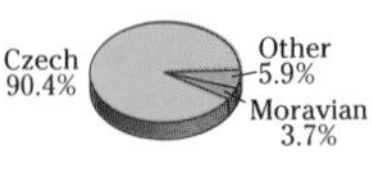

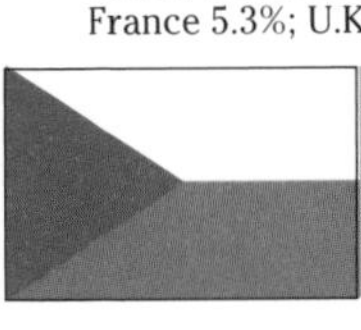

When Czechs, Slovaks, and Ruthenians united to form Czechoslovakia in 1918, a simple white-red bicolor flag was chosen; in 1920 it incorporated a blue triangle at the hoist. Czechoslovakia divided into Slovakia and the Czech Republic in 1993, but the latter country readopted the Czechoslovak flag as its own.

Official name: Kingdom of Denmark
Head of government: Prime Minister
Official language: Danish
Monetary unit: Danish krone
Area: 16,640 sq. mi. (43,098 sq. km.)
Population (2010): 5,546,000
GNI per capita (2009): U.S.$58,930
Principal exports (2008): machinery and apparatus 22.4%, food 15.7%, petroleum 8.9%, pharmaceuticals and medicine 6.9% *to:* Germany 17.5%; Sweden 14.6%; United Kingdom 8.1%; Norway 6.1%

Age Breakdown

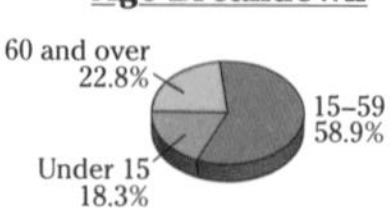

A traditional story claims that the Danish flag fell from heaven on June 15, 1219, but the previously existing war flag of the Holy Roman Empire was of a similar design, with its red field symbolizing battle and its white cross suggesting divine favor. In 1849 the state and military flag was altered and adopted as a symbol of the Danish people.

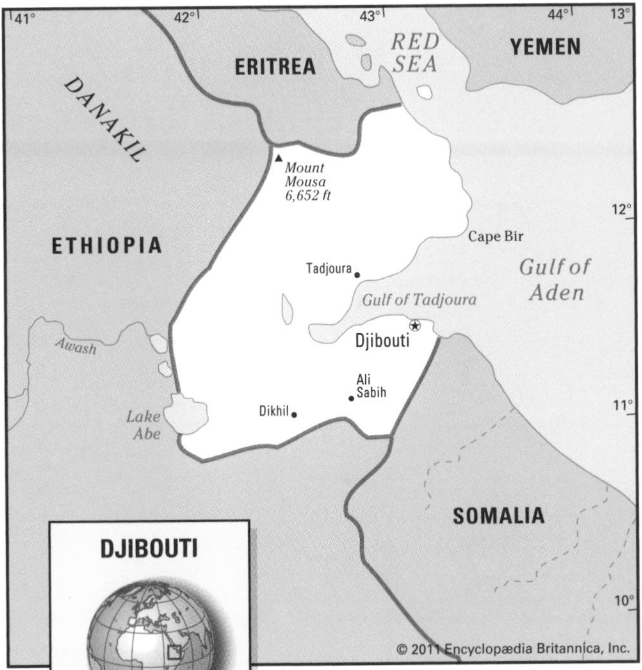

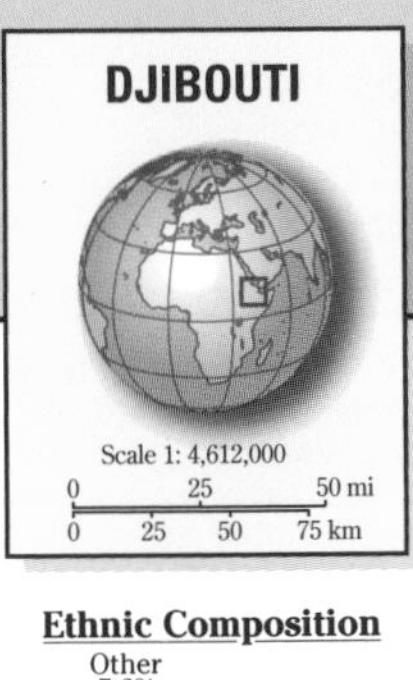

Official name: Republic of Djibouti
Head of state and government: President
Official languages: Arabic; French
Monetary unit: Djibouti franc
Area: 8,950 sq. mi. (23,200 sq. km.)
Population (2010): 833,000
GNI per capita (2009): U.S.$1,280
Principal exports: camels *c.* 32%, raw sugar *c.* 27%, cattle *c.* 26%, rice *c.* 6% *to* (2008): Somalia *c.* 80%; United Arab Emirates *c.* 4%; Yemen *c.* 4%

Ethnic Composition

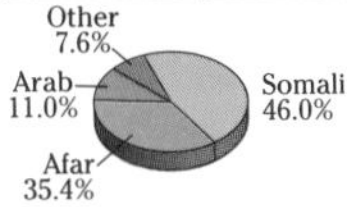

First raised by anti-French separatists, the flag was officially hoisted on June 27, 1977. The color of the Afar people, green, stands for prosperity. The color of the Issa people, light blue, symbolizes sea and sky, and recalls the flag of Somalia. The white triangle is for equality and peace; the red star is for unity and independence.

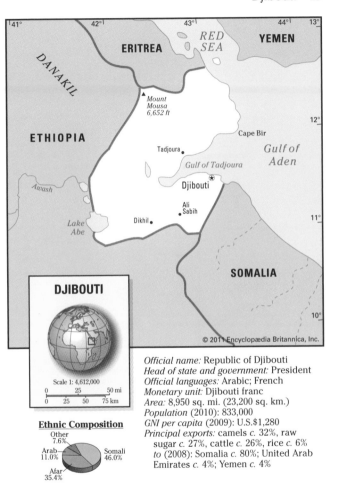

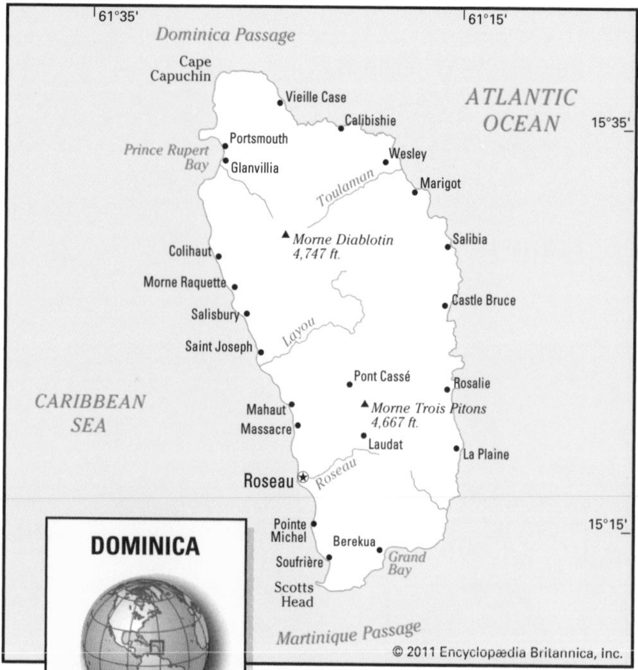

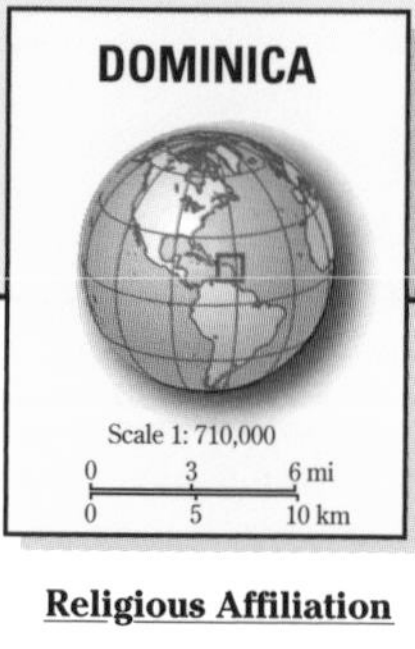

Official name: Commonwealth of Dominica
Head of government: Prime Minister
Official language: English
Monetary unit: East Caribbean dollar
Area: 285.3 sq. mi. (739.0 sq. km.)
Population (2010): 72,200
GNI per capita (2009): U.S.$4,900
Principal exports (2008): food 37.3%, soap 33.2%, pebbles/gravel/used cement aggregates 8.0% *to:* Jamaica 16.3%; Antigua and Barbuda 15.3%; France 13.8%; U.K. 13.3%; Trinidad and Tobago 8.8%

Religious Affiliation

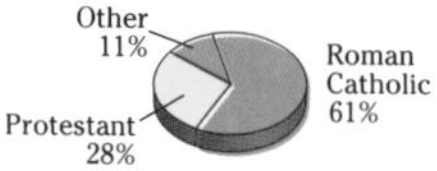

The flag was hoisted on Nov. 3, 1978, at independence from Britain. Its background symbolizes forests; its central disk is red for socialism and bears a sisserou (a rare local bird). The stars are for the parishes of the island. The cross of yellow, white, and black is for the Carib, Caucasian, and African peoples and for fruit, water, and soil.

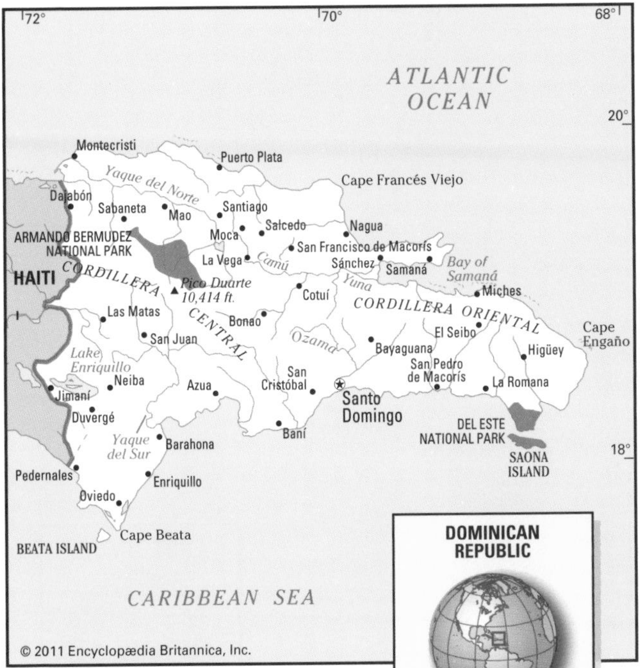

Official name: Dominican Republic
Head of state and government: President
Official language: Spanish
Monetary unit: Dominican peso
Area: 18,792 sq. mi. (48,671 sq. km.)
Population (2010): 9,884,000
GNI per capita (2009): U.S.$4,530
Principal exports (2008): food 11.1%, apparel and clothing accessories 11.0%, medical/surgical instruments 9.0% *to:* U.S. 61.0%; Haiti 10.2%; Netherlands 3.2%

Ethnic Composition

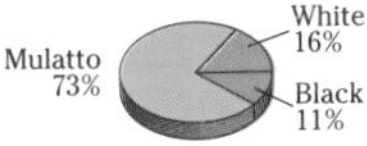

On Feb. 28, 1844, Spanish-speaking Dominican revolutionaries added a white cross to the simple blue-red flag of eastern Hispaniola, in order to emphasize their Christian heritage. On November 6 of that same year the new constitution established the flag, but with the colors at the fly end reversed so that the blue and red would alternate.

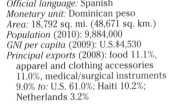

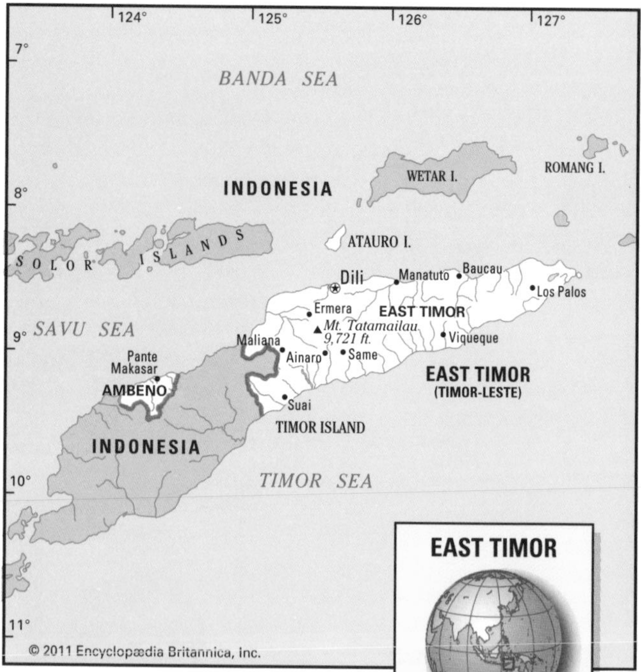

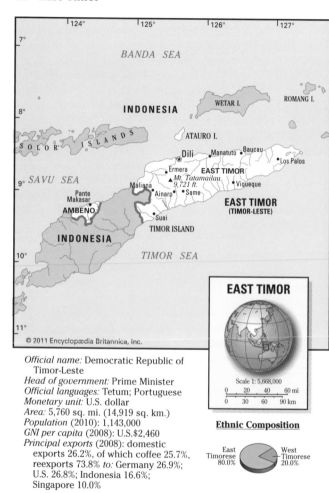

Official name: Democratic Republic of Timor-Leste
Head of government: Prime Minister
Official languages: Tetum; Portuguese
Monetary unit: U.S. dollar
Area: 5,760 sq. mi. (14,919 sq. km.)
Population (2010): 1,143,000
GNI per capita (2008): U.S.$2,460
Principal exports (2008): domestic exports 26.2%, of which coffee 25.7%, reexports 73.8% *to:* Germany 26.9%; U.S. 26.8%; Indonesia 16.6%; Singapore 10.0%

Ethnic Composition

After Indonesia's withdrawal in 1999, East Timor came under the UN flag. The new national flag was adopted on May 20, 2002, when East Timor gained full sovereignty. The black is for more than four centuries of colonial repression, the yellow the struggle for independence, and the red the suffering of the East Timorese. The white star symbolizes hope.

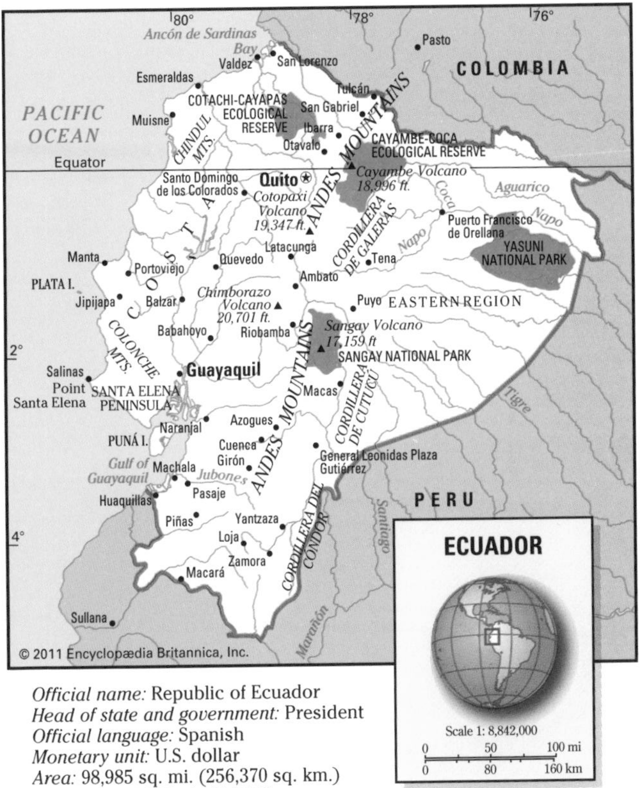

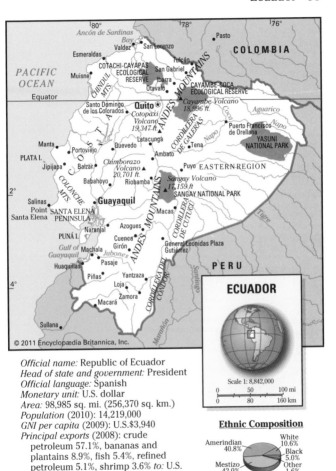

Official name: Republic of Ecuador
Head of state and government: President
Official language: Spanish
Monetary unit: U.S. dollar
Area: 98,985 sq. mi. (256,370 sq. km.)
Population (2010): 14,219,000
GNI per capita (2009): U.S.$3,940
Principal exports (2008): crude petroleum 57.1%, bananas and plantains 8.9%, fish 5.4%, refined petroleum 5.1%, shrimp 3.6% *to:* U.S. 45.3%; Peru 9.2%; Chile 8.1%; Panama 4.8%; Colombia 4.2%

Ethnic Composition

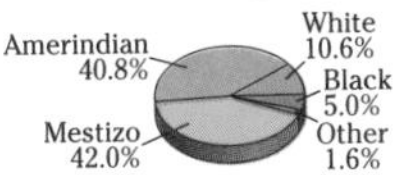

Victorious against the Spanish on May 24, 1822, Antonio José de Sucre hoisted a yellow-blue-red flag. Other flags were later used, but on Sept. 26, 1860, the current flag design was adopted. The coat of arms is displayed on the flag when it is used abroad or for official purposes, to distinguish it from the flag of Colombia.

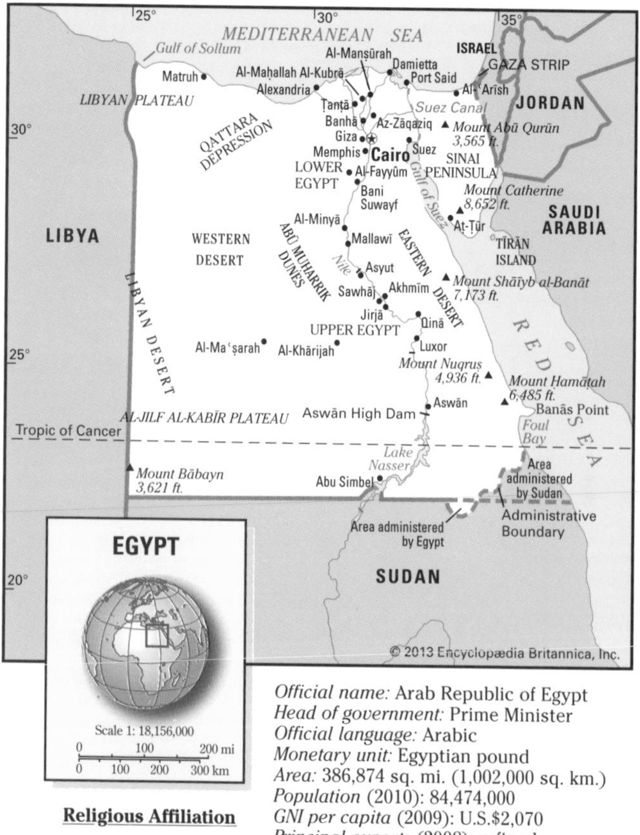

Official name: Arab Republic of Egypt
Head of government: Prime Minister
Official language: Arabic
Monetary unit: Egyptian pound
Area: 386,874 sq. mi. (1,002,000 sq. km.)
Population (2010): 84,474,000
GNI per capita (2009): U.S.$2,070
Principal exports (2008): refined petroleum 18.9%, LNG 13.7%, food products 9.6%, crude petroleum 8.4% *to:* India 6.3%; Spain 5.7%; Netherlands 5.7%; U.S. 4.9%

Religious Affiliation

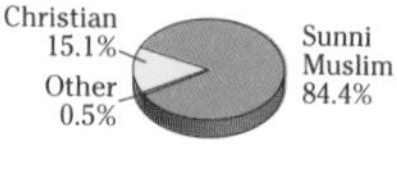

The 1952 revolt against British rule established the red-white-black flag with a central gold eagle. Two stars replaced the eagle in 1958, and in 1972 a federation with Syria and Libya was formed, adding instead the hawk of Quraysh (the tribe of Muhammad). On Oct. 9, 1984, the eagle of Saladin (a major 12th-century ruler) was substituted.

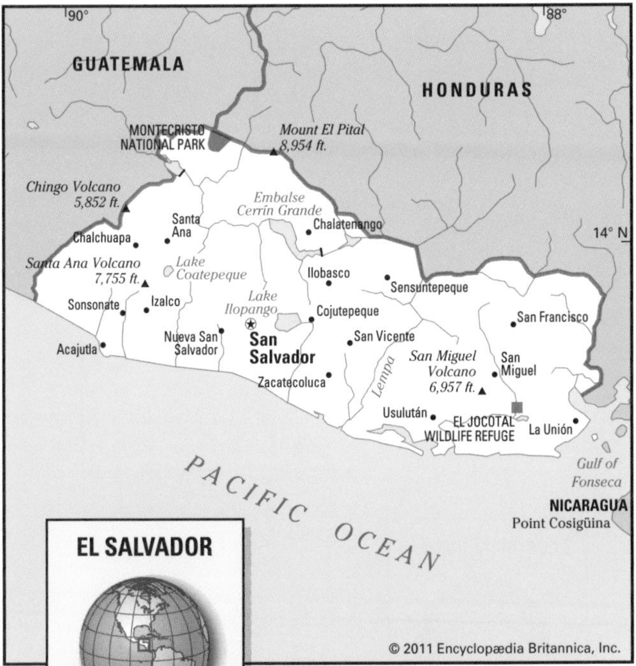

Age Breakdown

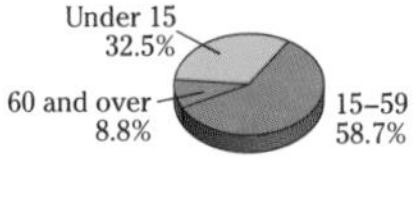

Official name: Republic of El Salvador
Head of state and government: President
Official language: Spanish
Monetary unit: U.S. dollar
Area: 8,124 sq. mi. (21,040 sq. km.)
Population (2010): 6,052,000
GNI per capita (2009): U.S.$3,370
Principal exports (2008): apparel and clothing accessories 34.7%, food 17.8%, paper and paper products 3.8% *to:* United States 48.1%; Guatemala 13.6%; Honduras 13.0%; Nicaragua 5.5%; Costa Rica 3.7%

In the early 19th century a blue-white-blue flag was designed for the short-lived United Provinces of Central America, in which El Salvador was a member. On Sept. 15, 1912, the flag was reintroduced in El Salvador. The coat of arms in the center resembles that used by the former federation and includes the national motto, "God, Union, Liberty."

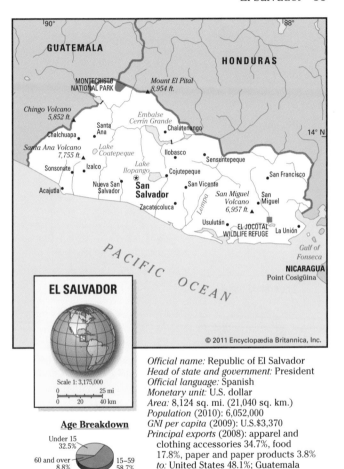

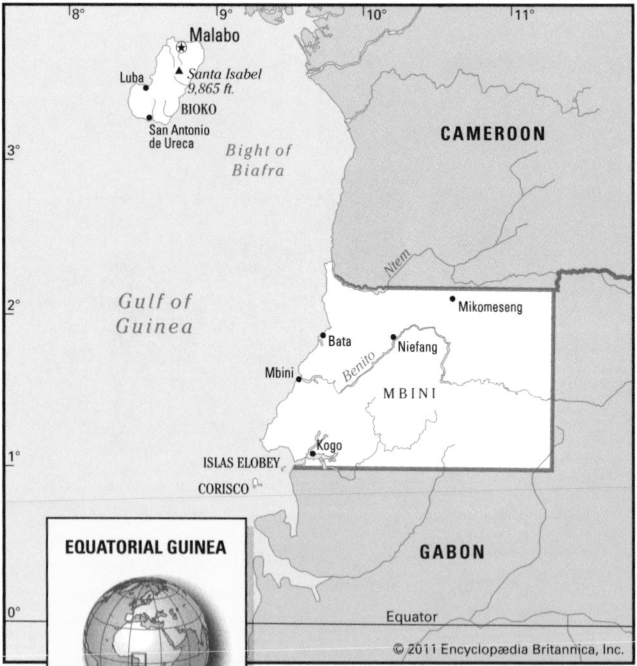

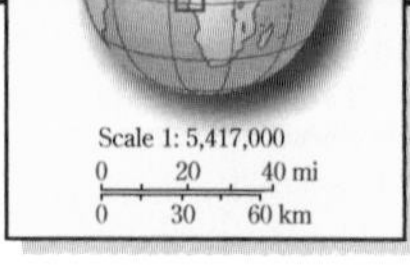

Ethnic Composition

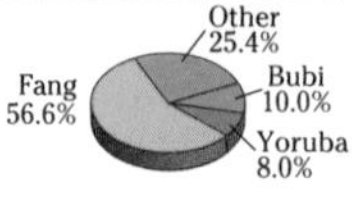

Official name: Republic of Equatorial Guinea
Head of state and government: Prime Minister
Official languages: Spanish, French
Monetary unit: CFA franc
Area: 10,831 sq. mi. (28,051 sq. km.)
Population (2010): 651,000
GNI per capita (2009): U.S.$12,420
Principal exports (2008): crude petroleum 78.1%, methol 21.2%, timber 0.4% *to:* U.S. *c.* 23%; Spain *c.* 18%; China *c.* 15%; Taiwan *c.* 11%; France *c.* 8%

The flag was first hoisted at independence (Oct. 12, 1968). Its coat of arms shows the silk-cotton tree, or god tree, which recalls early Spanish influence in the area. The sea, which links parts of the country, is reflected in the blue triangle. The green is for vegetation, white is for peace, and red is for the blood of martyrs in the liberation struggle.

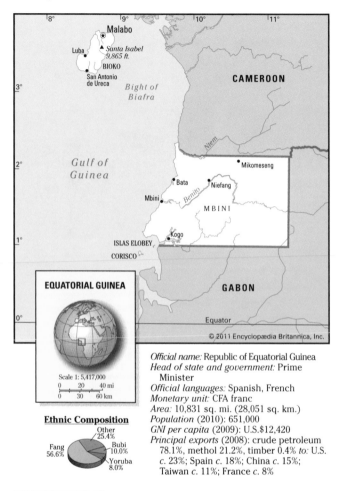

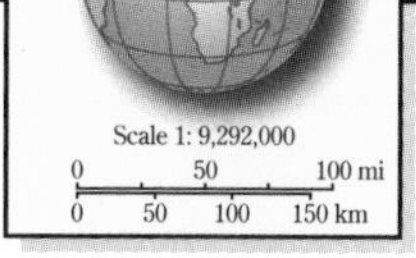

Ethnolinguistic Composition

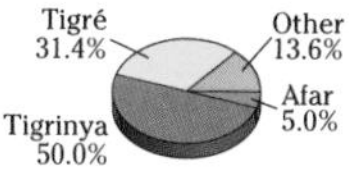

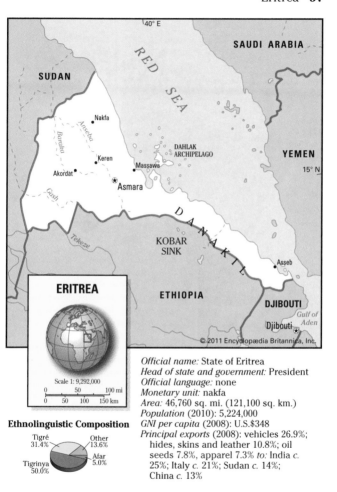

Official name: State of Eritrea
Head of state and government: President
Official language: none
Monetary unit: nakfa
Area: 46,760 sq. mi. (121,100 sq. km.)
Population (2010): 5,224,000
GNI per capita (2008): U.S.$348
Principal exports (2008): vehicles 26.9%; hides, skins and leather 10.8%; oil seeds 7.8%, apparel 7.3% *to:* India *c.* 25%; Italy *c.* 21%; Sudan *c.* 14%; China *c.* 13%

Officially hoisted at the proclamation of independence on May 24, 1993, the national flag was based on that of the Eritrean People's Liberation Front. The red triangle is for the blood of patriots, the green is for agriculture, and the blue is for maritime resources. Around a central branch is a circle of olive branches with 30 leaves.

Official name: Republic of Estonia
Head of government: Prime Minister
Official language: Estonian
Monetary unit: kroon
Area: 16,769 sq. mi. (43,432 sq. km.)
Population (2010): 1,340,000
GNI per capita (2009): U.S.$14,060
Principal exports (2004): machinery and apparatus 20.0%, sawn wood/wood manufactures 11.1%, refined petroleum 9.7%, road vehicles/parts 7.3% *to:* Finland 16.7%; Russia 15.1%; Sweden 12.6%; Latvia 9.1%

Ethnic Composition

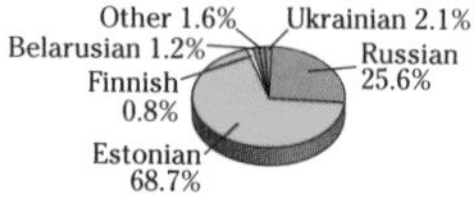

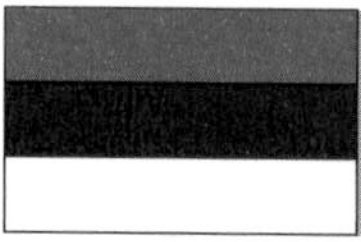

In the late 19th century an Estonian students' association adopted the blue-black-white flag. Blue was said to stand for the sky, black for the soil, and white for aspirations to freedom and homeland. The flag was officially recognized on July 4, 1920. It was replaced under Soviet rule, and readopted on Oct. 20, 1988.

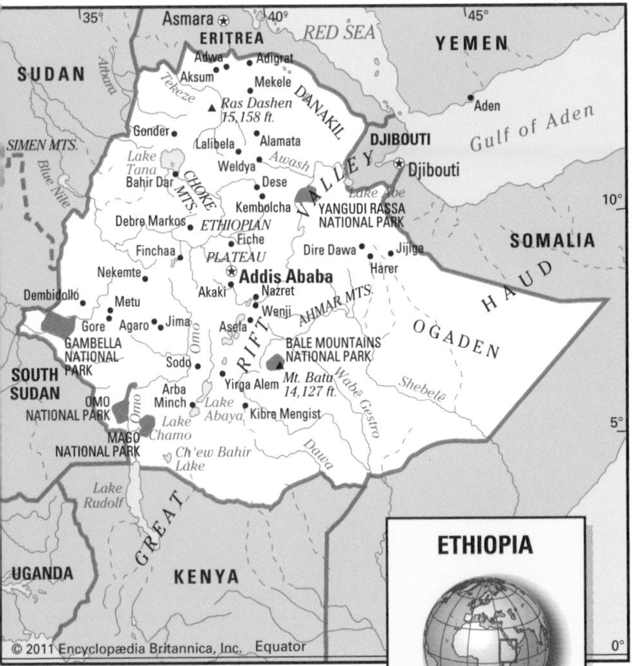

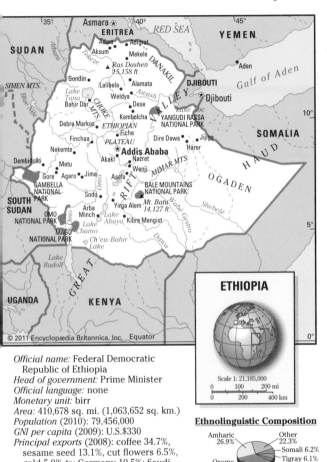

Official name: Federal Democratic Republic of Ethiopia
Head of government: Prime Minister
Official language: none
Monetary unit: birr
Area: 410,678 sq. mi. (1,063,652 sq. km.)
Population (2010): 79,456,000
GNI per capita (2009): U.S.$330
Principal exports (2008): coffee 34.7%, sesame seed 13.1%, cut flowers 6.5%, gold 5.0% *to:* Germany 10.5%; Saudi Arabia 7.7%; Netherlands 7.4%; U.S. 7.2%; Switzerland 6.2%

Ethnolinguistic Composition

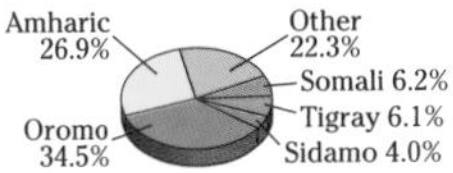

The flag is red (for sacrifice), green (for labor, development, and fertility), and yellow (for hope, justice, and equality). Tricolor pennants were used prior to the official flag of Oct. 6, 1897, and a tricolor was flown by antigovernment forces in 1991. On Feb. 6, 1996, the disk (for peace) and star (for unity and the future) were added.

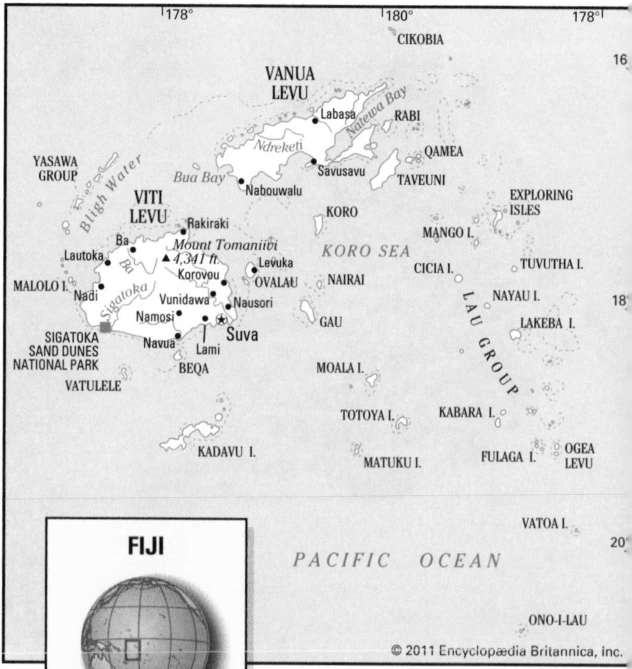

Official name: Republic of the Fiji Islands
Head of government: Prime Minister
Official languages: English, Fijian, and Hindustani have equal status
Monetary unit: Fiji dollar
Area: 7,055 sq. mi. (18,272 sq. km.)
Population (2010): 844,000
GNI per capita (2009): U.S.$3,950
Principal exports (2004): reexports [mostly petroleum products] 33.2%, sugar 16.9%, fish 9.1%, mineral water 9.1%, clothing 6.9% *to:* U.K. 14.9%; Australia 12.3%; U.S. 12.2%; other islands 10.5%; New Zealand 5.6%

Ethnic Composition

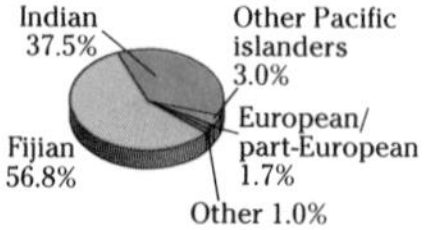

The national flag, introduced on Oct. 10, 1970, is a modified version of Fiji's colonial flag. It includes the Union Jack on a light blue field. The shield has the red cross of St. George on a white background, below a yellow lion, which holds a cocoa pod. Local symbols (sugar cane, coconuts, bananas, and the Fiji dove) are also shown.

Official name: Republic of Finland
Head of government: Prime Minister
National languages: Finnish; Swedish
Monetary unit: euro
Area: 130,666 sq. mi. (338,424 sq. km.)
Population (2010): 5,364,000
GNI per capita (2009): U.S.$45,680
Principal exports (2008): telecommunications equipment 13.4%, paper and cardboard 11.4%, iron and steel 7.0%, specialized machinery 6.7%, refined petroleum 6.5% *to:* Russia 11.6%; Sweden 10.1%; Germany 10.0%; U.S. 6.3%; U.K. 5.5%

Religious Affiliation

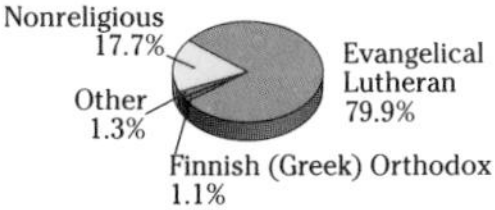

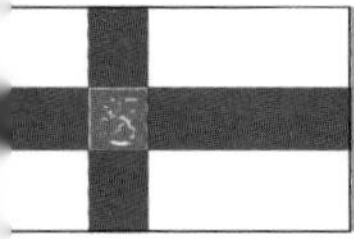

In 1862, while Finland was under Russian control, a flag was proposed that would have a white background for the snows of Finland and blue for its lakes. The blue was in the form of a "Nordic cross" similar to those used by other Scandinavian countries. The flag was officially adopted by the newly independent country on May 29, 1918.

Official name: French Republic
Head of government: Prime Minister
Official language: French
Monetary unit: euro
Area: 210,026 sq. mi. (543,965 sq. km.)
Population (2010): 62,962,000
GNI per capita (2009): U.S.$43,990
Principal exports (2008): machinery and apparatus 24.9%, chemical products 16.8%, road vehicles/parts 10.1%, food 8.2%; aircraft/parts 6.4%; mineral fuels 5.1% *to:* Germany 14.6%; Italy 8.8%; Spain 8.4%; U.K. 7.9%; Belguim 7.6%

Religious Affiliation

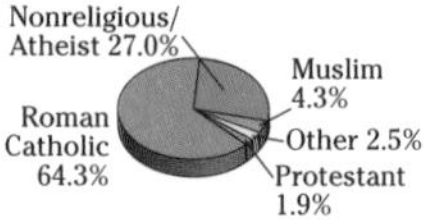

From 1789 blue and red, the traditional colors of Paris, were included in flags with Bourbon royal white. In 1794 the tricolor was made official. It embodied liberty, equality, fraternity, democracy, secularism, and modernization, but there is no symbolism attached to the individual colors. It has been the sole national flag since March 5, 1848.

Official name: Gabonese Republic
Head of government: Prime Minister
Official language: French
Monetary unit: CFA franc
Area: 103,347 sq. mi. (267,667 sq. km.)
Population (2010): 1,501,000
GNI per capita (2009): U.S.$7,370
Principal exports (2008): petroleum 76.4%, manganese ore 14.7%, wood 5.3% *to:* United States 51.8%; China 13.2%; India 6.4%; France 6.0%; Netherlands 3.6%

Ethnic Composition

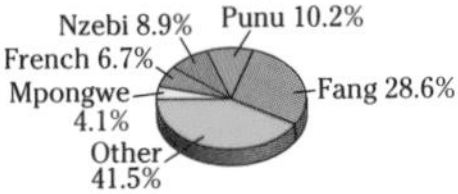

After proclaiming independence from France, Gabon adopted its national flag on Aug. 9, 1960. The central yellow stripe is for the Equator, which runs through the country. Green stands for the tropical forests that are one of Gabon's most important resources. Blue represents its extensive coast along the South Atlantic Ocean.

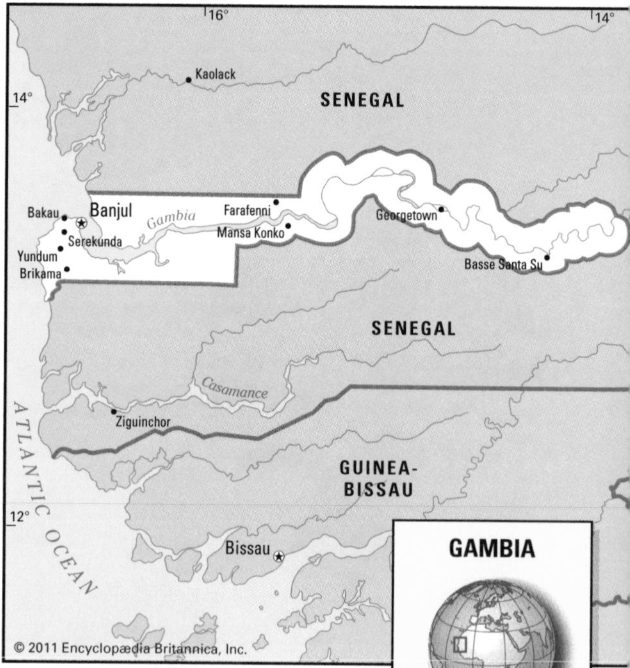

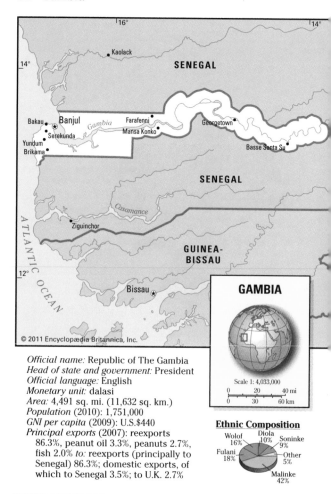

© 2011 Encyclopædia Britannica, Inc.

Official name: Republic of The Gambia
Head of state and government: President
Official language: English
Monetary unit: dalasi
Area: 4,491 sq. mi. (11,632 sq. km.)
Population (2010): 1,751,000
GNI per capita (2009): U.S.$440
Principal exports (2007): reexports 86.3%, peanut oil 3.3%, peanuts 2.7%, fish 2.0% *to:* reexports (principally to Senegal) 86.3%; domestic exports, of which to Senegal 3.5%; to U.K. 2.7%

Ethnic Composition

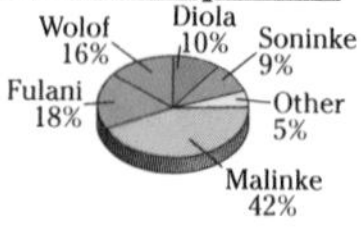

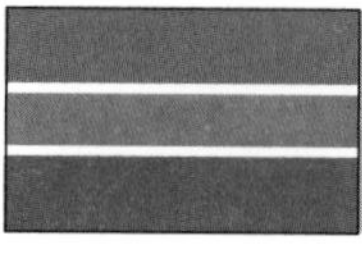

The Gambia achieved independence from Britain on Feb. 18, 1965, under the current flag. The center stripe is blue to symbolize the Gambia River. The red stripe is for the sun and the equator. The green stripe is for agricultural produce (peanuts, grains, and citrus fruits), while the white stripes are said to stand for peace and unity.

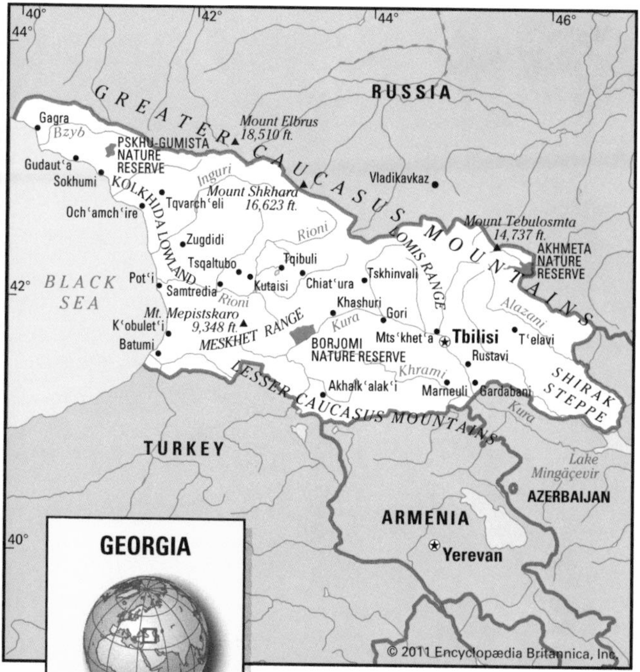

Ethnic Composition

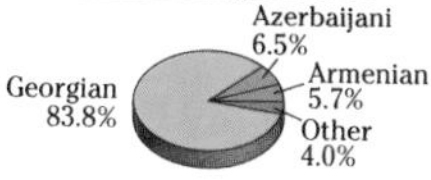

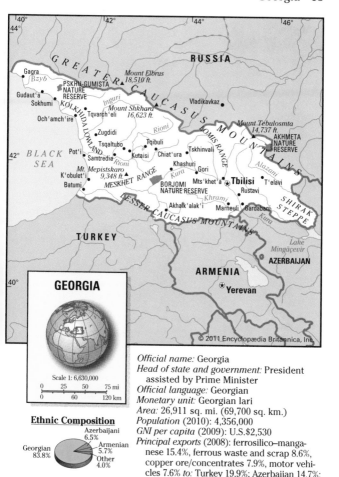

Official name: Georgia
Head of state and government: President assisted by Prime Minister
Official language: Georgian
Monetary unit: Georgian lari
Area: 26,911 sq. mi. (69,700 sq. km.)
Population (2010): 4,356,000
GNI per capita (2009): U.S.$2,530
Principal exports (2008): ferrosilico–manganese 15.4%, ferrous waste and scrap 8.6%, copper ore/concentrates 7.9%, motor vehicles 7.6% *to:* Turkey 19.9%; Azerbaijan 14.7%; Canada 10.3%; Armenia 8.2%; Ukraine 7.4%

Although independent from Russia in 1991, Georgia adopted this flag only on January 14, 2004, after the next government change. The Cross of St. George and four smaller ones on this flag probably first were used in the 14th century, but Russia suppressed all such designs when annexing Georgia in 1801. Cherry red is the national color, and white stands for hope.

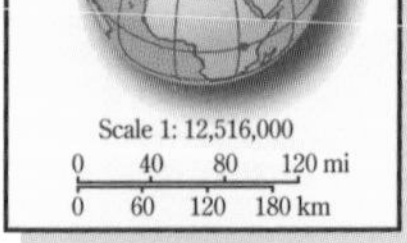

Official name: Federal Republic of Germany
Head of government: Chancellor
Official language: German
Monetary unit: euro
Area: 137,879 sq. mi. (357,104 sq. km.)
Population (2010): 81,644,000
GNI per capita (2009): U.S.$42,560
Principal exports (2008): machinery 27.9%, transport equipment 18.3%, chemicals and chemical products 14.6%, manufactured goods 13.8% *to:* France 9.7%; U.S. 7.2%; U.K. 6.7%; Netherlands 6.6%; Italy 6.4%; Austria 5.4%

Age Breakdown

In the early 19th century German nationalists displayed black, gold, and red on their uniforms and tricolor flags. The current flag was used officially from 1848 to 1852 and re-adopted by West Germany on May 9, 1949. East Germany flew a similar flag but only the flag of West Germany was maintained upon reunification in 1990.

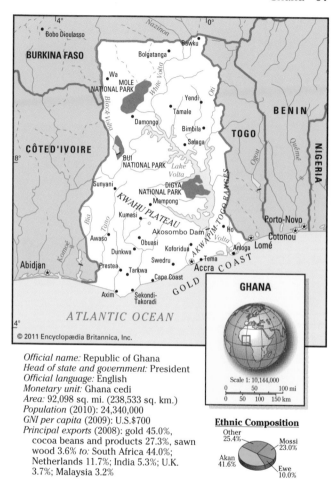

Official name: Republic of Ghana
Head of state and government: President
Official language: English
Monetary unit: Ghana cedi
Area: 92,098 sq. mi. (238,533 sq. km.)
Population (2010): 24,340,000
GNI per capita (2009): U.S.$700
Principal exports (2008): gold 45.0%, cocoa beans and products 27.3%, sawn wood 3.6% *to:* South Africa 44.0%; Netherlands 11.7%; India 5.3%; U.K. 3.7%; Malaysia 3.2%

Ethnic Composition

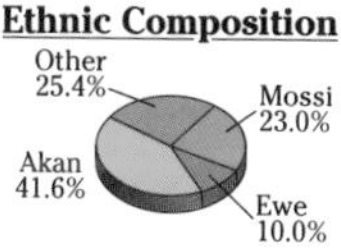

On March 6, 1957, independence from Britain was granted and a flag, based on the red-white-green tricolor of a nationalist organization, was hoisted. A black "lodestar of African freedom" was added and the white stripe was changed to yellow, symbolizing wealth. Green is for forests and farms, red for the independence struggle.

Official name: Hellenic Republic
Head of government: Prime Minister
Official language: Greek
Monetary unit: euro
Area: 50,949 sq. mi. (131,957 sq. km.)
Population (2010): 11,329,000
GNI per capita (2009): U.S.$28,630
Principal exports (2008): food 15.6%, of which fruits and vegetables 7.7%, machinery and apparatus 10.6%, refined petroleum 10.1%, apparel 6.0% *to:* Italy 11.5%; Germany 10.5%; Bulgaria 7.1%; Cyprus 6.4%; U.S. 5.1%

Age Breakdown

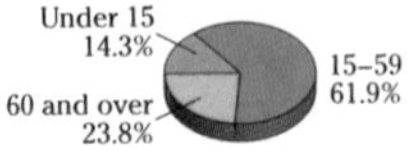

In March 1822, during the revolt against Ottoman rule, the first Greek national flags were adopted; the most recent revision to the flag was made on Dec. 22, 1978. The colors symbolize Greek Orthodoxy while the cross stands for "the wisdom of God, freedom and country." The stripes are for the battle cry for independence: "Freedom or Death."

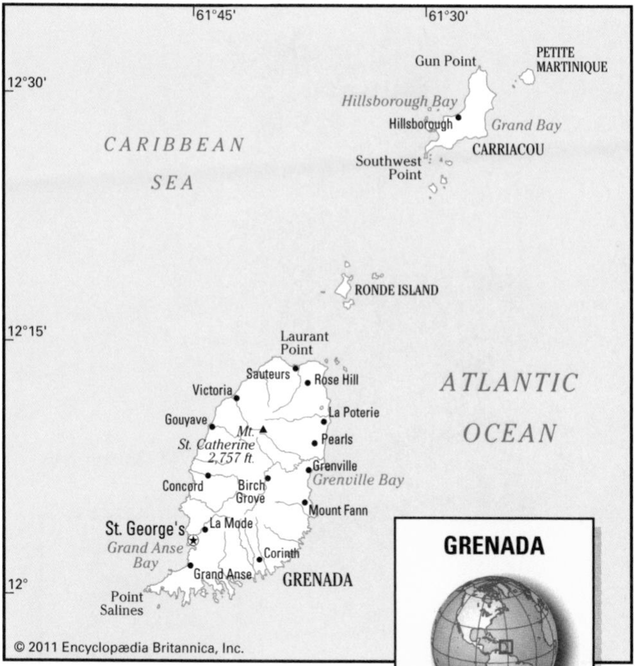

Official name: Grenada
Head of government: Prime Minister
Official language: English
Monetary unit: East Caribbean dollar
Area: 133 sq. mi. (344 sq. km.)
Population (2010): 108,000
GNI per capita (2009): U.S.$5,580
Principal exports (2008): food 57.0%, of which spices 8.9%, tuna 8.5%; toliet paper 9.5%; general industrial machinery 4.5% *to:* U.S. 16.4%; Dominica 16.4%; Saint Lucia 11.1%; Barbados 9.5%; St. Kitts and Nevis 8.5%

Religious Affiliation

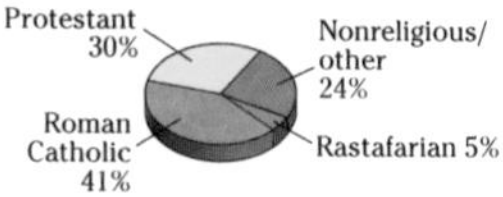

Grenada's flag was officially hoisted on Feb. 3, 1974. Its background is green for vegetation and yellow for the sun, and its red border is symbolic of harmony and unity. The seven stars are for the original administrative subdivisions of Grenada. Nutmeg, a crop for which the "Isle of Spice" is internationally known, is represented as well.

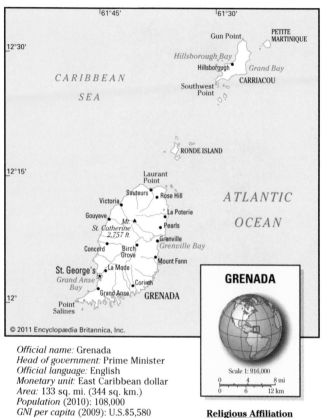

Official name: Republic of Guatemala
Head of state and government: President
Official language: Spanish
Monetary unit: quetzal
Area: 42,130 sq. mi. (109,117 sq. km.)
Population (2010): 14,377,000
GNI per capita (2009): U.S.$2,630
Principal exports (2008): food products 32.1%, of which coffee 8.4%, raw sugar 4.9%, bananas 4.4%; apparel 15.9%; crude petroleum 4.8% *to:* United States 39.4%; El Salvador 12.6%; Honduras 9.5%; Mexico 6.6%; Nicaragua 4.2%

Ethnic Composition

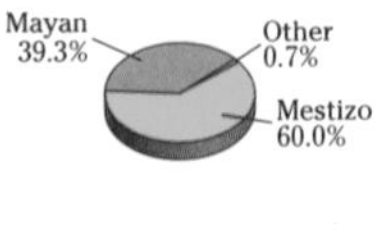

The flag was introduced in 1871. It has blue and white stripes (colors of the former United Provinces of Central America) and a coat of arms with the quetzal (the national bird), a scroll, a wreath, and crossed rifles and sabres. Different artistic variations have been used but on Sept. 12, 1968, the present pattern was established.

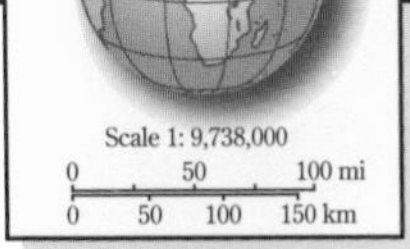

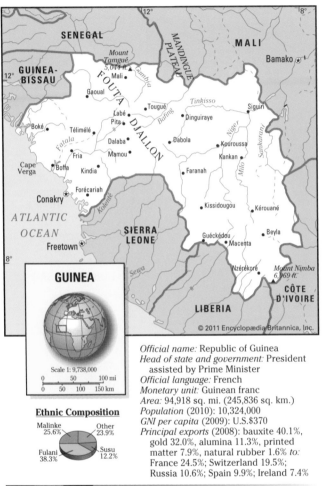

Official name: Republic of Guinea
Head of state and government: President assisted by Prime Minister
Official language: French
Monetary unit: Guinean franc
Area: 94,918 sq. mi. (245,836 sq. km.)
Population (2010): 10,324,000
GNI per capita (2009): U.S.$370
Principal exports (2008): bauxite 40.1%, gold 32.0%, alumina 11.3%, printed matter 7.9%, natural rubber 1.6% *to:* France 24.5%; Switzerland 19.5%; Russia 10.6%; Spain 9.9%; Ireland 7.4%

Ethnic Composition

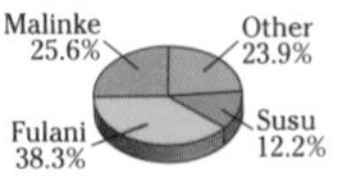

The flag was adopted on Nov. 12, 1958, one month after independence from France. Its simple design was influenced by the French tricolor. The red is said to be a symbol of sacrifice and labor, while the yellow is for mineral wealth, the tropical sun, and justice. Green symbolizes agricultural wealth and the solidarity of the people.

© 2011 Encyclopædia Britannica, Inc.

Official name: Republic of Guinea-Bissau
Head of state and government: President assisted by Prime Minister
Official language: Portuguese
Monetary unit: CFA franc
Area: 13,948 sq. mi. (36,125 sq. km.)
Population (2010): 1,593,000
GNI per capita (2009): U.S.$510
Principal exports (2008): cashews 86.3%, fish and shrimp 18.5% *to:* India *c.* 64%; Nigeria *c.* 30%

Ethnic Composition

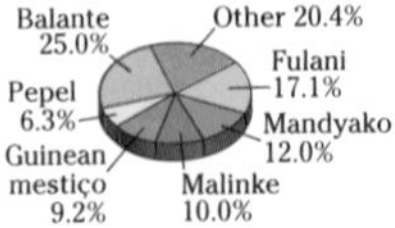

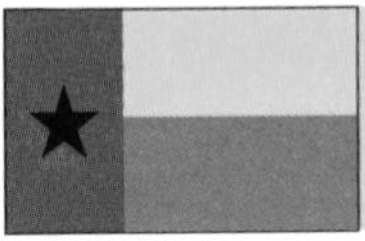

The flag has been used since the declaration of independence from Portugal on Sept. 24, 1973. The black star on the red stripe was for African Party leadership, the people, and their will to live in dignity, freedom, and peace. Yellow was for the harvest and other rewards of work, and green was for the nation's vast jungles and agricultural lands.

Official name: Co-operative Republic of Guyana
Head of state and government: President
Official language: English
Monetary unit: Guyanese dollar
Area: 83,012 sq. mi. (214,999 sq. km.)
Population (2010): 748,000
GNI per capita (2008): U.S.$1,420
Principal exports (2008): gold 22.7%, bauxite 22.3%, raw cane sugar 13.9%, rice 13.0%, shrimp 4.7%, Sawn wood 4.1%, diamonds 3.5% *to:* Canada 22.5%; U.S. 17.5%; U.K. 13.5%; Ukraine 5.4%; Jamaica 4.8%

Religious Affiliation

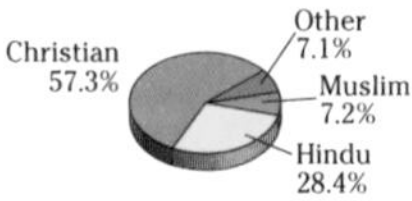

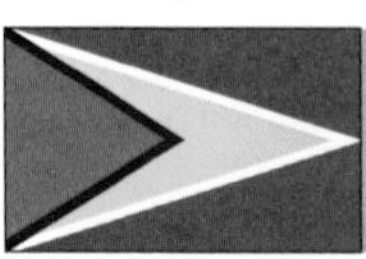

Upon independence from Britain on May 26, 1966, the flag was first hoisted. The green stands for jungles and fields, white suggests the rivers which are the basis for the Indian word guiana ("land of waters"), red is for zeal and sacrifice in nation-building, and black is for perseverance. The flag is nicknamed "The Golden Arrowhead."

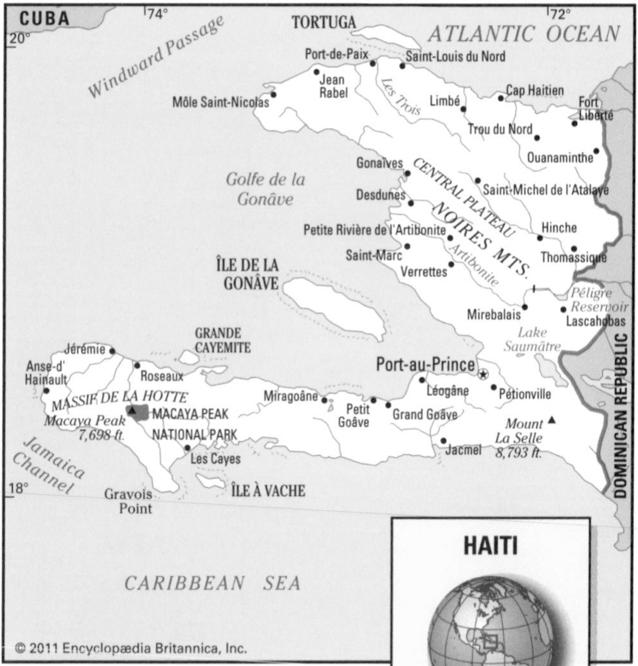

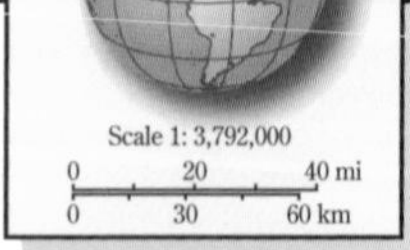

Official name: Republic of Haiti
Head of government: Prime Minister
Official languages: Haitian Creole; French
Monetary unit: gourde
Area: 10,695 sq. mi. (27,700 sq. km.)
Population (2010): 9,649,000
GNI per capita (2008): U.S.$660
Principal exports (2009): reassembled manufactures 89.3%, mangoes 1.9%, essentials oils 1.8%, cacao 1.4% *to:* United States *c.* 70%; Dominican Republic *c.* 9%; Canada *c.* 3%

Religious Affiliation

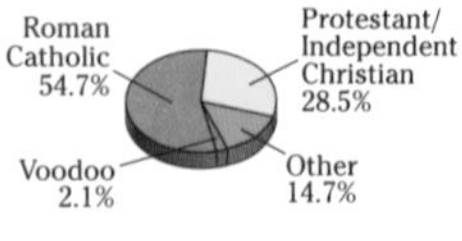

After the French Revolution of 1789 Haiti underwent a slave revolt, but the French tricolor continued in use until 1803. The new blue-red flag represented the black and mulatto populations only. A black-red flag was used by various dictators, including François "Papa Doc" Duvalier and his son, but on Feb. 25, 1986, the old flag was reestablished.

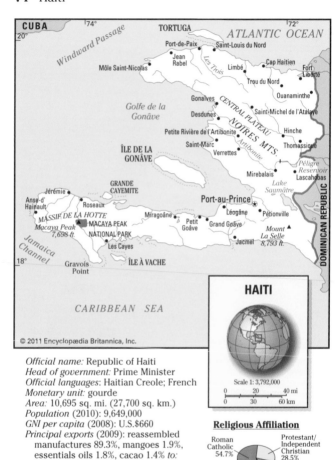

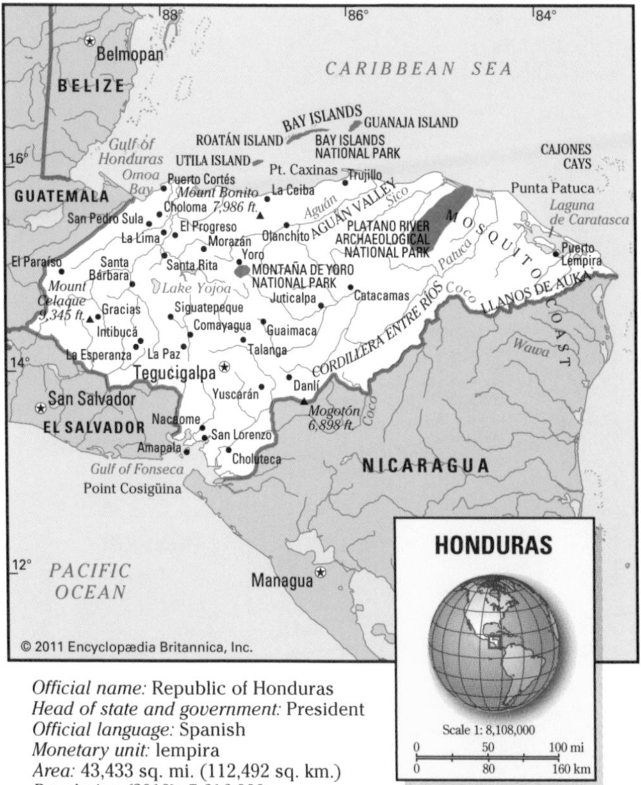

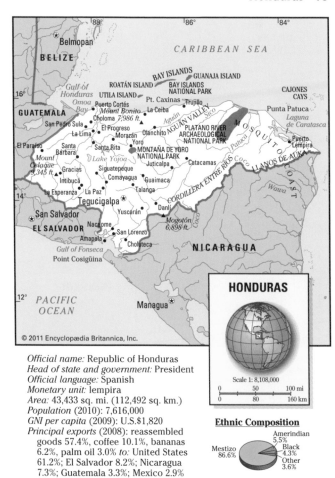

© 2011 Encyclopædia Britannica, Inc.

Official name: Republic of Honduras
Head of state and government: President
Official language: Spanish
Monetary unit: lempira
Area: 43,433 sq. mi. (112,492 sq. km.)
Population (2010): 7,616,000
GNI per capita (2009): U.S.$1,820
Principal exports (2008): reassembled goods 57.4%, coffee 10.1%, bananas 6.2%, palm oil 3.0% *to:* United States 61.2%; El Salvador 8.2%; Nicaragua 7.3%; Guatemala 3.3%; Mexico 2.9%

Ethnic Composition

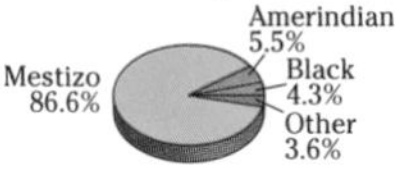

Since Feb. 16, 1866, the Honduran flag has retained the blue-white-blue design of the flag of the former United Provinces of Central America, but with five central stars symbolizing the states of Honduras, El Salvador, Nicaragua, Costa Rica, and Guatemala. The flag design has often been associated with Central American reunification attempts.

Official name: Republic of Hungary
Head of government: Prime Minister
Official language: Hungarian
Monetary unit: forint
Area: 35,919 sq. mi. (93,030 sq. km.)
Population (2010): 10,005,000
GNI per capita (2009): U.S.$12,980
Principal exports (2008): machinery and apparatus 46.1%, telecommunication equipment 11.6%, electrical machinery 9.6%, road vehicles/parts 10.8%, food 6.0% *to:* Germany 26.7%; Italy 5.3%; Romania 5.3%; Austria 4.9%; Slovakia 4.7%

Religious Affiliation

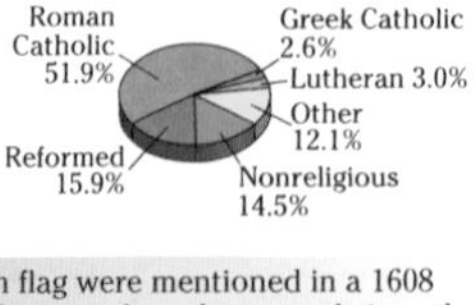

The colors of the Hungarian flag were mentioned in a 1608 coronation ceremony, but they may have been used since the 13th century. The tricolor was adopted on Oct. 12, 1957, after the abortive revolution of 1956. The white is said to symbolize Hungary's rivers, the green its mountains, and the red the blood shed in its many battles.

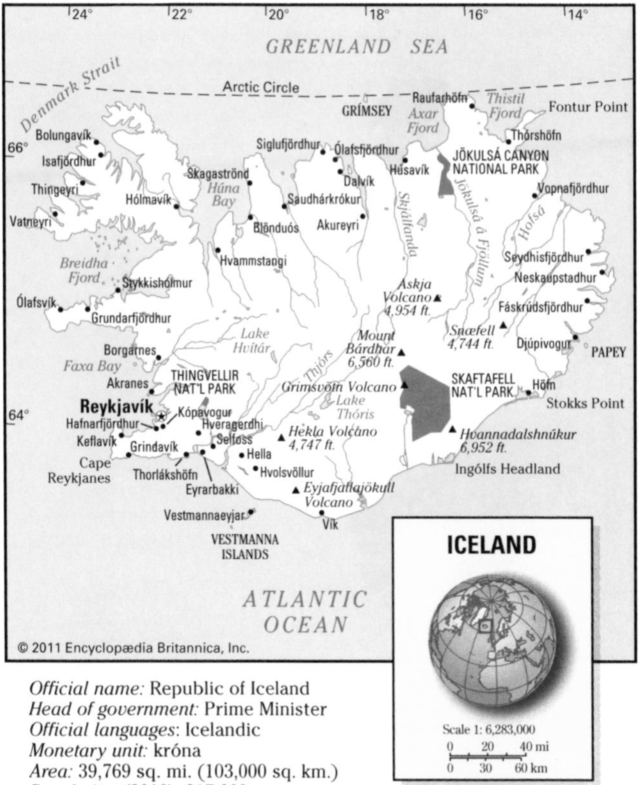

Official name: Republic of Iceland
Head of government: Prime Minister
Official languages: Icelandic
Monetary unit: króna
Area: 39,769 sq. mi. (103,000 sq. km.)
Population (2010): 317,000
GNI per capita (2009): U.S.$43,220
Principal exports (2008): aluminum 39.0%, fresh fish 21.7%, dried/salted fish 8.0%, aircraft 6.1% *to:* Netherlands 34.4%; United Kingdom 11.6%; Germany 11.3%; U.S. 5.6%; Japan 4.4%

Age Breakdown

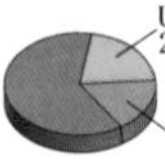

Approval for an Icelandic flag was given by the king of Denmark on June 19, 1915; it became a national flag on Dec. 1, 1918, when the separate kingdom of Iceland was proclaimed. The flag was retained upon the creation of a republic on June 17, 1944. The design has a typical "Scandinavian cross."

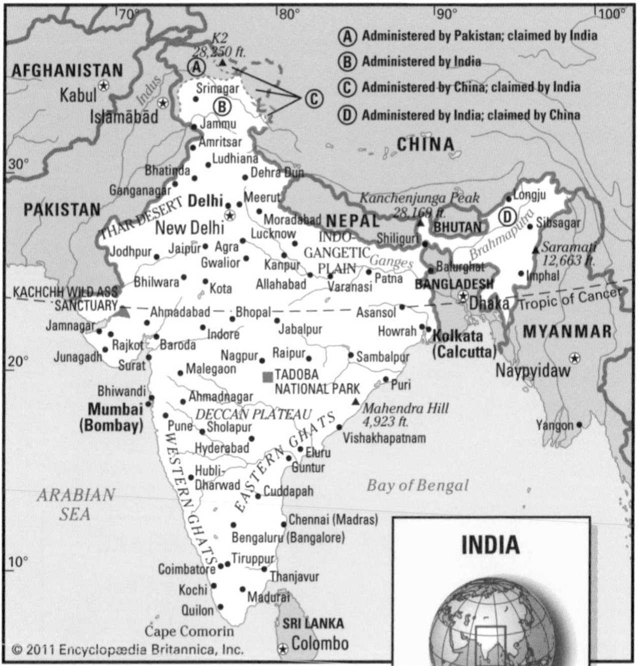

Official name: Republic of India
Head of government: Prime Minister
Official languages: Hindi; English
Monetary unit: Indian rupee
Area: 1,222,559 sq. mi. (3,166,414 sq. km.)
Population (2010): 1,173,108,000
GNI per capita (2009): U.S.$1,170
Principal exports (2008–09): gems and jewelry 15.1%, refined petroleum 14.9%, textiles and wearing apparel 10.8%, food, beverages and tobacco 9.5%, chemical products 8.4% *to:* U.A.E. 12.9%; U.S. 11.3%; China 5.0%; Singapore 4.4%; U.K. 3.6%; Hong Kong 3.6%

Linguistic Composition

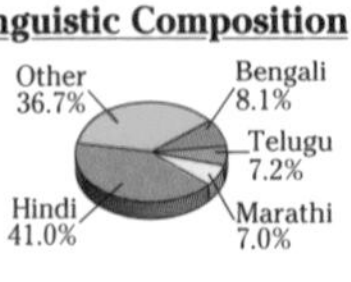

Earlier versions of the flag were used from the 1920s, but the current flag was hoisted officially on July 22, 1947. The orange was said to stand for courage and sacrifice, white for peace and truth, and green for faith and chivalry. The blue wheel is a chakra, associated with Emperor Asoka's attempts to unite India in the 3rd century BC.

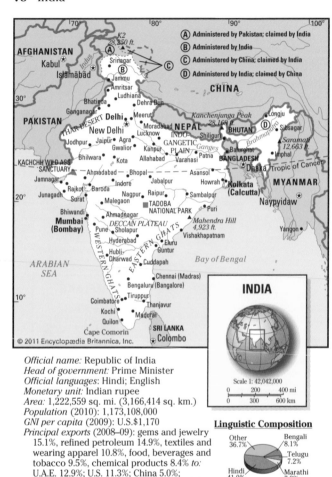

Official name: Republic of Indonesia
Head of state and government: President
Official language: Indonesian
Monetary unit: rupiah
Area: 737,815 sq. mi. (1,910,931 sq. km.)
Population (2010): 232,517,000
GNI per capita (2009): U.S.$2,230
Principal exports (2008): machinery and apparatus 9.9%, natural gas 9.5%, crude petroleum 9.1%, palm oil 9.0%, coal 7.7%, food 5.8% *to:* Japan 20.2%; U.S. 9.4%; Singapore 9.4%; China 8.5%

Ethnic Composition

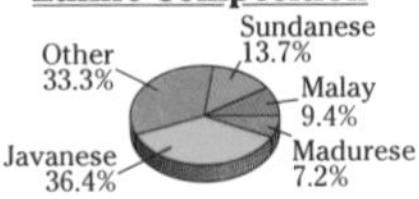

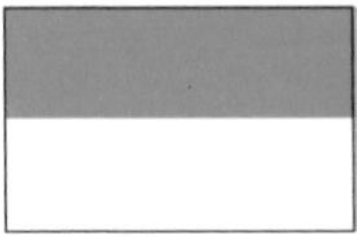

Indonesia's red and white flag was associated with the Majapahit empire which existed from the 13th to the 16th century. It was adopted on Aug. 17, 1945, and it remained after Indonesia won its independence from The Netherlands in 1949. Red is for courage and white for honesty. The flag is identical, except in dimensions, to the flag of Monaco.

Official name: Islamic Republic of Iran
Head of state and government: President
Official language: Farsi (Persian)
Monetary unit: rial
Area: 636,374 sq. mi. (1,648,200 sq. km.)
Population (2010): 73,887,000
GNI per capita (2009): U.S.$4,530
Principal exports (2008–09): petroleum/natural gas 85.2%, organic chemicals 3.1%, plastics 1.4%, pistachios 0.7%, carpets 0.4% *to:* China *c.* 15%; Japan *c.* 14%; India *c.* 9%; South Korea *c.* 6%; Turkey *c.* 6%

Ethnic Composition

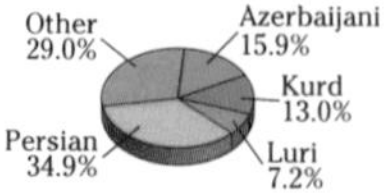

The tricolor flag was recognized in 1906 but altered after the revolution of 1979. Along the central stripe are the Arabic words Allahu akbar ("God is great"), repeated 22 times. The coat of arms can be read as a rendition of the word Allah, as a globe, or as two crescents. The green is for Islam, white is for peace, and red is for valor.

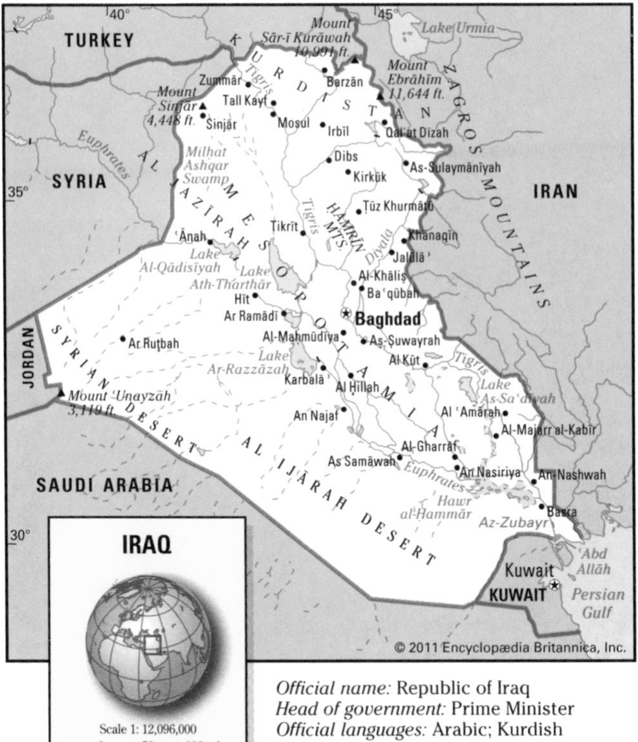

Official name: Republic of Iraq
Head of government: Prime Minister
Official languages: Arabic; Kurdish
Monetary unit: Iraqi dinar
Area: 167,618 sq. mi. (434,128 sq. km.)
Population (2010): 31,467,000
GNI per capita (2009): U.S.$2,210
Principal exports (2003): crude petroleum 97.1%, refined petroleum 2.4% *to:* U.S. *c.* 39%; India *c.* 12%; Italy *c.* 10%; South Korea *c.* 7%

Ethnic Composition

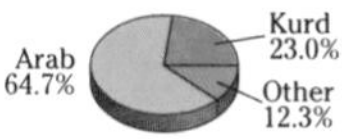

In 2004, about a year after the fall of the dictator Saddam Hussein, Iraq raised a flag with red, white, and black stripes. In the white stripe were three green stars and the Arabic inscription saying, "God is great." The colors honor a 13th-century poem by Sali al-Din al-Hilli (see Kuwait, p. 91). A new flag was raised on Jan. 28, 2008, with the stars removed.

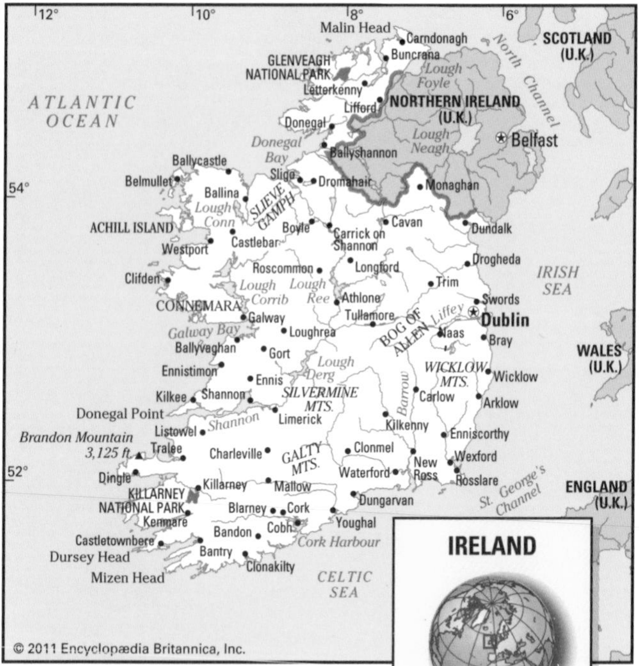

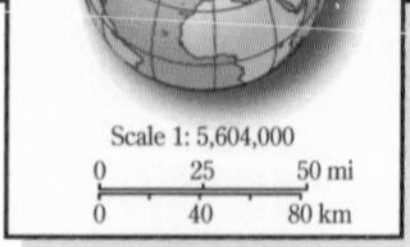

Official name: Ireland
Head of government: Prime Minister
Official languages: Irish; English
Monetary unit: euro
Area: 27,133 sq. mi. (70,273 sq. km.)
Population (2010): 4,451,000
GNI per capita (2009): U.S.$44,310
Principal exports (2008): organic chemicals 20.6%, medicinal and pharmaceuticals 19.3%, computers/office machines/ parts 10.8%, food 8.2% *to:* U.S. 19.3%; U.K. 18.4%; Belgium 14.2%; Germany 7.1%; France 5.8%

Age Breakdown

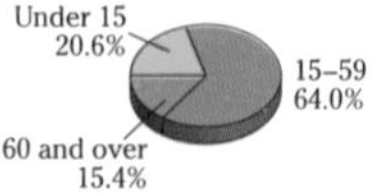

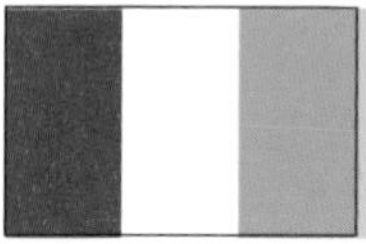

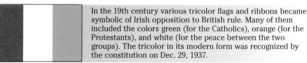

In the 19th century various tricolor flags and ribbons became symbolic of Irish opposition to British rule. Many of them included the colors green (for the Catholics), orange (for the Protestants), and white (for the peace between the two groups). The tricolor in its modern form was recognized by the constitution on Dec. 29, 1937.

Official name: State of Israel
Head of government: Prime Minister
Official languages: Hebrew; Arabic
Monetary unit: new (Israeli) sheqel
Area: 8,357 sq. mi. (21,643 sq. km.)
Population (2010): 7,302,000
GNI per capita (2009): U.S.$25,740
Principal exports (2008): polished diamonds 25.3%, chemical products 25.2%, machinery and apparatus 19.5%, rough diamonds 6.3% *to:* U.S. 32.6%; Belgium 7.5%; Hong Kong 6.8%; India 3.8%; Netherlands 3.3%

Religious Affiliation

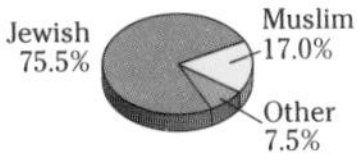

Symbolic of the traditional *tallit,* or Jewish prayer shawl, and including the Star of David, the flag was used from the late 19th century. It was raised when Israel proclaimed independence on May 14, 1948, and the banner was legally recognized on Nov. 12, 1948. A dark blue was also substituted for the traditional lighter shade of blue.

Official name: Italian Republic
Head of government: Prime Minister
Official language: Italian
Monetary unit: euro
Area: 116,346 sq. mi. (301,336 sq. km.)
Population (2010): 60,487,000
GNI per capita (2009): U.S.$35,080
Principal exports (2008): nonelectrical machinery and apparatus 21.0%, chemicals 9.9%, road vehicles/parts 7.7%, iron and steel 5.4%, electrical machinery 5.1% *to:* Germany 12.7%; France 11.1%; Spain 6.5%; U.S. 6.3%; U.K. 5.2%; Switzerland 4.0%

Age Breakdown

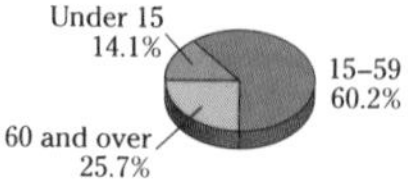

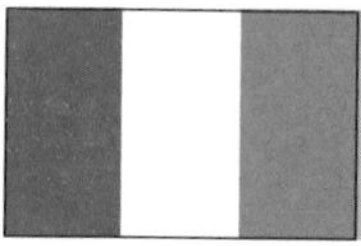

The first Italian national flag was adopted on Feb. 25, 1797, by the Cispadane Republic. Its stripes were vertically positioned on May 11, 1798, and thereafter it was honored by all Italian nationalists. The design was guaranteed by a decree (March 23, 1848) of King Charles Albert of Sardinia, ordering troops to carry the flag into battle.

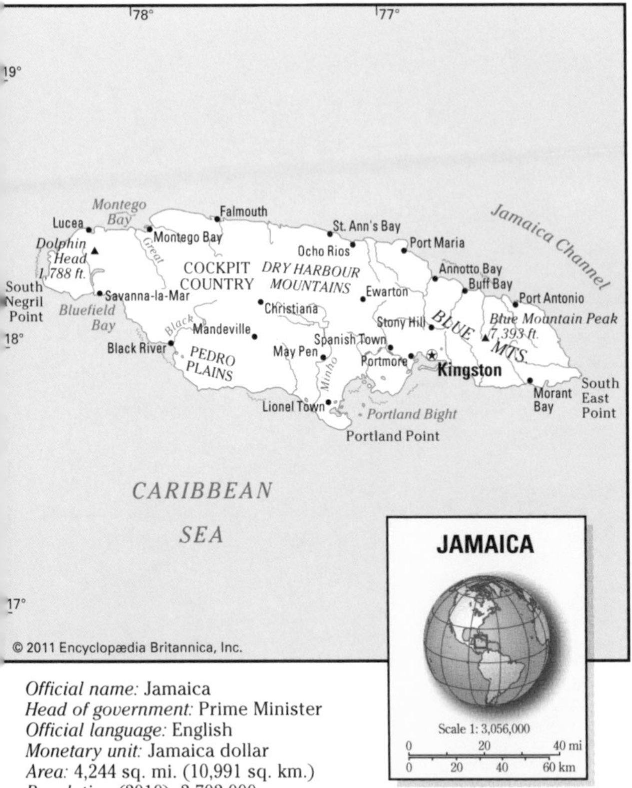

© 2011 Encyclopædia Britannica, Inc.

Official name: Jamaica
Head of government: Prime Minister
Official language: English
Monetary unit: Jamaica dollar
Area: 4,244 sq. mi. (10,991 sq. km.)
Population (2010): 2,702,000
GNI per capita (2009): U.S.$5,020
Principal exports (2008): alumina 50.5%, refined petroleum 17.9%, food 10.6%, coffee 1.1%, undernatured ethyl alcohol 6.2% *to:* United States 40.3%; Canada 10.6%; U.K. 9.2%

Religious Affiliation

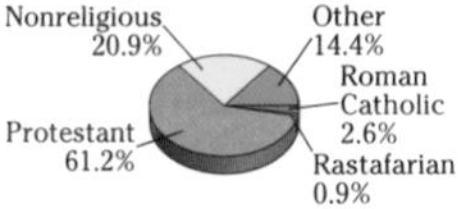

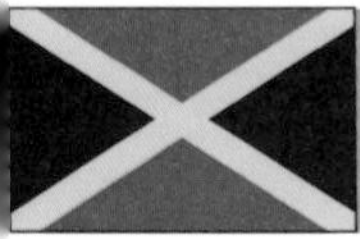

The flag was designed prior to independence from Britain (Aug. 6, 1962). The black color stood for hardships faced by the nation, green for agriculture and hope, and yellow for the natural wealth of Jamaica. This was summed up in the phrase, "Hardships there are, but the land is green and the sun shineth."

Official name: Japan
Head of government: Prime Minister
Official language: Japanese
Monetary unit: yen
Area: 145,898 sq. mi. (377,873 sq. km.)
Population (2010): 127,320,000
GNI per capita (2009): U.S.$37,870
Principal exports (2008): machinery and apparatus 37.2%, road vehicles and parts 21.8%; chemical products 8.8% *to:* United States 17.8%; China 16.0%; South Korea 7.6%; unspecified Asia (probably Taiwan) 5.9%; Hong Kong 5.2%

Age Breakdown

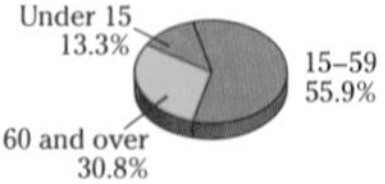

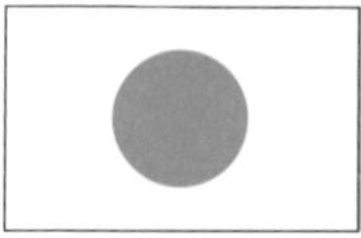

The flag features a red sun on a cool white background. Traditionally, the sun goddess founded Japan in the 7th century BC and gave birth to its first emperor, Jimmu. Even today the emperor is known as the "Son of the Sun" and the popular name for the country is "Land of the Rising Sun." The current flag design was adopted on Aug. 5, 1854.

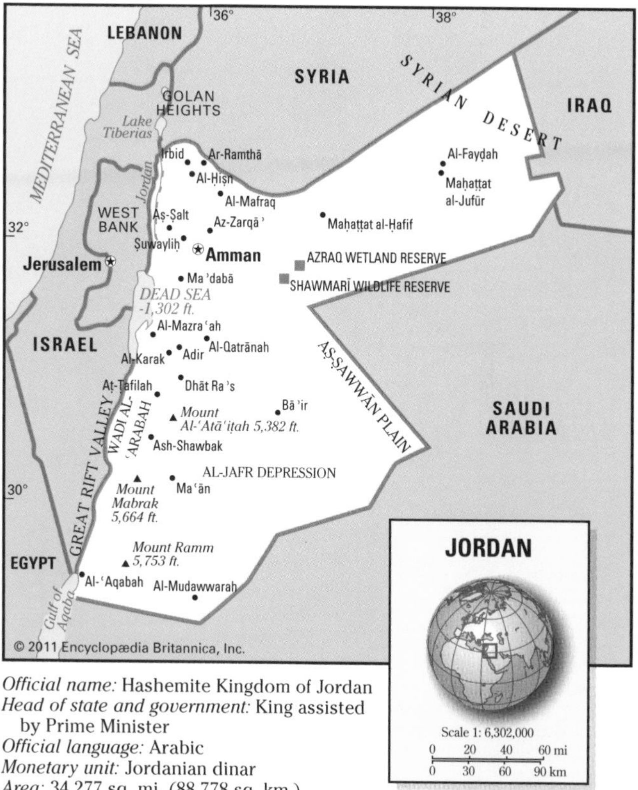

Official name: Hashemite Kingdom of Jordan
Head of state and government: King assisted by Prime Minister
Official language: Arabic
Monetary unit: Jordanian dinar
Area: 34,277 sq. mi. (88,778 sq. km.)
Population (2010): 6,046,000
GNI per capita (2009): U.S.$3,740
Principal exports (2008): fertilizer 24.3%, apparel/accessories 13.4%, food products 10.8%, machinery and apparatus 10.7%, medicines 6.6% *to:* Iraq 16.5%; India 16.5%; U.S. 13.5%; free zones 8.5%; Saudi Arabia 7.0%; U.A.E. 4.7%

Religious Affiliation

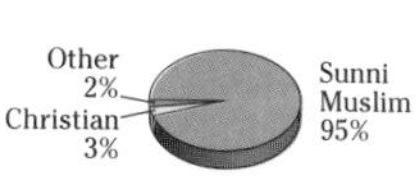

In 1917 Husayn ibn Ali raised the Arab Revolt flag. With the addition of a white seven-pointed star, this flag was adopted by Transjordan on April 16, 1928, and retained upon the independence of Jordan on March 22, 1946. White is for purity, black for struggle and suffering, red for bloodshed, and green for Arab lands.

Official name: Republic of Kazakhstan
Head of state and government: President assisted by Prime Minister
Official languages: Kazakh; Russian
Monetary unit: tenge
Area: 1,052,100 sq. mi. (2,724,900 sq. km.)
Population (2010): 16,310,000
GNI per capita (2009): U.S.$6,740
Principal exports (2008): crude petroleum 61.1%, iron and steel 8.3%, nonferrous metal 6.3%, metal ore and metal scrap 5.0%, food 4.0% *to:* Italy 16.7%; Switzerland 15.9%; China 10.8%; Russia 8.7%; France 7.6%

Ethnic Composition

The flag was adopted in June 1992. Light blue is a traditional color of the nomads of Central Asia; it symbolizes peace and well-being. The golden sun and eagle represent freedom and the high ideals of the Kazakhs. Along the edge is a band of traditional Kazakh ornamentation; the band was originally in red but is now in golden yellow.

Ethnic Composition

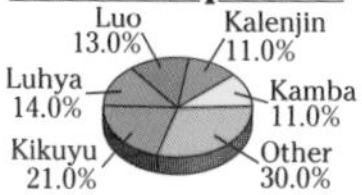

Official name: Republic of Kenya
Head of state and government: President assisted by Prime Minister
Official languages: Swahili; English
Monetary unit: Kenya shilling
Area: 224,961 sq. mi. (582,646 sq. km.)
Population (2010): 40,863,000
GNI per capita (2009): U.S.$770
Principal exports (2008): tea 18.6%, cut flowers 8.9%, vegetables 5.5%, apparel/ accessories 5.1%, inorganic chemicals 4.4% *to* (2001): Uganda 12.3%; United Kingdom 11.0%; Tanzania 8.5%; Netherlands 7.6%; U.S. 6.0%

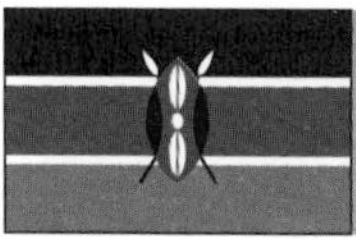

Upon independence from Britain (Dec. 12, 1963), the Kenyan flag became official. It was based on the flag of the Kenya African National Union. Black is for the people, red for humanity and the struggle for freedom, green for the fertile land, and white for unity and peace. The shield and spears are traditional weapons of the Masai people.

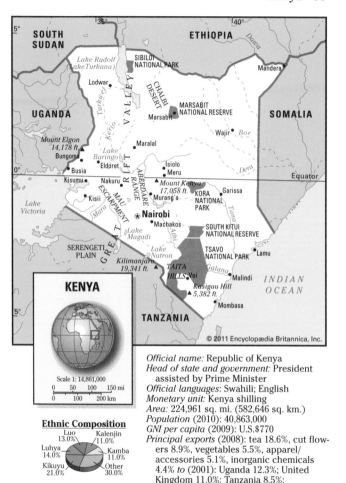

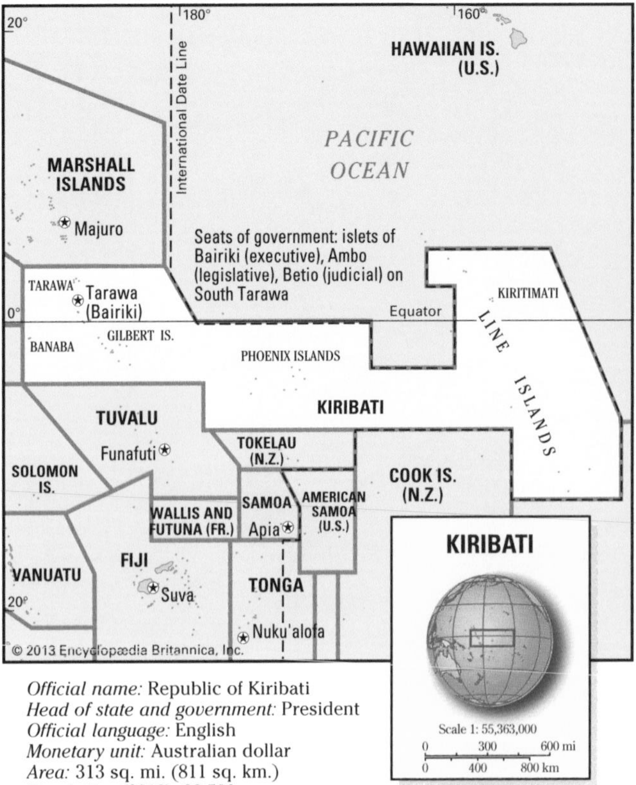

Official name: Republic of Kiribati
Head of state and government: President
Official language: English
Monetary unit: Australian dollar
Area: 313 sq. mi. (811 sq. km.)
Population (2010): 99,500
GNI per capita (2009): U.S.$1,890
Principal exports (2007): domestic exports 81.0%, of which crude coconut oil 45.7%, copra 14.4%, fish 10.7%, handicraft 8.3%, seaweed 1.9%, reexports 19.0% *to* (2005): free zones *c.* 34%; Australia *c.* 22%; Fiji *c.* 17%; other Asia (probably Taiwan) *c.* 14%

Age Breakdown

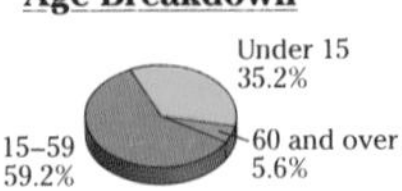

Great Britain acquired the Gilbert and Ellice Islands in the 19th century. In 1975 the Gilbert Islands separated from the Ellice Islands to form Kiribati, and a new flag was adopted based on the coat of arms granted to the islands in 1937. It has waves of white and blue, for the Pacific Ocean, as well as a yellow sun and a local frigate bird.

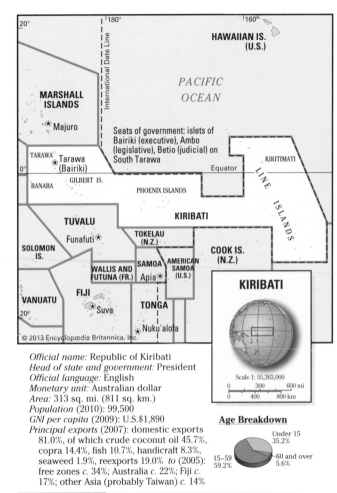

Official name: Republic of Kosovo
Head of government: Prime Minister
Official languages: Albanian; Serbian
Monetary unit: euro
Area: 4,212 sq. mi. (10,908 sq. km.)
Population (2010): 1,815,000
GNI per capita (2008): U.S.$2,752
Principal exports (2008): iron and steel [all forms] 63.3%[1], food products 11.0%, mineral fuels 9.1% *to:* Belgium 14.3%; Italy 13.0%; India 12.0%; Albania 10.8%; Macedonia 9.9%

[1]Nearly all scrap metal.

Age Breakdown

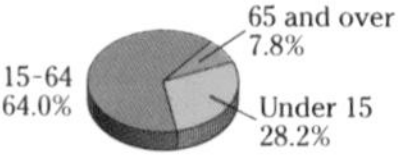

Kosovo declared independence on February 17, 2008. The flag chosen emphasizes Kosovo as a multiethnic country by featuring the colors of the European Union: a blue field and a yellow silhouette of the country, above which six white stars are said to represent the country's six main ethnic groups.

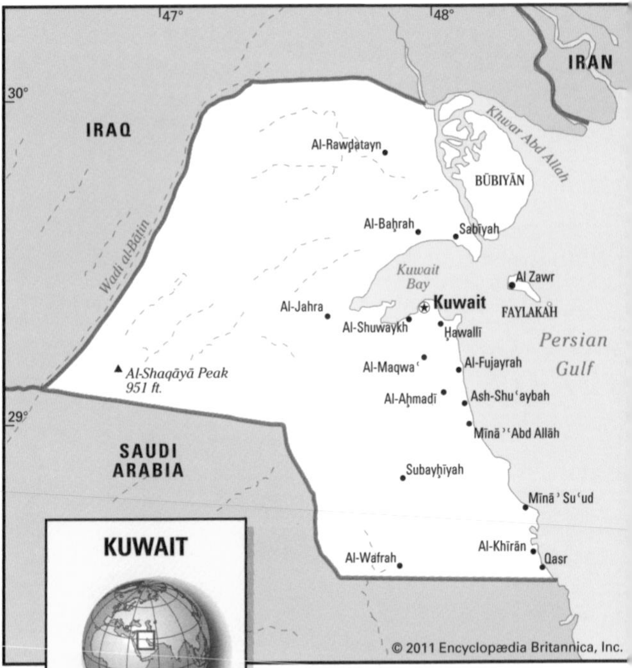

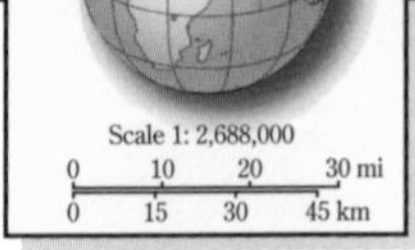

Official name: State of Kuwait
Head of state and government: Emir assisted by Prime Minister
Official language: Arabic
Monetary unit: Kuwaiti dinar
Area: 6,880 sq. mi. (17,818 sq. km.)
Population (2010): 3,524,000
GNI per capita (2008): U.S.$59,874
Principal exports (2003): crude petroleum 61.6%, refined petroleum 29.8%, liquefiec propane and butane 3.1% polyethylene 1.7% *to*: Japan *c.* 19%; South Korea *c.* 15% India *c.* 11%; Taiwan *c.* 10%; U.S. *c.* 9%

Religious Affiliation

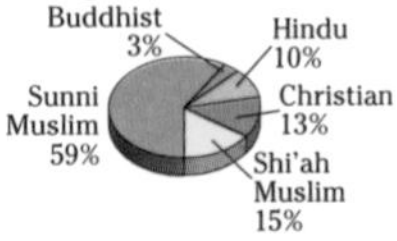

The red flag of Kuwait, in use since World War I, was replaced by the current flag on Oct. 24, 1961, shortly after independence from Britain. The symbolism is from a poem written over six centuries ago. The green stands for Arab lands, black is for battles, white is for the purity of the fighters, and red is for the blood on their swords.

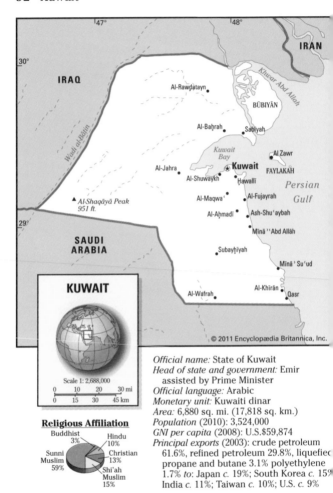

Official name: Kyrgyz Republic
Head of state and government: President (interim)
Official languages: Kyrgyz; Russian
Monetary unit: Kyrgyz som
Area: 77,199 sq. mi. (199,945 sq. km.)
Population (2010): 5,141,000
GNI per capita (2009): U.S.$870
Principal exports (2007): refined petroleum 20.8%, gold 19.8%, machinery and apparatus 6.2%; women's/girls' outerwear 5.5%, vegetables 4.2%, glass 3.5% *to:* Switzerland 31.7%; Russia 13.5%; Uzbekistan 11.9%; Kazakhstan 9.7%; U.A.E. 7.2%

Ethnic Composition

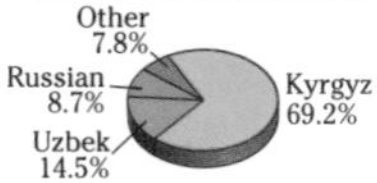

The Kyrgyz flag replaced a Soviet-era design on March 3, 1992. The red recalls the flag of the national hero Mansas the Noble. The central yellow sun has 40 rays, corresponding to the followers of Mansas and the tribes he united. On the sun is the stylized view of the roof of a yurt, a traditional nomadic home that is now seldom used.

Official name: Lao People's Democratic Republic
Head of government: Prime Minister
Official language: Lao
Monetary unit: kip
Area: 91,429 sq. mi. (236,800 sq. km.)
Population (2010): 6,258,000
GNI per capita (2009): U.S.$880
Principal exports (2008): copper 37.9%, garments 11.6%, timber 8.0%, gold 7.3%, electricity 7.2% *to:* Vietnam 13.2%; China 8.6%; South Korea 4.5%; U.K. 3.3%

Ethnic Composition

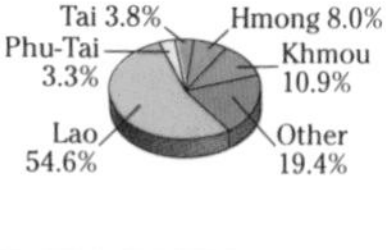

The Lao flag was first used by anticolonialist forces from the mid-20th century. The white disk honored the Japanese who had supported the Lao independence movement, but it also symbolized a bright future. Red was said to stand for the blood of patriots and blue was for the promise of future prosperity. The flag was adopted on Dec. 2, 1975.

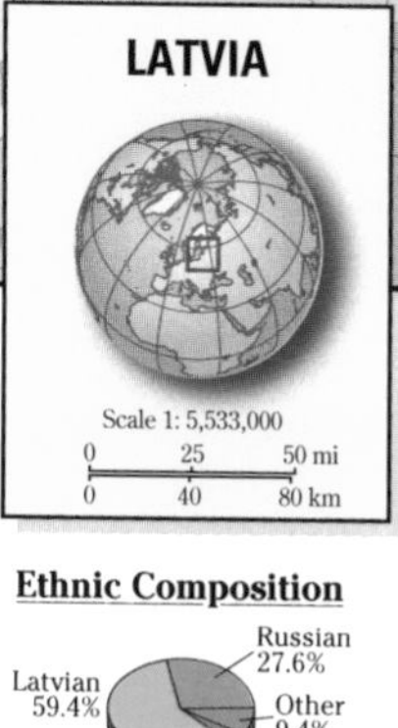

Ethnic Composition

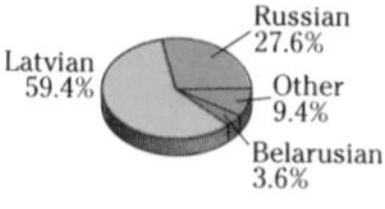

Official name: Republic of Latvia
Head of government: Prime Minister
Official language: Latvian
Monetary unit: lats
Area: 24,938 sq. mi. (64,589 sq. km.)
Population (2010): 2,238,000
GNI per capita (2009): U.S.$12,390
Principal exports (2008): machinery and apparatus 12.0%, food 10.9%, rough/sawn wood 9.9%, iron and steel 9.4%, chemical products 9.1% *to:* Lithuania 16.7%; Estonia 14.0%; Russia 10.0%; Germany 8.1%; Sweden 6.6%

The basic flag design was used by a militia unit in 1279, according to a 14th century source. Popularized in the 19th century among anti-Russian nationalists, the flag flew in 1918 and was legally adopted on Jan. 20, 1923. Under Soviet control the flag was suppressed, but it was again legalized in 1988 and flown officially from Feb. 27, 1990.

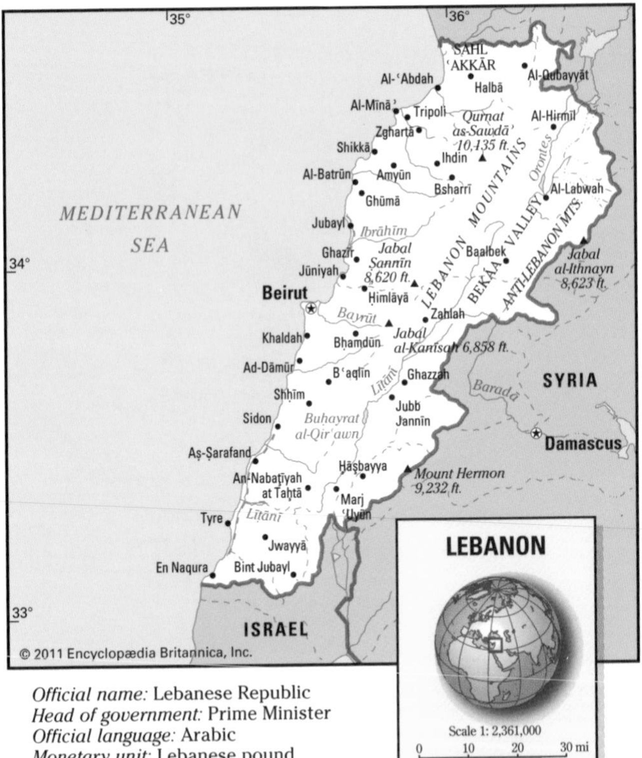

Official name: Lebanese Republic
Head of government: Prime Minister
Official language: Arabic
Monetary unit: Lebanese pound
Area: 4,005 sq. mi. (10,372 sq. km.)
Population (2010): 4,125,000
GNI per capita (2009): U.S.$7,970
Principal exports (2008): precious metal jewelry and stones 16.5%, electrical equipment 15.4%, base and fabricated metals 15.2%, chemicals 12.5% *to:* U.A.E. 10.0%; Switzerland 9.5%; Iraq 7.7%; Syria 6.4%; Saudi Arabia 6.0%

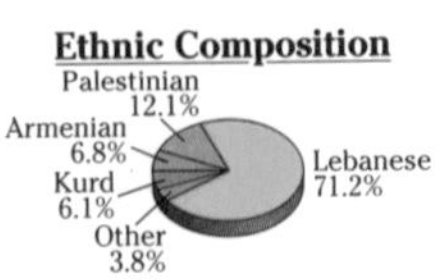

On Sept. 1, 1920, French-administered Lebanon adopted a flag based on the French tricolor. The current red-white flag was established by the constitution of 1943, which divided power among the Muslim and Christian sects. On the central stripe is a cedar tree, which is a biblical symbol for holiness, peace, and eternity.

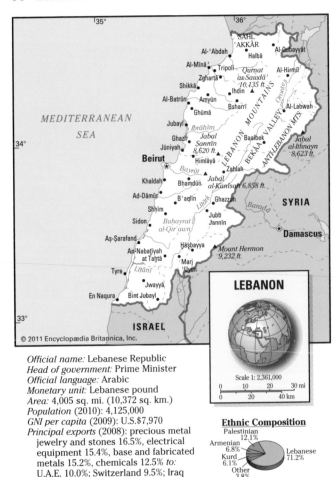

Official name: Kingdom of Lesotho
Head of government: Prime Minister
Official languages: Sotho; English
Monetary unit: loti
Area: 11,720 sq. mi. (30,355 sq. km.)
Population (2010): 1,920,000
GNI per capita: U.S.$1,020
Principal exports (2008): textiles and wearing apparel 50.4%, diamonds 24.0%, machinery and transportation equipment 14.0%, food, beverages, and tobacco 6.6% *to:* United States 59.7%; other SACU countries 19.0%; Belgium 17.0%

Ethnic Composition

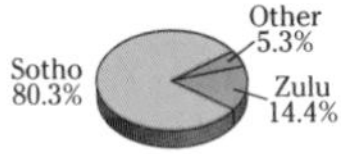

A flag adopted in 1987 contained a white triangle (for peace), a green triangle (for prosperity), and a central diagonal blue stripe (for rain). A new flag, hoisted on Oct. 4, 2006, has three horizontal stripes in the same colors as the previous flag but with the white stripe in the center, on which is depicted, in black, a traditional Sotho straw hat.

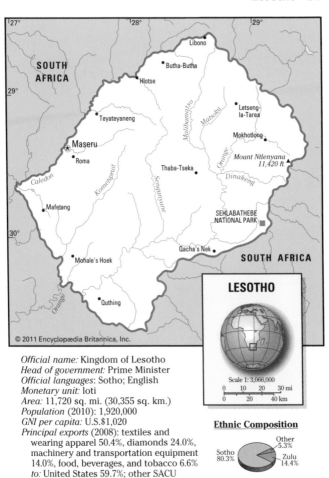

Official name: Republic of Liberia
Head of state and government: President
Official language: English
Monetary unit: Liberian dollar
Area: 37,420 sq. mi. (96,917 sq. km.)
Population (2010): 3,763,000
GNI per capita (2009): U.S.$160
Principal exports (2009): rubber 62.4%, gold 6.5%, diamonds 5.0%; cocoa beans/coffee 2.4% *to:* India *c.* 21%; U.S. *c.* 19%; Poland *c.* 15%; Germany *c.* 11%; Belgium *c.* 7%

Religious Affiliation

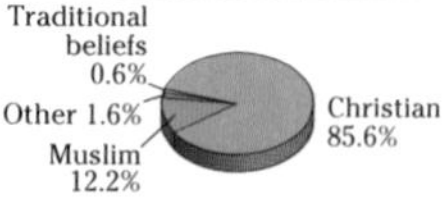

In the 19th century land was purchased on the African coast by the American Colonization Society, in order to return freed slaves to Africa. On April 9, 1827, a flag based on that of the United States was adopted, featuring a white cross. On Aug. 24, 1847, after independence, the cross was replaced by a star and the number of stripes was reduced.

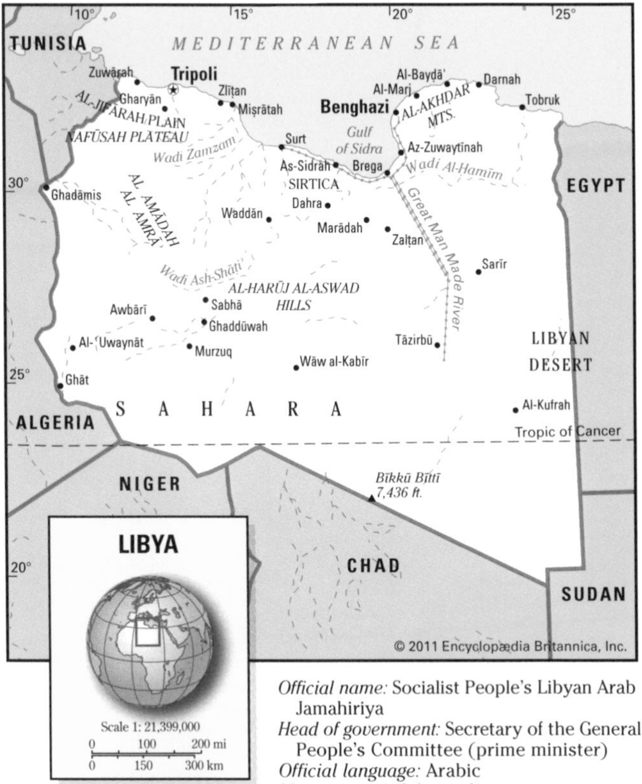

Official name: Socialist People's Libyan Arab Jamahiriya
Head of government: Secretary of the General People's Committee (prime minister)
Official language: Arabic
Monetary unit: Libyan dinar
Area: 686,126 sq. mi. (1,777,060 sq. km.)
Population (2010): 6,546,000
GNI per capita (2009): U.S.$12,020
Principal exports (2007): hydrocarbons [mostly crude petroleum] 97.5% *to:* Italy *c.* 38%; Germany *c.* 12%; Spain *c.* 7%; France *c.* 7%, U.S. *c.* 6%

Age Breakdown

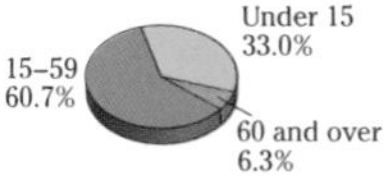

In 1947 three regions united to become the United Kingdom of Libya. A flag consisting of red, black, and green stripes with a centered white crescent and star became official in 1949. In 1969 the monarchy was overthrown by Muammar al-Qaddafi, who changed the flag to solid green. Following the overthrow of Qaddafi in 2011, the 1949 flag was reinstated.

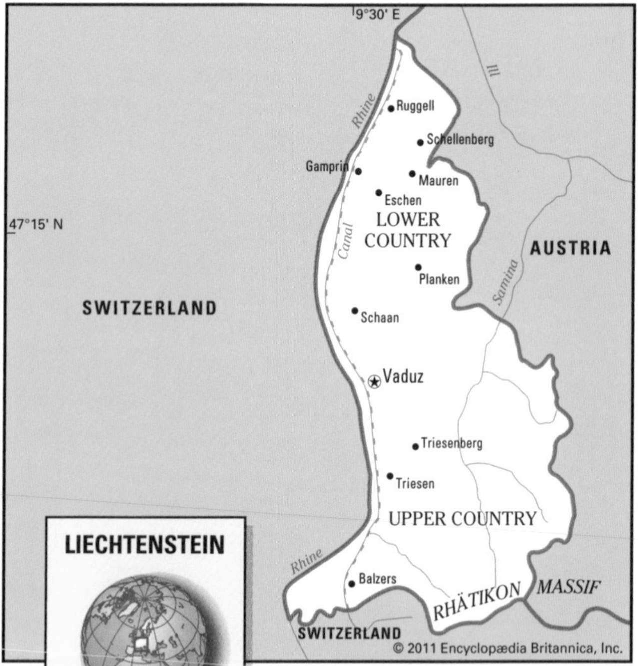

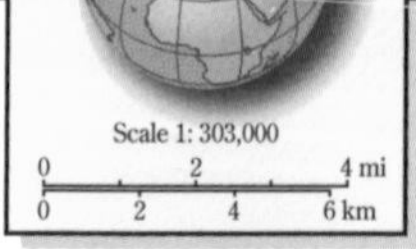

Official name: Principality of Liechtenstein
Head of government: Head of Government (Prime Minister)
Official language: German
Monetary unit: Swiss franc
Area: 62.0 sq. mi. (160.5 sq. km.)
Population (2010): 36,000
GNI per capita (2008): U.S.$121,509
Principal exports (2009): machinery and electronic goods 41.6%, fabricated metals/precision tools 18.7%, food and beverages 9.3%, transport equipment/parts 9.2%, glass and ceramic products 6.5% *to:* Germany 23.6%; U.S. 11.3%; Austria 11.0%; France 10.1%; Italy 6.5%

Religious Affiliation

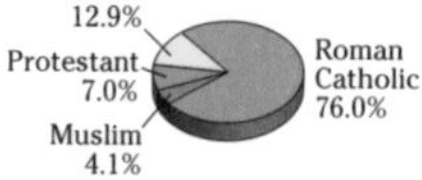

The blue-red flag was given official status in October 1921. At the 1936 Olympics it was learned that this same flag was used by Haiti; thus, in 1937 a yellow crown was added, which symbolizes the unity of the people and their prince. Blue stands for the sky, red for the evening fires in homes. The flag was last modified on Sept. 18, 1982.

Official name: Republic of Lithuania
Head of government: Prime Minister
Official language: Lithuanian
Monetary unit: litas
Area: 25,212 sq. mi. (65,300 sq. km.)
Population (2010): 3,297,000
GNI per capita (2009): U.S.$11,410
Principal exports (2008): refined petroleum 22.8%, food 13.3%, machinery and apparatus 10.5%, road vehicles/parts 6.7%, fertilizers 6.4% *to:* Russia 16.0%; Latvia 11.6%; Germany 7.2%; Poland 5.8%; Estonia 5.7%

Ethnic Composition

The tricolor flag of Lithuania was adopted on Aug. 1, 1922. It was long suppressed under Soviet rule until its reestablishment on March 20, 1989. The yellow color suggests ripening wheat and freedom from want. Green is for hope and the forests of the nation, while red stands for love of country, sovereignty, and valor in defense of liberty.

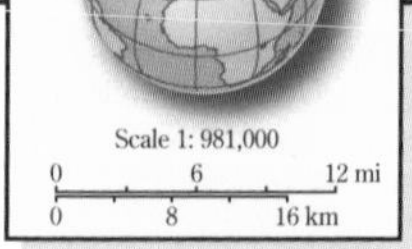

Official name: Grand Duchy of Luxembourg
Head of government: Prime Minister
Official language: none
Monetary unit: euro
Area: 999 sq. mi. (2,586 sq. km.)
Population (2010): 506,000
GNI per capita (2009): U.S.$74,430
Principal exports (2008): iron and steel 27.8%, machinery and apparatus 15.3%, plastics 6.8%, road vehicles 6.0%, food 4.8% *to:* Germany 27.7%; France 17.2%; Belgium 13.3%; Netherlands 5.3%; Italy 4.7%

Ethnic Composition

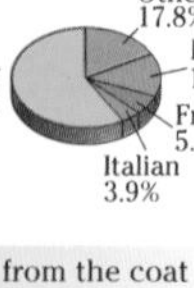

In the 19th century the national colors, from the coat of arms of the dukes of Luxembourg, came to be used in a tricolor of red-white-blue, coincidentally the same as the flag of The Netherlands. To distinguish it from the Dutch flag, the proportions were altered and the shade of blue was made lighter. It was recognized by law on Aug. 16, 1972.

Official name: Republic of Macedonia
Head of government: Prime Minister
Official languages: Macedonian; Albanian
Monetary unit: denar
Area: 9,928 sq. mi. (25,713 sq. km.)
Population (2010): 2,051,000
GNI per capita (2009): U.S.$4,400
Principal exports (2007): 37.6%, clothing 18.9%, food 7.4%, refined petroleum 4.7%, metal ore/metal scrap 3.8% *to:* Serbia 19.1%; Germany 14.4%; Greece 12.5%; Italy 10.3%; Bulgaria 7.2%

Ethnic Composition

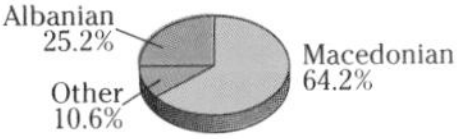

A "starburst" flag replaced the communist banner on Aug. 11, 1992. The starburst was a symbol of Alexander the Great and his father, Philip of Macedon, but its use by Macedonia was opposed by Greece. Thus on Oct. 6, 1995, the similar "golden sun" flag was chosen instead. The gold and red colors originated in an early Macedonian coat of arms.

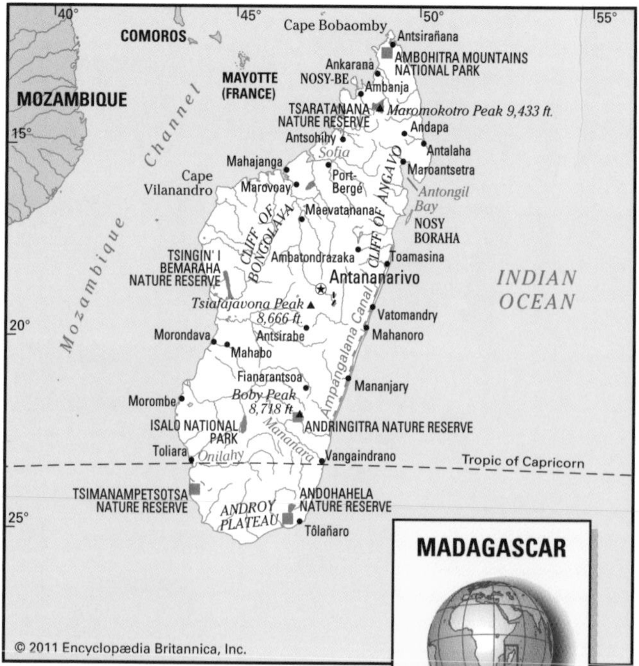

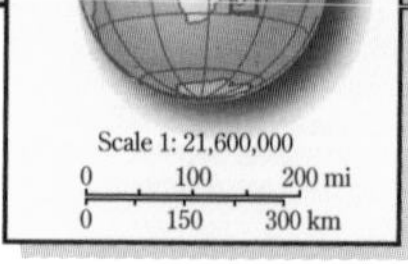

Official name: Republic of Madagascar
Head of government: President of High Authority of Transition
Official language: none
Monetary unit: ariary
Area: 226,662 sq. mi. (587,051 sq. km.)
Population (2010): 20,146,000
GNI per capita (2008): U.S.$410
Principal exports (2008): clothing 53.2%, food/spices 19.4%, of which shrimp 6.6%, vanilla 3.0%, cloves 1.8%, refined petroleum 5.4%
to: France 45.1%; U.S. 21.9%; Germany 6.5%; China 3.1%; Italy 2.4%

Religious Affiliation

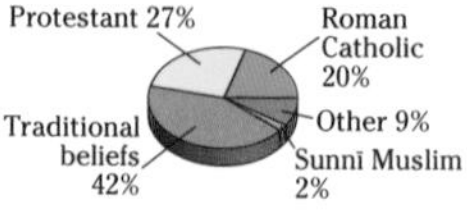

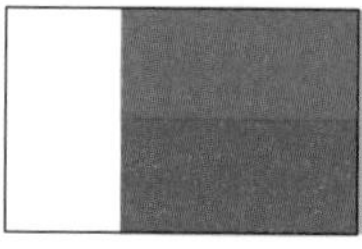

The Madagascar flag was adopted on Oct. 16, 1958, by the newly proclaimed Malagasy Republic, formerly a French colony. The flag combines the traditional Malagasy colors of white and red with a stripe of green. The white and red are said to stand for purity and sovereignty, while the green represents the coastal regions and symbolizes hope.

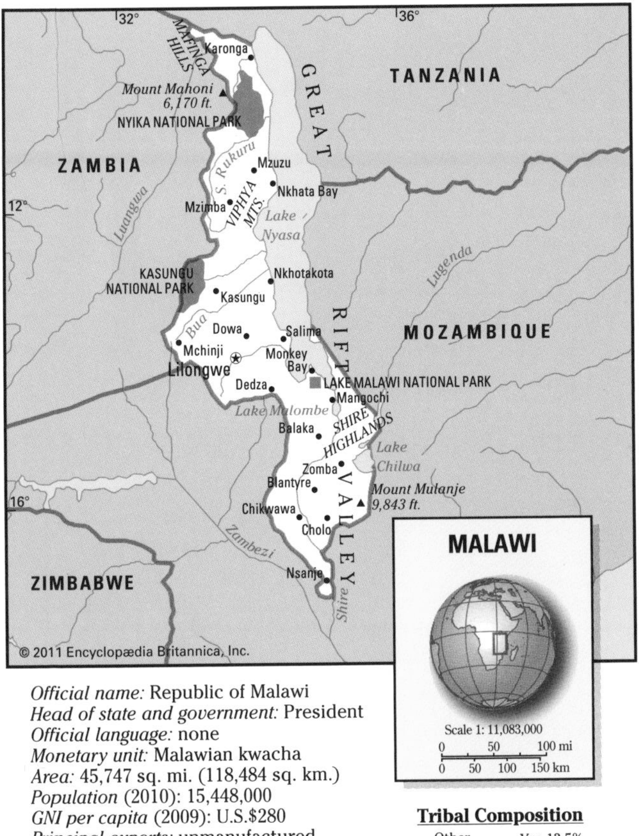

Official name: Republic of Malawi
Head of state and government: President
Official language: none
Monetary unit: Malawian kwacha
Area: 45,747 sq. mi. (118,484 sq. km.)
Population (2010): 15,448,000
GNI per capita (2009): U.S.$280
Principal exports: unmanufactured tobacco 67.1%, raw sugar 5.8%, tea 4.2%, apparel/clothing 2.9%, cotton 2.5% *to:* Belgium 13.0%; South Africa 10.1%; U.K. 8.9%; Netherlands 5.9%; U.S. 5.7%

Tribal Composition

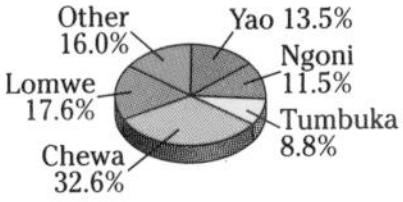

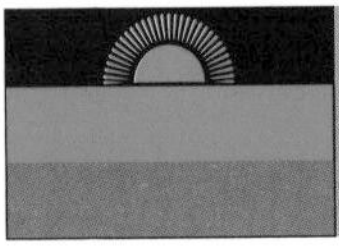

In 1964, independent Malawi adopted a flag that was striped black for the African people, red for the blood of the martyrs, and green for the vegetation and climate. A red setting sun was on the black stripe. A new flag in 2010, reordered the stripes to red-black-green and replaced the half sun with a full sun. The old flag was restored in 2012.

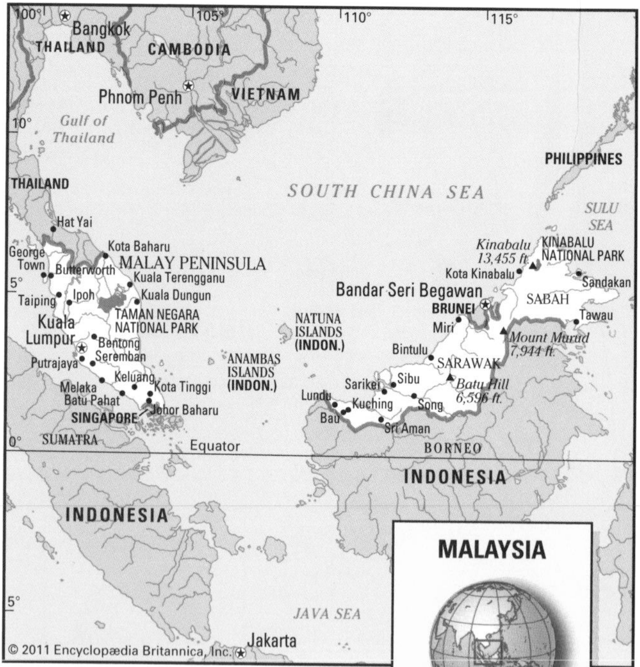

Official name: Malaysia
Head of government: Prime Minister
Official language: Malay
Monetary unit: ringgit
Area: 127,366 sq. mi. (329,876 sq. km.)
Population (2010): 28,275,000
GNI per capita (2009): U.S.$7,230
Principal exports (2008): computers/office machines 12.8%, petroleum 11.2%, electrical machinery/parts 10.0%, palm oil 6.4% *to:* Singapore 14.7%; U.S. 12.5%; Japan 10.8%; China 9.5%; Thailand 4.8%

Ethnic Composition

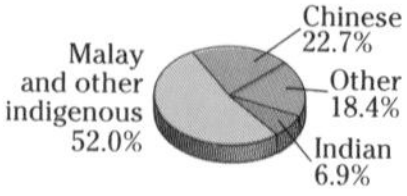

The flag hoisted on May 26, 1950, had 11 stripes, a crescent, and an 11-pointed star. The number of stripes and star points was increased to 14 on Sept. 16, 1963. Yellow is a royal color in Malaysia while red, white, and blue indicate connections with the Commonwealth. The crescent is a reminder that the population is mainly Muslim.

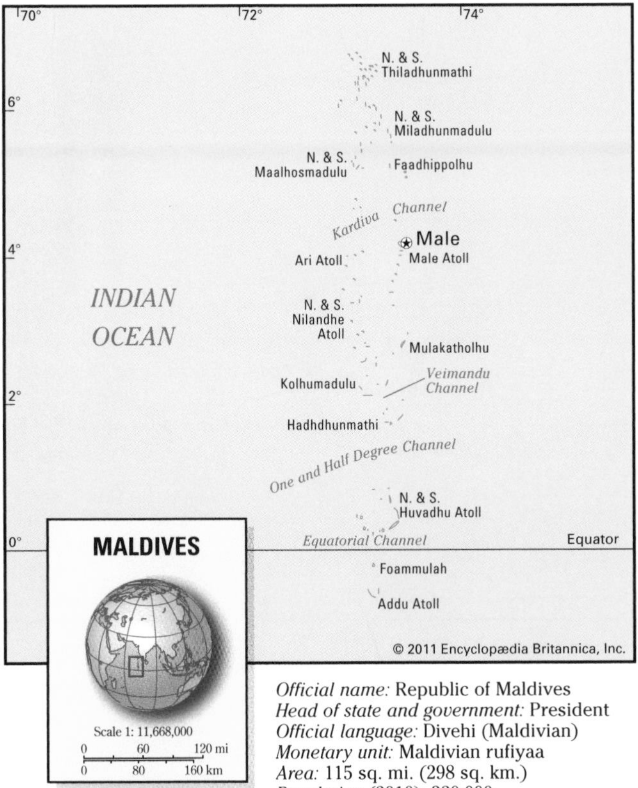

Age Breakdown

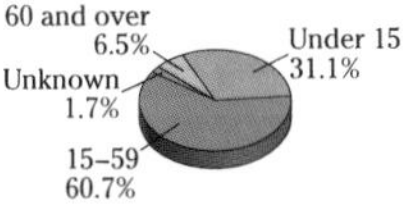

Official name: Republic of Maldives
Head of state and government: President
Official language: Divehi (Maldivian)
Monetary unit: Maldivian rufiyaa
Area: 115 sq. mi. (298 sq. km.)
Population (2010): 320,000
GNI per capita (2009): U.S.$3,870
Principal exports (2009): reexports [mostly jet fuel] 53.2%; fish 44.9%; of which fresh yellowfin tuna 18.3%, fresh skipjack tuna 10.7%, dried fish 6.5% *to:* Thailand 20.8%; Sri Lanka 17.9%; France 11.1%; U.K. 9.7%; Japan 3.9%

Maldivian ships long used a plain red ensign like those flown by Arabian and African nations. While a British protectorate in the early 20th century, the Maldives adopted a flag which was only slightly altered upon independence (July 26, 1965). The green panel and white crescent are symbolic of Islam, progress, prosperity, and peace.

Official name: Republic of Mali
Head of government: Prime Minister
Official language: French
Monetary unit: CFA franc
Area: 482,077 sq. mi. (1,248,574 sq. km.)
Population (2010): 15,022,000
GNI per capita (2009): U.S.$3,870
Principal exports (2008): gold 74.9%, raw cotton 10.6%, livestock 5.9% *to:* South Africa 72.5%; Senegal 6.8%; Cote d'Ivoire 2.6%; Switzerland 2.6%; China 1.8%

Ethnic Composition

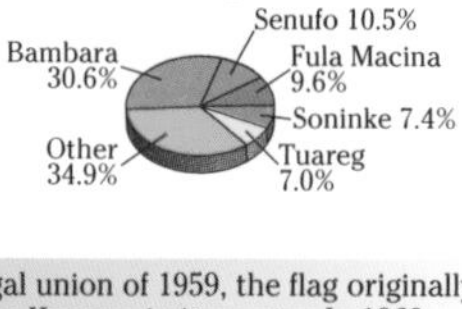

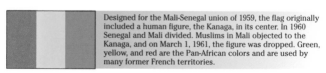

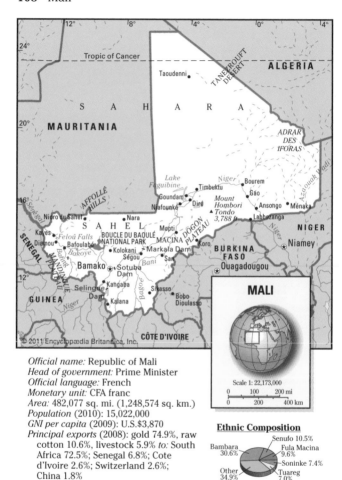

Designed for the Mali-Senegal union of 1959, the flag originally included a human figure, the Kanaga, in its center. In 1960 Senegal and Mali divided. Muslims in Mali objected to the Kanaga, and on March 1, 1961, the figure was dropped. Green, yellow, and red are the Pan-African colors and are used by many former French territories.

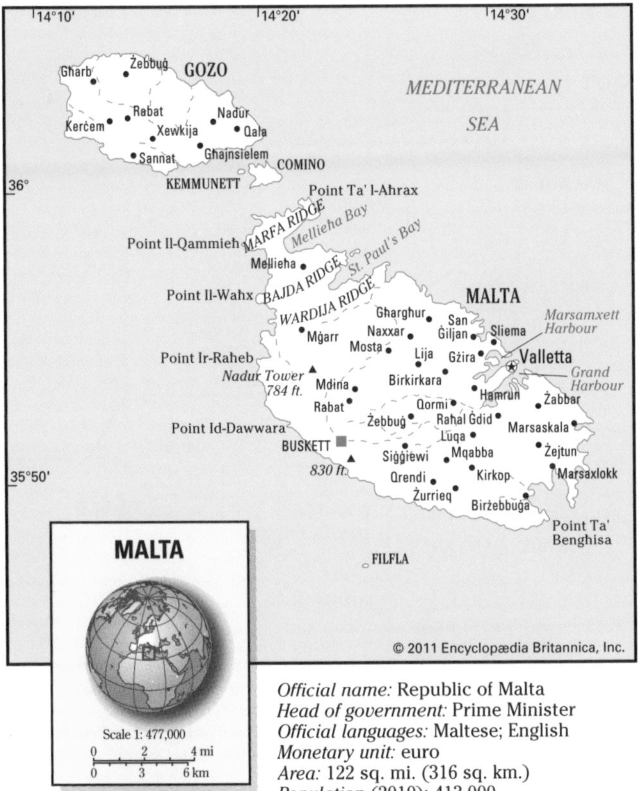

Official name: Republic of Malta
Head of government: Prime Minister
Official languages: Maltese; English
Monetary unit: euro
Area: 122 sq. mi. (316 sq. km.)
Population (2010): 413,000
GNI per capita (2008): U.S.$19,512
Principal exports (2008): machinery and apparatus 55.6%, medicines 8.3%, food 6.3%, printed matter 4.9%, children's toys 3.2% *to:* Singapore 13.6%; Germany 13.0%; France 11.6%; U.S. 9.0%; U.K. 8.2%

Age Breakdown

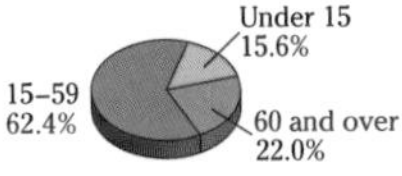

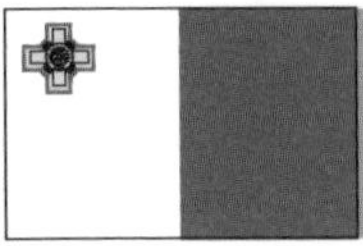

The Maltese flag was supposedly based on an 11th-century coat of arms, and a red flag with a white cross was used by the Knights of Malta from the Middle Ages. The current flag dates from independence within the Commonwealth (Sept. 21, 1964). The George Cross was granted by the British for the heroic defense of the island in World War II.

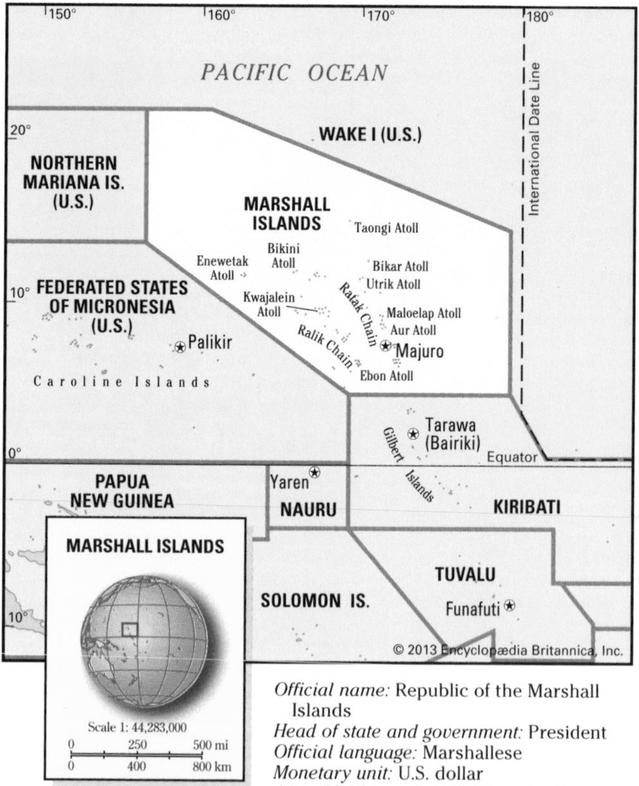

Religious Affiliation

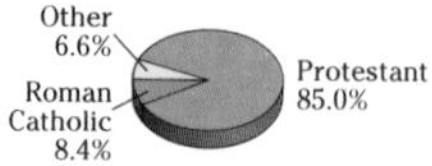

Official name: Republic of the Marshall Islands
Head of state and government: President
Official language: Marshallese
Monetary unit: U.S. dollar
Area: 70.05 sq. mi. (181.43 sq. km.)
Population (2010): 54,400
GNI per capita (2009): U.S.$3,060
Principal exports (2006): frozen fish 44.5%, reexports of diesel fuel 41.2%, crude coconut oil 9.9% *to:* mostly the U.S.

The island nation hoisted its flag on May 1, 1979. The blue stands for the ocean. The white is for brightness while the orange is for bravery and wealth. The two stripes joined symbolize the Equator, and they increase in width to show growth and vitality. The rays of the star are for the municipalities; its four long rays recall a Christian cross.

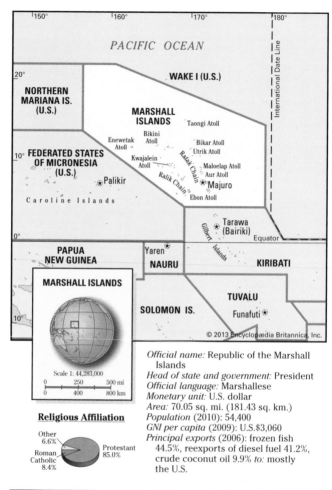

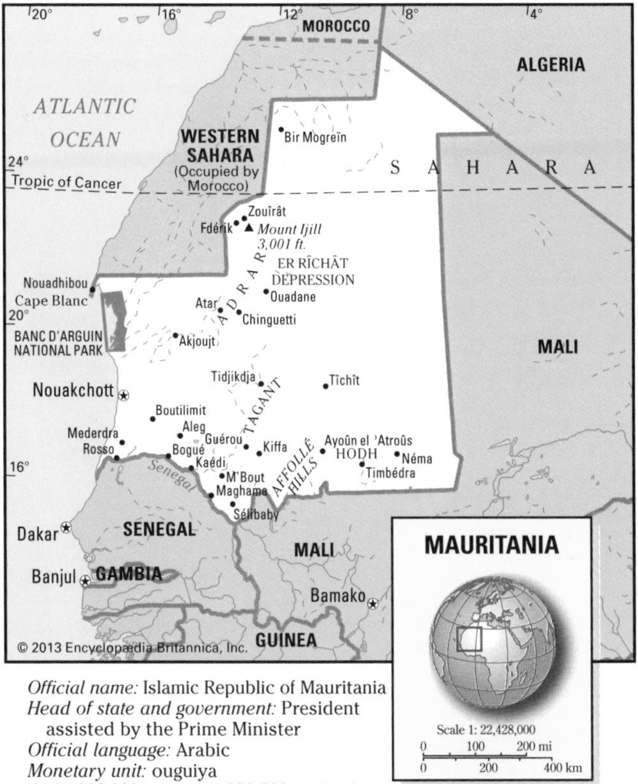

© 2013 Encyclopædia Britannica, Inc.

Official name: Islamic Republic of Mauritania
Head of state and government: President assisted by the Prime Minister
Official language: Arabic
Monetary unit: ouguiya
Area: 398,000 sq. mi. (1,030,700 sq. km.)
Population (2010): 3,205,000
GNI per capita (2009): U.S.$960
Principal exports (2002): iron ore 47.5%, crude petroleum 20.1%, fish 11.3%, copper ore 7.8%, gold 7.4% *to:* France 16.3%; Germany 8.2%; China 7.8%; Switzerland 7.4%; Italy 7.3%

Age Breakdown

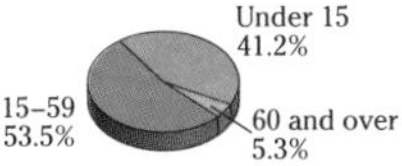

In 1958 Mauritania was granted autonomous status within the French Community. The current flag replaced the French tricolor on April 1, 1959, and no changes were made to the design at independence (Nov. 28, 1960). The green background of the flag and its star and crescent are traditional Muslim symbols that have been in use for centuries.

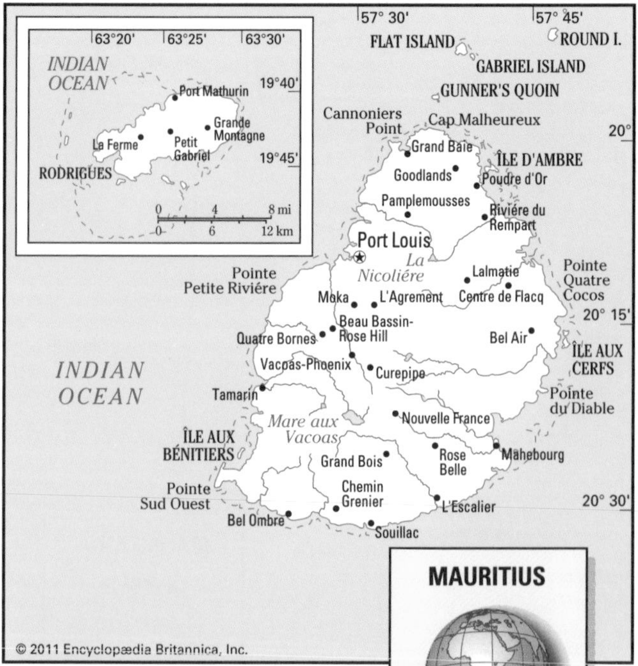

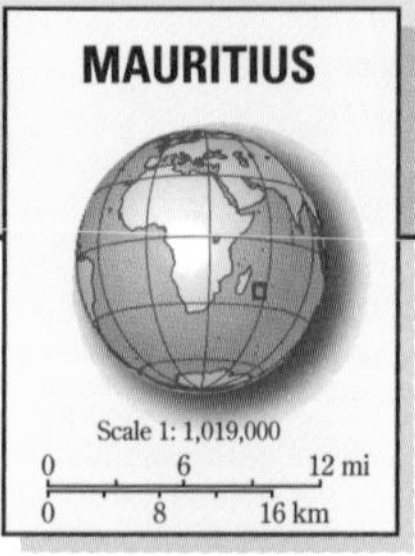

Official name: Republic of Mauritius
Head of government: Prime Minister
Official language: English
Monetary unit: Mauritian rupee
Area: 788 sq. mi. (2,040 sq. km.)
Population (2010): 1,282,000
GNI per capita (2009): U.S.$7,240
Principal exports (2008): clothing 35.2%, food 27.1%, telecommunication equipment 3.4% *to:* U.K. 29.5%; France 14.7%; U.S. 5.8%; Madagascar 5.1%

Ethnic Composition

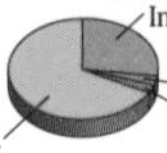

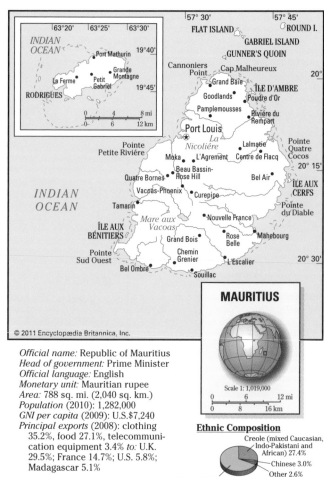

In 1968 this flag was first flown on March 12, at the time of Mauritius's independence from the United Kingdom. The flag's red stands for the struggle for freedom, while the blue represents the Indian Ocean. The light of independence is shown by yellow. Green is for agriculture and the year-round flourishing of the island's plant life.

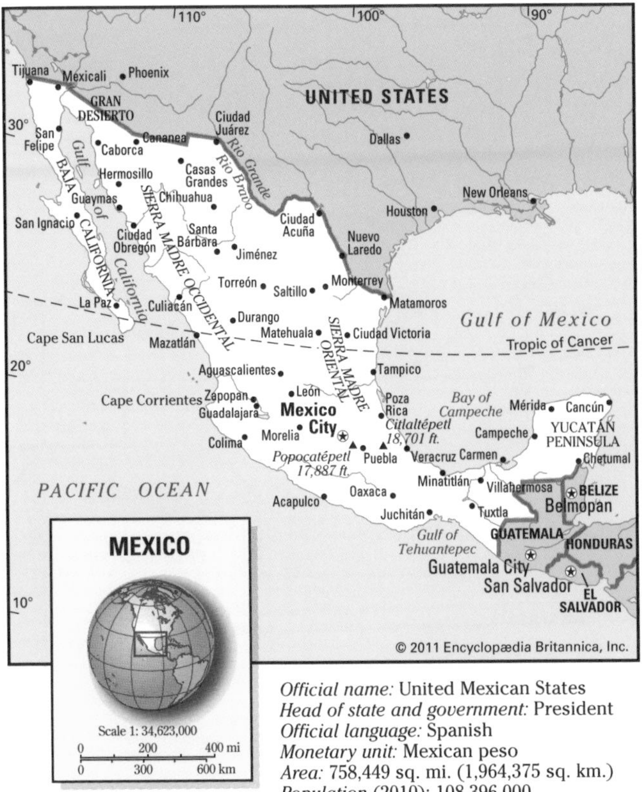

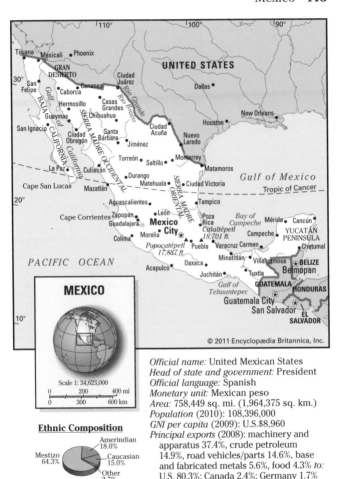

Official name: United Mexican States
Head of state and government: President
Official language: Spanish
Monetary unit: Mexican peso
Area: 758,449 sq. mi. (1,964,375 sq. km.)
Population (2010): 108,396,000
GNI per capita (2009): U.S.$8,960
Principal exports (2008): machinery and apparatus 37.4%, crude petroleum 14.9%, road vehicles/parts 14.6%, base and fabricated metals 5.6%, food 4.3% *to:* U.S. 80.3%; Canada 2.4%; Germany 1.7%

Ethnic Composition

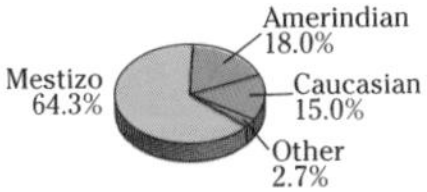

The green-white-red tricolor was officially established in 1821. Green is for independence, white for Roman Catholicism, and red for union. The emblem depicts the scene supposedly witnessed by the Aztecs in 1325: an eagle with a snake in its beak standing upon a cactus growing out of rocks in the water. The flag was modified on Sept. 17, 1968.

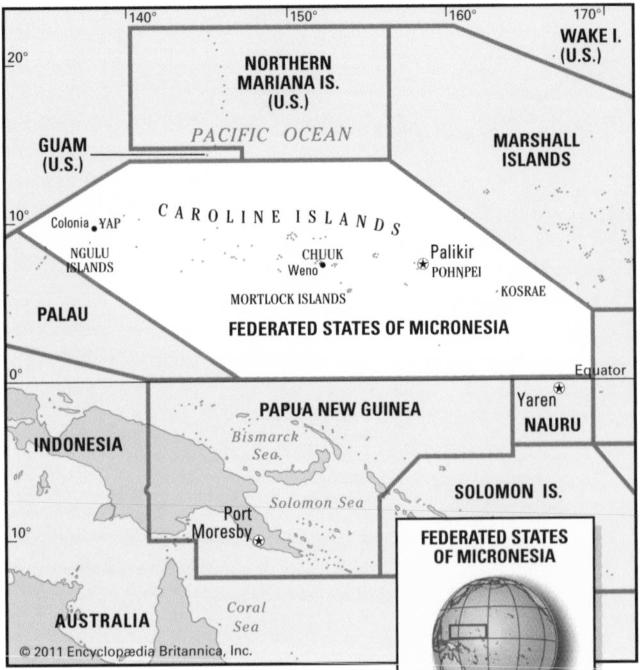

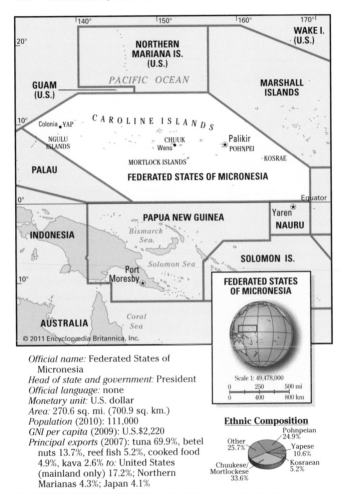

Official name: Federated States of Micronesia
Head of state and government: President
Official language: none
Monetary unit: U.S. dollar
Area: 270.6 sq. mi. (700.9 sq. km.)
Population (2010): 111,000
GNI per capita (2009): U.S.$2,220
Principal exports (2007): tuna 69.9%, betel nuts 13.7%, reef fish 5.2%, cooked food 4.9%, kava 2.6% *to:* United States (mainland only) 17.2%; Northern Marianas 4.3%; Japan 4.1%

Ethnic Composition

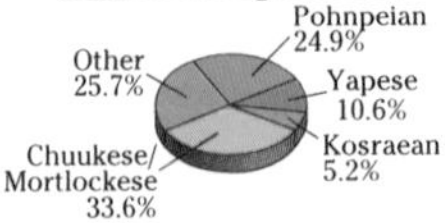

On Nov. 30, 1978, the flag of the former United States trust territory was approved by an interim congress. Based on the symbolism of the territory, the flag has stars for the four states of Micronesia. After sovereignty was granted in 1986, a dark blue background (for the Pacific Ocean) was substituted for the original "United Nations blue."

Ethnic Composition

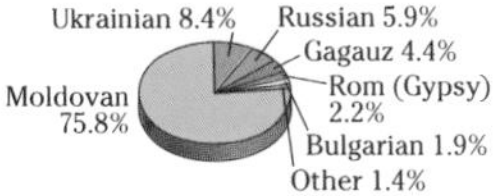

Official name: Republic of Moldova
Head of government: Prime Minister
Official language: Moldovan
Monetary unit: Moldovan leu
Area: 13,067 sq. mi. (33,843 sq. km.)
Population (2010): 3,941,000
GNI per capita (2009): U.S.$1,590
Principal exports (2008): apparel/clothing 16.8%, food 15.6%, wine 9.7%, oil seeds/vegetable oils 8.2%, insulated wire/cable 6.3% *to:* Romania 21.1%; Russia 19.7%; Italy 10.5%; Ukraine 9.0%; Belarus 5.8%

By 1989, Moldovans protested against communist rule, and the traditional tricolor of blue-yellow-red, which had flown briefly in 1917–18, became a popular symbol. It replaced the communist flag in May 1990 and remained after independence in 1991. The shield has an eagle on whose breast are an aurochs head, a crescent, a star, and a flower.

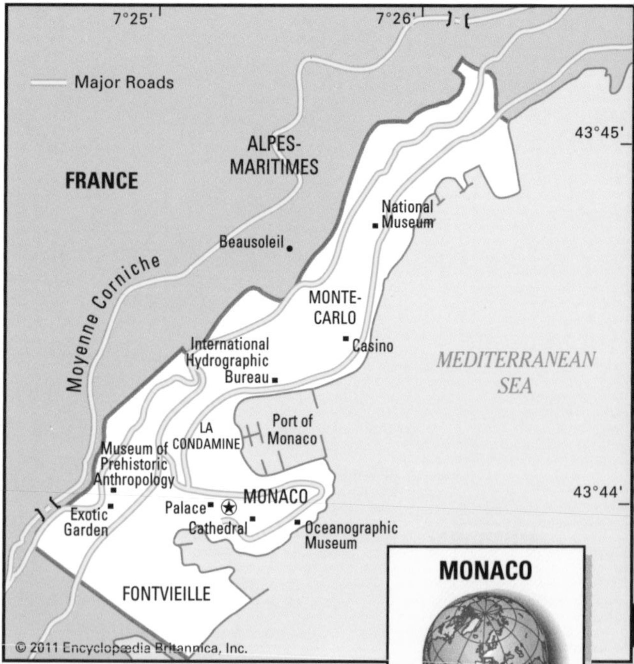

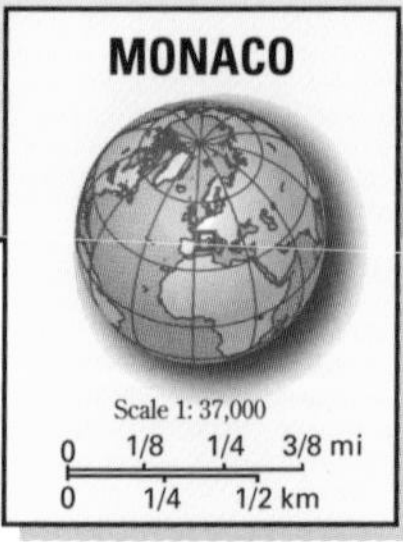

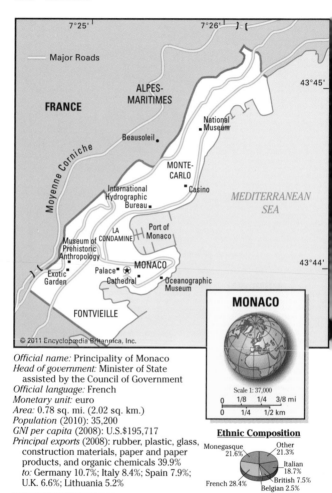

Official name: Principality of Monaco
Head of government: Minister of State assisted by the Council of Government
Official language: French
Monetary unit: euro
Area: 0.78 sq. mi. (2.02 sq. km.)
Population (2010): 35,200
GNI per capita (2008): U.S.$195,717
Principal exports (2008): rubber, plastic, glass, construction materials, paper and paper products, and organic chemicals 39.9% *to:* Germany 10.7%; Italy 8.4%; Spain 7.9%; U.K. 6.6%; Lithuania 5.2%

Ethnic Composition

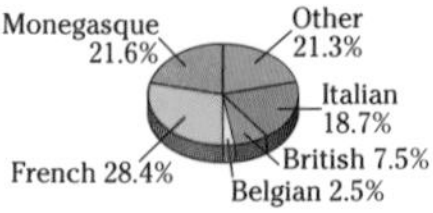

Used at the United Nations and by private citizens, Monaco's national flag's plain red and white are from the ruling Grimaldi family's coat of arms. The coat of arms shows a red and white shield flanked by Franciscan monks. Francois Grimaldi disguised himself as such a monk in capturing the fortress of Monaco in 1297.

Official name: Mongolia
Head of government: Prime Minister
Official language: Khalkha Mongolian
Monetary unit: tugrik
Area: 603,930 sq. mi. (1,564,160 sq. km.)
Population (2010): 2,763,000
GNI per capita (2009): U.S.$1,630
Principal exports (2007): copper ore/concentrate 43.0%, gold 12.5%, wool/find animal hair 10.2%, zinc ore/concentrate 9.3%, coal 6.1% *to:* China 74.2%; Canada 9.5%; U.S. 3.4%; Russia 3.0%; Italy 3.0%

Ethnic Composition

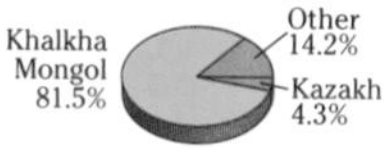

In 1945, the flag symbolizing communism (red) and Mongol nationalism (blue) was established. Near the hoist is a *soyonba,* a grouping of philosophical symbols (flame, sun, moon, yin-yang, triangles, and bars). Yellow traditionally stood for Lamaist Buddhism. On Jan. 12, 1992, a five-pointed star (for Communism) was removed from the flag.

Official name: Republic of Montenegro
Head of government: Prime Minister
Official language: Montenegrin[1]
Monetary unit: euro
Area: 5,333 sq. mi. (13,812 sq. km.)
Population (2010): 633,000
GNI per capita (2009): U.S.$6,550
Principal exports (2007): products of aluminum industry 47.0%, base metals 11.9%, beverages and tobacco 8.9%, mineral fuels 8.1% *to:* Italy 30.1%; Serbia 24.9%; Greece 12.3%; Slovenia 8.6%; Bos.–Her. 5.1%

Ethnic Composition

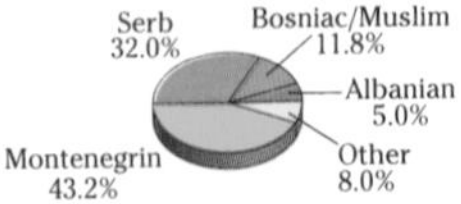

[1]Serbian, Bosnian, Albanian and Croatian can also be used as official languages per constitution.

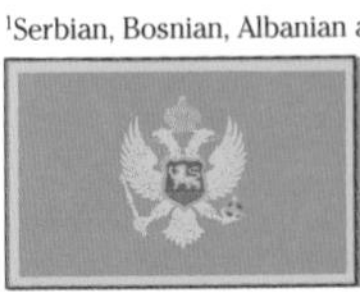

Independent in 1878, Montenegro flew the Russian-inspired red-blue-white flag. After World War I, it became part of Yugoslavia, without its own flag. Serbia-Montenegro stayed in Yugoslavia after the other republics seceded in the 1990s. In 2004, Montenegro adopted this new flag, showing the arms of the ancient Njegoš dynasty, and became independent in 2006.

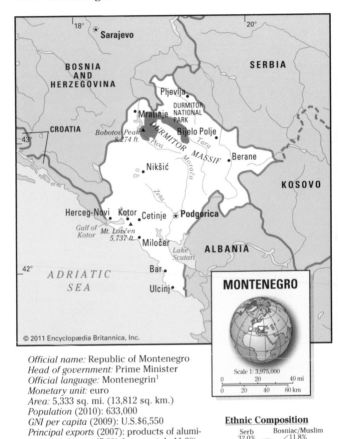

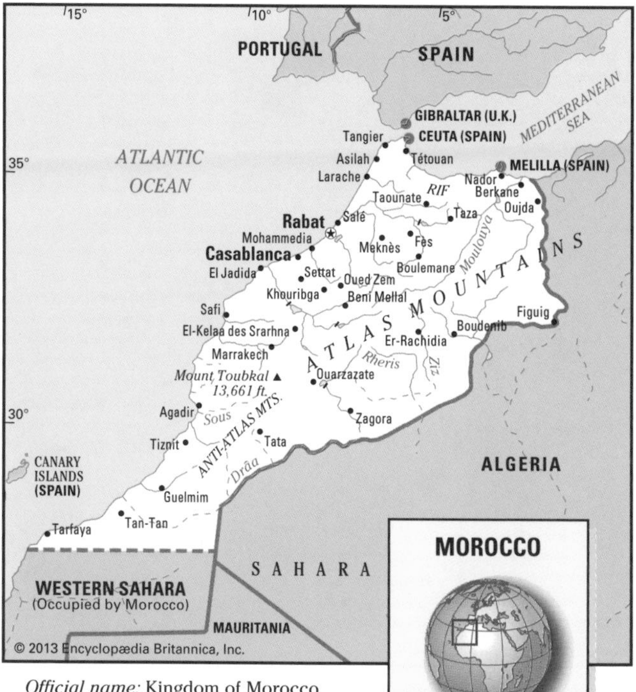

Official name: Kingdom of Morocco
Head of state and government: King assisted by Prime Minister
Official language: Arabic
Monetary unit: Moroccan dirham
Area: 170,773 sq. mi. (442,300 sq. km.)
Population (2010): 32,119,000
GNI per capita (2009): U.S.$2,790
Principal exports (2008): fertilizers [all kinds] 18.4%, inorganic chemicals 14.8%, outerwear 11.7%, fish/shrimp/octopuses 7.9%, insulated wire/cable 7.3% *to:* France 20.2%; Spain 17.9%; India 6.8%; Brazil 4.8%; Italy 4.7%

Ethnic Composition

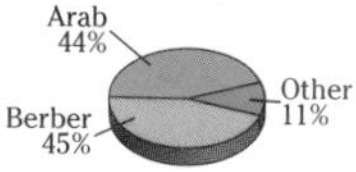

After Morocco was subjected to the rule of France and Spain in the 20th century, the plain red flag, which had been displayed on its ships, was modified on Nov. 17, 1915. To its center was added the ancient pentagram known as the "Seal of Solomon." The flag continued in use even after the French granted independence in 1956.

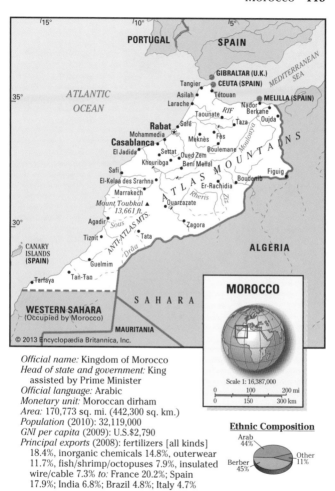

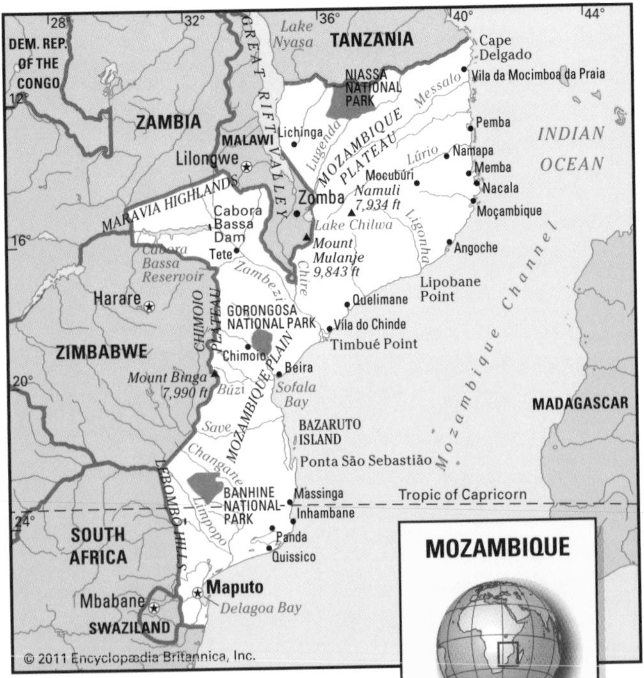

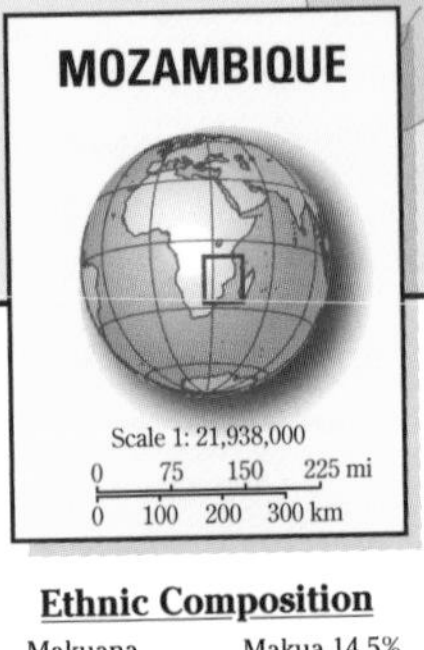

Official name: Republic of Mozambique
Head of state and government: President
Official language: Portuguese
Monetary unit: (new) metical
Area: 308,642 sq. mi. (799,379 sq. km.)
Population (2010): 22,426,000
GNI per capita (2009): U.S.$440
Principal exports (2008): aluminum 54.7%, electricity 8.5%, unmanufactured tobacco 7.3%, food 5.6% *to:* Netherlands 55.6%; South Africa 10.0%; Zimbabwe 3.0%; China 1.9%; Spain 1.9%

Ethnic Composition

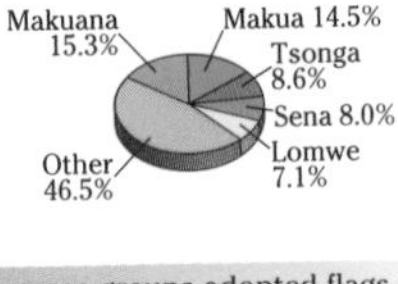

In the early 1960s, anti-Portuguese groups adopted flags of green (for forests), black (for the majority population), white (for rivers and the ocean), gold (for peace and mineral wealth), and red (for the blood of liberation). The current flag was readopted in 1983; on its star are a book, a hoe, and an assault rifle.

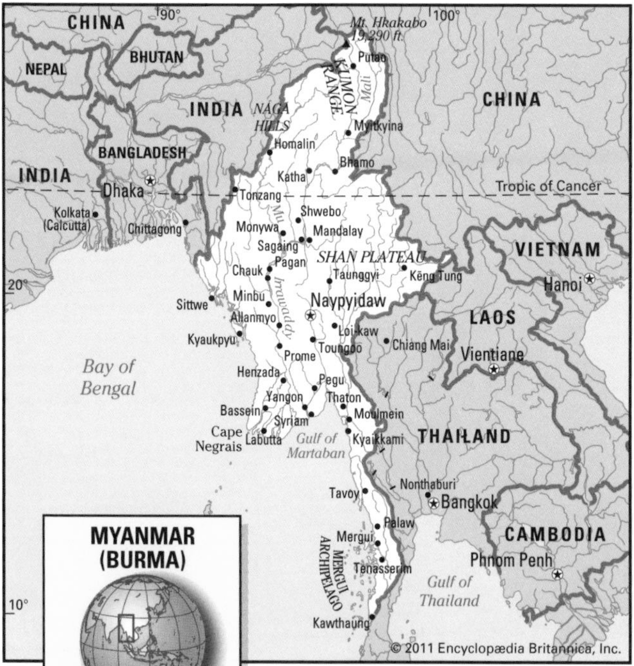

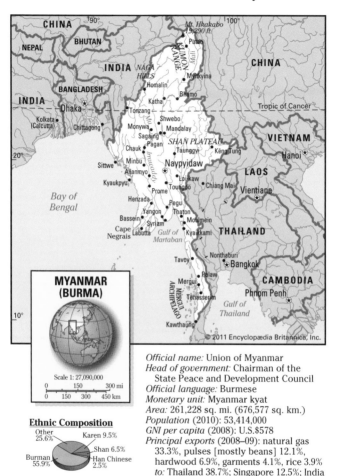

Official name: Union of Myanmar
Head of government: Chairman of the State Peace and Development Council
Official language: Burmese
Monetary unit: Myanmar kyat
Area: 261,228 sq. mi. (676,577 sq. km.)
Population (2010): 53,414,000
GNI per capita (2008): U.S.$578
Principal exports (2008–09): natural gas 33.3%, pulses [mostly beans] 12.1%, hardwood 6.9%, garments 4.1%, rice 3.9% *to:* Thailand 38.7%; Singapore 12.5%; India 11.9%; Hong Kong 9.8%; China 9.1%

Ethnic Composition

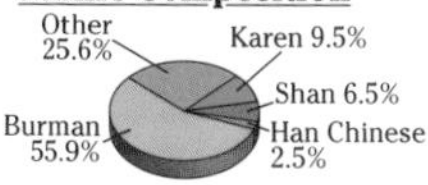

A flag, first used in Burma in 1943, had yellow, green, and red stripes. When Burma became independent from Britain (1948), it adopted a red flag with a blue canton containing white stars (later modified). Burma was renamed Myanmar in 1988. A new flag, hoisted on Oct. 21, 2010 again had yellow, green, and red stripes with a central white star.

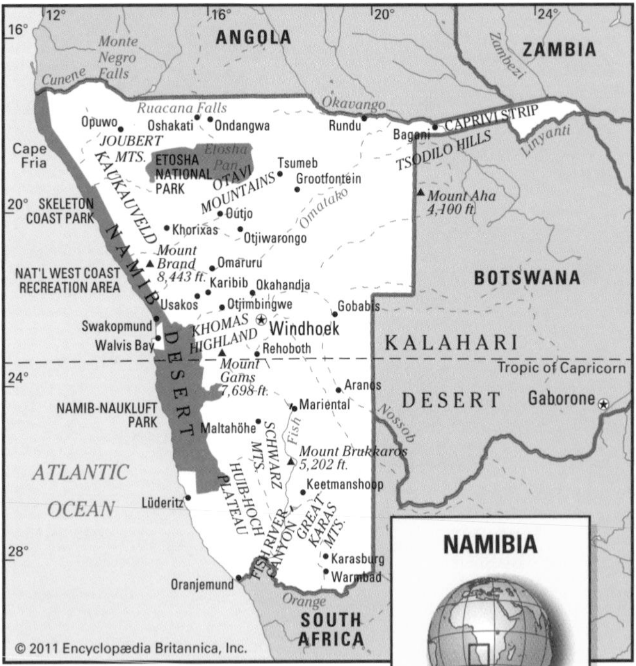

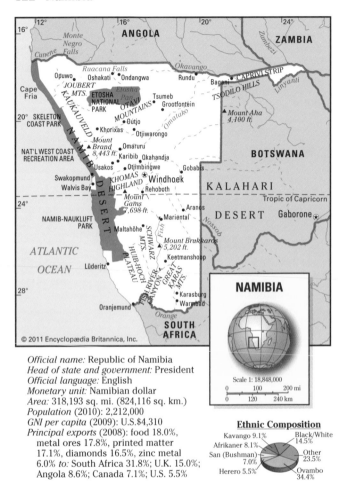

Official name: Republic of Namibia
Head of state and government: President
Official language: English
Monetary unit: Namibian dollar
Area: 318,193 sq. mi. (824,116 sq. km.)
Population (2010): 2,212,000
GNI per capita (2009): U.S.$4,310
Principal exports (2008): food 18.0%, metal ores 17.8%, printed matter 17.1%, diamonds 16.5%, zinc metal 6.0% *to:* South Africa 31.8%; U.K. 15.0%; Angola 8.6%; Canada 7.1%; U.S. 5.5%

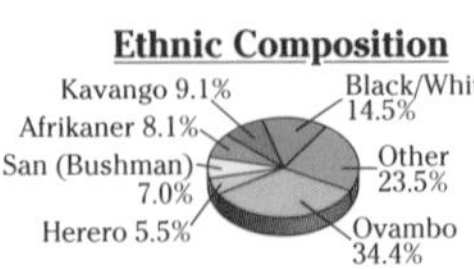

The flag was adopted on Feb. 2, 1990, and hoisted on independence from South Africa, March 21, 1990. Its colors are those of the South West Africa People's Organization: blue (for sky and ocean), red (for heroism and determination), and green (for agriculture). The gold sun represents life and energy while the white stripes are for water resources.

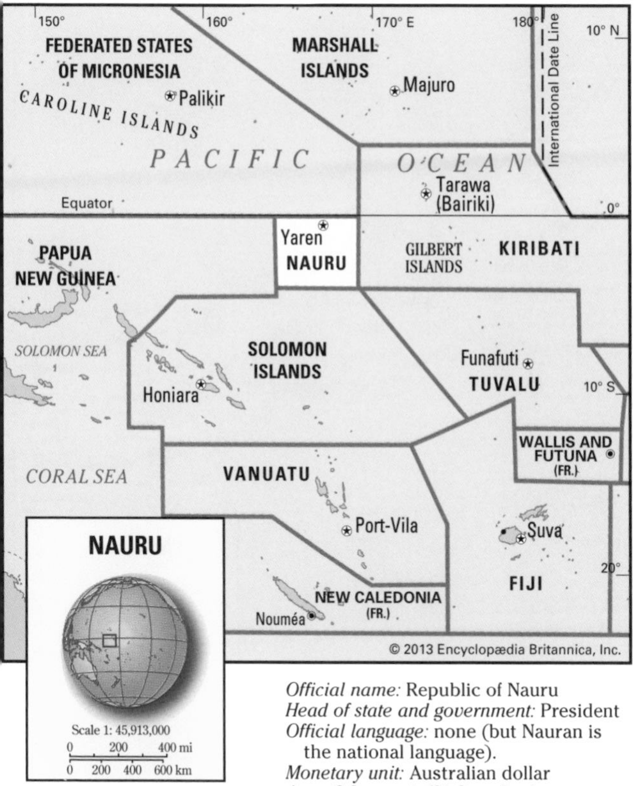

Ethnic Composition

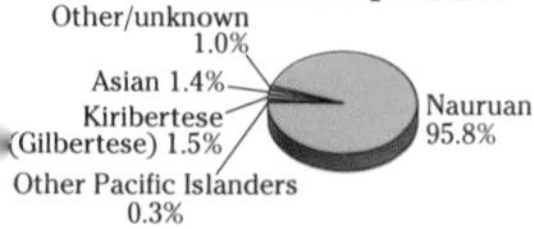

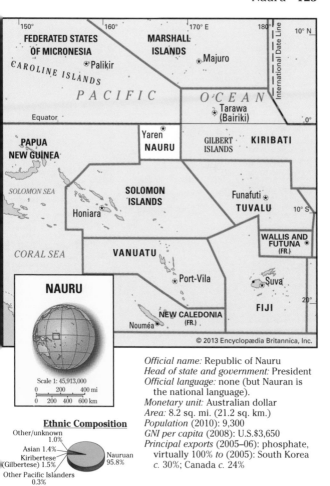

Official name: Republic of Nauru
Head of state and government: President
Official language: none (but Nauran is the national language).
Monetary unit: Australian dollar
Area: 8.2 sq. mi. (21.2 sq. km.)
Population (2010): 9,300
GNI per capita (2008): U.S.$3,650
Principal exports (2005–06): phosphate, virtually 100% *to* (2005): South Korea *c.* 30%; Canada *c.* 24%

Celebrating its independence from Australia on January 31, 1968, Nauru showed this flag chosen from a local competition. The blue field is for the Pacific Ocean. Its yellow horizontal stripe stands for the equator, which lies about 40 miles north of the island republic. Representing the original 12 tribes of Nauru is the 12-pointed white star beneath.

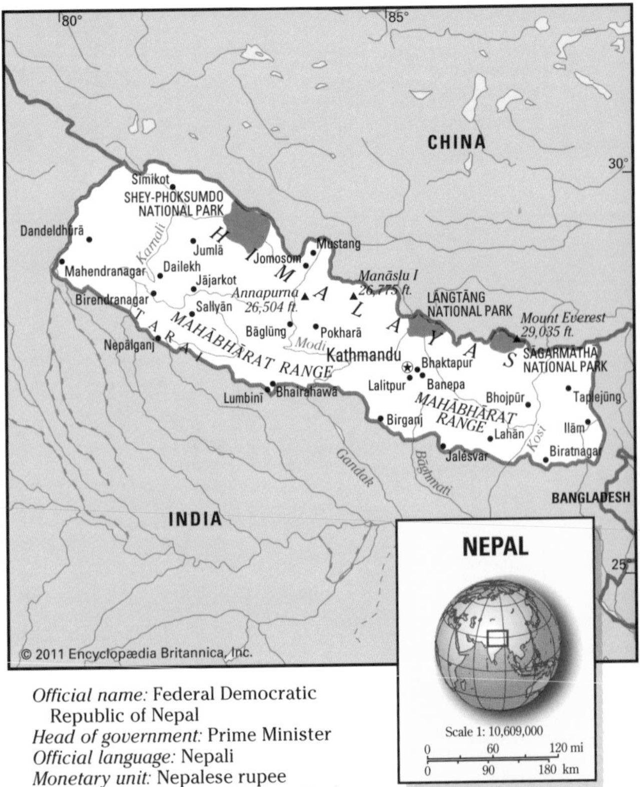

Official name: Federal Democratic Republic of Nepal
Head of government: Prime Minister
Official language: Nepali
Monetary unit: Nepalese rupee
Area: 56,827 sq. mi. (147,181 sq. km.)
Population (2010): 28,952,000
GNI per capita (2009): U.S.$440
Principal exports (2008–09): textiles/thread/yarn 12.2%, pulses 9.9%, garments 9.7%, woolen carpets 8.4% *to:* India *c.* 55%; U.S. *c.* 10%; Bangladesh *c.* 9%; Germany *c.* 5%

Religious Affiliation

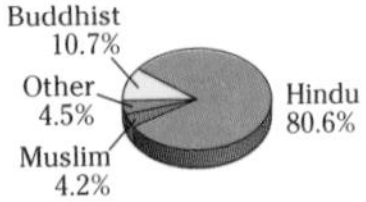

Established on Dec. 16, 1962, Nepal's flag consists of two united pennant shapes; it is the only non-rectangular national flag in the world. In the upper segment is a moon with a crescent attached below; in the bottom segment appears a stylized sun. The symbols are for different dynasties and express a hope for the immortality of the nation. The crimson and blue colors are common in Nepali art.

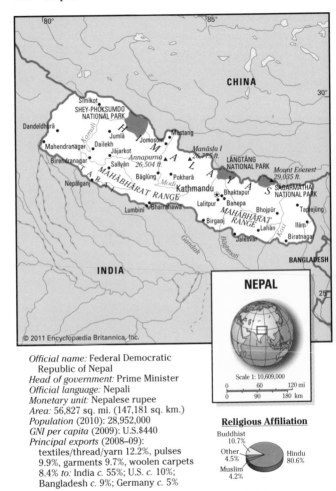

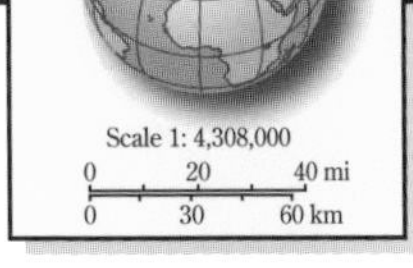

Official name: Kingdom of the Netherlands
Head of government: Prime Minister
Official language: Dutch
Monetary unit: euro
Area: 16,040 sq. mi. (41,543 sq. km.)
Population (2010): 16,602,000
GNI per capita (2009): U.S.$49,350
Principal exports (2008): machinery and apparatus 22.9%, chemicals 13.4%, food 10.1%, refined petroleum 9.7%, bulbs/plants/flowers 1.7% *to:* Germany 24.5%; Belgium 9.1%; U.K. 9.1%; France 8.7%

Religious Affiliation

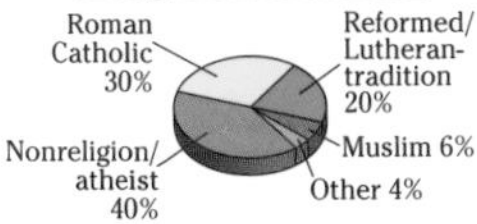

The history of the Dutch flag dates to the use of orange, white, and blue as the livery colors of William, Prince of Orange, and the use of the tricolor at sea in 1577. By 1660 the color red was substituted for orange. The flag was legalized by pro-French "patriots" on Feb. 14, 1796, and reaffirmed by royal decree on Feb. 19, 1937.

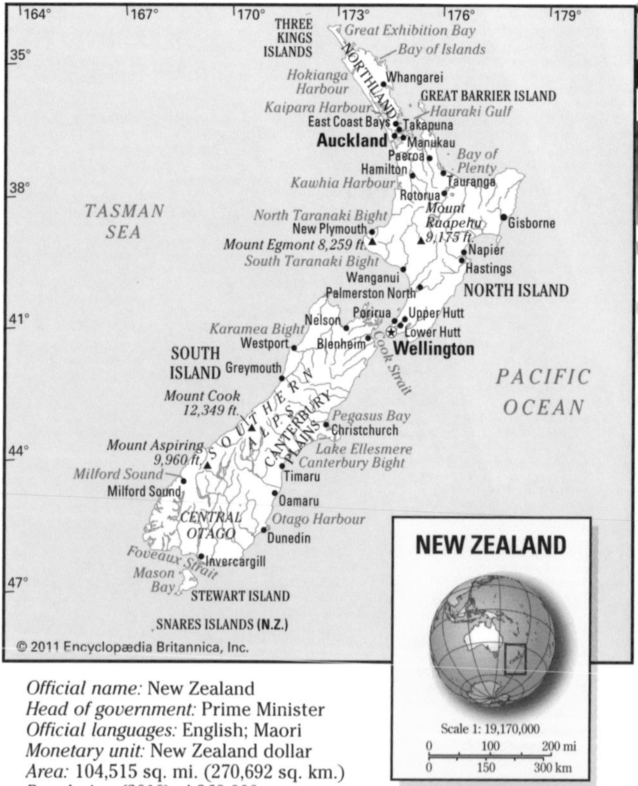

Official name: New Zealand
Head of government: Prime Minister
Official languages: English; Maori
Monetary unit: New Zealand dollar
Area: 104,515 sq. mi. (270,692 sq. km.)
Population (2010): 4,369,000
GNI per capita (2009–10): U.S.$26,754
Principal exports (2008): food 47.0%, of which meat 12.3%, milk/cream 11.3%; wood and paper products 7.8%; machinery and apparatus 6.9%, crude petroleum 6.5% *to:* Australia 23.3%; U.S. 10.2%; Japan 8.4%; China 5.9%; U.K. 3.9%

Ethnic Composition

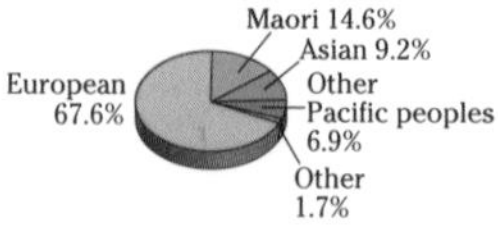

The Maori of New Zealand accepted British control in 1840, and a colonial flag was adopted on Jan. 15, 1867. It included the Union Jack in the canton and the letters "NZ" at the fly end. Later versions used the Southern Cross. Dominion status was granted on Sept. 26, 1907, and independence on Nov. 25, 1947, but the flag was unchanged.

Official name: Republic of Nicaragua
Head of state and government: President
Official language: Spanish
Monetary unit: córdoba
Area: 50,337 sq. mi. (130,373 sq. km.)
Population (2010): 5,822,000
GNI per capita (2009): U.S.$1,010
Principal exports (2007): coffee 15.8%, beef 15.0%, milk/cream/cheese 7.8%, raw sugar 6.1%, crustaceans 5.9%, gold 5.4% *to:* United States 31.2%; El Salvador 14.1%; Honduras 9.3%; Costa Rica 7.3%; Canada 5.8%

Ethnic Composition

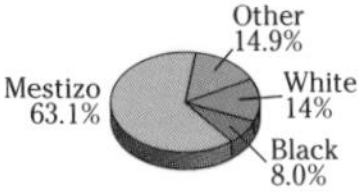

On Aug. 21, 1823, a blue-white-blue flag was adopted by the five member states of the United Provinces of Central America, which included Nicaragua. From the mid-19th century various flag designs were used in Nicaragua, but the old flag was readopted in 1908, with a modified coat of arms, and reaffirmed by law on Aug. 27, 1971.

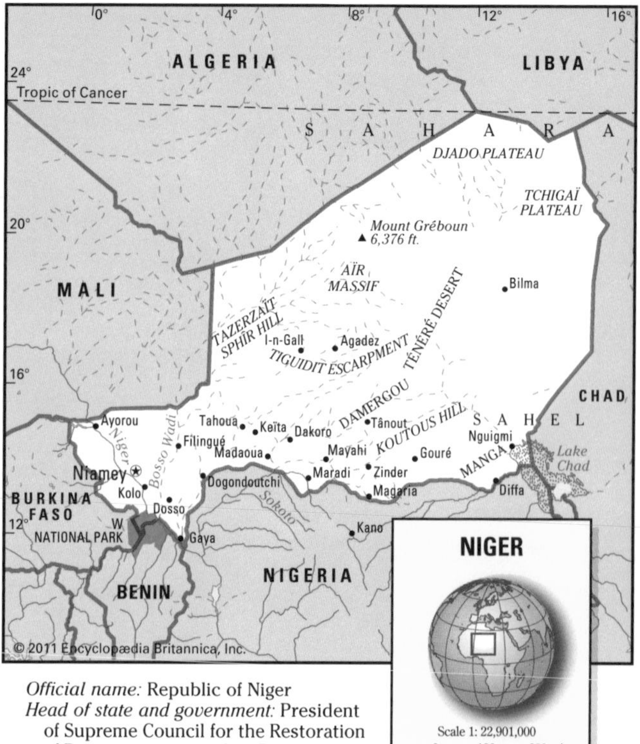

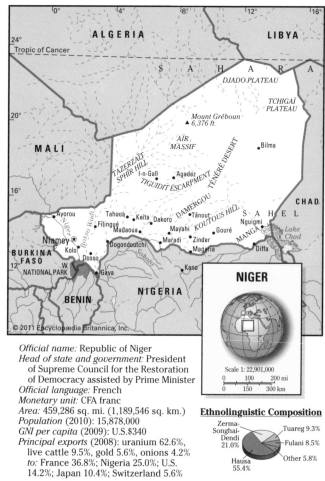

Official name: Republic of Niger
Head of state and government: President of Supreme Council for the Restoration of Democracy assisted by Prime Minister
Official language: French
Monetary unit: CFA franc
Area: 459,286 sq. mi. (1,189,546 sq. km.)
Population (2010): 15,878,000
GNI per capita (2009): U.S.$340
Principal exports (2008): uranium 62.6%, live cattle 9.5%, gold 5.6%, onions 4.2% *to:* France 36.8%; Nigeria 25.0%; U.S. 14.2%; Japan 10.4%; Switzerland 5.6%

Ethnolinguistic Composition

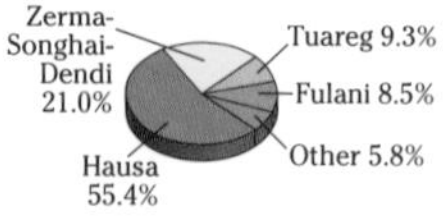

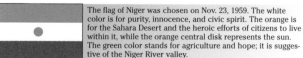

The flag of Niger was chosen on Nov. 23, 1959. The white color is for purity, innocence, and civic spirit. The orange is for the Sahara Desert and the heroic efforts of citizens to live within it, while the orange central disk represents the sun. The green color stands for agriculture and hope; it is suggestive of the Niger River valley.

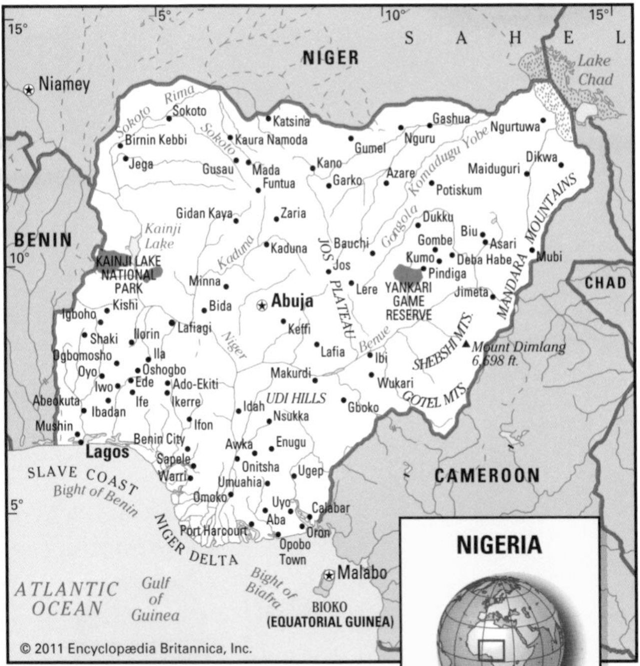

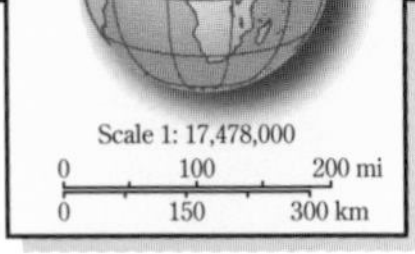

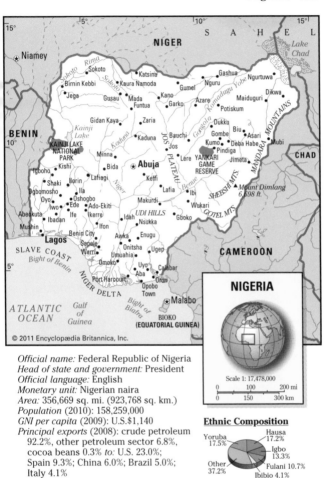

Official name: Federal Republic of Nigeria
Head of state and government: President
Official language: English
Monetary unit: Nigerian naira
Area: 356,669 sq. mi. (923,768 sq. km.)
Population (2010): 158,259,000
GNI per capita (2009): U.S.$1,140
Principal exports (2008): crude petroleum 92.2%, other petroleum sector 6.8%, cocoa beans 0.3% *to:* U.S. 23.0%; Spain 9.3%; China 6.0%; Brazil 5.0%; Italy 4.1%

Ethnic Composition

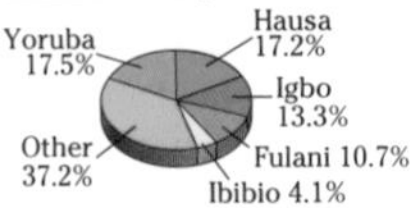

The Nigerian flag became official upon independence from Britain on Oct. 1, 1960. The flag design is purposefully simple in order not to favor the symbolism of any particular ethnic or religious group. Agriculture is represented by the green stripes while unity and peace are symbolized by the white stripe.

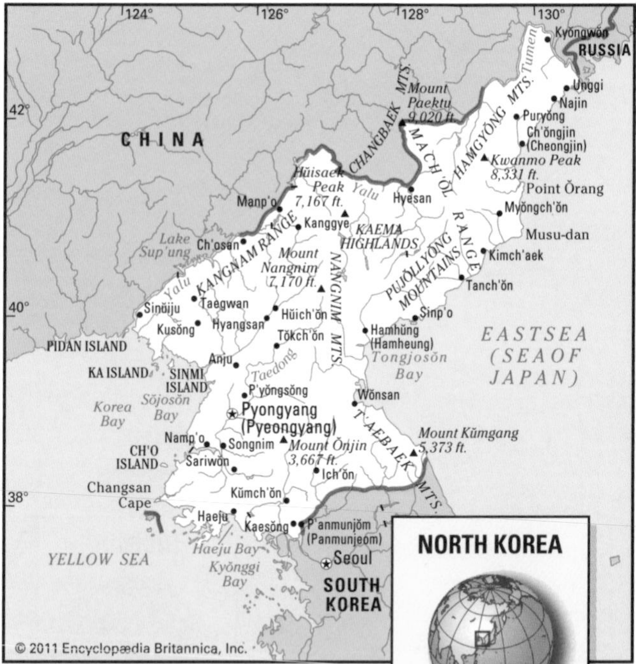

Official name: Democratic People's Republic of Korea
Head of state and government: Supreme Leader/Chairman of the National Defense Commission
Official language: Korean
Monetary unit: (new) North Korean won
Area: 47,399 sq. mi. (122,762 sq. km.)
Population (2010): 24,249,000
GNI per capita (2008): U.S.$1,033
Principal exports: agricultural products, textiles, machinery and apparatus, mineral fuels *to:* China; South Korea; India

Age Breakdown

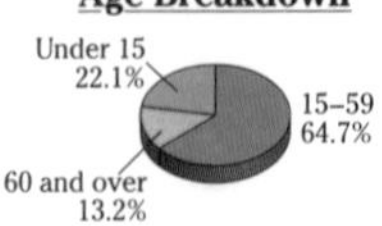

The traditional Korean Taeguk flag (still used by South Korea) was official in North Korea until July 10, 1948, when the current flag was introduced. Its red stripe and star are for the country's commitment to communism, while blue is said to stand for a commitment to peace. The white stripes stand for purity, strength, and dignity.

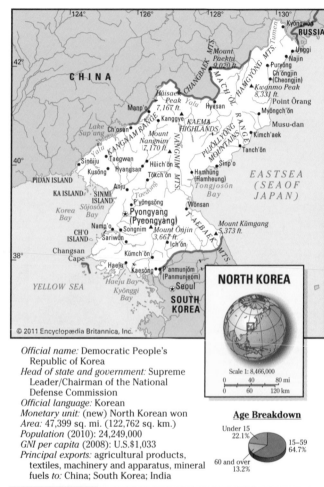

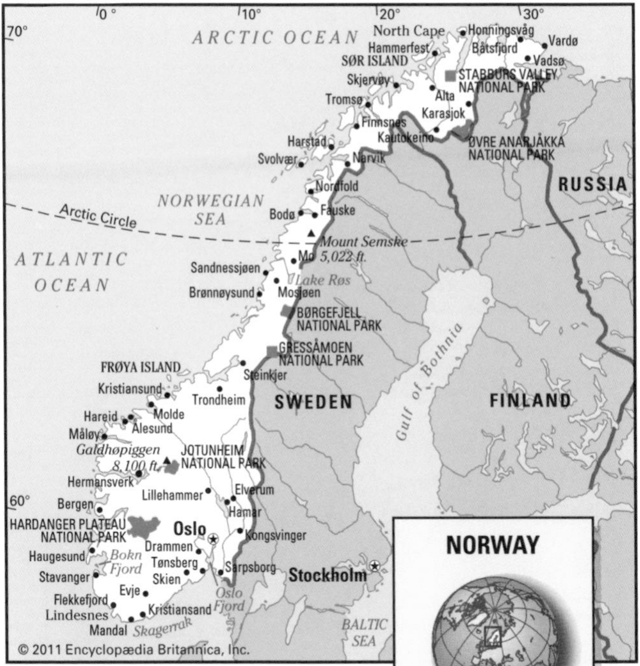

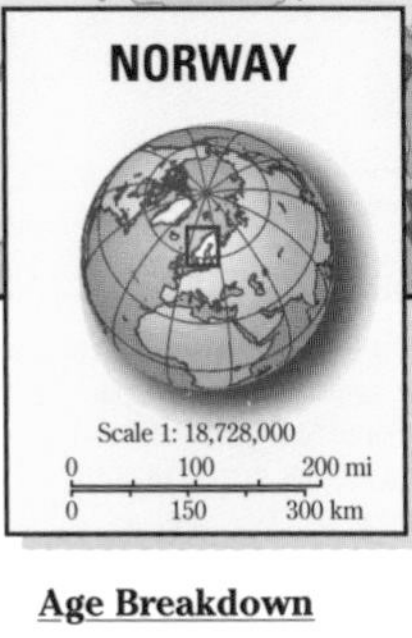

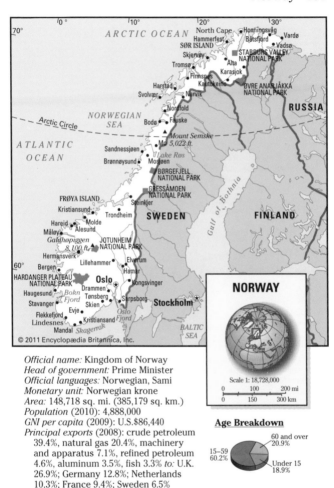

Official name: Kingdom of Norway
Head of government: Prime Minister
Official languages: Norwegian, Sami
Monetary unit: Norwegian krone
Area: 148,718 sq. mi. (385,179 sq. km.)
Population (2010): 4,888,000
GNI per capita (2009): U.S.$86,440
Principal exports (2008): crude petroleum 39.4%, natural gas 20.4%, machinery and apparatus 7.1%, refined petroleum 4.6%, aluminum 3.5%, fish 3.3% *to:* U.K. 26.9%; Germany 12.8%; Netherlands 10.3%; France 9.4%; Sweden 6.5%

Age Breakdown

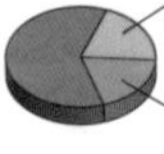

The first distinctive Norwegian flag was created in 1814 while the country was under Swedish rule. It was based on the red Danish flag with its white cross. In 1821 the Norwegian parliament developed the current flag design. From 1844 to 1899, six years before independence, the official flag included a symbol of Swedish-Norwegian union.

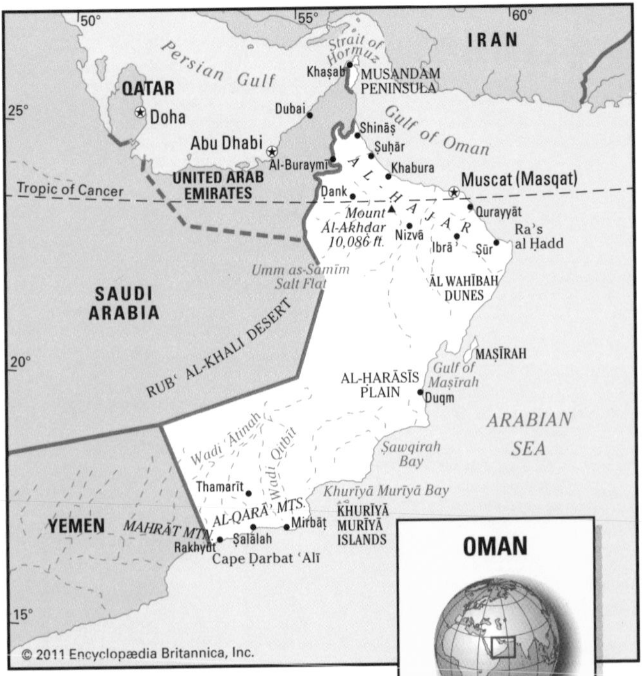

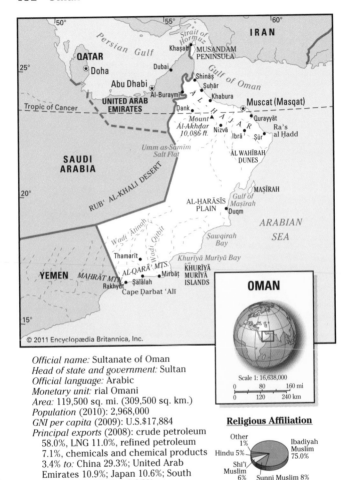

Official name: Sultanate of Oman
Head of state and government: Sultan
Official language: Arabic
Monetary unit: rial Omani
Area: 119,500 sq. mi. (309,500 sq. km.)
Population (2010): 2,968,000
GNI per capita (2009): U.S.$17,884
Principal exports (2008): crude petroleum 58.0%, LNG 11.0%, refined petroleum 7.1%, chemicals and chemical products 3.4% *to:* China 29.3%; United Arab Emirates 10.9%; Japan 10.6%; South Korea 9.6%; Thailand 6.8%

Religious Affiliation

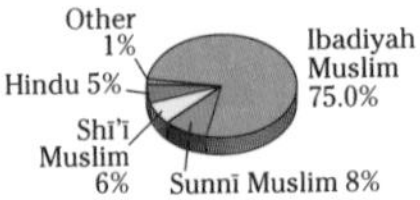

The flag dates to Dec. 17, 1970, and it was altered on Nov. 18, 1995. The white is for peace and prosperity, red is for battles, and green is for the fertility of the land. Unofficially, white recalls the imamate, red the sultanate, and green Al-Jabal Al-Akhdar ("The Green Mountain"). The coat of arms has two swords, a dagger, and a belt.

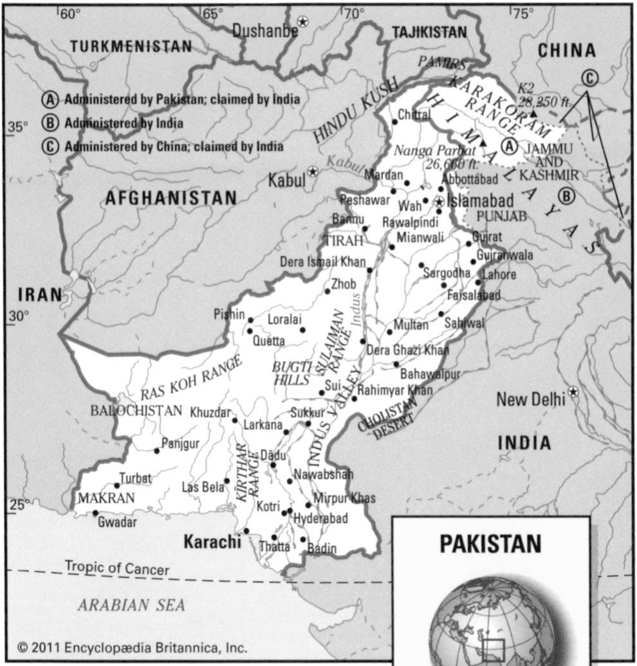

Official name: Islamic Republic of Pakistan
Head of government: Prime Minister
Official language: Urdū[1]
Monetary unit: Pakistan rupee
Area: 307,374 sq. mi. (796,096 sq. km.)
Population (2010): 184,405,000
GNI per capita (2009): U.S.$1,020
Principal exports (2008): apparel and accessories 19.3%, rice 12.0%, woven cotton fabrics 10.9%, bedding 10.1%, refined petroleum 5.7% *to* (2009): U.S. 16.1%; U.A.E. 11.7%; Afghanistan 8.6%; U.K. 4.5%; China 4.2%

Ethnic Composition

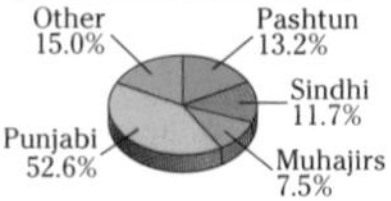

[1]English may be used for official purposes.

On Dec. 30, 1906, the All India Muslim League approved this typically Muslim flag, with its star and crescent. At independence (Aug. 14, 1947) a white stripe was added for minority religious groups. Also symbolized are prosperity and peace by the green and white colors, progress by the crescent, and knowledge and light by the star.

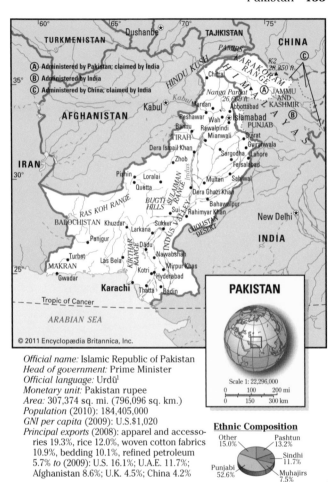

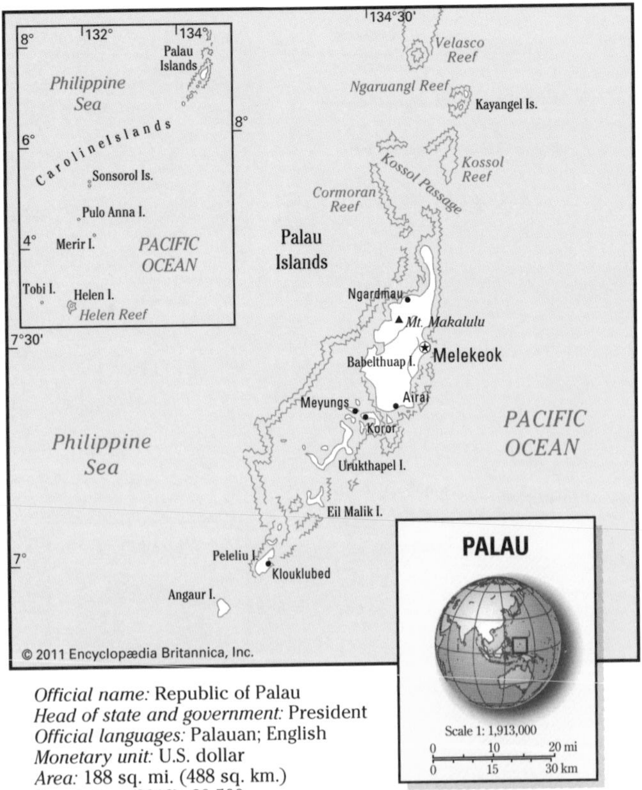

Official name: Republic of Palau
Head of state and government: President
Official languages: Palauan; English
Monetary unit: U.S. dollar
Area: 188 sq. mi. (488 sq. km.)
Population (2010): 20,500
GNI per capita (2008): U.S.$8,940
Principal exports (2006–07): mostly high grade tuna and garments *to* (2008): mostly Japan; far less significantly the Philippines and South Korea

Religious Affiliation

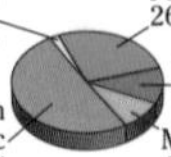

Approved on Oct. 22, 1980, and hoisted on Jan. 1, 1981, the Palauan flag was left unaltered at independence in 1994. The golden disk represents the full moon, which is said on Palau to be propitious for fishing, planting, and other activities and gives the people "a feeling of warmth, tranquillity, peace, love, and domestic unity."

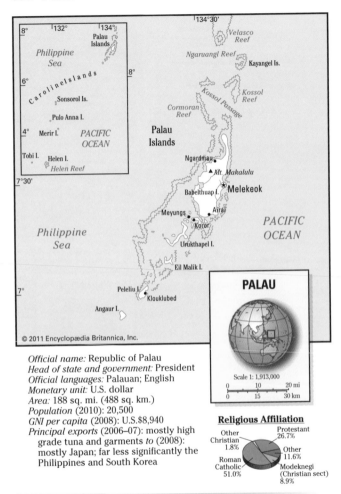

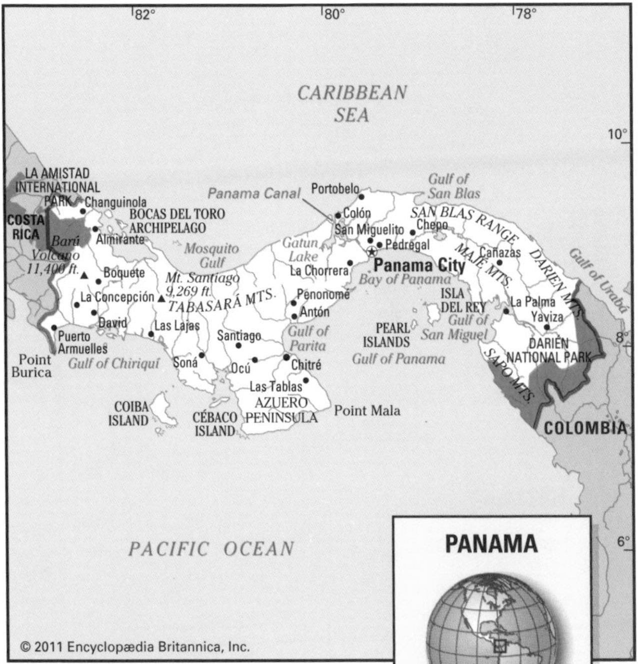

Official name: Republic of Panama
Head of state and government: President
Official language: Spanish
Monetary unit: balboa
Area: 29,157 sq. mi. (75,517 sq. km.)
Population (2010): 3,328,000
GNI per capita (2009): U.S.$6,740
Principal exports (2008): fish 29.3%, melons and papayas 18.8%, bananas 8.6%, crustaceans and mollusks 7.2%, metal scrap 4.7% *to:* U.S. 39.2%, Netherlands 10.7%; Costa Rica 5.8%; Sweden 5.5%; U.K. 5.4%

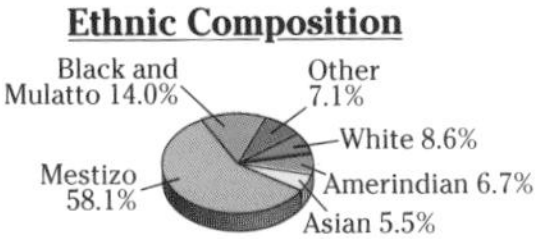

The Panamanian flag became official on July 4, 1904, after independence from Colombia was won through the intervention of the United States, which was determined to construct the Panama Canal. The flag was influenced by the United States, and its quartered design was said to symbolize the power sharing of Panama's two main political parties.

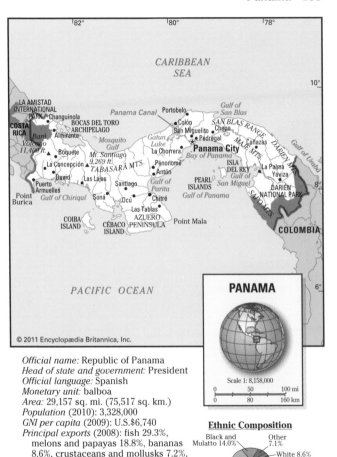

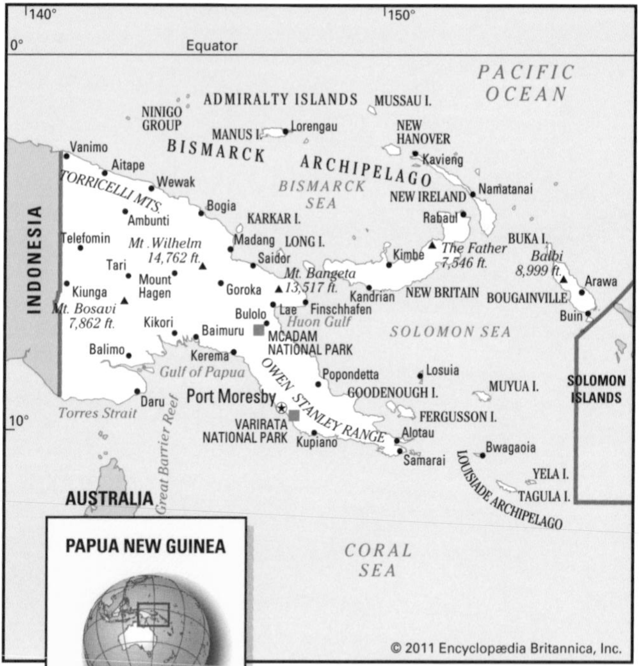

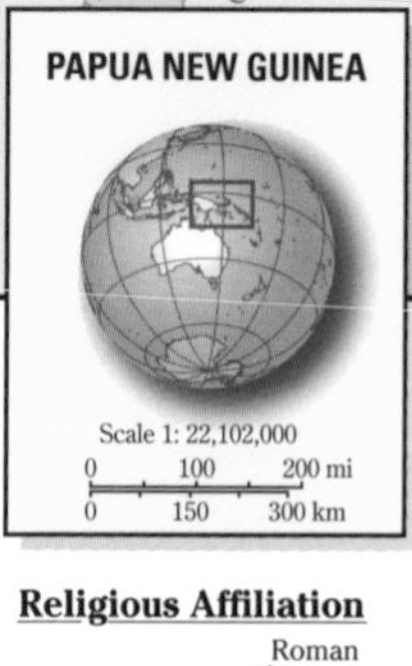

Official name: Independent State of Papua New Guinea
Head of government: Prime Minister
Official languages: English; Hiri Moto; Tuk Pisin
Monetary unit: kina
Area: 178,704 sq. mi. (462,840 sq. km.)
Population (2010): 6,065,000
GNI per capita (2009): U.S.$1,180
Principal exports (2009): gold 44.9%, copper 16.8%, crude oil 13.6%, palm oil 5.9% *to:* Australia 44.3%; Japan 13.3%; Philippines 7.8%; Germany 4.8%; South Korea 4.7%

Religious Affiliation

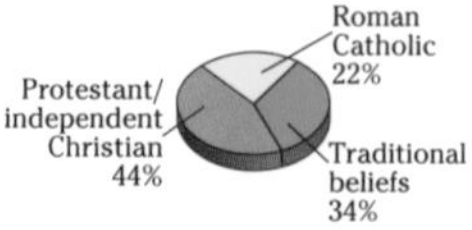

The formerly German-, British-, and Australian-controlled territory officially recognized its flag on March 11, 1971, and flag usage was extended to ships at independence (Sept. 16, 1975). The colors red and black are shown extensively in local art and clothing. Featured emblems are a bird of paradise and the Southern Cross constellation.

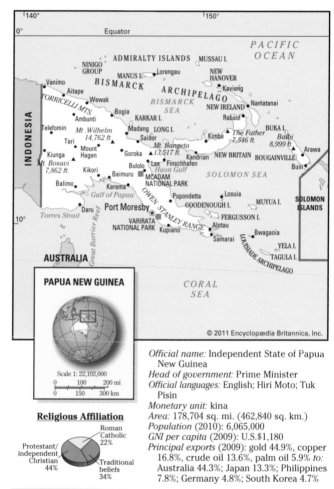

Official name: Republic of Paraguay
Head of state and government: President
Official languages: Spanish; Guaraní
Monetary unit: guaraní
Area: 157,048 sq. mi. (406,752 sq. km.)
Population (2010): 6,376,000
GNI per capita (2009): U.S.$2,280
Principal exports (2008): soybean 33.8%, bovine meat 13.6%, soybean oil cake (feed stuff for animals) 12.1%, soybean oil 11.1%, cereals 8.6% *to:* Uruguay 17.7%; Argentina 16.2%; Brazil 14.0%; Chile 8.4%; Russia 6.0%

Ethnic Composition

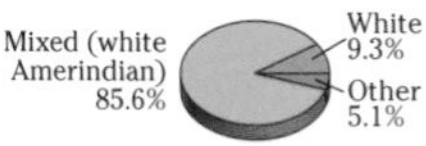

Under the dictator José Gaspar Rodríguez de Francia (1814–40) the French colors were adopted for the flag. The coat of arms (a golden star surrounded by a wreath) is on the obverse side, but the seal of the treasury (a lion, staff, and liberty cap, with the motto "Peace and Justice") is on the reverse; the flag is unique in this respect.

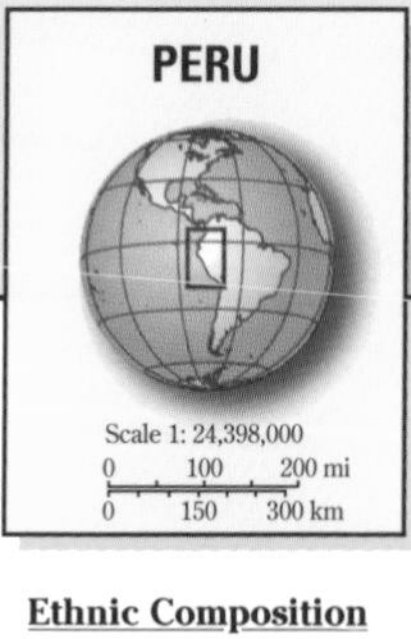

Official name: Republic of Peru
Head of state and government: President assisted by Prime Minister
Official languages: Spanish; Quechua; Aymara
Monetary unit: nuevo sol
Area: 496,218 sq. mi. (1,285,198 sq. km.)
Population (2010): 29,244,000
GNI per capita (2009): U.S.$4,160
Principal exports (2008): ore/concentrates 27.7%, gold 17.8%, food 14.4%, petroleum 9.1% *to:* U.S. 18.6%; China 12.0%; Switzerland 10.9%; Canada 6.3%; Japan 5.9%

Ethnic Composition

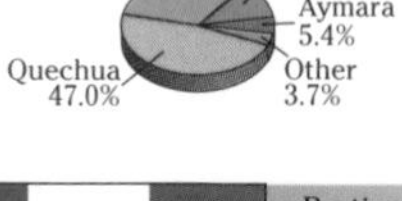

Partisans in the early 19th century adopted a red-white-red flag resembling that of Spain, but they soon made its stripes vertical. In 1825 the current design was established. The shield includes figures symbolic of national wealth—the vicuna (a relative of the alpaca), a cinchona tree, and a cornucopia with gold and silver coins.

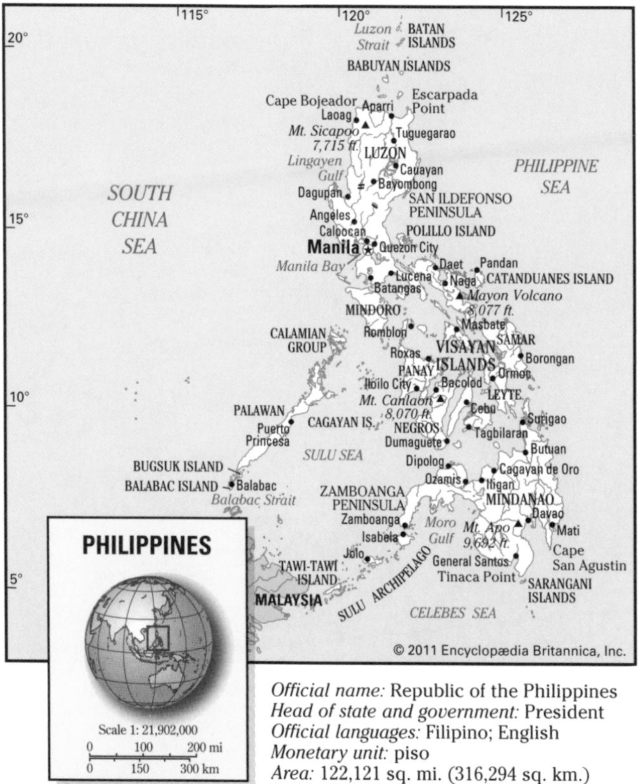

Official name: Republic of the Philippines
Head of state and government: President
Official languages: Filipino; English
Monetary unit: piso
Area: 122,121 sq. mi. (316,294 sq. km.)
Population (2010): 93,617,000
GNI per capita (2009): U.S.$1,790
Principal exports (2008): electronic integrated circuits/parts 22.7%, computers/office machines/parts 18.4%, food 4.8%, parts of road vehicles 4.2%, apparel 3.9% *to:* United States 16.7%; Japan 15.7%; China 11.1%; Hong Kong 10.2%; Netherlands 7.6%

Ethnic Composition

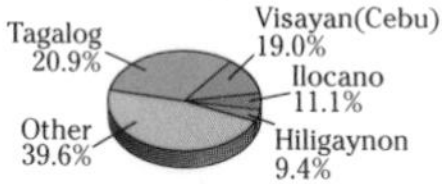

In 1898, during the Spanish-American War, Filipinos established the basic flag in use today; it was officially adopted in 1936. The white triangle is for liberty. The golden sun and stars are for the three main areas of the Philippines: Luzon, the Visayan Islands, and Mindanao. The red color is for courage and the blue color is for sacrifice.

Official name: Republic of Poland
Head of government: Prime Minister
Official language: Polish
Monetary unit: zloty
Area: 120,726 sq. mi. (312,679 sq. km.)
Population (2010): 38,183,000
GNI per capita (2009): U.S.$12,260
Principal exports (2008): transport equipment 17.4%, base and fabricated metals 12.9%, electrical equipment 12.4%, machinery and apparatus 12.3%, food products 10.1% *to:* Germany 25.1%; France 6.2%; Italy 6.0%; U.K. 5.8%

Age Breakdown

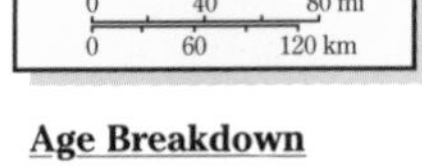

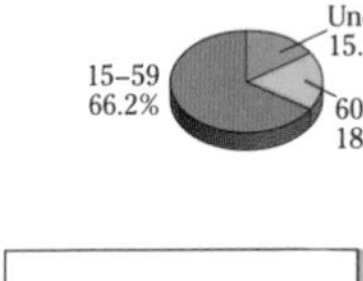

The colors of the Polish flag originated in its coat of arms, a white eagle on a red shield, dating from 1295. The precise symbolism of the colors is not known, however. Poland's simple flag of white-red horizontal stripes was adopted on Aug. 1, 1919. The flag was left unaltered under the Soviet-allied communist regime (1944 to 1990).

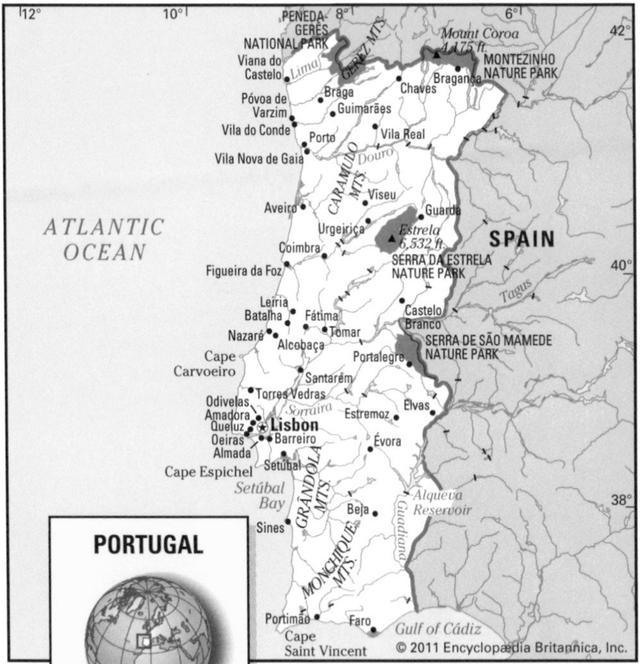

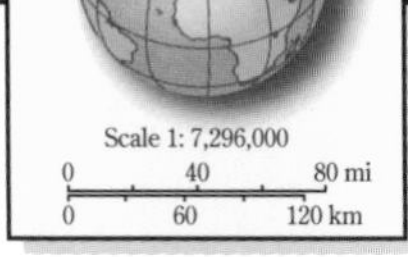

Age Breakdown

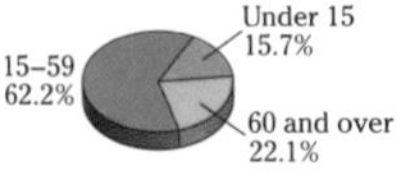

Official name: Portuguese Republic
Head of government: Prime Minister
Official language: Portuguese
Monetary unit: euro
Area: 35,558 sq. mi. (92,094 sq. km.)
Population (2010): 10,643,000
GNI per capita (2009): U.S.$20,940
Principal exports (2008): machinery and apparatus 18.0%, road vehicles/parts 11.2%, base and fabricated metals 7.7%, apparel 6.0% *to:* Spain 25.2%; Germany 12.3%; France 10.9%; Angola 6.0%; United Kingdom 5.2%

The central shield includes five smaller shields for a victory over the Moors in 1139, and a red border with gold castles. Behind the shield is an armillary sphere (an astronomical device) recalling world explorations and the kingdom of Brazil. Red and green were used in many early Portuguese flags. The current flag dates to June 30, 1911.

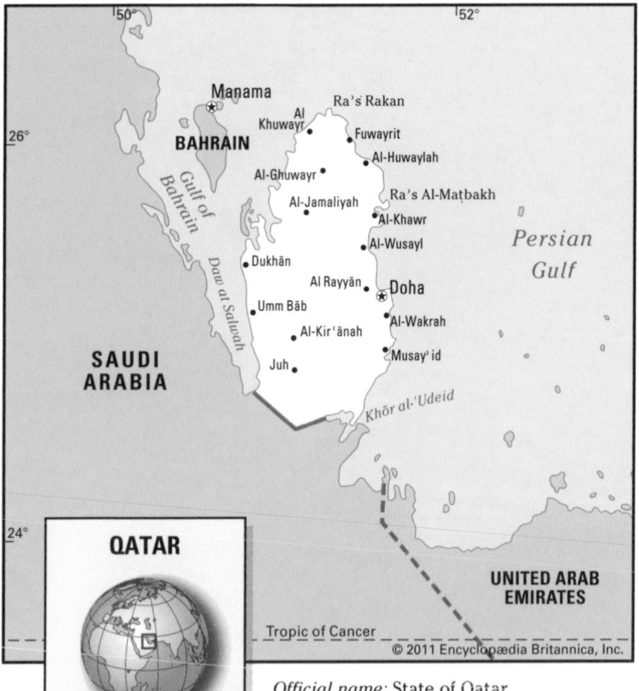

Ethnic Composition

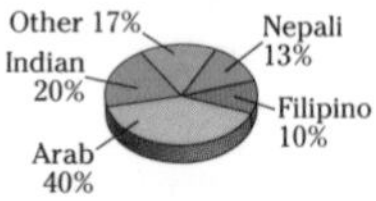

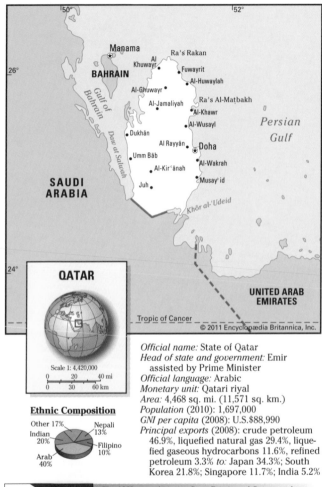

Official name: State of Qatar
Head of state and government: Emir assisted by Prime Minister
Official language: Arabic
Monetary unit: Qatari riyal
Area: 4,468 sq. mi. (11,571 sq. km.)
Population (2010): 1,697,000
GNI per capita (2008): U.S.$88,990
Principal exports (2008): crude petroleum 46.9%, liquefied natural gas 29.4%, liquefied gaseous hydrocarbons 11.6%, refined petroleum 3.3% *to:* Japan 34.3%; South Korea 21.8%; Singapore 11.7%; India 5.2%

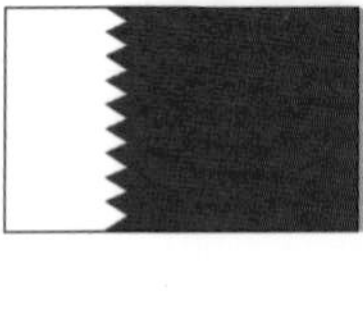

The 1868 treaty between Great Britain and Qatar may have inspired the creation of the flag. Qataris chose mauve or maroon instead of red (a more typical color among Arab countries) perhaps to distinguish it from the flag used in Bahrain. Passages from the Quran, in Arabic script, have sometimes been added to the flag.

Official name: Romania
Head of government: Prime Minister
Official language: Romanian
Monetary unit: (new) leu
Area: 92,043 sq. mi. (238,391 sq. km.)
Population (2010): 21,444,000
GNI per capita (2009): U.S.$8,330
Principal exports (2008): machinery and apparatus 23.4%, base and fabricated metals 12.0%, road vehicles/parts 8.2%, refined petroleum 7.9%, apparel 7.8% *to:* Germany 16.5%; Italy 15.5%; France 7.3%; Turkey 5.1%; Hungary 5.1%

Ethnic Composition

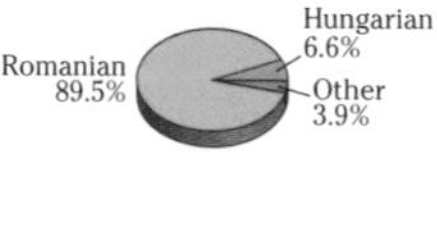

In 1834 Walachia, an ancient region of Romania, chose a naval ensign with stripes of red, blue, and yellow. The modern Romanian tricolor was created in 1848 and flown for a brief time. In 1867 Romania reestablished the vertical tricolor, and with the fall of the 20th-century communist regime, it was defined on Dec. 27, 1989.

Ethnic Composition

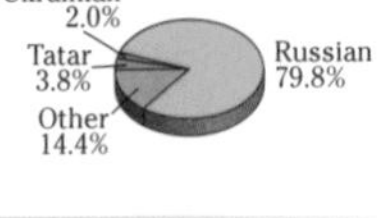

Tsar Peter the Great visited the Netherlands in order to modernize the Russian navy, and in 1699 he chose a Dutch-influenced flag for Russian ships. The flag soon became popular on land as well. After the Russian Revolution it was replaced by the communist red banner, but the tricolor again became official on Aug. 21, 1991.

Official name: Russian Federation
Head of government: President
Official language: Russian
Monetary unit: ruble
Area: 6,601,700 sq. mi. (17,098,200 sq. km.)
Population (2010): 141,892,000
GNI per capita (2009): U.S.$9,370
Principal exports (2008): mineral fuels, of which crude petroleum 32.4%, refined petroleum 16.8%, natural gas 14.2%; iron and steel 6.1%, chemicals and chemical products 4.8% *to:* Netherlands 12.2%; Germany 7.1%; Turkey 5.9%; Belarus 5.1%; Ukraine 5.0%; China 4.5%; Poland 4.3%

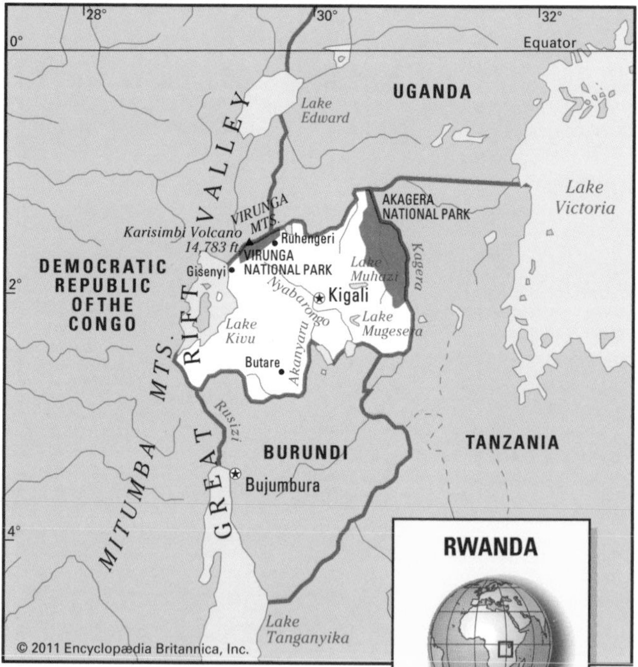

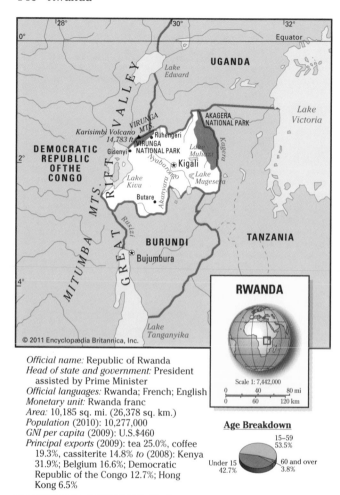

Official name: Republic of Rwanda
Head of state and government: President assisted by Prime Minister
Official languages: Rwanda; French; English
Monetary unit: Rwanda franc
Area: 10,185 sq. mi. (26,378 sq. km.)
Population (2010): 10,277,000
GNI per capita (2009): U.S.$460
Principal exports (2009): tea 25.0%, coffee 19.3%, cassiterite 14.8% *to* (2008): Kenya 31.9%; Belgium 16.6%; Democratic Republic of the Congo 12.7%; Hong Kong 6.5%

Age Breakdown

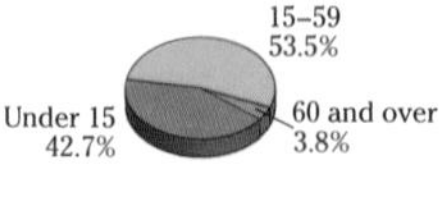

December 31, 2001 Rwanda raised this flag to promote unity, work ethic, heroism, and self-assurance. Under Belgium, minority Tutsi ruled feudally until 1959, when the Hutu majority revolted and took power. Rwanda won independence from Belgium in 1962. In 1994 Tutsis were back, after suffering hundreds of thousands of killings by Hutu.

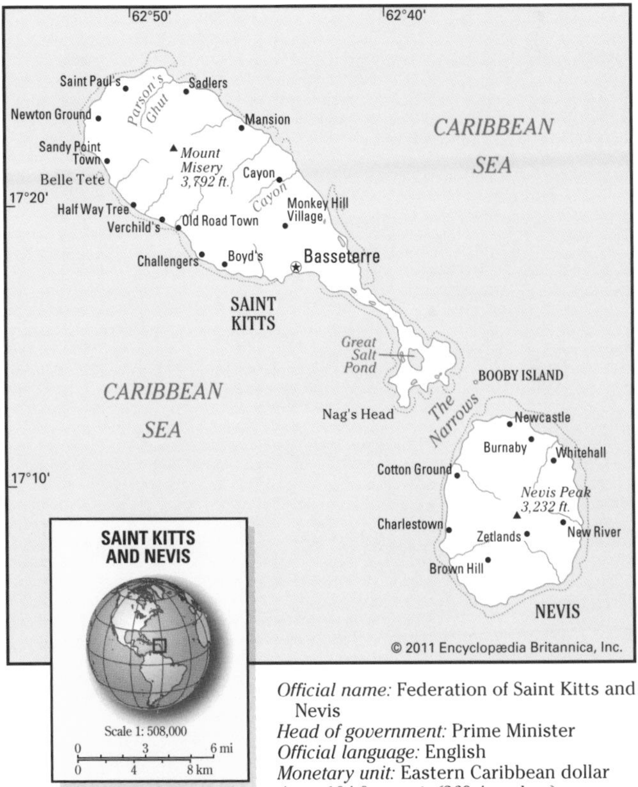

Official name: Federation of Saint Kitts and Nevis
Head of government: Prime Minister
Official language: English
Monetary unit: Eastern Caribbean dollar
Area: 104.0 sq. mi. (269.4 sq. km.)
Population (2010): 49,900
GNI per capita (2009): U.S.$10,150
Principal exports (2007): electrical switches 35%, telecommunication equipment/parts 34.0%, self-propelled shovels 5.0%, beer 4.4% *to:* United States 86.5%; U.K. 2.3%; Antigua and Barbuda 1.8%

Religious Affiliation

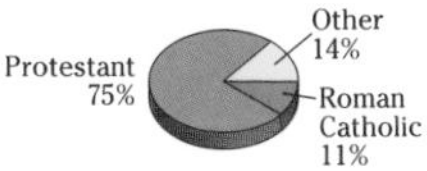

On Sept. 18, 1983, at the time of its independence from Britain, St. Kitts and Nevis hoisted the current flag. It has green (for fertility), red (for the struggle against slavery and colonialism), and black (for African heritage). The yellow flanking stripes are for sunshine, and the two stars, one for each island, are for hope and liberty.

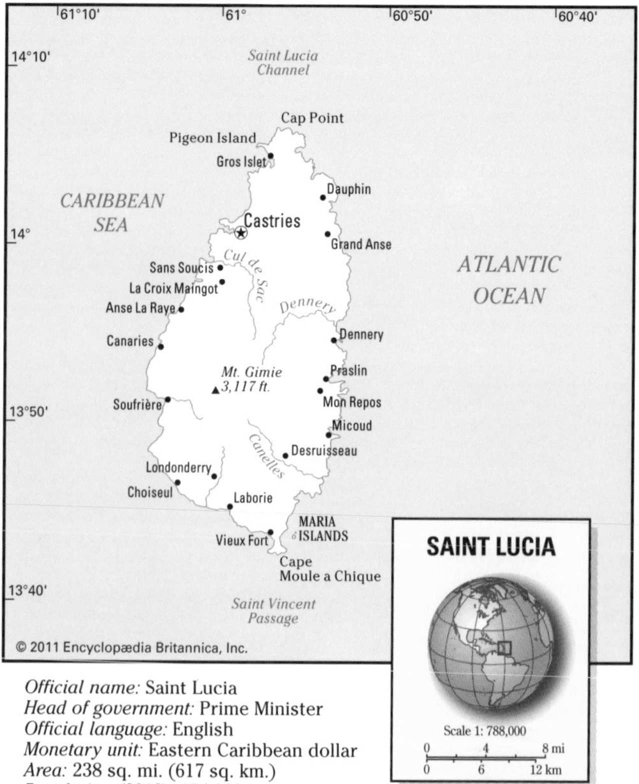

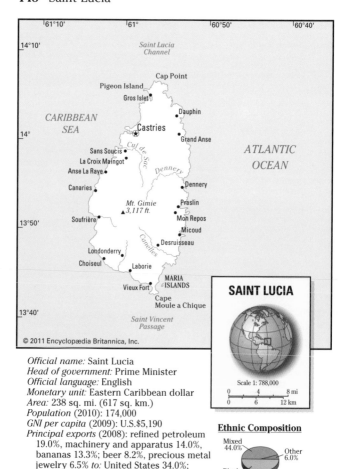

Official name: Saint Lucia
Head of government: Prime Minister
Official language: English
Monetary unit: Eastern Caribbean dollar
Area: 238 sq. mi. (617 sq. km.)
Population (2010): 174,000
GNI per capita (2009): U.S.$5,190
Principal exports (2008): refined petroleum 19.0%, machinery and apparatus 14.0%, bananas 13.3%; beer 8.2%, precious metal jewelry 6.5% *to:* United States 34.0%; Trinidad and Tobago 23.2%; Barbados 8.5%; St. Vincent and the Grenadines 3.9%

Ethnic Composition

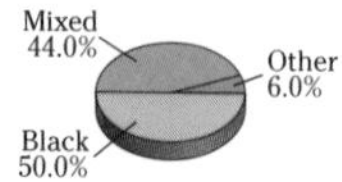

Upon independence from Britain, February 22, 1979, Saint Lucia raised this flag. The blue reflects the surrounding Atlantic Ocean and the Caribbena Sea. Its yellow triangle prepresents its tropical sunshine that tourists love, and its black triangle symbolizes the Pitons, ancient volcanic cones found in the southwest, while the adjoining white indicates racial harmony.

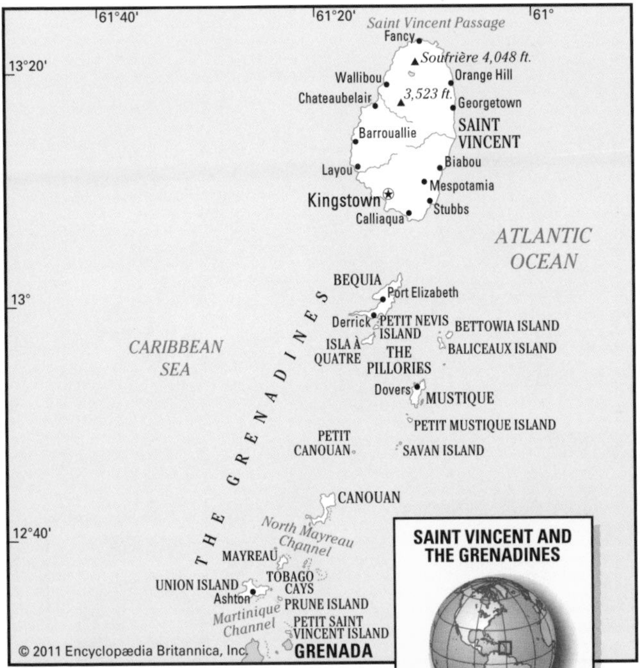

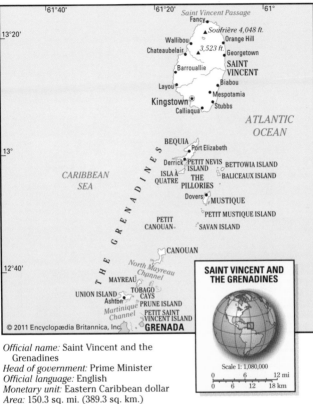

Official name: Saint Vincent and the Grenadines
Head of government: Prime Minister
Official language: English
Monetary unit: Eastern Caribbean dollar
Area: 150.3 sq. mi. (389.3 sq. km.)
Population (2010): 101,000
GNI per capita (2009): U.S.$5,130
Principal exports (2008): food 61.7% (bananas 15.9%, wheat flour 15.1%, rice 12.1%), machinery and apparatus 23.0% *to:* Grenada 18.2%; Trinidad and Tobago 17.4%; St. Lucia 14.8%; Barbados 10.7%; U.K. 9.0%

Ethnic Composition

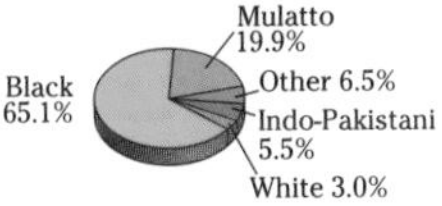

At independence from Britain in 1979 a national flag was designed, but it was replaced by the current flag on Oct. 22, 1985. The three green diamonds are arranged in the form of a V. Green is for the rich vegetation and the vitality of the people, yellow is for sand and personal warmth, and blue is for sea and sky.

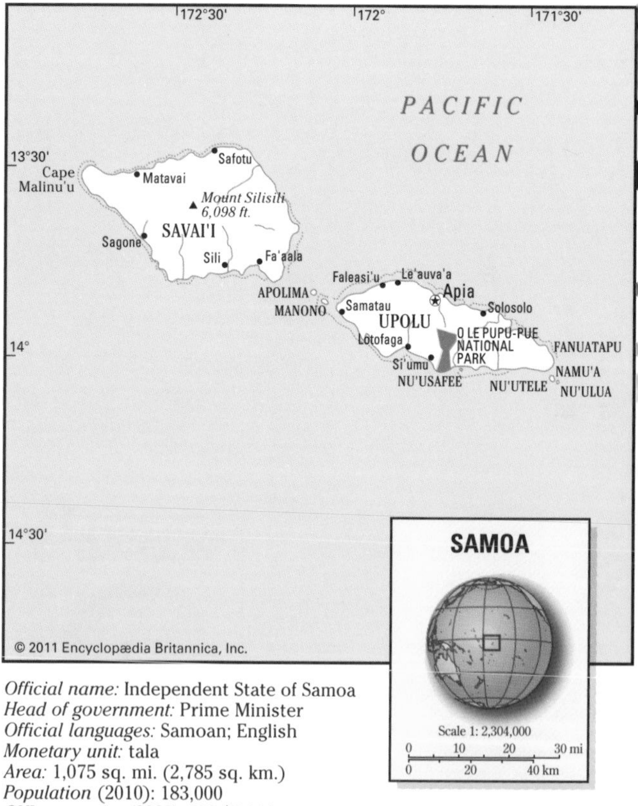

© 2011 Encyclopædia Britannica, Inc.

Official name: Independent State of Samoa
Head of government: Prime Minister
Official languages: Samoan; English
Monetary unit: tala
Area: 1,075 sq. mi. (2,785 sq. km.)
Population (2010): 183,000
GNI per capita (2009): U.S.$2,840
Principal exports (2008): ignition wiring sets 80.1%, tuna 6.8%, beer 1.8%, fruit juice 1.7%, coconut oil 1.4% *to:* Australia 81.7%; New Zealand 10.1%; American Samoa 3.6%; U.S. 1.9%

Religious Affiliation

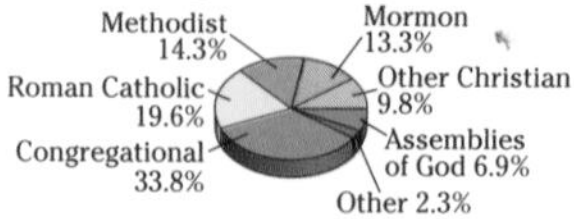

The first national flag of Samoa may date to 1873. Under British administration, a version of the current flag was introduced on May 26, 1948. On Feb. 2, 1949, a fifth star was added to the Southern Cross. White in the flag is said to stand for purity, blue for freedom, and red for courage. The flag was left unaltered upon independence in 1962.

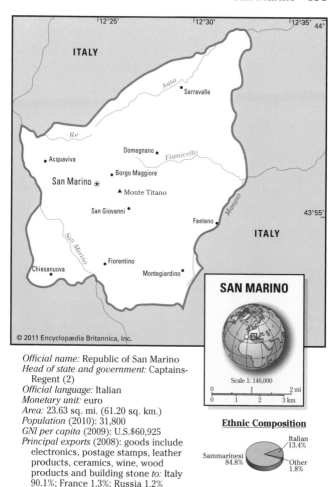

© 2011 Encyclopædia Britannica, Inc.

Official name: Republic of San Marino
Head of state and government: Captains-Regent (2)
Official language: Italian
Monetary unit: euro
Area: 23.63 sq. mi. (61.20 sq. km.)
Population (2010): 31,800
GNI per capita (2009): U.S.$60,925
Principal exports (2008): goods include electronics, postage stamps, leather products, ceramics, wine, wood products and building stone *to:* Italy 90.1%; France 1.3%; Russia 1.2%

Ethnic Composition

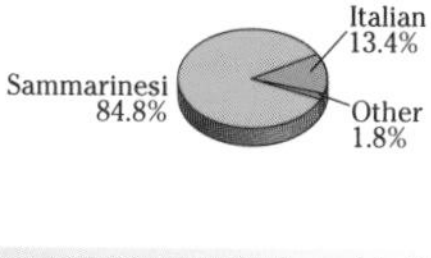

The colors of the flag, blue and white, were first used in the national cockade in 1797. The coat of arms in its present form was adopted on April 6, 1862, when the crown was added as a symbol of national sovereignty. Also in the coat of arms are three towers (Guaita, Cesta, and Montale) from the fortifications on Mount Titano.

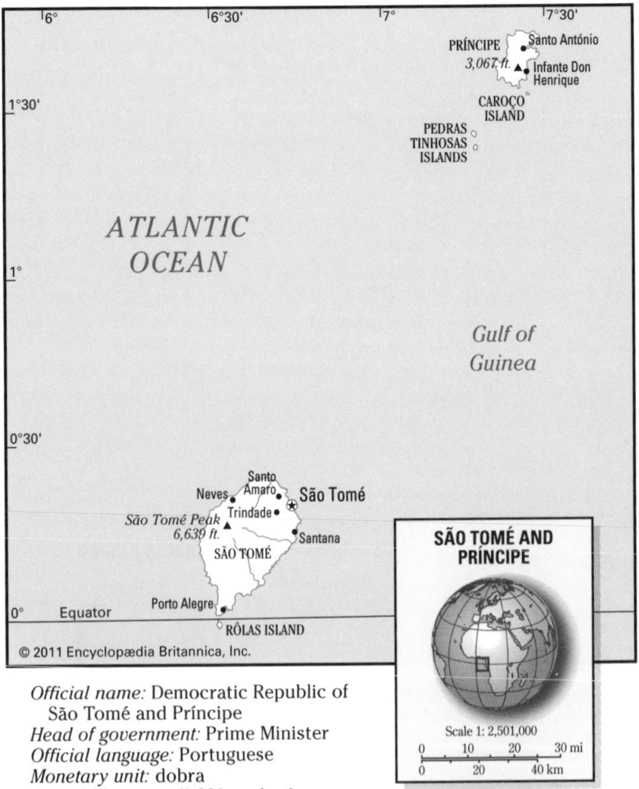

Official name: Democratic Republic of São Tomé and Príncipe
Head of government: Prime Minister
Official language: Portuguese
Monetary unit: dobra
Area: 386 sq. mi. (1,001 sq. km.)
Population (2010): 176,000
GNI per capita (2009): U.S.$1,140
Principal exports (2009): cocoa beans 98.3%, coconuts 0.6% *to:* Netherlands 34.7%; Portugal 29.3%; Belguim 19.2%

Age Breakdown

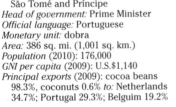

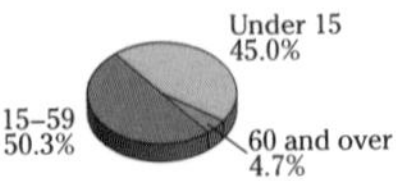

The national flag was adopted upon independence from Portugal on July 12, 1975. Its colors are associated with Pan-African independence. The red triangle stands for equality and the nationalist movement. The stars are for the African population living on the nation's two main islands. Green is for vegetation and yellow is for the tropical sun.

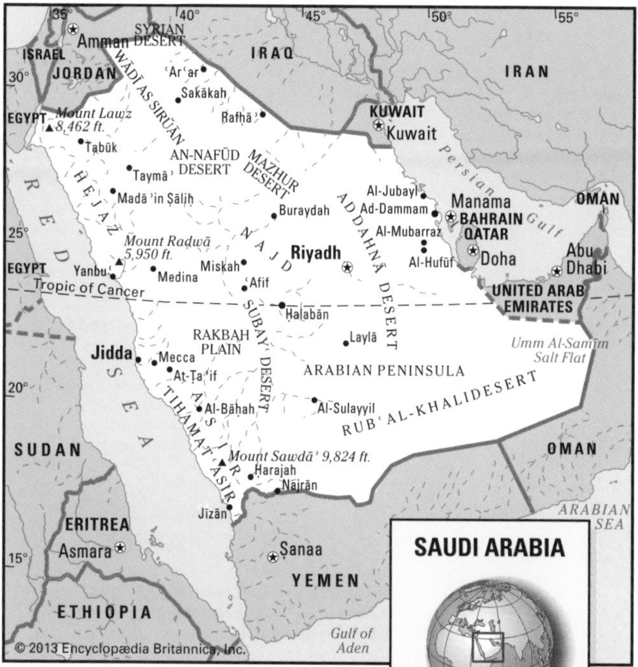

Official name: Kingdom of Saudi Arabia
Head of state and government: King
Official language: Arabic
Monetary unit: Saudi riyal
Area: 830,000 sq. mi. (2,149,690 sq. km.)
Population (2010): 25,732,000
GNI per capita (2008): U.S.$18,718
Principal exports (2008): petroleum 78.8%, refined petroleum products 10.8%, other mineral fuels 5.3% *to:* U.S. 16.3%; Japan 15.2%; China 8.9%; South Korea 8.6%; India 7.3%

Ethnic Composition

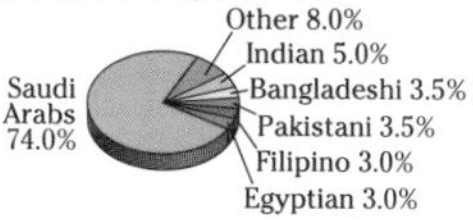

The Saudi flag, made official in 1932 but altered in 1968, originated in the military campaigns of Muhammad. The color green is associated with Fatima, the Prophet's daughter, and the Arabic inscription is translated as "There is no God but Allah and Muhammad is the Prophet of Allah." The saber symbolizes the militancy of the faith.

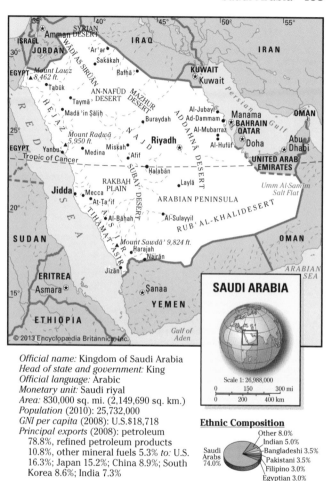

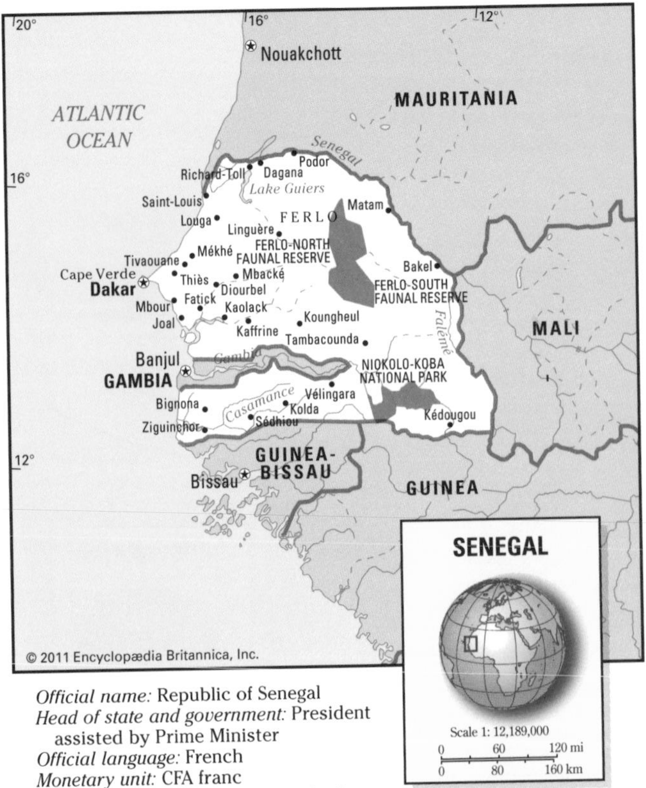

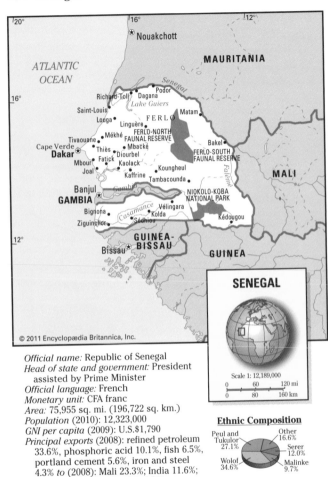

© 2011 Encyclopædia Britannica, Inc.

Official name: Republic of Senegal
Head of state and government: President assisted by Prime Minister
Official language: French
Monetary unit: CFA franc
Area: 75,955 sq. mi. (196,722 sq. km.)
Population (2010): 12,323,000
GNI per capita (2009): U.S.$1,790
Principal exports (2008): refined petroleum 33.6%, phosphoric acid 10.1%, fish 6.5%, portland cement 5.6%, iron and steel 4.3% *to* (2008): Mali 23.3%; India 11.6%; France 7.5%; The Gambia 4.2%

Ethnic Composition

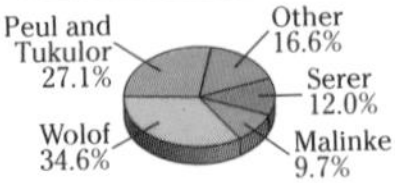

In a federation with French Sudan (now Mali) on April 4, 1959, Senegal used a flag with a human figure in the center. After the federation broke up in August 1960, Senegal substituted a green star for the central figure. Green is for hope and religion, yellow is for natural riches and labor, and red is for independence, life, and socialism.

Official name: Republic of Serbia
Head of government: Prime Minister
Official language: Serbian
Monetary unit: Serbian dinar
Area:[1] 29,922 sq. mi. (77,498 sq. km.)
Population (2010):[1] 7,293,000
GNI per capita (2009):[1] U.S.$5,990
Principal exports (2008):[1] base and fabricated metals 23.9%, food products 13.5%, machinery and apparatus 13.1% *to:* Bosnia and Herzegovina 12.2%; Montenegro 11.7%; Germany 10.4%; Italy 10.3%; Russia 5.0%

[1]Excludes Kosovo

Age Breakdown

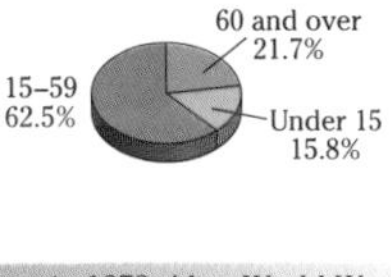

Serbia first became independent in 1878. After World War I, Serbia (with Montenegro), as part of Yugoslavia, had no flag of its own. Again independent in 2006 (from both Montenegro and Yugoslavia), Serbia now flies this flag, adopted in 2004. The four Cyrillic *C*s in the coat of arms are thought to mean, "Only unity will save the Serbs."

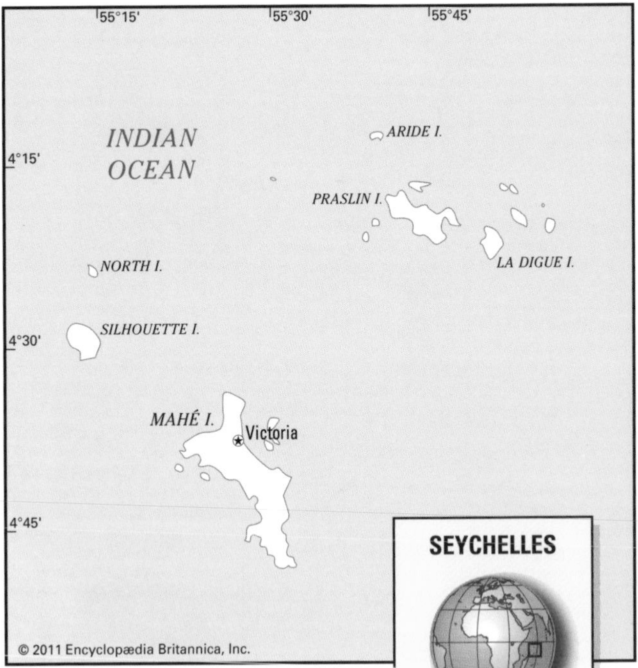

Official name: Republic of Seychelles
Head of state and government: President
Official language: none
Monetary unit: Seychelles rupee
Area: 174.4 sq. mi. (451.7 sq. km.)
Population (2010): 87,600
GNI per capita (2009): U.S.$8,480
Principal exports (2007): domestic exports 55.3%, of which canned tuna 50.6%, fish meal 1.2%, medicine and medical appliances 1.2%; reexports 44.7%, of which petroleum products to ships and aircraft 43.1% *to:* United Kingdom 40.1%; France 34.7%; Italy 10.0%; Germany 3.2%

Age Breakdown

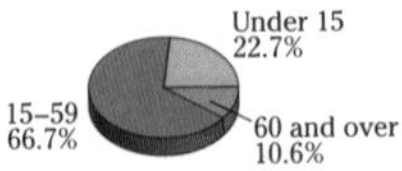

The former British colony underwent a revolution in 1977. The government was democratized in 1993, and on Jan. 8, 1996, a new flag was designed. The blue color is for sky and sea, yellow is for the sun, red is for the people and their work for unity and love, white is for social justice and harmony, and green is for the land and natural environment.

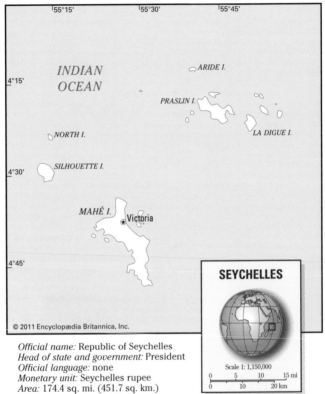

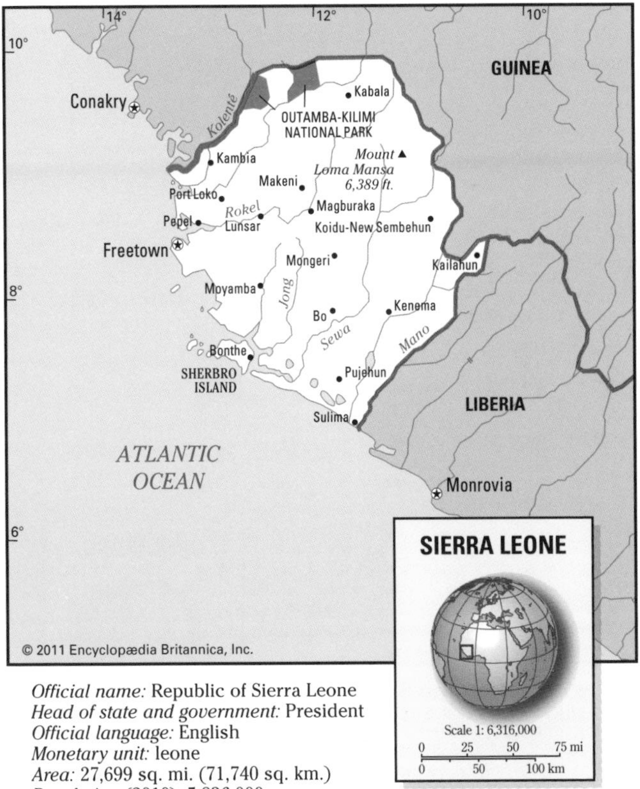

Official name: Republic of Sierra Leone
Head of state and government: President
Official language: English
Monetary unit: leone
Area: 27,699 sq. mi. (71,740 sq. km.)
Population (2010): 5,836,000
GNI per capita (2009): U.S.$340
Principal exports (2008): diamonds 45.8%, bauxite 13.0%, cacao 6.9%, reexports 6.8%, gold 1.9%, ilmenite 1.2% *to:* Belgium *c.* 39%; U.S. *c.* 22%; India *c.* 7%; France *c.* 5%

Ethnic Composition

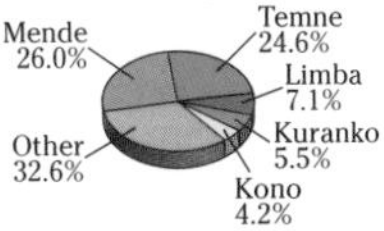

Under British colonial control Sierre Leone was founded as a home for freed slaves. With independence on April 27, 1961, the flag was hoisted. Its stripes stand for agriculture and the mountains (green); unity and justice (white); and the aspiration to contribute to world peace, especially through the use of the natural harbor at Freetown (blue).

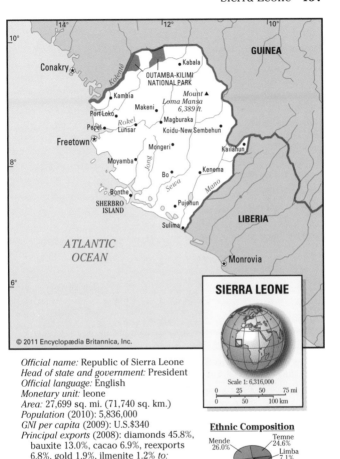

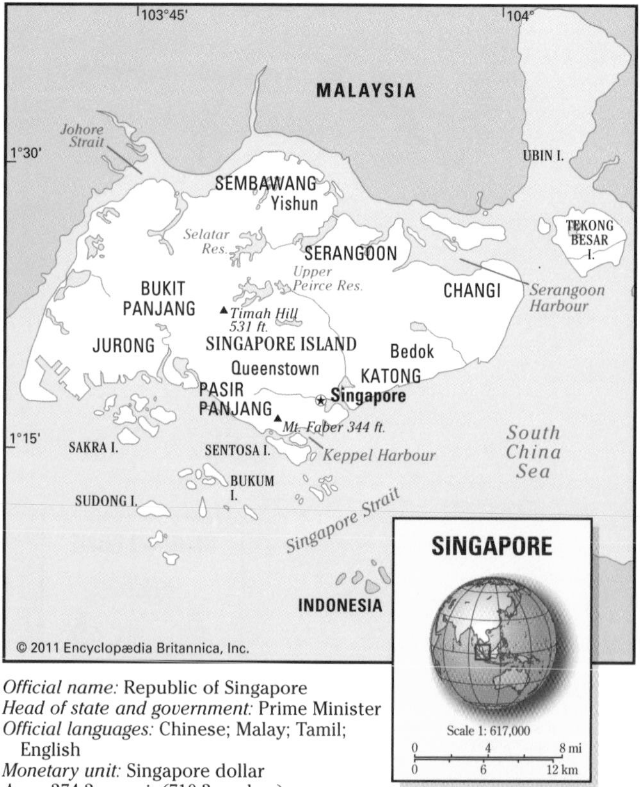

Official name: Republic of Singapore
Head of state and government: Prime Minister
Official languages: Chinese; Malay; Tamil; English
Monetary unit: Singapore dollar
Area: 274.2 sq. mi. (710.3 sq. km.)
Population (2010): 5,093,000
GNI per capita (2009): U.S.$37,220
Principal exports (2009): integrated circuits/parts 20.4%, petroleum 19.9%, nonelectrical machinery and equipment 15.5%, personal computers/parts 6.3% *to:* Hong Kong 11.6%; Malaysia 11.5%; Indonesia 9.7%; China 9.7%; U.S. 6.5%; South Korea 4.7%

Ethnic Composition

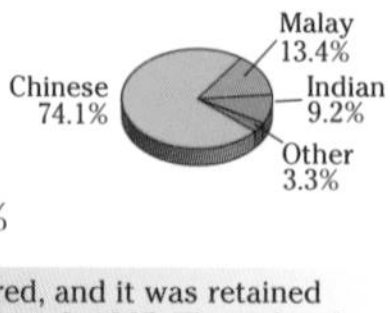

On Dec. 3, 1959, the flag was acquired, and it was retained after separation from Malaysia on Aug. 9, 1965. The red and white stripes stand for universal brotherhood, equality, purity, and virtue. The crescent symbolizes the growth of a young country, while the five stars are for democracy, peace, progress, justice, and equality.

Official name: Slovak Republic
Head of government: Prime Minister
Official language: Slovak
Monetary unit: euro
Area: 18,932 sq. mi. (49,034 sq. km.)
Population (2010): 5,431,000
GNI per capita (2009): U.S.$16,130
Principal exports (2008): machinery and apparatus 31.2% (television receivers 12.0%); road vehicles/parts 22.0%, base and fabricated metals 12.4% *to:* Germany 20.2%; Czech Republic 13.1%; France 6.8%; Poland 6.6%; Hungary 6.2%

Ethnic Composition

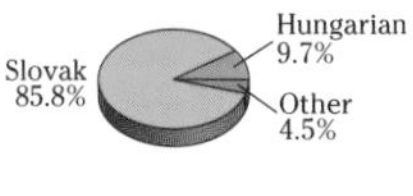

In 1189 the kingdom of Hungary (including Slovakia) introduced a double-barred cross in its coat of arms; this symbol was altered in 1848-49 by Slovak nationalists. After a period of communist rule, the tricolor was made official in 1989. On Sept. 3, 1992, the shield was added to the white-blue-red flag to differentiate it from the flag of Russia.

Official name: Republic of Slovenia
Head of government: Prime Minister
Official language: Slovene
Monetary unit: euro
Area: 7,827 sq. mi. (20,273 sq. km.)
Population (2010): 2,051,000
GNI per capita (2009): U.S.$23,520
Principal exports (2008): machinery and apparatus 24.2% (industrial machinery 6.2%), household-type equipment 4.6%; road vehicles/parts 14.5%; base and fabricated metals 13.1% *to:* Germany 18.9%; Italy 12.1%; Croatia 8.6%; Austria 7.8%; France 6.6%

Age Breakdown

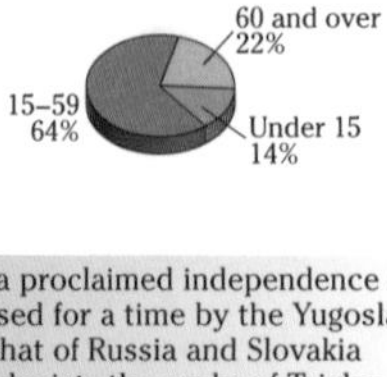

Under the current flag Slovenia proclaimed independence on June 25, 1991, but it was opposed for a time by the Yugoslav army. The flag is the same as that of Russia and Slovakia except for the coat of arms. It depicts the peaks of Triglav (the nation's highest mountain), the waves of the Adriatic coast, and three stars on a blue background.

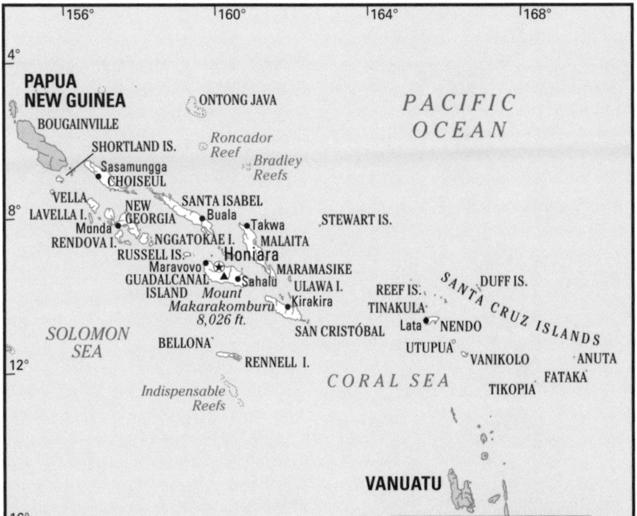

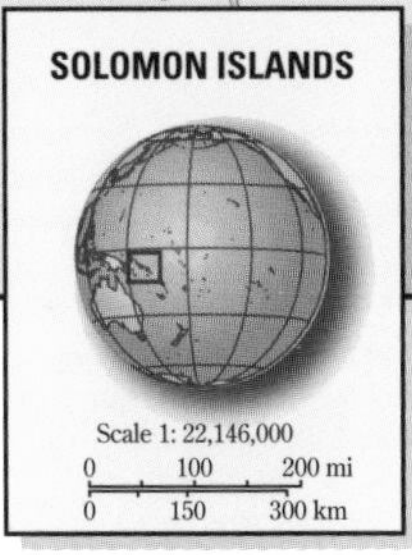

Official name: Solomon Islands
Head of government: Prime Minister
Official language: English
Monetary unit: Solomon Islands dollar
Area: 10,954 sq. mi. (28,370 sq. km.)
Population (2010): 536,000
GNI per capita (2009): U.S.$910
Principal exports (2008): timber 57.1%, copra 11.3%, palm oil 10.7%, fish products 7.8%, cacao beans 4.6% *to:* China 46.6%; Thailand 7.2%; Philippines 7.1%; Dem. Rep. of the Congo 6.1%; Japan 4.8%

Age Breakdown

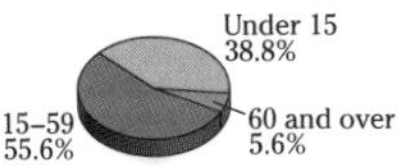

The flag was introduced on Nov. 18, 1977, eight months before independence from Britain. The yellow stripe stands for the sun. The green triangle is for the trees and crops of the fertile land, while the blue triangle symbolizes rivers, rain, and the ocean. The five stars represented the original five districts of the island.

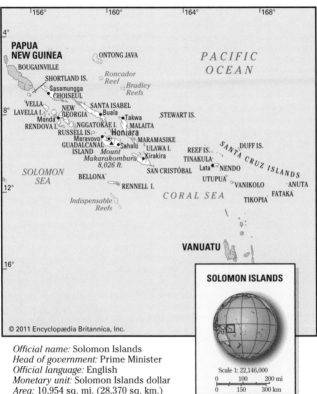

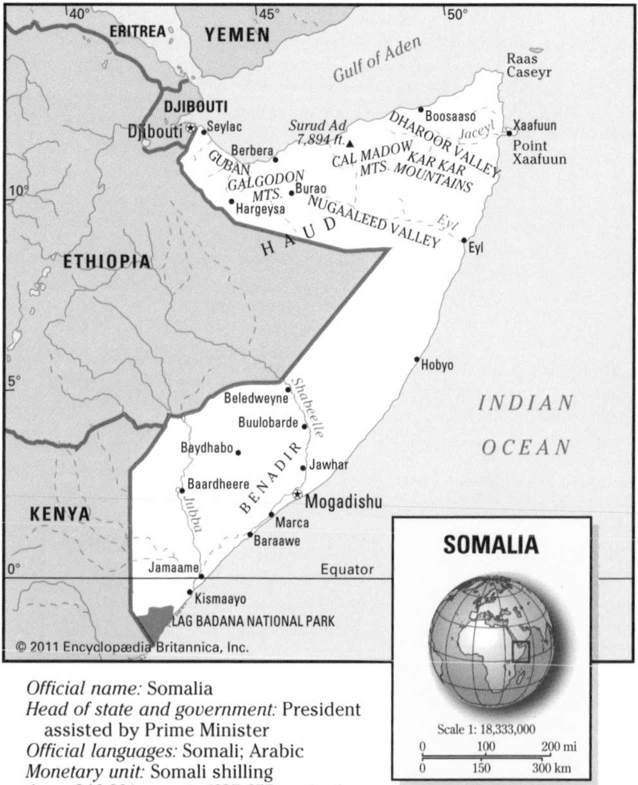

Official name: Somalia
Head of state and government: President assisted by Prime Minister
Official languages: Somali; Arabic
Monetary unit: Somali shilling
Area: 246,201 sq. mi. (637,657 sq. km.)
Population (2010): 9,359,000
GNI per capita (2008): U.S.$288
Principal exports (2007): goats 12.0%, sheep 6.4%, cattle 5.5%; other agricultural products 1.4%, unspecified 74.7% *to* (2008): U.A.E. *c.* 57%; Yemen *c.* 21%; Saudi Arabia *c.* 4%

Age Breakdown

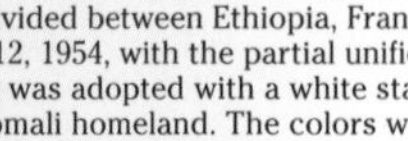

From the mid-19th century, areas in the Horn of Africa with Somali populations were divided between Ethiopia, France, Britain, and Italy. On Oct. 12, 1954, with the partial unification of these areas, the flag was adopted with a white star, each point referring to a Somali homeland. The colors were influenced by the colors of the United Nations.

Official name: Republic of South Africa
Head of state and government: President
Official languages: Afrikaans; English[1]
Monetary unit: rand
Area: 471,359 sq. mi. (1,220,813 sq. km.)
Population (2010): 49,991,000
GNI per capita (2009): U.S.$5,770
Principal exports (2008): platinum 12.3%; iron and steel 11.1%; road vehicles 9.4%, gold 7.4%, coal 5.9%, food 5.2% *to:* Japan 11.0%; U.S. 10.8%; Germany 7.8%; U.K. 6.6%; China 5.8%

[1]also Ndebele; Pedi; Sotho; Swazi; Tsonga; Tswana; Venda; Xhosa; Zulu

Ethnic Composition

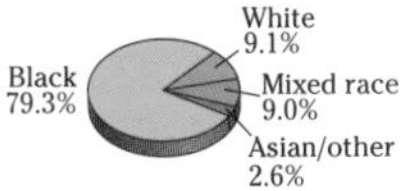

With the decline of apartheid, the flag was hoisted on April 27, 1994, and confirmed in 1996. Its six colors collectively represent Zulus, English or Afrikaners, Muslims, supporters of the African National Congress, and other groups. The Y-symbol stands for "merging history and present political realities" into a united and prosperous future.

Official name: Republic of Korea
Head of state and government: President, assisted by Prime Minister
Official language: Korean
Monetary unit: (South Korean) won
Area: 38,486 sq. mi. (99,678 sq. km.)
Population (2010): 49,169,000
GNI per capita (2009): U.S.$19,830
Principal exports (2008): machinery and apparatus 34.0%, transport equipment 21.4%, chemicals 10.1%, petroleum 9.1%
to: China 21.7%; United States 11.0%; Japan 6.8%; Hong Kong 4.9%; Singapore 3.9%

Age Breakdown

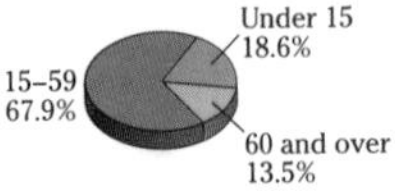

The flag was adopted in August 1882. Its white background is for peace, while the central emblem represents yin-yang (Korean: *um-yang*), the duality of the universe. The black bars recall sun, moon, earth, heaven and other Confucian principles. Outlawed under Japanese rule, the flag was revived in 1945 and slightly modified in 1950 and 1984.

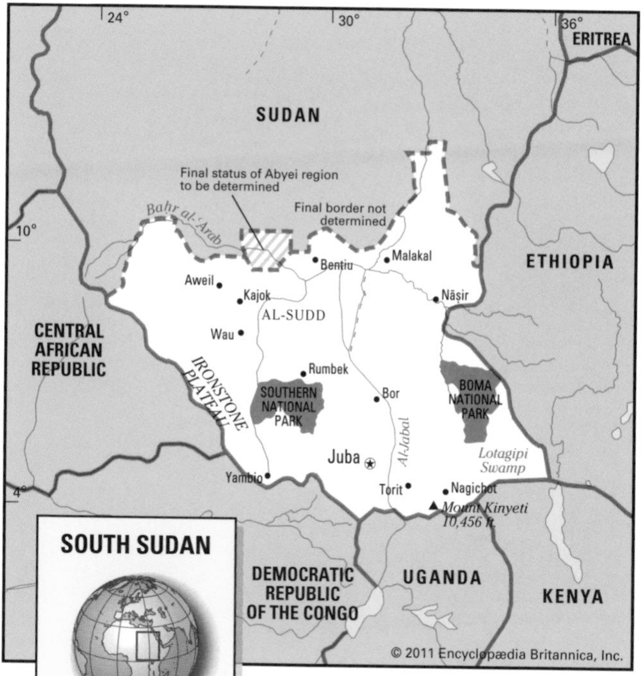

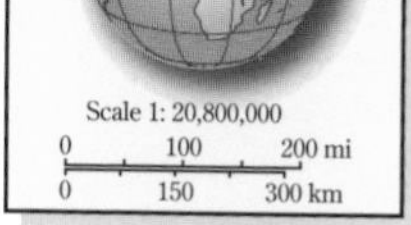

Official name: South Sudan
Head of state and government: President
Official language: English
Monetary unit: South Sudan pound
Area: 248,777 sq. mi. (644,330 sq. km.)
Population (2010): 8,974,000
GNI per capita (2007): U.S.$90
Principal exports n.a.

Ethnic Composition

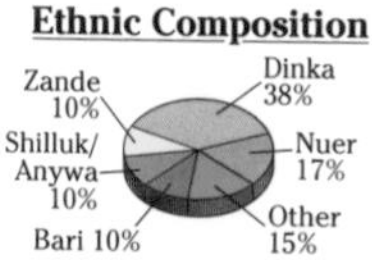

South Sudan became independent on July 9, 2011, and hoisted this six-color flag. The black recalls the country's black African ancestry. The white symbolizes peace and goodwill. Red stands for the blood and sacrifice of heroes and martyrs. Green symbolizes natural wealth, prosperity, and progress. The blue triangle represents the Nile River flowing through the land. Yellow symbolizes hope and determination.

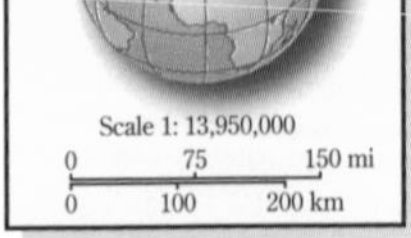

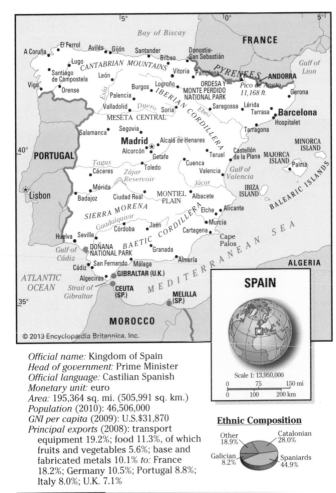

Official name: Kingdom of Spain
Head of government: Prime Minister
Official language: Castilian Spanish
Monetary unit: euro
Area: 195,364 sq. mi. (505,991 sq. km.)
Population (2010): 46,506,000
GNI per capita (2009): U.S.$31,870
Principal exports (2008): transport equipment 19.2%; food 11.3%, of which fruits and vegetables 5.6%; base and fabricated metals 10.1% *to:* France 18.2%; Germany 10.5%; Portugal 8.8%; Italy 8.0%; U.K. 7.1%

Ethnic Composition

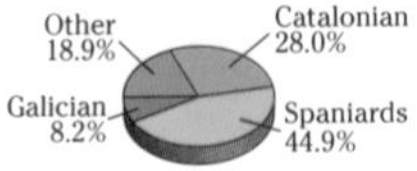

The colors of the flag have no official symbolic meaning. Introduced in 1785 by King Charles III, the flag was changed only under the Spanish Republic (1931–39). Under different regimes, however, the coat of arms has been altered. The current design dates from Dec. 18, 1981, with the death of Francisco Franco and the resurgence of democracy.

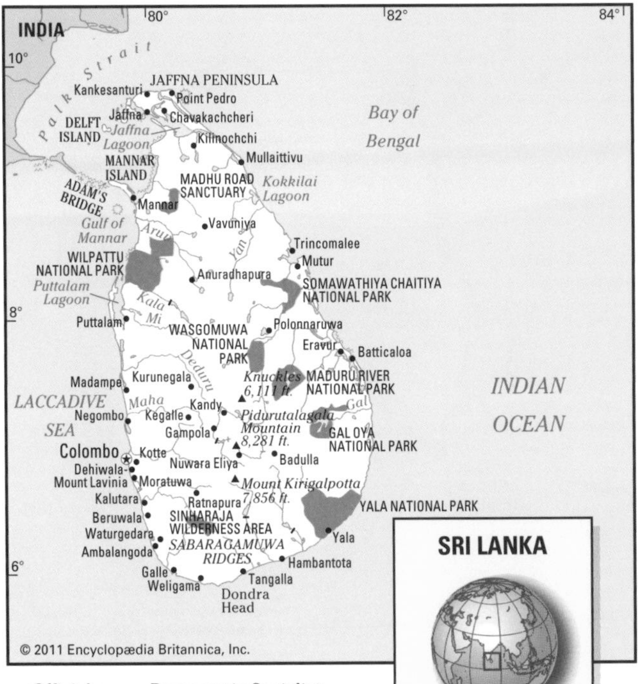

Official name: Democratic Socialist Republic of Sri Lanka
Head of state and government: President
Official languages: Sinhala; Tamil
Monetary unit: Sri Lanka rupee
Area: 25,332 sq. mi. (65,610 sq. km.)
Population (2010): 20,410,000
GNI per capita (2009): U.S.$1,990
Principal exports (2008): clothing and accessories 40.9%, tea 14.9%, precious and semiprecious stones 5.9%, rubber tires 4.0% *to:* U.S. 22.5%; U.K. 13.1%; Germany 5.5%; Italy 5.3%; India 5.3%

Ethnic Composition

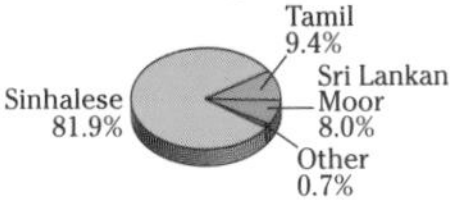

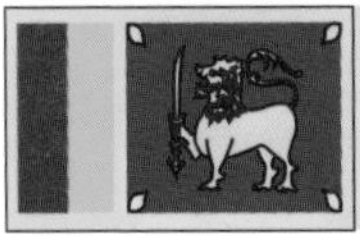

From the 5th century BCE the Lion flag was a symbol of the Sinhalese people. The flag was replaced by the Union Jack in 1815 but readopted upon independence in 1948. The stripes of green (for Muslims) and orange (for Hindus) were added in 1951. In 1972 four leaves of the Bo tree were added as a symbol of Buddhism; the leaves were altered in 1978.

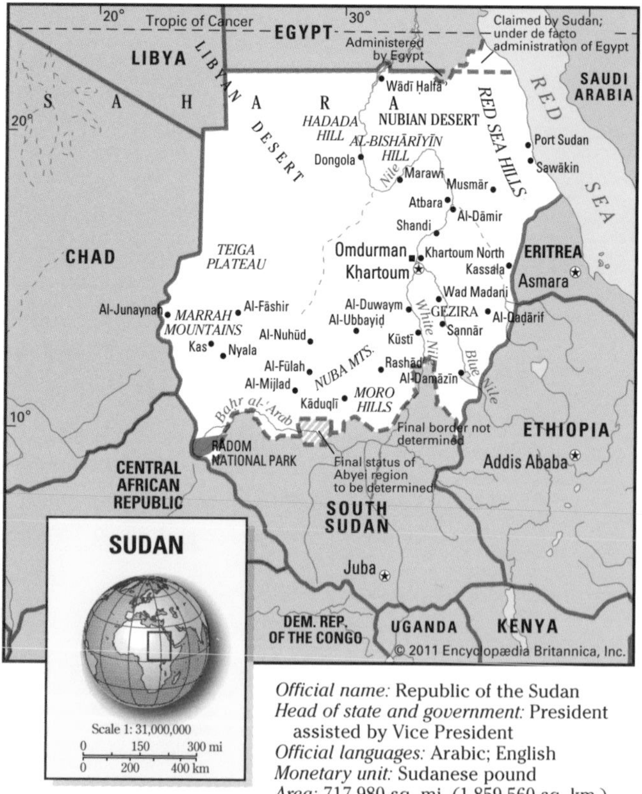

Ethnic Composition

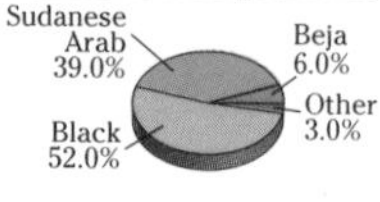

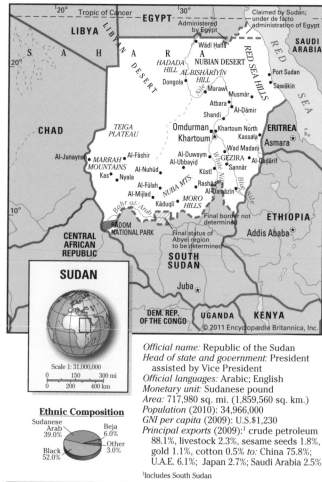

Official name: Republic of the Sudan
Head of state and government: President assisted by Vice President
Official languages: Arabic; English
Monetary unit: Sudanese pound
Area: 717,980 sq. mi. (1,859,560 sq. km.)
Population (2010): 34,966,000
GNI per capita (2009): U.S.$1,230
Principal exports (2009):[1] crude petroleum 88.1%, livestock 2.3%, sesame seeds 1.8%, gold 1.1%, cotton 0.5% *to:* China 75.8%; U.A.E. 6.1%; Japan 2.7%; Saudi Arabia 2.5%

[1]Includes South Sudan

The flag was first hoisted on May 20, 1970. It uses Pan-Arab colors. Black is for al-Mahdi (a leader in the 1800s) and the name of the country (sudan in Arabic means black); white recalls the revolutionary flag of 1924 and suggests peace and optimism; red is for patriotic martyrs, socialism, and progress; and green is for prosperity and Islam.

Official name: Republic of Suriname
Head of state and government: President
Official language: Dutch
Monetary unit: Suriname dollar
Area: 63,251 sq. mi. (163,820 sq. km.)
Population (2010): 524,000
GNI per capita (2008): U.S.$4,990
Principal exports (2007): alumina 41.9%, gold 31.7%, crude petroleum 7.0%, shrimp and fish 6.4%, rice 1.2% *to:* Canada 23.0%; Norway 14.4%; U.S. 12.1%; Trinidad and Tobago 7.2%; France 5.4%

Ethnic Composition

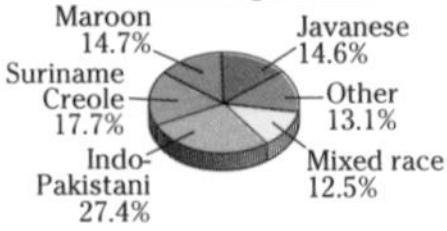

Adopted on Nov. 21, 1975, four days before independence from the Dutch, the flag of Suriname features green stripes for jungles and agriculture, white for justice and freedom, and red for the progressive spirit of a young nation. The yellow star is symbolic of the unity of the country, its golden future, and the people's spirit of sacrifice.

Official name: Kingdom of Swaziland
Head of state and government: King, assisted by Prime Minister
Official languages: Swazi; English
Monetary unit: lilangeni
Area: 6,704 sq. mi. (17,364 sq. km.)
Population (2010): 1,354,000
GNI per capita (2009): U.S.$2,350
Principal exports (2007): essential oils 29.4%, food 21.0%, silicates 19.9%; apparel/clothing accessories 4.4%, organic chemicals 4.3% *to:* South Africa 45.2%; Botswana 31.6%; U.K. 14.2%; United States 3.2%

Ethnic Composition

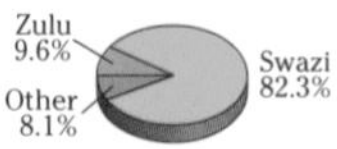

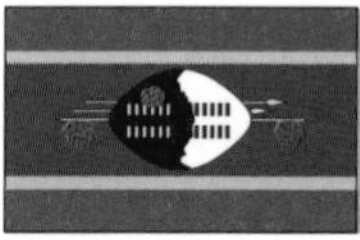

The flag dates to the creation of a military banner in 1941, when Swazi troops were preparing for the Allied invasion of Italy. On April 25, 1967, it was hoisted as the national flag. The crimson stripe stands for past battles, yellow for mineral wealth, and blue for peace. Featured are a Swazi war shield, two spears, and a "fighting stick."

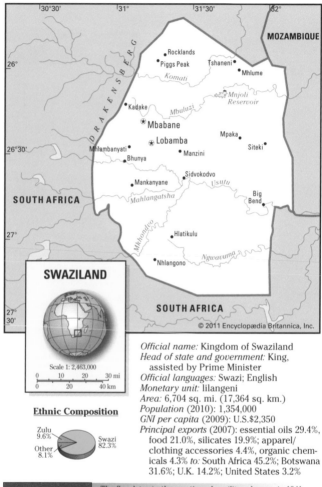

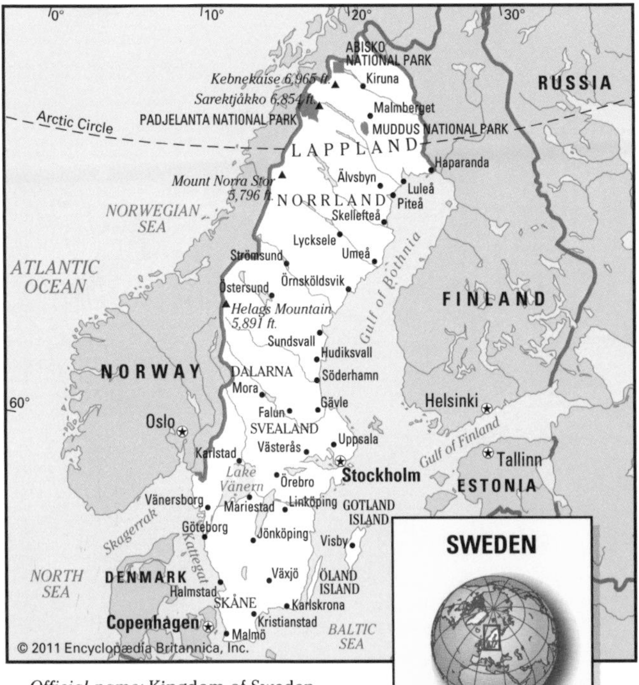

Official name: Kingdom of Sweden
Head of government: Prime Minister
Official language: Swedish
Monetary unit: Swedish krona
Area: 173,860 sq. mi. (450,295 sq. km.)
Population (2010): 9,381,000
GNI per capita (2009): U.S.$48,930
Principal exports (2008): machinery and apparatus 27.2%, road vehicles/parts 10.8%, refined petroleum 6.3%, iron and steel 5.9%, paper products 5.8%, pharmaceuticals 5.0% *to:* Norway 10.6%; Germany 10.2%; U.K. 7.4%; Denmark 7.3%; Finland 6.4%; U.S. 6.4%

Age Breakdown

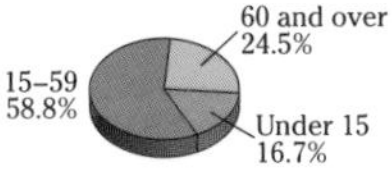

From the 14th century the coat of arms of Sweden had a blue field with three golden crowns, and the earlier Folkung dynasty used a shield of blue and white wavy stripes with a gold lion. The off-center "Scandinavian cross" was influenced by the flag of the rival kingdom of Denmark. The current flag law was adopted on July 1, 1906.

Official name: Swiss Confederation
Head of state and government: President of the Federal Council
Official languages: French; German; Italian
Monetary unit: Swiss franc
Area: 15,940 sq. mi. (41,285 sq. km.)
Population (2010): 7,807,000
GNI per capita (2008): U.S.$65,330
Principal exports (2008): medicine and pharmaceuticals 22.0%, machinery and apparatus 21.5%, wrist watches 7.3%, base and fabricated metals 6.9% *to:* Germany 19.7%; U.S. 9.6%; Italy 8.7%; France 8.6%; U.K. 5.1%

National Composition

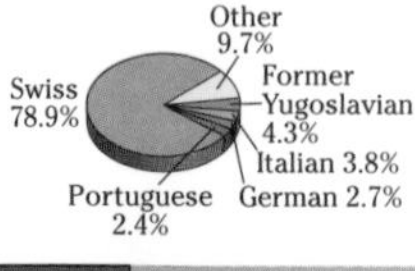

The Swiss flag is ultimately based on the war flag of the Holy Roman Empire. Schwyz, one of the original three cantons of the Swiss Confederation, placed a narrow white cross in the corner of its flag in 1240. This was also used in 1339 at the Battle of Laupen. Following the 1848 constitution, the flag was recognized by the army, and it was established as the national flag on land on Dec. 12, 1889.

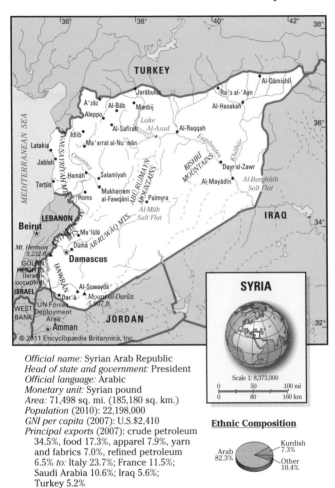

Official name: Syrian Arab Republic
Head of state and government: President
Official language: Arabic
Monetary unit: Syrian pound
Area: 71,498 sq. mi. (185,180 sq. km.)
Population (2010): 22,198,000
GNI per capita (2007): U.S.$2,410
Principal exports (2007): crude petroleum 34.5%, food 17.3%, apparel 7.9%, yarn and fabrics 7.0%, refined petroleum 6.5% *to:* Italy 23.7%; France 11.5%; Saudi Arabia 10.6%; Iraq 5.6%; Turkey 5.2%

Ethnic Composition

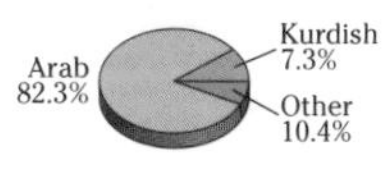

In 1918 the Arab Revolt flag flew over Syria, which joined Egypt in the United Arab Republic in 1958 and based its new flag on that of the Egyptian revolution of 1952; its stripes were red-white-black, with two green stars for the constituent states. In 1961 Syria broke from the union, but it readopted the flag on March 29, 1980.

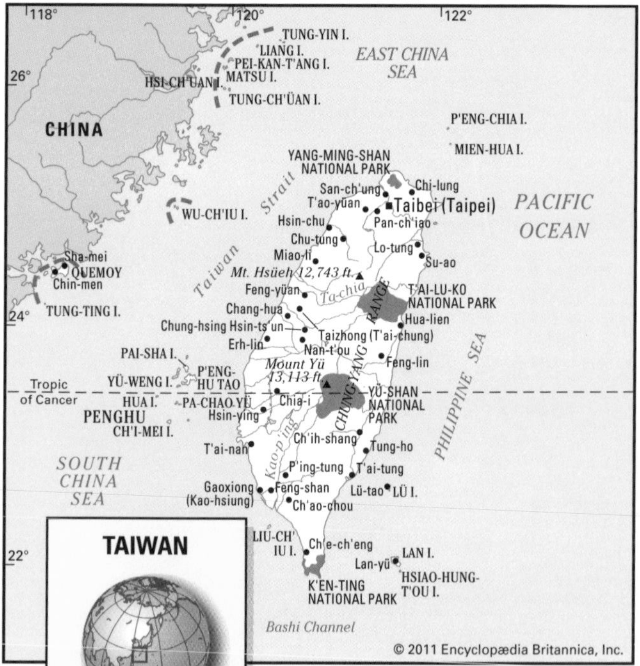

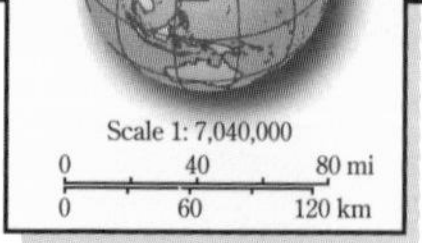

Official name: Republic of China
Head of government: Premier
Official language: Mandarin Chinese
Monetary unit: New Taiwan dollar
Area: 13,973 sq. mi. (36,191 sq. km.)
Population (2010): 23,138,000
GNI per capita (2009): U.S.$16,969
Principal exports (2009): machinery and electronic goods 46.7%, base and fabricated metals 9.5%, plastics and rubber products 8.1%, precision instruments, watches, and musical instruments 7.9% *to:* China 26.6%; Hong Kong 14.5%; U.S. 11.6%; Japan 7.1%; Singapore 4.2%

Religious Affiliation

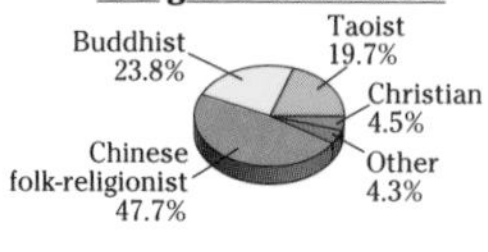

Under Chiang Kai-shek, a new Chinese national flag was adopted on Oct. 28, 1928, and it was carried to Taiwan in 1949–50 when the Nationalists fled the mainland. The three colors stand for the "Three Principles of the People" of the Nationalist (Kuomintang) Party—nationalism, democracy, and socialism.

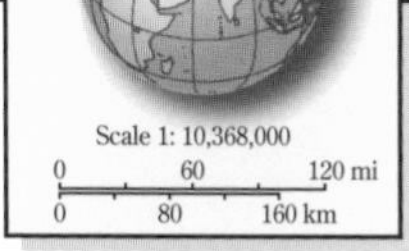

Ethnic Composition

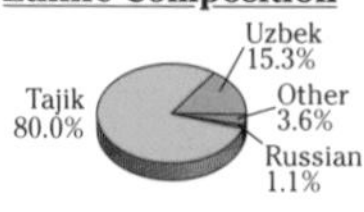

Official name: Republic of Tajikistan
Head of government: Prime Minister
Official language: Tajik
Monetary unit: somoni
Area: 55,300 sq. mi. (143,100 sq. km.)
Population (2010): 7,075,000
GNI per capita (2009): U.S.$700
Principal exports (2009): aluminum 58.5%, cotton fiber 9.9%, electricity 6.3% *to:* Israel 39.6%; Turkey 8.7%; Russia 7.6%; Italy 7.4%; Norway 7.2%

Following independence from the Soviet Union in 1991, Tajikistan developed a new flag on Nov. 24, 1992. The green stripe is for agriculture, while red is for sovereignty. White is for the main crop—cotton. The central crown contains seven stars representing unity among workers, peasants, intellectuals, and other social classes.

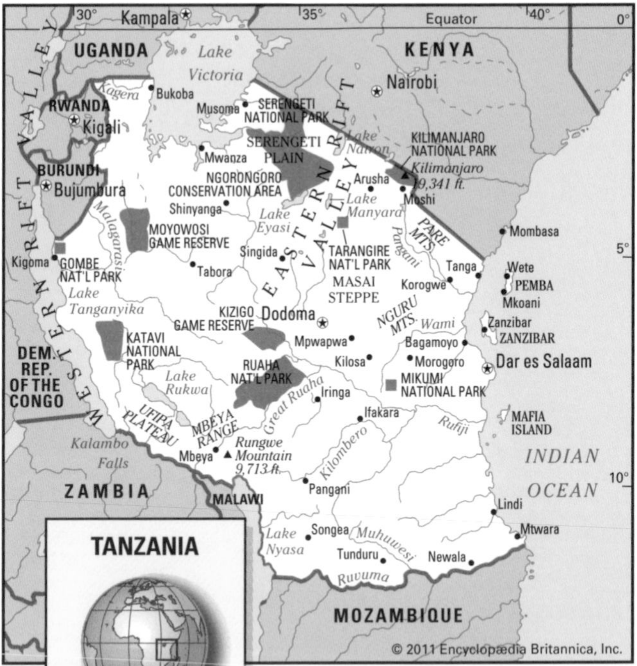

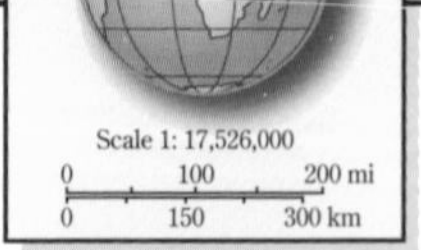

Official name: United Republic of Tanzania
Head of state and government: President
Official languages: Swahili; English
Monetary unit: Tanzanian shilling
Area: 364,017 sq. mi. (942,799 sq. km.)
Population (2010): 41,893,000
GNI per capita (2009): U.S.$500
Principal exports (2007): gold (and much less significantly copper and silver) 35.8%, fish 7.1%, coffee 5.3%, tobacco 4.5%, cotton fibre/worn clothing 4.5% *to:* Switzerland 20.8%; Kenya 8.6%; South Africa 8.5%; China 8.2%; India 6.3%

Religious Affiliation

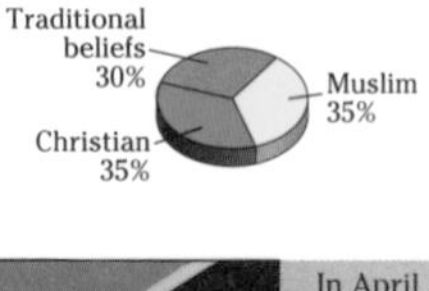

In April 1964 Tanganyika and Zanzibar united, and in July their flag traditions melded to create the current design. The black stripe is for the majority population, while green is for the rich agricultural resources of the land. Mineral wealth is reflected in the yellow fimbriations (narrow borders), while the Indian Ocean is symbolized by blue.

Official name: Kingdom of Thailand
Head of government: Prime Minister
Official language: Thai
Monetary unit: baht
Area: 198,117 sq. mi. (513,120 sq. km.)
Population (2010): 67,090,000
GNI per capita (2009): U.S.$3,760
Principal exports (2008): computers and parts 9.4%, transportation equipment 9.4%, agricultural products 9.0%, integrated circuits and parts 8.7%, electrical machinery and apparatus 6.8% *to:* U.S. 11.4%; Japan 11.3%; China 9.1%; Singapore 5.7%; Hong Kong 5.7%

Ethnic Composition

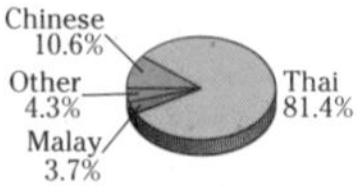

In the 17th century, the flag of Thailand was plain red, and Thai ships in 1855 displayed a flag with a central white elephant as a symbol of good fortune. The Thai king replaced the elephant with two white stripes in 1916 and added the blue stripe on Sept. 28, 1917. Red symbolizes the blood of patriots, white is for Buddhism, and blue is for royal guidance.

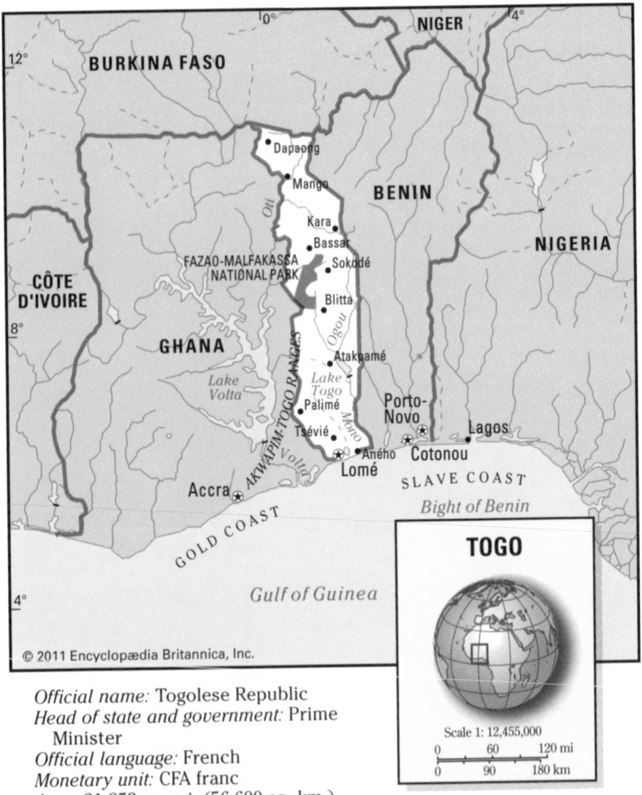

Official name: Togolese Republic
Head of state and government: Prime Minister
Official language: French
Monetary unit: CFA franc
Area: 21,853 sq. mi. (56,600 sq. km.)
Population (2010): 6,587,000
GNI per capita (2009): U.S.$440
Principal exports (2007): portland cement 24.1%, cement clinker 19.6%, iron and steel 12.5%, crude fertilizer 11.2%, food 9.5% *to:* Niger 12.7%; Benin 10.9%; India 9.8%; Burkina Faso 9.8%; Mali 7.1%

Religious Affiliation

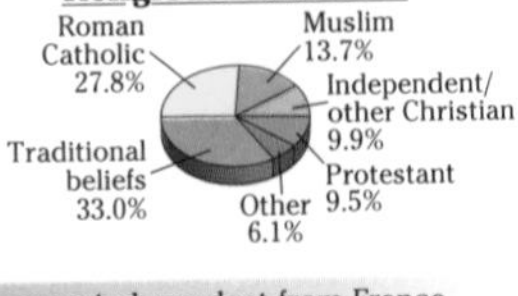

On April 27, 1960, Togo became independent from France under the current flag. Its stripes correspond to the administrative regions and symbolize that the population depends on the land for its sustenance (green) and its own labor for development (yellow). The red is for love, fidelity, and charity, while the white star is for purity and unity.

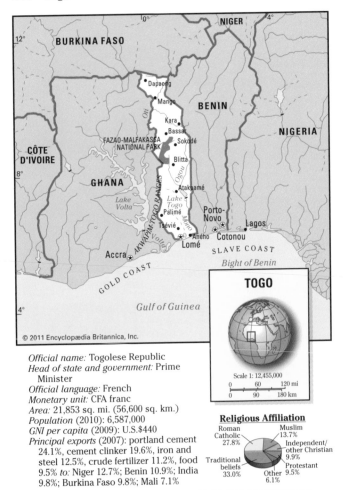

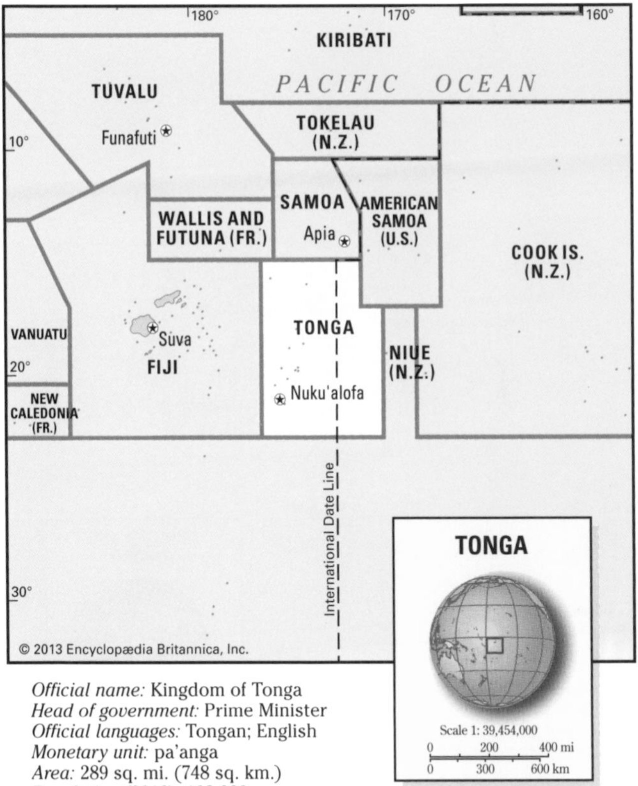

Official name: Kingdom of Tonga
Head of government: Prime Minister
Official languages: Tongan; English
Monetary unit: pa'anga
Area: 289 sq. mi. (748 sq. km.)
Population (2010): 103,000
GNI per capita (2009): U.S.$3,260
Principal exports (2008–09): fish 27.8%, root crops 20.5%, other agricultural products 23.8% *to:* New Zealand 36.2%; U.S. 17.1%; Japan 13.2%; Australia 11.8%

Religious Affiliation

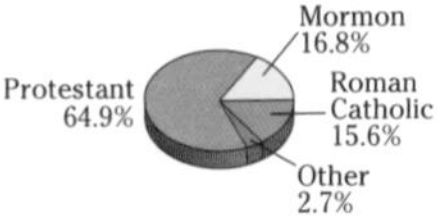

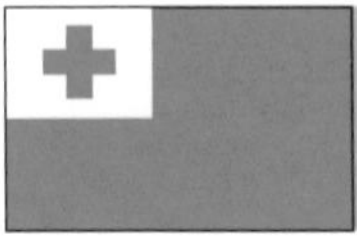

The colors red and white were popular in the Pacific long before the arrival of Europeans. The Tonga constitution (Nov. 4, 1875) established the flag, which was created by King George Tupou I with the advice of a missionary. The cross was chosen as a symbol of the widespread Christian religion, and the color red was related to the blood of Jesus

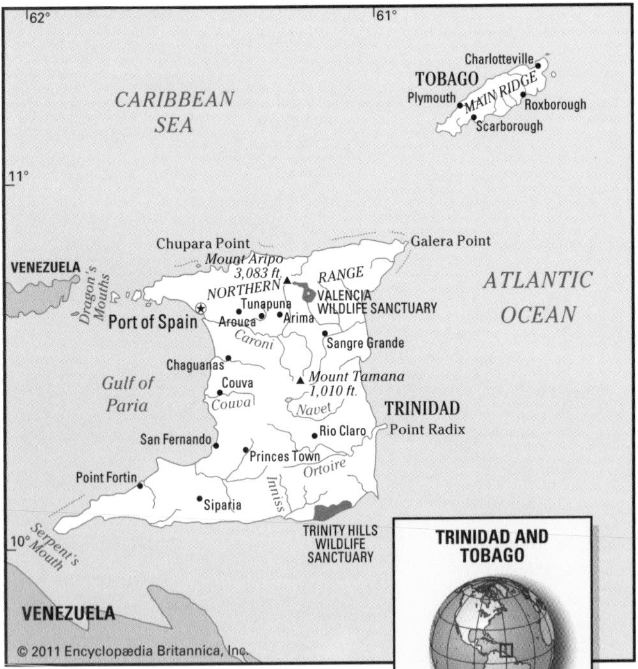

© 2011 Encyclopædia Britannica, Inc.

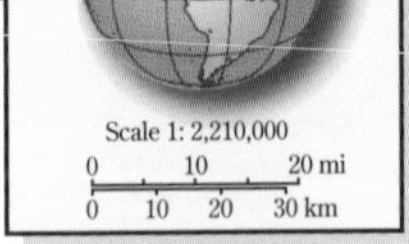

Official name: Republic of Trinidad and Tobago
Head of government: Prime Minister
Official language: English
Monetary unit: Trinidad and Tobago dollar
Area: 1,990 sq. mi. (5,155 sq. km.)
Population (2010): 1,312,000
GNI per capita (2009): U.S.$16,560
Principal exports (2008): refined petroleum 27.5%, LNG 26.1%, crude petroleum 11.1%, ammonia 9.5%, methanol 5.7% *to:* United States 46.0%; Jamaica 6.7%; Spain 6.2%; Mexico 3.2%; Netherlands 3.0%

Religious Affiliation

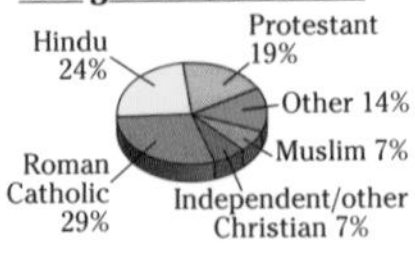

Hoisted on independence day, Aug. 31, 1962, the flag symbolizes earth, water, and fire as well as past, present, and future. Black also is a symbol of unity, strength, and purpose. White recalls the equality and purity of the people and the sea that unites them. Red is for the sun, the vitality of the people and nation, friendliness, and courage.

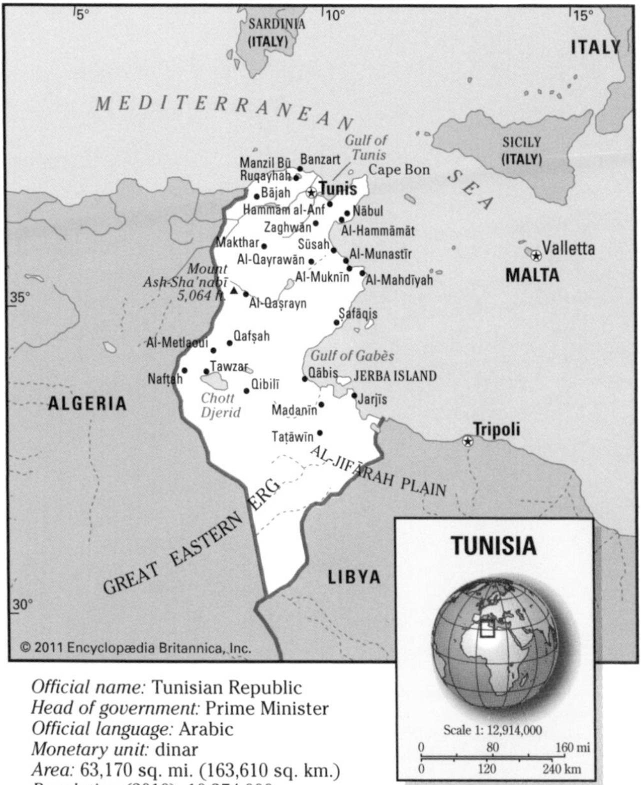

Official name: Tunisian Republic
Head of government: Prime Minister
Official language: Arabic
Monetary unit: dinar
Area: 63,170 sq. mi. (163,610 sq. km.)
Population (2010): 10,374,000
GNI per capita (2009): U.S.$3,720
Principal exports (2009): apparel (incl. knitwear) 21.4%, petroleum 13.6%, phosphate products 7.0%, electrical wires/cables 7.0%, footwear/leather goods 4.0% *to:* France 29.7%; Italy 21.0%; Germany 8.8%; Libya 5.8%; U.K. 4.8%

Age Breakdown

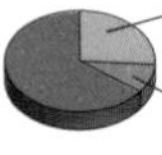

The Tunisian flag, established in 1835, contains the crescent and moon, a symbol used by the Ottoman Empire but dating from the ancient Egyptians and Phoenicians. More as a cultural than a religious symbol, the crescent and star came to be associated with Islam because of its widespread adoption in Muslim nations.

Official name: Republic of Turkey
Head of government: Prime Minister
Official language: Turkish
Monetary unit: New Turkish lira
Area: 303,224 sq. mi. (785,347 sq. km.)
Population (2010): 73,085,000
GNI per capita (2009): U.S.$8,730
Principal exports (2008): base and fabricated metals 18.0%, machinery and apparatus 13.8%, road vehicles 13.6%, apparel 8.8%, petroleum 5.4% *to:* Germany 9.8%; U.K. 6.2%; U.A.E. 6.0%; Italy 5.9%; France 5.0%

Religious Affiliation

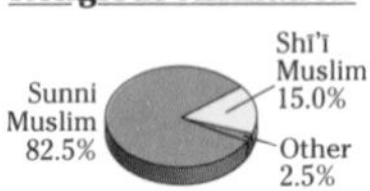

In June 1793 the flag was established for the navy, although its star had eight points instead of the current five (since about 1844). This design was reconfirmed in 1936 following the revolution led by Ataturk. Various myths are associated with the symbolism of the red color and the star and crescent, but none really explains their origins.

Official name: Turkmenistan
Head of state and government: President
Official language: Turkmen
Monetary unit: (new) manat
Area: 189,657 sq. mi. (491,210 sq. km.)
Population (2010): 4,941,000
GNI per capita (2009): U.S.$3,420
Principal exports (2005–06): natural gas 55.8%, petroleum (all forms) 24.7%, textile yarn 3.9%, ships/boats/floating structures 2.1% *to* (2008): Ukraine *c.* 40%; Iran *c.* 16%; Poland *c.* 9%; Hungary *c.* 8%

Ethnic Composition

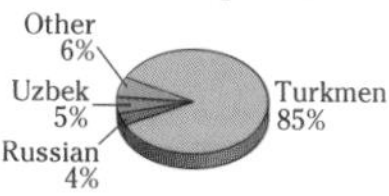

Raised on February 19, 1992, following Turkmenistan's independence from Russia, the flag's stripe holds a design of five carpet motifs associated with local tribes. Green is a symbol of Islam, the white crescent stands for hope, and the stars are for the five senses. In 1997, as a symbol of neutrality, an olive wreath was put on the vertical stripe.

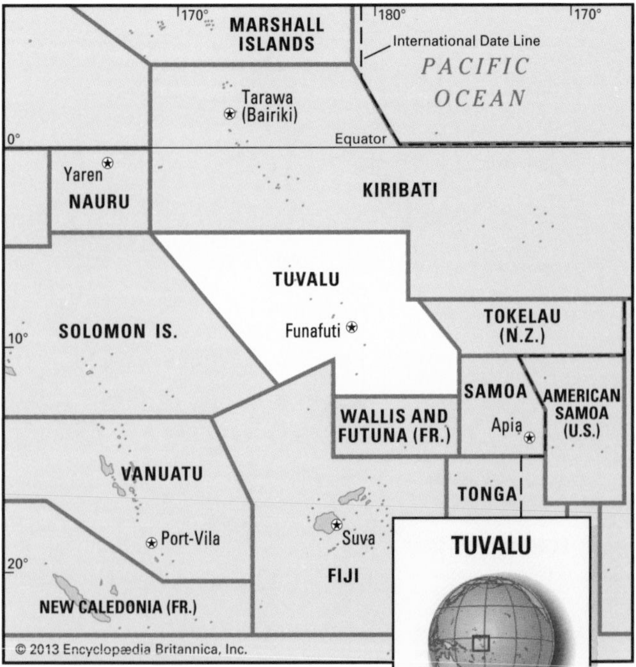

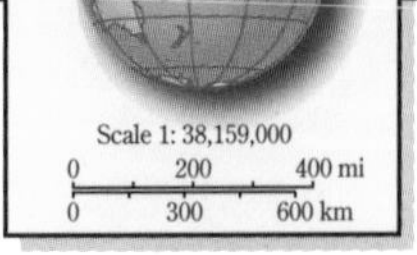

Official name: Tuvalu
Head of government: Prime Minister
Official language: none
Monetary unit: Tuvaluan dollar
Area: 9.90 sq. mi. (25.63 sq. km.)
Population (2010): 11,100
GNI per capita (2008): U.S.$2,889
Principal exports (2005): precision instruments 18.6%, machinery and apparatus 17.4%, base and fabricated metals 15.4%, wood and wood products 12.5% *to:* Fiji 93.1%; El Salvador 4.6%; New Zealand 2.2%; U.K. 0.1%

Ethnic Composition

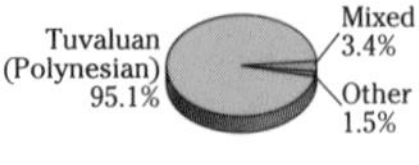

On Oct. 1, 1978, three years after separating from the Gilbert Islands, Tuvalu became independent under the current flag. The stars represent the atolls and islands of the country. The Union Jack recalls links with Britain and the Commonwealth. Replaced by supporters of republicanism on Oct. 1, 1995, the flag was reinstated on April 11, 1997.

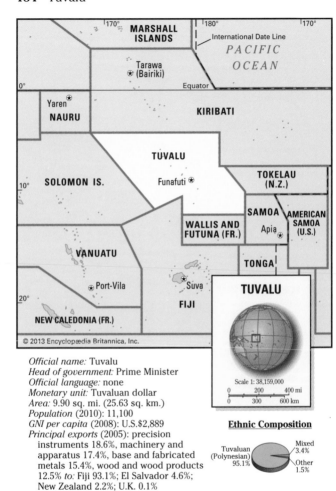

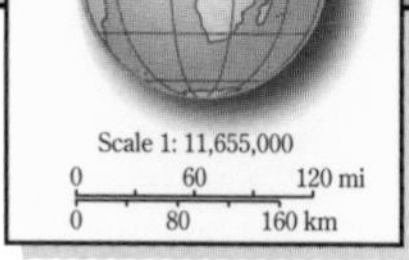

Official name: Republic of Uganda
Head of state and government: President assisted by the Prime Minister
Official languages: English; Swahili
Monetary unit: Ugandan shilling
Area: 93,263 sq. mi. (241,551 sq. km.)
Population (2010): 33,796,000
GNI per capita (2009): U.S.$460
Principal exports (2008): food products and beverages 49.6%, base metals 6.2%, electrical machinery 5.1%, cements, bricks and ceramics 5.0% *to:* Sudan 14.3%; Kenya 9.5%; Switzerland 9.0%; Rwanda 7.9%; U.A.E. 7.4%

Religious Affiliation

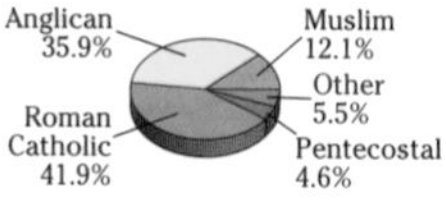

The crested crane symbol was selected by the British for Uganda. The flag, established for independence on Oct. 9, 1962, was based on the flag of the ruling Uganda People's Congress (which has three black-yellow-red stripes), with the addition of the crane in the center. Black stands for the people, yellow for sunshine, and red for brotherhood.

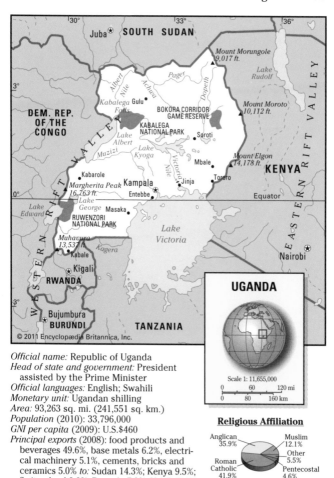

Official name: Ukraine
Head of government: Prime Minister
Official language: Ukrainian
Monetary unit: hryvnya
Area: 233,062 sq. mi. (603,628 sq. km.)
Population (2010): 45,858,000
GNI per capita (2009): U.S.$2,800
Principal exports (2008): iron and steel 38.0%, machinery and apparatus 9.6%, cereals 6.1%, metal ore/metal scrap 4.4%, petroleum 4.1% *to:* Russia 23.5%; Turkey 6.9%; Italy 4.3%; Poland 3.5%; Belarus 3.1%

Ethnic Composition

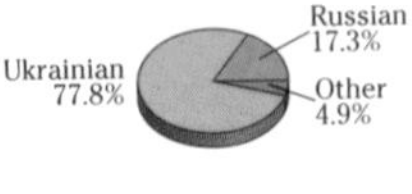

The first national flag of Ukraine, adopted in 1848, had equal stripes of yellow over blue and was based on the coat of arms of the city of Lviv. In 1918 the stripes were reversed to reflect the symbolism of blue skies over golden wheat fields. A red Soviet banner flew from 1949, but it was replaced by the blue-yellow bicolor on Jan. 28, 1992.

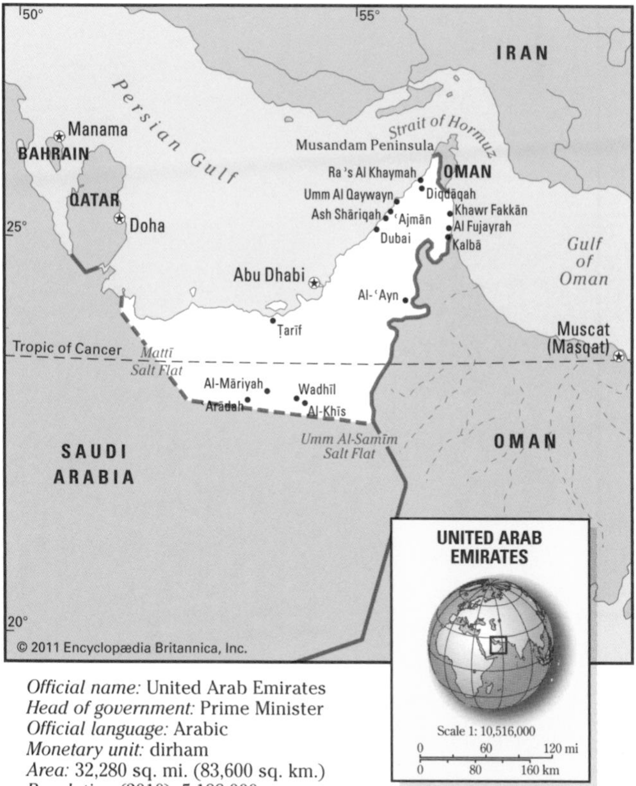

Official name: United Arab Emirates
Head of government: Prime Minister
Official language: Arabic
Monetary unit: dirham
Area: 32,280 sq. mi. (83,600 sq. km.)
Population (2010): 5,188,000
GNI per capita (2008): U.S.$57,094
Principal exports (2008): crude petroleum and refined petroleum 49.2%, gold 4.3%, unset diamonds 3.2%, road vehicles/ parts 3.0%, platinum-group metals 1.9% *to:* Japan *c.* 11%; South Korea *c.* 11%; India *c.* 11%; Iran *c.* 8%; Thailand *c.* 6%

Ethnic Composition

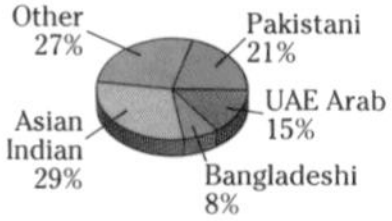

On Dec. 2, 1971, six small Arab states formed the United Arab Emirates, and a seventh state joined on Feb. 11, 1972. The flag took its colors from the Arab Revolt flag of 1917. The colors are included in a 13th-century poem which speaks of green Arab lands defended in black battles by blood-red swords of Arabs whose deeds are pure white.

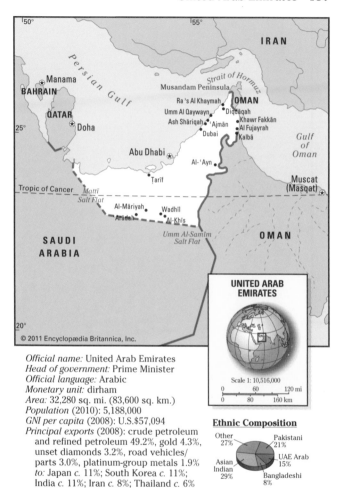

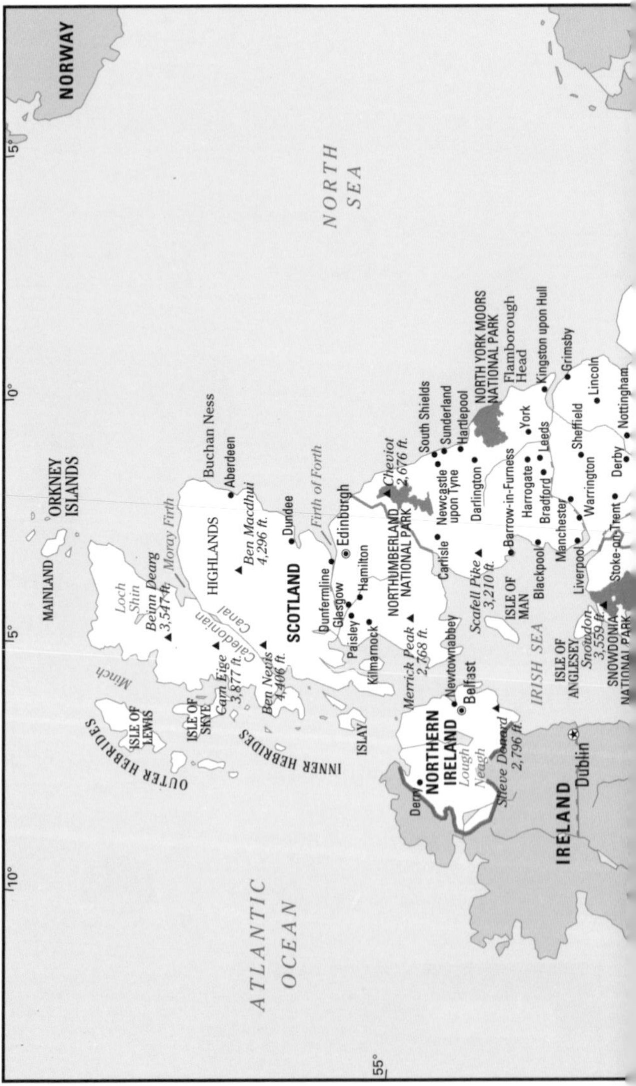
NORWAY
NORTH SEA
ORKNEY ISLANDS
MAINLAND
Buchan Ness
Aberdeen
Moray Firth
Loch Shin
Beinn Dearg 3,547 ft.
HIGHLANDS
Ben Macdhui 4,296 ft.
Dundee
Firth of Forth
Edinburgh
Caledonian Canal
SCOTLAND
Dunfermline
Glasgow
Hamilton
Paisley
Kilmarnock
Minch
OUTER HEBRIDES
ISLE OF LEWIS
ISLE OF SKYE
Carn Eige 3,877 ft.
Ben Nevis 4,406 ft.
INNER HEBRIDES
ISLAY
Cheviot 2,676 ft.
NORTHUMBERLAND NATIONAL PARK
South Shields
Sunderland
Hartlepool
Newcastle upon Tyne
Carlisle
Darlington
NORTH YORK MOORS NATIONAL PARK
Flamborough Head
Kingston upon Hull
Grimsby
Lincoln
York
Leeds
Harrogate
Bradford
Barrow-in-Furness
Scafell Pike 3,210 ft.
Merrick Peak 2,768 ft.
Newtownabbey
Belfast
NORTHERN IRELAND
Lough Neagh
Slieve Donard 2,796 ft.
Derry
IRELAND
Dublin
IRISH SEA
ISLE OF MAN
Blackpool
Manchester
Liverpool
Warrington
Sheffield
Nottingham
Derby
Stoke-on-Trent
ISLE OF ANGLESEY
Snowdon 3,559 ft.
SNOWDONIA NATIONAL PARK
ATLANTIC OCEAN
5°
0°
5°
10°
55°

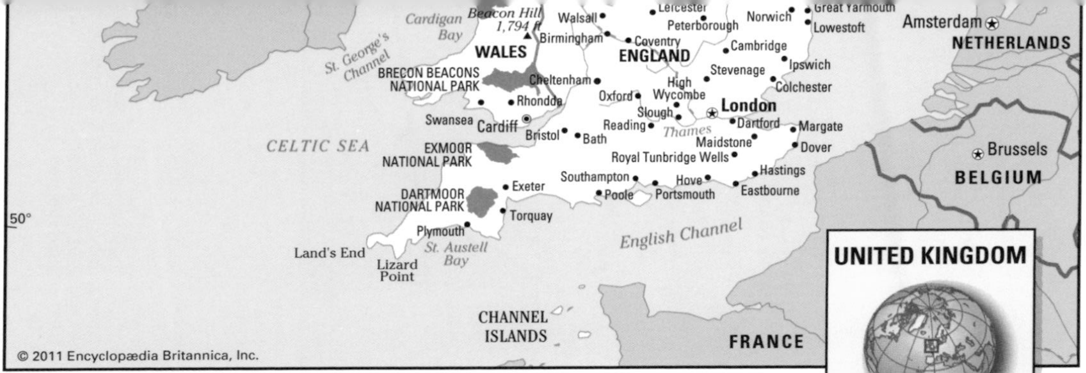

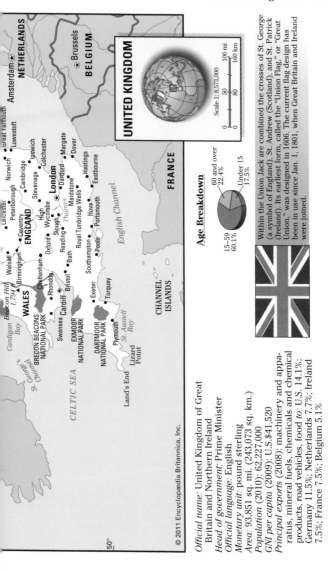

Official name: United Kingdom of Great Britain and Northern Ireland
Head of government: Prime Minister
Official language: English
Monetary unit: pound sterling
Area: 93,851 sq. mi. (243,073 sq. km.)
Population (2010): 62,227,000
GNI per capita (2009): U.S.$41,520
Principal exports (2008): machinery and apparatus, mineral fuels, chemicals and chemical products, road vehicles, food *to:* U.S. 14.1%; Germany 11.5%; Netherlands 7.7%; Ireland 7.5%; France 7.5%; Belgium 5.1%

Age Breakdown

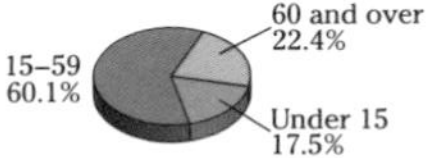

Within the Union Jack are combined the crosses of St. George (a symbol of England), St. Andrew (Scotland), and St. Patrick (Ireland). Its earliest form, called the "Union Flag," or "Great Union," was designed in 1606. The current flag design has been in use since Jan. 1, 1801, when Great Britain and Ireland were joined.

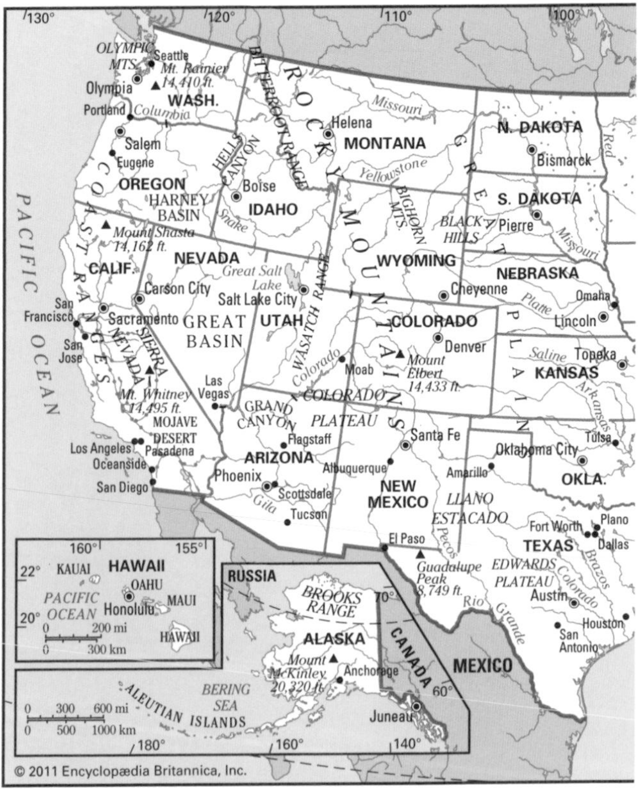

Official name: United States of America
Head of state and government: President
Official language: none
Monetary unit: dollar
Area: 3,678,190 sq. mi. (9,526,468 sq. km.)
Population (2010): 310,062,000
GNI per capita (2009): U.S.$47,240
Principal exports (2008): chemicals 13.8%, motor vehicles and parts 8.2%, electrical machinery 8.1%, agricultural commodities 6.6%, other transportation equipment 6.0% *to:* Canada 20.1%; Mexico 11.7%; China 5.5%; Japan 5.1%; Germany 4.2%; United Kingdom 4.1%; Netherlands 3.1%; South Korea 2.7%

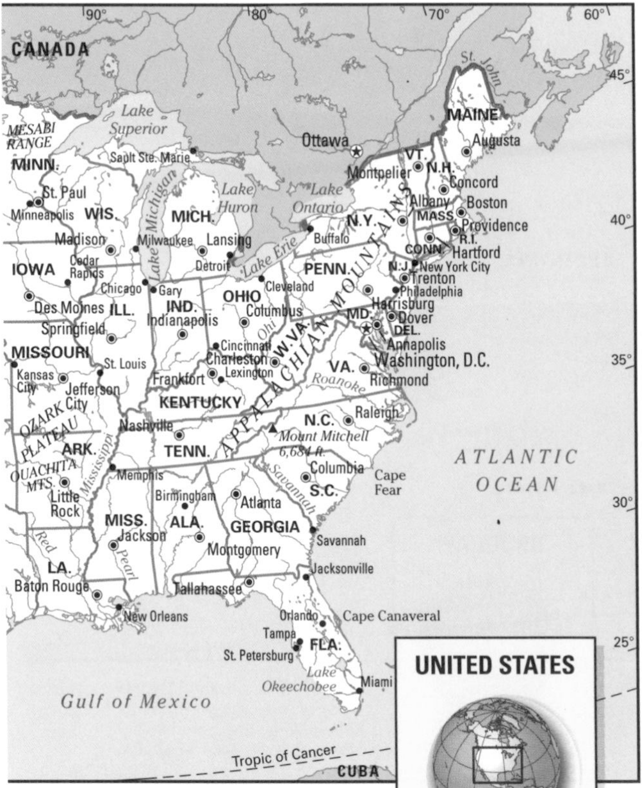

Religious Affiliation

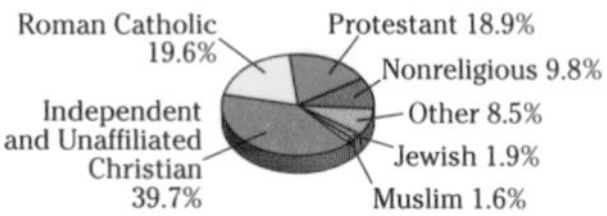

The Stars and Stripes has white stars corresponding to the states of the union (50 since July 4, 1960), as well as stripes for the 13 original states. The first unofficial national flag, hoisted on Jan. 1, 1776, had the British Union flag in the canton. The official flag dates to June 14, 1777; its design was standardized in 1912 and 1934.

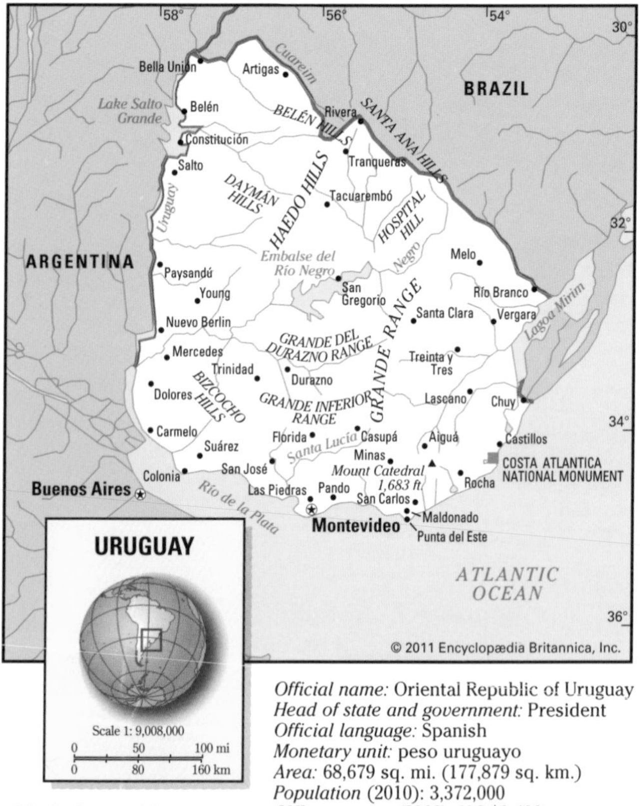

Official name: Oriental Republic of Uruguay
Head of state and government: President
Official language: Spanish
Monetary unit: peso uruguayo
Area: 68,679 sq. mi. (177,879 sq. km.)
Population (2010): 3,372,000
GNI per capita (2009): U.S.$9,400
Principal exports (2008): beef 20.1%, cereals 13.3%, milk/butter/cheese 7.2%, wood chips or particles/rough wood 6.3%, soybeans 5.5% *to:* Brazil 16.6%; free zones 9.6%; Argentina 8.5%; Russia 5.6%; Spain 4.0%

Ethnic Composition

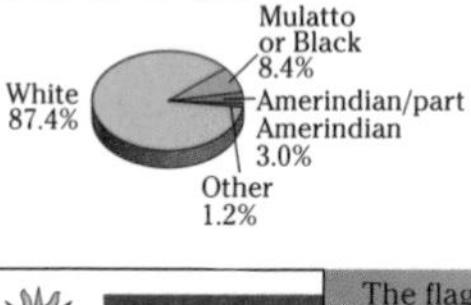

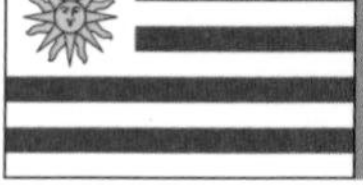

The flag adopted on Dec. 16, 1828, combined symbols of Argentina with the flag pattern of the United States. It was last altered on July 11, 1830. On the canton is the golden "Sun of May," which was seen on May 25, 1810, as a favorable omen for anti-Spanish forces in Buenos Aires, Arg. The stripes are for the original Uruguayan departments.

Official name: Republic of Uzbekistan
Head of state and government: President assisted by Prime Minister
Official language: Uzbek
Monetary unit: sum
Area: 171,469 sq. mi. (444,103 sq. km.)
Population (2010): 27,866,000
GNI per capita (2009): U.S.$1,100
Principal exports (2008): energy products 25.2%, gold (2007) *c.* 20%, cotton fiber 9.2%, machinery and apparatus 7.5% *to:* Russia 17.2%; Switzerland 8.9%; Ukraine 8.5%; Turkey 4.6%; Iran 4.6%

Ethnic Composition

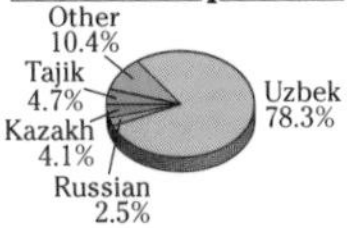

The flag of the former Soviet republic was legalized on Nov. 18, 1991. The blue is for water but also recalls the 14th-century ruler Timur. The green is for nature, fertility, and new life. The white is for peace and purity; red is for human life force. The stars are for the months and the Zodiac, while the moon is for the new republic and Islam.

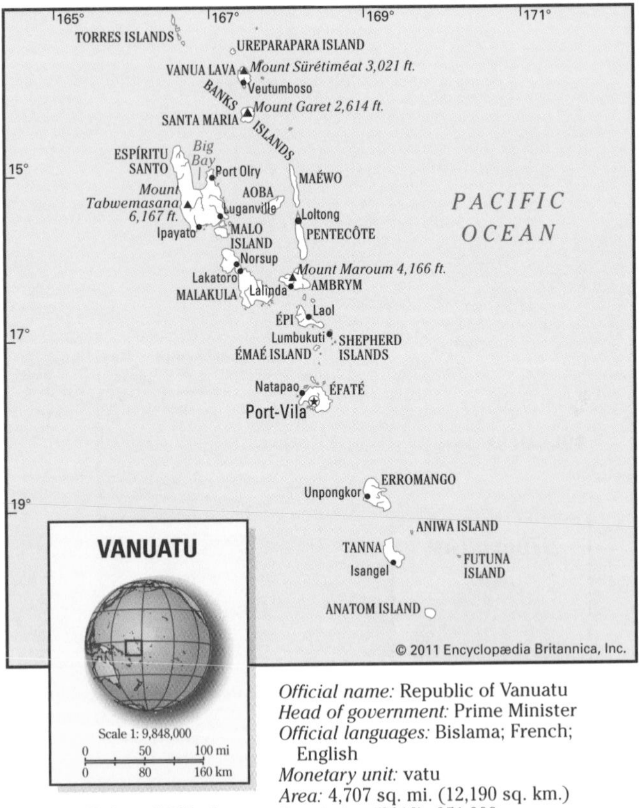

Religious Affiliation

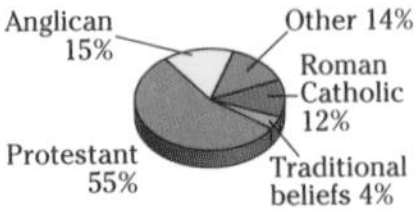

Official name: Republic of Vanuatu
Head of government: Prime Minister
Official languages: Bislama; French; English
Monetary unit: vatu
Area: 4,707 sq. mi. (12,190 sq. km.)
Population (2010): 251,000
GNI per capita (2009): U.S.$2,620
Principal exports (2008): copra 27.3%, coconut oil 19.0%, kava 14.1%, beef 10.9%, cocoa 5.7% *to:* Philippines 14.0%; New Caledonia 9.7%; Fiji 6.7%; Japan 5.4%; Singapore 5.4%

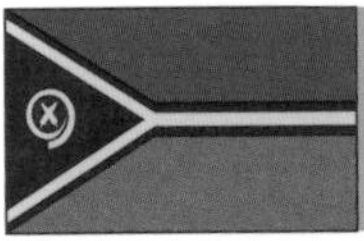

The flag was hoisted upon independence from France and Britain, on July 30, 1980. Black is for the soil and the people, green for vegetation, and red for local religious traditions such as the sacrifice of pigs. On the triangle are two crossed branches and a full-round pig's tusk, a holy symbol. The horizontal "Y" is for peace and Christianity.

Official name: Bolivarian Republic of Venezuela
Head of state and government: President
Official language: Spanish[1]
Monetary unit: bolívar
Area: 353,841 sq. mi. (916,445 sq. km.)
Population (2010): 29,044,000
GNI per capita (2009): U.S.$10,200
Principal exports (2008): crude petroleum and petroleum products 93.5%, iron and steel 1.9%, aluminum 1.1% *to:* U.S. 40.4%; Latin America 24.8%; Netherlands Antilles 20.2%

[1]Indigenous Indian languages are also official

Ethnic Composition

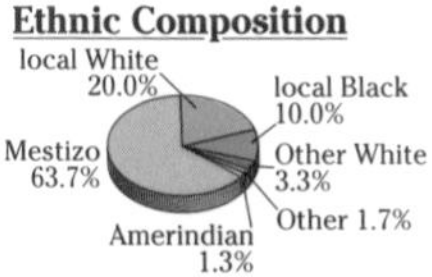

This flag was adopted March 7, 2006. Yellow stands for the gold of the New World, separated by the blue of the Atlantic Ocean from "bloody Spain," symbolized by red. The stars are for the original seven provinces plus the eighth for Guyana. In the upper hoist corner, the national arms are added to flags flown on government buildings.

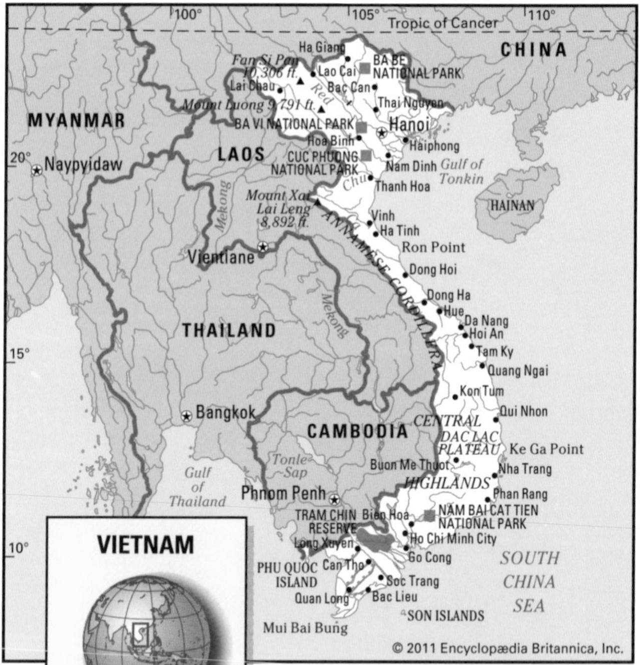

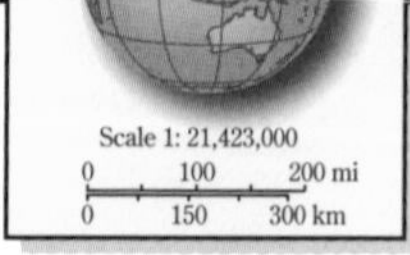

Official name: Socialist Republic of Vietnam
Head of government: Prime Minister
Official language: Vietnamese
Monetary unit: dong
Area: 127,882 sq. mi. (331,212 sq. km.)
Population (2010): 87,117,000
GNI per capita (2009): U.S.$2,850
Principal exports (2007): crude petroleum 17.5%, garments 14.6%, machinery and apparatus 10.4%, footwear, 8.4%, fish/crustaceans/mollusks 7.7% *to:* U.S. 20.8%; Japan 12.5%; Australia 7.8%; China 7.5%; Singapore 4.6%

Religious Affiliation

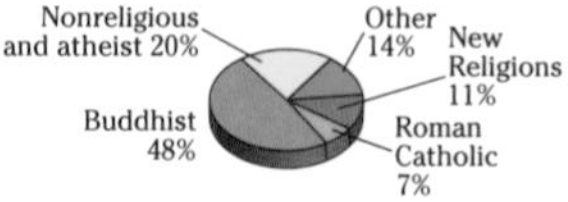

On Sept. 29, 1945, Vietnamese communists adopted the red flag in use today. On July 4, 1976, following the defeat of the American-sponsored government in the south, the flag became official throughout the nation. The five points of the star are said to stand for the proletariat, peasantry, military, intellectuals, and petty bourgeoisie.

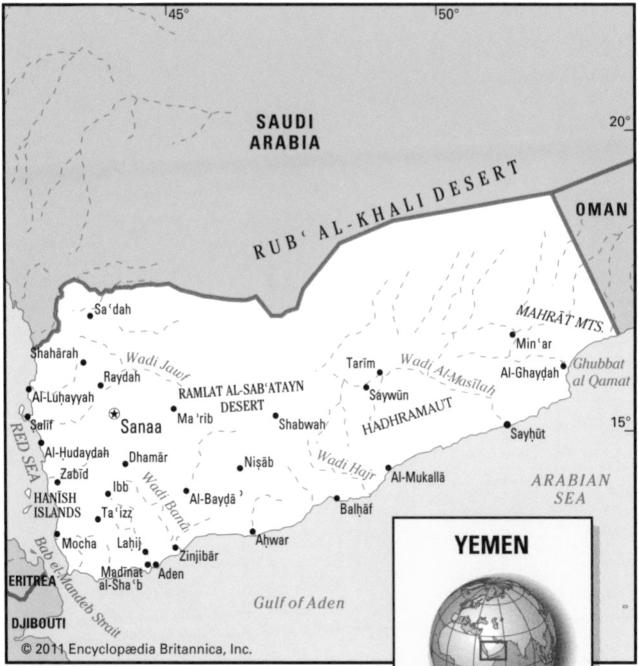

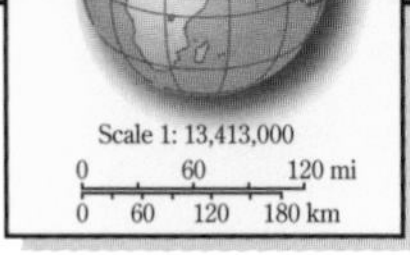

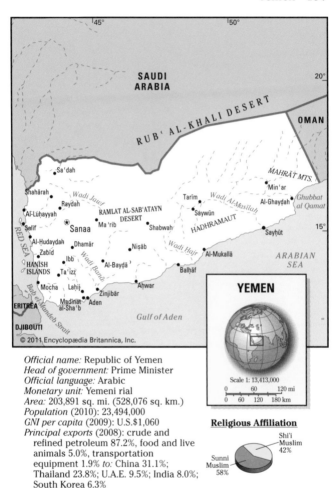

Official name: Republic of Yemen
Head of government: Prime Minister
Official language: Arabic
Monetary unit: Yemeni rial
Area: 203,891 sq. mi. (528,076 sq. km.)
Population (2010): 23,494,000
GNI per capita (2009): U.S.$1,060
Principal exports (2008): crude and refined petroleum 87.2%, food and live animals 5.0%, transportation equipment 1.9% *to:* China 31.1%; Thailand 23.8%; U.A.E. 9.5%; India 8.0%; South Korea 6.3%

Religious Affiliation

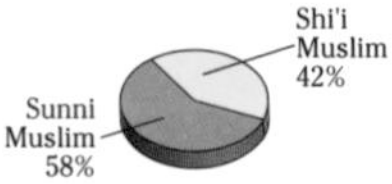

Revolutions broke out in North Yemen in 1962 and in South Yemen in 1967. In 1990 the two states unified, and that May 23 the tricolor was adopted, its design influenced by the former United Arab Republic. The black is for the dark days of the past, white for the bright future, and red for the blood shed for independence and unity.

Official name: Republic of Zambia
Head of state and government: President
Official language: English
Monetary unit: Zambian kwacha
Area: 290,585 sq. mi. (752,612 sq. km.)
Population (2010): 13,460,000
GNI per capita (2009): U.S.$970
Principal exports (2008): copper metal 64.2%, copper ore/concentrate 13.5%, cobalt 5.8%, food 3.9% *to:* Switzerland 49.8%; South Africa 10.4%; Egypt 7.5%; Dem. Rep. of the Congo 5.6%

Religious Affiliation

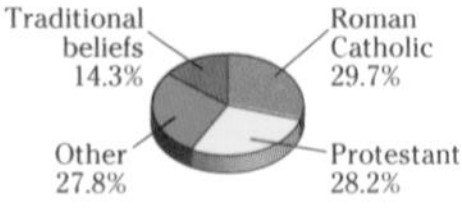

Zambia separated from Britain on Oct. 24, 1964. Its flag, based on the flag of the United National Independence Party, has a green background for agriculture, red for the freedom struggle, black for the African people, and orange for copper. The orange eagle appeared in the colonial coat of arms of 1939. It symbolizes freedom and success.

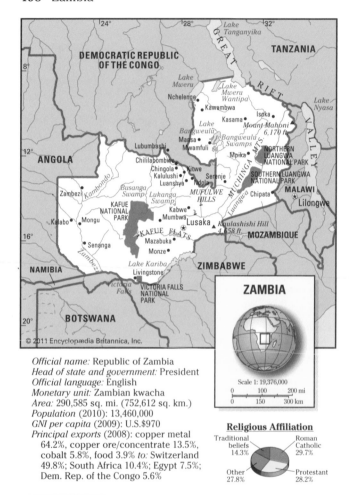

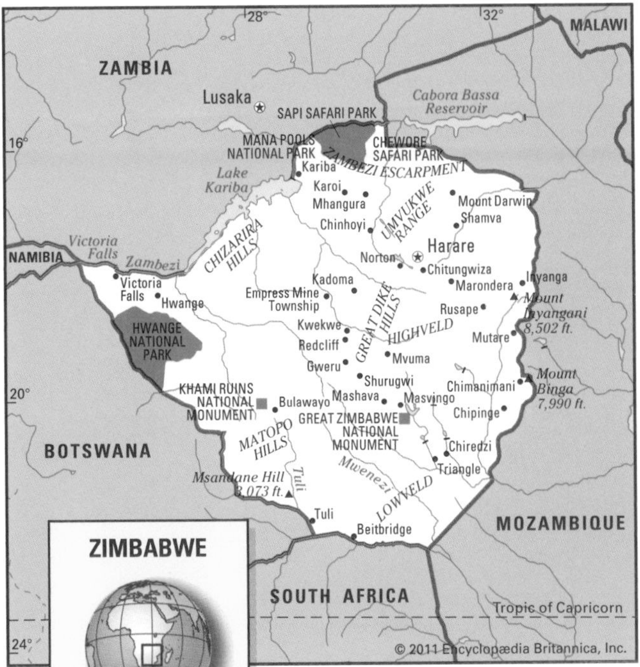

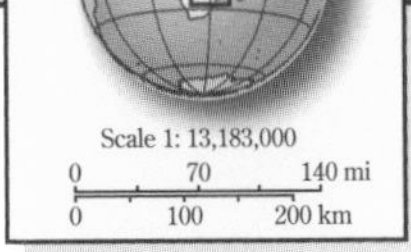

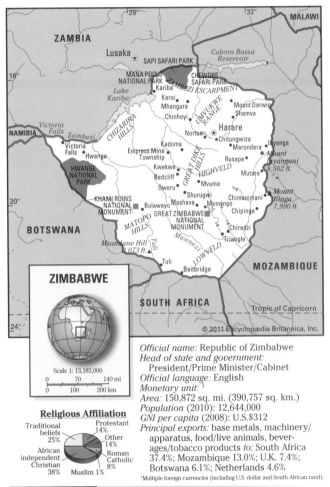

Official name: Republic of Zimbabwe
Head of state and government: President/Prime Minister/Cabinet
Official language: English
Monetary unit: [1]
Area: 150,872 sq. mi. (390,757 sq. km.)
Population (2010): 12,644,000
GNI per capita (2008): U.S.$312
Principal exports: base metals, machinery/apparatus, food/live animals, beverages/tobacco products *to:* South Africa 37.4%; Mozambique 13.0%; U.K. 7.4%; Botswana 6.1%; Netherlands 4.6%

[1]Multiple foreign currencies (including U.S. dollar and South African rand).

Religious Affiliation

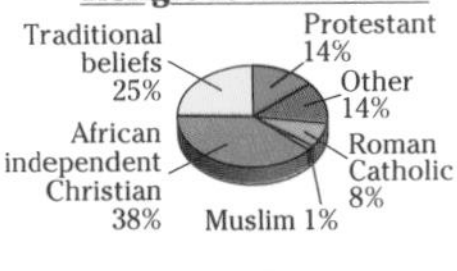

On April 18, 1980, elections brought the black majority to power under the current flag. The black color is for the ethnic majority, while red is for blood, green for agriculture, yellow for mineral wealth, and white for peace and progress. At the hoist is a red star (for socialism) and the ancient "Zimbabwe Bird" from the Great Zimbabwe ruins.

States of the United States

ALABAMA

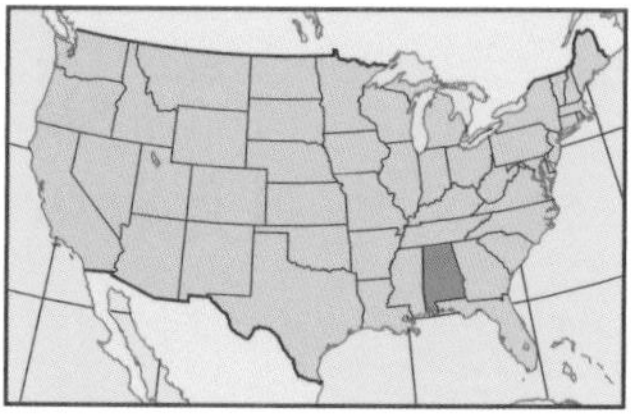

Official name: State of Alabama
Nickname: Cotton State, Yellowhammer State
State Capital: Montgomery
State flower: Camellia
Motto: We Dare Defend Our Rights
Admitted to the Union: 1819 (22nd)
Total area: 51,701 sq. mi. (133,905 sq. km.) (ranks 30th)
Population (2010): 4,779,736. (ranks 23rd)
Chief cities: Birmingham, Huntsville, Mobile, Montgomery, Tuscaloosa
Chief products/industries: Corn, soybeans, peanuts, livestock, coal, iron ore, petroleum, iron and steel, chemicals, textiles, historically notable cotton production.
Highest point: Cheaha Mountain 2405 ft. (733 m.)

State History

Original inhabitants were American Indians whose settlement sites and burial mounds are in evidence; the major groups were Cherokees, Chickasaws, Choctaws, and Creeks when area first explored by Spaniards, notably by Hernando de Soto 1539–40; first permanent settlement established 1711 by French at site of Mobile on Mobile Bay; became English 1763; southern part included in West Florida, retroceded to Spain in 1783 and claimed by U.S. as part of Louisiana Purchase 1803; rest of Alabama became part of U.S. 1783, with dividing line under dispute until 1795 when Spain ceded claim north of 31°; parts included in Territory South of the Ohio River 1790 and Mississippi Territory 1798 ff.; organized as a territory 1817; southern tip formally ceded to U.S. 1819; first constitutional convention July 1819; admitted to Union Dec. 14, 1819; 2nd constitutional convention Jan. 7–Mar. 20, 1861 passed ordinance of secession Jan. 11, 1861; government of Confederate States of America organized at Montgomery Feb. 4, 1861; 3rd constitutional convention Sept. 12–30, 1865 declared secession null and void, and abolished slavery; readmitted to Union 1868; present constitution, formulated by 6th constitutional convention, adopted 1901.

In the Civil War, the flag of the short-lived (Jan. 11–Feb. 8, 1861) Republic of Alabama showed the goddess of liberty with a sword and a single-starred flag, and the motto, "Independent Now and Forever." The present flag, adopted in 1895, recalls the Confederate battle flag, and so is usually square, not rectangular, but the law does not specify its dimensions.

TENNESSEE
MISSISSIPPI
GEORGIA
FLORIDA
88°
87°
86°
85°
35°
34°
33°
32°
31°
30°
0 20 40 mi
0 30 60 km
Florence
Athens
Huntsville
Tuscumbia
Decatur
Scottsboro
Fort Payne
Russellville
Moulton
Guntersville
Cullman
Hamilton
Centre
Double Springs
Gadsden
Oneonta
Jasper
Ashville
Vernon
Heflin
Berry
Pell City
Anniston
Bessemer
Birmingham
Talladega
Carrollton
Ashland
Wedowee
Columbiana
Tuscaloosa
Centreville
Rockford
Lafayette
Eutaw
Dadeville
Clanton
Greensboro
Auburn
Opelika
Marion
Wetumpka
Livingston
Selma
Prattville
Tuskegee
Phenix City
Montgomery
Linden
Union Springs
Hayneville
Butler
Camden
Clayton
Greenville
Luverne
Troy
Grove Hill
Abbeville
Monroeville
Chatom
Elba
Ozark
Evergreen
Dothan
Andalusia
Brewton
Geneva
Bay Minette
Prichard
Mobile
Mobile Bay
Pensacola Bay
Choctawhatchee Bay
Perdido Bay
Gulf of Mexico
© 2011 Encyclopædia Britannica, Inc.

ALASKA

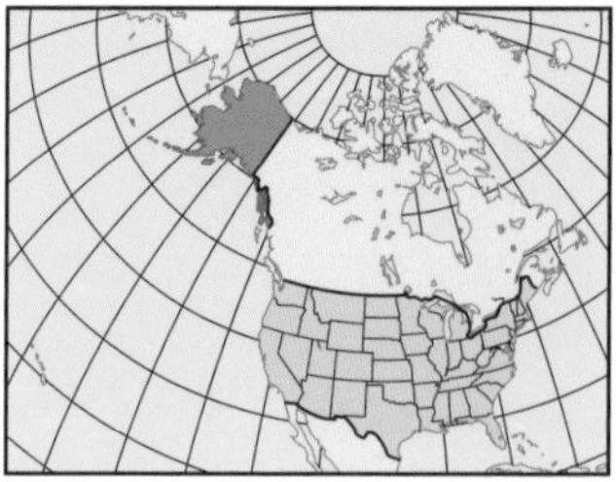

Official name: State of Alaska
Nickname: The Last Frontier
State Capital: Juneau
State flower: Forget-me-not
Motto: North to the Future (unofficial)
Admitted to the Union: 1959 (49th)
Total area: 590,693 sq. mi. (1,529,888 sq. km.) (ranks 1st)
Population (2010): 710,231 (ranks 47th)
Chief cities: Anchorage, Fairbanks, Juneau
Principal products/industries: Oil extraction, quarrying (sand and gravel), fishing, timber, tourism
Highest point: Mt. McKinley 20,320 ft. (6194 m.)

State History

Original inhabitants (American Indians and Inuits) thought to have immigrated over Beringia as well as from the Arctic area. Explored by Russian voyages, especially of Vitus Bering 1741; their first permanent settlement on Kodiak Island 1792; visited by British explorers James Cook, George Vancouver, and Sir Alexander Mackenzie and by Hudson Bay traders 1778–1847; under trade monopoly of Russian-American Fur Company 1799–1861, first managed by Aleksandr Baranov; ownership claimed by Russia; region south to 54°40′ ceded by Russia to U.S. for $7,200,000 by treaty of 1867 negotiated by Secretary of State William H. Seward (hence early nickname of Alaska, "Seward's Folly"); organized 1884; received final U.S. territorial status 1912; gold discoveries, including Klondike 1896; disputed boundary with British Columbia arbitrated in favor of U.S. 1903; restriction of seal fisheries by treaties with Great Britain, Russia, and Japan 1911; in WWII Aleutian islands of Attu and Kiska occupied by Japanese June 1942–Aug. 1943; present constitution adopted 1956; was granted statehood 1959; suffered severe earthquake damage 1964; large oil reserves discovered 1968; crude-oil pipeline south from North Slope to Valdez begun 1975, opened 1977.

Alaska held a territorial flag design competition in 1926, and the winning design was created by 13-year-old Benny Benson, who lived in an orphanage. The dark blue represents the Alaskan sky and the Big Dipper points to the North Star, for Alaska's being the northernmost part of the U.S.

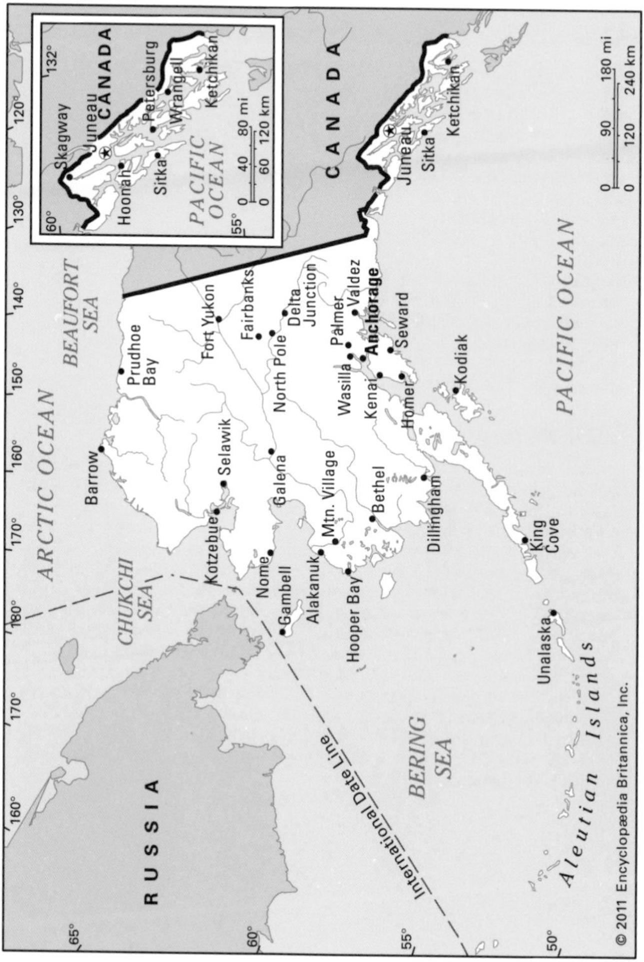
ARCTIC OCEAN
BEAUFORT SEA
CHUKCHI SEA
BERING SEA
PACIFIC OCEAN
RUSSIA
CANADA
International Date Line
Aleutian Islands
Barrow
Prudhoe Bay
Kotzebue
Selawik
Fort Yukon
Fairbanks
North Pole
Delta Junction
Galena
Nome
Gambell
Alakanuk
Mtn. Village
Hooper Bay
Bethel
Dillingham
Wasilla
Palmer
Valdez
Anchorage
Kenai
Homer
Seward
Kodiak
King Cove
Unalaska
Juneau
Sitka
Ketchikan
Skagway
Hoonah
Petersburg
Wrangell
PACIFIC OCEAN
0 40 80 mi
0 60 120 km
0 90 180 mi
0 120 240 km
60°
55°
132°
65°
60°
55°
50°
160°
170°
180°
170°
160°
150°
140°
130°
120°
© 2011 Encyclopædia Britannica, Inc.

ARIZONA

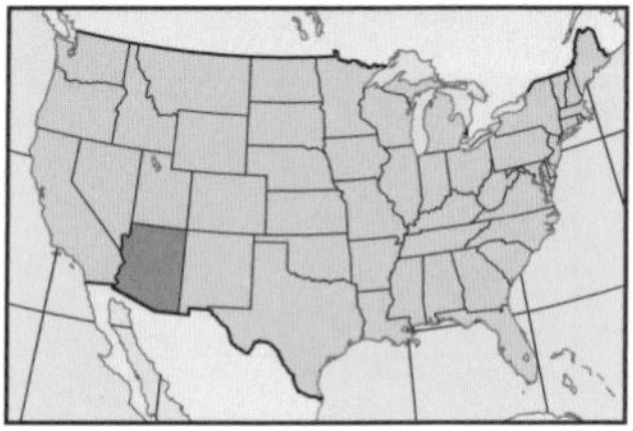

Official name: State of Arizona
Nickname: Grand Canyon State
State Capital: Phoenix
State Flower: Saguaro cactus blossom
Motto: Ditat Deus (God Enriches)
Admitted to the Union: 1912 (48th)
Total area: 113,991 sq. mi. (295,235 sq. km.) (ranks 6th)
Population (2010): 6,392,017 (ranks 16th)
Chief Cities: Chandler, Glendale, Mesa, Phoenix, Scottsdale, Tempe, Tucson
Principal products/industries: Cotton, wheat, sorghum, hay, citrus fruit, copper, molybdenum, gold, electronic equipment, food processing, tourism
Highest point: Humphreys Peak 12,633 ft. (3851 m.)

State History

Inhabited probably from 25,000 B.C. Notable early cultures Hohokum 300 B.C.–1400 A.D. and Anasazi after 100 A.D. Apache and Navajo came later c. 1300. Spanish exploration began with expedition of Franciscan friar Marcos de Niza 1539; Coronado followed 1540; ruled by Spain as part of New Spain 1598–1821; inauguration of Spanish missions to Hopis 1638; region acquired by U.S. by Treaty of Guadalupe Hidalgo 1848 and Gadsden Purchase 1853; included in New Mexico Territory 1850; organized as territory of Arizona 1863; Apache wars continued up to latter part of 19th century until Geronimo finally surrendered 1886; with New Mexico refused statehood 1906; submitted a constitution for congressional approval 1911; congressional resolution accepting this constitution vetoed by President William Howard Taft chiefly because of provision allowing recall of judges by popular vote; after objectionable matter withdrawn from constitution, admitted to Union Feb. 14, 1912; by state constitutional amendment restored the provision allowing recall of judges Nov. 1912.

Five years after attaining statehood, Arizona adopted its state flag. The rays suggest a colorful Arizona sunset over a desert in shadow, and the central star represents the state as a rich copper-producing area. The red and yellow are colors from the Spanish flag, recalling early explorers; the red and blue suggest the Stars and Stripes.

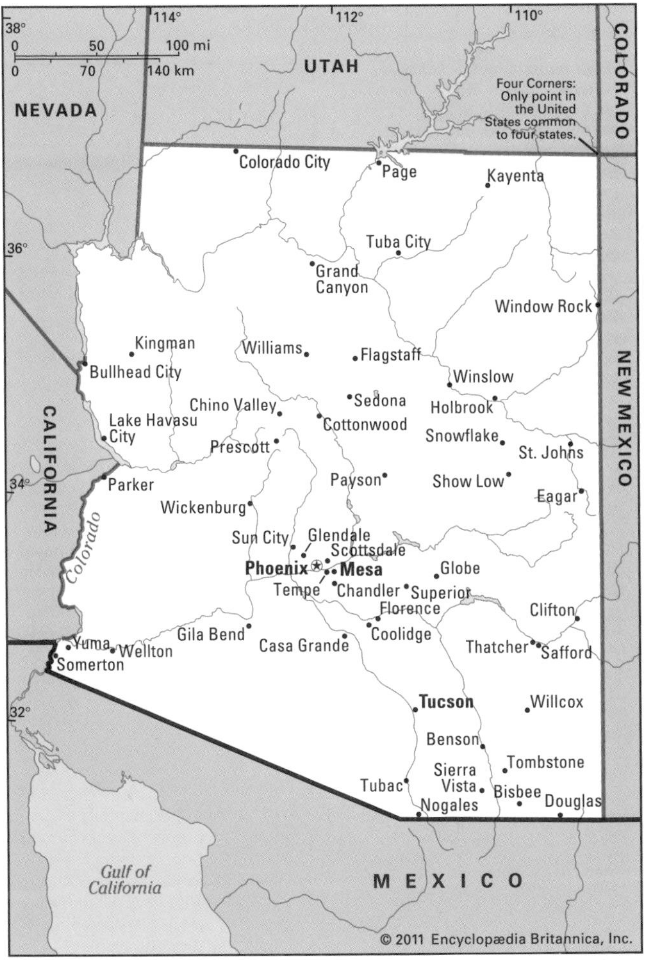

38°
36°
34°
32°
114°
112°
110°
0 50 100 mi
0 70 140 km
NEVADA
UTAH
COLORADO
NEW MEXICO
CALIFORNIA
MEXICO
Gulf of California
Colorado
Four Corners: Only point in the United States common to four states.
Colorado City
Page
Kayenta
Tuba City
Grand Canyon
Window Rock
Kingman
Williams
Flagstaff
Bullhead City
Winslow
Chino Valley
Sedona
Holbrook
Lake Havasu City
Cottonwood
Snowflake
Prescott
St. Johns
Parker
Payson
Show Low
Eagar
Wickenburg
Sun City
Glendale
Scottsdale
Phoenix
Mesa
Globe
Tempe
Chandler
Superior
Florence
Clifton
Gila Bend
Coolidge
Yuma
Wellton
Casa Grande
Thatcher
Safford
Somerton
Tucson
Willcox
Benson
Tombstone
Sierra Vista
Tubac
Bisbee
Douglas
Nogales
© 2011 Encyclopædia Britannica, Inc.

ARKANSAS

Official name: State of Arkansas
Nickname: The Natural State
State Capital: Little Rock
State Flower: Apple blossom
Motto: Regnat Populus (The People Rule)
Admitted to the Union: 1836 (25th)
Total area: 53,179 sq. mi. (137,733 sq. km.) (ranks 29th)
Population (2010): 2,915,918 (ranks 32nd)
Chief Cities: Fayetteville, Fort Smith, Jonesboro, Little Rock, North Little Rock, Springdale
Principal products/industries: Soybeans, corn, cotton, fruit, rice, livestock, bauxite, machinery, food processing
Highest point: Magazine Mountain 2753 ft. (839 m.)

State History

Early inhabitants, American Indians c. 500 A.D.; among first European explorers, Hernando de Soto 1541, Jacques Marquette and Louis Joliet 1673, Sieur de La Salle and Henry de Tonti 1682; Arkansas Post first permanent settlement (1686); in region claimed by France and yielded to Spain 1762; retroceded to France 1800; included in Louisiana Purchase 1803, Louisiana Territory 1805, and Missouri Territory 1812; Arkansas Territory organized 1819, which included current state plus most of what is now Oklahoma (except a strip along the northern boundary), and which was reduced to the current state's boundaries by 1828; adopted first constitution 1836 and admitted to Union June 15 of same year; seceded 1861; capture of Arkansas Post from Confederates 1863; readmitted into Union 1868; implementation of strict Jim Crow laws ensued; federal troops sent to Little Rock 1957 to enforce school desegregation laws.

The three stars originally appearing in the center recalled that Arkansas was the third state created from the Louisiana Territory and that it had been ruled by three different countries (France, Spain, and the U.S.). The flag was modified in 1923 by the addition of a fourth star to stand for the Confederate States of America.

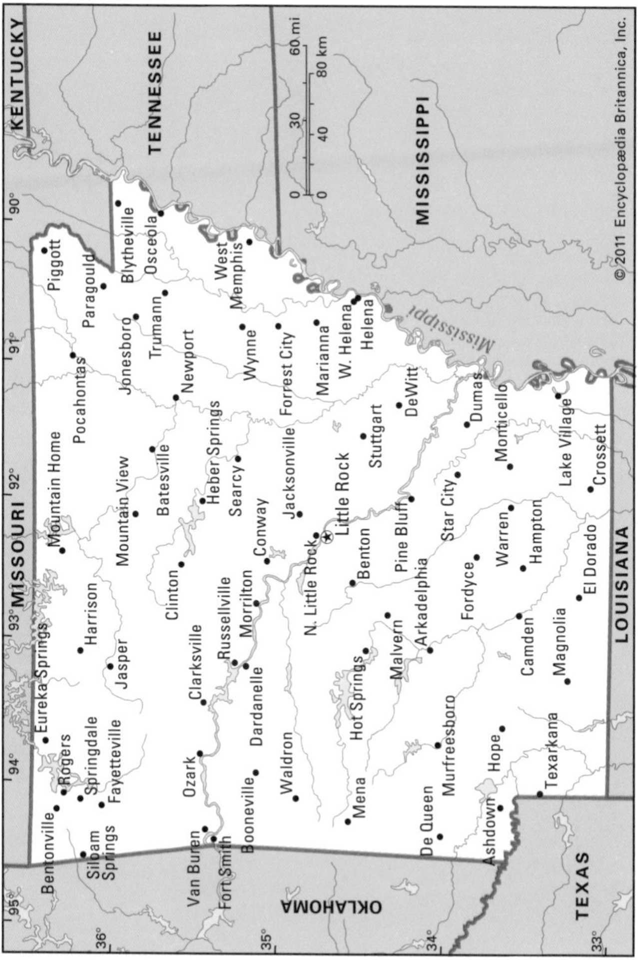
KENTUCKY
TENNESSEE
MISSISSIPPI
MISSOURI
LOUISIANA
TEXAS
OKLAHOMA
Mississippi
0 30 60 mi
0 40 80 km
90°
91°
92°
93°
94°
95°
36°
35°
34°
33°
Piggott
Paragould
Blytheville
Osceola
West Memphis
Trumann
Jonesboro
Pocahontas
Newport
Wynne
Forrest City
Marianna
W. Helena
Helena
DeWitt
Dumas
Monticello
Lake Village
Crossett
Stuttgart
Mountain Home
Mountain View
Batesville
Heber Springs
Searcy
Jacksonville
Little Rock
N. Little Rock
Conway
Pine Bluff
Star City
Warren
Hampton
El Dorado
Benton
Fordyce
Arkadelphia
Malvern
Camden
Magnolia
Harrison
Clinton
Morrilton
Russellville
Clarksville
Jasper
Eureka Springs
Rogers
Springdale
Fayetteville
Bentonville
Siloam Springs
Ozark
Van Buren
Fort Smith
Booneville
Dardanelle
Waldron
Hot Springs
Mena
De Queen
Murfreesboro
Hope
Ashdown
Texarkana
©2011 Encyclopædia Britannica, Inc.

CALIFORNIA

Official name: State of California
Nickname: Golden State
State Capital: Sacramento
State Flower: California poppy
Motto: Eureka (I Have Found It)
Admitted to the Union: 1850 (31st)
Total area: 158,608 sq. mi. (410,793 sq. km.) (ranks 3rd)
Population (2010): 37,253,956 (ranks 1st)
Chief Cities: Anaheim, Bakersfield, Fresno, Long Beach, Los Angeles, Oakland, Sacramento, San Diego, San Francisco, San Jose
Principal products/industries: Tomatoes, lettuce, broccoli, strawberries, grapes, oranges, and other fruits and vegetables, cotton, rice, flowers, oil, natural gas, gypsum, food products, soft drinks, transportation equipment, electrical machinery, electronics, movie and television industries, tourism
Highest point: Mt. Whitney 14,494 ft. (4419 m.)

State History

Inhabited originally by American Indians; first European coastal exploration by voyage of Spanish emissaries Juan Rodríguez Cabrillo and Bartolomé Ferrelo who established Spanish claim to region 1542–43; coast reached by English mariner Sir Francis Drake 1579; first Franciscan mission established by Junípero Serra at San Diego 1769; remained under Spanish control and later under Mexican control until conquered by U.S. forces during Mexican War (1846–47); ceded to U.S. by Treaty of Guadalupe Hidalgo 1848; settlement by Americans begun in 1841, greatly accelerated after discovery of gold at Coloma (Sutter's Mill) in 1848 which brought influx of miners and adventurers; admitted to Union Sept. 9, 1850 as a free state under Missouri Compromise; present constitution (many times amended) drawn up by constitutional convention 1878–79, ratified by people, and in force Jan. 1, 1880; with an already expanding population, state in 20th century grew even more with advent of the automobile; has more miles of freeway than any other state in U.S.; economy largest of all states in U.S.; subject to earthquakes, state suffered severe ones in north around San Francisco especially 1906 and 1989 and in south around Los Angeles 1994.

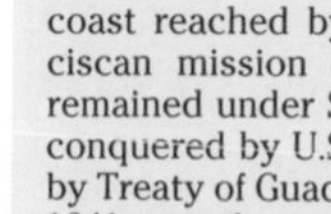

In 1846, during the Mexican-American War, Mexican-ruled California proclaimed independence and raised the original Bear Flag (June 14, 1846), featuring the now-extinct California grizzly bear. In 1911 the flag of the short-lived California Republic became the state flag. It is unusual in featuring a design used by a formerly independent country.

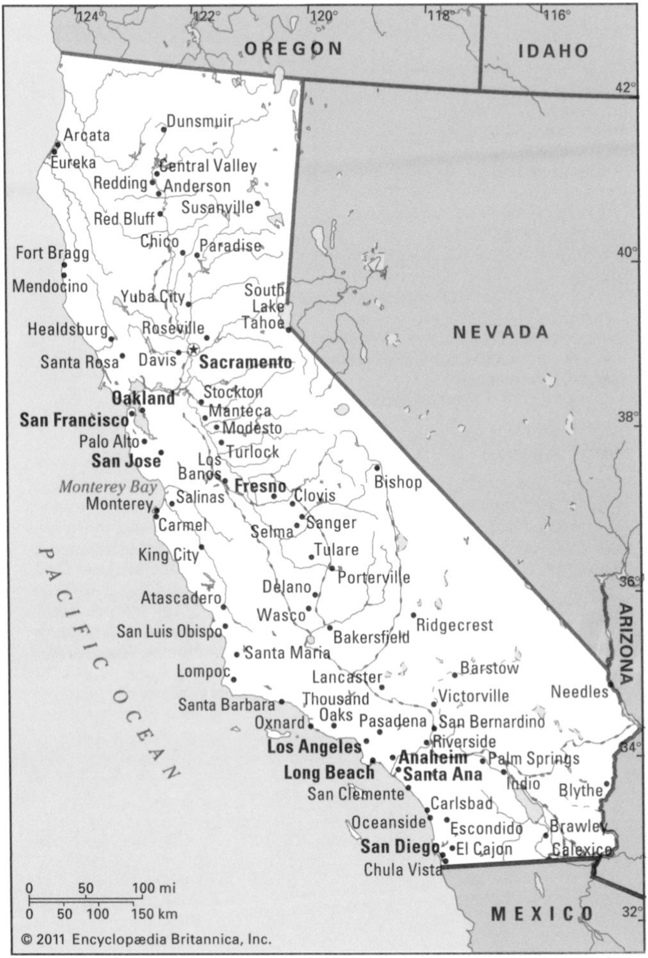
124°
122°
120°
118°
116°
42°
40°
38°
36°
34°
32°
OREGON
IDAHO
NEVADA
ARIZONA
MEXICO
PACIFIC OCEAN
Monterey Bay
Dunsmuir
Arcata
Eureka
Central Valley
Redding
Anderson
Susanville
Red Bluff
Chico
Paradise
Fort Bragg
Mendocino
Yuba City
South Lake Tahoe
Healdsburg
Roseville
Santa Rosa
Davis
Sacramento
Oakland
Stockton
Manteca
San Francisco
Modesto
Palo Alto
Turlock
San Jose
Los Banos
Bishop
Fresno
Clovis
Salinas
Monterey
Carmel
Sanger
Selma
Tulare
King City
Porterville
Delano
Atascadero
Wasco
Ridgecrest
San Luis Obispo
Bakersfield
Santa Maria
Barstow
Lompoc
Lancaster
Victorville
Needles
Santa Barbara
Thousand Oaks
Oxnard
Pasadena
San Bernardino
Riverside
Los Angeles
Anaheim
Palm Springs
Long Beach
Santa Ana
Indio
Blythe
San Clemente
Carlsbad
Oceanside
Escondido
Brawley
San Diego
El Cajon
Calexico
Chula Vista
0 50 100 mi
0 50 100 150 km
© 2011 Encyclopædia Britannica, Inc.

COLORADO

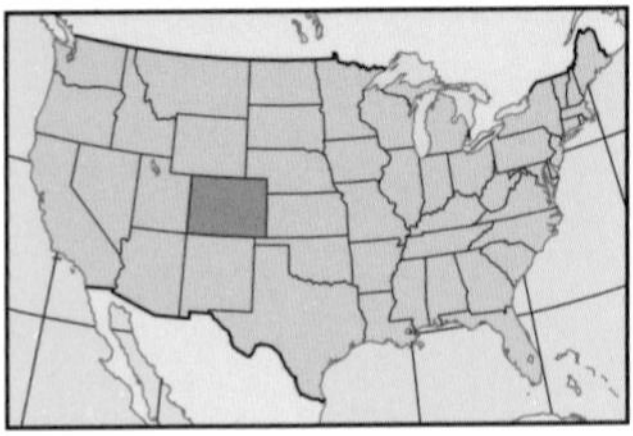

Official name: State of Colorado
Nickname: Centennial State
State Capital: Denver
State Flower: Columbine
Motto: Nil Sine Numine (Nothing Without Providence)
Admitted to the Union: 1876 (38th)
Total area: 104,095 sq. mi. (269,605 sq. km.) (ranks 8th)
Population (2010): 5,029,196 (ranks 22nd)
Chief Cities: Aurora, Colorado Springs, Denver, Fort Collins, Lakewood, Thornton
Principal products/industries: Wheat, sugar beets, corn, livestock, oil, molybdenum, coal, food processing, printing, semiconductors, tourism, outdoor recreation
Highest point: Mt. Elbert 14,433 ft. (4,399 m.)

State History

In early times, southwestern part of state inhabited by the Anasazi; when Europeans arrived, plains inhabited primarily by the Arapaho, Cheyenne, Comanche, and Kiowa; mountains inhabited mainly by the Utes; explored chiefly by 18th century Spaniards; claimed by Spain and also France; eastern part acquired by U.S. in Louisiana Purchase 1803, rest in territory yielded by Mexico 1845–48; explored for U.S. government by Zebulon Pike 1806, Stephen Long 1820, and John Frémont 1842; additional exploration by a host of fur trappers and traders; parts included in Louisiana, Missouri, Utah, New Mexico, Kansas, and Nebraska territories 1805–61; gold, discovered at Cherry Creek (in present-day Denver) in 1858, attracted American settlers; organized as territory of Colorado 1861; admitted as state Aug. 1, 1876; constitution adopted 1876.

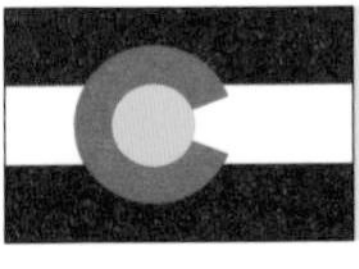

The red C stands not only for the name of the state but also for the state flower (columbine) and the state nickname ("Centennial State"). Colorado became a state in 1876, when the country was celebrating the centennial of its independence. The red, white, and blue suggest the U.S. flag; the blue, yellow, and white, the columbine colors.

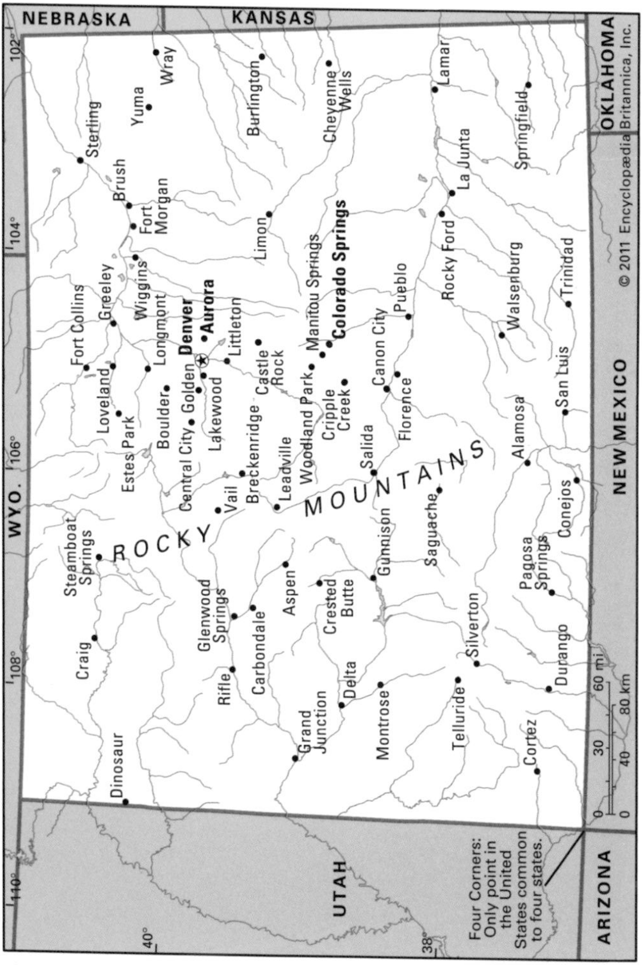
NEBRASKA
KANSAS
OKLAHOMA
NEW MEXICO
ARIZONA
UTAH
WYO.
ROCKY MOUNTAINS
Sterling
Yuma
Wray
Burlington
Cheyenne Wells
Lamar
Springfield
La Junta
Brush
Fort Morgan
Limon
Colorado Springs
Manitou Springs
Rocky Ford
Walsenburg
Trinidad
Fort Collins
Greeley
Wiggins
Longmont
Denver
Aurora
Littleton
Pueblo
Canon City
Castle Rock
Woodland Park
Cripple Creek
Florence
Loveland
Estes Park
Boulder
Golden
Lakewood
Central City
Breckenridge
Leadville
Salida
Vail
Gunnison
Saguache
Alamosa
San Luis
Conejos
Steamboat Springs
Craig
Glenwood Springs
Carbondale
Aspen
Crested Butte
Rifle
Grand Junction
Delta
Montrose
Telluride
Silverton
Pagosa Springs
Durango
Cortez
Dinosaur
Four Corners: Only point in the United States common to four states.
102°
104°
106°
108°
110°
40°
38°
0 30 60 mi
0 40 80 km
© 2011 Encyclopædia Britannica, Inc.

CONNECTICUT

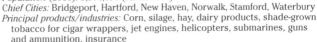

Official name: State of Connecticut
Nicknames: Constitution State, Nutmeg State
State Capital: Hartford
State Flower: Mountain laurel
Motto: Qui Transtulit Sustinet (He Who Transplanted Still Sustains)
Admitted to the Union: 1788; 5th of the original 13 colonies to ratify the U.S. Constitution
Total area: 5,004 sq. mi. (12,960 sq. km.) (ranks 48th)
Population (2010): 3,574,097 (ranks 29th)
Chief Cities: Bridgeport, Hartford, New Haven, Norwalk, Stamford, Waterbury
Principal products/industries: Corn, silage, hay, dairy products, shade-grown tobacco for cigar wrappers, jet engines, helicopters, submarines, guns and ammunition, insurance
Highest point: Mt. Frissell 2380 ft. (726 m.)

State History

Originally inhabited by the Algonquin Indians. Connecticut River explored 1614 by Dutch navigator Adriaen Block, and again 1632 by Edward Winslow of Plymouth; posts established 1633 by the Dutch at Hartford and by a Plymouth contingent at Windsor; a 3rd post established at Wethersfield 1634 following 1633 exploration of the area by John Oldham of Massachusetts Bay Colony; permanent settlements established at the three river towns of Hartford, Windsor, and Wethersfield 1635–36, primarily by colonists from Massachusetts Bay; Saybrook Colony established 1635; Pequot tribe nearly extinguished in Pequot War 1636–37; New Haven Colony established 1638; three river towns formed Connecticut Colony and adopted Fundamental Orders, considered by some to be the first American constitution based on the consent of the governed, 1638–39; in New England Confederation 1643–84; Connecticut Colony absorbed Saybrook Colony 1644; received charter 1662 which united Connecticut and New Haven colonies and granted strip of land extending to Pacific; included in Dominion of New England, the government of Connecticut was briefly taken over by British colonial governor Sir Edmund Andros 1687–89; relinquished claims to western lands 1786 except for Western Reserve (situated in what is now Ohio) to which it abandoned jurisdiction 1800; participated in Hartford Convention 1814–15; adopted state constitution 1818, in force until 1965, when it was replaced by another.

The coat of arms is based on the 1711 seal of the colony of Connecticut. Its three grapevines are thought to represent either the colonies of Connecticut, New Haven, and Saybrook or the first three area towns established by Europeans (Hartford, Wethersfield, and Windsor).

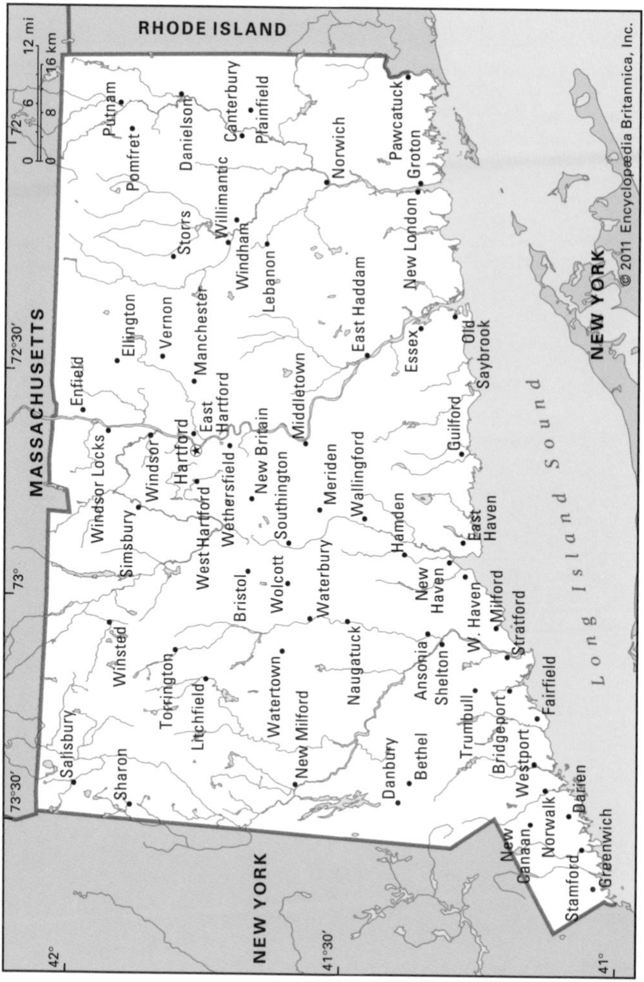
MASSACHUSETTS
RHODE ISLAND
NEW YORK
NEW YORK
Long Island Sound
0 6 12 mi
0 8 16 km
72°
72°30′
73°
73°30′
42°
41°30′
41°
Salisbury
Sharon
Winsted
Torrington
Litchfield
Watertown
New Milford
Danbury
Bethel
Naugatuck
Ansonia
Shelton
Trumbull
Bridgeport
Westport
Fairfield
Norwalk
Darien
New Canaan
Stamford
Greenwich
Stratford
Milford
W. Haven
New Haven
Waterbury
Wolcott
Bristol
Simsbury
Windsor Locks
Enfield
Windsor
West Hartford
Hartford
East Hartford
Wethersfield
New Britain
Southington
Meriden
Wallingford
Hamden
East Haven
Guilford
Middletown
Old Saybrook
Essex
East Haddam
Manchester
Vernon
Ellington
Storrs
Windham
Willimantic
Lebanon
New London
Groton
Norwich
Pawcatuck
Canterbury
Plainfield
Danielson
Pomfret
Putnam
© 2011 Encyclopædia Britannica, Inc.

DELAWARE

Official name: State of Delaware
Nicknames: First State, Diamond State
State Capital: Dover
State Flower: Peach blossom
Motto: Liberty and Independence
Admitted to the Union: 1787; 1st of the original 13 colonies to ratify the U.S. Constitution
Total area: 2,023 sq. mi. (5,240 sq. km.) (ranks 49th)
Population (2010): 897,934 (ranks 45th)
Chief Cities: Dover, Newark, Wilmington
Principal products/industries: Chemicals, food processing, poultry, fishing, soybeans, corn
Highest point: Ebright Azimuth 448 ft. (137 m.)

State History

Region originally inhabited by several Algonquian tribes; earliest European settlements made by Dutch 1631 at present site of Lewes; first permanent settlements made by Swedes 1638; New Sweden captured by Dutch 1655 and, as part of New Netherland, by English 1664; part of New York until it became part of a grant made to William Penn 1682; in 1704 received right to separate legislative assembly, but remained under governor of Pennsylvania until 1776; active in American Revolution; formulated first state constitution 1776, adopted present constitution 1897; remained in Union during Civil War.

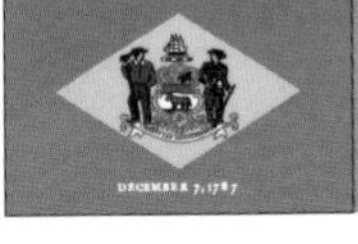

The diamond shape may represent the nickname "Diamond State." The coat of arms incorporates symbols appropriate for the late 18th century—a soldier, a farmer, agricultural produce (a sheaf of wheat and an ear of corn), an ox, and a ship.

76°
75°30′
75°
PENNSYLVANIA
NEW JERSEY
MARYLAND
39°30′
39°
38°30′
Chesapeake Bay
Delaware Bay
ATLANTIC OCEAN
Rehoboth Bay
Indian River Inlet
Arden
Claymont
Hockessin
Bellefonte
Elsmere
Edgemoor
Marshallton
Wilmington
Newport
Newark
New Castle
Bear
Glasgow
Delaware City
Port Penn
Odessa
Middletown
Smyrna
Clayton
Leipsic
Cheswold
Dupont Manor
Dover
Rodney Village
Kent Acres
Camden
Highland Acres
Rising Sun
Felton
Frederica
Harrington
Houston
Milford
Lincoln
Ellendale
Greenwood
Milton
Lewes
Bridgeville
Rehoboth Beach
Georgetown
Seaford
Millsboro
Laurel
Ocean View
Bethany Beach
Delmar
Selbyville
Fenwick Island
0 6 12 mi
0 5 10 15 km
© 2011 Encyclopædia Britannica, Inc.

FLORIDA

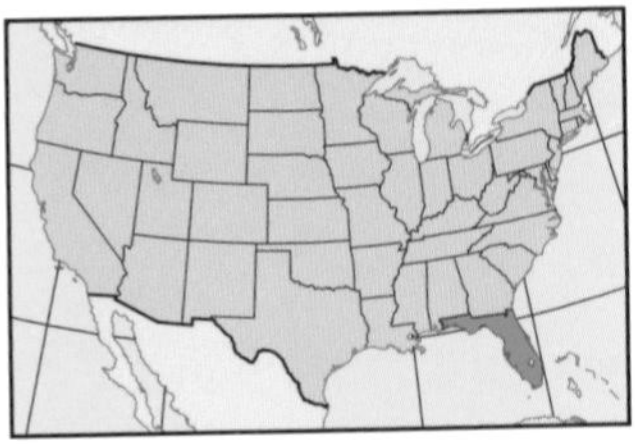

Official name: State of Florida
Nickname: Sunshine State
State Capital: Tallahassee
State Flower: Orange blossom
Motto: In God We Trust
Admitted to the Union: 1845 (27th)
Total area: 58,976 sq. mi. (152,747 sq. km.) (ranks 22nd)
Population (2010): 18,801,310 (ranks 4th)
Chief Cities: Fort Lauderdale, Hialeah, Jacksonville, Miami, Orlando, St. Petersburg, Tallahasse, Tampa
Principal products/industries: Citrus fruits, vegetables, dairy products, cattle, phosphates, food products, beverages, electronic equipment, tourism
Highest point: Britton Hill 345 ft. (105 m.)

State History

Spanish Florida, which included southeastern part of present U.S., sighted and explored by Juan Ponce de León 1513; St. Augustine settled 1565; following Seven Years' War, ceded to England by Spain in exchange for Havana 1763; divided into two provinces (known as the Floridas), East and West Florida; retroceded to Spain 1783; West Florida claimed by U.S. as part of Louisiana Purchase 1803; border crossed by Gen. Andrew Jackson who captured Pensacola 1814 and 1818; purchased for $5,000,000 by U.S. under Adams-Onís Treaty 1819; organized as territory of Florida 1822; most Seminole natives relocated to Indian Territory (now Oklahoma) following war (1835–42); admitted to Union as slave state Mar. 3, 1845; passed ordinance of secession Jan. 10, 1861; annulled ordinance of secession Oct. 28, 1865 and abolished slavery; readmitted to Union 1868; present constitution adopted 1885, much amended 1968.

After the Civil War, Florida designated the state seal to appear in the center of a white flag; the design showed an American Indian woman on a promontory extending into water where a steamboat was sailing. Later, a red saltire (similar to that of the Confederate Battle Flag) was added so that it would not resemble a flag of surrender.

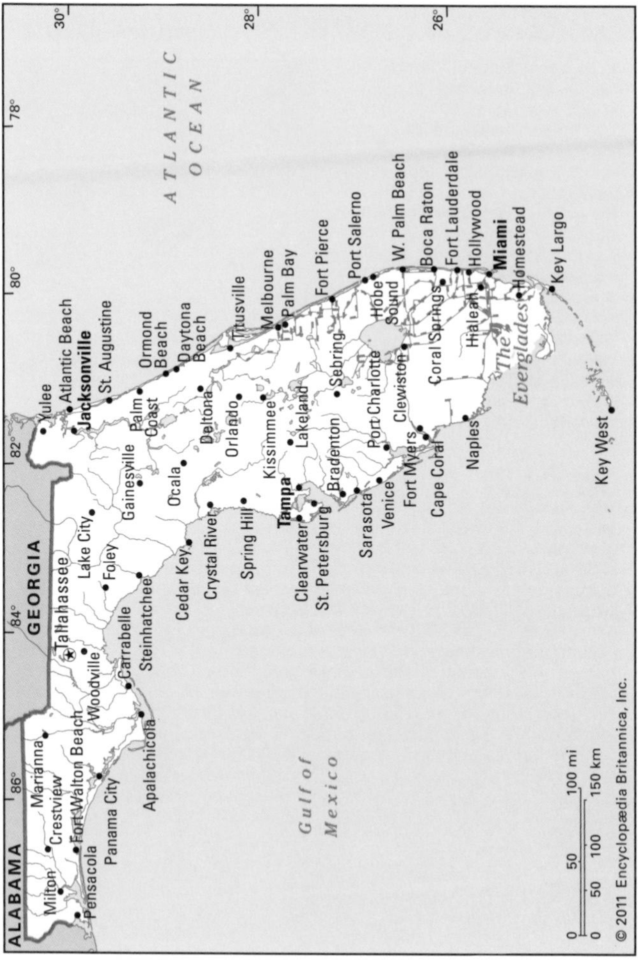
ALABAMA
GEORGIA
ATLANTIC OCEAN
Gulf of Mexico
The Everglades
30°
28°
26°
78°
80°
82°
84°
86°
Milton
Pensacola
Crestview
Fort Walton Beach
Marianna
Panama City
Apalachicola
Woodville
Tallahassee
Carrabelle
Steinhatchee
Lake City
Foley
Cedar Key
Crystal River
Spring Hill
Clearwater
St. Petersburg
Tampa
Gainesville
Ocala
Yulee
Atlantic Beach
Jacksonville
St. Augustine
Palm Coast
Ormond Beach
Daytona Beach
Deltona
Orlando
Kissimmee
Lakeland
Titusville
Melbourne
Palm Bay
Fort Pierce
Sebring
Bradenton
Sarasota
Venice
Port Charlotte
Fort Myers
Cape Coral
Clewiston
Port Salerno
Hobe Sound
W. Palm Beach
Boca Raton
Coral Springs
Fort Lauderdale
Hollywood
Hialeah
Miami
Homestead
Naples
Key Largo
Key West
0 50 100 mi
0 50 100 150 km
© 2011 Encyclopædia Britannica, Inc.

GEORGIA

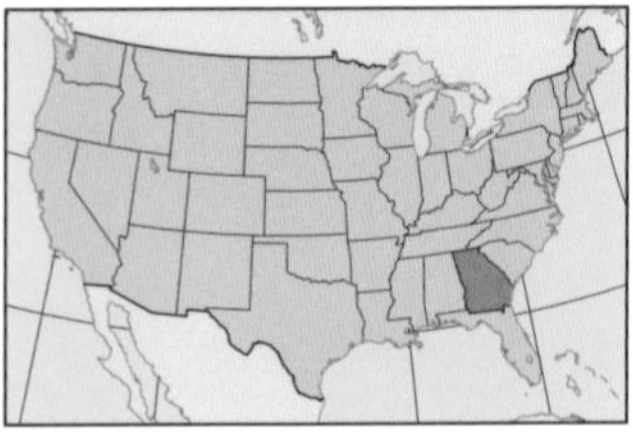

Official name: State of Georgia
Nicknames: Empire State of the South, Peach State
State Capital: Atlanta
State Flower: Cherokee rose, azalea
Motto: Wisdom, Justice, Moderation
Admitted to the Union: 1788; 4th of the original 13 colonies to ratify the U.S. Constitution
Total area: 58,921 sq. mi. (152,605 sq. km.) (ranks 24th)
Population (2010): 9,687,653 (ranks 9th)
Chief Cities: Athens, Atlanta, Augusta, Columbus, Macon, Sandy Springs, Savannah
Principal products/industries: Processed foods, peanuts, pecans, peaches, tobacco, poultry, livestock, clays, textiles, pulp, carpets and rugs, automobile assembly
Highest point: Brasstown Bald 4784 ft. (1459 m.)

State History

Inhabited by Creek and Cherokee peoples when explored by Spanish and penetrated by Spanish missions 16th century; English colony, last of original 13 colonies to be founded, chartered 1732 and settled 1733 at Savannah by English philanthropist James E. Oglethorpe as refuge for debtors and as buffer state between Spanish Florida and the Carolinas; surrendered charter to crown 1752; became royal colony 1754; Savannah held by British 1778–82; chartered University of Georgia 1785, the oldest state university; first southern state to ratify U.S. Constitution Jan. 2, 1788; ceded claims to western lands (now Alabama and Mississippi) 1802; Creek and Cherokee tribes forcibly removed to Indian Territory 1830s; seceded from Union Jan. 19, 1861; scene of battle of Chickamauga 1863, campaign between Chattanooga and Atlanta, and Gen. William T. Sherman's "March to the Sea" 1864; ordinance of secession repealed Oct. 30, 1865 and slavery abolished; last state to be readmitted to Union July 15, 1870; adopted present constitution 1945.

Approved in March 2004, Georgia's flag is reminiscent of the Confederate Stars and Bars, with three broad red-white-red stripes and a blue canton. The state coat of arms (from the seal) and the motto "In God we trust" below it in yellow within the canton are surrounded by a circle of 13 white stars, symbolizing Georgia's position as one of the 13 original U.S. states.

85°
84°
83°
82°
81°
35°
34°
33°
32°
31°
30°
TENNESSEE
NORTH CAROLINA
SOUTH CAROLINA
ALABAMA
FLORIDA
ATLANTIC OCEAN
Gulf of Mexico
Savannah River
Dalton
Blue Ridge
Blairsville
Clayton
Ellijay
La Fayette
Cleveland
Calhoun
Dahlonega
Jasper
Toccoa
Summerville
Dawsonville
Homer
Hartwell
Rome
Cartersville
Canton
Gainesville
Jefferson
Elberton
Cedartown
Roswell
Winder
Athens
Marietta
Lexington
Smyrna
Monroe
Lincolnton
Buchanan
Atlanta
Decatur
Washington
Carrollton
East Point
Madison
Greensboro
Martinez
Covington
Thomson
Augusta
Newnan
Jackson
Griffin
Sparta
Eatonton
Waynesboro
Milledgeville
Zebulon
La Grange
Barnesville
Gray
Louisville
Thomaston
Sandersville
Macon
Irwinton
Sylvania
Talbotton
Wrightsville
Warner Robins
Swainsboro
Butler
Columbus
Fort Valley
Dublin
Statesboro
Buena Vista
Perry
Cochran
Metter
Springfield
Cusseta
Oglethorpe
Vidalia
Lyons
Claxton
Andersonville
Eastman
Vienna
Reidsville
Savannah
Lumpkin
Americus
McRae
Cordele
Abbeville
Hazlehurst
Hinesville
Cuthbert
Fitzgerald
Baxley
Dawson
Leesburg
Jesup
Ludowici
Fort Gaines
Albany
Sylvester
Douglas
Alma
Tifton
Darien
Pearson
Blackshear
Newton
Camilla
Moultrie
Nashville
Brunswick
Colquitt
Waycross
Nahunta
Adel
Woodbine
Lakeland
Homerville
Bainbridge
Cairo
Thomasville
Valdosta
Folkston
Quitman
Statenville
0 20 40 mi
0 30 60 km
© 2011 Encyclopædia Britannica, Inc.

HAWAII

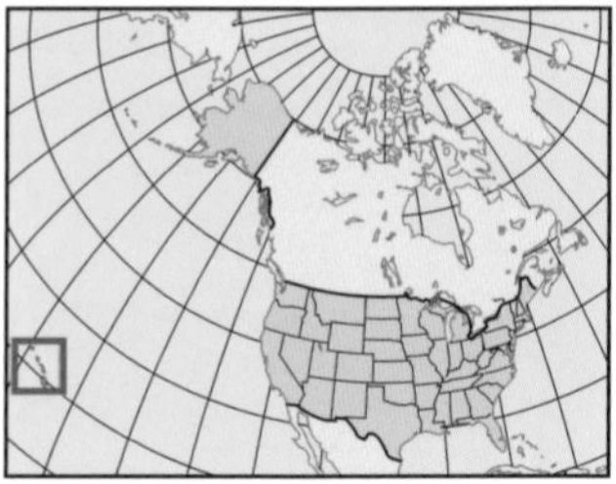

Official name: State of Hawaii
Nickname: Aloha State
State Capital: Honolulu
State Flower: Yellow hibiscus
Motto: Ua Mau Ke Ea O Ka Aina I Ka Pono (The Life of the Land is Perpetuated in Righteousness)
Admitted to the Union: 1959 (50th)
Total area: 6,468 sq. mi. (16,752 sq. km.) (ranks 47th)
Population (2010): 1,360,301 (ranks 40th)
Chief Cities/settlements: Hilo (on island of Hawaii), Honolulu (on island of Oahu), Lihue (on island of Kauai), Wailuku (on island of Maui)
Principal products/industries: Sugarcane production, food processing, tourism, military bases
Highest point: Mauna Kea 13,796 ft. (4208 m.) on island of Hawaii

State History

Original settlers came from the Marquesas Islands c. 400 A.D.; groups from Tahiti arrived c. 900–1000 A.D.; first European encounter 1778 with English Capt. James Cook who named it the Sandwich Islands and was killed here 1779; most of island group united under rule (1795–1819) of King Kamehameha I; frequented by American whalers from early 19th century; first visited by Christian missionaries from New England 1820; recognized as independent by U.S., Great Britain, and France 1840s; secured reciprocity treaty with U.S. 1875; Queen Liliuokalani overthrown and provisional government established with U.S. assistance 1893; declared republic 1894; annexed to U.S. by joint resolution 1898; established as U.S. territory 1900; scene of Japanese attack on Pearl Harbor Dec. 7, 1941; admitted as a state Aug. 21, 1959.

In 1793 Captain George Vancouver from Great Britain presented the Union Jack to the conquering king Kamehameha I, who was then uniting the islands into a single state; the Union Jack flew unofficially as the flag of Hawaii until 1816, when red, white, and blue stripes were added.

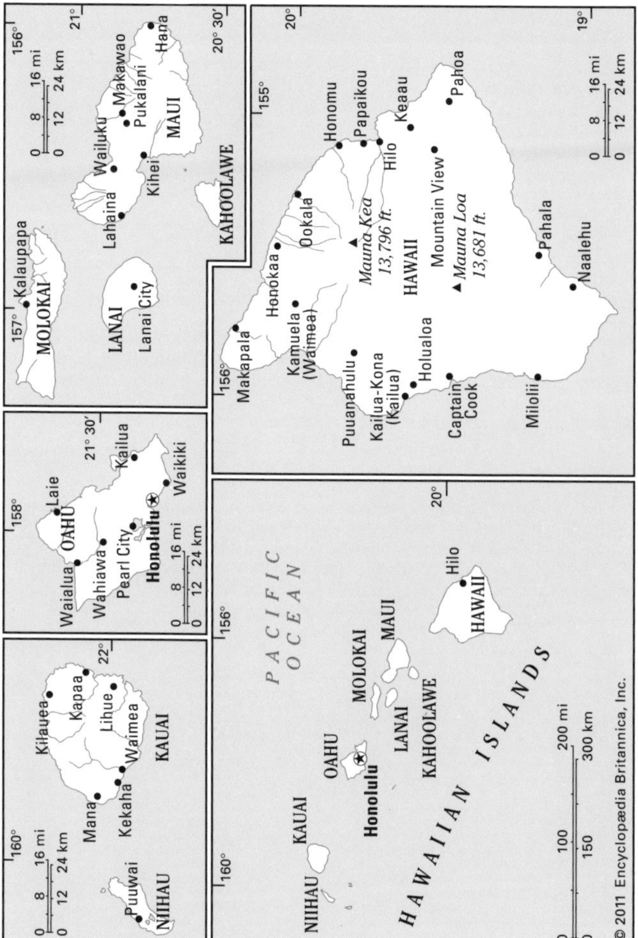
MOLOKAI
Kalaupapa
LANAI
Lanai City
MAUI
Lahaina
Wailuku
Kihei
Makawao
Pukalani
Hana
KAHOOLAWE
HAWAII
Makapala
Honokaa
Kamuela (Waimea)
Ookala
Honomu
Papaikou
Hilo
Keaau
Pahoa
Mauna Kea 13,796 ft.
Mauna Loa 13,681 ft.
Mountain View
Puuanahulu
Kailua-Kona (Kailua)
Holualoa
Captain Cook
Milolii
Pahala
Naalehu
OAHU
Waialua
Laie
Wahiawa
Pearl City
Honolulu
Kailua
Waikiki
KAUAI
Kilauea
Kapaa
Lihue
Waimea
Kekaha
Mana
NIIHAU
Puuwai
PACIFIC OCEAN
HAWAIIAN ISLANDS
© 2011 Encyclopædia Britannica, Inc.

IDAHO

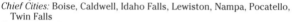

Official name: State of Idaho
Nickname: Gem State
State Capital: Boise
State Flower: Syringa
Motto: Esto Perpetua (Let It Be Perpetual)
Admitted to the Union: 1890 (43rd)
Total area: 83,569 sq. mi. (216,443 sq. km.) (ranks 14th)
Population (2010): 1,567,582 (ranks 39th)
Chief Cities: Boise, Caldwell, Idaho Falls, Lewiston, Nampa, Pocatello, Twin Falls
Principal products/industries: Potatoes, sugar beets, wheat, alfalfa, Kentucky bluegrass seed, cattle, antimony, silver, phosphates, lead, wood products, chemicals, food products, fishing, hunting, outdoor recreation
Highest point: Borah Peak, 12,662 ft. (3862 m.)

State History

First inhabited by American Indians; explored by Lewis and Clark expedition 1805; part of Oregon Country; ceded to U.S. by British 1846; included in Oregon Territory 1848; became part of Washington Territory in 1850s, and part of Idaho Territory 1863; gold discovered 1860; crossed by Oregon Trail; admitted to Union July 3, 1890.

On March 5, 1866, Idaho Territory adopted its first official seal, representing mountains below a new moon, a steamer on the Shoshone River, figures of Liberty and Peace, an elk's head, and agricultural produce. A similar seal was adopted for the new state on March 14, 1891.

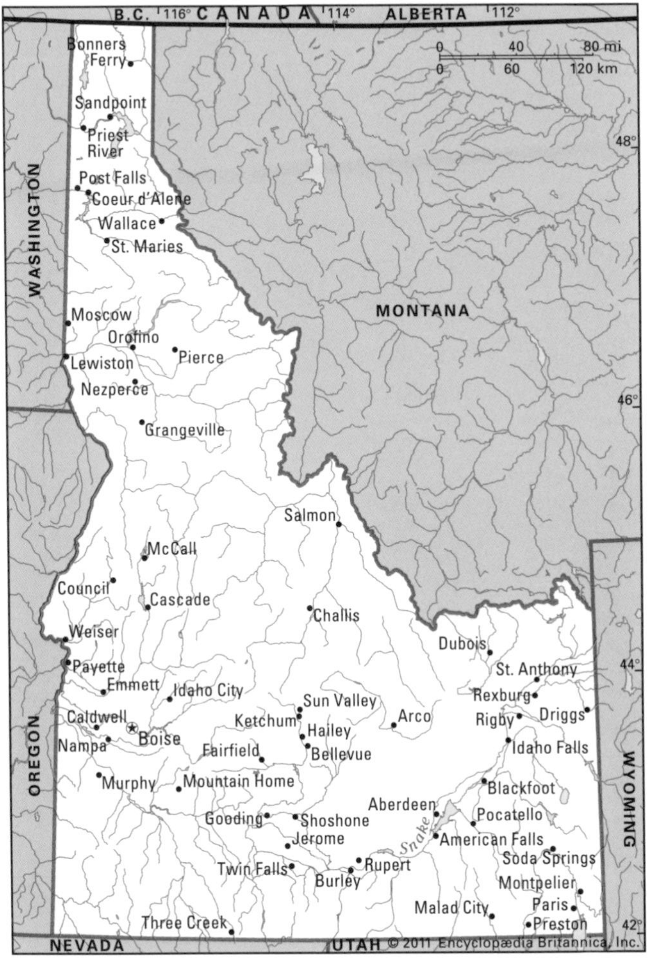
B.C.
116°
CANADA
114°
ALBERTA
112°
0 40 80 mi
0 60 120 km
48°
46°
44°
42°
WASHINGTON
OREGON
MONTANA
WYOMING
NEVADA
UTAH
Bonners Ferry
Sandpoint
Priest River
Post Falls
Coeur d'Alene
Wallace
St. Maries
Moscow
Orofino
Pierce
Lewiston
Nezperce
Grangeville
Salmon
McCall
Council
Cascade
Challis
Weiser
Payette
Emmett
Idaho City
Caldwell
Boise
Nampa
Sun Valley
Ketchum
Hailey
Bellevue
Fairfield
Arco
Dubois
St. Anthony
Rexburg
Rigby
Driggs
Idaho Falls
Blackfoot
Pocatello
Aberdeen
American Falls
Soda Springs
Montpelier
Paris
Preston
Malad City
Murphy
Mountain Home
Gooding
Shoshone
Jerome
Snake
Twin Falls
Burley
Rupert
Three Creek
© 2011 Encyclopædia Britannica, Inc.

ILLINOIS

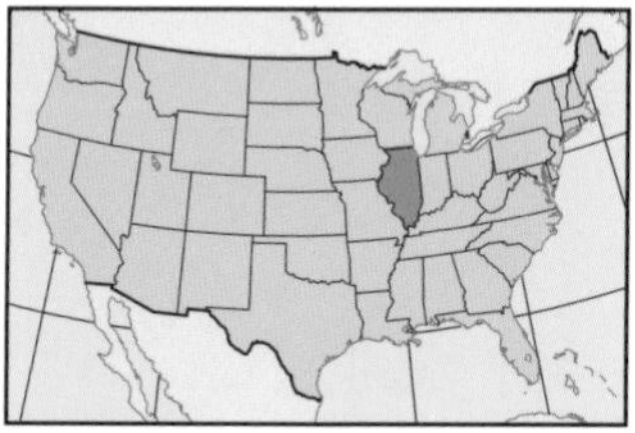

Official name: State of Illinois
Nickname: Prairie State, Land of Lincoln
State Capital: Springfield
State Flower: Violet
Motto: State Sovereignty—National Union
Admitted to the Union: 1818 (21st)
Total area: 57,916 sq. mi. (150,002 sq. km.) (ranks 25th)
Population (2010): 12,830,632 (ranks 5th)
Chief Cities: Aurora, Chicago, Joliet, Naperville, Peoria, Rockford, Springfield
Principal products/industries: Corn, soybeans, wheat, oats, dairy products, livestock, oil, coal, machinery, chemicals, metal products, food products, printing and publishing
Highest point: Charles Mound, 1235 ft. (377 m.)

State History

Explored by Père Jacques Marquette and Louis Jolliet 1673 and by René-Robert Cavelier de La Salle who erected Fort Crèvecœur on Illinois River 1680; included in French Louisiana; ceded by France to England 1763 and by England to U.S. 1783; Virginia claims to territory given up by 1786; part of Northwest Territory 1787, of Indiana Territory 1800, and of Illinois Territory 1809; admitted to the Union Dec. 3, 1818 with capital at Kaskaskia (capital transferred to Vandalia 1820 and to Springfield 1837); adopted present constitution 1970.

On July 6, 1915, the legislature adopted a flag that had been developed in a contest. The flag showed design elements from the state seal—a rock on a stretch of land with water and the rising sun behind it, plus a shield bearing the national stars and stripes in the claws of a bald eagle.

92°
91°
90°
89°
WISCONSIN
88°
87°
0 20 40 mi
0 30 60 km
IOWA
Galena
Harvard
Waukegan
Lake Michigan
Rockford
Belvidere
Highland Park
Freeport
Mount Carroll
Schaumburg
Evanston
42°
Oregon
De Kalb
Elgin
Oak Park
Wheaton
Chicago
Morrison
Dixon
Aurora
Naperville
Yorkville
Joliet
Rock Island
Moline
Princeton
La Salle
Morris
Aledo
Cambridge
Peru
Ottawa
Toulon
Kankakee
Lacon
41°
Galesburg
Monmouth
Pontiac
Watseka
Peoria
Eureka
Pekin
Normal
Carthage
Lewistown
Paxton
Macomb
Bloomington
Rantoul
Havana
INDIANA
Lincoln
Champaign
Danville
Mount Sterling
Beardstown
Clinton
Urbana
40°
Quincy
Virginia
Petersburg
Monticello
Decatur
Tuscola
Jacksonville
Springfield
Pittsfield
Winchester
Sullivan
Paris
Taylorville
Charleston
Mississippi
Carrollton
Carlinville
Shelbyville
Marshall
Hardin
Toledo
Hillsboro
Effingham
Jerseyville
39°
Newton
Robinson
MISSOURI
Alton
Vandalia
Greenville
Lawrenceville
Edwardsville
Louisville
Olney
E. St. Louis
Carlyle
Salem
Belleville
Mount Vernon
Albion
Mount Carmel
Waterloo
Nashville
Fairfield
Pinckneyville
McLeansboro
Carmi
38°
Chester
Benton
Harrisburg
Murphysboro
Marion
Shawneetown
Jonesboro
Elizabethtown
Vienna
Golconda
Mound City
Metropolis
KENTUCKY
37°
Cairo
© 2011 Encyclopædia Britannica, Inc.

INDIANA

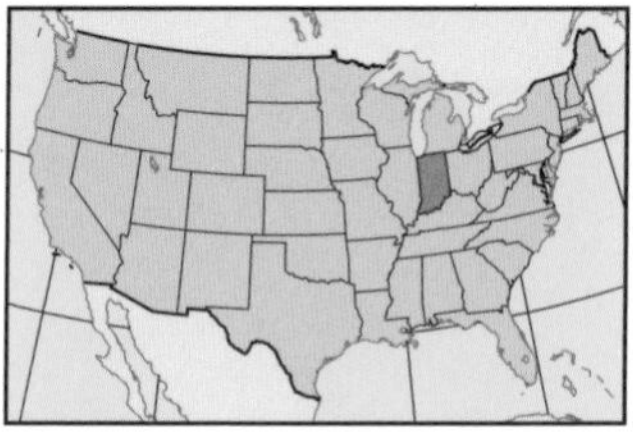

Official name: State of Indiana
Nickname: Hoosier State
State Capital: Indianapolis
State Flower: Peony
Motto: The Crossroads of America
Admitted to the Union: 1816 (19th)
Total area: 36,417 sq. mi. (94,320 sq. km.) (ranks 38th)
Population (2010): 6,483,802 (ranks 15th)
Chief Cities: Bloomington, Evansville, Fort Wayne, Gary, Hammond, Indianapolis, South Bend
Principal products/industries: Corn, soybeans, wheat, popcorn, tobacco, livestock, coal, building stone, steel, machinery, chemicals
Highest point: Hoosier Hill Point 1257 ft. (383 m.)

State History

Inhabited early perhaps by Mound Builders; the Miami, among other American Indians in area when Europeans first arrived; French settlement at Vincennes c. 1700; included in territory ceded by France to England 1763; ceded by England to U.S. by Treaty of Paris 1783; included in Northwest Territory 1787 and Indiana Territory 1800; admitted to the Union Dec. 11, 1816; capital removed from Corydon to Indianapolis 1825; adopted present constitution 1851.

In 1916, celebrating Indiana's centennial, a competition yielded this "state banner," approved on May 31, 1917. The torch is symbolic of enlightenment and liberty. A total of 19 stars ring the torch, recalling that the state was the 19th to join the Union. In 1955 the General Assembly changed its classification from state banner to state flag.

42°
88°
87°
86°
85°
41°
40°
39°
38°
Lake Michigan
MICHIGAN
ILLINOIS
OHIO
KENTUCKY
Ohio
Michigan City
South Bend
Elkhart
Angola
Gary
Hammond
Portage
Mishawaka
Lagrange
La Porte
Goshen
Merrillville
Hobart
Crown Point
Valparaiso
Nappanee
Albion
Auburn
Knox
Plymouth
Warsaw
Columbia City
Rochester
Fort Wayne
Rensselaer
Winamac
Huntington
Decatur
Kentland
Logansport
Wabash
Monticello
Peru
Bluffton
Fowler
Delphi
Kokomo
Marion
Geneva
West Lafayette
Hartford City
Portland
Lafayette
Tipton
Williamsport
Frankfort
Muncie
Winchester
Covington
Lebanon
Anderson
Crawfordsville
Noblesville
Carmel
New Castle
Newport
Indianapolis
Greenfield
Richmond
Rockville
Danville
Greenwood
Rushville
Connersville
Greencastle
Brazil
Franklin
Shelbyville
Terre Haute
Martinsville
Greensburg
Brookville
Spencer
Nashville
Columbus
Lawrenceburg
Sullivan
Bloomington
Seymour
North Vernon
Bloomfield
Rising Sun
Brownstown
Bedford
Vevay
Madison
Vincennes
Shoals
Scottsburg
Washington
Paoli
Salem
French Lick
Charlestown
Jasper
English
New Albany
Clarksville
Princeton
Huntingburg
Jeffersonville
Corydon
New Harmony
Boonville
Evansville
Mt. Vernon
Tell City
Newburgh
0 20 40 mi
0 30 60 km
© 2011 Encyclopædia Britannica, Inc.

IOWA

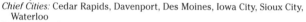

Official name: State of Iowa
Nickname: Hawkeye State, Corn State
State Capital: Des Moines
State Flower: Wild prairie rose
Motto: Our Liberties We Prize, and Our Rights We Will Maintain
Admitted to the Union: 1846 (29th)
Total area: 56,273 sq. mi. (145,746 sq. km.) (ranks 26th)
Population (2010): 3,046,355 (ranks 30th)
Chief Cities: Cedar Rapids, Davenport, Des Moines, Iowa City, Sioux City, Waterloo
Principal products/industries: Corn, soybeans, oats, milk, eggs, hay, cattle, hogs, cement, food products, farm machinery, chemicals
Highest point: Hawkeye Point 1670 ft. (509 m.)

State History

Traces found of early inhabitation by Mound Builders, among others; French explorers Louis Jolliet and Jacques (Père) Marquette among first Europeans to visit 1673; became part of U.S. by Louisiana Purchase 1803; part of Louisiana Territory 1805, of Missouri Territory 1812, unorganized territory c. 1821–34, of Michigan Territory 1834, of Wisconsin Territory 1836, and of Iowa Territory 1838; first permanent settlement made 1833 at Dubuque; held first constitutional convention 1844; present constitution dates from 1857. Admitted to Union Dec. 28, 1846; capital moved from Iowa City to Des Moines 1857.

In 1921 the legislature approved a state banner—rather than a state flag—with a blue stripe along the hoist and a red stripe in the fly, recalling the French Tricolor, which had flown over Iowa before the Louisiana Purchase of 1803. In the center is a flying bald eagle and a ribbon emblazoned with the state motto.

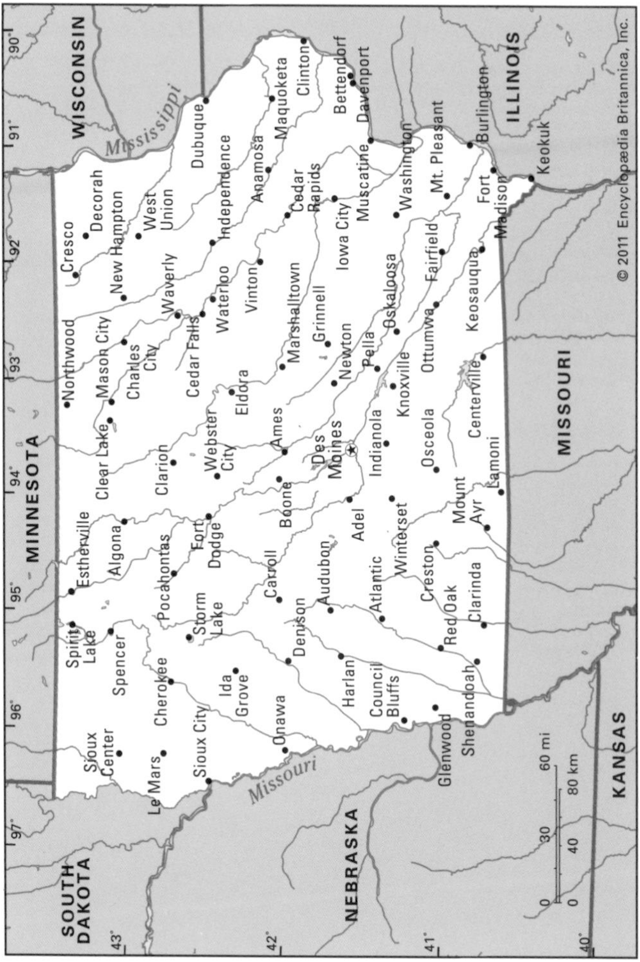
MINNESOTA
WISCONSIN
ILLINOIS
MISSOURI
KANSAS
NEBRASKA
SOUTH DAKOTA
Mississippi
Missouri
Dubuque
Maquoketa
Clinton
Bettendorf
Davenport
Muscatine
Burlington
Keokuk
Fort Madison
Mt. Pleasant
Washington
Iowa City
Cedar Rapids
Anamosa
Independence
West Union
Decorah
Cresco
New Hampton
Waverly
Waterloo
Cedar Falls
Vinton
Marshalltown
Grinnell
Newton
Pella
Oskaloosa
Fairfield
Ottumwa
Keosauqua
Centerville
Knoxville
Indianola
Des Moines
Ames
Eldora
Charles City
Mason City
Northwood
Clear Lake
Clarion
Webster City
Boone
Osceola
Lamoni
Mount Ayr
Creston
Winterset
Adel
Fort Dodge
Algona
Estherville
Pocahontas
Carroll
Audubon
Atlantic
Clarinda
Red Oak
Shenandoah
Glenwood
Council Bluffs
Harlan
Denison
Storm Lake
Spirit Lake
Spencer
Cherokee
Ida Grove
Onawa
Sioux City
Le Mars
Sioux Center
43°
42°
41°
40°
97°
96°
95°
94°
93°
92°
91°
90°
0
30
60 mi
0
40
80 km
© 2011 Encyclopædia Britannica, Inc.

KANSAS

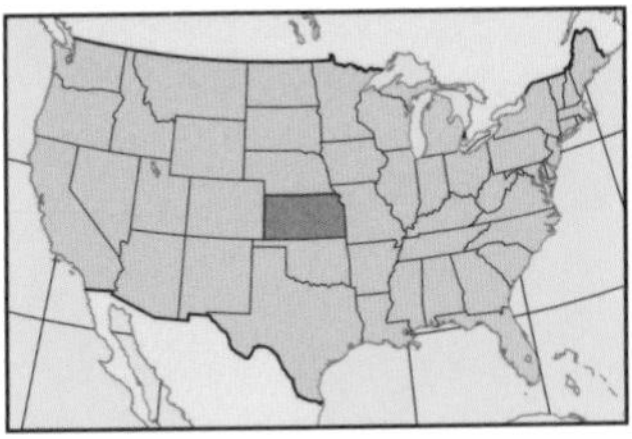

Official name: State of Kansas
Nickname: Sunflower State, Jayhawker State
State Capital: Topeka
State Flower: Sunflower
Motto: Ad Astra per Aspera (To the Stars Through Difficulty)
Admitted to the Union: 1861 (34th)
Total area: 82,278 sq. mi. (213,099 sq. km.) (ranks 15th)
Population (2010): 2,853,118 (ranks 33rd)
Chief Cities: Kansas City, Olathe, Overland Park, Topeka, Wichita
Principal products/industries: Wheat, sorghum, corn, cattle, oil, salt, transportation equipment, machinery, chemicals, soap and cleaning products
Highest point: Mt. Sunflower 4039 ft. (1232 m.)

State History

Before coming of Europeans, inhabited sparsely by both nomadic and settled American Indians, among them, the Kansa; probably entered by Spanish explorer Francisco de Coronado's expedition 1541; came to U.S. as part of Louisiana Purchase 1803; included in Louisiana Territory 1805 and Missouri Territory 1812; southwestern corner lost to Spanish in 1819 treaty; in unorganized territory c. 1821–54; regained southwestern corner with annexation of Texas 1845; by Kansas-Nebraska Act 1854, Kansas Territory organized, including Kansas and central portion of eastern Colorado; admitted to Union with present boundaries as free state Jan. 29, 1861.

In the center of the Kansas flag is a version of the seal, the original of which is dated 1861. Some of the state's features are: commerce, shown by the river and boat; agriculture, by the plowing farmer; and westward settlement, by the wagon train and the homesteader's cabin (which stopped pouring chimney smoke in 1985). The sunflower became the state flower in 1903.

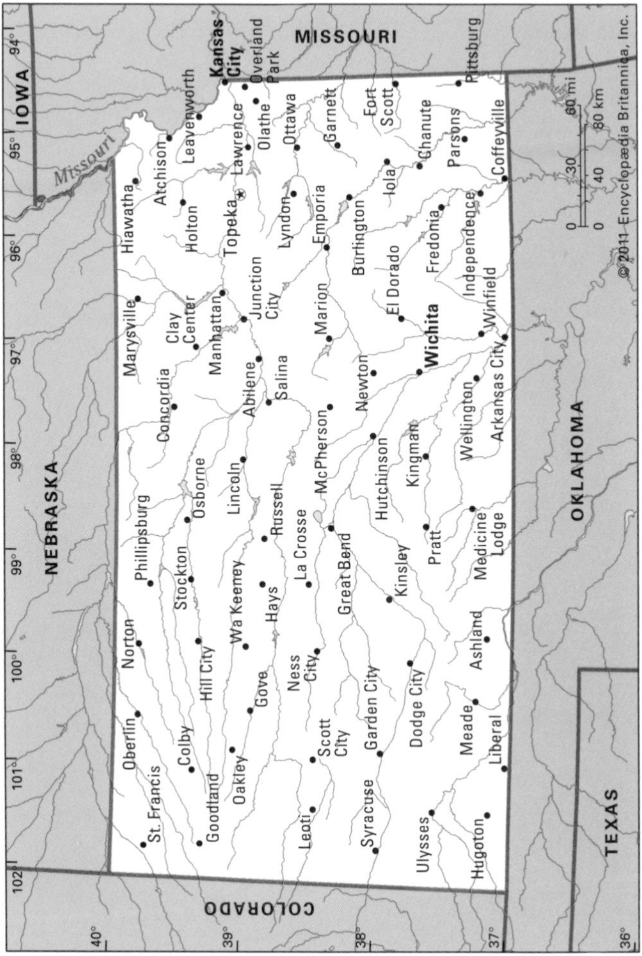
IOWA
NEBRASKA
MISSOURI
OKLAHOMA
TEXAS
COLORADO
Missouri
Kansas City
Overland Park
Leavenworth
Atchison
Hiawatha
Holton
Topeka
Lawrence
Olathe
Ottawa
Garnett
Fort Scott
Pittsburg
Chanute
Parsons
Coffeyville
Iola
Burlington
Emporia
Lyndon
Junction City
Manhattan
Clay Center
Marysville
Concordia
Abilene
Salina
Marion
El Dorado
Fredonia
Independence
Winfield
Wichita
Newton
McPherson
Hutchinson
Kingman
Wellington
Arkansas City
Lincoln
Osborne
Phillipsburg
Stockton
Russell
La Crosse
Great Bend
Pratt
Medicine Lodge
Kinsley
Hays
Wa Keeney
Norton
Hill City
Ness City
Garden City
Dodge City
Ashland
Meade
Liberal
Gove
Oakley
Colby
Oberlin
Goodland
St. Francis
Scott City
Leoti
Syracuse
Ulysses
Hugoton
94°
95°
96°
97°
98°
99°
100°
101°
102°
40°
39°
38°
37°
36°
0 30 60 mi
0 40 80 km
© 2011 Encyclopædia Britannica, Inc.

KENTUCKY

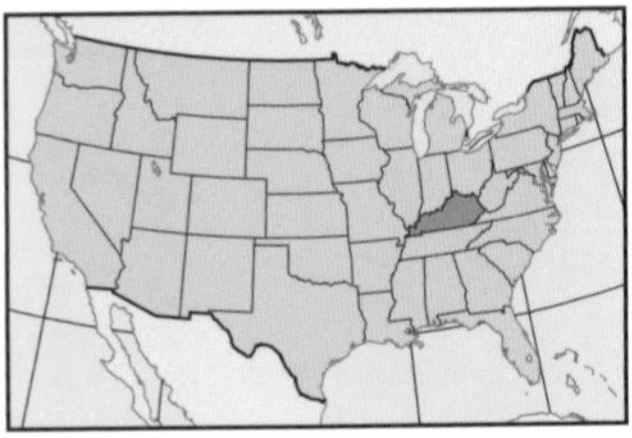

Official name: Commonwealth of Kentucky
Nickname: Bluegrass State
State Capital: Frankfort
State Flower: Goldenrod
Motto: United We Stand, Divided We Fall
Admitted to the Union: 1792 (15th)
Total area: 40,411 sq. mi. (104,664 sq. km.) (ranks 37th)
Population (2010): 4,339,367 (ranks 26th)
Chief Cities: Bowling Green, Covington, Lexington, Louisville, Owensboro
Principal products/industries: Tobacco, soybeans, corn, wheat, thoroughbred horses, cattle, hogs, oil, natural gas, coal, bourbon whiskey, farm equipment, chemicals, wearing apparel, printing
Highest point: Black Mt. 4139 ft. (2162 m.)

State History

Inhabited by American Indian peoples before arrival of European explorers; entered by American explorer Thomas Walker 1750; included in territory ceded by French 1763; explored by expeditions under American pioneer Daniel Boone from 1769; first permanent English settlement at Boonesborough made by Transylvania Company 1775; because of its many Indian wars known as the "Dark and Bloody Ground"; organized as county of Virginia 1776; included in territory of U.S. by Treaty of Paris 1783; received consent of Virginia to statehood 1789; admitted to Union June 1, 1792; as border state during Civil War torn between North and South, providing troops to both sides; despite an attempt to be neutral, invaded by Confederate troops 1862; suffered skirmishes thereafter but remained in Union; adopted present constitution 1891.

At the time of its admission to the Union in 1792, Kentucky was considered the nation's western frontier, and this was reflected in the symbolism of the state seal: two men embracing, one a frontiersman in buckskins and the other a gentleman in formal frock coat, suggesting Westerners and Easterners in national unity.

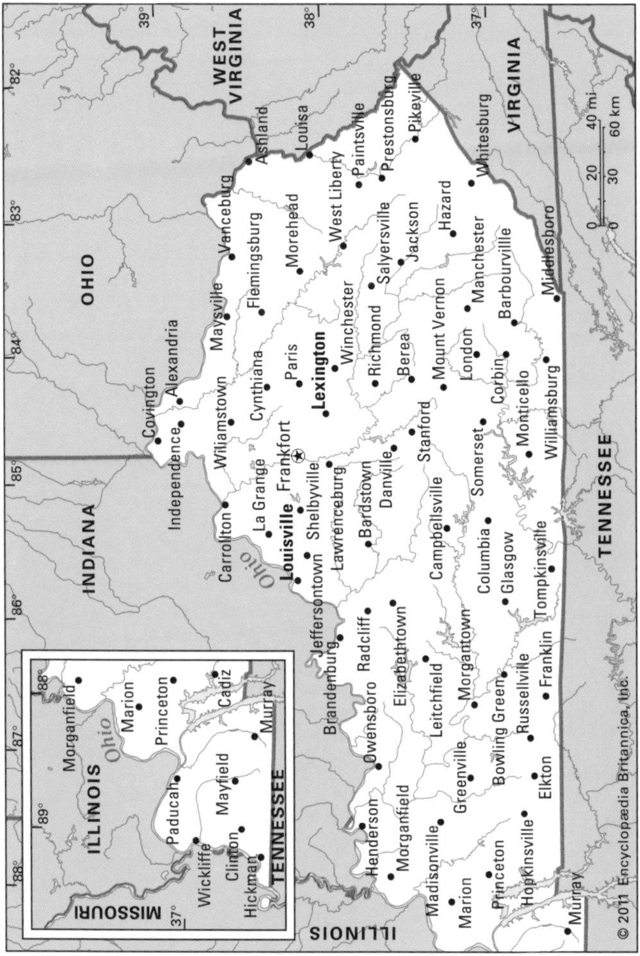
OHIO
INDIANA
ILLINOIS
WEST VIRGINIA
VIRGINIA
TENNESSEE
Ohio
Louisville
Lexington
Frankfort
Covington
Alexandria
Independence
Williamstown
Maysville
Vanceburg
Ashland
Louisa
Flemingsburg
Cynthiana
Paris
Morehead
West Liberty
Paintsville
Prestonsburg
Pikeville
Winchester
Salyersville
Jackson
Hazard
Whitesburg
Richmond
Berea
Mount Vernon
Manchester
London
Corbin
Barbourville
Middlesboro
Williamsburg
Monticello
Somerset
Stanford
Danville
Carrollton
La Grange
Shelbyville
Lawrenceburg
Bardstown
Jeffersontown
Campbellsville
Columbia
Glasgow
Tompkinsville
Brandenburg
Radcliff
Elizabethtown
Leitchfield
Morgantown
Bowling Green
Russellville
Franklin
Owensboro
Henderson
Morganfield
Greenville
Elkton
Madisonville
Hopkinsville
Marion
Princeton
Murray
MISSOURI
Morganfield
Marion
Princeton
Cadiz
Paducah
Mayfield
Murray
Wickliffe
Clinton
Hickman
0 20 40 mi
0 30 60 km
© 2011 Encyclopædia Britannica, Inc.

LOUISIANA

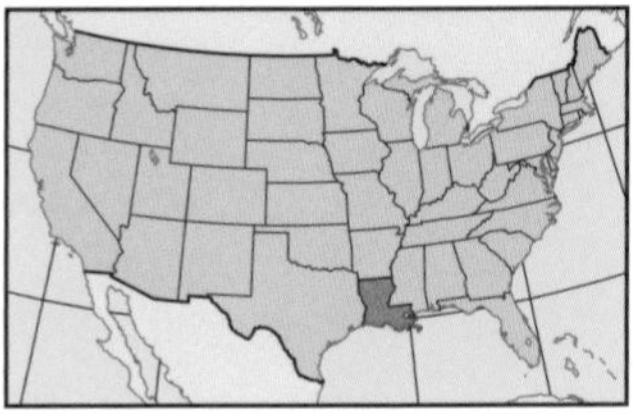

Official name: State of Louisiana
Nickname: Pelican State, Creole State, Sugar State
State Capital: Baton Rouge
State Flower: Magnolia, Iris
Motto: Union, Justice, Confidence
Admitted to the Union: 1812 (18th)
Total area: 47,632 sq. mi. (123,366 sq. km.) (ranks 31st)
Population (2010): 4,533,372 (ranks 25th)
Chief Cities: Baton Rouge, Lafayette, Metairie, New Orleans, Shreveport
Principal products/industries: Rice, soybeans, cotton, sugarcane, sweet potatoes, seafood, oil, natural gas, sulfur, salt, chemicals, transportation equipment, lumber, tourism
Highest point: Driskill Mt. 535 ft. (163 m.)

State History

Inhabited by native peoples for thousands of years prior to European exploration, which began in the 16th century; name "Louisiana" originally applied to entire Mississippi River basin, claimed for France by explorer René-Robert Cavelier, Sieur de La Salle 1682; Natchitoches, first settlement within area of present state, founded 1714; New Orleans founded 1718; except for New Orleans, region east of Mississippi River ceded by France to Great Britain 1763; West Florida (incl. portion of present state of Louisiana east of Mississippi River north of Lake Pontchartrain) returned to Spain 1783 and claimed by U.S. as part of Louisiana Purchase 1803; New Orleans and region west of Mississippi River ceded to Spain 1762–63; returned to France 1800–03, and sold to U.S. in Louisiana Purchase; Orleans Territory organized 1804 and admitted to Union Apr. 30, 1812 as state of Louisiana, the first to be carved out of Louisiana Purchase; passed ordinance of secession Jan. 26, 1861; abolished slavery 1864; readmitted to Union 1868; present constitution adopted 1974.

A pelican tearing at its breast to feed its young is the central emblem of the flag. Real pelicans never perform this activity, but from the Middle Ages this symbol has represented the spirit of self-sacrifice and dedication to progeny. As early as 1812 the pelican was used as a Louisiana symbol.

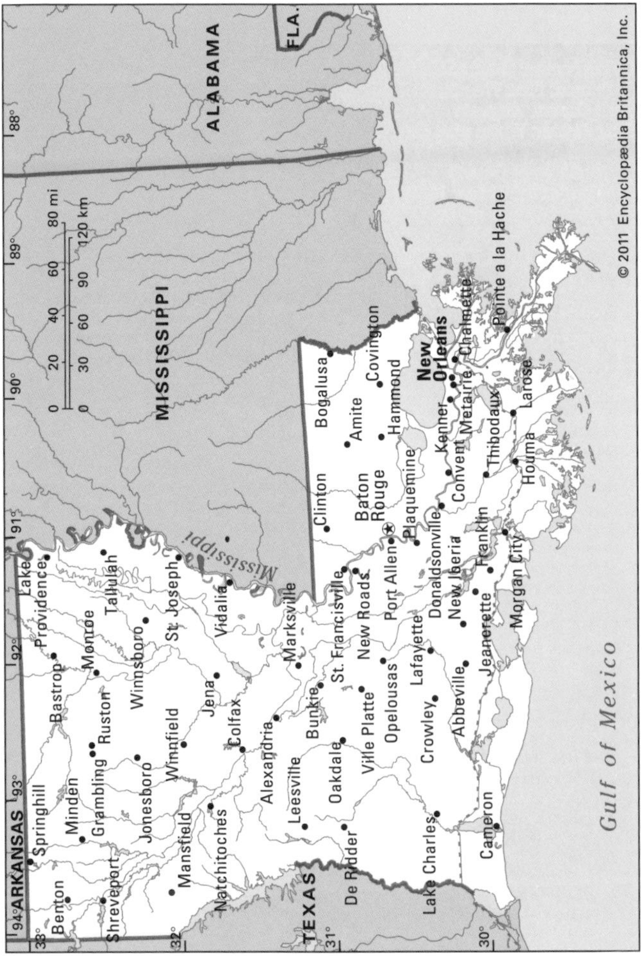
ARKANSAS
MISSISSIPPI
ALABAMA
FLA.
TEXAS
Gulf of Mexico
Mississippi
0 20 40 60 80 mi
0 30 60 90 120 km
94° 93° 92° 91° 90° 89° 88°
33° 32° 31° 30°
Benton
Shreveport
Springhill
Minden
Grambling
Ruston
Jonesboro
Mansfield
Natchitoches
Winnfield
Bastrop
Monroe
Winnsboro
Lake Providence
Tallulah
St. Joseph
Vidalia
Jena
Colfax
Alexandria
Leesville
De Ridder
Oakdale
Bunkie
Marksville
Ville Platte
Opelousas
St. Francisville
New Roads
Port Allen
Baton Rouge
Clinton
Lafayette
Crowley
Lake Charles
Cameron
Abbeville
Jeanerette
New Iberia
Franklin
Morgan City
Donaldsonville
Plaquemine
Convent
Thibodaux
Houma
Kenner
Metairie
New Orleans
Chalmette
Larose
Pointe a la Hache
Hammond
Amite
Bogalusa
Covington
© 2011 Encyclopædia Britannica, Inc.

MAINE

Official name: State of Maine
Nickname: Pine Tree State
State Capital: Augusta
State Flower: White pine cone and tassel
Motto: Dirigo (I Direct)
Admitted to the Union: 1820 (23rd)
Total area: 33,123 sq. mi. (85,788 sq. km.) (ranks 39th)
Population (2010): 1,328,361 (ranks 41st)
Chief Cities: Auburn, Augusta, Bangor, Biddeford, Lewiston, Portland, South Portland
Principal products/industries: Potatoes, blueberries, apples, cranberries, poultry, gravel, tourism, fishing (esp. lobstering), food products, leather goods, paper, wood products
Highest point: Mt. Katahdin 5267 ft. (1606 m.)

State History

Evidence of prehistoric inhabitants; inhabited by Algonquians (especially Penobscot and Passamaquoddy tribes) at time of European settlement; claimed and settled by both English and French; included in grant to Plymouth Company 1606; first settlement by English at mouth of the Sagadahoc (Kennebec) 1607 failed, but city of Saco and Monhegan Island were settled c. 1622; through series of grants, beginning in 1622, claimed by Massachusetts Bay Colony and English proprietor Sir Ferdinando Gorges; annexed to Massachusetts (1652) which bought out Gorges's claim 1677; northern parts frequently attacked by French 17th–18th centuries; a district of Massachusetts until 1820; admitted to Union as free state as part of Missouri Compromise Mar. 15, 1820; boundary with Canada settled by treaty with Great Britain 1842.

Until 1820 Maine was a district of Massachusetts, and its early symbols were based on that connection. The pine tree emblem was used for the Massachusetts naval flag in 1776. The current state flag, established in 1909, has its coat of arms showing a moose-and-pine tree emblem on a shield supported by a farmer and a sailor.

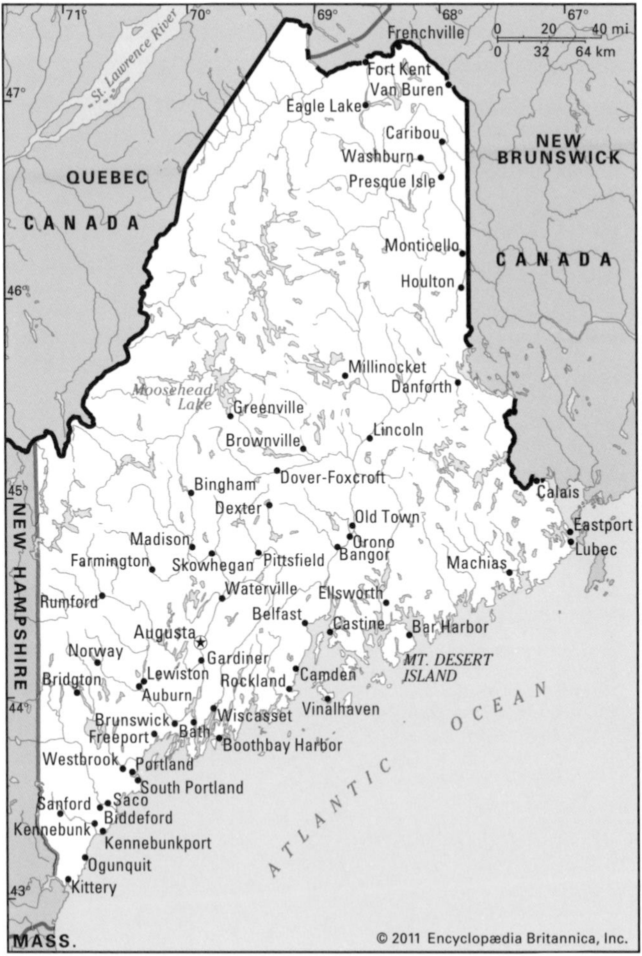
71°
70°
69°
68°
67°
47°
46°
45°
44°
43°
0 20 40 mi
0 32 64 km
St. Lawrence River
QUEBEC
CANADA
NEW BRUNSWICK
CANADA
NEW HAMPSHIRE
MASS.
Frenchville
Fort Kent
Van Buren
Eagle Lake
Caribou
Washburn
Presque Isle
Monticello
Houlton
Millinocket
Danforth
Moosehead Lake
Greenville
Lincoln
Brownville
Dover-Foxcroft
Bingham
Calais
Dexter
Old Town
Eastport
Orono
Lubec
Madison
Bangor
Farmington
Skowhegan
Pittsfield
Machias
Waterville
Ellsworth
Rumford
Belfast
Castine
Bar Harbor
Augusta
Norway
Gardiner
MT. DESERT ISLAND
Lewiston
Bridgton
Camden
Rockland
Auburn
Vinalhaven
Wiscasset
Brunswick
Bath
Freeport
Boothbay Harbor
Westbrook
Portland
South Portland
Sanford
Saco
Biddeford
Kennebunk
Kennebunkport
Ogunquit
Kittery
ATLANTIC OCEAN
© 2011 Encyclopædia Britannica, Inc.

MARYLAND

Official name: State of Maryland
Nickname: Free State, Old Line State
State Capital: Annapolis
State Flower: Black-eyed Susan
Motto: Fatti Maschii, Parole Femine (Manly Deeds, Womanly Words)
Admitted to the Union: 1788; 7th of the original 13 colonies to ratify the U.S. Constitution
Total area: 10,441 sq. mi. (27,042 sq. km.) (ranks 42nd)
Population (2010): 5,773,552 (ranks 19th)
Chief Cities: Annapolis, Baltimore, Columbia, Germantown, Silver Spring
Principal products/industries: Dairy products, corn, soybeans, food products, tobacco, chickens and other livestock, fishing especially for crabs, stone, sand and gravel, tourism, primary metals, transportation equipment, chemicals, electrical equipment
Highest point: Backbone Mt. 3360 ft. (1025 m.)

State History

Originally inhabited by American Indians; English first visited early 17th century; granted to George Calvert (Lord Baltimore) as proprietary colony 1632; first American colony to achieve religious freedom; first settled at St. Marys 1634, which was its capital 1634–94; colony under rule of British crown 1689–1715; its long-standing boundary dispute with Pennsylvania settled by drawing of Mason-Dixon Line 1760s; first state constitution adopted 1776; adopted Articles of Confederation 1781; ceded territory for District of Columbia; during Civil War remained in the Union, but was subjected to suspension of habeas corpus; invaded by Confederate forces 1862; abolished slavery 1864; adopted present constitution 1867.

Maryland has a state flag that was flown when the colony was under British rule: the personal banner of Sir George Calvert, the first Lord Baltimore. It has six vertical yellow and black stripes, with a matching diagonal. It is combined with the arms of the Crossland family (maternal family of Sir George Calvert): a quartered white-and-red shield.

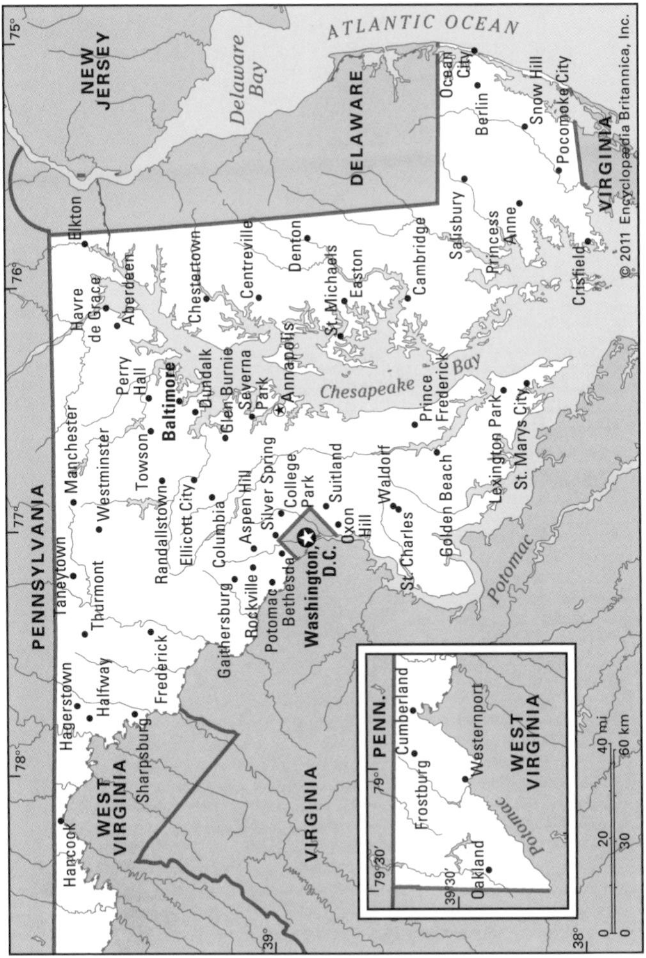
PENNSYLVANIA
NEW JERSEY
DELAWARE
WEST VIRGINIA
VIRGINIA
ATLANTIC OCEAN
Delaware Bay
Chesapeake Bay
Potomac
Washington, D.C.
Baltimore
Annapolis
Elkton
Havre de Grace
Aberdeen
Chestertown
Centreville
Denton
St. Michaels
Easton
Cambridge
Salisbury
Princess Anne
Crisfield
Ocean City
Berlin
Snow Hill
Pocomoke City
Manchester
Westminster
Taneytown
Thurmont
Hagerstown
Halfway
Frederick
Sharpsburg
Hancock
Perry Hall
Towson
Randallstown
Ellicott City
Columbia
Dundalk
Glen Burnie
Severna Park
Gaithersburg
Rockville
Aspen Hill
Silver Spring
College Park
Potomac
Bethesda
Suitland
Oxon Hill
Waldorf
St. Charles
Prince Frederick
Golden Beach
Lexington Park
St. Marys City
PENN.
Cumberland
Frostburg
Westernport
Oakland
75°
76°
77°
78°
79°
79°30′
39°30′
39°
38°
0 20 40 mi
0 30 60 km
© 2011 Encyclopædia Britannica, Inc.

MASSACHUSETTS

Official name: Commonwealth of Massachusetts
Nickname: Bay State, Old Colony State
State Capital: Boston
State Flower: Mayflower
Motto: Ense Petit Placidam Sub Libertate Quietem (By the Sword We Seek Peace, but Peace Only Under Liberty)
Admitted to the Union: 1788; 6th of the original 13 colonies to ratify the U.S. Constitution
Total area: 8,262 sq. mi. (21,398 sq. km.) (ranks 43rd)
Population (2010): 6,547,629 (ranks 14th)
Chief Cities: Boston, Cambridge, Lowell, New Bedford, Springfield, Worcester
Principal products/industries: Dairy products, tobacco, cranberries and other fruit, potatoes, vegetables, vegetables, electronic equipment, electrical equipment, printing and publishing, pharmaceuticals, tourism, education, fishing
Highest point: Mt. Greylock 3487 ft. (1064 m.)

State History

Perhaps explored by Norse c. 11th century; coast skirted by Florentine explorer Giovanni da Verrazano 1524; Cape Cod discovered by Englishman Bartholomew Gosnold 1602 who made first (temporary) European settlement within present limits of state; at time of European settlement, region inhabited by several Algonquin tribes; Plymouth settled by Pilgrims 1620; Massachusetts Bay Colony, founded and governed by Massachusetts Bay Company 1629–84; Harvard College founded 1636; joined New England Confederation 1643; acquired province of Maine 1652; after loss of first charter 1684, governed as part of Dominion of New England 1686; by its 2nd charter 1691, received jurisdiction over Maine and Plymouth colonies; in 18th century, gradually became a center of resistance to imperial colonial policy; British troops withdrawn to Boston after colonial uprisings at Lexington and Concord 1775; battle of Bunker Hill 1775; British evacuated Boston 1776; gave up claims to western lands 1785–86; western Massachusetts scene of Shays' Rebellion, an uprising in protest of harsh government economic policies 1786–87; eastern Massachusetts early center of American cotton manufacture. Maine became separate state 1820.

The seal of the Massachusetts Bay Colony of 1629 showed an Indian and pine trees, and both of these symbols have continued to be used up to the present time. The Indian appears in gold on a blue shield together with a silver star indicative of statehood.

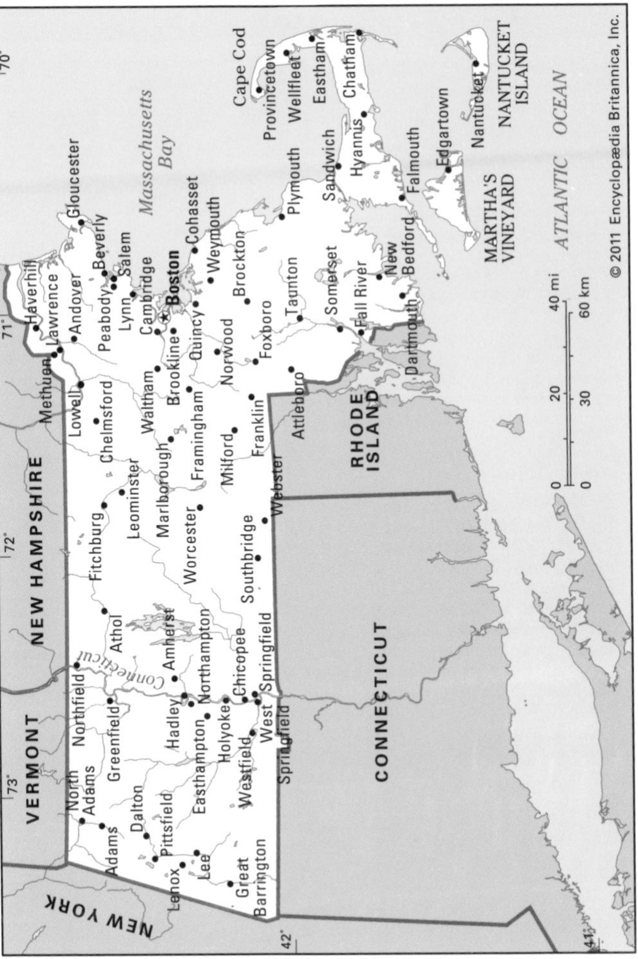

VERMONT
NEW HAMPSHIRE
NEW YORK
CONNECTICUT
RHODE ISLAND
MARTHA'S VINEYARD
NANTUCKET ISLAND
ATLANTIC OCEAN
Massachusetts Bay
Cape Cod
Connecticut
73°
72°
71°
70°
42°
41°
Haverhill
Lawrence
Methuen
Andover
Gloucester
Beverly
Peabody
Salem
Lynn
Cambridge
Boston
Brookline
Quincy
Cohasset
Weymouth
Brockton
Norwood
Foxboro
Taunton
Somerset
Fall River
New Bedford
Dartmouth
Attleboro
Franklin
Milford
Framingham
Waltham
Lowell
Chelmsford
Marlborough
Leominster
Fitchburg
Worcester
Southbridge
Webster
Athol
Amherst
Northampton
Chicopee
Springfield
West Springfield
Holyoke
Westfield
Easthampton
Hadley
Northfield
Greenfield
North Adams
Adams
Dalton
Pittsfield
Lenox
Lee
Great Barrington
Plymouth
Sandwich
Hyannis
Falmouth
Edgartown
Nantucket
Chatham
Eastham
Wellfleet
Provincetown
0 20 40 mi
0 30 60 km
© 2011 Encyclopædia Britannica, Inc.

MICHIGAN

Official name: State of Michigan
Nickname: Wolverine State, Great Lake State
State Capital: Lansing
State Flower: Apple blossom, Dwarf lake iris
Motto: Si Quaeris Paeninsulam Amoenam Circumspice (If You Seek a Beautiful Peninsula, Look Around You)
Admitted to the Union: 1837 (26th)
Total area: 96,716 sq. mi. (250,486 sq. km.) (ranks 11th)
Population (2010): 9,883,640 (ranks 8th)
Chief Cities: Ann Arbor, Dearborn, Detroit, Flint, Grand Rapids, Lansing, Livonia, Sterling Heights, Warren
Principal products/industries: Dairy products, fruit, iron ore, limestone, copper, natural gas, motor vehicles and parts, tourism
Highest point: Mt. Arvon 1979 ft. (604 m.)

State History

Inhabited especially by Algonquian tribes prior to arrival of Europeans; first European to visit the region was French adventurer Étienne Brulé in early 17th century; first settled at Sault Sainte Marie by French explorer and missionary Père Marquette 1668; military post of Detroit founded 1701; ceded to England 1763 following French and Indian War and to U.S. 1783; included in Northwest Territory 1787 and in Indiana Territory 1800, 1803; Michigan Territory organized on the Lower Peninsula, 1805; boundaries extended 1818 to include Upper Peninsula and beyond; Upper Peninsula briefly included in Wisconsin Territory 1836; boundary dispute with Ohio (Toledo War) settled by U.S. Congress in favor of Ohio, with Michigan receiving as compensation the Upper Peninsula and statehood (admitted as free state Jan. 26, 1837); Lansing became capital 1847; adopted present constitution 1963.

The bald eagle of the U.S. serves as a crest to the state shield, while an elk and a moose, supposedly based on the coat of arms of the Hudson's Bay Company, serve as supporters. The central design of the shield shows a man with a rifle standing on a peninsula and the sun setting over surrounding waters.

88°
87°
86°
85°
84°
83°
82°
89°
48°
ISLE ROYALE
Lake Superior
90°
89°
47°
Lake Superior
Houghton
Ontonagon
L'Anse
Bessemer
Ironwood
WISCONSIN
Iron River
Eagle River
Calumet
Houghton
Lake Superior
0 20 40 60 80 mi
0 30 60 90 120 km
47°
L'Anse
Grand Marais
Marquette
Ishpeming
Munising
Newberry
Sault Ste. Marie
CANADA
ONTARIO
Crystal Falls
46°
Manistique
Iron Mountain
Gladstone
St. Ignace
Mackinaw City
Cheboygan
Escanaba
Rogers City
Petoskey
Charlevoix
Menominee
Leland
Bellaire
Gaylord
Alpena
45°
Atlanta
Lake Huron
Traverse City
Kalkaska
Mio
Frankfort
Beulah
Grayling
Harrisville
WISCONSIN
Lake City
West Branch
Manistee
Cadillac
Tawas City
44°
Harrison
Gladwin
Ludington
Reed City
Clare
Bad Axe
Baldwin
Big Rapids
Lake Michigan
Midland
Hart
Bay City
Mt. Pleasant
Sandusky
Caro
Whitehall
Alma
Saginaw
Frankenmuth
Muskegon
Grand Rapids
Greenville
St. Johns
43°
Owosso
Lapeer
Grand Haven
Ionia
Flint
Port Huron
Corunna
Wyoming
Lansing
Waterford
Holland
East Lansing
Sterling Heights
Hastings
Charlotte
Pontiac
South Haven
Mason
Livonia
Warren
Battle Creek
Benton Harbor
Kalamazoo
Ann Arbor
Detroit
CANADA
ONTARIO
Portage
Marshall
Jackson
42°
St. Joseph
Dowagiac
Coldwater
Tecumseh
Monroe
Three Rivers
Lake Erie
Niles
Sturgis
Hillsdale
Adrian
ILLINOIS
INDIANA
OHIO
© 2011 Encyclopædia Britannica, Inc.

MINNESOTA

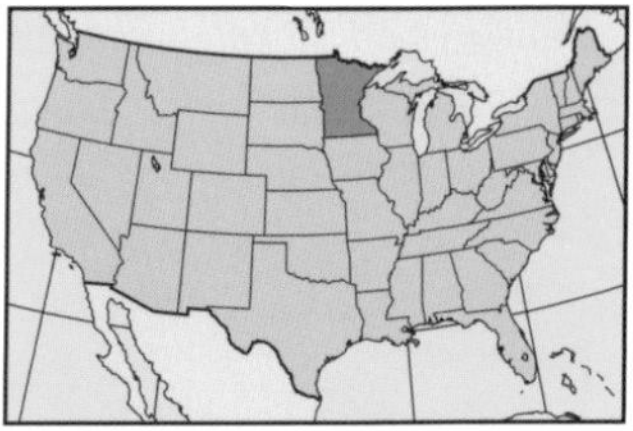

Official name: State of Minnesota
Nicknames: North Star State, Gopher State, Land of 10,000 Lakes
State Capital: St. Paul
State Flower: Pink and white lady's slipper
Motto: L'étoile du Nord (Star of the North)
Admitted to the Union: 1858 (32nd)
Total area: 86,935 sq. mi. (225,161 sq. km.) (ranks 12th)
Population (2010): 5,303,925 (ranks 21st)
Chief Cities: Bloomington, Brooklyn Park, Duluth, Minneapolis, Rochester, St. Paul
Principal products/industries: Oats, corn, soybeans, sugar beets, wild rice, turkeys, hogs, dairy products, malt beverages and other alcoholic beverages, iron ore, granite, limestone, electronic equipment, pulp and paper products, food processing, tourism
Highest point: Eagle Mt. 2301 ft. (702 m.)

State History

Evidence of prehistoric habitation; at time of European arrival, inhabited by Algonquian Ojibwa and Siouan Dakota American Indian tribes; probably visited by French explorers Pierre Radisson and Seigneur Chouart des Groseilliers 1654–60; Upper Mississippi Valley explored by Frenchmen René-Robert, Sieur de La Salle and Louis Hennepin 1680, and became extensive fur-trading region under the French; part northeast of the Mississippi ceded to British 1763 and to U.S. 1783, and included in Northwest Territory 1787; southwestern part acquired by U.S. in Louisiana Purchase 1803; northwestern part ceded to U.S. in border treaty with British 1818; Fort Snelling, first U.S. outpost in the region, established 1819; included in various territories before organization of Minnesota Territory Mar. 3, 1849, which included present Minnesota and the parts of North and South Dakota that lie east of the Missouri River; admitted to Union (with present boundaries) May 11, 1858; Sioux uprising occurred in southern Minnesota 1862; an early center of the Grange movement from 1867 on.

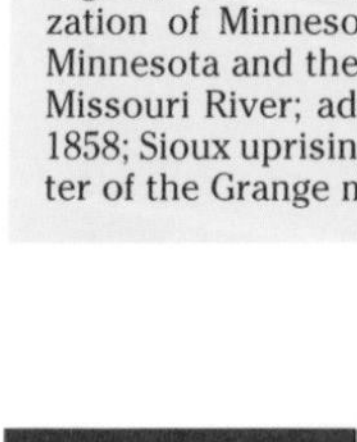

The central design of the flag has the state seal in circular form. Around the seal are 19 gold stars (arranged in 5 groups) symbolizing Minnesota as the 19th state to follow the original 13, and a border of lady's slipper flowers. Inside is a mounted Indian, a representation of St. Anthony Falls, and a setting sun.

97° 96° 95° 94° 93° 92° 91°
0 20 40 60 80 mi
0 30 60 90 120 km
MANITOBA
CANADA
ONTARIO
Angle Inlet
91° 90° 48°
Grand Portage
Grand Marais
Lake Superior
49°
Hallock
Roseau
Baudette
International Falls
Warren
Thief River Falls
Big Falls
48°
Red Lake Falls
Crookston
Ely
Tower
NORTH DAKOTA
Bagley
Bemidji
Chisolm
Virginia
Hibbing
Ada
Mahnomen
Grand Rapids
Lake Superior
Walker
Two Harbors
Moorhead
Park Rapids
Detroit Lakes
Proctor
Duluth
Carlton
Aitkin
Wadena
Brainerd
Fergus Falls
Breckenridge
46°
Elbow Lake
Long Prairie
Little Falls
Hinckley
Mississippi
Alexandria
Mora
Wheaton
Sauk Centre
Foley
Pine City
Morris
Glenwood
St. Cloud
Cambridge
WISCONSIN
Elk River
Ortonville
Benson
Coon Rapids
Willmar
Litchfield
Buffalo
Madison
45°
Minneapolis
St. Paul
SOUTH DAKOTA
Granite Falls
Montevideo
Hutchinson
Chaska
Bloomington
Canby
Olivia
Glencoe
Shakopee
Hastings
Gaylord
Red Wing
Redwood Falls
Le Sueur
Ivanhoe
Marshall
St. Peter
Mississippi
Wabasha
Northfield
New Ulm
Faribault
Mankato
Owatonna
Winona
44°
Slayton
Waseca
Pipestone
St. James
Rochester
Windom
Luverne
Albert Lea
Preston
Caledonia
Worthington
Fairmont
Blue Earth
Austin
IOWA
© 2011 Encyclopædia Britannica, Inc.

MISSISSIPPI

Official name: State of Mississippi
Nickname: Magnolia State
State Capital: Jackson
State Flower: Magnolia
Motto: Virtute et Armis (By Valor and Arms)
Admitted to the Union: 1817 (20th)
Total area: 47,692 sq. mi. (123,522 sq. km.) (ranks 32nd)
Population (2010): 2,967,297 (ranks 31st)
Chief Cities: Biloxi, Gulfport, Hattiesburg, Jackson, Meridian, Southhaven
Principal Products: Cotton, soybeans, grains, livestock, petroleum, natural gas, chemicals, apparel, wood products, transportation equipment
Highest point: Woodall Mt. 806 ft. (246 m.)

State History

Evidence of prehistoric inhabitants (Mound Builders); prior to European settlement inhabited by several tribes including the Choctaw, Natchez, and Chickasaw; became part of French-controlled Louisiana; Biloxi settled by French colonist Pierre Le Moyne d'Iberville 1699; except for southern part (British West Florida), region ceded to U.S. 1783; northern section included in Territory South of the Ohio River 1790; southern part included in Mississippi Territory 1798, which was expanded 1804 to include most of current state; western part of the territory admitted to the Union with its present boundaries Dec. 10, 1817 as state of Mississippi, but its southernmost strip of land not formally ceded by Spain until 1819; seceded Jan. 9, 1861; scene of important battles during Civil War; readmitted to Union Feb. 23, 1870; adopted present constitution 1890.

After the Civil War, a new state constitution was adopted, the product of a white majority that wished to minimize the influence in state affairs of local blacks and of the federal government. The new flag, still in use, has three stripes that recall the Stars and Bars of the Confederacy, and the Confederate Battle Flag as its canton.

TENNESSEE
ARKANSAS
LOUISIANA
LOUISIANA
ALABAMA
Mississippi
Mississippi
Gulf of Mexico
Mobile Bay
0 30 60 mi
0 40 80 km
92° 91° 90° 89° 88°
35° 34° 33° 32° 31° 30°
Southaven
Hernando
Holly Springs
Ashland
Corinth
Iuka
Tunica
Senatobia
Ripley
Booneville
Sardis
New Albany
Oxford
Marks
Batesville
Pontotoc
Tupelo
Fulton
Clarksdale
Water Valley
Sumner
Okolona
Rosedale
Charleston
Houston
Amory
Grenada
Aberdeen
Cleveland
Walthall
West Point
Indianola
Greenwood
Columbus
Greenville
Winona
Starkville
Leland
Vaiden
Mississippi State
Belzoni
Ackerman
Lexington
Louisville
Kosciusko
Macon
Mayersville
Rolling Fork
Yazoo City
Carthage
Philadelphia
De Kalb
Canton
Decatur
Vicksburg
Jackson
Forest
Meridian
Raymond
Brandon
Crystal Springs
Raleigh
Quitman
Port Gibson
Mendenhall
Bay Springs
Fayette
Hazelhurst
Laurel
Brookhaven
Prentiss
Collins
Waynesboro
Natchez
Meadville
Monticello
Ellisville
Hattiesburg
New Augusta
Liberty
McComb
Columbia
Woodville
Magnolia
Tylertown
Pervis
Leakesville
Poplarville
Wiggins
Lucedale
Picayune
Gulfport
Biloxi
Bay Saint Louis
Pascagoula
© 2011 Encyclopædia Britannica, Inc.

MISSOURI

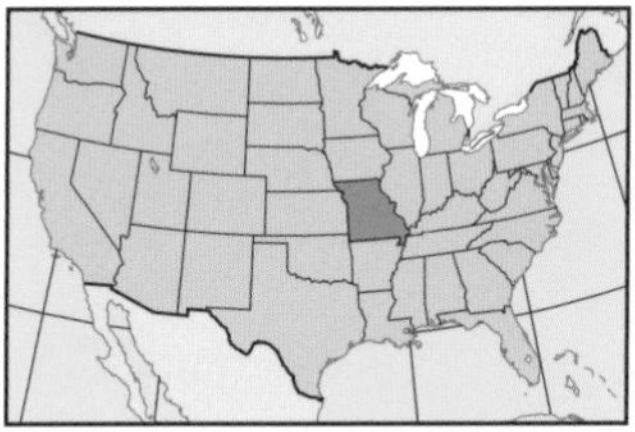

Official name: State of Missouri
Nickname: Show Me State
State Capital: Jefferson City
State Flower: Hawthorn
Motto: Salus Populi Suprema Lex Esto (Let the Welfare of the People Be the Supreme Law)
Admitted to the Union: 1821 (24th)
Total area: 69,703 sq. mi. (180,530 sq. km.) (ranks 21st)
Population (2010): 5,988,927 (ranks 18th)
Chief Cities: Columbia, Independence, Kansas City, Springfield, St. Louis
Principal products/industries: Soybeans, corn, wheat, cotton, livestock, cement, lead, iron ore, coal, transportation and aerospace equipment, chemicals, fabricated metal products
Highest point: Taum Sauk Mt. 1772 ft. (540 m.)

State History

Evidence of prehistoric inhabitants (Mound Builders); prior to European settlement inhabited by several Algonquian and Siouan tribes, including the Osage and the Missouri; visited by French explorers Père Marquette 1673 and Louis Jolliet 1683; probably first settled by French at Ste. Genevieve 1735; part of Louisiana Purchase 1803; included in Louisiana Territory 1805, and in Missouri Territory 1812; Missouri's application for admission as slave state 1817 caused bitter controversy which was settled by Missouri Compromise 1820 (Missouri admitted as slave state Aug. 10, 1821, Maine as free, no slavery above 36°30′—later repealed); did not secede from Union 1861; scene of fighting during Civil War 1861–64; adopted present constitution 1945.

The flag has the state coat of arms, which is divided vertically, with the arms of the United States on one side and a crescent and bear on the other. The crescent, a traditional symbol in heraldry of a 2nd son, was intended to indicate that Missouri was the 2nd state carved out of the Louisiana Territory.

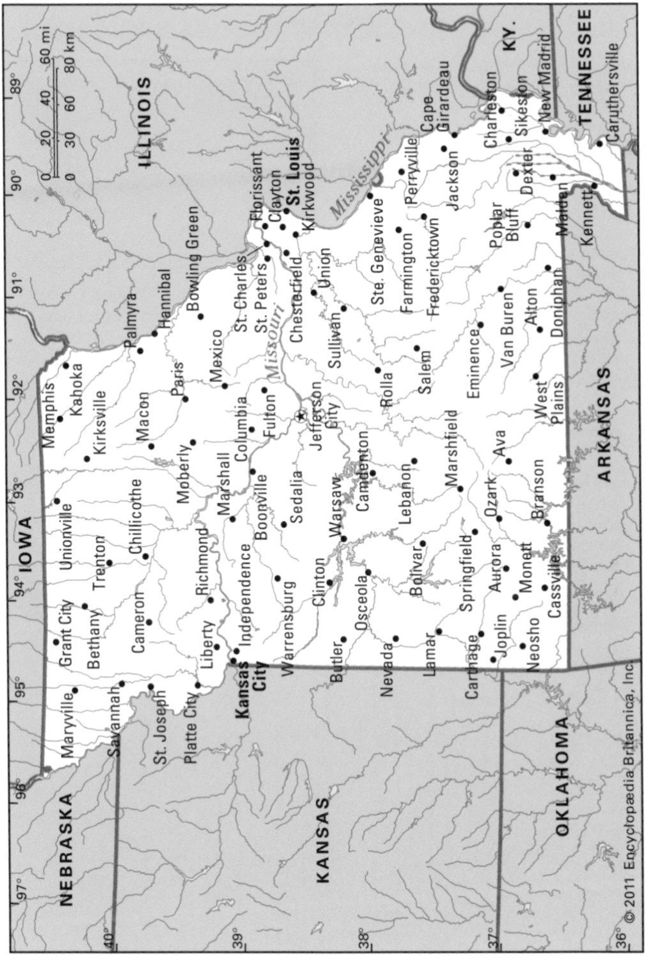
ILLINOIS
IOWA
NEBRASKA
KANSAS
OKLAHOMA
ARKANSAS
TENNESSEE
KY.
0 20 40 60 mi
0 30 60 80 km
89°
90°
91°
92°
93°
94°
95°
96°
97°
40°
39°
38°
37°
36°
Missouri
Mississippi
Memphis
Kahoka
Kirksville
Unionville
Grant City
Maryville
Bethany
Trenton
Savannah
St. Joseph
Cameron
Chillicothe
Macon
Palmyra
Hannibal
Paris
Moberly
Mexico
Bowling Green
Platte City
Liberty
Richmond
Marshall
Columbia
Fulton
Kansas City
Independence
Boonville
Sedalia
Jefferson City
St. Charles
St. Peters
Florissant
Clayton
St. Louis
Kirkwood
Chesterfield
Union
Sullivan
Warrensburg
Clinton
Warsaw
Camdenton
Butler
Osceola
Nevada
Lamar
Bolivar
Lebanon
Rolla
Salem
Ste. Genevieve
Farmington
Fredericktown
Perryville
Cape Girardeau
Jackson
Springfield
Marshfield
Carthage
Joplin
Neosho
Aurora
Monett
Cassville
Ozark
Branson
Ava
West Plains
Eminence
Van Buren
Alton
Doniphan
Poplar Bluff
Dexter
Malden
Kennett
Charleston
Sikeston
New Madrid
Caruthersville
© 2011 Encyclopædia Britannica, Inc.

MONTANA

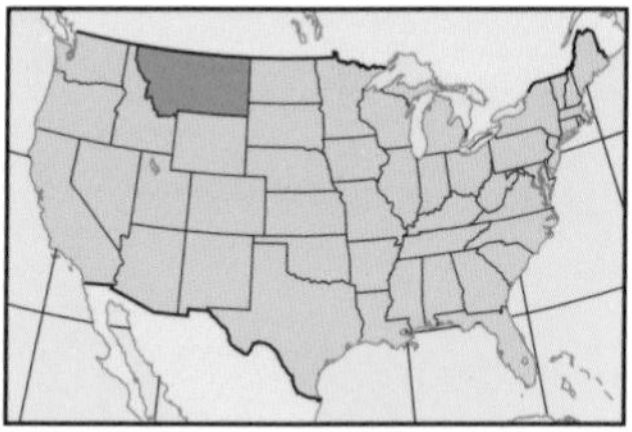

Official name: State of Montana
Nickname: Treasure State, Big Sky Country
State Capital: Helena
State Flower: Bitterroot
Motto: Oro y Plata (Gold and Silver)
Admitted to the Union: 1889 (41st)
Total area: 147,039 sq. mi. (380,829 sq. km.) (ranks 4th)
Population (2010): 989,415 (ranks 44th)
Chief Cities: Billings, Bozeman, Butte, Great Falls, Helena, Missoula
Principal products/industries: Wheat, sunflowers, sugar beets, corn, livestock, copper, petroleum, phosphate rock, food processing, lumber, primary metals
Highest point: Granite Peak 12,799 ft. (3904 m.)

State History

Inhabited by several native tribes prior to European settlement, including Blackfoot, Cheyenne, Arapaho, and Flathead Indians; all except a small area in northwest was part of Louisiana Purchase 1803; crossed by American explorers Meriwether Lewis and William Clark 1805–06; its boundary with Canada settled by treaties 1818 and 1846; part west of the Rocky Mountains acquired in Oregon Country; parts included in various territories of the U.S. prior to organization of territory of Montana 1864; first crossed by rail (Northern Pacific) 1883; admitted to Union Nov. 8, 1889; adopted new state constitution 1972.

The state flag has at its center a seal that includes a representation of the Rocky Mountains, fundamental to the state's topography and to its name, from the Spanish montaña ("mountain"). The seal also depicts a river and forests and Great Falls, a distinctive landmark.

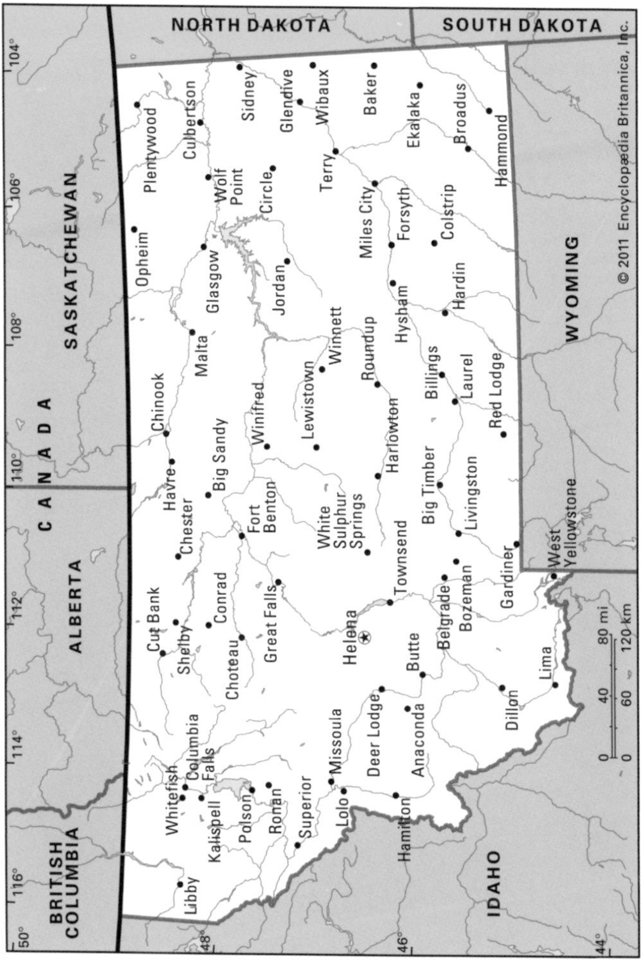
CANADA
BRITISH COLUMBIA
ALBERTA
SASKATCHEWAN
NORTH DAKOTA
SOUTH DAKOTA
WYOMING
IDAHO
50°
48°
46°
44°
116°
114°
112°
110°
108°
106°
104°
Libby
Whitefish
Columbia Falls
Kalispell
Polson
Ronan
Superior
Lolo
Missoula
Hamilton
Deer Lodge
Anaconda
Butte
Dillon
Lima
Cut Bank
Shelby
Choteau
Conrad
Great Falls
Helena
Belgrade
Bozeman
Townsend
Chester
Havre
Big Sandy
Fort Benton
White Sulphur Springs
Livingston
Gardiner
West Yellowstone
Big Timber
Chinook
Winifred
Lewistown
Harlowton
Red Lodge
Laurel
Billings
Roundup
Winnett
Malta
Glasgow
Jordan
Hysham
Hardin
Opheim
Forsyth
Colstrip
Miles City
Plentywood
Wolf Point
Circle
Terry
Culbertson
Sidney
Glendive
Wibaux
Baker
Ekalaka
Broadus
Hammond
0 40 80 mi
0 60 120 km
© 2011 Encyclopædia Britannica, Inc.

NEBRASKA

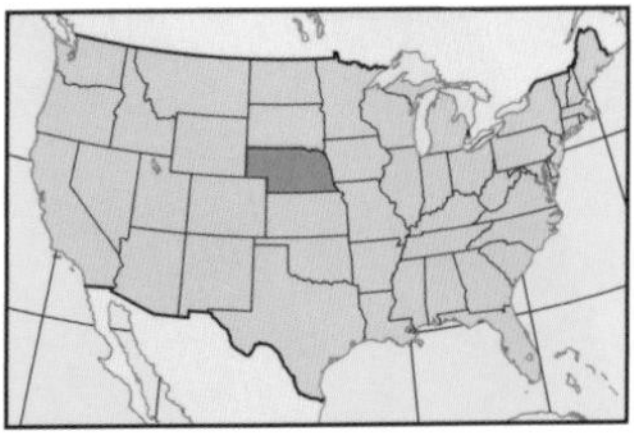

Official name: State of Nebraska
Nickname: Cornhusker State
State Capital: Lincoln
State Flower: Goldenrod
Motto: Equality Before the Law
Admitted to the Union: 1867 (37th)
Total area: 77,349 sq. mi. (200,333 sq. km.) (ranks 16th)
Population (2010): 1,826,341 (ranks 38th)
Chief Cities: Lincoln, Omaha
Principal products/industries: Corn, wheat, livestock, oil, food processing, machinery, fabricated metal products, grain products, livestock feeds
Highest point: Panorama Point 5424 ft. (1654 m.)

State History

Part of Louisiana Purchase 1803, of Louisiana Territory 1805, and of Missouri Territory 1812; part of unorganized U.S. territory c. 1821–54; part of Nebraska Territory organized 1854 as result of Kansas-Nebraska Act; territory reduced to area of present state by 1863; held first constitutional convention 1866; admitted to Union Mar. 1, 1867; established one-house legislature, the nation's only one, 1937.

In 1925, Nebraska became the last of the conterminous 48 states to adopt a flag of its own. In the design is the seal, which shows the Missouri River with a steamboat, a blacksmith in the foreground, a settler's cabin surrounded by wheat sheaves and growing corn, and a railroad train heading toward the Rocky Mountains.

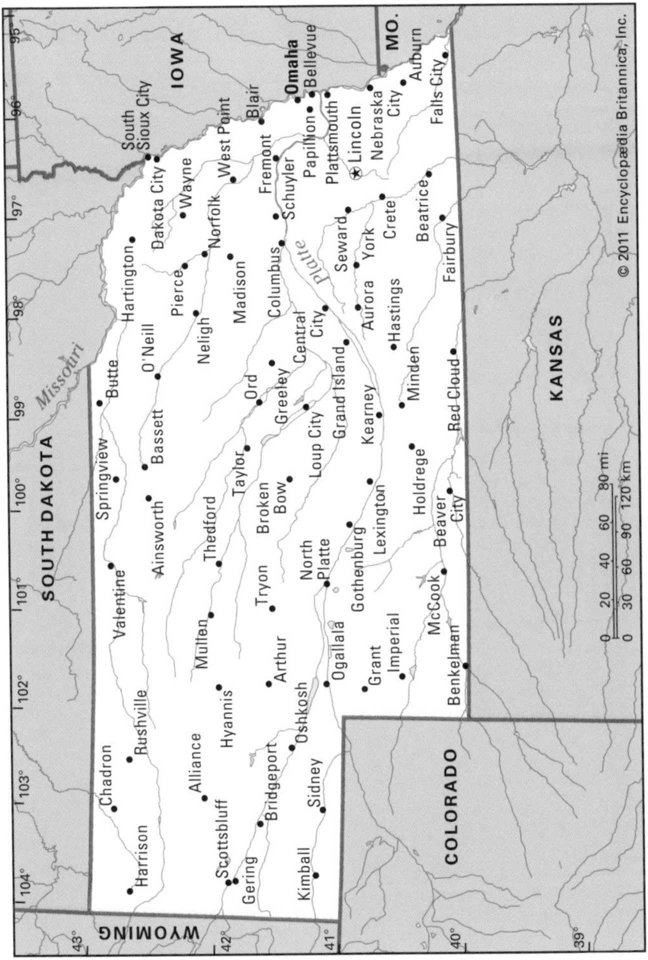
SOUTH DAKOTA
IOWA
MO.
KANSAS
COLORADO
WYOMING
Missouri
Platte
Omaha
Lincoln
South Sioux City
Dakota City
Wayne
West Point
Blair
Bellevue
Papillion
Plattsmouth
Fremont
Schuyler
Nebraska City
Auburn
Falls City
Beatrice
Crete
Seward
York
Fairbury
Hartington
Pierce
Norfolk
Madison
Columbus
Neligh
O'Neill
Butte
Central City
Aurora
Hastings
Grand Island
Greeley
Ord
Loup City
Kearney
Minden
Red Cloud
Holdrege
Springview
Bassett
Ainsworth
Valentine
Taylor
Broken Bow
Thedford
Mullen
Tryon
North Platte
Gothenburg
Lexington
Beaver City
McCook
Imperial
Grant
Ogallala
Arthur
Hyannis
Benkelman
Oshkosh
Rushville
Chadron
Alliance
Bridgeport
Sidney
Scottsbluff
Gering
Kimball
Harrison
95°
96°
97°
98°
99°
100°
101°
102°
103°
104°
43°
42°
41°
40°
39°
0 20 40 60 80 mi
0 30 60 90 120 km
© 2011 Encyclopædia Britannica, Inc.

NEVADA

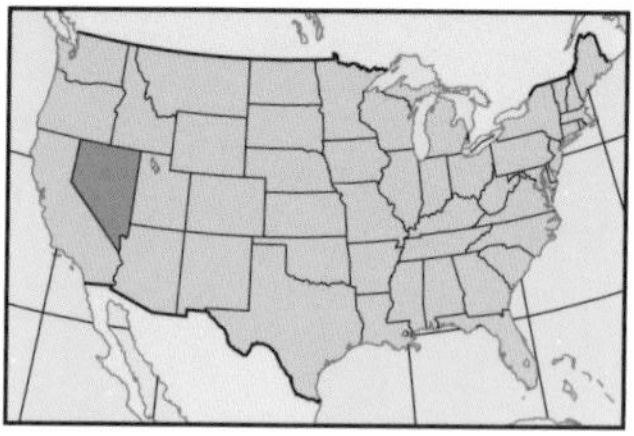

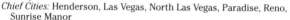

Official name: State of Nevada
Nickname: Silver State; Sagebrush State
State Capital: Carson City
State Flower: Sagebrush
Motto: All For Our Country
Admitted to the Union: 1864 (36th)
Total area: 110,572 sq. mi. (286,380 sq. km.) (ranks 7th)
Population (2010): 2,700,551 (ranks 35th)
Chief Cities: Henderson, Las Vegas, North Las Vegas, Paradise, Reno, Sunrise Manor
Principal products/industries: Wheat, livestock, gold, barite, mercury, lumber and wood products, chemicals, tourism and gambling
Highest point: Boundary Peak 13,140 ft. (4007 m.)

State History

Evidence of prehistoric inhabitants in the region (since about 20,000 years ago) includes projectile points, rock art, and dwelling remains; some Anasazi sites in southeast; at time of European contact (c. 18th century) region inhabited by several Indian tribes including Shoshoni and Paiute; some exploration by Spanish (18th century), fur traders (1820s), and others; major exploration and mapping by John C. Frémont and Kit Carson 1843–45; included in region ceded by Mexico to U.S. 1848; included in Utah Territory 1850–61; first permanent settlement made c. 1850 at Mormon Station (now Genoa); settlement increased after discovery of Comstock Lode 1859; organized as Territory of Nevada 1861; admitted to Union as state Oct. 31, 1864; enlarged slightly 1866 to present boundaries.

An early state flag, honoring the mining industry in the state, had silver and gold stars and the words "silver," "Nevada," and "gold" on a blue field. Today's flag features a wreath of sagebrush surrounding a silver star and the motto "Battle Born," honoring Nevada's admission to the Union during the Civil War.

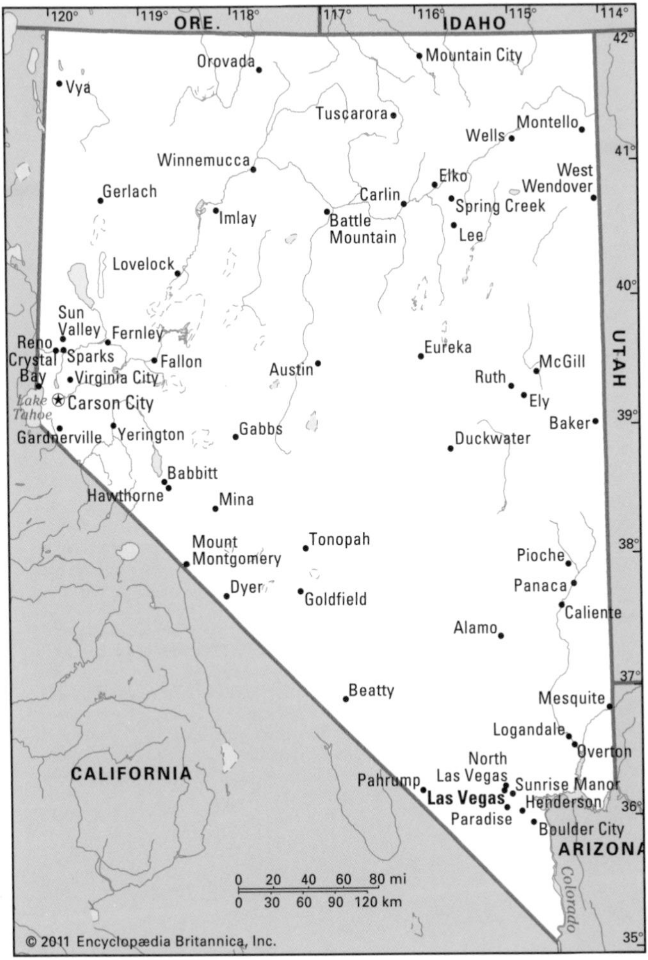
120°
119°
ORE.
118°
117°
116°
IDAHO
115°
114°
42°
41°
40°
39°
38°
37°
36°
35°
UTAH
ARIZONA
CALIFORNIA
Orovada
Mountain City
Vya
Tuscarora
Montello
Wells
Winnemucca
West Wendover
Elko
Gerlach
Carlin
Spring Creek
Imlay
Battle Mountain
Lee
Lovelock
Sun Valley
Fernley
Reno
Crystal Bay
Sparks
Fallon
Virginia City
Eureka
McGill
Austin
Ruth
Ely
Lake Tahoe
Carson City
Baker
Gardnerville
Yerington
Gabbs
Duckwater
Babbitt
Hawthorne
Mina
Tonopah
Mount Montgomery
Pioche
Panaca
Dyer
Goldfield
Caliente
Alamo
Beatty
Mesquite
Logandale
Overton
North Las Vegas
Pahrump
Sunrise Manor
Las Vegas
Henderson
Paradise
Boulder City
Colorado
0 20 40 60 80 mi
0 30 60 90 120 km
© 2011 Encyclopædia Britannica, Inc.

NEW HAMPSHIRE

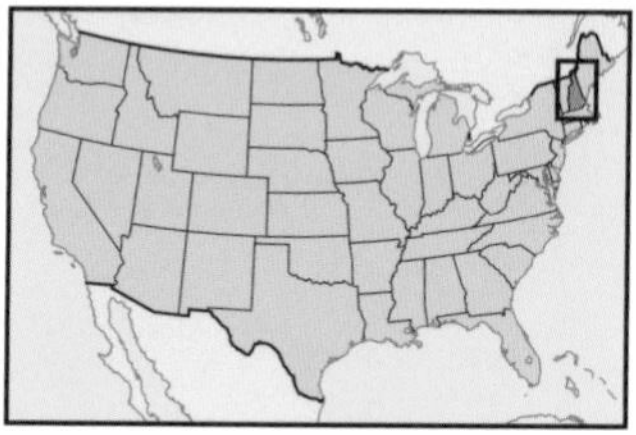

Official name: State of New Hampshire
Nickname: Granite State
State Capital: Concord
State Flower: Purple lilac
Motto: Live Free Or Die
Admitted to the Union: 1788; 9th of the original 13 colonies to ratify the U.S. Constitution
Total area: 9,280 sq. mi. (24,035 sq. km.) (ranks 45th)
Population (2010): 1,316,470 (ranks 42nd)
Chief Cities: Concord, Manchester, Nashua
Principal products/industries: Dairy products, apples, maple syrup, vegetables, Christmas trees, nursery plants, tourism, electrical products, electronic equipment, paper products, leather goods, once an important center of granite quarrying
Highest point: Mt. Washington 6288 ft. (1918 m.)

State History

Prior to European settlement, inhabited by numerous Algonquin tribes, especially of the Pennacook confederacy; coast explored by several English explorers early 17th century; area east of the Merrimack River included in grant to John Mason and Sir Ferdinando Gorges 1622 and in New Hampshire grant to Mason 1629; first settled by English near Portsmouth 1623; controlled by Massachusetts 1641–79; made a separate royal province 1679 but under same governor as Massachusetts 1699–1741; area of Vermont settled under New Hampshire jurisdiction, which New York disputed; area of Vermont awarded 1764 by royal order to jurisdiction of New York (final claims to area not relinquished by New Hampshire until 1782); first colony to declare independence from Great Britain 1776; adopted first constitution 1776, present constitution 1784 which later was frequently amended; Dartmouth College case decided 1819 in U.S. Supreme Court, confirming right of private corporations against excessive state regulation.

The 1909 flag law provided for the state seal in the center, framed by a wreath of laurel with nine stars interspersed, signifying the rank of New Hampshire as the ninth state to ratify the U.S. Constitution. The seal, modified in 1931, features the frigate Raleigh being built at Portsmouth in 1776.

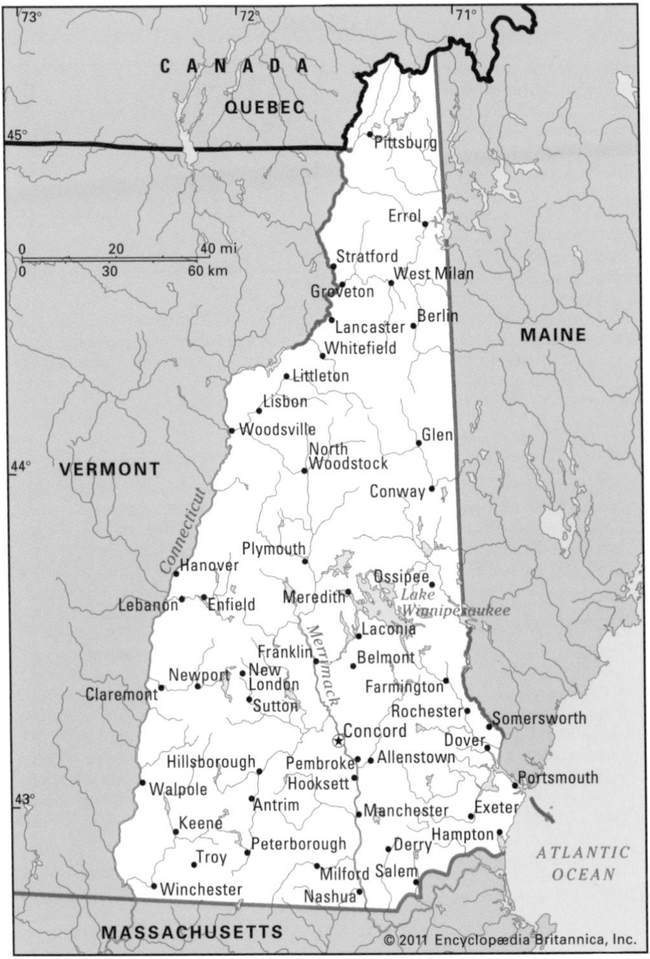
73°
72°
71°
CANADA
QUEBEC
45°
Pittsburg
Errol
0 20 40 mi
0 30 60 km
Stratford
West Milan
Groveton
Lancaster
Berlin
MAINE
Whitefield
Littleton
Lisbon
Woodsville
Glen
North Woodstock
44°
VERMONT
Conway
Connecticut
Plymouth
Hanover
Ossipee
Lake Winnipesaukee
Lebanon
Enfield
Meredith
Merrimack
Laconia
Franklin
Belmont
Newport
New London
Farmington
Claremont
Sutton
Rochester
Somersworth
Concord
Dover
Hillsborough
Pembroke
Allenstown
Portsmouth
Walpole
Hooksett
43°
Antrim
Manchester
Exeter
Keene
Hampton
Peterborough
Derry
ATLANTIC OCEAN
Troy
Milford
Salem
Winchester
Nashua
MASSACHUSETTS
© 2011 Encyclopædia Britannica, Inc.

NEW JERSEY

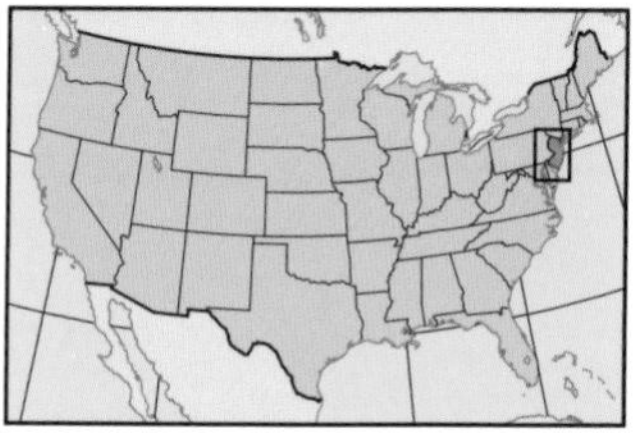

Official name: State of New Jersey
Nickname: Garden State
State Capital: Trenton
State Flower: Violet
Motto: Liberty and Prosperity
Admitted to the Union: 1787; 3rd of the original 13 colonies to ratify the U.S. Constitution
Total area: 7,812 sq. mi. (20,233 sq. km.) (ranks 46th)
Population (2010): 8,791,894 (ranks 11th)
Chief Cities: Edison, Elizabeth, Jersey City, Newark, Paterson
Principal products/industries: Blueberries, corn, cranberries, peppers, tomatoes, nursery plants, chemical products, electronic equipment, apparel, electrical machinery
Highest point: High Point 1803 ft. (550 m.)

State History

Prior to European colonization, region inhabited especially by Delaware tribes; sighted by Florentine navigator Giovanni da Verrazano 1524 and English navigator Henry Hudson 1609; first settled by Dutch and along Delaware River by Swedes; ceded to English as part of New Netherland 1664 and given the Latin name of Nova Caesarea; its eastern and northern part (East Jersey) became a proprietary colony regranted by Duke of York to Sir George Carteret and was sold to William Penn and associates 1682; its western and southern part (West Jersey), or the lower counties on Delaware River, held by William Penn 1676–1702; became royal province 1702; governed by governor of New York until 1738; declared independence from England and adopted first state constitution 1776; scene of numerous battles during the Revolutionary War, especially the important battles at Trenton, Princeton, and Monmouth; delegates to Constitutional Convention 1787 forwarded New Jersey Plan for small states; Trenton became state capital 1790; adopted new state constitution 1844 which included several democratic reforms; present constitution adopted 1947.

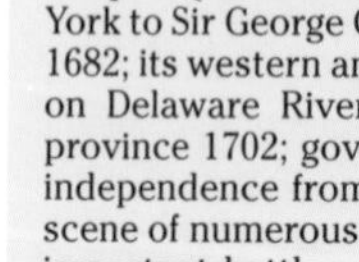

The state flag was adopted in 1896. The coat of arms depicts three plows that stand for agriculture, which is also represented by the goddess Ceres (one of the supporters). The other supporter is Liberty. The horse's head in the crest was shown on early New Jersey coins.

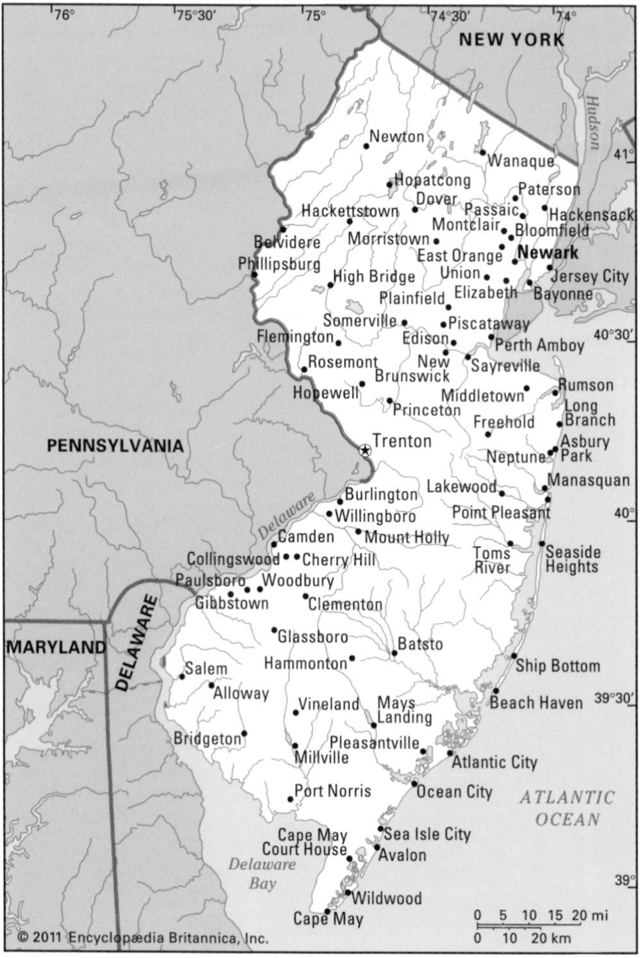
76°
75°30′
75°
74°30′
74°
41°
40°30′
40°
39°30′
39°
NEW YORK
PENNSYLVANIA
MARYLAND
DELAWARE
Hudson
Delaware
Delaware Bay
ATLANTIC OCEAN
Newton
Wanaque
Hopatcong
Paterson
Dover
Passaic
Hackensack
Hackettstown
Montclair
Bloomfield
Belvidere
Morristown
East Orange
Newark
Phillipsburg
High Bridge
Union
Jersey City
Elizabeth
Bayonne
Plainfield
Somerville
Piscataway
Flemington
Edison
Perth Amboy
Rosemont
New Brunswick
Sayreville
Hopewell
Middletown
Rumson
Princeton
Long Branch
Freehold
Trenton
Asbury Park
Neptune
Manasquan
Lakewood
Burlington
Point Pleasant
Willingboro
Camden
Mount Holly
Toms River
Seaside Heights
Collingswood
Cherry Hill
Paulsboro
Woodbury
Gibbstown
Clementon
Glassboro
Batsto
Hammonton
Ship Bottom
Salem
Alloway
Beach Haven
Vineland
Mays Landing
Bridgeton
Pleasantville
Millville
Atlantic City
Port Norris
Ocean City
Cape May Court House
Sea Isle City
Avalon
Wildwood
Cape May
0 5 10 15 20 mi
0 10 20 km
© 2011 Encyclopædia Britannica, Inc.

NEW MEXICO

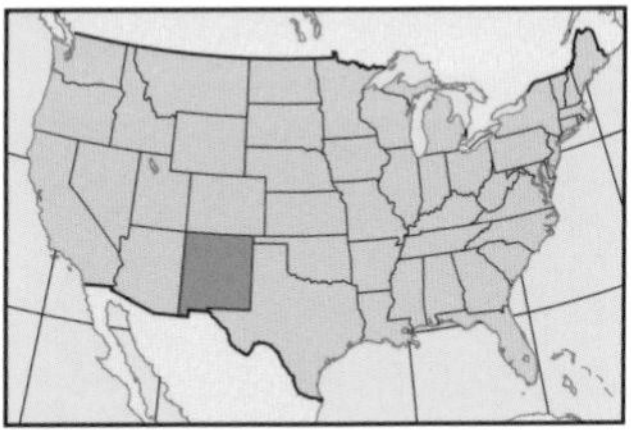

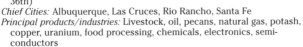

Official name: State of New Mexico
Nickname: Land of Enchantment
State Capital: Santa Fe
State Flower: Yucca
Motto: Crescit Eundo (It Grows As It Goes)
Admitted to the Union: 1912 (47th)
Total area: 121,590 sq. mi. (314,915 sq. km.) (ranks 5th)
Population (2010): 2,059,179 (ranks 36th)
Chief Cities: Albuquerque, Las Cruces, Rio Rancho, Santa Fe
Principal products/industries: Livestock, oil, pecans, natural gas, potash, copper, uranium, food processing, chemicals, electronics, semiconductors
Highest point: Wheeler Peak 13,161 ft. (4014 m.)

State History

Evidence of prehistoric inhabitants, especially Mogollon and Anasazi peoples; at time of European arrival inhabited mainly by Pueblo tribes (such as the Zuni) and Athabascan tribes (such as the Apache and the Navajo); first European visitor to area was missionary Marcos de Niza sent from Mexico (New Spain) 1539; explored by Spanish explorer Francisco Vásquez de Coronado's expedition 1540–42; Spanish settlement begun by explorer Juan de Oñate 1598; Santa Fe founded in 1609–10; governed by Mexico after 1821; part east of Rio Grande included in annexation of Texas 1845; rest ceded to U.S. by Mexico 1848 (Treaty of Guadalupe Hidalgo) except for southern strip which was included in Gadsden Purchase 1853; first bid for statehood 1850 denied in favor of organization of New Mexico Territory; territory reduced to area of present state by 1863; held several constitutional conventions before finally being admitted to Union as state Jan. 6, 1912.

The flag was officially adopted in March 1925 as a result of a design competition. The colors are based on the flag of Spain, which had ruled New Mexico until the early 19th century. Today the Zia sun is widely recognized as a state symbol, and the design of the capitol building of New Mexico was influenced by its shape.

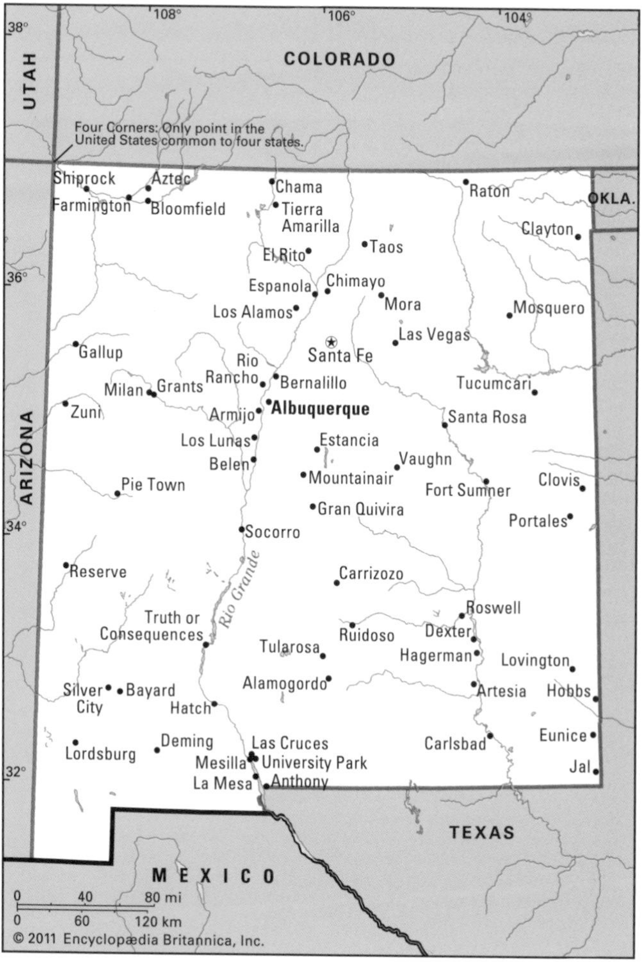
COLORADO
UTAH
ARIZONA
OKLA.
TEXAS
MEXICO
108°
106°
104°
38°
36°
34°
32°
Four Corners: Only point in the United States common to four states.
Shiprock
Aztec
Farmington
Bloomfield
Chama
Tierra Amarilla
Raton
Clayton
Taos
El Rito
Espanola
Chimayo
Mora
Los Alamos
Mosquero
Las Vegas
Gallup
Santa Fe
Rio Rancho
Bernalillo
Milan
Grants
Tucumcari
Zuni
Armijo
Albuquerque
Santa Rosa
Los Lunas
Estancia
Belen
Vaughn
Mountainair
Fort Sumner
Clovis
Pie Town
Gran Quivira
Portales
Socorro
Rio Grande
Reserve
Carrizozo
Roswell
Truth or Consequences
Ruidoso
Dexter
Tularosa
Hagerman
Lovington
Alamogordo
Artesia
Hobbs
Silver City
Bayard
Hatch
Deming
Las Cruces
Carlsbad
Eunice
Lordsburg
Mesilla
University Park
Jal
La Mesa
Anthony
0 40 80 mi
0 60 120 km
© 2011 Encyclopædia Britannica, Inc.

NEW YORK

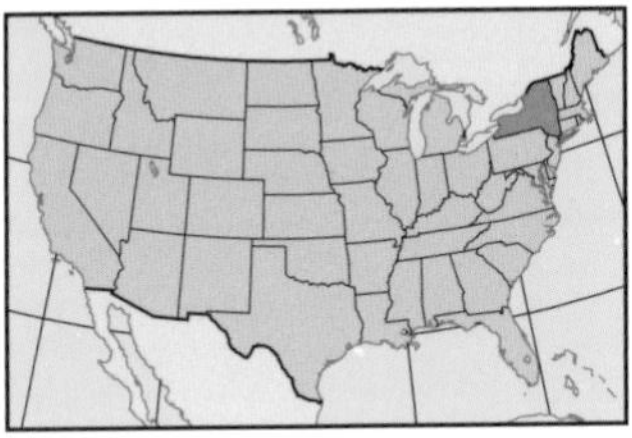

Official name: State of New York
Nickname: Empire State
State Capital: Albany
State Flower: Rose
Motto: Excelsior (Ever Upward)
Admitted to the Union: 1788; 11th of the original 13 colonies to ratify the U.S. Constitution
Total area: 53,095 sq. mi. (137,515 sq. km.) (ranks 27th)
Population (2010): 19,378,102 (ranks 3rd)
Chief Cities: Albany, Buffalo, New York City, Rochester, Syracuse, Yonkers
Principal products/industries: Vegetables, fruit, dairy products, zinc, gravel, salt, apparel, computers and software, primary metals, electrical machinery, chemicals, finance, printing and publishing, food processing
Highest point: Mt. Marcy 5344 ft. (1630 m.)

State History

Prior to European colonization inhabited by Algonquins (Mahican, Wappinger) and Iroquois (Mohawk, Oneida, Onondaga, Cayuga, and Seneca); New York Bay visited by Florentine navigator Giovanni da Verrazano 1524; explored 1609 by English navigator Henry Hudson (Hudson River) and French explorer Samuel de Champlain (northern New York to Lake Champlain); Dutch trading posts, established on Manhattan Island and at Fort Nassau, were taken over by Dutch West India Company under which early colonization occurred; opened 1629 to patroon colonization for several years; formed part of Dutch colony of New Netherland, surrendered without resistance to English 1664 and renamed New York after its proprietor, Duke of York; briefly recaptured by Dutch 1673–74; scene of much fighting during French and Indian War, in which the Iroquois Confederacy became allied with the British; after ratifying Declaration of Independence, held first state constitutional convention 1776, adopted first state constitution 1777; scene of numerous engagements of the American Revolution including Ticonderoga, Long Island, White Plains, Saratoga, and Kingston, and also of Benedict Arnold's treason at West Point; ratified U.S. Constitution 1788; state capital moved 1797 from New York City to Albany; Canadian frontier scene of several engagements during War of 1812; opening of Erie Canal 1825 spurred development of western New York; adopted present constitution 1894.

The coat of arms features a sun symbol, two supporters, and the state motto. The scene depicted under the sun is a view of the Hudson River. The supporters of the shield are Liberty (with her liberty cap on a staff) and Justice. An American eagle surmounts the globe at the top.

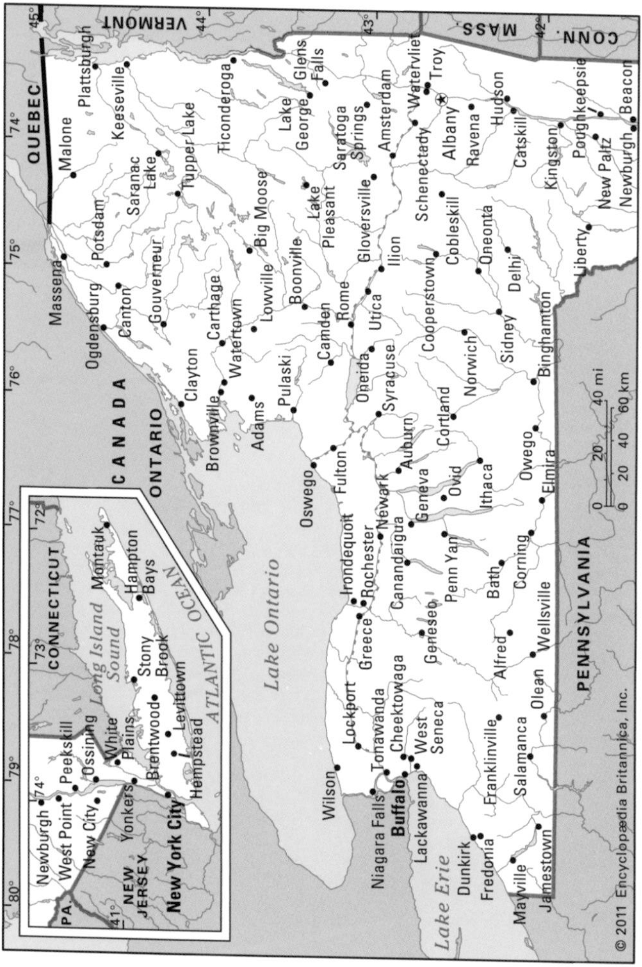
QUEBEC
VERMONT
CANADA
ONTARIO
MASS.
CONN.
PENNSYLVANIA
Lake Ontario
Lake Erie
45°
44°
43°
42°
74°
75°
76°
77°
78°
79°
80°
Malone
Plattsburgh
Keeseville
Massena
Potsdam
Saranac Lake
Tupper Lake
Ticonderoga
Ogdensburg
Canton
Gouverneur
Clayton
Carthage
Watertown
Brownville
Adams
Big Moose
Lowville
Boonville
Pulaski
Lake George
Glens Falls
Lake Pleasant
Saratoga Springs
Camden
Rome
Oswego
Fulton
Oneida
Utica
Gloversville
Amsterdam
Ilion
Syracuse
Auburn
Schenectady
Watervliet
Troy
Albany
Cooperstown
Cobleskill
Ravena
Hudson
Norwich
Cortland
Oneonta
Catskill
Irondequoit
Rochester
Newark
Geneva
Ovid
Ithaca
Sidney
Delhi
Kingston
Poughkeepsie
Greece
Canandaigua
Penn Yan
Owego
Binghamton
Liberty
New Paltz
Newburgh
Beacon
Geneseo
Bath
Corning
Elmira
Lockport
Tonawanda
Cheektowaga
West Seneca
Alfred
Wellsville
Wilson
Niagara Falls
Buffalo
Lackawanna
Franklinville
Olean
Salamanca
Dunkirk
Fredonia
Mayville
Jamestown
0 20 40 mi
0 20 40 60 km
CONNECTICUT
NEW JERSEY
PA.
41°
72°
73°
74°
Newburgh
West Point
New City
Peekskill
Ossining
White Plains
Yonkers
New York City
Brentwood
Hempstead
Levittown
Stony Brook
Hampton Bays
Montauk
Long Island Sound
ATLANTIC OCEAN
© 2011 Encyclopædia Britannica, Inc.

NORTH CAROLINA

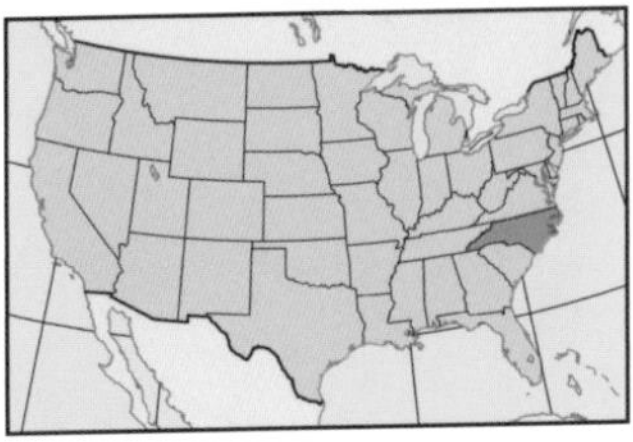

Official name: State of North Carolina
Nicknames: Tar Heel State, Old North State
State Capital: Raleigh
State Flower: Dogwood
Motto: To Be Rather Than To Seem
Admitted to the Union: 1789; 12th of the original 13 colonies to ratify the U.S. Constitution
Total area: 52,663 sq. mi. (136,397 sq. km.) (ranks 28th)
Population (2010): 9,535,483 (ranks 10th)
Chief Cities: Charlotte, Durham, Fayetteville, Greensboro, Raleigh, Winston-Salem
Principal products/industries: Tobacco, corn, fruit, soybeans, peanuts, livestock, gravel, feldspar, tourism, textiles, cigarettes, food products, chemicals, furniture, electronics and electrical equipment
Highest point: Mt. Mitchell 6684 ft. (2039 m.)

State History

Inhabited by several Algonquin, Siouan, and Iroquoian tribes prior to European contact, especially the Cherokee, Catawba, and Tuscarora; coast explored by Florentine navigator Giovanni da Verrazano (under French employ) 1524, and others; first English settlement in the New World established 1585 at Roanoke Island; region of Albemarle Sound settled mid-17th century by Virginia colonists; formed a part of Carolina grant given 1663 (expanded 1665) by King Charles II to eight noblemen of his court; governed largely separately from South Carolina from late 17th century, and officially separated 1712; Regulator movement (1768–71) against excessive taxation and government corruption suppressed by colonial forces at Alamance 1771; first Revolutionary battle in the state occurred at "Moores Creek Bridge" Feb. 27, 1776; Provincial Congress adopted Apr. 12, 1776 the Halifax Resolves that authorized the delegates for North Carolina to the Continental Congress "to concur with the delegates of the other colonies in declaring independency"—the first explicit sanction of independence by an American colony; adopted state constitution 1776; passed ordinance of secession May 20, 1861; secession ordinance annulled and slavery abolished 1865; new state constitution 1868; readmitted to Union July 11, 1868; latest state constitution 1971.

One of the ribbons in the flag has "May 20th, 1775," the date on which some local citizens were supposedly first to proclaim their independence from Great Britain. The other ribbon has "April 12th, 1776," date of the Halifax Resolves, authorizing North Carolina delegates to approve the U.S. Declaration of Independence.

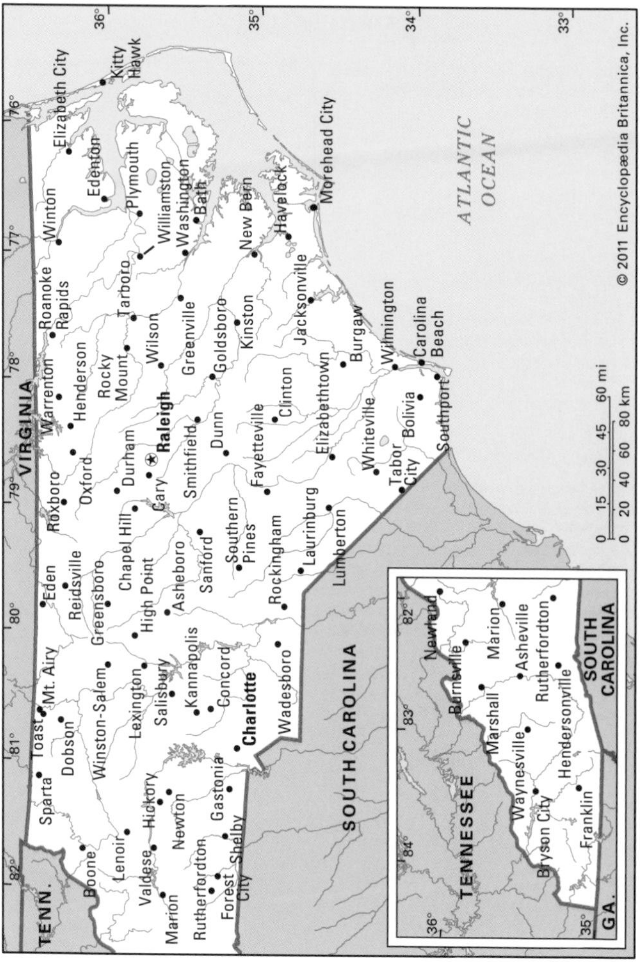
VIRGINIA
TENN.
SOUTH CAROLINA
ATLANTIC OCEAN
Elizabeth City
Kitty Hawk
Edenton
Plymouth
Winton
Williamston
Washington
Bath
New Bern
Havelock
Morehead City
Roanoke Rapids
Tarboro
Greenville
Kinston
Jacksonville
Warrenton
Henderson
Rocky Mount
Wilson
Goldsboro
Burgaw
Wilmington
Carolina Beach
Southport
Bolivia
Whiteville
Tabor City
Clinton
Elizabethtown
Fayetteville
Dunn
Smithfield
Raleigh
Oxford
Durham
Cary
Roxboro
Chapel Hill
Southern Pines
Sanford
Laurinburg
Lumberton
Rockingham
Eden
Reidsville
Greensboro
High Point
Asheboro
Mt. Airy
Winston-Salem
Lexington
Salisbury
Kannapolis
Concord
Wadesboro
Charlotte
Toast
Dobson
Sparta
Hickory
Newton
Gastonia
Boone
Lenoir
Valdese
Marion
Rutherfordton
Forest City
Shelby
0 15 30 45 60 mi
0 20 40 60 80 km
76° 77° 78° 79° 80° 81° 82°
36° 35° 34° 33°
© 2011 Encyclopædia Britannica, Inc.
TENNESSEE
GA.
SOUTH CAROLINA
Newland
Burnsville
Marion
Marshall
Asheville
Rutherfordton
Waynesville
Hendersonville
Bryson City
Franklin
82° 83° 84°
36° 35°

NORTH DAKOTA

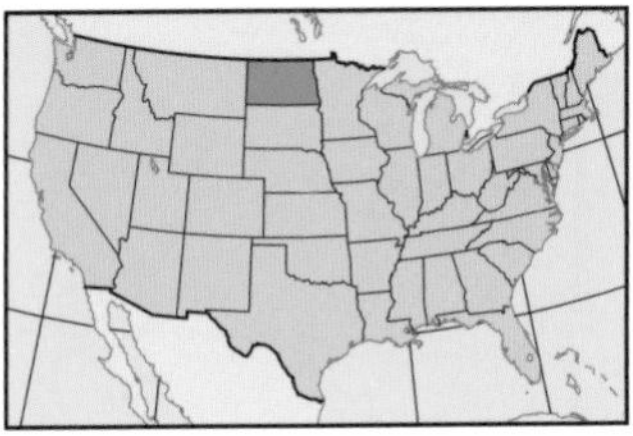

Official name: State of North Dakota
Nicknames: Peace Garden State, Flickertail State
State Capital: Bismarck
State Flower: Wild prairie rose
Motto: Liberty and Union, Now and Forever, One and Inseparable
Admitted to the Union: 1889 (39th)
Total area: 70,698 sq. mi. (183,107 sq. km.) (ranks 19th)
Population (2010): 672,591 (ranks 48th)
Chief Cities: Bismarck, Fargo, Grand Forks, Minot
Principal products/industries: Wheat, barley, flaxseed, canola, dry beans, oats, livestock, oil, coal, food processing, wood products, refined petroleum
Highest point: White Butte 3506 ft. (1069 m.)

State History

Evidence of prehistoric inhabitants throughout the state; at time of European contact was inhabited by native Algonquin (Cheyenne and Ojibwa), Caddoan (Arikara), and especially Siouan (Assiniboin, Dakota, Hidatsa, and Mandan) peoples; first visited by La Vérendrye brothers 1742–43; greater part included in Louisiana Purchase 1803; northern limit of northeast section determined by treaty with Great Britain 1818; parts included in several U.S. territories 1805–61; Dakota Territory (capital Yankton 1861–83, Bismark 1883–89) organized Mar. 2, 1861 including North and South Dakota and much of Wyoming and Montana; reduced in 1868 to area of present two states of North and South Dakota; settlement hastened by discovery of gold c. 1874 in the Black Hills; separated from South Dakota and admitted to Union as state Nov. 2, 1889; constitution passed 1889.

In the late 19th century the Dakota Territorial Guard displayed a blue flag with the coat of arms of the U.S. in the center. After North Dakota joined the Union in 1889, a similar design was used by the state's National Guard. In 1911 the design was approved for the official state flag.

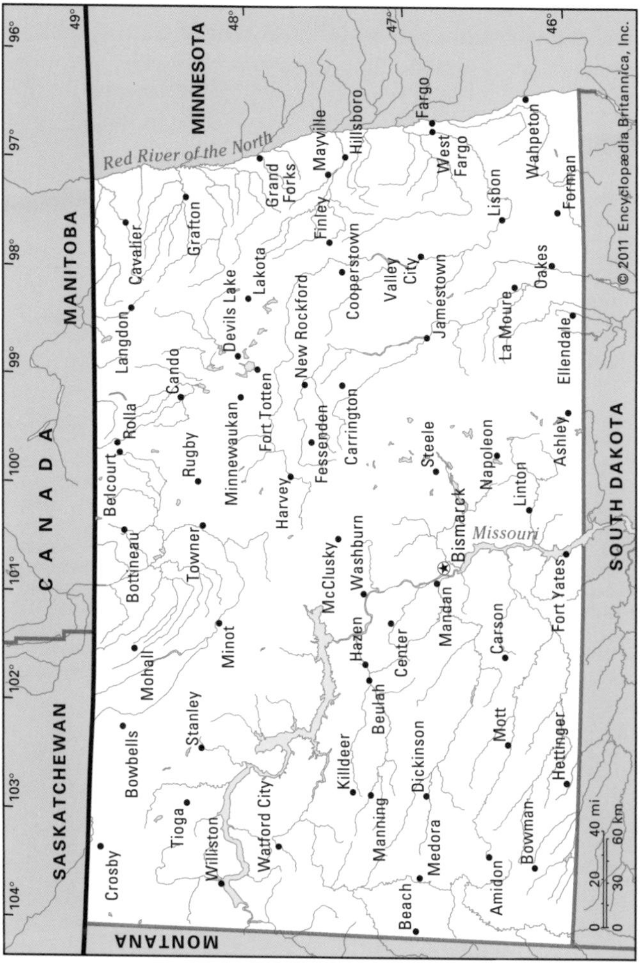
CANADA
SASKATCHEWAN
MANITOBA
MINNESOTA
MONTANA
SOUTH DAKOTA
Red River of the North
Missouri
Crosby
Bowbells
Tioga
Williston
Stanley
Mohall
Minot
Watford City
Killdeer
Manning
Beulah
Hazen
Dickinson
Medora
Beach
Amidon
Bowman
Hettinger
Mott
Carson
Center
Mandan
Bismarck
Washburn
McClusky
Towner
Bottineau
Belcourt
Rolla
Rugby
Cando
Langdon
Cavalier
Grafton
Devils Lake
Minnewaukan
Fort Totten
Lakota
New Rockford
Harvey
Fessenden
Carrington
Cooperstown
Finley
Mayville
Grand Forks
Hillsboro
Fargo
West Fargo
Valley City
Jamestown
Steele
Napoleon
Linton
Fort Yates
Ashley
Ellendale
La Moure
Oakes
Lisbon
Forman
Wahpeton
104°
103°
102°
101°
100°
99°
98°
97°
96°
49°
48°
47°
46°
0 20 40 mi
0 30 60 km
© 2011 Encyclopædia Britannica, Inc.

OHIO

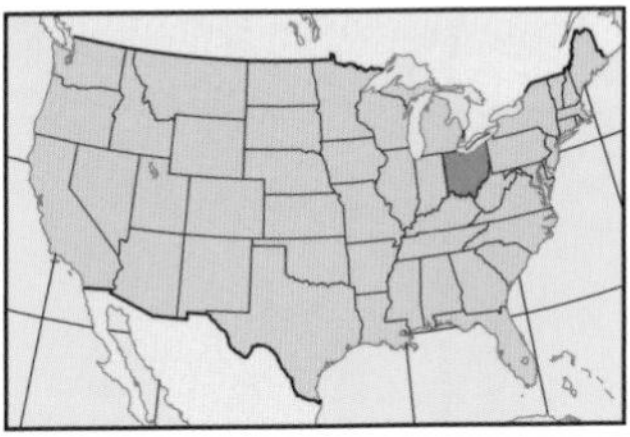

Official name: State of Ohio
Nickname: Buckeye State
State Capital: Columbus
State Flower: Scarlet carnation
Motto: With God, All Things Are Possible
Admitted to the Union: 1803 (17th)
Total area: 44,825 sq. mi. (116,096 sq. km.) (ranks 34th)
Population (2010): 11,536,504 (ranks 7th)
Chief Cities: Akron, Cincinnati, Cleveland, Columbus, Dayton, Toledo
Principal products/industries: Corn, soybeans, grapes, apples, tobacco, oats, livestock, natural gas, coal, iron and steel, rubber products, machinery, food products
Highest point: Campbell Hill 1549 ft. (472 m.)

State History

Has many earthwork mounds of prehistoric Mound Builders; inhabited by various Indian tribes (including Miami, Shawnee, Delaware, and Wyandot) when Europeans began settling the area; claimed by both France and Britain in colonial times; ceded to Britain 1763 following French and Indian War; became part of U.S. by Treaty of Paris 1783 following American Revolution; included 1787 in Northwest Territory; first permanent white settlement at Marietta 1788; western boundary with Indian lands determined by Maj. Gen. Anthony Wayne's defeat of Indians 1794 at Fallen Timbers and by Treaty of Greenville 1795; Western Reserve incorporated 1800; first constitution 1802; unofficially entered Union Feb. 19, 1803. In 1953, by resolution of U.S. Congress, Mar. 1, 1803 declared official day of admission to Union.

The red disk at the hoist end suggests the seed of the buckeye, the official state tree. The white O is the initial letter of the state name, while the use of stars and stripes and the colors red, white, and blue clearly honor the national flag. The 17 stars in the flag recall that Ohio was the 17th state to join the Union.

85°
84°
83°
82°
81°
CANADA
ONTARIO
MICHIGAN
Lake Erie
42°
41°
40°
39°
38°
PENNSYLVANIA
INDIANA
KENTUCKY
WEST VIRGINIA
Ohio
Ohio River
Conneaut
Ashtabula
Painesville
Jefferson
Toledo
Wauseon
Port Clinton
Sandusky
Cleveland
Chardon
Lorain
Bryan
Napoleon
Bowling Green
Fremont
Elyria
Parma
Warren
Defiance
Clyde
Norwalk
Cuyahoga Falls
Niles
New Bavaria
Medina
Ravenna
Tiffin
Paulding
Findlay
Willard
Akron
Youngstown
Barberton
Ottawa
Van Wert
Shelby
Alliance
Salem
Upper Sandusky
Bucyrus
Ashland
Canton
Delphos
Lima
Wooster
Lisbon
Massillon
Galion
Mansfield
Kenton
Millersburg
East Liverpool
Celina
Marion
Dover
New Philadelphia
Wapakoneta
Mount Gilead
Mount Vernon
Bellefontaine
Cadiz
Steubenville
Marysville
Delaware
Coshocton
Sidney
Martins Ferry
St. Clairsville
Upper Arlington
Greenville
Newark
Urbana
Troy
Cambridge
Columbus
Zanesville
London
Grove City
New Lexington
Springfield
Dayton
Caldwell
Lancaster
Kettering
Woodsfield
Washington Court House
Xenia
Circleville
McConnelsville
Middletown
Logan
Marietta
Hamilton
Lebanon
Wilmington
Chillicothe
Athens
Fairfield
McArthur
Hillsboro
Cincinnati
Waverly
Pomeroy
Batavia
Jackson
Georgetown
Gallipolis
West Union
Portsmouth
Ironton
South Point
0 20 40 mi
0 30 60 km
© 2011 Encyclopædia Britannica, Inc.

OKLAHOMA

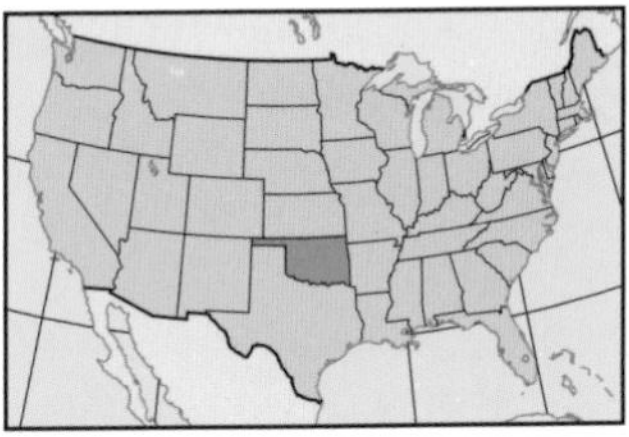

Official name: State of Oklahoma
Nickname: Sooner State
State Capital: Oklahoma City
State Flower: Mistletoe, Oklahoma hybrid rose
Motto: Labor Omnia Vincit (Labor Conquers All Things)
Admitted to the Union: 1907 (46th)
Total area: 69,899 sq. mi. (181,038 sq. km.) (ranks 20th)
Population (2010): 3,751,351 (ranks 28th)
Chief Cities: Broken Arrow, Oklahoma City, Norman, Tulsa
Principal products/industries: Wheat, cotton, sorghum, beef cattle, electronics and electrical equipment, gas and petroleum, food processing, fabricated metal products
Highest point: Black Mesa 4973 ft. (1517 m.)

State History

Except for Panhandle, formed part of Louisiana Purchase 1803; southern part nominally included in Arkansas Territory 1819–28; settled by Indians as unorganized Indian Territory c. 1820–40, especially following the 1830 Indian Removal Act and subsequent forced migration of tribes from the East; part opened to white settlement 1889; western part organized as Oklahoma Territory 1890; rest gradually opened to whites; on Nov. 16, 1907, Indian Territory and Oklahoma Territory were merged and admitted to Union as state.

The blue background symbolizes loyalty and devotion; the traditional bison-hide shield of the Osage Indians suggests the defense of the state. The shield has small crosses, standing for stars (common in Native American art), and an olive branch and calumet as emblems of peace for whites and Native Americans.

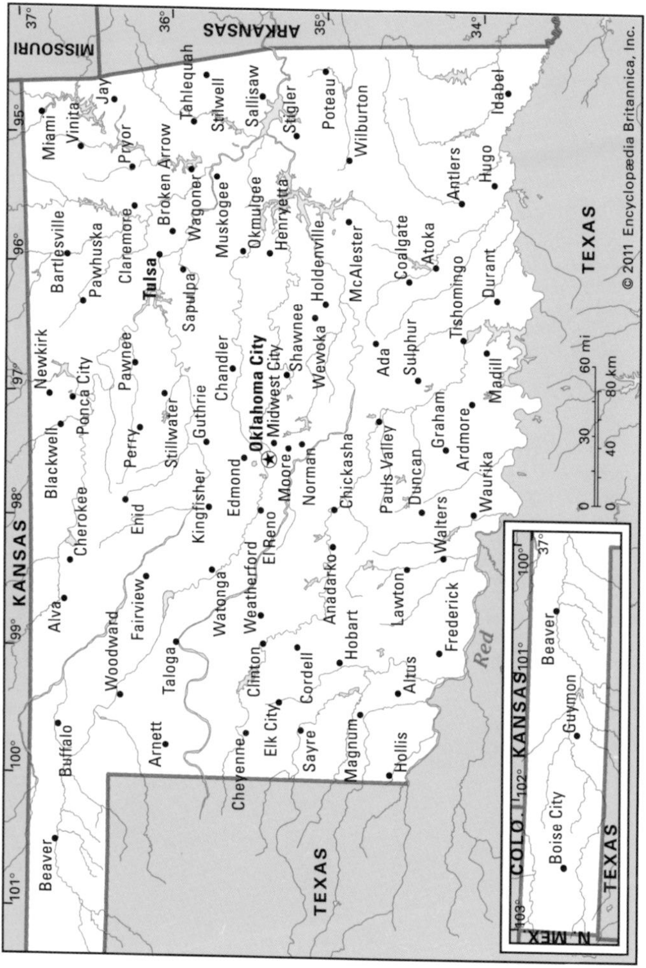
MISSOURI
ARKANSAS
KANSAS
TEXAS
TEXAS
Red
37°
36°
35°
34°
95°
96°
97°
98°
99°
100°
101°
Miami
Vinita
Jay
Pryor
Tahlequah
Stilwell
Sallisaw
Stigler
Poteau
Wilburton
Idabel
Hugo
Antlers
Broken Arrow
Wagoner
Muskogee
Okmulgee
Henryetta
Holdenville
McAlester
Coalgate
Atoka
Tishomingo
Durant
Bartlesville
Pawhuska
Claremore
Tulsa
Sapulpa
Shawnee
Wewoka
Ada
Sulphur
Madill
Ardmore
Graham
Newkirk
Ponca City
Blackwell
Pawnee
Perry
Stillwater
Guthrie
Chandler
Oklahoma City
Midwest City
Edmond
Moore
Norman
Chickasha
Pauls Valley
Duncan
Waurika
Walters
Lawton
Frederick
Altus
Hollis
Magnum
Sayre
Elk City
Cheyenne
Clinton
Cordell
Hobart
Anadarko
El Reno
Weatherford
Watonga
Kingfisher
Enid
Cherokee
Alva
Fairview
Woodward
Taloga
Arnett
Buffalo
Beaver
0
30
60 mi
0
40
80 km
© 2011 Encyclopædia Britannica, Inc.
N. MEX.
COLO.
KANSAS
TEXAS
103°
102°
101°
100°
37°
Boise City
Guymon
Beaver

OREGON

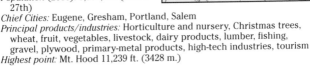

Official name: State of Oregon
Nickname: Beaver State
State Capital: Salem
State Flower: Oregon grape
Motto: Alis Volat Propriis (She Flies With Her Own Wings)
Admitted to the Union: 1859 (33rd)
Total area: 97,048 sq. mi. (251,353 sq. km.) (ranks 9th)
Population (2010): 3,381,074 (ranks 27th)
Chief Cities: Eugene, Gresham, Portland, Salem
Principal products/industries: Horticulture and nursery, Christmas trees, wheat, fruit, vegetables, livestock, dairy products, lumber, fishing, gravel, plywood, primary-metal products, high-tech industries, tourism
Highest point: Mt. Hood 11,239 ft. (3428 m.)

State History

Inhabited by numerous American Indian peoples when Europeans arrived; coast first sighted by Spanish sailors; region claimed for England by Sir Francis Drake 1579; visited by Capt. James Cook 1778; Columbia River explored by Capt. Robert Gray of Boston 1792, giving U.S. a claim to the region; mouth of Columbia River reached by Meriwether Lewis and William Clark's overland expedition 1805; for a time jointly occupied by England and U.S.; first white settlement founded at Astoria by American fur trader John Jacob Astor 1811, but lost to British during War of 1812; region dominated by Britain's Hudson's Bay Company under John McLoughlin (often called "the father of Oregon") 1820s through 1840s; first permanent settlement in the Willamette Valley established 1834 by Methodist missionaries; settlement accelerated from c. 1843 with mass migration of Americans over the Oregon Trail; Great Britain relinquished claim to region 1846; part of Oregon Territory 1848; admitted to Union with present boundaries Feb. 14, 1859.

The elements in the seal are ships, mountains, and symbols of agriculture, as well as a pioneer covered wagon and the phrase "The Union." The 33 stars correspond to Oregon's order of admission to the Union. A beaver symbol on the reverse recalls the importance of the animal to early trappers and hunters in the Pacific Northwest.

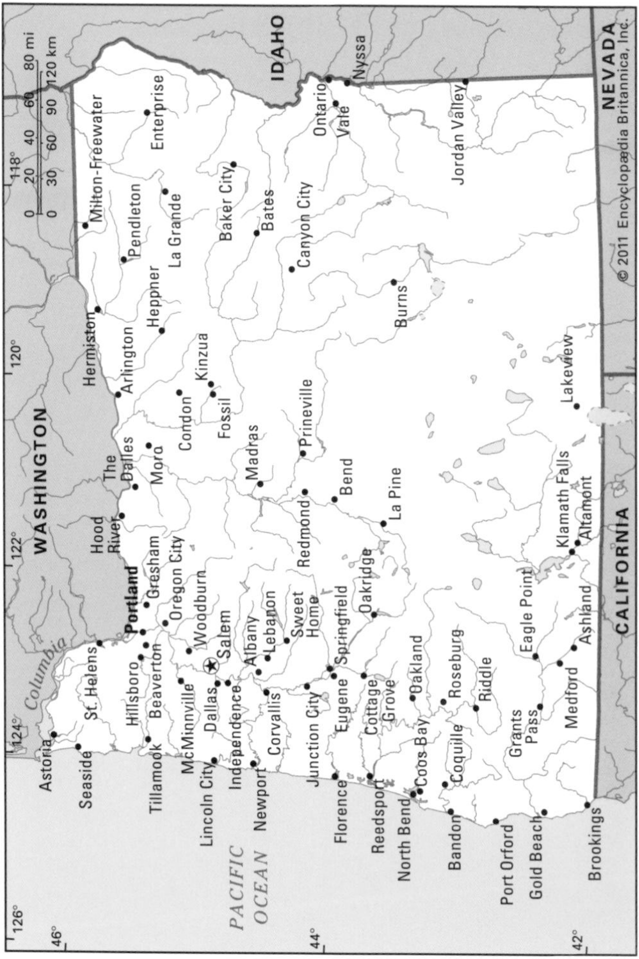
WASHINGTON
IDAHO
NEVADA
CALIFORNIA
PACIFIC OCEAN
Columbia
0 20 40 60 80 mi
0 30 60 90 120 km
118°
120°
122°
124°
126°
46°
44°
42°
Astoria
Seaside
St. Helens
Tillamook
Hillsboro
Beaverton
Portland
Gresham
Oregon City
Hood River
The Dalles
Mora
McMinnville
Woodburn
Salem
Dallas
Lincoln City
Independence
Newport
Corvallis
Albany
Lebanon
Sweet Home
Junction City
Eugene
Springfield
Florence
Reedsport
Cottage Grove
Oakridge
North Bend
Coos Bay
Oakland
Bandon
Coquille
Roseburg
Riddle
Port Orford
Gold Beach
Brookings
Grants Pass
Medford
Ashland
Eagle Point
Klamath Falls
Altamont
Lakeview
La Pine
Bend
Redmond
Prineville
Madras
Fossil
Kinzua
Condon
Arlington
Hermiston
Heppner
Pendleton
Milton-Freewater
La Grande
Enterprise
Baker City
Bates
Canyon City
Burns
Ontario
Vale
Nyssa
Jordan Valley
© 2011 Encyclopædia Britannica, Inc.

PENNSYLVANIA

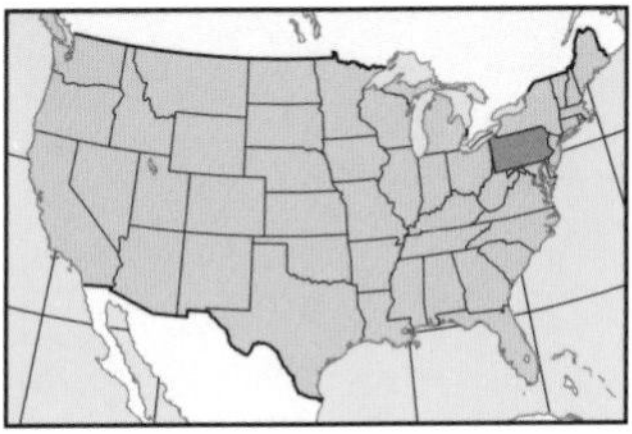

Official name: Commonwealth of Pennsylvania
Nickname: Keystone State
State Capital: Harrisburg
State Flower: Mountain laurel
Motto: Virtue, Liberty, and Independence
Admitted to the Union: 1787; 2nd of the original 13 colonies to ratify the U.S. Constitution
Total area: 46,055 sq. mi. (119,283 sq. km.) (ranks 33rd)
Population (2010): 12,702,379 (ranks 6th)
Chief Cities: Allentown, Erie, Harrisburg, Philadelphia, Pittsburgh
Principal products/industries: Corn, mushrooms, apples, tobacco, wheat, oats, dairy products, coal, iron ore, iron and steel, electrical machinery, apparel, chemicals, transportation equipment
Highest point: Mt. Davis 3213 ft. (980 m.)

State History

French adventurer Étienne Brulé probably first European to visit this area 1615–16, inhabited principally by Delaware, Susquehanna, and Shawnee tribes; first European settlement made by Swedes on Tinicum Island 1643; rights to land granted by British crown to William Penn, who established Quaker colony 1682; first hospital in U.S. established in Philadelphia 1751; Pennsylvania-Maryland boundary line determined 1763–67; Declaration of Independence pronounced in Philadelphia 1776; delegation headed by Benjamin Franklin represented Pennsylvania in Constitutional Convention in Philadelphia 1787; ratified U.S. Constitution Dec. 12, 1787; flood disaster at Johnstown May 31, 1889.

Agriculture and commerce are represented in the coat of arms by the ship and the wheat sheaves, the plow, the wreath of corn and olive, and the horses in harness. The state motto, "Virtue, Liberty, and Independence," is inscribed on the ribbon below the arms.

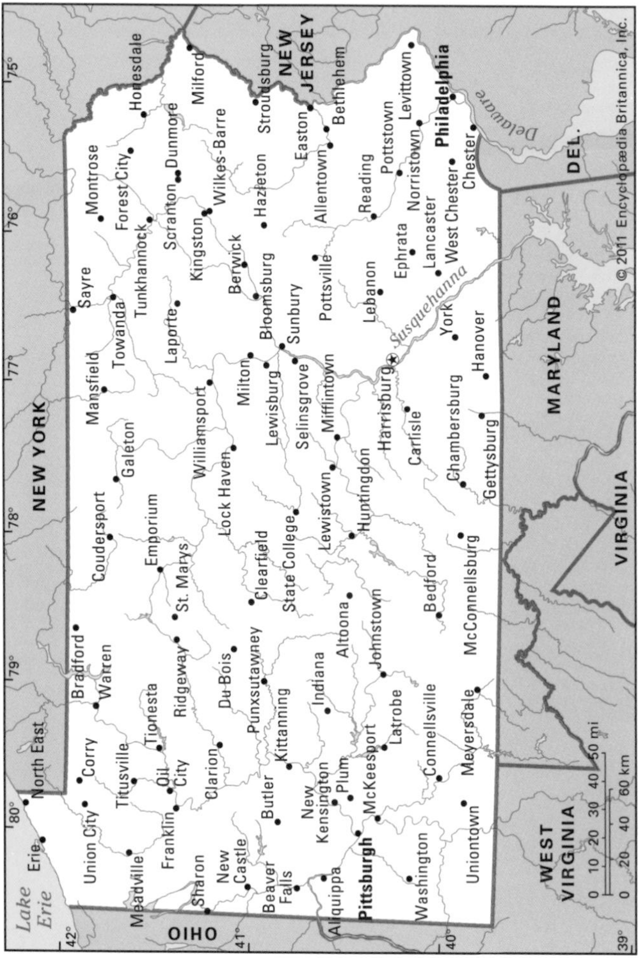
NEW YORK
NEW JERSEY
DEL.
MARYLAND
VIRGINIA
WEST VIRGINIA
OHIO
Lake Erie
Delaware
Susquehanna
75°
76°
77°
78°
79°
80°
42°
41°
40°
39°
Erie
North East
Union City
Corry
Meadville
Titusville
Warren
Bradford
Franklin
Oil City
Tionesta
Sharon
New Castle
Clarion
Ridgeway
Beaver Falls
Butler
Kittanning
Punxsutawney
Du Bois
St. Marys
Emporium
Coudersport
Galeton
Mansfield
Sayre
Towanda
Montrose
Forest City
Tunkhannock
Honesdale
Scranton
Dunmore
Milford
Kingston
Wilkes-Barre
Laporte
Williamsport
Lock Haven
Clearfield
State College
Altoona
Johnstown
Indiana
Latrobe
McKeesport
Plum
New Kensington
Aliquippa
Pittsburgh
Washington
Connellsville
Meyersdale
Uniontown
McConnellsburg
Bedford
Huntingdon
Lewistown
Mifflintown
Selinsgrove
Lewisburg
Milton
Sunbury
Bloomsburg
Berwick
Hazleton
Stroudsburg
Easton
Bethlehem
Allentown
Pottsville
Reading
Pottstown
Norristown
Levittown
Philadelphia
Chester
West Chester
Lancaster
Ephrata
Lebanon
Harrisburg
Carlisle
York
Hanover
Gettysburg
Chambersburg
0 10 20 30 40 50 mi
0 20 40 60 km
© 2011 Encyclopædia Britannica, Inc.

RHODE ISLAND

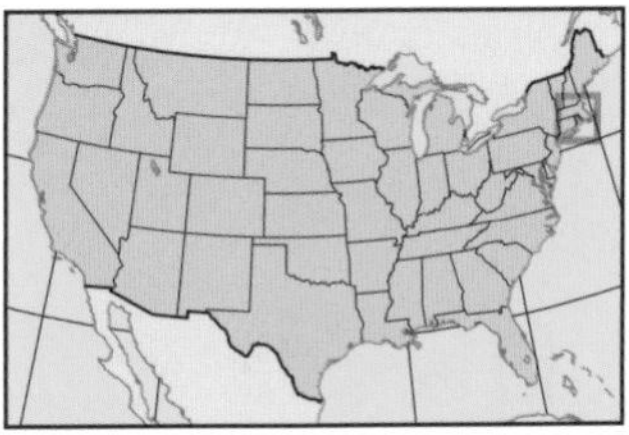

Official name: State of Rhode Island and Providence Plantations
Nicknames: Ocean State, Little Rhody
State Capital: Providence
State Flower: Violet
Motto: Hope
Admitted to the Union: 1790; 13th of the original 13 colonies to ratify the U.S. Constitution
Total area: 1,221 sq. mi. (3,162 sq. km.) (ranks 50th)
Population (2010): 1,052,567 (ranks 43rd)
Chief Cities: Cranston, Newport, Pawtucket, Providence, Warwick
Principal products/industries: Apples, peaches, dairy products, jewelry making, electronics, tourism, historically important textile industry
Highest point: Jerimoth Hill 812 ft. (248 m.)

State History

Originally settled by Narragansett Indians; Narragansett Bay explored by Florentine navigator Giovanni da Verrazano 1524; first permanent nonnative settlement founded by Roger Williams for religious dissenters at Providence 1636; scattered settlements united when charter granted by British King Charles II to Roger Williams 1663; charter provisions continued in effect until Dorr's Rebellion 1842, led by political activist Thomas Dorr, whose attempts to form an alternate government providing for extension of suffrage resulted in new state constitution 1843.

The Rhode Island legislature adopted an anchor for its colonial seal in 1647. The anchor was used on military flags by the time of the American Revolutionary War. The flag's anchor and motto were represented in Rococo style and encircled by stars corresponding to the number of original states in the Union.

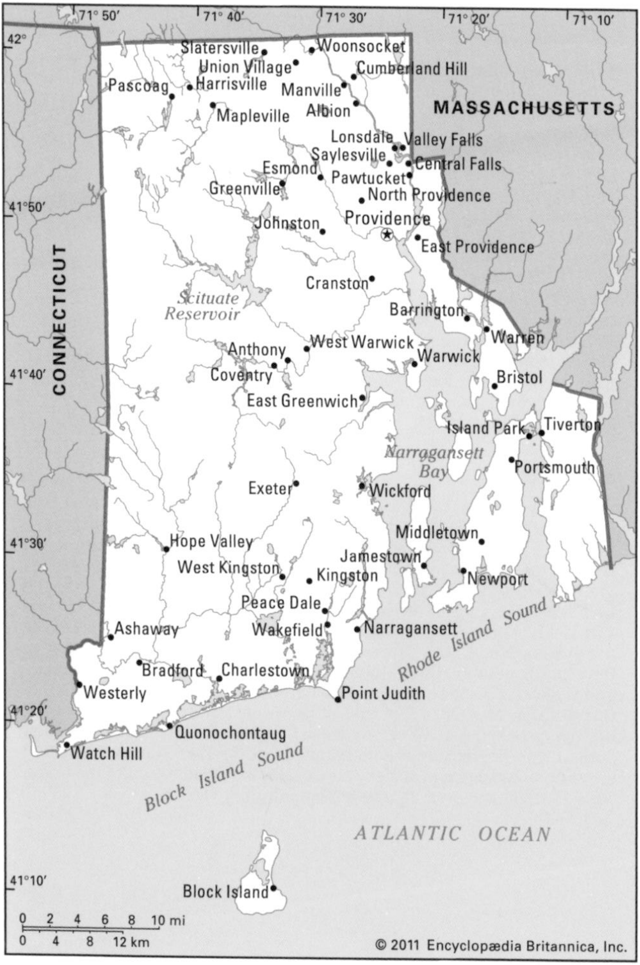

71° 50′
71° 40′
71° 30′
71° 20′
71° 10′
42°
41°50′
41°40′
41°30′
41°20′
41°10′
MASSACHUSETTS
CONNECTICUT
Slatersville
Woonsocket
Union Village
Cumberland Hill
Pascoag
Harrisville
Manville
Mapleville
Albion
Lonsdale
Valley Falls
Saylesville
Central Falls
Esmond
Pawtucket
Greenville
North Providence
Johnston
Providence
East Providence
Cranston
Scituate Reservoir
Barrington
Warren
Anthony
West Warwick
Warwick
Coventry
Bristol
East Greenwich
Island Park
Tiverton
Narragansett Bay
Portsmouth
Exeter
Wickford
Middletown
Hope Valley
Jamestown
West Kingston
Kingston
Newport
Peace Dale
Ashaway
Wakefield
Narragansett
Rhode Island Sound
Bradford
Charlestown
Westerly
Point Judith
Quonochontaug
Watch Hill
Block Island Sound
ATLANTIC OCEAN
Block Island
0 2 4 6 8 10 mi
0 4 8 12 km
© 2011 Encyclopædia Britannica, Inc.

SOUTH CAROLINA

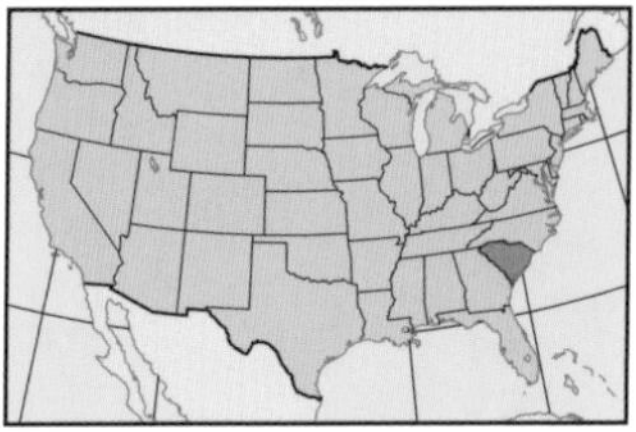

Official name: State of South Carolina
Nickname: Palmetto State
State Capital: Columbia
State Flower: Yellow jessamine
Mottos: Dum Spiro Spero
(While I breathe, I hope)
and Animis Opibusque Parati
(Prepared in Mind and Resources)
Admitted to the Union: 1788; 8th of the original 13 colonies to ratify the U.S. Constitution
Total area: 31,114 sq. mi. (80,585 sq. km.) (ranks 40th)
Population (2010): 4,625,364 (ranks 24th)
Chief Cities: Charleston, Columbia, North Charleston
Principal products/industries: Tobacco, cotton, barley, soybeans, fruit, peanuts, livestock, lumbering, sand, gravel, stone, textiles, chemicals, paper products, cement, clothing, tourism
Highest point: Sassafras Mt. 3560 ft. (1086 m.)

State History

Evidence of Mound Builder inhabitants in western part of state; at time of European contact, inhabited by Siouan, Iroquoian, and Muskogean Indians; coast explored by Spanish 1521; unsuccessful attempts at settlement made by Spanish and French 16th century; included in Carolina grant given 1663 by Charles II to eight noblemen of his court; Charleston founded 1670; English settlements harassed by Spanish and Indians 17th–18th centuries; overthrew proprietary rule 1719 in favor of rule as a crown province 1729; scene of several engagements during American Revolution, notably Kings Mountain, Cowpens, Eutaw Springs, Camden, and Guilford Courthouse; ceded western lands to U.S. 1787; ratified U.S. Constitution May 23, 1788; first state to secede from Union, passing ordinance of secession Dec. 20, 1860; Confederate forces attacked Fort Sumter Apr. 12, 1861, in the initial action of the Civil War; ordinance of secession repealed and slavery abolished 1865; readmitted to the Union June 25, 1868; adopted its present constitution 1895.

On September 13, 1775, a blue flag with a white crescent was raised by anti-British forces at a fort in Charleston Harbor. The fortification was protected by palmetto logs that caused British cannonballs to bounce off. Consequently the palmetto was adopted by South Carolinians as their chief state symbol.

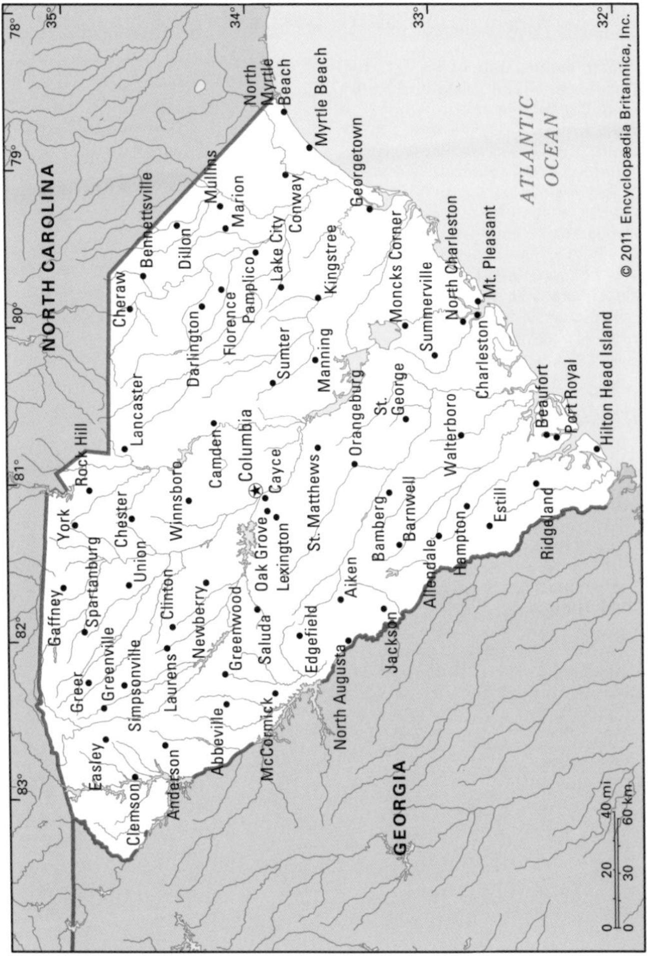
NORTH CAROLINA
GEORGIA
ATLANTIC OCEAN
78°
79°
80°
81°
82°
83°
35°
34°
33°
32°
Rock Hill
Lancaster
Cheraw
Bennettsville
Dillon
Mullins
Marion
North Myrtle Beach
Myrtle Beach
Conway
Georgetown
Lake City
Pamplico
Darlington
Florence
Kingstree
Sumter
Manning
Moncks Corner
Summerville
North Charleston
Mt. Pleasant
Charleston
Camden
Columbia
Cayce
Orangeburg
St. George
Walterboro
Beaufort
Port Royal
Hilton Head Island
York
Chester
Winnsboro
Gaffney
Spartanburg
Union
Clinton
Newberry
Oak Grove
Lexington
St. Matthews
Bamberg
Barnwell
Estill
Ridgeland
Hampton
Allendale
Aiken
Jackson
North Augusta
Edgefield
Saluda
Greenwood
Greenville
Greer
Simpsonville
Laurens
Abbeville
McCormick
Easley
Anderson
Clemson
0 20 40 mi
0 30 60 km
© 2011 Encyclopædia Britannica, Inc.

SOUTH DAKOTA

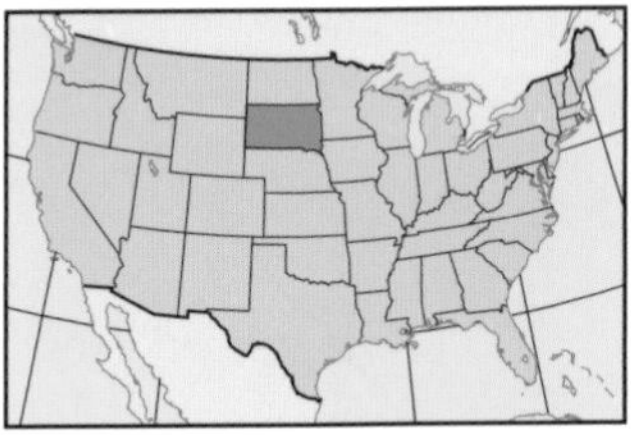

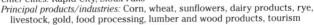

Official name: State of South Dakota
Nickname: Mount Rushmore State
State Capital: Pierre
State Flower: Pasqueflower
Motto: Under God the People Rule
Admitted to the Union: 1889 (40th)
Total area: 77,116 sq. mi. (199,730 sq. km.) (ranks 17th)
Population (2010): 814,180 (ranks 46th)
Chief Cities: Rapid City, Sioux Falls
Principal products/industries: Corn, wheat, sunflowers, dairy products, rye, livestock, gold, food processing, lumber and wood products, tourism
Highest point: Harney Peak 7242 ft. (2209 m.)

State History

Evidence of prehistoric Mound Builders' settlements; at time of European contact, inhabited by several Indian tribes, including especially the Arikara, who soon moved north, and several Dakota tribes; explored somewhat by French in 18th century; included in Louisiana Purchase 1803 and traversed by Lewis and Clark expedition 1804, 1806; fur trade with Indians conducted throughout 19th century until outbreak of Civil War; first permanent European settlement founded 1817, on future site of Fort Pierre, as a trading post; after several attempts, organized as part of Dakota Territory 1861 with capital at Yankton; latter 19th century characterized by conflict with Indians, several insect plagues, and Black Hills gold rush (discovery 1874); admitted to Union Nov. 2, 1889 upon division of Dakota Territory into two states; Pierre selected as state capital 1889; state constitution dates from 1889.

The South Dakota seal is represented over a sun in such a way that only the sun's rays are visible. The seal repeats the name of the state and the date of admission to the Union. Around the seal is the state name and nickname. The seal depicts a farmer, cattle, crops, a smelting furnace, and a steamship.

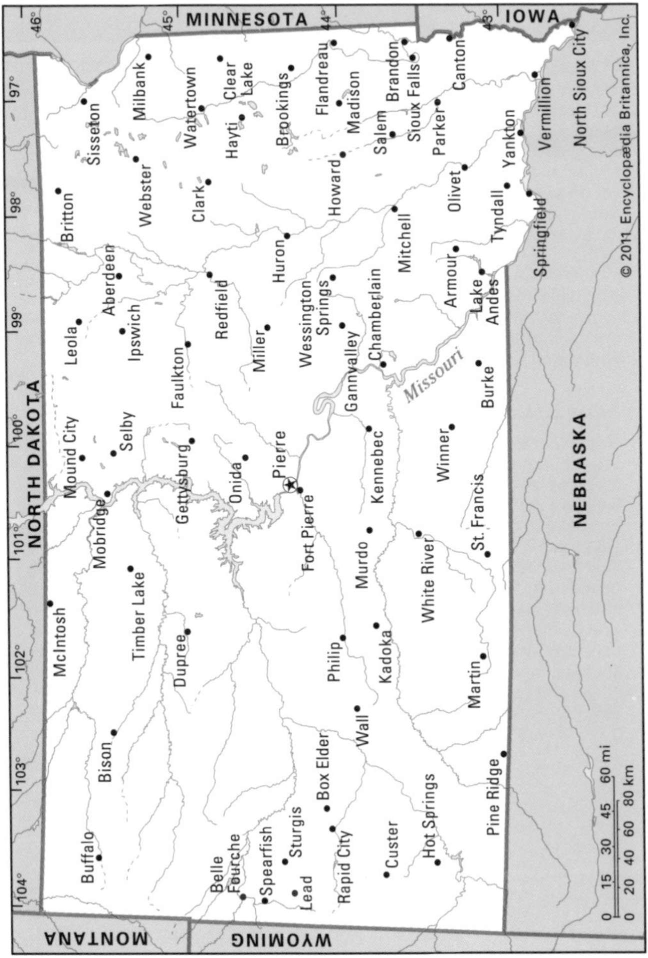

NORTH DAKOTA
MINNESOTA
IOWA
NEBRASKA
WYOMING
MONTANA
Missouri
46°
45°
44°
43°
97°
98°
99°
100°
101°
102°
103°
104°
Britton
Sisseton
Milbank
Webster
Watertown
Clear Lake
Hayti
Clark
Brookings
Flandreau
Madison
Howard
Brandon
Sioux Falls
Salem
Canton
Parker
Huron
Aberdeen
Leola
Ipswich
Redfield
Faulkton
Miller
Wessington Springs
Chamberlain
Mitchell
Olivet
Yankton
Vermillion
North Sioux City
Tyndall
Springfield
Armour
Lake Andes
Gannvalley
Burke
Mound City
Selby
Gettysburg
Onida
Pierre
Fort Pierre
Kennebec
Winner
Mobridge
St. Francis
Timber Lake
Murdo
White River
McIntosh
Dupree
Philip
Kadoka
Martin
Bison
Wall
Pine Ridge
Buffalo
Box Elder
Hot Springs
Custer
Rapid City
Sturgis
Spearfish
Belle Fourche
Lead
0 15 30 45 60 mi
0 20 40 60 80 km
© 2011 Encyclopædia Britannica, Inc.

TENNESSEE

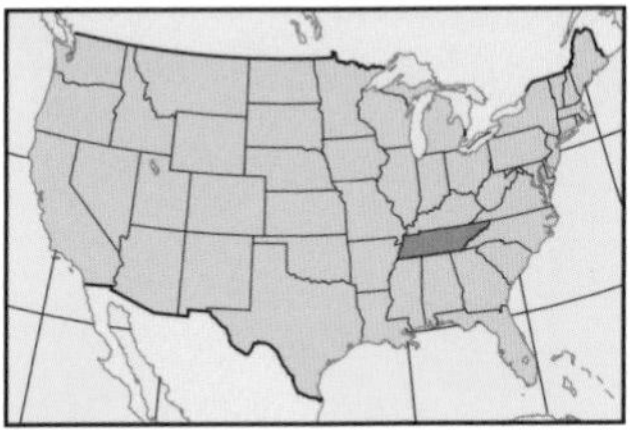

Official name: State of Tennessee
Nickname: Volunteer State
State Capital: Nashville
State Flower: Iris
Motto: Agriculture and Commerce
Admitted to the Union: 1796 (16th)
Total area: 42,145 sq. mi. (109,155 sq. km.) (ranks 36th)
Population (2010): 6,346,105 (ranks 17th)
Chief Cities: Chattanooga, Clarksville, Knoxville, Memphis, Murfreeboro, Nashville
Principal products/industries: Cotton, tobacco, soybeans, corn, livestock, coal, phosphate rock, chemicals, textiles, cement, electrical machinery
Highest point: Clingmans Dome 6643 ft. (2026 m.)

State History

Original inhabitants included Chicksaw, Cherokee, and Shawnee, among others; region visited by Spanish explorer Hernando de Soto c. 1540; included in British charter of Carolina and in French Louisiana claim late 17th century; claim to region ceded by France to Great Britain after French and Indian War; first permanent settlements made in Watauga Valley c. 1770; acknowledged by Great Britain as a part of United States after Revolutionary War; temporary state of Franklin formed c. 1784; included in Territory South of the Ohio River after North Carolina relinquished claims 1790; admitted to Union with present boundaries June 1, 1796; passed ordinance of secession June 8, 1861; scene of battles in Civil War, notably Shiloh, Chattanooga, Stones River, Nashville; slavery abolished and ordinance of secession declared null and void 1865; first of seceding states to be reorganized and readmitted to Union (July 24, 1866). Constitution dates from 1870.

The current flag design features three stripes and three stars. These were said by the designer to refer to "the three grand divisions of the State," but they have also been said to represent the three presidents who lived in Tennessee (Andrew Jackson, James Polk, and Andrew Johnson).

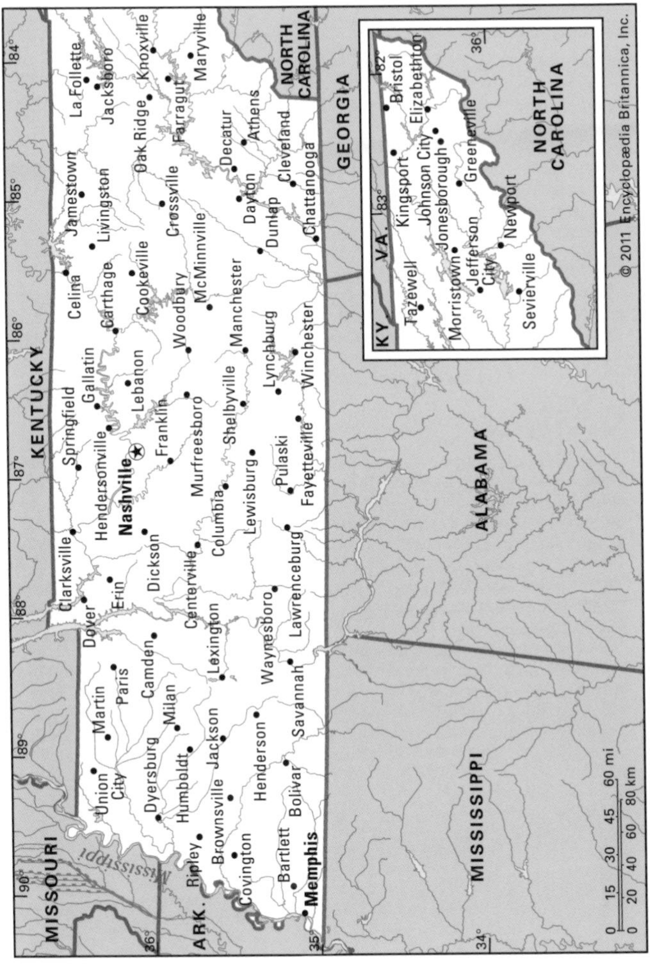
KENTUCKY
MISSOURI
ARK.
MISSISSIPPI
ALABAMA
GEORGIA
NORTH CAROLINA
Mississippi
Nashville
Memphis
Knoxville
Chattanooga
Clarksville
Springfield
Hendersonville
Gallatin
Lebanon
Franklin
Murfreesboro
Columbia
Shelbyville
Lewisburg
Pulaski
Fayetteville
Lynchburg
Winchester
Manchester
Woodbury
McMinnville
Cookeville
Carthage
Celina
Livingston
Jamestown
Crossville
Dayton
Dunlap
Cleveland
Decatur
Athens
Oak Ridge
Farragut
Maryville
La Follette
Jacksboro
Dickson
Erin
Dover
Centerville
Lawrenceburg
Waynesboro
Lexington
Camden
Paris
Martin
Union City
Dyersburg
Milan
Humboldt
Jackson
Henderson
Savannah
Bolivar
Brownsville
Ripley
Covington
Bartlett
KY.
VA.
Bristol
Kingsport
Elizabethton
Johnson City
Jonesborough
Greeneville
Tazewell
Morristown
Jefferson City
Newport
Sevierville
84°
85°
86°
87°
88°
89°
90°
82°
83°
36°
35°
34°
0 15 30 45 60 mi
0 20 40 60 80 km
© 2011 Encyclopædia Britannica, Inc.

TEXAS

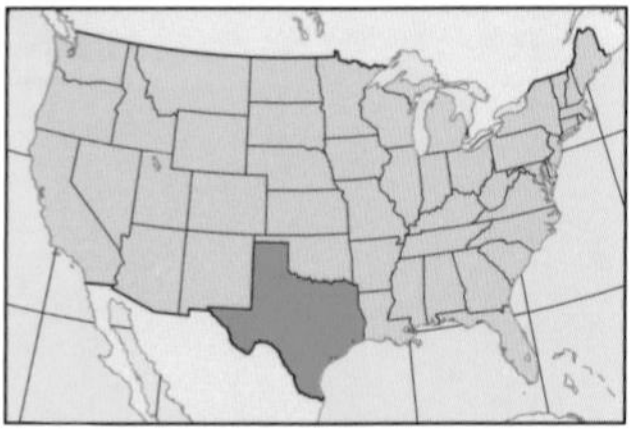

Official name: State of Texas
Nickname: Lone Star State
Capital: Austin
State flower: Bluebonnet
Motto: Friendship
Admitted to the Union: 1845 (28th)
Total area: 266,833 sq. mi. (691,094 sq. km.) (ranks 2nd)
Population (2010): 25,145,561 (ranks 2nd)
Chief cities: Arlington, Austin, Corpus Christi, Dallas, El Paso, Fort Worth, Houston, Plano, San Antonio
Principal products/industries: Cotton, apples, greenhouse and nursery products, rice, sorghum grain, wheat, livestock, oil, natural gas, sulfur, chemicals, electronics, food processing
Highest point: Guadalupe Peak 8749 ft. (2668 m.)

State History

Originally inhabited by Indians including Apaches, several tribes of the Caddo group, and others; explored by Spaniards early 16th–late 17th centuries; French explorer René-Robert Cavelier, Sieur de La Salle, attempted settlement at Matagorda Bay 1685, laying basis for French claim to region as part of Louisiana; effective Spanish occupation began c. 1700; U.S. acquired French claim in Louisiana Purchase 1803; U.S. claim to Texas relinquished by treaty with Spain 1819; became part of Mexico after Mexico gained independence from Spain 1821; Declaration of Independence from Mexico Mar. 1836; Texan army under commander Sam Houston won decisive battle against Mexican forces at San Jacinto Apr. 1836, gaining independence for the Republic of Texas; sought annexation to U.S. and was admitted to Union Dec. 29, 1845; boundary with Mexico along the Rio Grande fixed after Mexican War by Treaty of Guadalupe Hidalgo 1848; passed ordinance of secession Feb. 1, 1861; readmitted to Union Mar. 30, 1870; adopted constitution 1876.

The first official (though nonnational) Texas flag was based on the green-white-red vertical tricolor of Mexico. The present state flag was originally adopted in 1839 as the second national flag of the Republic of Texas. There was no change when Texas became a state of the United States in 1845.

© 2011 Encyclopædia Britannica, Inc.

UTAH

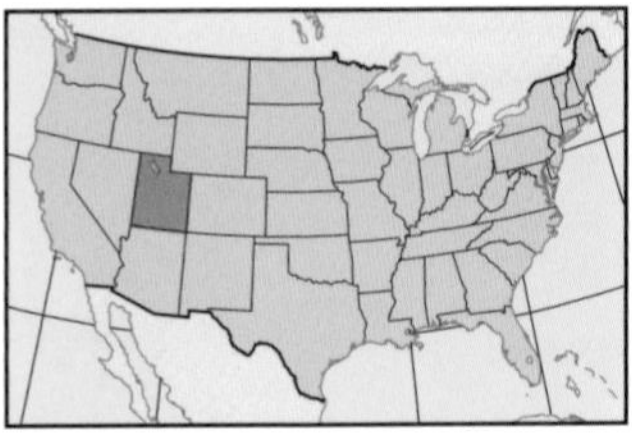

Official name: State of Utah
Nickname: Beehive State
State Capital: Salt Lake City
State Flower: Sego lily
Motto: Industry
Admitted to the Union: 1896 (45th)
Total area: 84,897 sq. mi. (219,882 sq. km.) (ranks 13th)
Population (2010): 2,763,885 (ranks 34th)
Chief Cities: Ogden, Orem, Provo, Salt Lake City, Sandy, West Jordan, West Valley City
Principal products/industries: Peaches, cherries, onions, wheat, hay, livestock, turkeys, dairy products, copper, gold, silver, molybdenum, high-tech products, aerospace products, food products, tourism
Highest point: Kings Peak 13,528 ft. (4126 m.)

State History

Originally inhabited by American Indian peoples including the Shoshoni, Ute, and Paiute. Possibly explored by Spaniards sent out by explorer Francisco Vásquez de Coronado 1540; visited by Spanish missionaries 1776; Great Salt Lake discovered by American pioneer James Bridger 1824; acquired by U.S. from Mexico in Treaty of Guadalupe Hidalgo 1848; first permanent white settlers were Mormons, led to valley of Great Salt Lake by Brigham Young, head of Mormon Church, in 1847; part of Utah Territory organized 1850; territory reduced to area of present state by 1868; conflict between Mormon authorities and U.S. government, known as Utah War (1857–58); admitted to Union Jan. 4, 1896.

The design carries the state seal, which features a bald eagle over a beehive and crossed U.S. flags to indicate the protection of the U.S. and Utah's loyalty to the nation. The dates 1847 and 1896 refer to the settlement of the original Mormon community at Salt Lake City and the achievement of statehood.

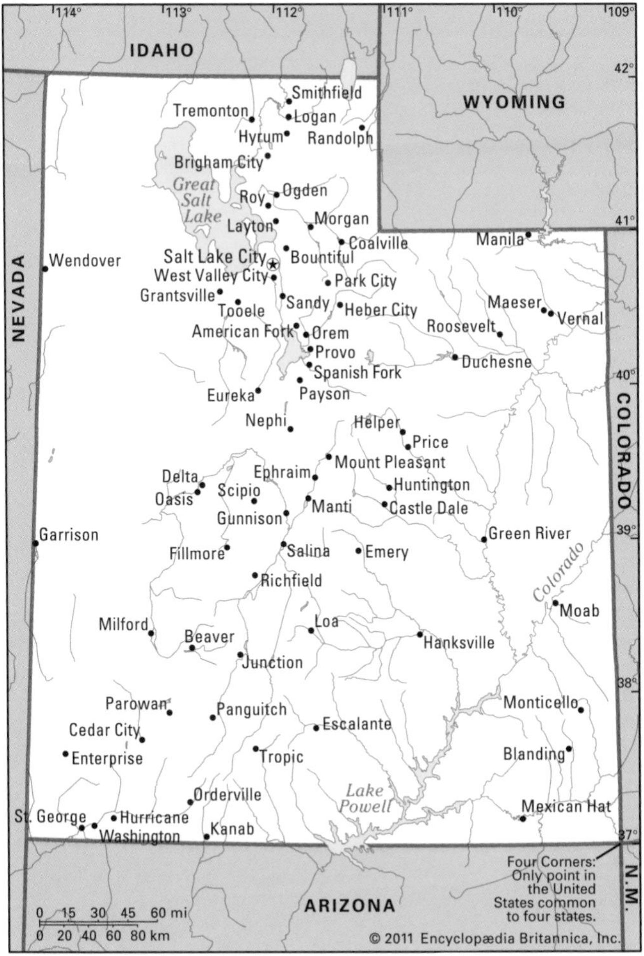
114°
113°
112°
111°
110°
109°
42°
41°
40°
39°
38°
37°
IDAHO
WYOMING
NEVADA
COLORADO
ARIZONA
N.M.
Smithfield
Tremonton
Logan
Hyrum
Randolph
Brigham City
Great Salt Lake
Ogden
Roy
Morgan
Layton
Coalville
Manila
Wendover
Salt Lake City
Bountiful
West Valley City
Park City
Grantsville
Tooele
Sandy
Heber City
Maeser
Vernal
Roosevelt
American Fork
Orem
Provo
Duchesne
Spanish Fork
Eureka
Payson
Nephi
Helper
Price
Mount Pleasant
Ephraim
Delta
Huntington
Scipio
Oasis
Manti
Castle Dale
Gunnison
Garrison
Green River
Fillmore
Salina
Emery
Colorado
Richfield
Moab
Milford
Loa
Beaver
Hanksville
Junction
Monticello
Parowan
Panguitch
Escalante
Cedar City
Enterprise
Tropic
Blanding
Lake Powell
Orderville
Mexican Hat
St. George
Hurricane
Washington
Kanab
Four Corners: Only point in the United States common to four states.
0 15 30 45 60 mi
0 20 40 60 80 km
© 2011 Encyclopædia Britannica, Inc.

VERMONT

Official name: State of Vermont
Nickname: Green Mountain State
State Capital: Montpelier
State Flower: Red clover
Motto: Freedom and Unity
Admitted to the Union: 1791 (14th)
Total area: 9,617 sq. mi. (24,908 sq. km.) (ranks 44th)
Population (2010): 625,741 (ranks 49th)
Chief Cities/Towns: Burlington, Rutland
Principal products/industries: Dairy products, maple syrup, apples, greenhouse and nursery products, food products, marble, talc, metalworking, textiles, furniture, electronics, fabricated metals, paper goods, tourism
Highest point: Mt. Mansfield 4393 ft. (1340 m.)

State History

Inhabited originally by American Indians, the Abnaki; explored 1609 by French expedition led by Samuel de Champlain, who discovered the lake now bearing his name; temporary settlement by French at Fort Ste. Anne on Isle La Motte 1666; English established Fort Dummer near site of present Brattleboro 1724; disputes arose between New Hampshire and New York concerning jurisdiction of area, New Hampshire having awarded grants to settlers; Green Mountain Boys organized by Ethan Allen 1770 to repel encroachers from west, New York having won its appeal to crown for rights to settle; when Revolutionary War intervened, Allen and Green Mountain Boys fighting for colonies captured Fort Ticonderoga from British 1775; declared itself independent republic 1777; claims to the region later dropped by New Hampshire and New York; admitted to Union Mar. 4, 1791; present constitution adopted 1793 (since amended).

The flag design has the Vermont coat of arms which shows a pastoral scene with the Green Mountains in the background, a large pine tree in the foreground, wheat sheaves, and a cow. The inscription "Freedom and Unity," the word "Vermont," a wreath, and the head of a deer as the crest complete the design.

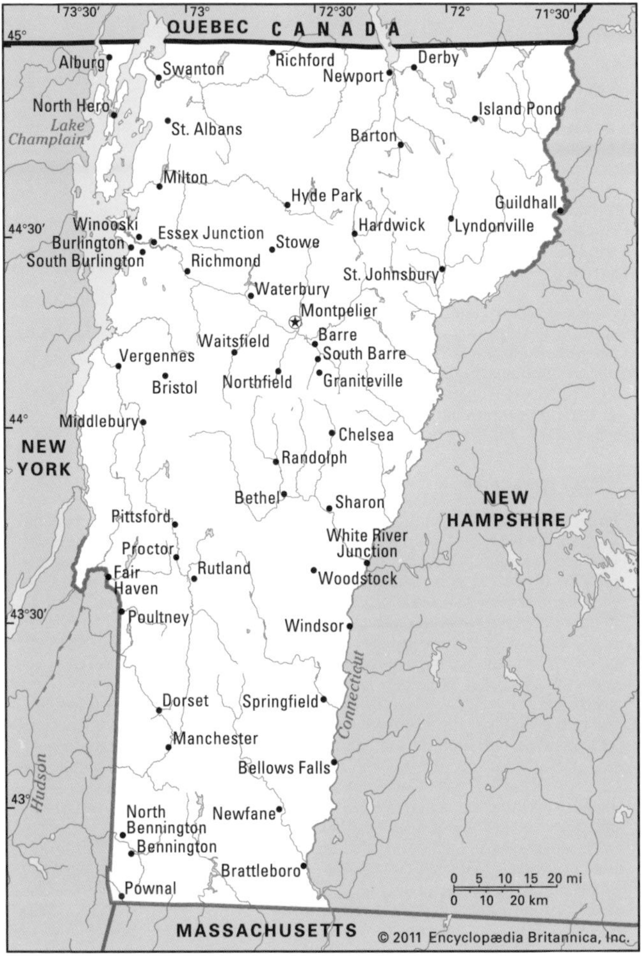
73°30′
73°
72°30′
72°
71°30′
45°
44°30′
44°
43°30′
43°
QUEBEC
CANADA
Alburg
Swanton
Richford
Newport
Derby
North Hero
Lake Champlain
St. Albans
Island Pond
Barton
Milton
Hyde Park
Guildhall
Winooski
Essex Junction
Hardwick
Lyndonville
Burlington
South Burlington
Stowe
Richmond
St. Johnsbury
Waterbury
Montpelier
Barre
South Barre
Waitsfield
Vergennes
Bristol
Northfield
Graniteville
Middlebury
Chelsea
NEW YORK
Randolph
Bethel
Sharon
NEW HAMPSHIRE
Pittsford
Proctor
White River Junction
Rutland
Fair Haven
Woodstock
Poultney
Windsor
Connecticut
Dorset
Springfield
Manchester
Bellows Falls
Hudson
North Bennington
Newfane
Bennington
Brattleboro
Pownal
0 5 10 15 20 mi
0 10 20 km
MASSACHUSETTS
© 2011 Encyclopædia Britannica, Inc.

VIRGINIA

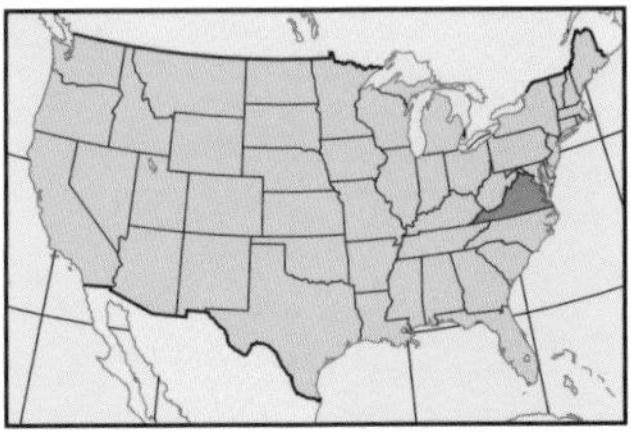

Official name: Commonwealth of Virginia
Nickname: Old Dominion
State Capital: Richmond
State Flower: Flowering dogwood
Motto: Sic Semper Tyrannis (Thus Always to Tyrants)
Admitted to the Union: 1788; 10th of the original 13 colonies to ratify the U.S. Constitution
Total area: 40,599 sq. mi. (105,151 sq. km.) (ranks 35th)
Population (2010): 8,001,024 (ranks 12th)
Chief Cities: Alexandria, Arlington, Chesapeake, Hampton, Newport News, Norfolk, Richmond, Virginia Beach
Principal products/industries: Dairy products, tobacco, vegetables, livestock, coal, chemicals, food products, transportation equipment, electrical equipment, textiles, federal government employment
Highest point: Mt. Rogers 5729 ft. (1747 m.)

State History

Originally inhabited by American Indians when futile attempts were made by English navigator Sir Walter Raleigh to found settlements 1584–87; first royal charter to London (Virginia) Company followed by first permanent settlement, made by colonists sent out by this company, at Jamestown 1607; first popular assembly in America convened 1619; colony finally thrived primarily on successful tobacco cultivation introduced to settlers by Indians; one of the first colonies to express resistance to the Stamp Act and other British taxes 1765; active in movement for independence during the Revolution; scene of surrender of British Lord Charles Cornwallis at Yorktown 1781; northwestern part of western lands ceded to U.S. 1784, southern part admitted to the Union as the state of Kentucky 1792; ratified the U.S. Constitution June 25, 1788; although slavery had been outlawed, it continued to be important part of economy; tensions heightened between slaveholders and abolitionists during first half of 19th century; passed ordinance of secession 1861; western counties remained loyal to the Union, separated from Virginia 1861 and admitted to the Union as the state of West Virginia 1863; scene of many battles of the Civil War, among them Bull Run (first and second), Fair Oaks, Chancellorsville, Fredericksburg, the Wilderness, Cold Harbor, and many engagements in Shenandoah Valley; readmitted to Union Jan. 26, 1870. New constitution promulgated 1902, revised 1971.

The design of the seal features a woman personifying virtue and dressed as an Amazon. She wears a helmet and holds a spear and sword above the Latin motto "Sic semper tyrannis" ("Thus always to tyrants"). She is standing on the prostrate figure of a fallen king, his crown lying to one side.

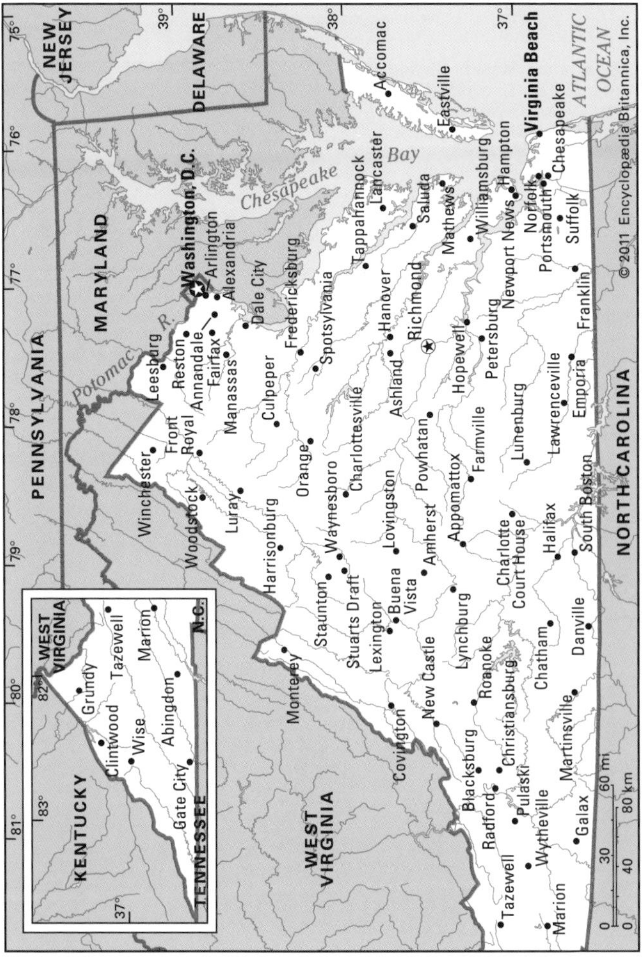
PENNSYLVANIA
NEW JERSEY
DELAWARE
MARYLAND
Washington, D.C.
Chesapeake Bay
Potomac R.
ATLANTIC OCEAN
WEST VIRGINIA
NORTH CAROLINA
KENTUCKY
TENNESSEE
N.C.
75°
76°
77°
78°
79°
80°
81°
82°
83°
39°
38°
37°
Accomac
Eastville
Virginia Beach
Chesapeake
Norfolk
Portsmouth
Suffolk
Hampton
Newport News
Williamsburg
Mathews
Saluda
Lancaster
Tappahannock
Arlington
Alexandria
Dale City
Fredericksburg
Spotsylvania
Hanover
Richmond
Ashland
Hopewell
Petersburg
Franklin
Emporia
Lawrenceville
Lunenburg
Farmville
Powhatan
Charlottesville
Culpeper
Manassas
Fairfax
Annandale
Reston
Leesburg
Front Royal
Winchester
Woodstock
Luray
Orange
Harrisonburg
Waynesboro
Staunton
Stuarts Draft
Lovingston
Amherst
Appomattox
Charlotte Court House
South Boston
Halifax
Buena Vista
Lexington
Monterey
Lynchburg
Chatham
Danville
Covington
New Castle
Roanoke
Christiansburg
Martinsville
Blacksburg
Radford
Pulaski
Wytheville
Galax
Tazewell
Marion
Grundy
Clintwood
Wise
Abingdon
Gate City
0 30 60 mi
0 40 80 km
© 2011 Encyclopædia Britannica, Inc.

WASHINGTON

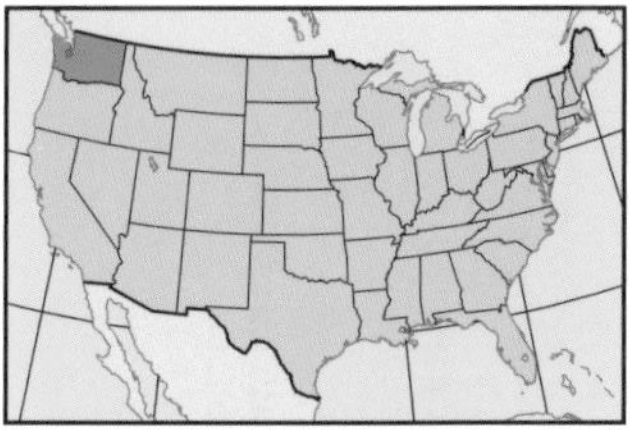

Official name: State of Washington
Nickname: Evergreen State
State Capital: Olympia
State Flower: Rhododendron
Motto: Alki (By and By)
Admitted to the Union: 1889 (42nd)
Total area: 68,095 sq. mi. (176,365 sq. km.) (ranks 18th)
Population (2010): 6,724,540 (ranks 13th)
Chief Cities: Bellevue, Everett, Seattle, Spokane, Tacoma, Vancouver
Principal products/industries: Wheat, fruit, dairy products, fishing, zinc, lead, gravel, aircraft and other transportation equipment, lumber, chemicals
Highest point: Mt. Rainier 14,410 ft. (4395 m.)

State History

Area inhabited by Pacific coast Indians when region visited by Spanish, Russian, British, and French explorers 1543–1792 (short-lived settlement 1791 at Neah Bay); explored by Lewis and Clark, who sailed down Columbia River 1805; part of Oregon Country; occupied jointly by Great Britain and U.S. 1818–46; first permanent settlement at Tumwater 1845; by treaty with Great Britain 1846 northern boundary set at 49th parallel; part of Oregon Territory 1848; settlement at Seattle 1851, at Tacoma 1852; became part of Washington Territory 1853; territory reduced to area of present state 1863; admitted to Union as state Nov. 11, 1889.

The flag contains the state seal with the name of the state, the date of its admission to the Union, and a bust of George Washington. In 1915 a background of green for the flag of the "Evergreen State" was chosen.

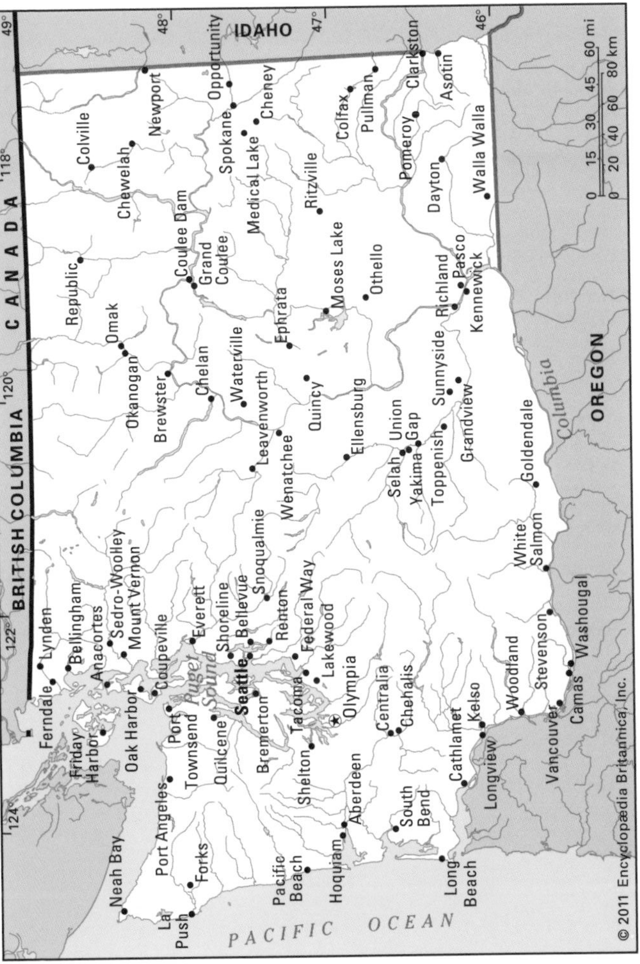
BRITISH COLUMBIA
CANADA
IDAHO
OREGON
PACIFIC OCEAN
Puget Sound
Columbia
49°
48°
47°
46°
124°
122°
120°
118°
Colville
Newport
Chewelah
Republic
Omak
Okanogan
Brewster
Chelan
Coulee Dam
Grand Coulee
Opportunity
Spokane
Cheney
Medical Lake
Colfax
Pullman
Clarkston
Asotin
Pomeroy
Dayton
Walla Walla
Ritzville
Moses Lake
Othello
Ephrata
Waterville
Quincy
Leavenworth
Wenatchee
Ellensburg
Selah
Union Gap
Yakima
Toppenish
Sunnyside
Grandview
Richland
Pasco
Kennewick
Goldendale
White Salmon
Washougal
Stevenson
Camas
Vancouver
Woodland
Kelso
Longview
Cathlamet
Long Beach
South Bend
Centralia
Chehalis
Olympia
Lakewood
Tacoma
Federal Way
Renton
Snoqualmie
Bellevue
Shoreline
Seattle
Everett
Bremerton
Shelton
Aberdeen
Hoquiam
Pacific Beach
Quilcene
Port Townsend
Port Angeles
Forks
La Push
Neah Bay
Oak Harbor
Coupeville
Mount Vernon
Sedro-Woolley
Anacortes
Friday Harbor
Ferndale
Bellingham
Lynden
0 15 30 45 60 mi
0 20 40 60 80 km
© 2011 Encyclopædia Britannica, Inc.

WEST VIRGINIA

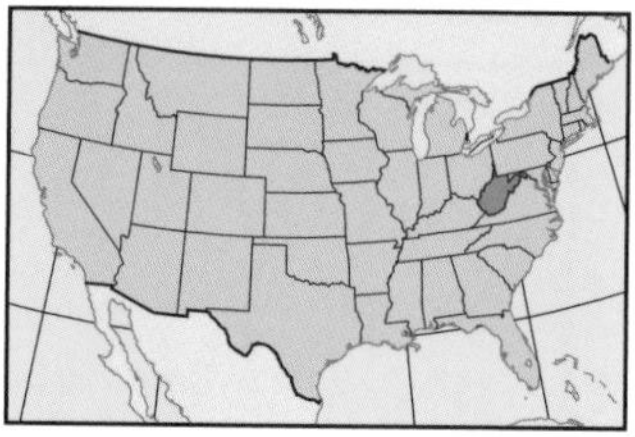

Official name: State of West Virginia
Nickname: Mountain State
State Capital: Charleston
State Flower: Great laurel
Motto: Montani Semper Liberi (Mountaineers Are Always Free)
Admitted to the Union: 1863 (35th)
Total area: 24,230 sq. mi. (62,755 sq. km.) (ranks 41st)
Population (2010): 1,852,994 (ranks 37th)
Chief Cities: Charleston, Huntington, Morgantown
Principal products/industries: Corn, tobacco, apples, dairy products, cattle, coal, stone, primary metals, chemicals, automobile parts, recreation
Highest point: Spruce Knob 4861 ft. (1483 m.)

State History

Inhabited originally by Mound Builders and later by other American Indian peoples; European arrival 17th–18th centuries brought conflicts among French, British, and Indians; although part of Virginia, rugged terrain restricted settlement; after American Revolution, concerns of inhabitants who were less likely to have slaves differed from those in eastern Virginia; dissatisfaction with Virginia government grew, as did sentiment for separation from eastern part of state; with outbreak of Civil War, residents from western Virginia voted against ordinance of secession May 1861; government loyal to U.S. federal government organized at Wheeling June 1861; population voted to create new state 1861 and a state constitution ratified 1862; admitted to Union June 20, 1863; state constitution adopted 1872 (since amended).

Last modified in 1929, West Virginia's flag shows a farmer, a miner and a rock with the date of statehood, June 20, 1863. The motto, "Mountaineers are always free," refers to the secession of the citizens of the mountains of western Virginia in 1861 when slave-holding Virginia joined the Confederacy.

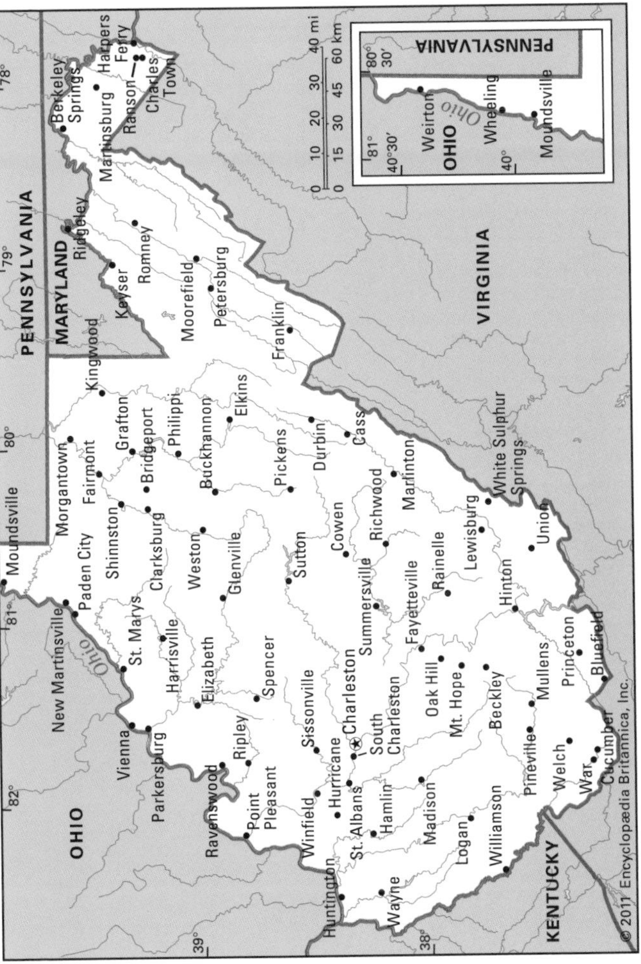
PENNSYLVANIA
MARYLAND
OHIO
VIRGINIA
KENTUCKY
Ohio
78°
79°
80°
81°
82°
39°
38°
0 10 20 30 40 mi
0 15 30 45 60 km
Berkeley Springs
Harpers Ferry
Martinsburg
Ranson
Charles Town
Ridgeley
Romney
Keyser
Moorefield
Petersburg
Franklin
Kingwood
Morgantown
Fairmont
Grafton
Bridgeport
Philippi
Buckhannon
Elkins
Pickens
Durbin
Cass
Marlinton
Richwood
Moundsville
Paden City
Shinnston
Clarksburg
Weston
Glenville
Sutton
Cowen
Summersville
Rainelle
Lewisburg
White Sulphur Springs
Union
New Martinsville
St. Marys
Harrisville
Elizabeth
Spencer
Sissonville
Charleston
South Charleston
Fayetteville
Oak Hill
Mt. Hope
Beckley
Hinton
Mullens
Princeton
Bluefield
Vienna
Parkersburg
Ravenswood
Ripley
Point Pleasant
Winfield
Hurricane
St. Albans
Hamlin
Madison
Logan
Williamson
Pineville
Welch
War
Cucumber
Huntington
Wayne
80° 30′
81°
40°30′
40°
Weirton
Wheeling
Moundsville
© 2011 Encyclopædia Britannica, Inc.

WISCONSIN

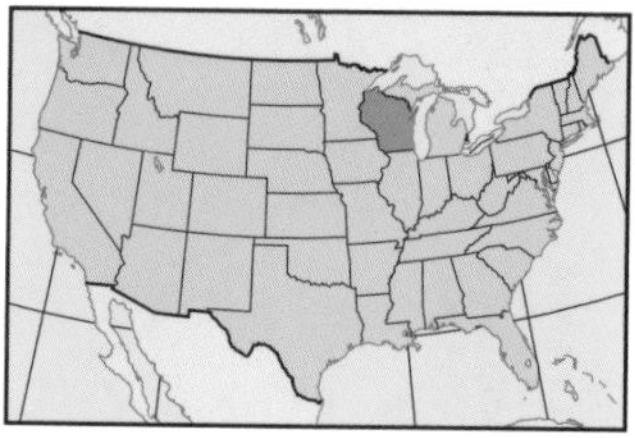

Official name: State of Wisconsin
Nickname: Badger State (unofficial)
State Capital: Madison
State Flower: Violet
Motto: Forward
Admitted to the Union: 1848 (30th)
Total area: 65,496 sq. mi. (169,634 sq. km.) (ranks 23rd)
Population (2010): 5,686,986 (ranks 20th)
Chief Cities: Green Bay, Kenosha, Madison, Milwaukee, Racine
Principal products/industries: Dairy products, corn, cranberries, honey, maple syrup, potatoes, strawberries, livestock, machinery, paper products, metal products, recreation
Highest point: Timms Hill 1951 ft. (595 m.)

State History

Originally inhabited by prehistoric Mound Builders; by time of European arrival, several different Indian tribes were inhabiting the region; area visited by French explorer Jean Nicolet 1634; first permanent European settlement 1717; French settlement at Green Bay 1745; throughout 18th century some Indian tribes sided with French while others sided with English, provoking general unrest; French claim ceded to Great Britain 1763 after French and Indian War; recognized by Great Britain as part of U.S. 1783; claims relinquished during 1780s by Virginia, Massachusetts, and Connecticut; part of Northwest Territory 1787, Indiana Territory 1800, Illinois Territory 1809, and Michigan Territory 1818; conflicts between Indians and settlers continued into 19th century culminating in Black Hawk War 1832, in which Indians suffered massacre; included in Wisconsin Territory 1836; admitted to Union May 29, 1848; constitution ratified 1848 (since amended).

The flag features the U.S. motto and national shield in the center, surrounded by symbols of typical 19th-century occupations—farming, mining, manufacturing, and shipping. A miner and sailor serve as supporters to the shield, above which appears a badger as a crest honoring "the Badger State," a nickname referring to early miners.

93°
92°
91°
90°
89°
88°
87°
47°
46°
45°
44°
43°
42°
MINNESOTA
Lake Superior
MICHIGAN
Washburn
Superior
Ashland
Hurley
Hayward
Eagle River
Florence
Grantsburg
Shell Lake
Phillips
Rhinelander
Crandon
Balsam Lake
Rice Lake
Ladysmith
Barron
Merrill
Antigo
Medford
Peshtigo
Marinette
Sturgeon Bay
New Richmond
Wausau
Keshena
Oconto
Hudson
Chippewa Falls
Green Bay
Menomonie
Eau Claire
Marshfield
Shawano
Ellsworth
Algoma
Durand
Neillsville
Wisconsin Rapids
Stevens Point
Green Bay
Kewaunee
Plover
De Pere
Alma
Whitehall
Appleton
Kaukauna
Two Rivers
Mississippi River
Black River Falls
Neenah
Tomah
Wautoma
Oshkosh
Manitowoc
Sparta
Berlin
Ripon
Fond du Lac
Sheboygan
MINNESOTA
La Crosse
Mauston
Wisconsin Dells
Plymouth
Waupun
Viroqua
Reedsburg
Portage
West Bend
Beaver Dam
Port Washington
Baraboo
Columbus
Richland Center
Watertown
Menomonee Falls
Spring Green
Madison
Milwaukee
Waukesha
Prairie du Chien
Dodgeville
Jefferson
West Allis
Stoughton
Whitewater
IOWA
Lancaster
Platteville
Janesville
Elkhorn
Racine
Monroe
Beloit
Lake Geneva
Kenosha
Lake Michigan
ILLINOIS
0 40 80 mi
0 50 100 km
© 2011 Encyclopædia Britannica, Inc.

WYOMING

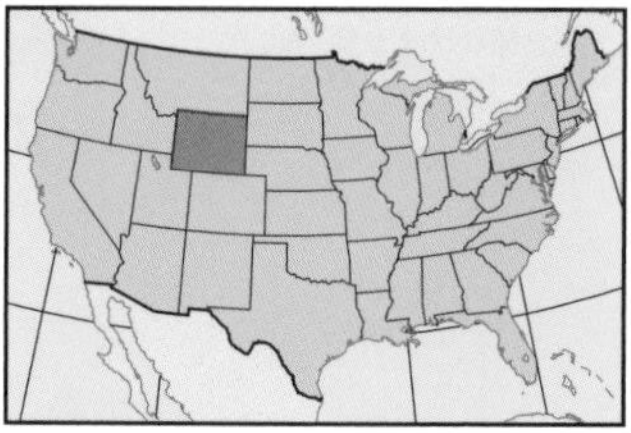

Official name: State of Wyoming
Nicknames: Equality State, Cowboy State
State Capital: Cheyenne
State Flower: Indian paintbrush
Motto: Equal Rights
Admitted to the Union: 1890 (44th)
Total area: 97,812 sq. mi. (253,332 sq. km.) (ranks 10th)
Population (2010): 563,626 (ranks 50th)
Chief Cities: Casper, Cheyenne, Laramie
Principal products/industries: Sugar beets, beans, barley, hay, wheat, livestock, oil, natural gas, uranium, coal, oil refining, lumber, tourism
Highest point: Gannett Peak 13,804 ft. (4210 m.)

State History

Inhabited by Plains Indians when first visited by white explorers during 18th century; originally a part of Louisiana region claimed by France; greater part acquired by U.S. in Louisiana Purchase 1803; remainder acquired with annexation of Texas 1845, British cession of Oregon Country 1846, and cession of Mexican territory to U.S. 1848; included in several U.S. territories prior to organization of Wyoming 1868; adopted women's suffrage, first instance in U.S., 1869; admitted to Union July 10, 1890; constitution adopted 1890; Nellie Tayloe Ross governor 1925–27, first woman governor of a U.S. state.

The seal, adopted in 1893, includes the motto, "Equal rights," recalling that in 1869 Wyoming was first to give equal voting and office-holding rights to women. Adopted on January 31, 1917, the design's white is said to stand for purity and uprightness, and blue for sky, fidelity, justice, and virility. The red is for the blood shed by both early pioneers and the original native population.

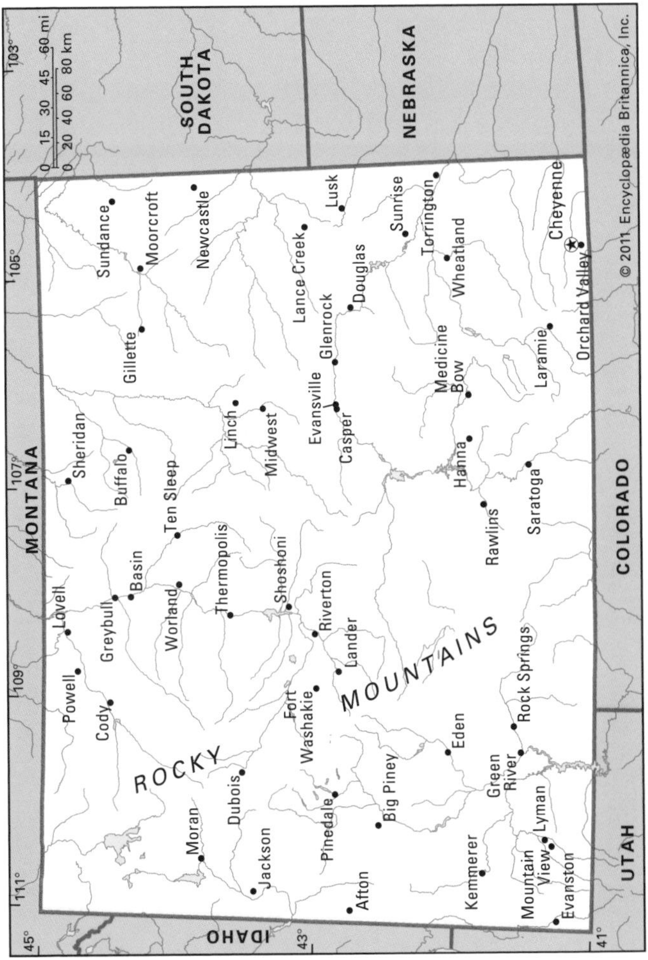
MONTANA
SOUTH DAKOTA
NEBRASKA
COLORADO
UTAH
IDAHO
ROCKY MOUNTAINS
0 15 30 45 60 mi
0 20 40 60 80 km
45°
43°
41°
111°
109°
107°
105°
103°
Sheridan
Buffalo
Sundance
Moorcroft
Newcastle
Gillette
Lance Creek
Lusk
Sunrise
Torrington
Douglas
Glenrock
Evansville
Casper
Linch
Midwest
Ten Sleep
Thermopolis
Basin
Greybull
Worland
Lovell
Powell
Cody
Shoshoni
Riverton
Lander
Fort Washakie
Dubois
Moran
Jackson
Pinedale
Big Piney
Afton
Kemmerer
Eden
Green River
Rock Springs
Lyman
Mountain View
Evanston
Rawlins
Saratoga
Hanna
Medicine Bow
Wheatland
Laramie
Cheyenne
Orchard Valley
© 2011 Encyclopædia Britannica, Inc.

The District of Columbia and the Territories of the United States

THE DISTRICT OF COLUMBIA

Official name: District of Columbia
Nickname: D.C.
State Flower: American beauty rose
Motto: Justitia Omnibus (Justice to all)
Admitted to the Union: February 21, 1871 (as a municipal corporation)
Total area: 68 sq. mi. (176 sq. km.)
Population (2010): 601,723
Principal industries: government and tourism
Highest point: Tenleytown, at Reno Reservoir 410 ft. (125 m.)

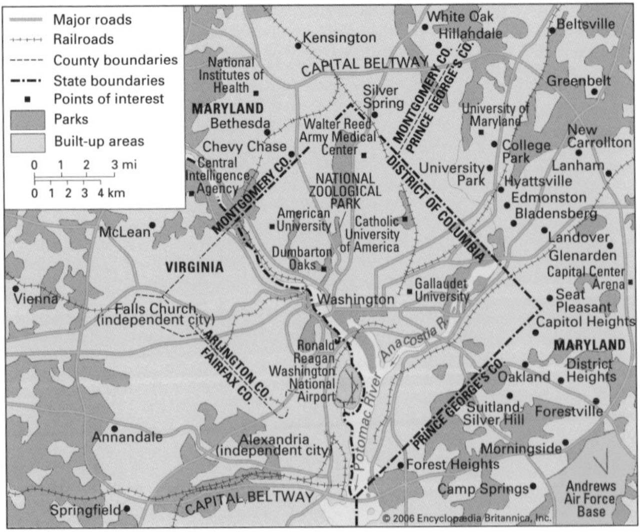

First flown on October 23, 1938, the District's flag was adapted by designer Charles Dunn from the coat of arms of George Washington's family, dating to the 1500s in England. Speculation is that the three stars stand for the three commissioners who once ran the District, and that the Washington family arms' design (with its blue stars, not red) inspired the Stars and Stripes.

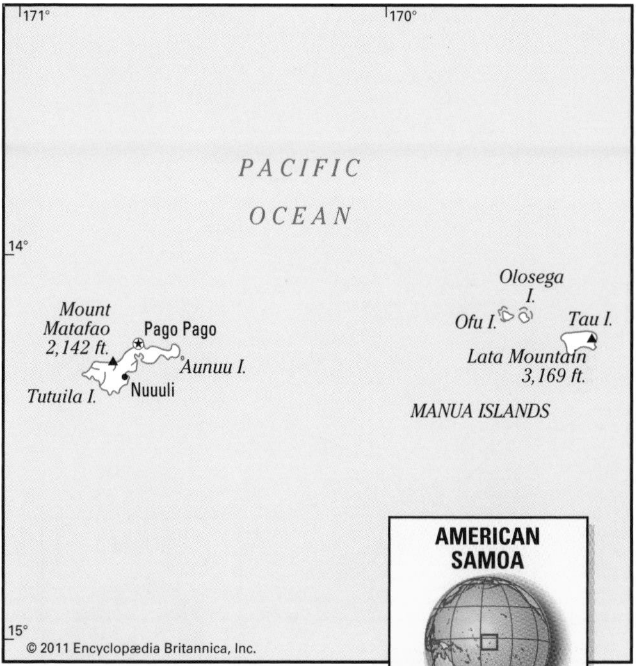

Official name: American Samoa
Head of government: Governor
Official languages: English; Samoan
Monetary unit: U.S. dollar
Area: 84 sq. mi. (219 sq. km.)
Population (2010): 65,900
GDP per capita (2007): U.S.$7,801
Principal exports (2008): tuna 94.3%, pet food 1.7% *to:* nearly all to the United States

Ethnic Composition

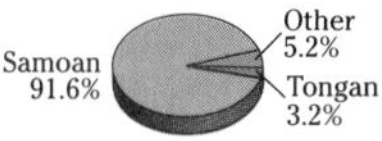

In 1900, part of Samoa became a U.S. territory. This flag, based on heraldric ideas by the Samoans, became official on April 27, 1960. The red, white, and blue are traditional in both Samoa and the United States. The eagle holds in its talons two Samoan emblems, a fly whisk, symbol of the wisdom of traditional chiefs, and a war club, representing state power.

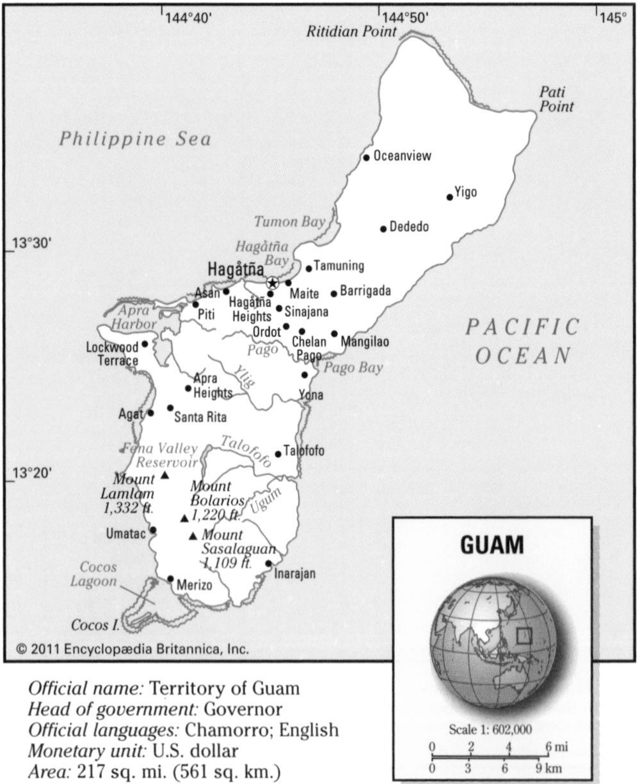

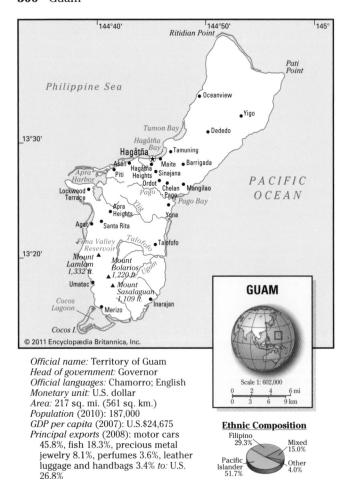

Official name: Territory of Guam
Head of government: Governor
Official languages: Chamorro; English
Monetary unit: U.S. dollar
Area: 217 sq. mi. (561 sq. km.)
Population (2010): 187,000
GDP per capita (2007): U.S.$24,675
Principal exports (2008): motor cars 45.8%, fish 18.3%, precious metal jewelry 8.1%, perfumes 3.6%, leather luggage and handbags 3.4% *to:* U.S. 26.8%

Ethnic Composition

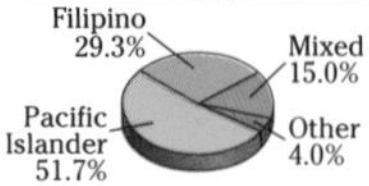

U.S. administered Guam after the 1898 Spanish-American War, and it became a territory in 1950. This flag was adopted in 1917, and reconfirmed in 1931. The lozenge's red border commemorates nearly three years of Japanese occupation endured in World War II, and the shape recalls stones used by ancient Chamorros for hunting. They used the type of canoe shown.

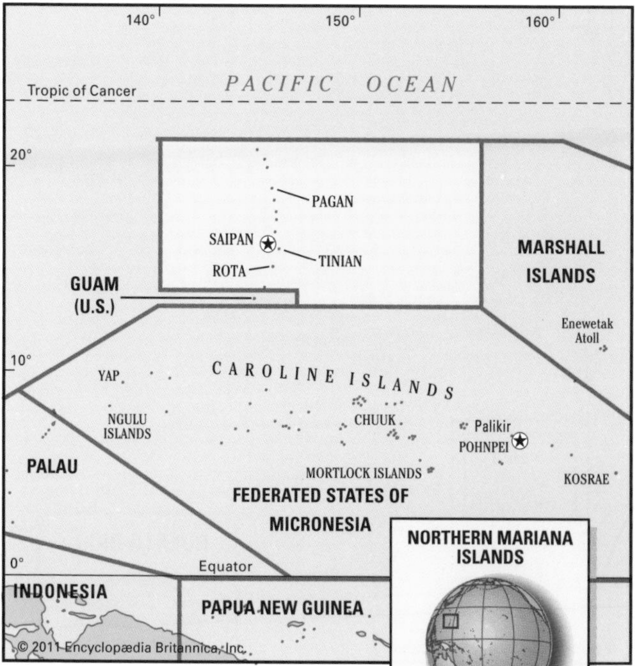

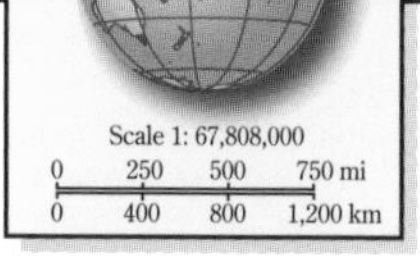

Official name: Commonwealth of the Northern Mariana Islands
Head of government: Governor
Official languages: Chamorro; Carolinian; English
Monetary unit: U.S. dollar
Area: 177 sq. mi. (457 sq. km.)
Population (2010): 48,300
GDP per capita (2007): U.S.$16,408
Principal exports (2008): apparel and clothing accessories 53.7%; iron and steel 16.3%, fish, crustaceans, and mollusks 11.8% *to:* mostly to the U.S.

Ethnic Composition

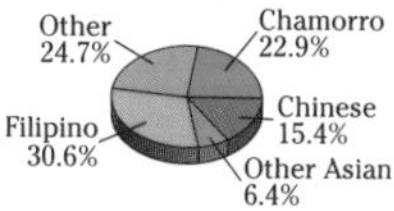

Once the Ladrone Islands, these 15 islands were under Japan from 1914. The U.S. occupied them in 1944, and in 1986 they became a U.S. commonwealth. The latte stones, used as housing supports and burial markers, are revered. The original flag, adopted March 31, 1972, lacked the wreath, added in 1981; the current flag was adopted in the mid-1990s.

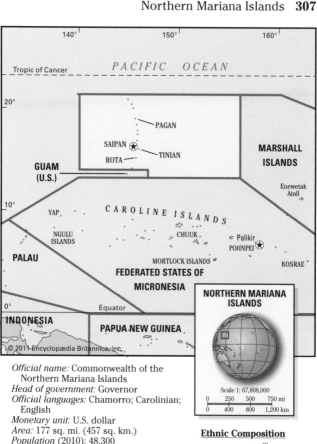

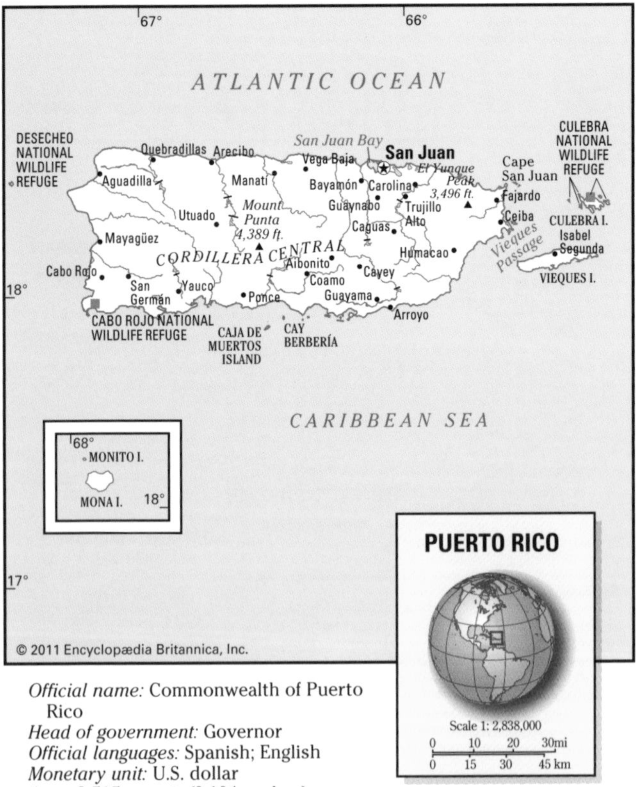

Official name: Commonwealth of Puerto Rico
Head of government: Governor
Official languages: Spanish; English
Monetary unit: U.S. dollar
Area: 3,515 sq. mi. (9,104 sq. km.)
Population (2010): 3,979,000
GNI per capita (2008): U.S.$15,399
Principal exports (2007–08): pharmaceutical and medicine 66%, food 7.0%, computer/electronic products 6.4% *to:* U.S. 71.6%; U.S. Virgin Islands 0.2%

Ethnic Composition

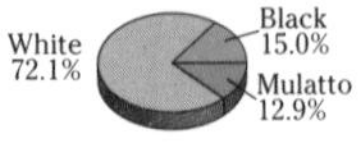

The flag chosen by exiled Puerto Ricans in 1895 was the Cuban flag with red and blue reversed. Raised on July 25, 1952, when Puerto Rico became a U.S. commonwealth, the star is for the commonwealth; the white stripes are for individual rights and freedom. The red stripes, as well as the corners of the triangle, correspond to the three branches of government.

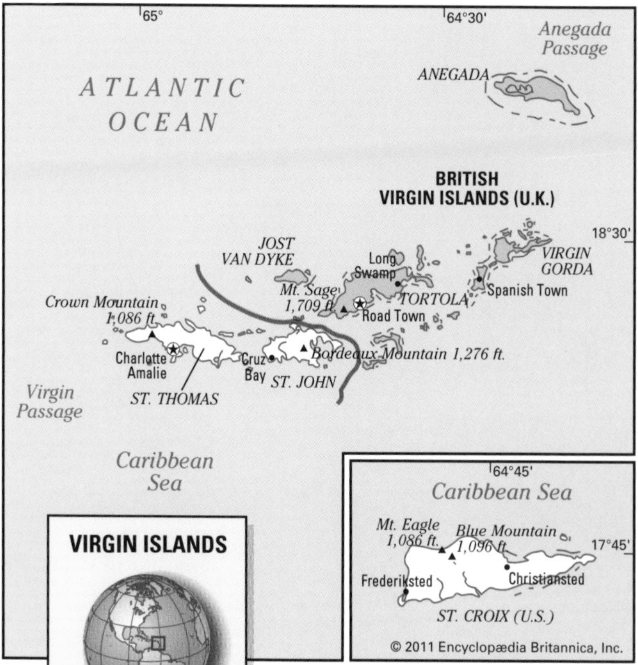

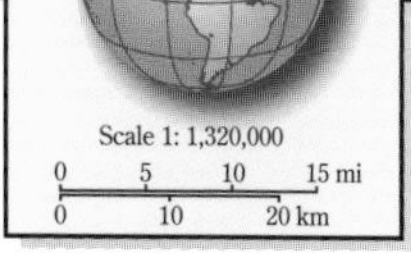

Official name: United States Virgin Islands
Head of government: Governor
Official language: English
Monetary unit: U.S. dollar
Area: 138 sq. mi. (353 sq. km.)
Population (2010): 118,000
GDP per capita (2007): U.S.$39,915
Principal exports (2009): refined petroleum 85.6% *to:* United States 87.3%; other countries 12.7%

Ethnic Composition

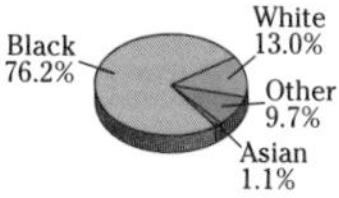

The islands, bought by the U.S. in 1917, flew the U.S. flag until May 17, 1921, when the territorial governor authorized this flag. The arrows are thought to represent the main islands of Saint Croix, Saint John, and Saint Thomas. In 1493, Columbus named the islands for St. Ursula, the legendary 4th-century leader of virgins who reputedly were martyred in Germany by the Huns.

Dependencies and Areas of Special Sovereignty

Name	Formal Name	Sovereignty	Administrative Center	Location	Position
Akrotiri (see note 15)	Akrotiri	United Kingdom	Episkopi (see note 16)	Mediterranean Sea (on island of Cyprus)	34°36' N 32°57' E
American Samoa (see note 1)				western Pacific Ocean	
Anguilla	Anguilla	United Kingdom	The Valley	Caribbean Sea	18°15' N 63°05' W
Antarctica	Antarctica	(none) (see note 2)	(none)	surrounding South Pole	87°00' S 60°00' E
Aruba	Aruba	Netherlands	Oranjestad	Caribbean Sea	12°30' N 69°58' W
Ashmore and Cartier Islands	Territory of Ashmore and Cartier Islands	Australia	Administered from Canberra	Indian Ocean	12°25' S 123°20' E
Baker Island	Baker Island	United States	Administered from Washington, D.C.	central Pacific Ocean	0°15' N 176°27' W
Bermuda	Bermuda	United Kingdom	Hamilton	North Atlantic Ocean	32°20' N 64°45' W
Bouvet Island	Bouvet Island	Norway	Administered from Oslo	South Atlantic Ocean	54°26' S 3°24' E
British Indian Ocean Territory (see note 3)	British Indian Ocean Territory	United Kingdom	(none)	Indian Ocean	7°00' S 72°00' E
Cayman Islands	Cayman Islands	United Kingdom	George Town	Caribbean Sea	19°30' N 80°40' W
Christmas Island	Territory of Christmas Island	Australia	The Settlement (Flying Fish Cove)	Indian Ocean	10°30' S 105°40' E
Clipperton Island	Clipperton Island	France	Administered from Paris	eastern Pacific Ocean	10°17' N 109°13' W
Cocos (Keeling) Islands	Territory of Cocos (Keeling) Islands	Australia	West Island	Indian Ocean	12°10' N 96°55' E
Cook Islands	Cook Islands	New Zealand	Avarua	South Pacific Ocean	20°00' S 158°00' W

Name	Formal Name	Sovereignty	Administrative Center	Location	Position
Coral Sea	Coral Sea Islands Territory	Australia	Administered from Canberra	Coral Sea (off eastern Australia)	18°30' S 152°00' E
Curaçao (see note 11)	Curaçao	Netherlands	Willemstad	Caribbean Sea	12°11' N 69°00' W
Dhekelia (see note 15)	Dhekelia	United Kingdom	Episkopi (see note 16)	Mediterranean Sea (on island of Cyprus)	35°01' N 33°46' E
Falkland Islands (Islas Malvinas)	Falkland Islands (Islas Malvinas)	United Kingdom (see note 4)	Stanley	South Atlantic Ocean	51°45' S 59°00' W
Faroe Islands	Faroe Islands	Denmark	Tórshavn	North Atlantic Ocean	62°00' N 7°00' W
French Guiana (see note 5)				northern South America	4°00' N 53°00' W
French Polynesia	French Polynesia	France	Papeete	South Pacific Ocean	15°00' S 140°00' W
French Southern and Antarctic Lands (see note 6)	French Southern and Antarctic Lands	France	Administered from Paris	southern Indian Ocean	49°30' S 69°30' E
Gibraltar	Gibraltar	United Kingdom	Gibraltar	Iberian Peninsula (south of Spain)	36°08' N 5°21' W
Greenland	Greenland	Denmark	Nuuk (Godthab)	North Atlantic Ocean/Arctic Ocean	70°00' N 40°00' W
Guadeloupe (see note 5)				Caribbean Sea	16°15' N 61°35' W
Guam (see note 1)				western Pacific Ocean	
Guernsey (see note 7)	Bailiwick of Guernsey	British Crown Dependency	Saint Peter Port	English Channel (off northern France)	49°28' N 2°35' W
Heard Island and McDonald Islands	Territory of Heard Island and McDonald Islands	Australia	Administered from Canberra	southern Indian Ocean	53°00' S 73°00' E

Name	Formal Name	Sovereignty	Administrative Center	Location	Position
Hong Kong	Hong Kong Special Administrative Region	China (see note 8)	(none)	South China Sea	22°15' N 114°11' W
Howland Island	Howland Island	United States	Administered from Washington, D.C.	central Pacific Ocean	0°48' N 176°38' W
Isle of Man	Isle of Man	British Crown Dependency	Douglas	Irish Sea (off western Great Britain)	54°15' N 4°30' W
Jan Mayen	Jan Mayen	Norway	Administered from Oslo (see note 9)	Arctic Ocean (east of Greenland)	71°00' N 8°20' W
Jarvis Island	Jarvis Island	United States	Administered from Washington, D.C.	central Pacific Ocean	0°23' S 160°02' W
Jersey	Bailiwick of Jersey	British Crown Dependency	Saint Helier	English Channel (off northern France)	49°15' N 2°10' W
Johnston Atoll	Johnston Atoll	United States	Administered from Washington, D.C.	North Pacific Ocean	16°45' N 169°32' W
Kingman Reef	Kingman Reef	United States	Administered from Washington, D.C.	North Pacific Ocean	6°24' N 162°22' W
Macau	Macau Special Administrative Region	China (see note 10)	Macau	southeastern China	22°10' N 113°33' E
Martinique (see note 5)				Caribbean Sea	14°40' N 61°00' W
Mayotte	Departmental Collectivity of Mayotte	France	Mamoudzou	Mozambique Channel (southeastern Africa)	12°50' S 45°10' E
Midway Islands	Midway Islands	United States	Administered from Washington, D.C.	North Pacific Ocean	28°13' N 177°22' W

Name	Formal Name	Sovereignty	Administrative Center	Location	Position
Montserrat	Montserrat	United Kingdom	Plymouth	Caribbean Sea	16°45' N 62°12' W
Navassa Island	Navassa Island	United States	Administered from Washington, D.C.	Caribbean Sea	18°24' N 75°01' W
New Caledonia	New Caledonia	France	Nouméa	South Pacific Ocean	21°30' S 165°30' E
Niue	Niue	New Zealand	Alofi	South Pacific Ocean	19°02' S 169°52' W
Norfolk Island	Territory of Norfolk Island	Australia	Kingston	South Pacific Ocean	29°02' S 167°57' E
Northern Mariana Islands (see note 1)				western Pacific Ocean	
Palmyra Atoll	Palmyra Atoll	United States	Administered from Washington, D.C.	central Pacific Ocean	5°52' N 162°06' W
Paracel Islands	Paracel Islands	undetermined (see note 12)	(none)	South China Sea	16°30' N 112°15' E
Pitcairn Islands	Pitcairn, Henderson, Ducie and Oeno Islands	United Kingdom	Adamstown	South Pacific Ocean	25°04' S 130°05' W
Puerto Rico (see note 1)				eastern Caribbean Sea	
Reunion (see note 5)				Indian Ocean	21°06' S 55°36' E
Saint Barthelemy	Saint Barthelemy	France	Gustavia	Caribbean Sea	17°54' N 62°50' W
Saint Helena (see note 13)	Saint Helena, Ascension, and Tristan da Cunha	United Kingdom	Jamestown	South Atlantic Ocean	15°57' S 5°42' W
Saint Martin (see note 17)	Saint Martin	France	Marigot	Caribbean Sea	18°04' N 63°04' W
Saint Pierre and Miquelon	Territorial Collectivity of Saint Pierre and Miquelon	France	Saint-Pierre	North Atlantic Ocean (off eastern Canada)	46°55' N 56°20' W
Sint Maarten (see note 11)	Sint Maarten	Netherlands	Philipsburg	Caribbean Sea	18°04' N 63°04' W

Name	Formal Name	Sovereignty	Administrative Center	Location	Position
South Georgia and the South Sandwich Islands	South Georgia and the South Sandwich Islands	United Kingdom (see note 4)	(none)	South Atlantic Ocean	54°00' S 38°00' W
Spratly Islands	Spratly Islands	undetermined (see note 14)	(none)	South China Sea	10°00' N 114°00' E
Svalbard	Svalbard	Norway	Longyearbyen	Arctic Ocean	78°00' N 20°00' E
Tokelau	Tokelau	New Zealand	(none)	South Pacific Ocean	9°00' S 171°45' W
Turks and Caicos Islands	Turks and Caicos Islands	United Kingdom	Grand Turk	Atlantic Ocean (bordering Caribbean Sea)	21°45' N 71°35' W
Virgin Islands, British	Virgin Islands, British	United Kingdom	Road Town	eastern Caribbean Sea	18°20' N 64°50' W
Virgin Islands, U.S. (see note 1)				eastern Caribbean Sea	
Wake Island	Wake Island	United States	Administered from Washington, D.C.	North Pacific Ocean	19°17' N 166°36' E
Wallis and Futuna	Wallis and Futuna	France	Matâ'utu	west central Pacific Ocean	14°00' S 177°00' W
Western Sahara	Western Sahara	(to be determined)	(none)	northwest Africa	24°30' N 13°00' W

NOTES

Note 1: The U.S. dependences of American Samoa, Guam, North Mariana Islands, Puerto Rico, and U.S. Virgin Islands will be found on their own pages following the states.

Note 2: Antarctica consists of the territory south of 60 degrees south latitude. This area includes claims by Argentina, Australia, Chile, France, New Zealand, Norway, and the United Kingdom, the legal status of which remains in suspense under the terms of the Antarctic Treaty of 1959. The United States recognizes no claims to Antarctica.

Note 3: Chagos Archipelago (including Diego Garcia).

Note 4: U.K. Overseas Territory (also claimed by Argentina).

Note 5: French Guiana, Guadeloupe, Martinique and Reunion are departments (first-order administrative units) of France, and are therefore not dependencies or areas of special sovereignty. They are included in this list only for the convenience of the user. The Department of Guadeloupe includes the nearby islands of Marie-Galante, La Desirade, and Iles des Saintes.

Note 6: The French Southern and Antarctic Lands includes Île Amsterdam, Île Saint-Paul, Îles Crozet, and Îles Kerguelen in the southern Indian Ocean; the "Îles Eparses" (Bassas da India, Europa Island, Glorioso

Islands, Juan de Nova Island and Tromelin Island) in the Mozambique Channel and western Indian Ocean; and the French-claimed sector of Antarctica, "Terre Adélie." The United States does not recognize the French claim to "Terre Adélie" (see note 2).

Note 7: The Bailiwick of Guernsey includes the islands of Alderney, Guernsey, Herm, Sark, and nearby smaller islands.

Note 8: Under a Sino-British declaration of September 1984, Hong Kong reverted to Chinese control on July 1, 1997. It is now a semi-autonomous entity that exists pursuant to international agreement and maintains its own government apart from the People's Republic of China.

Note 9: Administered from Oslo, Norway, through a governor resident in Longyearbyen, Svalbard.

Note 10: Under the Sino-Portuguese Joint Declaration on the Question of Macau signed in 1987, Macau reverted to Chinese control on December 20, 1999. It is now a semi-autonomous entity that exists pursuant to international agreement and maintains its own government apart from the People's Republic of China.

Note 11: The Netherlands Antilles dissolved on October 10, 2010. Curaçao and Sint Maarten (the Dutch two-fifths of the island of Saint Martin) became autonomous territories of the Kingdom of the Netherlands. Bonaire, Saba, and Sint Eustatius now fall under the direct administration of the Netherlands.

Note 12: South China Sea islands occupied by China but claimed by Vietnam.

Note 13: The territory of Saint Helena includes the Island group of Tristan da Cunha; Saint Helena also administers Ascension Island.

Note 14: South China Sea islands claimed in entirety by China and Vietnam and in part by the Philippines and Malaysia; each of these states occupies some part of the islands.

Note 15: United Kingdom sovereign base area on the island of Cyprus.

Note 16: The joint force headquarters, under the Commander of the British Forces Cyprus, administers both sovereign base areas from Episkopi.

Note 17: The island of Saint Martin is divided: the North three-fifths form the French collectivity of Saint-Martin, while the southern two-fifths (Sint Maarten) is an autonomous territory of the Kingdom of the Netherlands.

Source: Office of The Geographer and Global Issues, Bureau of Intelligence and Research, U.S. Department of State, Washington, D.C.

Outlying Islands Not Shown on Main Country Maps

Island or islands name	Sovereignty	Location	Position
Saint Peter and Saint Paul Archipelago	Brazil	central Atlantic Ocean	00°56' N, 29°22' W
Arquipélago de São Pedro e São Paulo	Brazil	central Atlantic Ocean	00°56' N, 29°22' W
Fernando de Noronha archipelago	Brazil	central Atlantic Ocean	03°51' S, 32°25' W
Trinidad Island (Ilha da Trindade)	Brazil	South Atlantic Ocean	20°31' S, 29°19' W
Martin Vaz Islands (Ilhas Martin Vaz)	Brazil	South Atlantic Ocean	20°30' S, 28°51' W
Desventuradas Islands (Islas Desventurados)	Chile	South Pacific Ocean	26°00' S, 80°00' W
Juan Fernandez Archipelago (Archipiélago Juan Fernández)	Chile	South Pacific Ocean	33°00' S, 80°00' W
Providencia Island (Isla de Providencia)	Colombia	Caribbean Sea (east of Nicaragua)	13°21' N, 81°22' W
San Andres Island (Isla de San Andrés)	Colombia	Caribbean Sea (east of Nicaragua)	12°33' N, 81°43' W
Cayos del Este Sudeste	Colombia	Caribbean Sea (east of Nicaragua)	12°25' N, 81°29' W
Albuquerque Cays (Cayos de Albuquerque)	Colombia	Caribbean Sea (east of Nicaragua)	12°10' N, 81°52' W
Galapagos Islands (Islas Galápagos)	Ecuador	central Pacific Ocean	00°00' S, 90°30' W
Andaman and Nicobar Islands	India	Indian Ocean (west of Myanmar)	10°00' N, 93°00' E
Chatham Islands	New Zealand	South Pacific Ocean	44°00' S, 176°35' W
Bounty Islands	New Zealand	South Pacific Ocean	47°45' S, 179°03' E
Antipodes Islands	New Zealand	South Pacific Ocean	49°42' S, 178°46' E
Campbell Island	New Zealand	South Pacific Ocean	52°30' S, 169°05' E
Auckland Islands	New Zealand	South Pacific Ocean	50°40' S, 166°30' E
Azores (Açores)	Portugal	North Atlantic Ocean	38°30' N, 28°00' W
Madeira	Portugal	North Atlantic Ocean (off Africa)	32°40' N, 16°45' W
Canary Islands (Islas Canarias)	Spain	North Atlantic Ocean (off Africa)	28°00' N, 15°30' W
Socotra Island	Yemen	Indian Ocean (east of Somalia)	12°30' N, 54°00' E

Country Capitals and Their Populations

Country	National Capital	Population of National Capital	United Nations (date of admission)	Common-wealth of Nations
Afghanistan	Kābul	2,536,300	1946	
Albania	Tiranë	400,000	1955	
Algeria	Algiers	2,740,000	1962	
Andorra	Andorra la Vella	21,609	1993	
Angola	Luanda	2,783,000	1976	
Antigua and Barbuda	Saint John's	31,000	1981	•
Argentina	Buenos Aires	2,776,138	1945	
Armenia	Yerevan	1,104,900	1992	
Australia	Canberra	356,120	1945	•
Austria	Vienna	1,687,271	1955	
Azerbaijan	Baku	1,145,000	1992	
Bahamas, The	Nassau	226,100	1973	•
Bahrain	Al-Manamah	157,000	1971	
Bangladesh	Dhākā (Dacca)	6,732,968	1974	•
Barbados	Bridgetown	5,996	1966	•
Belarus	Minsk	1,836,808	1945	
Belgium	Brussels	148,873	1945	
Belize	Belmopan	16,435	1981	•
Benin	Cotonou (official)	762,000	1960	
	Porto-Novo (de facto)	257,000		
Bhutan	Thimphu	79,185	1971	
Bolivia	La Paz (administrative)	835,300	1945	
	Sucre (judicial)	265,300		
Bosnia and Herzegovina	Sarajevo	392,000	1992	
Botswana	Gaborone	224,000	1966	•
Brazil	Brasília	2,606,885	1945	
Brunei	Bandar Seri Begawan	32,331	1984	•
Bulgaria	Sofia	1,162,898	1955	
Burkina Faso	Ouagadougou	1,475,233	1960	
Burundi	Bujumbura	429,000	1962	
Cambodia	Phnom Penh	1,242,992	1955	
Cameroon	Yaoundé	1,739,000	1960	•
Canada	Ottawa	812,129	1945	•
Cape Verde	Praia	125,000	1975	
Central African Republic	Bangui	622,771	1960	
Chad	N'Djamena	721,000	1960	
Chile	Santiago	200,792	1945	
China	Beijing (Peking)	8,580,376	1945	
Colombia	Bogotá	7,243,698	1945	
Comoros	Moroni	46,000	1975	
Congo, Democratic Republic of the	Kinshasha	7,273,947	1960	
Congo, Republic of the	Brazzaville	1,355,000	1960	
Costa Rica	San José	356,174	1945	
Cote d'Ivoire	Abidjan	3,802,000	1960	
Croatia	Zagreb	690,000	1992	

Country Capitals and Their Populations

Country	National Capital	Population of National Capital	United Nations (date of admission)	Common-wealth of Nations
Cuba	Havana	2,148,132	1945	
Cyprus	Nicosia	206,200	1960	•
Czech Republic	Prague	1,212,097	1993	
Denmark	Copenhagen	1,167,569	1945	
Djibouti	Djibouti	325,000	1977	
Dominica	Roseau	20,200	1978	•
Dominican Republic	Santo Domingo	2,154,000	1945	
East Timor	Dili	159,000	2002	
Ecuador	Quito	1,701,000	1945	
Egypt	Cairo	6,758,581	1945	
El Salvador	San Salvador	316,090	1945	
Equatorial Guinea	Malabo	96,000	1968	
Eritrea	Asmara	601,000	1993	
Estonia	Tallinn	398,594	1991	
Ethiopia	Addis Ababa	3,100,000	1945	
Fiji	Suva	85,691	1970	
Finland	Helsinki	576,632	1955	
France	Paris	2,181,374	1945	
Gabon	Libreville	576,000	1960	
Gambia	Banjul	34,828	1965	•
Georgia	Tbilisi	1,106,700	1992	
Germany	Berlin	3,431,675	1973	
Ghana	Accra	2,121,000	1957	•
Greece	Athens	745,514	1945	
Grenada	Saint George's	4,300	1974	•
Guatemala	Guatemala City	1,024,000	1945	
Guinea	Conakry	1,494,000	1958	
Guinea-Bissau	Bissau	330,000	1974	
Guyana	Georgetown	35,440	1966	•
Haiti	Port-au-Prince	703,023	1945	
Honduras	Tegucigalpa	944,400	1945	
Hungary	Budapest	1,721,556	1955	
Iceland	Reykjavik	118,665	1946	
India	New Delhi	302,363	1945	•
Indonesia	Jakarta	9,558,198	1950	
Iran	Tehrān	7,873,000	1945	
Iraq	Baghdad	5,054,000	1945	
Ireland	Dublin	506,211	1955	
Israel	Jerusalem (Yerushalayim, Al-Quds)	747,600	1949	
Italy	Rome (Roma)	2,718,768	1955	
Jamaica	Kingston	96,052	1962	•
Japan	Tokyo	8,717,529	1956	
Jordan	Amman	1,036,330	1955	
Kazakhstan	Astana	684,018	1992	
Kenya	Nairobi	2,864,700	1963	•
Kiribati	Bairiki	36,717	1999	•
Kosovo	Pristina (Prishtinë)	107,614	—	

Country	National Capital	Population of National Capital	United Nations (date of admission)	Common-wealth of Nations
Kuwait	Kuwait (Al-Kuwayt)	32,403	1963	
Kyrgyzstan	Bishkek (Frunze)	822,000	1992	
Laos	Vientiane (Viangchan)	194,200	1955	
Latvia	Rīga	713,019	1991	
Lebanon	Beirut (Bayrūt)	1,846,000	1945	
Lesotho	Maseru	210,000	1966	•
Liberia	Monrovia	1,010,970	1945	
Libya	Tripoli (Ṭarābulus)	1,113,000	1955	
Liechtenstein	Vaduz	5,111	1990	
Lithuania	Vilnius	548,835	1991	
Luxembourg	Luxembourg	85,467	1945	
Macedonia	Skopje (Skopije)	506,926	1993	
Madagascar	Antananarivo	1,697,000	1960	
Malawi	Lilongwe	674,448	1964	•
Malaysia	Kuala Lumpur	1,305,792	1957	•
Maldives	Male	103,693	1965	•
Mali	Bamako	1,494,000	1960	
Malta	Valletta	6,319	1964	•
Marshall Islands	Majuro	20,800	1991	
Mauritania	Nouakchott	673,000	1961	•
Mauritius	Port Louis	148,878	1968	•
Mexico	Mexico City	8,463,906	1945	
Micronesia, Federated States of	Palikir	7,000	1991	
Moldova	Chişinău	630,300	1992	
Monaco	Monaco	32,543	1993	
Mongolia	Ulaanbaatar (Ulan Bator)	1,031,200	1961	
Montenegro	Podgorica	173,000		•
Morocco	Rabat	1,622,860	1956	
Mozambique	Maputo (Lourenço Marques)	1,099,102	1975	•
Myanmar	Naypyidaw	418,000	1948	
Namibia	Windhoek	289,000	1990	
Nauru	Yaren	632	1999	•
Nepal	Kāthmāndu	671,846	1955	
Netherlands	Amsterdam (capital) The Hague (seat of gov.)	747,584 475,932	1945	
New Zealand	Wellington	379,100	1945	•
Nicaragua	Managua	937,489	1945	
Niger	Niamey	915,000	1960	
Nigeria	Abuja	1,576,000	1960	•
North Korea	P'yˇongyang	2,581,076	1991	
Norway	Oslo	575,475	1945	
Oman	Muscat	27,477	1971	
Pakistan	Islāmābād	780,000	1947	•
Palau	Melekeok	632	1994	
Panama	Panama City	415,964	1945	

Country	National Capital	Population of National Capital	United Nations (date of admission)	Commonwealth of Nations
Papua New Guinea	Port Moresby	299,000	1975	•
Paraguay	Asunción	519,661	1945	
Peru	Lima	289,855	1945	
Philippines	Manila	1,660,714	1945	
Poland	Warsaw (Warszawa)	1,709,781	1945	
Portugal	Lisbon	489,562	1955	
Qatar	Doha	370,700	1971	
Romania	Bucharest	1,944,367	1955	
Russia	Moscow	10,470,318	1991	
Rwanda	Kigali	860,000	1962	
St. Kitts and Nevis	Basseterre	12,900	1983	•
St. Lucia	Castries	13,191	1979	•
St. Vincent and The Grenadines	Kingstown	26,000	1980	•
Samoa	Apia	37,237	1976	•
San Marino	San Marino	4,376	1992	
São Tomé and Príncipe	São Tomé	3,666	1975	
Saudi Arabia	Riyadh (Ar-Riyadh)	4,087,152	1945	
Senegal	Dakar	2,243,400	1960	
Serbia	Belgrade	1,119,020	1945	
Seychelles	Victoria	25,501	1976	•
Sierra Leone	Freetown	786,901	1961	•
Singapore	Singapore	4,436,001	1965	•
Slovakia	Bratislava	428,792	1993	
Slovenia	Ljubljana	278,315	1992	
Solomon Islands	Honiara	66,000	1978	•
Somalia	Mogadishu	1,100,000	1960	
South Africa	Bloemfontein (judicial)	397,000	1945	•
	Cape Town (legislative)	3,103,000		
	Pretoria (executive)	1,282,000		
South Korea	Seoul (Sŏul)	10,456,034	1991	
South Sudan	Juba	368,000	2011	
Spain	Madrid	3,132,463	1955	
Sri Lanka	Colombo	672,743	1955	•
Sudan	Khartoum	4,754,000	1956	
Sudan, South	Juba	82,346		
Suriname	Paramaribo	268,000	1975	
Swaziland	Mbabane	78,000	1968	•
Sweden	Stockholm	810,120	1946	
Switzerland	Bern (Berne)	123,466	2002	
Syria	Damascus (Dimashq)	1,614,500	1956	
Taiwan	Taipei (T'ai-pei)	2,607,428	-	
Tajikistan	Dushanbe	660,900	1992	
Tanzania	Dodoma	149,180	1961	•
Thailand	Bangkok	6,355,144	1946	
Togo	Lomé	921,000	1960	
Tonga	Nuku'alofa	23,658	1999	•

Country	National Capital	Population of National Capital	United Nations (date of admission)	Common-wealth of Nations
Trinidad and Tobago	Port-of-Spain	54,000	1962	•
Tunisia	Tunis	728,453	1956	
Turkey	Ankara	3,763,591	1945	
Turkmenistan	Ashkhabad (Ashgabat)	827,500	1992	
Tuvalu	Funafuti	4,492	2000	•
Uganda	Kampala	1,480,200	1962	•
Ukraine	Kiev (Kyyiv)	2,765,531	1945	
United Arab Emirates	Abu Dhabi (Abū Z̧aby)	633,136	1971	
United Kingdom	London (Greater London)	7,517,700	1945	•
United States	Washington, D.C.	572,059	1945	
Uruguay	Montevideo	1,513,000	1945	
Uzbekistan	Tashkent	2,201,000	1992	
Vanuatu	Port-Vila	44,040	1981	•
Venezuela	Caracas	1,836,000	1945	
Vietnam	Hanoi	2,644,536	1977	
Yemen	Sanaa	1,707,531	1947	
Zambia	Lusaka	1,328,000	1964	•
Zimbabwe	Harare	1,572,000	1980	

List of Selected Cities

AFGHANISTAN .... page 1

Adraskan	33°39' N,	062°16' E
Almār	35°50' N,	064°32' E
Anār Darreh	32°46' N,	061°39' E
Andkhvoy	36°56' N,	065°08' E
Āqchah	36°56' N,	066°11' E
Baghlān	36°13' N,	068°46' E
Bāghrān	33°04' N,	065°05' E
Bagrām	34°58' N,	069°17' E
Bālā Bolūk	32°38' N,	062°28' E
Bāmīān (Bāmyān)	34°50' N,	067°50' E
Barg-e Matāl	35°40' N,	071°21' E
Bāzār-e Panjvā'i	31°32' N,	065°28' E
Chaghcharān	34°31' N,	065°15' E
Chahār Borjak	30°17' N,	062°03' E
Chakhānsūr	31°10' N,	062°04' E
Delārām	32°11' N,	063°25' E
Do Qal'eh	32°08' N,	061°27' E
Dowlātabād	36°26' N,	064°55' E
Dūrāj	37°56' N,	070°43' E
Eslām Qal'eh	34°40' N,	061°04' E
Farāh (Farrah, Ferah)	32°22' N,	062°07' E
Feyẕābād (Faizābād)	37°06' N,	070°34' E
Ghaznī	33°33' N,	068°26' E
Ghūrīān	34°21' N,	061°30' E
Gīzāb	33°23' N,	066°16' E
Golestān	32°37' N,	063°39' E
Golrān	35°06' N,	061°41' E
Gowmal Kalay	32°31' N,	068°51' E
Herāt (Harāt)	34°20' N,	062°12' E
Jabal os Sarāj	35°07' N,	069°14' E
Jalālābād	34°26' N,	070°28' E
Jaldak	31°58' N,	066°43' E
Jawand	35°04' N,	064°09' E
Kabul	34°31' N,	069°12' E
Kajakī	32°16' N,	065°03' E
Kandahār (Qandahār)	31°35' N,	065°45' E
Khadīr	33°55' N,	065°56' E
Khānābād	36°41' N,	069°07' E
Kholm	36°42' N,	067°41' E
Khowst	33°22' N,	069°57' E
Kondūz (Qonduz)	36°45' N,	068°51' E
Koshk	34°57' N,	062°15' E
Kūhestānāt	35°49' N,	065°52' E
Lashkar Gāh (Bust)	31°35' N,	064°21' E
Maḥmūd-e Rāqī	35°01' N,	069°20' E
Mazār-e Sharif	36°42' N,	067°06' E
Nāvor	33°53' N,	067°57' E
Orgūn	32°57' N,	069°11' E
Orūzgān	32°56' N,	066°38' E
Owbeh	34°22' N,	063°10' E
Palālak	30°14' N,	062°54' E
Pol-e 'Alam	33°59' N,	069°02' E
Porchaman	33°08' N,	063°51' E
Qalāt	32°07' N,	066°54' E
Qal'eh-ye Now	34°59' N,	063°08' E
Sar-e Pol	36°14' N,	065°55' E
Sayghān	35°11' N,	067°42' E
Shāh Jūy	32°31' N,	067°25' E
Shahrak	34°06' N,	064°18' E
Shīndand (Sabzevār)	33°18' N,	062°08' E
Shīr Khān	37°11' N,	068°36' E
Yangī Qal'eh	37°28' N,	069°36' E
Zaranj	30°58' N,	061°53' E

ALBANIA .... page 2

Berat	40°42' N,	019°57' E
Burrel	41°36' N,	020°01' E
Cërrik	41°02' N,	019°57' E
Çorovodë	40°30' N,	020°13' E
Durrës	41°19' N,	019°26' E
Elbasan	41°06' N,	020°05' E
Ersekë	40°22' N,	020°40' E
Fier	40°43' N,	019°34' E
Gjirokastër	40°05' N,	020°10' E
Gramsh	40°52' N,	020°11' E
Himarë	40°07' N,	019°44' E
Kavajë	41°11' N,	019°33' E
Korçë (Koritsa)	40°37' N,	020°46' E
Krujë	41°30' N,	019°48' E
Kukës	42°05' N,	020°24' E
Laç	41°38' N,	019°43' E
Lezhë	41°47' N,	019°39' E
Librazhd	41°11' N,	020°19' E
Lushnje	40°56' N,	019°42' E
Patos	40°38' N,	019°39' E
Përmet	40°14' N,	020°21' E
Peshkopi	41°41' N,	020°25' E
Pogradec	40°54' N,	020°39' E
Pukë	42°03' N,	019°54' E
Rrëshen	41°47' N,	019°54' E
Sarandë	39°52' N,	020°00' E
Shkodër (Scutari)	42°05' N,	019°30' E
Tepelenë	40°19' N,	020°01' E
Trana (Tirana)	41°20' N,	019°50' E

Vlorë	40°27' N,	019°30' E
Vorë	41°23' N,	019°40' E

ALGERIA .... page 3

Adrar (Timmi)	27°54' N,	000°17'W
Aïn Beïda (Daoud)	35°48' N,	007°24' E
Algiers (or Al-Jaza'ir)	36°47' N,	003°03' E
Annaba (Bone)	36°54' N,	007°46' E
Batna	35°34' N,	006°11' E
Béchar (Colomb-Bechar)	31°37' N,	002°13' W
Bejaïa (Bougie)	36°45' N,	005°05' E
Beni Abbès	30°08' N,	002°10' W
Biskra (Beskra)	34°51' N,	005°44' E
Bordj Bou Arréridj	36°04' N,	004°47' E
Chlef (El-Asnam or Orleansville)	36°10' N,	001°20' E
Constantine (Qacentina)	36°22' N,	006°37' E
Djelfa	34°40' N,	003°15' E
El-Oued	33°20' N,	006°53' E
Ghardaïa	32°29' N,	003°40' E
In Salah (Aïn Salah)	27°13' N,	002°28' E
Kenadsa	31°34' N,	002°26' E
Médéa (Lemdiyya)	36°16' N,	002°45' E
Mostaganem (Mestghanem)	35°56' N,	000°05' E
Oran (Wahran)	35°42' N,	000°38' W
Ouargla (Warqla)	31°57' N,	005°20' E
Saïda	34°50' N,	000°09' E
Sétif (Stif)	36°12' N,	005°24' E
Sidi Bel Abbés	35°12' N,	000°38' W
Skikda (Philippeville)	36°52' N,	006°54' E
Souk-Ahras	36°17' N,	007°57' E
Tamanrasset (Fort Laperrine)	22°47' N,	005°31' W
Tébessa (Tbessa or Theveste)	35°24' N,	008°07' E
Tiaret (Tihert or Tagdempt)	35°22' N,	001°19' E
Tindouf	27°42' N,	008°09' W
Tlemcen (Tlemsen)	34°52' N,	001°19' W
Touggourt	33°06' N,	006°04' E

ANDORRA .... page 4

Andorra la Vella	42°30' N,	001°30' E
Canillo	42°34' N,	001°35' E
Encamp	42°32' N,	001°35' E
La Massana	42°33' N,	001°31' E
Les Escaldes	42°30' N,	001°32' E
Ordino	42°34' N,	001°30' E
Sant Julià de Lòria	42°28' N,	001°30' E
Soldeu	42°35' N,	001°40' E

ANGOLA .... page 5

Benguela (São Félipe de Benguela)	12°35' S,	013°24' E
Caála (Robert Williams)	12°51' S,	015°34' E
Cabinda	05°33' S,	012°12' E
Cacolo	10°08' S,	019°16' E
Caconda	13°44' S,	015°04' E
Caluquembe	13°52' S,	014°26' E
Camacupa (General Machado)	12°01' S,	017°29' E
Cangamba	13°41' S,	019°52' E
Catumbela	12°26' S,	013°33' E
Cubal	13°02' S,	014°15' E
Cuchi	14°39' S,	016°54' E
Damba	06°41' S,	015°08' E
Gabela	10°51' S,	014°22' E
Ganda (Mariano Machado)	13°01' S,	014°38' E
Huambo (Nova Lisboa)	12°46' S,	015°44' E
Kuito (Silva Porto)	12°23' S,	016°56' E
Lobito	12°21' S,	013°33' E
Luanda (São Paulo de Luanda)	08°49' S,	013°15' E
Luau	10°42' S,	022°14' E
Lubango (Sá da Bandeira)	14°55' S,	013°30' E
Lucapa	08°25' S,	020°45' E
Luena (Vila Luso)	11°47' S,	019°55' E
Malanje	09°32' S,	016°20' E
Mavinga	15°48' S,	020°21' E
M'banza Congo (São Salvador)	06°16' S,	014°15' E
Menongue (Serpa Pinto)	14°40' S,	017°42' E
Namibe (Moçâmedes, or Mossamedes)	15°10' S,	012°09' E
N'dalatando (Dalatando, or Salazar)	09°18' S,	014°55' E
Negage	07°46' S,	015°16' E
Nóqui	05°51' S,	013°26' E
Ondjiva	17°04' S,	015°44' E
Porto Amboin	10°44' S,	013°45' E
Quimbele	06°31' S,	016°13' E
Saurimo (Henrique de Carvalho)	09°39' S,	020°24' E
Soyo	06°08' S,	012°22' E
Sumbe (Novo Redondo)	11°12' S,	013°50' E
Tombua (Porto Alexandre)	15°48' S,	011°51' E
Uige (Carmona)	07°37' S,	015°03' E
Waku Kungo (Santa Comba)	11°21' S,	015°07' E

ANTIGUA AND BARBUDA . . . . page 6

Codrington	17°38' N,	061°50' W
St. John's	17°06' N,	061°51' W

ARGENTINA . . . . page 7

Avellaneda	29°07' S,	059°40' W
Bahía Blanca	38°43' S,	062°17' W
Buenos Aires	34°36' S,	058°27' W
Comodoro Rivadavia	45°52' S,	067°30' W
Concordia	31°24' S,	058°02' W
Córdoba	31°24' S,	064°11' W
Corrientes	27°28' S,	058°50' W
Formosa	26°11' S,	058°11' W
La Plata	34°55' S,	057°57' W
La Rioja	29°26' S,	066°51' W
Luján	34°34' S,	059°07' W
Mar del Plata	38°00' S,	057°33' W
Mercedes	33°40' S,	065°28' W
Neuquén	38°57' S,	068°04' W
Paraná	31°44' S,	060°32' W
Posadas	27°23' S,	055°53' W
Rawson	43°18' S,	065°06' W
Resistencia	27°27' S,	058°59' W
Río Gallegos	51°38' S,	069°13' W
Salta	24°47' S,	065°25' W
San Miguel de Tucumán	26°49' S,	065°13' W
San Rafael	34°36' S,	068°20' W
Santa Fe	31°38' S,	060°42' W
Santa Rosa	36°37' S,	064°17' W
Santiago del Estero	27°47' S,	064°16' W
Tandil	37°19' S,	059°09' W
Tigre	34°25' S,	058°34' W
Ushuaia	54°48' S,	068°18' W
Viedma	40°48' S,	063°00' W
Villa María	32°25' S,	063°15' W

ARMENIA . . . . page 8

Abovyan	40°15' N,	044°35' E
Alaverdi	41°08' N,	044°39' E
Ararat	39°50' N,	044°42' E
Artashat (Artaxata)	39°57' N,	044°33' E
Artik	40°37' N,	043°59' E
Charentsavan	40°24' N,	044°38' E
Dilijan	40°44' N,	044°52' E
Ejmiadzin (Echmiadzin)	40°10' N,	044°18' E
Goris (Geryusy)	39°30' N,	046°23' E
Gyumri (Kumayri, Alexandropol, or Leninakan)	40°48' N,	043°50' E
Hoktemberyan (Oktemberyan)	40°09' N,	044°02' E
Hrazdan (Razdan)	40°29' N,	044°46' E
Ijevan	40°51' N,	045°09' E
Kamo (Nor-Bayazet)	40°21' N,	045°08' E
Kapan	39°12' N,	046°24' E
Sevan	40°32' N,	044°56' E
Spitak	40°49' N,	044°16' E
Stepanavan	41°01' N,	044°23' E
Vanadzor	40°48' N,	044°30' E
Yerevan (Erevan)	40°11' N,	044°30' E

AUSTRALIA . . . . page 9

Adelaide	34°56' S,	138°36' E
Alice Springs	23°42' S,	133°53' E
Bowral	34°28' S,	150°25' E
Brisbane	27°30' S,	153°01' E
Broken Hill	31°57' S,	141°26' E
Bunbury	33°20' S,	115°38' E
Bundaberg	24°51' S,	152°21' E
Cairns	16°55' S,	145°46' E
Canberra	35°20' S,	149°10' E
Darwin	12°28' S,	130°50' E
Devonport	41°10' S,	146°21' E
Geelong	38°09' S,	144°21' E
Geraldton	28°46' S,	114°36' E
Gladstone	23°51' S,	151°15' E
Gold Coast	28°06' S,	153°27' E
Goulburn	34°45' S,	149°43' E
Hobart	42°55' S,	147°20' E
Kalgoorlie-Boulder	30°45' S,	121°28' E
Lismore	28°48' S,	153°16' E
Mackay	21°09' S,	149°12' E
Maryborough	25°32' S,	152°42' E
Melbourne	37°50' S,	145°00' E
Mount Gambier	37°50' S,	140°46' E
Mount Isa	20°44' S,	139°30' E
Newcastle	32°55' S,	151°45' E
Perth	31°56' S,	115°50' E
Port Macquarie	31°26' S,	152°55' E
Rockingham	32°17' S,	115°43' E
Sydney	33°53' S,	151°12' E
Toowoomba	27°33' S,	151°58' E
Warrnambool	38°23' S,	142°29' E
Whyalla	33°02' S,	137°35' E
Wollongong	34°25' S,	150°54' E

AUSTRIA . . . . page 10

Amstetten	48°07' N,	014°52' E
Baden	48°01' N,	016°14' E
Branau [am Inn]	48°16' N,	013°02' E
Bregenz	47°30' N,	009°46' E
Bruck [an der Leitha]	47°25' N,	015°17' E
Dornbirn	47°25' N,	009°44' E

Eisenstadt	47°51' N,	016°31' E
Feldkirch	47°14' N,	009°36' E
Freistadt	48°30' N,	014°30' E
Fürstenfeld	47°03' N,	016°05' E
Gmünd	48°46' N,	014°59' E
Gmunden	47°55' N,	013°48' E
Graz	47°04' N,	015°27' E
Hallein	47°41' N,	013°06' E
Innsbruck	47°16' N,	011°24' E
Kapfenberg	47°26' N,	015°18' E
Klagenfurt	46°38' N,	014°18' E
Klosterneuburg	48°18' N,	016°19' E
Köflach	47°04' N,	015°05' E
Krems an der Donau	48°25' N,	015°36' E
Kufstein	47°35' N,	012°10' E
Laa [an der Thaya]	48°43' N,	016°23' E
Landeck	47°08' N,	010°34' E
Leibnitz	46°46' N,	015°32' E
Leoben (Donawitz)	47°23' N,	015°06' E
Leonding	48°16' N,	014°15' E
Liezen	47°34' N,	014°14' E
Linz	48°18' N,	014°18' E
Neunkirchen	47°43' N,	016°05' E
Oberwart	47°17' N,	016°12' E
Radenthein	46°48' N,	013°43' E
Salzburg	47°48' N,	013°02' E
Sankt Pölten	48°12' N,	015°38' E
Schrems	48°47' N,	015°04' E
Steyr	48°03' N,	014°25' E
Telfs	47°18' N,	011°04' E
Ternitz	47°43' N,	016°02' E
Traun	48°13' N,	014°14' E
Trofaiach	47°25' N,	015°00' E
Vienna (Wien)	48°12' N,	016°22' E
Villach	46°36' N,	013°50' E
Vöcklabruck	48°01' N,	013°39' E
Völkermarkt	46°39' N,	014°38' E
Weiner Neustadt	47°48' N,	016°15' E
Wolfsberg	46°50' N,	014°50' E

AZERBAIJAN ..... page 11

Ağcabädi	40°02' N,	047°28' E
Ağdam	39°59' N,	046°57' E
Ağstafa	41°07' N,	045°27' E
Ağsu	40°34' N,	048°24' E
Äli-Bayramli	39°55' N,	048°56' E
Astara	38°26' N,	048°53' E
Baku (Bakı)	40°23' N,	049°51' E
Balakän	41°43' N,	046°24' E
Bärdä	40°24' N,	047°10' E
Daīkäsän	40°32' N,	046°07' E
Däväçi	41°12' N,	048°59' E
Füzuli	39°36' N,	047°09' E
Gäncä (Gyandzha, Gandzha, Kirovabad, or Yelizavetpol)	40°41' N,	046°22' E
Göyçay	40°39' N,	047°45' E
İmişli	40°47' N,	048°09' E
İsmayıllı	40°47' N,	048°09' E
Kürdämir	40°21' N,	048°11' E
Länkäran	38°45' N,	048°50' E
Masallı	39°03' N,	048°40' E
Mingäçevir (Mingechaur)	40°45' N,	047°03' E
Nakhichevan (Naxcivan)	39°12' N,	045°24' E
Neftçala	39°23' N,	049°16' E
Ordubad	38°54' N,	046°01' E
Qäbälä (Kutkashen)	40°58' N,	047°52' E
Qax	41°25' N,	046°55' E
Qazax	41°05' N,	045°22' E
Qazimämmäd	40°03' N,	048°56' E
Şäki (Sheki, Nukha)	41°12' N,	047°12' E
Salyan	39°35' N,	048°59' E
Şamaxı	40°38' N,	048°39' E
Şämkir	40°50' N,	046°02' E
Siyäzän	41°04' N,	049°02' E
Sumqayit	40°36' N,	049°38' E
Tovuz	40°59' N,	045°36' E
Ucar	40°31' N,	047°39' E
Xaçmaz	41°28' N,	048°48' E
Xankändi (Stepanakert)	39°50' N,	046°46' E
Xudat	41°38' N,	048°41' E
Yevlax	40°37' N,	047°09' E
Zaqatala	41°38' N,	046°39' E

BAHAMAS, THE .. page 12

Dunmore Town	25°30' N,	076°39' W
Freeport	26°32' N,	078°42' W
Matthew Town	20°57' N,	073°40' W
Nassau	25°05' N,	077°21' W
Old Bight	24°15' N,	075°21' W
West End	26°41' N,	078°58' W

BAHRAIN......... page 13

Ad Dūr	25°59' N,	050°37' E
Al-Ḥadd	26°15' N,	050°39' E
Al Jasrah	26°10' N,	050°27' E
Al Mālikīyah	37°10' N,	042°08' E
Al-Muharraq	26°16' N,	050°37' E
Ar-Rifa'	26°07' N,	050°33' E
Ar-Rifā'ash-Sharqī	26°07' N,	050°34' E
Ar-Rumaythah	25°55' N,	050°33' E
'Awālī	26°05' N,	050°33' E

Bārbaār	26°14' N,	050°29' E
Madīnat Ḩamad	26°08' N,	050°30' E
Madīnat 'Īsā	26°10' N,	050°33' E
Manama	26°13' N,	050°35' E

BANGLADESH .... page 14

Azmiriganj	24°33' N,	091°14' E
Bāgerhāt	22°40' N,	089°48' E
Bājitpur	24°13' N,	090°57' E
Barisāl	22°42' N,	090°22' E
Bhairab Bāzār	24°04' N,	090°58' E
Bogra	24°51' N,	089°22' E
Brāhmanbāria	23°59' N,	091°07' E
Chālna Port (Mongla Port)	22°28' N,	089°35' E
Chāndpur	23°13' N,	090°39' E
Chaumuhāni (Chowmohani)	22°56' N,	091°07' E
Chittagong	22°20' N,	091°50' E
Chuadānga	23°38' N,	088°51' E
Comilla (Kumillā)	23°27' N,	091°12' E
Cox's Bāzār	21°26' N,	091°59' E
Dhaka (Dacca or Dhakal)	23°43' N,	090°25' E
Dinājpur	25°38' N,	088°38' E
Farīdpur	23°36' N,	089°50' E
Gopālpur	24°50' N,	090°06' E
Ishurdi (Ishurda)	24°08' N,	089°05' E
Jamālpur	24°55' N,	089°56' E
Jessore	23°10' N,	089°13' E
Jhenida	23°33' N,	089°10' E
Khulna	22°48' N,	089°33' E
Kishorganj	24°26' N,	090°46' E
Kurigrām	25°49' N,	089°39' E
Kushtia	23°55' N,	089°07' E
Lākshām	23°14' N,	091°08' E
Lakshmipur	22°57' N,	090°50' E
Lālmanir Hāt (Lalmonirhat)	25°54' N,	089°27' E
Mādārīpur	23°10' N,	090°12' E
Mymensingh (Nasirābād)	24°45' N,	090°24' E
Naogaon	24°47' N,	088°56' E
Nārāyanganj	23°37' N,	090°30' E
Narsinghdi (Narsingdi)	23°55' N,	090°43' E
Nawābganj	24°36' N,	088°17' E
Noākhāli (Sudhárám)	22°49' N,	091°06' E
Pābna (Pubna)	24°00' N,	089°15' E
Patuākhāli	22°21' N,	090°21' E
Rājshāhi	24°22' N,	088°36' E
Rāngāmāti	22°38' N,	092°12' E
Rangpur	25°45' N,	089°15' E
Saidpur	25°47' N,	088°54' E
Sātkhira	22°43' N,	089°06' E
Sherpur	24°41' N,	089°25' E
Sherpur	25°01' N,	090°01' E
Sirajganj (Seraganj)	24°27' N,	089°43' E
Sylhet	24°54' N,	091°52' E
Tangail	24°15' N,	089°55' E

BARBADOS .... page 15

Bennetts	13°10' N,	059°36' W
Bridgetown	13°06' N,	059°37' W
Holetown	13°11' N,	059°39' W
Marchfield	13°07' N,	059°28' W
Massiah	13°10' N,	059°29' W
Oistins	13°04' N,	059°32' W
Portland	13°16' N,	059°36' W
Prospect	13°08' N,	059°36' W
Speightstown	13°15' N,	059°39' W
Westmoreland	13°13' N,	059°37' W

BELARUS .... page 16

Baranovichi	53°08' N,	026°02' E
Beloözersk (Beloozyorsk)	52°28' N,	025°10' E
Bobruysk	53°09' N,	029°14' E
Borisov (Barysaw)	54°15' N,	028°30' E
Braslav	55°38' N,	027°02' E
Brest (Brest-Litovsk)	52°06' N,	023°42' E
Bykhov	53°31' N,	030°15' E
Chashniki	54°52' N,	029°10' E
Cherikov	53°34' N,	031°23' E
Cherven	53°42' N,	028°26' E
Dobrush	52°25' N,	031°19' E
Dokshitsy	54°54' N,	027°46' E
Drogichin	52°11' N,	025°09' E
Dyatlovo	53°28' N,	025°24' E
Dzerzhinsk	53°41' N,	027°08' E
Gantsevichi	52°45' N,	026°26' E
Glubokoye	55°08' N,	027°41' E
Gorki	54°17' N,	030°59' E
Gorodok	55°28' N,	029°59' E
Grodno (Hrodna)	53°41' N,	023°50' E
Homyel' (Gomel)	52°25' N,	031°00' E
Kletsk	53°04' N,	026°38' E
Klimovichi	53°37' N,	031°58' E
Kobrin	52°13' N,	024°21' E
Kossovo	52°45' N,	025°09' E
Kostyukovichi	53°20' N,	032°03' E
Lepel	54°53' N,	028°42' E
Lida	53°53' N,	025°18' E
Luninets	52°15' N,	026°48' E
Mahilyow (Mogilyov, Mahilyou)	53°54' N,	030°21' E

Malorita	51°47' N,	024°05' E
Minsk (Mensk)	53°54' N,	027°34' E
Molodechno (Maladzyechna)	54°19' N,	026°51' E
Mosty	53°25' N,	024°32' E
Mozyr (Mazyr)	52°03' N,	029°16' E
Mstislavl	54°02' N,	031°44' E
Narovlya	51°48' N,	029°30' E
Nesvizh	53°13' N,	026°40' E
Novolukomi	54°39' N,	029°13' E
Orsha	54°31' N,	030°26' E
Oshmyany	54°25' N,	025°56' E
Osipovichi	53°18' N,	028°38' E
Petrikov	52°08' N,	028°30' E
Pinsk	52°07' N,	026°07' E
Polotsk (Polatsk)	55°29' N,	028°47' E
Pruzhany	52°33' N,	024°28' E
Rechitsa (Rechytsa)	52°22' N,	030°23' E
Slutsk	53°01' N,	027°33' E
Soligorsk (Salihorsk)	52°48' N,	027°32' E
Starye Dorogi	53°02' N,	028°16' E
Stolbtsy	53°29' N,	026°44' E
Stolin	51°53' N,	026°51' E
Svetlogorsk (Svetlahorsk)	52°38' N,	029°46' E
Verkhnedvinsk	55°47' N,	027°56' E
Vetka	52°33' N,	031°10' E
Vileyka	54°30' N,	026°55' E
Vitebsk (Vitsyebsk)	55°12' N,	030°11' E
Volkovysk	53°10' N,	024°28' E
Vysokoye	52°22' N,	023°22' E
Yelsk	51°48' N,	029°09' E
Zaslavl	54°00' N,	027°17' E
Zhitkovichi	52°14' N,	027°52' E
Zhodino	54°06' N,	028°21' E

BELGIUM .... page 17

Aalst (Alost)	50°56' N,	004°02' E
Aalter	51°05' N,	003°27' E
Antwerp (Antwerpen, Anvers)	51°13' N,	004°25' E
Arlon (Aarlen)	49°41' N,	005°49' E
Ath	50°38' N,	003°47' E
Athus	49°34' N,	005°50' E
Bastogne	50°00' N,	005°43' E
Bouillon	49°48' N,	005°04' E
Boussu	50°26' N,	003°48' E
Braine-l'Alleud	50°41' N,	004°22' E
Brecht	51°21' N,	004°38' E
Bree	51°08' N,	005°36' E
Brugge (Bruges)	51°13' N,	003°14' E
Brussels (Brussel, Bruxelles)	50°50' N,	004°20' E
Charleroi	50°25' N,	004°26' E
Ciney	50°18' N,	005°06' E
Couvin	50°03' N,	004°29' E
Dinant	50°16' N,	004°55' E
Eeklo	51°11' N,	003°34' E
Enghien (Edingen)	50°42' N,	004°02' E
Eupen	50°38' N,	006°02' E
Florenville	49°42' N,	005°18' E
Geel (Gheel)	51°10' N,	005°00' E
Genk (Genck)	50°58' N,	005°30' E
Ghent (Gand, Gent)	51°03' N,	003°43' E
Hasselt	50°56' N,	005°20' E
Ixelles (Elsene)	50°50' N,	004°22' E
Kapellen	51°19' N,	004°26' E
Kortrijk (Courtrai)	50°50' N,	003°16' E
La Louviere	50°28' N,	004°11' E
Liège (Luttich)	50°38' N,	005°34' E
Louvain (Leuven)	50°53' N,	004°42' E
Marche-en-Famenne	50°12' N,	005°20' E
Mechelen (Malines)	51°02' N,	004°28' E
Mons (Bergen)	50°27' N,	003°56' E
Mouscron (Moeskroen)	50°44' N,	003°13' E
Namur (Namen)	50°28' N,	004°52' E
Neerpelt	51°13' N,	005°25' E
Ostend (Oostende)	51°13' N,	002°55' E
Peer	51°08' N,	005°28' E
Péruwelz	50°31' N,	003°35' E
Philippeville	50°12' N,	004°32' E
Riemst	50°48' N,	005°36' E
Roeselare (Roulers)	50°57' N,	003°08' E
Saint-Hubert	50°01' N,	005°23' E
Schaerbeek (Schaarbeek)	50°51' N,	004°23' E
Seraing	50°36' N,	005°29' E
Sint-Niklaas	51°10' N,	004°08' E
Spa	50°30' N,	005°52' E
Spy	50°29' N,	004°42' E
Staden	50°59' N,	003°01' E
Tessenderlo	51°04' N,	005°05' E
Thuin	50°20' N,	004°17' E
Tienen	50°48' N,	004°57' E
Torhout	51°04' N,	003°06' E
Tournai (Doornik)	50°36' N,	003°23' E
Turnhout	51°19' N,	004°57' E
Uccle (Ukkel)	50°48' N,	004°19' E
Verviers	50°35' N,	005°52' E
Wanze	50°32' N,	005°13' E
Waremme	50°41' N,	005°15' E
Waterloo	50°43' N,	004°23' E
Zwijndrecht	51°13' N,	004°20' E

BELIZE .... page 18

Belize City	17°30' N,	088°12' W
Belmopan	17°15' N,	088°46' W
Benque Viejo	17°05' N,	089°08' W
Bermudian Landing	17°33' N,	088°31' W
Corozal	18°24' N,	088°24' W

Dangriga (Stann Creek)	16°58' N, 088°13' W
Monkey River	16°22' N, 088°29' W
Orange Walk	18°06' N, 088°33' W
Pembroke Hall	18°17' N, 088°27' W
Punta Gorda	16°07' N, 088°48' W
San Ignacio (El Cavo)	17°10' N, 089°04' W

BENIN .... page 19

Abomey	07°11' N, 001°59' E
Cotonou	06°21' N, 002°26' E
Djougou	09°42' N, 001°40' E
Kandi	11°08' N, 002°56' E
Natitingou	10°19' N, 001°22' E
Parakou	09°21' N, 002°37' E
Porto-Novo	06°29' N, 002°37' E
Savalou	07°56' N, 001°58' E
Savé	08°02' N, 002°29' E

BHUTAN .... page 20

Bumthang (Byakar or Jakar)	27°32' N, 090°43' E
Chhukha	27°04' N, 089°35' E
Chima Kothi	27°03' N, 089°35' E
Chirang	27°04' N, 090°06' E
Dagana (Taga)	27°03' N, 089°55' E
Deothang (Dewangiri)	26°52' N, 091°28' E
Domphu (Damphu)	27°01' N, 090°08' E
Gaylegphug (Gelekphu, Hatisar or Hatsar)	26°51' N, 090°29' E
Ha	27°22' N, 089°17' E
Kanglung (Kanglum)	27°16' N, 091°30' E
Lhuntsi	27°39' N, 091°09' E
Mongar	27°15' N, 091°12' E
Paro	27°26' N, 089°25' E
Pema Gatsel	26°59' N, 091°26' E
Phuntsholing	26°52' N, 089°26' E
Punakha	27°37' N, 089°52' E
Samchi (Tori Bari)	26°53' N, 089°07' E
Samdrup Jongkhar	26°47' N, 091°30' E
Shemgang	27°12' N, 090°38' E
Shompangkha (Sarbhang)	26°52' N, 090°16' E
Sibsoo	27°01' N, 088°55' E
Tashigang	27°20' N, 091°32' E
Thimphu	27°28' N, 089°38' E
Tongsa	27°31' N, 090°30' E
Wangdü Phodrang	27°29' N, 089°54' E

BOLIVIA .... page 21

Apolo	14°43' S, 068°31' W
Benavides	12°38' S, 067°20' W
Bermejo	22°44' S, 064°21' W
Camargo	20°39' S, 065°13' W
Camiri	20°03' S, 063°31' W
Caranavi	15°46' S, 067°36' W
Chulumani	16°24' S, 067°31' W
Cobija	11°02' S, 068°44' W
Cochabamba	17°24' S, 066°09' W
Concepción	16°15' S, 062°04' W
Copacabana	16°10' S, 069°05' W
Corocoro	17°12' S, 068°29' W
Cuevo	20°27' S, 063°32' W
El Carmen	18°49' S, 058°33' W
Fortaleza	10°37' S, 066°13' W
Guayaramerin	10°48' S, 065°23' W
Huacaya	20°45' S, 063°43' W
Huachacalla	18°45' S, 068°17' W
Ixiamas	13°45' S, 068°09' W
La Esperanza	14°34' S, 062°10' W
La Horquilla	12°34' S, 064°25' W
La Paz	16°30' S, 068°09' W
Llallagua	18°25' S, 066°38' W
Llica	19°52' S, 068°16' W
Loreto	15°13' S, 064°40' W
Magdalena	13°20' S, 064°08' W
Monteagudo	19°49' S, 063°59' W
Montero	17°20' S, 063°15' W
Oruro	17°59' S, 067°09' W
Porvenir	11°15' S, 068°41' W
Potosí	19°35' S, 065°45' W
Puerto Acosta	15°32' S, 069°15' W
Puerto Rico	11°05' S, 067°38' W
Punata	17°33' S, 065°50' W
Quetena	22°10' S, 067°25' W
Quillacollo	17°26' S, 066°17' W
Reyes	14°19' S, 067°23' W
Riberalta	10°59' S, 066°06' W
Roboré	18°20' S, 059°45' W
Samaipata	18°09' S, 063°52' W
San Ignacio	16°23' S, 060°59' W
San José	17°51' S, 060°47' W
San Matías	16°22' S, 058°24' W
San Pablo	15°41' S, 063°15' W
San Ramón	13°17' S, 064°43' W
Santa Cruz	17°48' S, 063°10' W
Santiago	19°22' S, 060°51' W
Siglo Veinte	18°22' S, 066°38' W
Sucre	19°02' S, 065°17' W
Tarabuco	19°10' S, 064°57' W
Tarija	21°31' S, 064°45' W
Tiahuanacu (Tiwanacu)	16°33' S, 068°42' W
Trinidad	14°47' S, 064°47' W
Tupiza	21°27' S, 065°43' W
Uyuni	20°28' S, 066°50' W
Villazón	22°06' S, 065°36' W
Yacuiba	22°02' S, 063°45' W

BOSNIA AND HERZEGOVINA ... page 22

Banja Luka	44°46' N,	017°10' E
Bihać	44°49' N,	015°52' E
Bijeljina	44°45' N,	019°13' E
Bosanska Gradiška	45°09' N,	017°15' E
Bosanski Šamac	45°04' N,	018°28' E
Brčko	44°52' N,	018°49' E
Derventa	44°59' N,	017°55' E
Goražde	43°40' N,	018°59' E
Jablanica	43°39' N,	017°45' E
Jajce	44°21' N,	017°17' E
Kladanj	44°14' N,	018°42' E
Ključ	44°32' N,	016°47' E
Konjic	43°39' N,	017°58' E
Mostar	43°21' N,	017°49' E
Prijedor	44°59' N,	016°42' E
Sanski Most	44°46' N,	016°40' E
Sarajevo	43°50' N,	018°25' E
Srebrenica	44°06' N,	019°18' E
Travnik	44°14' N,	017°40' E
Tuzla	44°33' N,	018°41' E
Vareš	44°10' N,	018°20' E
Zenica	44°13' N,	017°55' E

BOTSWANA ...... page 23

Francistown	21°13' S,	027°31' E
Gaborone	24°40' S,	025°54' E
Ghanzi	21°34' S,	021°47' E
Kanye	24°59' S,	025°21' E
Kasane	17°49' S,	025°09' E
Letlhakane	21°25' S,	025°35' E
Lobatse	25°13' S,	025°40' E
Mahalapye	23°04' S,	026°50' E
Maun	19°59' S,	023°25' E
Mochudi	24°25' S,	026°09' E
Orapa	21°17' S,	025°22' E
Palapye (Palapye Road)	22°33' S,	027°08' E
Ramotswa	24°52' S,	025°49' E
Selebi-Phikwe	22°01' S,	027°50' E
Serowe	22°23' S,	026°43' E
Shashe	21°26' S,	027°27' E
Tlokweng	24°32' S,	025°58' E
Tshabong	26°03' S,	022°27' E
Tshane	24°05' S,	021°54' E

BRAZIL .... page 24

Aracaju	10°55' S,	037°04' W
Belém (Para)	01°27' S,	048°29' W
Belo Horizonte	19°55' S,	043°56' W
Boa Vista	02°49' N,	060°30' W
Brasília	15°47' S,	047°55' W
Campina Grande	07°13' S,	035°53' W
Campo Grande	20°27' S,	054°37' W
Canoas	29°56' S,	051°11' W
Caxias do Sul	29°10' S,	051°11' W
Curitiba	25°25' S,	049°15' W
Duque de Caxias	22°47' S,	043°18' W
Florianópolis	27°35' S,	048°34' W
Fortaleza	03°43' S,	038°30' W
Goiânia	16°40' S,	049°16' W
Itabuna	14°48' S,	039°16' W
João Pessoa	07°07' S,	034°52' W
Macapá	00°02' N,	051°03' W
Maceió	09°40' S,	035°43' W
Manaus	03°08' S,	060°01' W
Natal	05°47' S,	035°13' W
Nova Iguaçu	22°45' S,	043°27' W
Novo Hamburgo	29°41' S,	051°08' W
Passo Fundo	28°15' S,	052°24' W
Pôrto Alegre	30°04' S,	051°11' W
Pôrto Velho	08°46' S,	063°54' W
Recife	08°03' S,	034°54' W
Rio Branco	09°58' S,	067°48' W
Rio de Janeiro	22°54' S,	043°14' W
Rio Grande	32°02' S,	052°05' W
Salvador	12°59' S,	038°31' W
Santarém	02°26' S,	054°42' W
Santo André	23°40' S,	046°31' W
São Gonçalo	22°51' S,	043°04' W
São José do Rio Prêto	20°48' S,	049°23' W
São Luís	02°31' S,	044°16' W
São Paulo	23°32' S,	046°37' W
Tefé	03°22' S,	064°42' W
Teresina	05°05' S,	042°49' W
Vitória	20°19' S,	040°21' W

BRUNEI .... page 25

Badas	04°36' N,	114°27' E
Bandar Seri Begawan (Brunei)	04°53' N,	114°56' E
Bangar	04°43' N,	115°04' E
Kuala Belait	04°36' N,	114°14' E
Labi	04°23' N,	114°27' E
Labu	04°45' N,	115°11' E
Muara	05°02' N,	115°04' E
Seria	04°37' N,	114°19' E
Sukang	04°19' N,	114°37' E
Tutong	04°48' N,	114°39' E

BULGARIA .... page 26

Balchik	43°25' N,	028°10' E
Berkovitsa	43°14' N,	023°07' E
Blagoevgrad	42°01' N,	023°06' E
Burgas	42°30' N,	027°28' E

Dimitrovgrad	42°03' N,	025°36' E
Dobrich (Tolbukhin)	43°34' N,	027°50' E
Dulovo	43°49' N,	027°09' E
Gabrovo	42°52' N,	025°19' E
Grudovo	42°21' N,	027°10' E
Kazanlŭk	42°37' N,	025°24' E
Khaskovo	41°56' N,	025°33' E
Kŭrdzhali	41°39' N,	025°22' E
Kyustendil	42°17' N,	022°41' E
Lom	43°49' N,	023°14' E
Lovech	43°08' N,	024°43' E
Montana (Mikhaylovgrad)	43°25' N,	023°13' E
Nikopol	43°42' N,	024°54' E
Pazardzhik	42°12' N,	024°20' E
Pernik (Dimitrovo)	42°36' N,	023°02' E
Petrich	41°24' N,	023°13' E
Pleven	43°25' N,	024°37' E
Plovdiv	42°09' N,	024°45' E
Razgrad	43°32' N,	026°31' E
Ruse	43°50' N,	025°57' E
Shumen (Kolarovgrad)	43°16' N,	026°55' E
Silistra	44°07' N,	027°16' E
Sliven	42°40' N,	026°19' E
Sofia	42°41' N,	023°19' E
Stara Zagora	42°25' N,	025°38' E
Troyan	42°53' N,	024°43' E
Varna	43°13' N,	027°55' E
Veliko Tŭrnovo	43°04' N,	025°39' E
Velingrad	42°01' N,	024°00' E
Vidin	43°59' N,	022°52' E
Vratsa (Vraca)	43°12' N,	023°33' E
Vrŭv	44°11' N,	022°44' E
Yambol	42°29' N,	026°30' E

BURKINA FASO . . . page 27

Banfora	10°38' N,	004°46' W
Bobo-Dioulasso	11°12' N,	004°18' W
Boulsa	12°39' N,	000°34' W
Dédougou	12°28' N,	003°28' W
Diébougou	10°58' N,	003°15' W
Dori	14°02' N,	000°02' W
Fada Ngourma	12°04' N,	000°21' W
Faramana	12°03' N,	004°40' W
Gaoua	10°20' N,	003°11' W
Kaya	13°05' N,	001°05' W
Koudougou	12°15' N,	002°22' W
Koupéla	12°11' N,	000°21' W
Léo	11°06' N,	002°06' W
Nouna	12°44' N,	003°52' W
Orodara	10°59' N,	004°55' W
Ouagadougou	12°22' N,	001°31' W
Ouahigouya	13°35' N,	002°25' W
Pô	11°10' N,	001°09' W
Réo	12°19' N,	002°28' W
Tenkodogo	11°47' N,	000°22' W
Yako	12°58' N,	002°16' W

BURUNDI . . . . page 28

Bubanza	03°06' S,	029°23' E
Bujumbura	03°23' S,	029°22' E
Bururi	03°57' S,	029°37' E
Gitega	03°26' S,	029°56' E
Muramvya	03°16' S,	029°37' E
Ngozi	02°54' S,	029°50' E
Nyanza-Lac	04°21' S,	029°36' E

CAMBODIA . . . . page 29

Ânlóng Vêng	14°14' N,	104°05' E
Bâ Kêv	13°42' N,	107°12' E
Battambang (Batdambang)	13°06' N,	103°12' E
Chbar	12°46' N,	107°10' E
Chŏâm Khsant	14°13' N,	104°56' E
Chŏng Kal	13°57' N,	103°35' E
Kâmpóng Cham	12°00' N,	105°27' E
Kâmpóng Chhnăng	12°15' N,	104°40' E
Kâmpóng Kdei	13°07' N,	104°21' E
Kâmpóng Saôm (Sihanoukville)	10°38' N,	103°30' E
Kâmpóng Spoe	11°27' N,	104°32' E
Kâmpóng Thum	12°42' N,	104°54' E
Kampot (Kâmpôt)	10°37' N,	104°11' E
Krâchéh (Kratie)	12°29' N,	106°01' E
Krâkôr	12°32' N,	104°12' E
Krŏng Kaôh Kŏng	11°37' N,	102°59' E
Lumphăt (Lomphat)	13°30' N,	106°59' E
Mémót	11°49' N,	106°11' E
Moŭng Roessei	12°46' N,	103°27' E
Ŏdŏngk	11°48' N,	104°45' E
Péam Prus	12°19' N,	103°09' E
Phnom Penh (Phnum Penh or Pnom Penh)	11°33' N,	104°55' E
Phnum Tbêng Méanchey	13°49' N,	104°58' E
Phsar Réam (Ream)	10°30' N,	103°37' E
Prey Vêng	11°29' N,	105°19' E
Pursat (Poŭthĭsăt)	12°32' N,	103°55' E
Rôviĕng Tbong	13°21' N,	105°07' E
Sândăn	12°42' N,	106°01' E
Senmonorom	12°27' N,	107°12' E
Siĕmpang	14°07' N,	106°23' E
Siem Reap (Siĕmréab)	13°22' N,	103°51' E
Sisŏphŏn	13°35' N,	102°59' E
Stoeng Trêng (Stung Treng)	13°31' N,	105°58' E
Svay Chék	13°48' N,	102°58' E

Takêv (Takéo)	10°59' N,	104°47' E
Tăng Krâsăng	12°34' N,	105°03' E
Virôchey	13°59' N,	106°49' E

CAMEROON ...... page 30

Bafang	05°09' N,	010°11' E
Bafia	04°45' N,	011°14' E
Bafoussam	05°28' N,	010°25' E
Bamenda	05°56' N,	010°10' E
Banyo	06°45' N,	011°49' E
Batibo	05°50' N,	009°52' E
Batouri	04°26' N,	014°22' E
Bertoua	04°35' N,	013°41' E
Bétaré-Oya	05°36' N,	014°05' E
Douala	04°03' N,	009°42' E
Ebolowa	02°54' N,	011°09' E
Edéa	03°48' N,	010°08' E
Eséka	03°39' N,	010°46' E
Foumban	05°43' N,	010°55' E
Garoua	09°18' N,	013°24' E
Guider	09°56' N,	013°57' E
Kaélé	10°07' N,	014°27' E
Kribi	02°57' N,	009°55' E
Kumba	04°38' N,	009°25' E
Loum	04°43' N,	009°44' E
Mamfe	05°46' N,	009°17' E
Maroua	10°36' N,	014°20' E
Mbalmayo	03°31' N,	011°30' E
Meiganga	06°31' N,	014°18' E
Mora	11°03' N,	014°09 E
Ngaoundéré	07°19' N,	013°35' E
Nkambe	06°38' N,	010°40' E
Nkongsamba	04°57' N,	009°56' E
Obala	04°10' N,	011°32' E
Sangmélima	02°56' N,	011°59' E
Tcholliré	08°24' N,	014°10' E
Tibati	06°28' N,	012°38' E
Wum	06°23' N,	010°24' E
Yagoua	10°20' N,	015°14' E
Yaoundé	03°52' N,	011°31' E
Yokadouma	03°31' N,	015°03' E

CANADA .... page 31

Amos	48°35' N,	078°07' W
Arctic Bay	73°02' N,	085°11' W
Baie-Comeau	49°13' N,	068°09' W
Baker Lake	64°15' N,	096°00' W
Banff	51°10' N,	115°34' W
Barrie	44°24' N,	079°40' W
Battleford	52°44' N,	108°19' W
Beauport	46°52' N,	071°11' W
Bonavista	48°39' N,	053°07' W
Brandon	49°50' N,	099°57' W
Bridgewater	44°23' N,	064°31' W
Brooks	50°35' N,	111°53' W
Buchans	48°49' N,	056°52' W
Burlington	43°19' N,	079°47' W
Burnaby	49°16' N,	122°57' W
Calgary	51°03' N,	114°05' W
Cambridge Bay	69°03' N,	105°05' W
Camrose	53°01' N,	112°50' W
Carbonear	47°44' N,	053°13' W
Carmacks	62°05' N,	136°17' W
Charlesbourg	46°51' N,	071°16' W
Charlottetown	46°14' N,	063°08' W
Chatham	42°24' N,	082°11' W
Chibougamau	49°55' N,	074°22' W
Chicoutimi	48°26' N,	071°04' W
Churchill	58°46' N,	094°10' W
Churchill Falls	53°33' N,	064°01' W
Cranbrook	49°30' N,	115°46' W
Dartmouth	44°40' N,	063°34' W
Dauphin	51°09' N,	100°03' W
Dawson	64°04' N,	139°26' W
Dawson Creek	55°46' N,	120°14' W
Duck Lake	52°49' N,	106°14' W
Edmonton	53°33' N,	113°28' W
Elliot Lake	46°23' N,	082°42' W
Enderby	50°33' N,	119°09' W
Eskimo Point	61°07' N,	094°03' W
Esterhazy	50°39' N,	102°05' W
Estevan	49°08' N,	102°59' W
Faro	62°14' N,	133°20' W
Fernie	49°30' N,	115°04' W
Flin Flon	54°46' N,	101°53' W
Fogo	49°43' N,	054°17' W
Fort Liard	60°15' N,	123°28' W
Fort MacLeod	49°43' N,	113°25' W
Fort McMurray	56°44' N,	111°23' W
Fort McPherson	67°27' N,	134°53' W
Fort Qu'Appelle	50°46' N,	103°48' W
Fort St. John	56°15' N,	120°51' W
Fort Smith	60°00' N,	111°53' W
Fredericton	45°58' N,	066°39' W
Gagnon	51°53' N,	068°10' W
Gander	48°57' N,	054°37' W
Gaspe	48°50' N,	064°29' W
Glace Bay	46°12' N,	059°57' W
Granby	45°24' N,	072°43' W
Grand Bank	47°06' N,	055°46' W
Grande Prairie	55°10' N,	118°48' W
Grand Falls	48°56' N,	055°40' W
Grimshaw	56°11' N,	117°36' W
Grise Fiord	76°25' N,	082°55' W
Haines Junction	60°45' N,	137°30' W
Halifax	44°39' N,	063°36' W
Hamilton	43°15' N,	079°51' W
Happy Valley-Goose Bay	53°19' N,	060°20' W

Harbour Grace.......... 47°42' N, 053°13' W
Hay River.............. 60°49' N, 115°47' W
Inuvik.................. 68°21' N, 133°43' W
Iqaluit (Frobisher Bay)... 63°45' N, 068°31' W
Iroquois Falls........... 48°46' N, 080°41' W
Jasper.................. 52°53' N, 118°05' W
Joliette................. 46°01' N, 073°27' W
Jonquiere.............. 48°25' N, 071°13' W
Kamloops.............. 50°40' N, 120°19' W
Kapuskasing........... 49°25' N, 082°26' W
Kelowna............... 49°53' N, 119°29' W
Kenora................ 49°47' N, 094°29' W
Kindersley............. 51°28' N, 109°10' W
Kirkland Lake.......... 48°09' N, 080°02' W
Kitchener.............. 43°27' N, 080°29' W
Kuujjuaq (Fort-Chimo)... 58°06' N, 068°25' W
La Baie................ 48°20' N, 070°52' W
Labrador City.......... 52°57' N, 066°55' W
La Tuque.............. 47°26' N, 072°47' W
Lethbridge............. 49°42' N, 112°49' W
Lewisporte............. 49°14' N, 055°03' W
Liverpool.............. 44°02' N, 064°43' W
Lloydminster........... 53°17' N, 110°00' W
London................ 42°59' N, 081°14' W
Longueuil.............. 45°32' N, 073°30' W
Lynn Lake.............. 56°51' N, 101°03' W
Maple Creek............ 49°55' N, 109°29' W
Marystown............. 47°10' N, 055°09' W
Mayo.................. 63°36' N, 135°54' W
Medicine Hat........... 50°03' N, 110°40' W
Mississauga............ 43°35' N, 079°39' W
Moncton............... 46°07' N, 064°48' W
Montmagny............ 46°59' N, 070°33' W
Montreal............... 45°30' N, 073°36' W
Moose Jaw............. 50°24' N, 105°32' W
Mount Pearl............ 47°31' N, 052°47' W
Nanaimo............... 49°10' N, 123°56' W
Nelson................ 49°30' N, 117°17' W
Nepean................ 45°16' N, 075°46' W
New Liskeard........... 47°30' N, 079°40' W
Niagara Falls........... 43°06' N, 079°04' W
Nickel Centre........... 46°34' N, 080°49' W
Nipawin............... 53°22' N, 104°00' W
North Battleford........ 52°47' N, 108°17' W
North Bay.............. 46°19' N, 079°28' W
North West River....... 53°32' N, 060°08' W
Old Crow.............. 67°34' N, 139°50' W
Oshawa................ 43°54' N, 078°51' W
Ottawa................ 45°25' N, 075°42' W
Pangnirtung............ 66°08' N, 065°43' W
Parry Sound............ 45°21' N, 080°02' W
Peace River............ 56°14' N, 117°17' W
Perce.................. 48°32' N, 064°13' W
Peterborough.......... 44°18' N, 078°19' W
Pine Point.............. 60°50' N, 114°28' W
Portage la Prairie....... 49°59' N, 098°18' W
Port Alberni............ 49°14' N, 124°48' W
Port Hawkesbury....... 45°37' N, 061°21' W
Prince Albert........... 53°12' N, 105°46' W
Prince George.......... 53°55' N, 122°45' W
Prince Rupert.......... 54°19' N, 130°19' W
Quebec................ 46°49' N, 071°14' W
Quesnel............... 53°00' N, 122°30' W
Rae-Edzo.............. 62°50' N, 116°03' W
Rankin Inlet............ 62°49' N, 092°05' W
Red Deer.............. 52°16' N, 113°48' W
Regina................. 50°27' N, 104°37' W
Resolute Bay........... 74°41' N, 094°54' W
Revelstoke............. 50°59' N, 118°12' W
Rimouski.............. 48°26' N, 068°33' W
Roberval............... 48°31' N, 072°13' W
Ross River............. 61°59' N, 132°26' W
Sachs Harbour.......... 72°00' N, 125°13' W
Saint Albert............ 53°38' N, 113°38' W
Sainte-Foy............. 46°47' N, 071°17' W
Saint John............. 45°16' N, 066°03' W
Saint John's............ 47°34' N, 052°43' W
Saskatoon.............. 52°07' N, 106°38' W
Sault Ste. Marie......... 46°31' N, 084°20' W
Scarborough........... 43°47' N, 079°15' W
Schefferville............ 54°48' N, 066°50' W
Selkirk................. 50°09' N, 096°52' W
Senneterre............. 48°23' N, 077°14' W
Sept-Îles............... 50°12' N, 066°23' W
Shawinigan............. 46°33' N, 072°45' W
Shelburne.............. 43°46' N, 065°19' W
Sherbrooke............ 45°25' N, 071°54' W
Snow Lake............. 54°53' N, 100°02' W
Springdale............. 49°30' N, 056°04' W
Sturgeon Falls.......... 46°22' N, 079°55' W
Sudbury............... 46°30' N, 081°00' W
Surrey................. 49°06' N, 122°47' W
Swan River............. 52°07' N, 101°16' W
Sydney................ 46°09' N, 060°11' W
Teslin.................. 60°10' N, 132°43' W
The Pas................ 53°50' N, 101°15' W
Thompson............. 55°45' N, 097°52' W
Thunder Bay........... 48°24' N, 089°19' W
Timmins............... 48°28' N, 081°20' W
Toronto............... 43°39' N, 079°23' W
Trois-Rivieres.......... 46°21' N, 072°33' W
Truro................. 45°22' N, 063°16' W
Tuktoyaktuk............ 69°27' N, 133°02' W
Val-d'Or............... 48°06' N, 077°47' W
Vancouver............. 49°15' N, 123°07' W
Vernon................ 50°16' N, 119°16' W
Victoria................ 48°26' N, 123°22' W
Wabush............... 52°55' N, 066°52' W
Watson Lake........... 60°04' N, 128°42' W
Weyburn............... 49°40' N, 103°51' W
Whitehorse............ 60°43' N, 135°03' W
Williams Lake.......... 52°08' N, 122°09' W

Windsor	42°18' N,	083°01' W
Windsor	44°59' N,	064°08' W
Winnipeg	49°53' N,	097°09' W
Yarmouth	43°50' N,	066°07' W
Yellowknife	62°27' N,	114°22' W
Yorkton	51°13' N,	102°28' W

CAPE VERDE...... page 32

Mindelo	16°53' N,	025°00' W
Porto Novo	17°01' N,	025°04' W
Praia	14°55' N,	023°31' W
São Filipe	14°54' N,	024°31' W

CENTRAL AFRICAN REPUBLIC .... page 33

Alindao	05°02' N,	021°13' E
Baboua	05°48' N,	014°49' E
Bambari	05°45' N,	020°40' E
Bangassou	04°44' N,	022°49' E
Bangui	04°22' N,	018°35' E
Batangafo	07°18' N,	018°18' E
Berbérati	04°16' N,	015°47' E
Bimbo	04°18' N,	018°33' E
Birao	10°17' N,	022°47' E
Boda	04°19' N,	017°28' E
Bossangoa	06°29' N,	017°27' E
Bossembélé	05°16' N,	017°39' E
Bouar	05°57' N,	015°36' E
Bouca	06°30' N,	018°17' E
Bozoum	06°19' N,	016°23' E
Bria	06°32' N,	021°59' E
Carnot	04°56' N,	015°52' E
Dekóa	06°19' N,	019°04' E
Ippy	06°15' N,	021°12' E
Kaga Bandoro	06°59' N,	019°11' E
Mbaïki	03°53' N,	018°00' E
Mobaye	04°19' N,	021°11' E
Mouka	07°16' N,	021°52' E
Ndélé	08°24' N,	020°39' E
Nola	03°32' N,	016°04' E
Obo	05°24' N,	026°30' E
Ouadda	08°04' N,	022°24' E
Ouanda Djallé	08°54' N,	022°48' E
Sibut	05°44' N,	019°05' E
Zinga	03°43' N,	018°35' E

CHAD .... page 34

Abéché	13°49' N,	020°49' E
Adre	13°28' N,	022°12' E
Am Dam	12°46' N,	020°29' E
Am Timan	11°02' N,	020°17' E
Am Zoer	14°13' N,	021°23' E
Aozou	21°49' N,	017°25' E
Arada	15°01' N,	020°40' E
Ati	13°13' N,	018°20' E
Biltine	14°32' N,	020°55' E
Bol	13°28' N,	014°43' E
Bongor	10°17' N,	015°22' E
Doba	08°39' N,	016°51' E
Gélengdeng	10°56' N,	015°32' E
Goré	07°55' N,	016°38' E
Goz Beïda	12°13' N,	021°25' E
Koro Toro	16°05' N,	018°30' E
Laï	09°24' N,	016°18' E
Largeau (Faya-Largeau)	17°55' N,	019°07' E
Mao	14°07' N,	015°19' E
Massenya	11°24' N,	016°10' E
Mongo	12°11' N,	018°42' E
Moundou	08°34' N,	016°05' E
N'Djamena (Fort Lamy)	12°07' N,	015°03' E
Pala	09°22' N,	014°54' E
Sarh (Fort-Archambault)	09°09' N,	018°23' E

CHILE .... page 35

Antofagasta	23°39' S,	070°24' W
Arica	18°29' S,	070°20' W
Castro	42°29' S,	073°46' W
Chillán	36°36' S,	072°07' W
Chuquicamata	22°19' S,	068°56' W
Coihaique	45°34' S,	072°04' W
Concepción	36°50' S,	073°03' W
Copiapó	27°22' S,	070°20' W
Coquimbo	29°58' S,	071°21' W
Iquique	20°13' S,	070°10' W
La Serena	29°54' S,	071°16' W
Porvenir	53°18' S,	070°22' W
Potrerillos	26°26' S,	069°29' W
Puerto Aisén	45°24' S,	072°42' W
Puerto Montt	41°28' S,	072°57' W
Punta Arenas	53°09' S,	070°55' W
Purranque	40°55' S,	073°10' W
San Pedro	33°54' S,	071°28' W
Santiago	33°27' S,	070°40' W
Talca	35°26' S,	071°40' W
Talcahuano	36°43' S,	073°07' W
Temuco	38°44' S,	072°36' W
Tocopilla	22°05' S,	070°12' W
Valdivia	39°48' S,	073°14' W
Valparaíso	33°02' S,	071°38' W
Viña del Mar	33°02' S,	071°34' W

CHINA .... page 36-7

Anshan	41°07' N,	122°57' E
Beijing	39°56' N,	116°24' E

Changchun	43°52' N,	125°21' E
Changsha	28°12' N,	112°58' E
Chengdu	30°40' N,	104°04' E
Chongqing (locally Yuzhou)	29°34' N,	106°35' E
Dalian (Lüda)	38°55' N,	121°39' E
Fushun	41°52' N,	123°53' E
Fuzhou	26°05' N,	119°18' E
Guangzhou	23°07' N,	113°15' E
Guiyang	26°35' N,	106°43' E
Haikou	20°03' N,	110°19' E
Hangzhou	30°15' N,	120°10' E
Harbin	45°45' N,	126°39' E
Hefei	31°51' N,	117°17' E
Hohhot	40°47' N,	111°37' E
Jinan	36°40' N,	117°00' E
Kunming	25°04' N,	102°41' E
Lanzhou	36°03' N,	103°41' E
Lhasa	29°39' N,	091°06' E
Nanchang	28°41' N,	115°53' E
Nanjing	32°03' N,	118°47' E
Nanning	22°49' N,	108°19' E
Qingdao	36°04' N,	120°19' E
Shanghai	31°14' N,	121°28' E
Shaoxing	30°00' N,	120°35' E
Shenyang	41°48' N,	123°27' E
Shijiazhuang	38°03' N,	114°29' E
Tai'an	36°12' N,	117°07' E
Taiyuan	37°52' N,	112°33' E
Tianjin	39°08' N,	117°12' E
Ürümqi	43°48' N,	087°35' E
Wuhan	30°35' N,	114°16' E
Xi'an	34°16' N,	108°54' E
Xining	36°37' N,	101°46' E
Yinchuan	38°28' N,	106°19' E
Zhengzhou	34°45' N,	113°40' E

COLOMBIA .... page 38

Armenia	04°31' N,	075°41' W
Barranquilla	10°59' N,	074°48' W
Bello	06°20' N,	075°33'W
Bisinaca	04°30' N,	069°40' W
Bogotá	04°36' N,	074°05' W
Bolívar	01°50' N,	076°58' W
Bucaramanga	07°08' N,	073°09' W
Buenaventura	03°53' N,	077°04' W
Cali	03°27' N,	076°31'W
Caranacoa	02°25' N,	068°57' W
Cartagena	10°25' N,	075°32' W
Cúcuta	07°54' N,	072°31' W
Duitama	05°50' N,	073°02' W
El Dorado	01°11' N,	071°52' W
El Yopal	05°21' N,	072°23' W
Florencia	01°36' N,	075°36' W
Ibagué	04°27' N,	075°14' W
Macujer	00°24' N,	073°07' W
Magangué	09°14' N,	074°45' W
Manizales	05°05' N,	075°32' W
Matarca	00°30' S,	072°38' W
Medellín	06°15' N,	075°35' W
Mitú	01°08' N,	070°03' W
Montería	08°46' N,	075°53' W
Ocaña	08°15' N,	073°20' W
Palmira	03°32' N,	076°16' W
Pasto	01°13' N,	077°17' W
Pereira	04°49' N,	075°43' W
Popayán	02°27' N,	076°36' W
Puerto Berrío	06°29' N,	074°24' W
Puerto Carreño	06°12' N,	067°22' W
Puerto Inírida	03°51' N,	067°55' W
Quibdó	05°42' N,	076°40' W
Ríohacha	11°33' N,	072°55' W
San José de Guaviare	02°35' N,	072°38' W
San Martín	03°42' N,	073°42' W
Santa Marta	11°15' N,	074°13' W
Sincelejo	09°18' N,	075°24' W
Sogamoso	05°43' N,	072°56' W
Tuluá	04°06' N,	076°11' W
Tumaco	01°49' N,	078°46' W
Tunja	05°31' N,	073°22' W
Urrao	06°20' N,	076°11'W
Valledupar	10°29' N,	073°15' W
Villa Rosario	07°50' N,	072°28' W
Villavicencio	04°09' N,	073°37' W
Zipaquirá	05°02' N,	074°00' W

COMOROS .... page 39

Fomboni	12°18' S,	043°46' E
Mitsamiouli	11°22' S,	043°21' E
Moroni	11°41' S,	043°16' E
Mutsamudu	12°10' S,	044°25' E

CONGO, DEMOCRATIC REPUBLIC OF THE page 40

Aketi	02°44' N,	023°46' E
Banana	06°01' S,	012°24' E
Bandundu	03°19' S,	017°22' E
Beni	00°30' N,	029°28' E
Boende	00°13' S,	020°52' E
Boma	05°51' S,	013°03' E
Buta	02°48' N,	024°44' E
Butembo	00°09' N,	029°17' E
Gandajika	06°45' S,	023°57' E
Gemena	03°15' N,	019°46' E
Ilebo	04°19' S,	020°35' E
Isiro	02°46' N,	027°37' E
Kabinda	06°08' S,	024°29' E
Kalemi (Albertville)	05°56' S,	029°12' E

Kamina	08°44' S,	025°00' E
Kananga (Luluabourg)	05°54' S,	022°25' E
Kikwit	05°02' S,	018°49' E
Kindu	02°57' S,	025°56' E
Kinshasa (Leopoldville)	04°18' S,	015°18' E
Kisangani (Stanleyville)	00°30' N,	025°12' E
Kolwezi	10°43' S,	025°28' E
Kutu	02°44' S,	018°09' E
Likasi	10°59' S,	026°44' E
Lubumbashi (Elisabethville)	11°40' N,	027°28' E
Manono	07°18' S,	027°25' E
Matadi	05°49' S,	013°27' E
Mbandaka	00°04' N,	018°16' E
Mbanza-Ngungu	05°15' S,	014°52' E
Mbuji-Mayi	06°09' S,	023°36' E
Mwene-Ditu	07°03' S,	023°27' E
Samba	04°38' S,	026°22' E
Tshikapa	06°25' S,	020°48' E
Yangambi	00°47' N,	024°28' E

CONGO, REPUBLIC OF THE . . . . page 41

Brazzaville	04°16' S,	015°17' E
Djambala	02°33' S,	014°45' E
Gamboma	01°53' S,	015°51' E
Impfondo	01°37' N,	018°04' E
Kayes	04°25' S,	011°41' E
Liranga	00°40' S,	017°36' E
Loubomo	04°12' N,	012°41' E
Madingou	04°09' S,	013°34' E
Makabana	02°48' S,	012°29' E
Makoua	00°01' N,	015°39' E
Mossendjo	02°57' S,	012°44' E
Mpouya	02°37' S,	16°013' E
Nkayi	04°11' S,	013°18' E
Ouesso	01°37' N,	016°04' E
Owando	00°29' S,	015°55' E
Pointe-Noire	04°48' S,	011°51' E
Sibiti	03°41' S,	013°21' E
Souanké	02°05' N,	014°03' E
Zanaga	02°15' S,	013°50' E

COSTA RICA . . . . . page 42

Alajuela	10°01' N,	084°13' W
Cañas	10°26' N,	085°06' W
Desamparados	09°54' N,	084°05' W
Golfito	08°39' N,	083°09' W
Heredia	10°00' N,	084°07' W
Ipís	09°58' N,	084°01' W
La Cruz	11°04' N,	085°38' W
Liberia	10°38' N,	085°26' W
Miramar	10°06' N,	084°44' W
Nicoya	10°09' N,	085°27' W
Puerto Limón (Limón)	10°00' N,	083°02' W
Puntarenas	09°58' N,	084°50' W
Quesada	10°20' N,	084°26' W
San Isidro	09°23' N,	083°42' W
San José	09°56' N,	084°05' W
San Ramón	10°05' N,	084°28' W
Santa Cruz	10°16' N,	085°35' W
Siquirres	10°06' N,	083°31' W
Tilarán	10°28' N,	084°58' W

COTE D´IVOIRE . . page 43

Abengourou	06°44' N,	003°29' W
Abidjan	05°19' N,	004°02' W
Aboisso	05°28' N,	003°12' W
Adzopé	06°06' N,	003°52' W
Agboville	05°56' N,	004°13' W
Anyama	05°30' N,	004°03' W
Arrah	06°40' N,	003°58' W
Biankouma	07°44' N,	007°37' W
Bondoukou	08°02' N,	002°48' W
Bouaflé	06°59' N,	005°45' W
Bouaké	07°41' N,	005°02' W
Bouna	09°16' N,	003°00' W
Boundiali	09°31' N,	006°29' W
Daloa	06°53' N,	006°27' W
Daoukro	07°03' N,	003°58' W
Dimbokro	06°39' N,	004°42' W
Divo	05°50' N,	005°22' W
Duékoué	06°45' N,	007°21' W
Ferkéssédougou	09°36' N,	005°12' W
Gagnoa	06°08' N,	005°56' W
Grand-Bassam	05°12' N,	003°44' W
Guiglo	06°33' N,	007°29' W
Katiola	08°08' N,	005°06' W
Kong	09°09' N,	004°37' W
Korhogo	09°27' N,	005°38' W
Lakota	05°51' N,	005°41' W
Man	07°24' N,	007°33' W
Odienné	09°30' N,	007°34' W
Oumé	06°23' N,	005°25' W
San-Pédro	04°44' N,	006°37' W
Sassandra	04°57' N,	006°05' W
Séguéla	07°57' N,	006°40' W
Sinfra	06°37' N,	005°55' W
Tabou	04°25' N,	007°21' W
Tengréla	10°26' N,	006°20' W
Tortiya	08°46' N,	005°41' W
Yamoussoukro	06°49' N,	005°17' W

CROATIA .... page 44

Bjelovar	45°54' N,	016°51' E
Đakovo	45°19' N,	018°25' E
Dubrovnik	42°39' N,	018°07' E
Jasenovav	45°16' N,	016°54' E
Karlovac	45°29' N,	015°33' E
Knin	44°02' N,	016°12' E
Makarska	43°18° N,	017°02' E
Nin	44°14' N,	015°11' E
Opatija	45°20' N,	014°19' E
Osijek	45°33' N,	018°42' E
Ploče	43°04' N,	017°26' E
Pula	44°52' N,	013°50' E
Sesvete	45°50' N,	016°10' E
Rijeka	45°21' N,	014°24' E
Sisak	45°29' N,	016°22' E
Slavonski Brod	45°09' N,	018°02' E
Slavonska Požega (Požega)	45°20' N,	017°41' E
Split	43°31' N,	016°26' E
Trogir	43°32' N,	016°15' E
Varaždin	46°18' N,	016°20' E
Vinkovci	45°17' N,	018°49' E
Vukovar	45°21' N,	019°00' E
Zadar	44°07' N,	015°15' E
Zagreb	45°48' S,	016°00' E

CUBA .... page 45

Banes	20°58' N,	075°43' W
Baracoa	20°21' N,	074°30' W
Bayamo	20°23' N,	076°39' W
Camagüey	21°23' N,	077°55' W
Cárdenas	23°02' N,	081°12' W
Ciego de Avila	21°51' N,	078°46' W
Cienfuegos	22°09' N,	080°27' W
Colón	22°43' N,	080°54' W
Florida	21°32' N,	078°14' W
Guantánamo	20°08' N,	075°12' W
Güines	22°50' N,	082°02' W
Havana (La Habana)	23°08' N,	082°22' W
Holguín	20°53' N,	076°15' W
Jagüey Grande	22°32' N,	081°08' W
Jovellanos	22°48' N,	081°12' W
Las Tunas	20°58' N,	076°57' W
Manzanillo	20°21' N,	077°07' W
Matanzas	23°03' N,	081°35' W
Mayarí	20°40' N,	075°41' W
Morón	22°06' N,	078°38' W
Nueva Gerona	21°53' N,	082°48' W
Nuevitas	21°33' N,	077°16' W
Palma Soriano	20°13' N,	076°00' W
Pinar del Río	22°25' N,	083°42' W
Placetas	22°19' N,	079°40' W
Puerto Padre	21°12' N,	076°36' W
Sagua la Grande	22°49' N,	080°05' W
San Antonio de los Baños	22°53' N,	082°30' W
Sancti Spíritus	21°56' N,	079°27' W
Santa Clara	22°24' N,	079°58' W
Santa Cruz del Sur	20°43' N,	078°00' W
Santiago de Cuba	20°01' N,	075°49' W

CYPRUS .... page 46

Akanthou	35°22' N,	033°45' E
Akrotiri	34°36' N,	032°57' E
Athna	35°03' N,	033°47' E
Ayios Amvrosios	35°20' N,	033°35' E
Ayios Theodhoros	34°48' N,	033°23' E
Famagusta	35°07' N,	033°57' E
Kalokhorio	34°55' N,	033°32' E
Kouklia	34°42' N,	032°34' E
Kyrenia	35°20' N,	033°19' E
Larnaca	34°55' N,	033°38' E
Laxia	35°06' N,	033°22' E
Leonarisso	35°28' N,	034°08' E
Limassol	34°40' N,	033°02' E
Livadhia	35°24' N,	034°02' E
Liveras	35°23' N,	032°57' E
Mari	34°44' N,	033°18' E
Morphou	35°12' N,	032°59' E
Nicosia (Lefkosia)	35°10' N,	033°22' E
Ora	34°51' N,	033°12' E
Ormidhia	34°59' N,	033°47' E
Pakhna	34°46' N,	032°48' E
Pano Lakatamia	35°06' N,	033°18' E
Paphos	34°45' N,	032°25' E
Paralimni	35°02' N,	033°59' E
Patriki	35°22' N,	033°59' E
Perivolia	34°49' N,	033°35' E
Pomos	35°09' N,	032°33' E
Prastio	35°10' N,	033°45' E
Trikomo	35°17' N,	033°52' E
Tsadha	34°50' N,	032°28' E
Varosha	35°06' N,	033°57' E
Vroisha	35°04' N,	032°40' E
Yialoussa	35°32' N,	034°11' E

CZECH REPUBLIC .... page 47

Břeclav	48°46' N,	016°53' E
Brno	49°12' N,	016°38' E
Česká Lípa	50°41' N,	014°33' E
České Budějovice	48°59' N,	014°28' E
Český Těšín	49°45' N,	018°37' E
Cheb	50°04' N,	012°22' E
Chomutov	50°27' N,	013°26' E

Děčín	50°47' N,	014°13' E
Frýdek Místek	49°41' N,	018°21' E
Havířov	49°47' N,	018°22' E
Havlíčkův Brod	49°37' N,	015°35' E
Hodonín	48°52' N,	017°08' E
Hradec Králové	50°13' N,	015°50' E
Jablonec	50°43' N,	015°11' E
Jihlava	49°24' N,	015°35' E
Karlovy Vary	50°13' N,	012°54' E
Karviná	49°52' N,	018°33' E
Kladno	50°09' N,	014°06' E
Kolín	50°02' N,	015°12' E
Krnov	50°06' N,	017°43' E
Kroměříž	49°18' N,	017°24' E
Liberec	50°47' N,	015°03' E
Litvínov	50°36' N,	013°37' E
Mladá Boleslav	50°25' N,	014°54' E
Most	50°32' N,	013°39' E
Nový Jičín	49°36' N,	018°01' E
Olomouc	49°35' N,	017°15' E
Opava	49°57' N,	017°55' E
Orlová	49°51' N,	018°25' E
Ostrava	49°50' N,	018°17' E
Pardubice	50°02' N,	015°47' E
Písek	49°18' N,	014°09' E
Plzeň	49°45' N,	013°22' E
Prague (Praha)	50°05' N,	014°28' E
Přerov	49°27' N,	017°27' E
Příbram	49°42' N,	014°01' E
Prostějov	49°28' N,	017°07' E
Šumperk	49°58' N,	016°58' E
Tábor	49°25' N,	014°40' E
Teplice	50°38' N,	013°50' E
Třebíč	49°13' N,	015°53' E
Trinec	49°41' N,	018°39' E
Trutnov	50°34' N,	015°54' E
Uherské Hradiště	49°04' N,	017°27' E
Ústí nad Labem	50°40' N,	014°02' E
Valašské Meziříči	49°28' N,	017°58' E
Vsetín	49°20' N,	018°00' E
Žd'ár nad Sázavou	49°35' N,	015°56' E
Zlín	49°13' N,	017°40' E
Znojmo	48°51' N,	016°03' E

DENMARK . . . . page 48

Ålborg (Aalborg)	57°03' N,	009°56' E
Århus (Aarhus)	56°09' N,	010°13' E
Års	56°48' N,	009°32' E
Brønderslev	57°16' N,	009°58' E
Brørup	55°29' N,	009°01' E
Copenhagen (København)	55°40' N,	012°35' E
Esbjerg	55°28' N,	008°27' E
Fakse	55°15' N,	012°08' E
Fredericia	55°35' N,	009°46' E
Frederiksberg	55°41' N,	012°32' E
Frederikshavn	57°26' N,	010°32' E
Gilleleje	56°07' N,	012°19' E
Give	55°51' N,	009°15' E
Grenå	56°25' N,	010°53' E
Hadsund	56°43' N,	010°07' E
Helsingǿr	56°02' N,	012°37' E
Herning	56°08' N,	008°59' E
Hillerød	55°56' N,	012°19' E
Hirtshals	57°35' N,	009°58' E
Hjørring	57°28' N,	009°59' E
Holstebro	56°21' N,	008°38' E
Hornslet	56°19' N,	010°20' E
Horsens	55°52' N,	009°52' E
Jyderup	55°40' N,	011°26' E
Klarup	57°01' N,	010°03' E
Køge	55°27' N,	012°11' E
Kolding	55°29' N,	009°29' E
Lemvig	56°32' N,	008°18' E
Løgstør	56°58' N,	009°15' E
Næstved	55°14' N,	011°46' E
Nakskov	54°50' N,	011°09' E
Nykøbing	54°46' N,	011°53' E
Nykøbing	55°55' N,	011°41' E
Nykøbing	56°48' N,	008°52' E
Odense	55°24' N,	010°23' E
Ølgod	55°49' N,	008°37' E
Otterup	55°31' N,	010°24' E
Padborg	54°49' N,	009°22' E
Randers	56°28' N,	010°03' E
Ribe	55°21' N,	008°46' E
Ringkøbing	56°05' N,	008°15' E
Rǿnne	55°06' N,	014°42' E
Roskilde	55°39' N,	012°05' E
Rudkøbing	54°56' N,	010°43' E
Skagen	57°44' N,	010°36' E
Skive	56°34' N,	009°02' E
Skjern	55°57' N,	008°30' E
Slagelse	55°24' N,	011°22' E
Sønderborg	54°55' N,	009°47' E
Struer	56°29' N,	008°37' E
Svendborg	55°03' N,	010°37' E
Thisted	56°57' N,	008°42' E
Tilst	56°12' N,	010°07' E
Toftlund	55°11' N,	009°04' E
Tønder	54°56' N,	008°54' E
Varde	55°38' N,	008°29' E
Vejle	55°42' N,	009°32' E
Viborg	56°26' N,	009°24' E
Vodskov	57°06' N,	010°02' E
Vordingborg	55°01' N,	011°55' E

DJIBOUTI . . . . page 49

Ali Sabih	11°10' N,	042°42' E
Dikhil	11°06' N,	042°23' E

Djibouti	11°36' N, 043°09' E
Tadjoura	11°47' N, 042°53' E

DOMINICA .... page 50

Castle Bruce	15°26' N, 061°16' W
Colihaut	15°30' N, 061°29' W
La Plaine	15°20' N, 061°15' W
Marigot	15°32' N, 061°18' W
Portsmouth	15°35' N, 061°28' W
Rosalie	15°22' N, 061°16' W
Roseau	15°18' N, 061°24' W
Saint Joseph	15°24' N, 061°26 W
Salibia	15°29' N, 061°16' W
Soufrière	15°13' N, 061°22' W
Vieille Case	15°36' N, 061°24' W

DOMINICAN REPUBLIC .... page 51

Azua	18°27' N, 070°44' W
Baní	18°17' N, 070°20' W
Barahona	18°12' N, 071°06' W
Bayaguana	18°58' N, 069°00' W
Bonao	18°56' N, 070°25' W
Cotuí	19°03' N, 070°09' W
Dajabón	19°33' N, 071°42' W
Duvergé	18°22' N, 071°31' W
El Seibo	18°46' N, 069°02' W
Enriquillo	17°54' N, 071°14' W
Higüey	18°37' N, 068°42' W
Jimaní	18°28' N, 071°51' W
La Romana	18°25' N, 068°58' W
La Vega	19°13' N, 070°31' W
Las Matas	18°52' N, 071°31' W
Mao	19°34' N, 071°05' W
Miches	18°59' N, 069°03' W
Moca	19°24' N, 070°31' W
Montecristi	19°52' N, 071°39' W
Nagua (Julia Molina)	19°23' N, 069°50' W
Neiba	18°28' N, 071°25' W
Pedernales	18°02' N, 071°45' W
Puerto Plata	19°48' N, 070°41' W
Sabaneta	19°28' N, 071°20' W
Salcedo	19°23' N, 070°25' W
Samaná	19°13' N, 069°19' W
San Cristóbal	18°25' N, 070°06' W
San Francisco de Macorís	19°18' N, 070°15' W
San Juan	18°48' N, 071°14' W
San Pedro de Macorís	18°27' N, 069°18' W
Sánchez	19°14' N, 069°36' W
Santiago	19°27' N, 070°42' W
Santo Domingo	18°28' N, 069°54' W

EAST TIMOR ..... page 52

Dili	08°33' S, 125°35' E
Manatuto	08°30' S, 126°01' E
Viqueque	08°52' S, 126°22' E

ECUADOR .... page 53

Ambato	01°15' S, 078°37' W
Azogues	02°44' S, 078°50' W
Babahoyo	01°49' S, 079°31' W
Balzar	01°22' S, 079°54' W
Cuenca	02°53' S, 078°59' W
Esmeraldas	00°59' N, 079°42' W
General Leonidas Plaza Gutiérrez	02°58' S, 078°25' W
Girón	03°10' S, 079°08' W
Guayaquil	02°10' S, 079°54' W
Huaquillas	03°29' S, 080°14' W
Ibarra	00°21' N, 078°07' W
Jipijapa	01°20' S, 080°35' W
Latacunga	00°56' S, 078°37' W
Loja	04°00' S, 079°13' W
Macará	04°23' S, 079°57' W
Macas	02°19' S, 078°07' W
Machala	03°16' S, 079°58' W
Manta	00°57' S, 080°44' W
Milagro	02°07' S, 079°36' W
Muisne	00°36' N, 080°02' W
Naranjal	02°40' S, 079°37' W
Otavalo	00°14' N, 078°16' W
Pasaje	03°20' S, 079°49' W
Piñas	03°40' S, 079°39' W
Portoviejo	01°03' S, 080°27' W
Puerto Francisco de Orellana (Coca)	00°28' S, 076°58' W
Puyo	01°28' S, 077°59' W
Quevedo	01°02' S, 079°27' W
Quito	00°13' S, 078°30' W
Riobamba	01°40' S, 078°38' W
Salinas	02°13' S, 080°58' W
San Gabriel	00°36' N, 077°49' W
San Lorenzo	01°17' N, 078°50' W
Santo Domingo de los Colorados (Santo Domingo)	00°15' S, 079°09' W
Tena	00°59' S, 077°49' W
Tulcán	00°48' N, 077°43' W
Valdez	01°15' N, 079°00' W
Yantzaza	03°51' S, 078°45' W
Zamora	04°04' S, 078°58' W
Zaruma	03°41' S, 079°37' W

EGYPT . . . . page 54

Akhmīm	26°34' N, 031°44' E
Al-'Arish	31°08' N, 033°48' E
Alexandria (Al-Iskandariyah)	31°12' N, 029°54' E
Al-Fayyûm	29°19' N, 030°50' E
Al-Khārijah	25°26' N, 030°33' E
Al-Maḥallah Al-Kubrā	30°58' N, 031°10' E
Al-Manṣūrah	31°03' N, 031°23' E
Al-Ma'ṣarah	25°30' N, 029°04' E
Al-Minyā	28°06' N, 030°45' E
Aswān	24°05' N, 032°53' E
Asyut	27°11' N, 031°11' E
Aṭ-Ṭur	28°14' N, 033°37' E
Az-Zāqaziq	30°35' N, 031°31' E
Banhā	30°28' N, 031°11' E
Bani Suwayf	29°05' N, 031°05' E
Cairo (Al-Qahirah)	30°03' N, 031°15' E
Damanhūr	31°02' N, 030°28' E
Damietta (Dumyāṭ)	31°25' N, 031°48' E
Giza (Al-Jīzah)	30°01' N, 031°13' E
Jirjā	26°20' N, 031°53' E
Luxor (Al-Uqsur)	25°41' N, 032°39' E
Mallawī	27°44' N, 030°50' E
Matruh	31°21' N, 027°14' E
Port Said (Bur Sa'id)	31°16' N, 032°18' E
Qinā	26°10' N, 032°43' E
Sawhāj	26°33' N, 031°42' E
Shibīn al-Kawm	30°33' N, 031°01' E
Suez (As-Suways)	29°58' N, 032°33' E
Ṭanṭā	30°47' N, 031°00' E

EL SALVADOR . . . page 55

Acajutla	13°35' N, 089°50' W
Chalatenango	14°02' N, 088°56' W
Chalchuapa	13°59' N, 089°41' W
Cojutepeque	13°43' N, 088°56' W
Ilobasco	13°51' N, 088°51' W
Izalco	13°45' N, 089°40' W
La Unión	13°20' N, 087°51' W
Nueva San Salvador (Santa Tecla)	13°41' N, 089°17' W
San Francisco (San Francisco Gotera)	13°42' N, 088°06' W
San Miguel	13°29' N, 088°11' W
San Salvador	13°42' N, 089°12' W
Santa Ana	13°59' N, 089°34' W
San Vincente	13°38' N, 088°48' W
Sensuntepeque	13°52' N, 088°38' W
Sonsonate	13°43' N, 089°44' W
Usulatán	13°21' N, 088°27' W
Zacatecoluca	13°20' N, 088°52' W

EQUATORIAL GUINEA . . . . page 56

Bata	01°51' N, 009°45' E
Kogo	01°05' N, 009°42' E
Malabo (Santa Isabel)	03°21' N, 008°40' E
Mbini	01°34' N, 009°37' E
Mikomeseng	02°08' N, 010°37' E
Niefang	01°51' N, 010°15' E
San Antonio de Ureca	03°16' N, 008°32' E

ERITREA . . . . page 57

Akordat	15°33' N, 037°53' E
Aseb (Assab)	13°00' N, 042°44' E
Asmara (Asmera)	15°20' N, 038°56' E
Keren	15°47' N, 038°28' E
Massawa (Mitsiwa)	15°36' N, 039°28' E
Nakfa	16°40' N, 038°29' E

ESTONIA . . . . page 58

Abja-Paluoja	58°08' N, 025°21' E
Ambla	59°11' N, 025°51' E
Antsla	57°50' N, 026°32' E
Haapsalu	58°56' N, 023°33' E
Järva-Jaani	59°02' N, 025°53' E
Järvakandi	58°47' N, 024°49' E
Jõgeva	58°45' N, 026°24' E
Käina	58°50' N, 022°47' E
Kallaste	58°39' N, 027°09' E
Kärdla	59°00' N, 022°45' E
Kehra	59°20' N, 025°20' E
Keila	59°18' N, 024°25' E
Kilingi-Nõmme	58°09' N, 024°58' E
Kiviõli	59°21' N, 026°57' E
Kohtla-Järve	59°24' N, 027°15' E
Kunda	59°29' N, 026°32' E
Kuressaare (Kingissepa)	58°15' N, 022°28' E
Lavassaare	58°31' N, 024°22' E
Lihula (Lihula)	58°41' N, 023°50' E
Loksa	59°35' N, 025°42' E
Maardu	59°25' N, 024°59' E
Märjamaa	58°54' N, 024°26' E
Mõisaküla	58°06' N, 025°11' E
Mustla	58°14' N, 025°52' E
Narva	59°23' N, 028°12' E
Nuia	58°06' N, 025°33' E
Orissaare	58°34' N, 023°05' E
Otepää	58°03' N, 026°30' E
Paide	58°54' N, 025°33' E
Paldiski	59°20' N, 024°06' E
Pärnu	58°24' N, 024°32' E
Põlva	58°03' N, 027°03' E

Püssi	59°22' N,	027°03' E
Rakvere	59°22' N,	026°20' E
Räpina	58°06' N,	027°27' E
Rapla	59°01' N,	024°47' E
Saue	59°18' N,	024°34' E
Sindi	58°24' N,	024°40' E
Suure-Jaani	58°33' N,	025°28' E
Tallinn	59°25' N,	024°45' E
Tapa	59°16' N,	025°58' E
Tartu	58°23' N,	026°43' E
Tootsi	58°34' N,	024°49' E
Tõrva	58°00' N,	025°56' E
Türi	58°48' N,	025°26' E
Valga	57°47' N,	026°02' E
Viivikonna	59°19' N,	027°42' E
Viljandi	58°24' N,	025°36' E
Võsu	59°35' N,	025°58' E

ETHIOPIA . . . . page 59

Addis Ababa (Adis Abeba)	09°02' N,	038°42' E
Adigrat	14°17' N,	039°28' E
Adwa (Adowa or Aduwa)	14°10' N,	038°54' E
Agaro	07°51' N,	036°39' E
Akaki	09°05' N,	039°00' E
Aksum	14°08' N,	038°43' E
Alamata	12°25' N,	039°33' E
Arba Minch (Arba Mench)	06°02' N,	037°33' E
Bahir Dar	11°36' N,	037°23' E
Debre Markos	10°21' N,	037°44' E
Debre Zeyit	08°45' N,	038°59' E
Dembidollo	08°32' N,	038°48' E
Dese (Dase)	11°08' N,	039°38' E
Dire Dawa	09°35' N,	041°52' E
Finchaa	09°33' N,	037°21' E
Gonder	12°36' N,	037°28' E
Gore	08°09' N,	035°32' E
Harer (Harar)	09°19' N,	042°07' E
Jijiga	09°21' N,	042°48' E
Jima (Jimma)	07°40' N,	036°50' E
Kembolcha (Kombolcha)	11°05' N,	039°44' E
Kibre Mengist	05°53' N,	038°59' E
Lalibela	12°02' N,	039°02' E
Mekele	13°30' N,	039°28' E
Metu	08°18' N,	035°35' E
Nazret	08°33' N,	039°16' E
Nekemte	09°05' N,	036°33' E
Sodo	06°54' N,	037°45' E
Weldya	11°50' N,	039°41' E
Yirga Alem	06°45' N,	038°25' E

FIJI . . . . page 60

Ba	17°33' S,	177°41' E
Lami	18°07' S,	178°25' E
Lautoka	17°37' S,	177°28' E
Nadi	17°48' S,	177°25' E
Suva	18°08' S,	178°25' E

FINLAND . . . . page 61

Espoo (Esbo)	60°13' N,	024°40' E
Forssa	60°49' N,	023°38' E
Hämeenlinna (Tavastehus)	61°00' N,	024°27' E
Hanko	59°50' N,	022°57' E
Haukipudas	65°11' N,	025°21' E
Heinola	61°13' N,	026°02' E
Helsinki	60°10' N,	024°58' E
Ilmajoki	62°44' N,	022°34' E
Ivalo	68°39' N,	027°36' E
Jämsä	61°52' N,	025°12' E
Joensuu	62°36' N,	029°46' E
Jyväskylä	62°14' N,	025°44' E
Kangasala	61°28' N,	024°05' E
Kaskinen	62°23' N,	021°13' E
Kemi	65°44' N,	024°34' E
Kittilä	67°40' N,	024°54' E
Kotka	60°28' N,	026°55' E
Kouvola	60°52' N,	026°42' E
Kuhmo	64°08' N,	029°31' E
Kuopio	62°54' N,	027°41' E
Lahti	60°58' N,	025°40' E
Lappeenranta (Villmanstrand)	61°04' N,	028°11' E
Lapua	62°57' N,	023°00' E
Lohja	60°15' N,	024°05' E
Mariehamn (Maarianhamina)	60°06' N,	019°57' E
Mikkeli (Sankt Michel)	61°41' N,	027°15' E
Nivala	63°55' N,	024°58' E
Nurmes	63°33' N,	029°07' E
Oulu (Uleåborg)	65°01' N,	025°28' E
Pello	66°47' N,	023°55' E
Pietarsaari	63°40' N,	022°42' E
Pori (Björneborg)	61°29' N,	021°47' E
Posio	66°06' N,	028°09' E
Raahe	64°41' N,	024°29' E
Rauma	61°08' N,	021°30' E
Rovaniemi	66°30' N,	025°43' E
Salla	66°50' N,	028°40' E
Salo	60°23' N,	023°08' E
Sotkamo	64°08' N,	028°25' E
Tampere (Tammerfors)	61°30' N,	023°45' E
Turku (Åbo)	60°27' N,	022°17' E
Vaasa (Vasa)	63°06' N,	021°36' E
Vantaa (Vanda)	60°18' N,	024°51' E

FRANCE .... page 62

Ajaccio	41°55' N,	008°44' E
Amiens	49°54' N,	002°18' E
Angers	47°28' N,	000°33' W
Annecy	45°54' N,	006°07' E
Auch	43°39' N,	000°35' E
Aurillac	44°55' N,	002°27' E
Auxerre	47°48' N,	003°34' E
Avignon	43°57' N,	004°49' E
Bar-le-Duc	48°47' N,	005°10' E
Bastia	42°42' N,	009°27' E
Beauvais	49°26' N,	002°05' E
Belfort	47°38' N,	006°52' E
Bonifacio	41°23' N,	009°09' E
Bordeaux	44°50' N,	000°34' W
Bourges	47°05' N,	002°24' E
Brest	48°24' N,	004°29' W
Caen	49°11' N,	000°21' W
Cahors	44°26' N,	001°26' E
Calais	50°57' N,	001°50' E
Charleville-Mézières	49°46' N,	004°43' E
Chartres	48°27' N,	001°30' E
Clermont-Ferrand	45°47' N,	003°05' E
Colmar	48°05' N,	007°22' E
Dijon	47°19' N,	005°01' E
Dunkirk (Dunkerque)	51°03' N,	002°22' E
Épinal	48°11' N,	006°27' E
Grenoble	45°10' N,	005°43' E
Guéret	46°10' N,	001°52' E
La Rochelle	46°10' N,	001°09' W
Le Havre	49°30' N,	000°08' E
Le Mans	48°00' N,	000°12' E
Lille	50°38' N,	003°04' E
Limoges	45°45' N,	001°20' E
Lyon	45°45' N,	004°51' E
Marseille	43°18' N,	005°24' E
Metz	49°08' N,	006°10' E
Mont-de-Marsan	43°53' N,	000°30' W
Moulins	46°34' N,	003°20' E
Nancy	48°41' N,	006°12' E
Nantes	47°13' N,	001°33' W
Nevers	46°59' N,	003°10' E
Nice	43°42' N,	007°15' E
Nîmes	43°50' N,	004°21' E
Niort	46°19' N,	000°28' W
Orléans	47°55' N,	001°54' E
Paris	48°52' N,	002°20' E
Pau	43°18' N,	000°22' W
Périgueux	45°11' N,	000°43' E
Perpignan	42°41' N,	002°53' E
Poitiers	46°35' N,	000°20' E
Quimper	48°00' N,	004°06' W
Rennes	48°05' N,	001°41' W
Saint-Brieuc	48°31' N,	002°47' W
Strasbourg	48°35' N,	007°45' E
Tarbes	43°14' N,	000°05' E
Toulon	43°07' N,	005°56' E
Toulouse	43°36' N,	001°26' E
Tours	47°23' N,	000°41' E
Troyes	48°18' N,	004°05' E
Tulle	45°16' N,	001°46' E
Valence	44°56' N,	004°54' E
Vannes	47°40' N,	002°45' W
Versailles	48°48' N,	002°08' E
Vesoul	47°38' N,	006°10' E

GABON .... page 63

Bitam	02°05' N,	011°29' E
Booué	00°06' S,	011°56' E
Fougamou	01°13' S,	010°36' E
Franceville	01°38' S,	013°35' E
Kango	00°09' N,	010°08' E
Koula-Moutou	01°08' S,	012°29' E
Lambaréné	00°42' S,	010°13' E
Lastoursville	00°49' S,	012°42' E
Léconi	01°35' S,	014°14' E
Libreville	00°23' N,	009°27' E
Makokou	00°34' N,	012°52' E
Mayumba	03°25' S,	010°39' E
Mekambo	01°01' N,	013°56' E
Mimongo	01°38' S,	011°39' E
Minvoul	02°09' N,	012°08' E
Mitzic	00°47' N,	011°34' E
Mouila	01°52' S,	011°01' E
Ndjolé	00°11' S,	010°45' E
Okondja	00°41' S,	013°47' E
Omboué	01°34' S,	009°15' E
Ovendo	00°17' N,	009°30' E
Oyem	01°37' N,	011°35' E
Port-Gentil	00°43' S,	008°47' E
Setté Cama	02°32' S,	009°45' E
Tchibanga	02°51' S,	011°02' E

GAMBIA .... page 64

Banjul	13°27' N,	016°35' W
Basse Santa Su	13°19' N,	014°13' W
Brikama	13°16' N,	016°39' W
Georgetown	13°32' N,	014°46' W
Mansa Konko	13°28' N,	015°33' W
Serekunda	13°26' N,	016°34' W
Yundum	13°20' N,	016°41' W

GEORGIA .... page 65

Akhalk'alak'i	41°24' N,	043°29' E
Batumi	41°38' N,	041°38' E
Chiat'ura	42°19' N,	043°18' E
Gagra	43°20' N,	040°15' E

Gardabani	41°28' N,	045°05' E
Gori	41°58' N,	044°07' E
Gudaut'a	43°06' N,	040°38' E
Khashuri	41°59' N,	043°36' E
K'obulet'i	41°50' N,	041°45' E
Kutaisi	42°15' N,	042°40' E
Marneuli	41°27' N,	044°48' E
Och'amch'ire	42°43' N,	041°28' E
Pot'i	42°09' N,	041°40' E
Rustari	41°33' N,	045°03' E
Samtredia	42°11' N,	042°20' E
Sokhumi	43°00' N,	041°02' E
Tbilisi (Tiflis)	41°42' N,	044°45' E
T'elavi	41°55' N,	045°28' E
Tqibuli	42°22' N,	042°59' E
Tqvarch'eli (Tkvarchely)	42°51' N,	041°41' E
Ts'khinvali (Staliniri)	42°14' N,	043°58' E
Tsqaltubo	42°20' N,	042°34' E
Zugdidi	42°30' N,	041°53' E

GERMANY .... page 66

Aachen	50°46' N,	006°06' E
Augsburg	48°22' N,	010°53' E
Aurich	53°28' N,	007°29' E
Baden-Baden	48°45' N,	008°15' E
Berlin	52°30' N,	013°22' E
Bielefeld	52°02' N,	008°32' E
Bonn	50°44' N,	007°06' E
Brandenburg	52°25' N,	012°33' E
Bremen	53°05' N,	008°48' E
Bremerhaven	53°33' N,	008°35' E
Chemnitz (Karl-Marx-Stadt)	50°50' N,	012°55' E
Cologne (Köln)	50°56' N,	006°57' E
Cottbus	51°46' N,	014°20' E
Dessau	51°50' N,	012°15' E
Dortmund	51°31' N,	007°27' E
Dresden	51°03' N,	013°45' E
Duisburg	51°26' N,	006°45' E
Düsseldorf	51°13' N,	006°46' E
Erfurt	50°59' N,	011°02' E
Erlangen	49°36' N,	011°01' E
Essen	51°27' N,	007°01' E
Frankfurt am Main	50°07' N,	008°41' E
Freiburg	48°00' N,	007°51' E
Göttingen	51°32' N,	009°56' E
Halle	51°30' N,	012°00' E
Hamburg	53°33' N,	010°00' E
Hannover	52°22' N,	009°43' E
Heidelberg	49°25' N,	008°42' E
Jena	50°56' N,	011°35' E
Kassel	51°19' N,	009°30' E
Kiel	54°20' N,	010°08' E
Leipzig	51°18' N,	012°20' E
Lübeck	53°52' N,	010°42' E
Magdeburg	52°10' N,	011°40' E
Mainz	50°00' N,	008°15' E
Mannheim	49°29' N,	008°28' E
Munich	48°09' N,	011°35' E
Nürnberg (Nuremberg)	49°27' N,	011°05' E
Oldenburg	54°18' N,	010°53' E
Osnabrück	52°16' N,	008°03' E
Potsdam	52°24' N,	013°04' E
Regensburg	49°01' N,	012°06' E
Rostock	54°05' N,	012°08' E
Saarbrücken	49°14' N,	007°00' E
Schwerin	53°38' N,	011°23' E
Siegen	50°52' N,	008°02' E
Stuttgart	48°46' N,	009°11' E
Ulm	48°24' N,	010°00' E
Wiesbaden	50°05' N,	008°15' E
Würzburg	49°48' N,	009°56' E
Zwickau	50°44' N,	012°30'E

GHANA .... page 67

Accra	05°33' N,	000°13' E
Anloga	05°48' N,	000°54' E
Awaso	06°14' N,	002°16' W
Axim	04°52' N,	002°14' W
Bawku	11°03' N,	000°15' W
Bolgatanga	10°47' N,	000°51' W
Cape Coast	05°06' N,	001°15' W
Damongo	09°05' N,	001°49' W
Dunkwa	05°58' N,	001°47' W
Koforidua	05°14' N,	001°20' W
Kumasi	06°41' N,	001°37' W
Mampong	07°04' N,	001°24' W
Obuasi	06°12' N,	001°40' W
Prestea	05°26' N,	002°09' W
Salaga	08°33' N,	000°31' W
Sekondi-Takoradi	04°53' N,	001°45' W
Sunyani	07°20' N,	002°20' W
Swedru	05°32' N,	000°42' W
Tamale	09°24' N,	000°50' W
Tarkwa	05°18' N,	001°59' W
Tema	05°37' N,	000°01' W
Wa	10°03' N,	002°29' W
Yendi	09°26' N,	000°01' W

GREECE .... page 68

Alexandroúpolis (Alexandhroupolis)	40°51' N,	025°52' E
Ándros	37°50' N,	024°56' E
Árgos	37°38' N,	022°44' E
Árta	39°09' N,	020°59' E
Áyios Nikólaos	35°11' N,	025°43' E
Drama	41°09' N,	024°09' E
Edessa (Edhessa)	40°48' N,	022°03' E

Ermoúpolis (Hermoúpolis)	37°27' N,	024°56' E
Flórina	40°47' N,	021°24' E
Hydra (Ídhra)	37°21' N,	023°28' E
Igoumenítsa	39°30' N,	020°16' E
Ioánnina (Yannina)	39°40' N,	020°50' E
Ios	36°44' N,	025°17' E
Iráklion (Candia or Heraklion)	35°20' N,	025°08' E
Kalamariá	40°35' N,	022°58' E
Kalamata (Kalámai)	37°02' N,	022°07' E
Kálimnos	36°57' N,	026°59' E
Karditsa	39°22' N,	021°55' E
Kariaí	40°15' N,	024°15' E
Karpenísion	38°55' N,	021°47' E
Kateríni	40°16' N,	022°30' E
Kavála (Kaválla or Neapolis)	40°56' N,	024°25' E
Kéa	37°38' N,	024°21' E
Kérkira	39°36' N,	019°55' E
Khalkís (Chalcis)	38°28' N,	023°36' E
Khaniá (Canea)	35°31' N,	024°02' E
Khíos (Chios)	38°22' N,	026°08' E
Kilkís	41°00' N,	022°52' E
Komotiní	41°07' N,	025°24' E
Lamía	38°54' N,	022°26' E
Larissa (Lárisa)	39°38' N,	022°25' E
Laurium (Lávrion)	37°43' N,	024°03' E
Mégara	38°00' N,	023°21' E
Mesolóngion (Missolonghi)	38°22' N,	021°26' E
Mitilíni (Mytilene)	39°06' N,	026°33' E
Monemvasía	36°41' N,	023°03' E
Náuplia(Navplion)	37°34' N,	022°48' E
Náxos	37°06' N,	025°23' E
Néa Ionía	38°02' N,	023°45' E
Pátrai	38°15' N,	021°44' E
Piraeus (Piraievs)	37°57' N,	028°38' E
Préveza	38°57' N,	020°45' E
Pylos (Pílos)	36°55' N,	021°42' E
Pyrgos (Pírgos)	37°41' N,	021°27' E
Réthimnon	35°22' N,	024°28' E
Rhodes (Ródhos)	36°26' N,	028°13' E
Sámos	37°45' N,	026°58' E
Samothráki	40°29' N,	025°31' E
Sérrai	41°05' N,	023°33' E
Sparta (Spárti)	37°05' N,	022°26' E
Thásos	40°47' N,	024°43' E
Thebes (Thívai)	38°19' N,	023°19' E
Thessaloníki (Salonika)	40°38' N,	022°56' E
Tríkala	39°33' N,	021°46' E
Trípolis	37°31' N,	022°22' E
Vólos	39°22' N,	022°57' E
Yithion (Githion)	36°45' N,	022°34' E
Xánthi	41°08' N,	024°53' E
Zákinthos	37°47' N,	020°54' E

GRENADA . . . . page 69

Birch Grove	12°07' N,	061°40' W
Concord	12°07' N,	061°44' W
Corinth	12°02' N,	061°40' W
Gouyave	12°10' N,	061°44 W
Grand Anse	12°01' N,	061°45' W
Grenville	12°07' N,	061°37' W
Hillsborough	12°29' N,	061°28' W
La Poterie	12°10' N,	061°36' W
Rose Hill	12°12' N,	061°37' W
St. George's	12°03' N,	061°45' W
Sauteurs	12°14' N,	061°38' W
Victoria	12°12' N,	061°42' W

GUATEMALA . . . . . page 70

Amatitlán	14°29' N,	090°37' W
Antigua Guatemala (Antigua)	14°34' N,	090°44' W
Champerico	14°18' N,	091°55' W
Coatepeque	14°42' N,	091°52' W
Cobán	15°29' N,	090°22' W
Cuilapa (Cuajiniquilapa)	14°17' N,	090°18' W
El Estor	15°32' N,	089°21' W
Escuintla	14°18' N,	090°47' W
Esquipulas	14°34' N,	089°21' W
Flores	16°56' N,	089°53' W
Gualán	15°08' N,	089°22' W
Guatemala City (Guatemala)	14°38' N,	090°31' W
Huehuetenango	15°20' N,	091°28' W
Jalapa	14°38' N,	089°59' W
Jutiapa	14°17' N,	089°54' W
Mazatenango	14°32' N,	091°30' W
Poptún	16°21' N,	089°26' W
Pueblo Nuevo Tiquisate	14°17' N,	091°22' W
Puerto Barrios	15°43' N,	088°36' W
Puerto San José	13°55' N,	090°49' W
Quezaltenango	14°50' N,	091°31' W
Salamá	15°06' N,	090°16' W
San Benito	16°55' N,	089°54' W
San Cristóbal Verapaz	15°23' N,	090°24' W
Santa Cruz del Quiché	15°02' N,	091°08' W
Sololá	14°46' N,	091°11' W
Todos Santos Cuchumatán	15°31' N,	091°37' W
Villa Nueva	14°31' N,	090°35' W
Zacapa	14°58' N,	089°32' W
Zunil	14°47' N,	091°29' W

GUINEA . . . . page 71

Beyla	08°41' N,	008°38' W
Boffa	10°10' N,	014°02' W
Boké	10°56' N,	014°18' W
Conakry	09°31' N,	013°43' W
Dabola	10°45' N,	011°07' W
Dalaba	10°42' N,	012°15' W
Dinguiraye	11°18' N,	010°43' W
Faranah	10°02' N,	010°44' W
Forécariah	09°26' N,	013°06' W
Fria	10°27' N,	013°32' W
Gaoual	11°45' N,	013°12' W
Guéckédou	08°33' N,	010°09' W
Kankan	10°23' N,	009°18' W
Kérouané	09°16' N,	009°01' W
Kindia	10°04' N,	012°51' W
Kissidougou	09°11' N,	010°06' W
Kouroussa	10°39' N,	009°53' W
Labé	11°19' N,	012°17' W
Macenta	08°33' N,	009°28' W
Mamou	10°23' N,	012°05' W
Nzérékoré	07°45' N,	008°49' W
Pita	11°05' N,	012°24' W
Siguiri	11°25' N,	009°10' W
Télimélé	10°54' N,	013°02' W
Tougué	11°27' N,	011°41' W

GUINEA-BISSAU . . . page 72

Bafatá	12°10' N,	014°40' W
Bambadinca	12°02' N,	014°52' W
Bedanda	11°21' N,	015°07' W
Béli	11°51' N,	013°56' W
Bissau	11°51' N,	015°35' W
Bissorã	12°03' N,	015°26' W
Bolama	11°35' N,	015°28' W
Buba	11°35' N,	015°00' W
Bula	12°07' N,	015°43' W
Buruntuma	12°26' N,	013°39' W
Cacheu	12°16' N,	016°10' W
Catió	11°17' N,	015°15' W
Empada	11°33' N,	015°14' W
Farim	12°29' N,	015°13' W
Fulacunda	11°46' N,	015°10' W
Gabú (Nova Lamego)	12°17' N,	014°13' W
Galomaro	11°57' N,	014°38' W
Jolmete	12°13' N,	015°52' W
Madina do Boé	11°45' N,	014°13' W
Mansôa	12°04' N,	015°19' W
Nhacra	11°58' N,	015°33' W
Piche	12°20' N,	013°57' W
Pirada	12°40' N,	014°10' W
Quebo	11°20' N,	014°56' W
Quinhámel	11°53' N,	015°51' W
Safim	11°57' N,	015°39' W
Sangonhá	11°10' N,	014°53' W
São Domingos	12°24' N,	016°12' W
Teixeira Pinto	12°04' N,	016°02' W
Tite	11°47' N,	015°24' W
Xitole	11°44' N,	014°49' W

GUYANA . . . . page 73

Apoteri	04°02' N,	058°34' W
Bartica	06°24' N,	058°37' W
Charity	07°24' N,	058°36' W
Corriverton	05°52' N,	057°10' W
Georgetown	06°48' N,	058°10' W
Isherton	02°19' N,	059°22' W
Ituni	05°30' N,	058°14' W
Karasabai	04°02' N,	059°32' W
Karmuda Village	05°38' N,	060°18' W
Lethem	03°23' N,	059°48' W
Linden	06°00' N,	058°18' W
Mabaruma	08°12' N,	059°47' W
Mahaicony Village	06°36' N,	057°48' W
Matthews Ridge	07°30' N,	060°10' W
New Amsterdam	06°15' N,	057°31' W
Orinduik	04°42' N,	060°01' W
Parika	06°52' N,	058°25' W
Port Kaituma	07°44' N,	059°53' W
Rose Hall	06°16' N,	057°21' W
Suddie	07°07' N,	058°29' W
Vreed en Hoop	06°48' N,	058°11' W

HAITI . . . . page 74

Anse-d'Hainault	18°30' N,	074°27' W
Cap-Haïtien	19°45' N,	072°12' W
Desdunes	19°17' N,	072°39' W
Gonaïves	19°27' N,	072°41' W
Grand Goâve	18°26' N,	072°46' W
Hinche	19°09' N,	072°01' W
Jean Rabel	18°15' N,	072°40' W
Lascahobas	18°50' N,	071°56' W
Léogâne	18°31' N,	072°38' W
Limbé	19°42' N,	072°24' W
Miragoâne	18°27' N,	073°06' W
Mirebalais	18°55' N,	072°06' W
Môle Saint-Nicolas	19°48' N,	073°23' W
Ouanaminthe	19°33' N,	071°44' W
Pètionville	18°31' N,	072°17' W
Petite Rivière de l'Artibonite	19°08' N,	072°29' W
Port-au-Prince	18°32' N,	072°20' W
Roseaux	18°36' N,	074°01' W
Saint-Louis du Nord	19°56' N,	072°43' W
Saint-Michel de l'Atalaye	19°22' N,	072°20' W

Thomasique	19°05' N, 071°50' W
Trou du Nord	19°38' N, 072°01' W
Verrettes	19°03' N, 072°28' W

HONDURAS ...... page 75

Amapala	13°17' N, 087°39' W
Catacamas	14°48' N, 085°54' W
Choloma	15°37' N, 087°57' W
Choluteca	13°18' N, 087°12' W
Comayagua	14°27' N, 087°38' W
Danlí	14°02' N, 086°35' W
El Paraíso	15°01' N, 088°59' W
El Progreso	15°24' N, 087°48' W
Gracias	14°35' N, 088°35' W
Guaimaca	14°32' N, 086°49' W
Intibucá	14°19' N, 088°10' W
Juticalpa	14°39' N, 086°12' W
La Ceiba	15°47' N, 086°48' W
La Esperanza	14°18' N, 088°11' W
La Lima	15°26' N, 087°55' W
La Paz	14°19' N, 087°41' W
Morazán	15°19' N, 087°36' W
Nacaome	13°32' N, 087°29' W
Olanchito	15°30' N, 086°34' W
Puerto Cortés	15°50' N, 087°50' W
Puerto Lempira	15°16' N, 083°46' W
San Lorenzo	13°25' N, 087°27' W
San Marcos de Colón	13°26' N, 086°48' W
San Pedro Sula	15°30' N, 088°02' W
Santa Bárbara	14°55' N, 088°14' W
Santa Rita	15°12' N, 087°53' W
Signatapeque	14°36' N, 087°57' W
Talanga	14°24' N, 087°05' W
Tegucigalpa	14°06' N, 087°13' W
Trujillo	15°55' N, 86°00' W
Yoro	15°08' N, 087°08' W
Yuscarán	13°56' N, 086°51' W

HUNGARY........ page 76

Baja	46°11' N, 018°58' E
Balmazújváros	47°37' N, 021°21' E
Barcs	45°58' N, 017°28' E
Békéscsaba	46°41' N, 021°06' E
Berettyóújfalu	47°13' N, 021°33' E
Budapest	47°30' N, 019°05' E
Cegléd	47°10' N, 019°48' E
Debrecen	47°32' N, 021°38' E
Dunaújváros (Sztálinváros)	46°59' N, 018°56' E
Eger	47°54' N, 020°23' E
Esztergom	47°48' N, 018°45' E
Fertőd (Eszterháza)	47°37' N, 016°52' E
Gyomaendrőd	46°56' N, 020°50' E
Gyöngyös	47°47' N, 019°56' E
Gyor	47°41' N, 017°38' E
Gyula	46°39' N, 021°17' E
Hódmezovásárhely	46°25' N, 020°20' E
Kalocsa	46°32' N, 019°00' E
Kaposvár	46°22' N, 017°48' E
Kazincbarcika	48°15' N, 020°38' E
Kecskemét	46°54' N, 019°42' E
Keszthely	46°46' N, 017°15' E
Kisvárda	48°13' N, 022°05' E
Körmend	47°01' N, 016°36' E
Kőszeg	47°23' N, 016°33' E
Lenti	46°37' N, 016°33' E
Makó	46°13' N, 020°29' E
Marcali	46°35' N, 017°25' E
Miskolc	48°06' N, 020°47' E
Mohács	45°59' N, 018°42' E
Nagyatád	46°13' N, 017°22' E
Nagykanizsa	46°27' N, 016°59' E
Nagykőrös	47°02' N, 019°47' E
Nyirbátor	47°50' N, 022°08' E
Nyíregyháza	47°57' N, 021°43' E
Orosháza	46°34' N, 020°40' E
Ózd	48°13' N, 020°18' E
Paks	46°38' N, 018°52' E
Pápa	47°20' N, 017°28' E
Pécs	46°05' N, 018°14' E
Salgótarján	48°07' N, 019°49' E
Sarkad	46°45' N, 021°23' E
Sárospatak	48°19' N, 021°35' E
Sátoraljaújhely	48°24' N, 021°40' E
Siklós	45°51' N, 018°18' E
Sopron	47°41' N, 016°36' E
Szeged	46°15' N, 020°10' E
Szeghalom	47°02' N, 021°10' E
Székesfehérvár	47°12' N, 018°25' E
Szekszárd	46°21' N, 018°43' E
Szigetvár	46°03' N, 017°48' E
Szolnok	47°11' N, 020°12' E
Szombathely	47°14' N, 016°37' E
Tamási	46°38' N, 018°17' E
Tatabánya	47°34' N, 018°25' E
Vác	47°47' N, 019°08' E
Veszprém	47°06' N, 017°55' E
Zalaegerszeg	46°50' N, 016°51' E

ICELAND......... page 77

Akureyri	65°40' N, 018°06' W
Reykjavík	64°09' N, 021°57' W
Vestmannaeyjar	62°26' N, 020°16' W

INDIA . . . . page 78

Agra	27°11' N,	078°01' E
Ahmadabad (Ahmedabad)	23°02' N,	072°37' E
Ahmadnāgār (Ahmednagar)	19°05' N,	074°44' E
Allahabad	25°27' N,	081°51' E
Amritsar	31°35' N,	074°53' E
Āsānsol	23°41' N,	086°59' E
Balurghat	25°13' N,	088°46' E
Bangalore	12°59' N,	077°35' E
Baroda (Vadodara)	22°18' N,	073°12' E
Bathinda (Bhatinda)	30°12' N,	074°57' E
Bhilwara	25°21' N,	074°38' E
Bhiwandi	19°18' N,	073°04' E
Bhopal	23°16' N,	077°24' E
Bombay (Mumbai)	18°58' N,	072°50' E
Calcutta	22°32' N,	088°22' E
Coimbatore	11°00' N,	076°58' E
Cuddapah	14°28' N,	078°49' E
Dehra Dun	30°19' N,	078°02' E
Delhi	28°40' N,	077°13' E
Eluru (Ellore)	16°42' N,	081°06' E
Gangānagar (Sri Gangānagar)	29°55' N,	073°53' E
Guntur	16°18' N,	080°27' E
Gwalior	26°13' N,	078°10' E
Howrah (Haora)	22°35' N,	088°20' E
Hubli-Dharwad	15°21' N,	075°10' E
Hyderabad	17°23' N,	078°28' E
Imphal	24°49' N,	093°57' E
Indore	22°43' N,	075°50' E
Jabalpur (Jubbulpore)	23°10' N,	079°57' E
Jaipur	26°55' N,	075°49' E
Jammu	32°44' N,	074°52' E
Jamnagar	22°28' N,	070°04' E
Jodhpur	26°17' N,	073°02' E
Jūnāgadh	21°31' N,	070°28' E
Kanpur (Cawnpore)	26°28' N,	080°21' E
Khambhat (Cambay)	22°18' N,	072°37' E
Kochi	09°58' N,	076°14' E
Kota (Kotah)	25°11' N,	075°50' E
Longju	28°45' N,	093°35' E
Lucknow	26°51' N,	080°55' E
Ludhiana	30°54' N,	075°51' E
Madras (Chennai)	13°05' N,	080°17' E
Madurai (Madura)	09°56' N,	078°07' E
Malegaon	20°33' N,	074°32' E
Meerut	28°59' N,	077°42' E
Nagpur	21°09' N,	079°06' E
New Delhi	28°36' N,	077°12' E
Patna	25°36' N,	085°07' E
Pune (Poona)	18°32' N,	073°52' E
Puri	19°48' N,	085°51' E
Quilon	08°53' N,	076°36' E
Raipur	21°14' N,	081°38' E
Rajkot	22°18' N,	070°47' E
Sambalpur	21°27' N,	083°58' E
Shiliguri (Siliguri)	26°42' N,	088°26' E
Sholapur (Solapur)	17°41' N,	075°55' E
Sibsāgar	26°59' N,	094°38' E
Srinagar	34°05' N,	074°49' E
Surat	21°10' N,	072°50' E
Thanjavur (Tanjore)	10°48' N,	079°09' E
Tiruppur (Tirupper)	11°06' N,	077°21' E
Vadodara (Baroda)	22°18' N,	073°12' E
Vārānasi (Banāras, Benares)	25°20' N,	083°00' E
Vishākhapatnam (Visākhāpatam)	17°42' N,	083°18' E

INDONESIA . . . . page 79

Ambon	03°43' S,	128°12' E
Balikpapan	01°17' S,	116°50' E
Banda Aceh (Kuta Raja)	05°34' N,	095°20' E
Bandung	06°54' S,	107°36' E
Banjarmasin	03°20' S,	114°35' E
Cilacap	07°44' S,	109°00' E
Jakarta	06°10' S,	106°48' E
Jambi	01°36' S,	103°37' E
Kendari	03°57' S,	122°35' E
Kupang	10°10' S,	123°35' E
Malang	07°59' S,	112°37' E
Manado	01°29' N,	124°51' E
Mataram	08°35' S,	116°07' E
Medan	03°35' N,	098°40' E
Padang	00°57' S,	100°21' E
Palembang	02°55' S,	104°45' E
Palu	00°53' S,	119°53' E
Samarinda	00°30' S,	117°09' E
Semarang	06°58' S,	110°25' E
Surabaya	07°15' S,	112°45' E
Ujungpandang	05°07' S,	119°24' E

IRAN . . . . page 80

Ahvāz	31°19' N,	048°42' E
Āmol	36°28' N,	052°21' E
Arāk	34°05' N,	049°41' E
Ardabīl	38°15' N,	048°18' E
Bakhtarān	34°19' N,	047°04' E
Bandar 'Abbās	27°11' N,	056°17' E
Behbahān	30°35' N,	050°14' E
Bīrjand	32°53' N,	059°13' E
Būshehr	28°59' N,	050°50' E
Dārāb	28°45' N,	054°34' E

Dezfūl	32°23' N,	048°24' E
Eṣfahān	32°40' N,	051°38' E
Gorgān	36°50' N,	054°29' E
Hamadān	34°48' N,	048°30' E
Kāshān	33°59' N,	051°29' E
Kāzerūn	29°37' N,	051°38' E
Kermān	30°17' N,	057°05' E
Khorramābād	33°30' N,	048°20' E
Khvoy	38°33' N,	044°58' E
Mahābād	36°45' N,	045°43' E
Mashhad	36°18' N,	059°36' E
Orūmīyeh	37°33' N,	045°04' E
Qā'en	33°44' N,	059°11' E
Qom	34°39' N,	050°54' E
Quchan	37°06' N,	058°30' E
Rafsanjān	30°24' N,	056°00' E
Rasht	37°16' N,	049°36' E
Sanandaj	35°19' N,	047°00' E
Shīrāz	29°36' N,	052°32' E
Tabrīz	38°05' N,	046°18' E
Tehran	35°40' N,	051°26' E
Yazd	31°53' N,	054°22' E
Zāhedān	29°30' N,	060°52' E
Zanjān	36°40' N,	048°29' E

IRAQ . . . . page 81

Ad-Diwaniyah	31°59' N,	044°56' E
Al-'Amarah	31°50' N,	047°09' E
Al-Gharrāf	31°21' N,	046°17' E
Al-Hillah	32°29' N,	044°25' E
Al-Khāliṣ	33°49' N,	044°32' E
Al-Kūt	32°30' N,	045°49' E
Al-Maḥmūdiya	33°03' N,	044°21' E
Al-Majarr al-Kabir	31°34' N,	047°00' E
'Ānah	34°28' N,	041°56' E
An-Najaf	31°59' N,	044°20' E
An-Nashwah	30°49' N,	047°36' E
An-Nasiriyah	31°02' N,	046°16' E
Ar-Ramādī	33°25' N,	043°17' E
Ar-Ruṭbah	33°02' N,	040°17' E
As-Samawah	31°18' N,	045°17' E
As-Sulaymaniyah	35°33' N,	045°26' E
Aṣ-Ṣuwayrah	32°55' N,	044°47' E
Baghdad	33°21' N,	044°25' E
Ba'qubah	33°45' N,	044°38' E
Barzān	36°55' N,	044°03' E
Basra (Al-Basrah)	30°30' N,	047°47' E
Dibs	35°40' N,	044°04' E
Hīt	33°38' N,	042°49' E
Irbil (Arbela, Arbil, or Erbil)	36°11' N,	044°01' E
Jalūlā'	34°16' N,	045°10' E
Karbala'	32°36' N,	044°02' E
Khānaqin	34°21' N,	045°22' E
Kirkuk	35°28' N,	044°23' E
Mosul (Al-Mawsil)	36°20' N,	043°08' E
Qal'at Dizah	36°11' N,	045°07' E
Sinjār	36°19' N,	041°52' E
Tall Kayf	36°29' N,	043°08' E
Tikrīt	34°36' N,	043°42' E
Ṭūz Khurmātū (Touz Hourmato)	34°53' N,	044°38' E
Zummār	36°47' N,	042°38' E

IRELAND . . . . page 82

Arklow (An tinbhear Mor)	52°48' N,	006°09' W
Athlone	53°26' N,	007°57' W
Ballina	54°07' N,	009°10' W
Ballycastle	54°17' N,	009°22' W
Ballycotton	51°50' N,	008°01' W
Ballymote	54°05' N,	008°31' W
Ballyvaghan	53°07' N,	009°09' W
Bandon (Droichead na Bandan)	51°45' N,	008°44' W
Bantry	51°41' N,	009°27' W
Belmullet	54°13' N,	010°00' W
Blarney	51°56' N,	008°34' W
Boyle	53°58' N,	008°18' W
Bray (Bre)	53°12' N,	006°06' W
Buncrana	55°08' N,	007°27' W
Carlow (Ceatharlach)	52°50' N,	006°56' W
Carndonagh	55°15' N,	007°16' W
Carrick on Shannon	53°57' N,	008°05' W
Castlebar	53°51' N,	009°18' W
Castletownbere	51°39' N,	009°55' W
Cavan (Cabhan, An)	54°00' N,	007°22' W
Charleville (Rath Luirc)	52°21' N,	008°41' W
Clifden	53°29' N,	010°01' W
Clonakilty	51°37' N,	008°53' W
Clonmel (Cluain Meala)	52°21' N,	007°42' W
Cobh	51°51' N,	008°17' W
Cork (Corcaigh)	51°54' N,	008°28' W
Dingle	52°08' N,	010°15' W
Donegal	54°39' N,	008°07' W
Drogheda (Droichead Atha)	53°43' N,	006°21' W
Dublin	53°20' N,	006°15' W
Dundalk (Dun Dealgan)	54°00' N,	006°25' W
Dungarvan	52°05' N,	007°37' W
Ennis (Inis)	52°51' N,	008°59' W
Enniscorthy	52°30' N,	006°34' W
Ennistimon	52°56' N,	009°18' W
Galway (Gaillimh)	53°17' N,	009°03' W
Gort	53°04' N,	008°49' W
Kenmare	51°53' N,	009°35' W
Kilkee	52°41' N,	009°38' W
Kilkenny (Cill Chainnigh)	52°39' N,	007°15' W
Killarney (Cill Airne)	52°03' N,	009°31' W

Letterkenny	54°57' N,	007°44' W
Lifford	54°50 N,	007°29' W
Limerick (Luimneach)	52°40' N,	008°37' W
Listowel	52°27' N,	009°29' W
Longford	53°44' N,	007°48' W
Loughrea	53°12' N,	008°34' W
Mallow	52°08' N,	008°38' W
Monaghan	54°15' N,	006°58' W
Naas (Nas, An)	53°13' N,	006°40' W
New Ross (Ros Mhic Thriuin)	52°23' N,	006°56' W
Portlaoise (Maryborough, Portlaoighise)	53°02' N,	007°18' W
Portumna	53°05' N,	008°13' W
Roscommon	53°38' N,	008°11' W
Rosslare	52°17' N,	006°23' W
Shannon	52°42' N,	008°52' W
Sligo	54°16' N,	008°29' W
Swords	53°27' N,	006°13' W
Tralee	52°16' N,	009°43' W
Trim	53°33' N,	006°48' W
Tullamore	53°16' N,	007°29' W
Waterford (Port Lairge)	52°15' N,	007°06' W
Westport	53°48' N,	009°31' W
Wexford (Loch Garman)	52°20' N,	006°28' W
Wicklow (Cill Mhantain)	52°59' N,	006°03' W
Youghal	51°57' N,	007°51' W

ISRAEL . . . . page 83

ʻArad	31°15' N,	035°13' E
Ashdod	31°49' N,	034°39' E
Ashqelon	31°40' N,	034°35' E
Bat Yam	32°01' N,	034°45' E
Beersheba (Be'er Shevaʻ)	31°14' N,	034°47' E
Bet She'an	32°30' N,	035°30' E
Bet Shemesh	31°45' N,	035°00' E
Dimona	31°04' N,	035°02' E
Elat	29°33' N,	034°57' E
ʻEn Yahav	30°38' N,	035°11' E
H̱adera	32°26' N,	034°55' E
Haifa (H̱efa)	32°50' N,	035°00' E
Haẕeva	30°48' N,	035°15' E
Herzliyya	32°10' N,	034°51' E
H̱olon	32°01' N,	034°46' E
Jerusalem (Yerushalayim)	31°46' N,	035°14' E
Karmi'el	32°55' N,	035°18' E
Nazareth (Naẕerat)	32°42' N,	035°18' E
Netanya	32°20' N,	034°51' E
Nir Yizẖaq	31°14' N,	034°22' E
Petaẖ Tiqwa	32°05' N,	034°53' E
Qiryat Ata	32°48' N,	035°06' E
Qiryat Shemona	33°13' N,	035°34' E
Rama	32°56' N,	035°22' E
Reẖovot	31°54' N,	034°49' E
Tel Aviv-Yafo	32°04' N,	034°46' E

ITALY . . . . page 84

Agrigento (Girgenti)	37°19' N,	013°34' E
Ancona	43°38' N,	013°30' E
Aosta	45°44' N,	007°20' E
Arezzo	43°25' N,	011°53' E
Bari	41°08' N,	016°51' E
Bologna	44°29' N,	011°20' E
Bolzano	46°31' N,	011°22' E
Brescia	45°33' N,	010°15' E
Cagliari	39°13' N,	009°07' E
Catania	37°30' N,	015°06' E
Catanzaro	38°54' N,	016°35' E
Crotone	39°05' N,	017°08' E
Cuneo (Coni)	44°23' N,	007°32' E
Fermo	43°09' N,	013°43' E
Florence (Firenze or Florentia)	43°46' N,	011°15' E
Foggia	41°27' N,	015°34' E
Genoa (Genova)	44°25' N,	008°57' E
Grosseto	42°46' N,	011°08' E
Iglesias	39°19' N,	008°32' E
Latina	41°28' N,	012°52' E
Manfredonia	41°38' N,	015°55' E
Marsala	37°48' N,	012°26' E
Milan (Milano)	45°28' N,	009°12' E
Naples (Napoli or Neapolis)	40°50' N,	014°15' E
Oristano	39°54' N,	008°36' E
Padua (Padova)	45°25' N,	011°53' E
Palermo	38°07' N,	013°22' E
Perugia (Perusia)	43°08' N,	012°22' E
Pescara	42°28' N,	014°13' E
Piombino	42°55' N,	010°32' E
Pisa	43°43' N,	010°23' E
Porto Torres	40°50' N,	008°24' E
Potenza	40°38' N,	015°48' E
Ragusa	36°55' N,	014°44' E
Ravenna	44°25' N,	012°12' E
Rome (Roma)	41°54' N,	012°29' E
Salerno	40°41' N,	014°47' E
San Remo	43°49' N,	007°46' E
Sassari	40°43' N,	008°34' E
Siena	43°19' N,	011°21' E
Syracuse (Siracusa)	37°04' N,	015°18' E
Taranto (Taras or Tarentum)	40°28' N,	017°14' E
Trapani	38°01' N,	012°29' E
Trento	46°04' N,	011°08' E
Trieste	45°40' N,	013°46' E
Turin (Torino)	45°03' N,	007°40' E

Udine	46°03' N,	013°14' E
Venice (Venezia)	45°27' N,	012°21' E
Verona	45°27' N,	011°00' E

JAMAICA .... page 85

Annotto Bay	18°16' N,	076°46' W
Kingston	17°58' N,	076°48' W
Lucea	18°27' N,	078°10' W
Mandeville	18°02' N,	077°30' W
May Pen	17°58' N,	077°14' W
Montego Bay	18°28' N,	077°55' W
Port Antonio	18°11' N,	076°28' W
St. Ann's Bay	18°26' N,	077°08' W
Savanna-la-Mar	18°13' N,	078°08' W
Spanish Town	17°59' N,	076°57' W

JAPAN .... page 86

Akita	39°43' N,	140°07' E
Aomori	40°49' N,	140°45' E
Asahikawa	43°46' N,	142°22' E
Chiba	35°36' N,	140°07' E
Fukui	36°04' N,	136°13' E
Fukuoka	33°35' N,	130°24' E
Fukushima	37°45' N,	140°28' E
Funabashi	35°42' N,	139°59' E
Gifu	35°25' N,	136°45' E
Hachinohe	40°30' N,	141°29' E
Hakodate	41°45' N,	140°43' E
Hiroshima	34°24' N,	132°27' E
Hofu	34°03' N,	131°34' E
Iwaki	37°05' N,	140°50' E
Kagoshima	31°36' N,	130°33' E
Kanazawa	36°34' N,	136°39' E
Kawasaki	35°32' N,	139°43' E
Kita-Kyushu	33°50' N,	130°50' E
Kōbe	34°41' N,	135°10' E
Kōchi	33°33' N,	133°33' E
Kumamoto	32°48' N,	130°43' E
Kushiro	42°58' N,	144°23' E
Kutchan	42°54' N,	140°45' E
Kyōto	35°00' N,	135°45' E
Matsue	35°28' N,	133°04' E
Matsuyama	33°50' N,	132°45' E
Mito	36°22' N,	140°28' E
Miyazaki	31°52' N,	131°25' E
Morioka	39°42' N,	141°09' E
Muroran	42°18' N,	140°59' E
Nagano	36°39' N,	138°11' E
Nagasaki	32°48' N,	129°55' E
Nagoya	35°10' N,	136°55' E
Naha	26°13' N,	127°40' E
Niigata	37°55' N,	139°03' E
Obihiro	42°55' N,	143°12' E
Okayama	34°39' N,	133°55' E
Ōsaka	34°40' N,	135°30' E
Otaru	43°13' N,	141°00' E
Sakai	34°35' N,	135°28' E
Sapporo	43°03' N,	141°21' E
Sendai	31°49' N,	130°18' E
Shizuoka	34°58' N,	138°23' E
Tokyo	35°42' N,	139°46' E
Tomakomai	42°38' N,	141°36' E
Tottori	35°30' N,	134°14' E
Toyama	36°41' N,	137°13' E
Utsunomiya	36°33' N,	139°52' E
Wakayama	34°13' N,	135°11' E
Wakkanai	45°25' N,	141°40' E
Yaizu	34°52' N,	138°20' E
Yamagata	38°15' N,	140°20' E
Yokohama	35°27' N,	139°39' E

JORDAN .... page 87

Adir	31°12' N,	035°46' E
Al-'Aqabah	29°31' N,	035°00' E
Al-Fayḍah	32°35' N,	038°13' E
Al-Ḥiṣn	32°29' N,	035°53' E
Al-Karak	31°11' N,	035°42' E
Al-Mafraq	32°21' N,	036°12' E
Al-Mazra'ah	31°16' N,	035°31' E
Al-Mudawwarah	29°19' N,	035°59' E
Al-Qaṭrānah	31°15' N,	036°03' E
Amman ('Ammān)	31°57' N,	035°56' E
Ar-Ramthā	32°34' N,	036°00' E
Ash-Shawbak	30°32' N,	035°34' E
Aṣ Ṣalt	32°03' N,	035°44' E
At-Ṭafilah	30°50' N,	.035°36' E
Az-Zarqā'	32°05' N,	036°06' E
Bā'ir	30°46' N,	036°41' E
Dhāt Ra's	31°00' N,	035°46' E
Irbid	32°33' N,	035°51' E
Ma'ān	30°12' N,	035°44' E
Ma'dabā	31°43' N,	035°48' E
Maḥaṭṭat al-Ḥafif	32°12' N,	037°08' E
Maḥaṭṭat al-Jufūr	32°30' N,	038°12' E
Ṣuwayliḥ	32°02' N,	035°50' E

KAZAKHSTAN .... page 88

Almaty (Alma-Ata)	43°15' N,	076°57' E
Aqtau (Aktau, or Shevchenko)	43°39' N,	051°12' E
Aqtöbe (Aktyubinsk)	50°17' N,	057°10' E
Arqalyq	50°13' N,	066°50' E
Astana (Akmola, Akmolinsk, Aqmola, or Tselinograd)	51°10' N,	071°30' E

Atyraū (Atenau, Gurjev, or Guryev)	47°07' N,	051°53' E
Ayaguz	47°56' N,	080°23' E
Balqash (Balkhash or Balchas)	46°49' N,	075°00' E
Dzhezkazgan	47°47' N,	067°46' E
Kokchetav	53°17' N,	069°30' E
Leningor (Leninogorsk or Ridder)	50°22' N,	083°32' E
Oral (Uralsk)	51°14' N,	051°22' E
Öskemen (Ust-Kamenogorsk)	49°58' N,	082°40' E
Panfilov (Zharkent)	44°10' N,	080°01' E
Pavlodar	52°18' N,	076°57' E
Petropavl (Petropavlovsk)	54°52' N,	069°06' E
Qaraghandy (Karaganda)	49°50' N,	073°10' E
Qostanay (Kustanay)	53°10' N,	063°35' E
Qyzylorda(Kzyl-Orda)	44°48' N,	065°28' E
Rūdnyy (Rudny)	52°57' N,	063°07' E
Semey (Semipalatinsk	50°28' N,	080°13' E
Shchūchinsk	52°56' N,	070°12' E
Shymkent (Chimkent or Cimkent)	42°18' N,	069°36' E
Taldyqorghan (Taldy -Kurgan)	45°00' N,	078°24' E
Talghar	43°19' N,	077°15' E
Termirtaū (Samarkand)	50°05' N,	072°56' E
Türkistan	43°20' N,	068°15' E
Tyuratam (Turaram or Leninsk)	45°40' N,	063°20' E
Zhambyl (Dzhambul)	42°54' N,	071°22' E
Zhangatas	43°34' N,	069°45' E
Zhetiqara	52°11' N,	061°12' E
Zhezqazghan	47°47' N,	067°46' E
Zyryan	49°43' N,	084°20' E

KENYA . . . . page 89

Bungoma	00°34' N,	034°34' E
Busia	00°28' N,	034°06' E
Eldoret	00°31' N,	035°17' E
Embu	00°32' S,	037°27' E
Garissa	00°28' S,	039°38' E
Isiolo	00°21' N,	037°35' E
Kisii	00°41' S,	034°46' E
Kisumu	00°06' S,	034°45' E
Lamu	02°16' S,	040°54' E
Lodwar	03°07' N,	035°36' E
Machakos	01°31' S,	037°16' E
Malindi	03°13' S,	040°07' E
Mandera	03°56' N,	041°52' E
Maralal	01°06' N,	036°42' E
Marsabit	02°20' N,	037°59' E
Meru	00°03' N,	037°39' E
Mombasa	04°03' N,	039°40' E
Murang'a	00°43' N,	037°09' E
Nairobi	01°17' S,	036°49' E
Nakuru	00°17' S,	036°04' E
Nanyuki	00°01' N,	037°04' E
Wajir	01°45' N,	040°04' E

KIRIBATI . . . . page 90

Bairiki	01°20' N,	173°01' E

KOSOVO . . . . page 91

Kosovska Mitrovica (Titova Mitrovica)	42°53' N,	020°52' E
Priština	42°40' N,	021°10' E
Prizren	42°13' N,	020°45' E

KUWAIT . . . . page 92

Al-Aḥmadī	29°05' N,	048°04' E
Al-Jahrah	29°20' N,	047°40' E
Ash-Shu'aybah	29°03' N,	048°08' E
Ḥawallī	29°19' N,	048°02' E
Kuwait	29°20' N,	047°59' E

KYRGYZSTAN . . . . page 93

Bishkek (Frunze)	42°54' N,	074°36' E
Dzhalal-Abad	40°56' N,	073°00' E
Irkeshtam	39°41' N,	073°55' E
Kara-Balta	42°50' N,	073°52' E
Karakol (Przhevalsk)	42°33' N,	078°18' E
Kök-Janggak	41°02' N,	073°12' E
Kyzyl-Kyya	40°16' N,	072°08' E
Mayly-Say	41°17' N,	072°24' E
Naryn	41°26' N,	075°58' E
Osh	40°32' N,	072°48' E
Sülüktü	39°56' N,	069°34' E
Talas	42°32' N,	072°14' E
Tash-Kömür	41°21' N,	072°14' E
Tokmok	42°52' N,	075°18' E
Ysyk-Kül (Rybachye)	42°26' N,	076°12' E

LAOS . . . . page 94

Attapu	14°48' N,	106°50' E
Ban Houayxay	20°18' N,	100°26' E
Champasak	14°53' N,	105°52' E

Louang Namtha	20°57' N,	101°25' E
Louangphrabang	19°52' N,	102°08' E
Muang Khammouan (Muang Thakhek)	17°24' N,	104°48' E
Muang Pek	19°35' N,	103°19' E
uang Xaignabouri (Sayaboury)	19°15' N,	101°45' E
Muang Xay	20°42' N,	101°59' E
Pakxé	15°07' N,	105°47' E
Phôngsali	21°41' N,	102°06' E
Saravan	15°43' N,	106°25' E
Savannakhét	16°33' N,	104°45' E
Vientiane (Viangchan)	17°58' N,	102°36' E
Xam Nua	20°25' N,	104°02' E

LATVIA .... page 95

Aizpute	56°43' N,	021°36' E
Alūksne	57°25' N,	027°03' E
Auce	56°28' N,	022°53' E
Balvi	57°08' N,	027°15' E
Bauska	56°24' N,	024°11' E
Cēsis	57°18' N,	025°15' E
Daugavpils	55°53' N,	026°32' E
Dobele	56°37' N,	023°16' E
Gulbene	57°11' N,	026°45' E
Ilūkste	55°58' N,	026°18' E
Jaunjelgava	56°37' N,	025°05' E
Jēkabpils	56°29' N,	025°51' E
Jelgava	56°39' N,	023°42' E
Jūrmala	56°58' N,	023°34' E
Kandava	57°02' N,	022°46' E
Kārsava	56°47' N,	027°40' E
Ķegums	56°44' N,	024°43' E
Krāslava	55°54' N,	027°10' E
Liepāja	56°31' N,	021°01' E
Limbaži	57°31' N,	024°42' E
Ludza	56°33' N,	027°43' E
Malta	56°23' N,	027°07' E
Mazsalace	57°52' N,	025°03' E
Ogre	56°49' N,	024°36' E
Piltene	57°13' N,	021°40' E
Preili	56°18' N,	026°43' E
Priekulė	55°33' N,	021°19' E
Rēzekne	56°30' N,	027°19' E
Riga (Rīga)	56°57' N,	024°06' E
Rujiena	57°54' N,	025°19' E
Sabile	57°03' N,	022°35' E
Salacgrīva	57°45' N,	024°21' E
Saldus	56°40' N,	022°30' E
Sigulda	57°09' N,	024°51' E
Stučka	56°35' N,	025°12' E
Talsi	57°15' N,	022°36' E
Valdemārpils	57°22' N,	022°35' E
Valmiera	57°33' N,	025°24' E
Ventspils	57°24' N,	021°31' E
Viesīte	56°21' N,	025°33' E
Viļaka	57°11' N,	027°41' E
Viļāni	56°33' N,	026°57' E
Zilupe	56°23' N,	028°07' E

LEBANON .... page 96

Ad-Dāmūr	33°44' N,	035°27' E
Al-ʻAbdah	34°31' N,	035°58' E
Al-Batrūn	34°15' N,	035°39' E
Al-Hirmīl	34°23' N,	036°23' E
Al-Labwah	34°12' N,	036°21' E
Al-Qubayyāt	34°34' N,	036°17' E
Amyūn	34°18' N,	035°49' E
An-Nabaṭīyah at-Taḥtā	33°23' N,	035°29' E
Aṣ-Ṣarafand	33°27' N,	035°18' E
Baalbek (Baʻlabakk)	34°00' N,	036°12' E
Bʻaqlīn	33°41' N,	035°33' E
Beirut (Bayrut)	33°53' N,	035°30' E
Bḥamdūn	33°48' N,	035°39' E
Bint Jubayl	33°07' N,	035°26' E
Bsharri	34°15' N,	036°01' E
En-Nāqūrah	33°07' N,	035°08' E
Ghazir	34°01' N,	035°40' E
Ghazzah	33°40' N,	035°49' E
Ghūmāh	34°13' N,	035°42' E
Halbā	34°33' N,	036°05' E
Ḥaṣbayya	33°24' N,	035°41' E
Ḥimlāyā	33°56' N,	035°42' E
Ihdin	34°17' N,	035°58' E
Jubayl (Byblos)	34°07' N,	035°39' E
Jubb Jannin	33°37' N,	035°47' E
Jūniyah	33°59' N,	035°58' E
Jwayyā	33°14' N,	035°19' E
Khaldah	33°47' N,	035°29' E
Marj ʻUyūn	33°22' N,	035°35' E
Shḥim	33°37' N,	035°29' E
Shikkā	34°20' N,	035°44' E
Sidon (Sayda)	33°33' N,	035°22' E
Tripoli (Tarabulus)	34°26' N,	035°51' E
Tyre (Ṣūr)	33°16' N,	035°11' E
Zaḥlah	33°51' N,	035°53' E
Zghartā	34°24' N,	035°54' E

LESOTHO .... page 97

Butha-Butha	28°45' S,	028°15' E
Libono	28°38' S,	028°35' E
Mafeteng	29°49' S,	027°15' E
Maseru	29°19' S,	027°29' E
Mohales Hoek	30°09' S,	027°28' E
Mokhotlong	29°22' S,	029°02' E
Qacha's Nek	30°08' S,	028°41' E
Quthing	30°24' S,	027°43' E
Roma	29°27' S,	027°42' E
Teyateyaneng	29°09' S,	027°44' E

LIBERIA . . . . page 98

Bentol	06°26' N,	010°36' W
Bopolu	06°54' N,	010°46' W
Buchanan (Grand Bassa)	05°53' N,	010°03' W
Careysburg	06°24' N,	010°33' W
Gbarnga	07°00' N,	009°29' W
Grand Cess (Grand Sesters)	04°34' N,	008°13' W
Greenville (Sino)	05°00' N,	009°02' W
Harbel	06°16' N,	010°21' W
Harper	04°22' N,	007°23' W
Kle	06°42' N,	010°53' W
Monrovia	06°19' N,	010°48' W
Robertsport	06°45' N,	011°22' W
Saniquellie (Sangbui)	07°22' N,	008°43' W
Tubmanburg (Vaitown)	06°52' N,	010°49' W
Voinjama	08°25' N,	009°45' W
Yekepa	07°35' N,	008°32' W
Zorzor	07°47' N,	009°26' W
Zwedru (Tchien)	06°04' N,	008°08' W

LIBYA . . . . page 99

Al-Bayḍā (Baida or Zāwiyat al-Bayḍā)	32°46' N,	021°43' E
Al-Kufrah	24°10' N,	023°15' E
Al-Marj (Barce)	32°30' N,	020°50' E
Al-ʿUwaynāt (Sardalas)	25°48' N,	010°33' E
As-Sidrah (Es-Sidre)	30°39' N,	018°22' E
Awbāri (Ubari)	26°35' N,	012°46' E
Az-Zuwaytinah	30°58' N,	020°07' E
Benghazi (Banghazi or Bengasi)	32°07' N,	020°04' E
Dahra	29°30' N,	017°50' E
Darnah (Dērna)	32°46' N,	022°39' E
Ghadāmis (Ghadāmes)	30°08' N,	009°30' E
Ghaddūwah (Goddua)	26°26' N,	014°18' E
Gharyān (Garian)	32°10' N,	013°01' E
Ghāt	24°58' N,	010°11' E
Marādah	29°14' N,	019°13' E
Miṣrātah (Misurata)	32°23' N,	015°06' E
Murzuq	25°55' N,	013°55' E
Sabhā (Sebha)	27°02' N,	014°26' E
Sarīr	27°30' N,	022°30' E
Surt (Sirte)	31°13' N,	016°35' E
Tarabulus, see Tripoli		
Tāzirbū	25°45' N,	021°00' E
Tobruk (Ṭubruq)	32°05' N,	023°59' E
Tripoli (Ṭarābulus)	32°54' N,	013°11' E
Waddān	29°10' N,	016°08' E
Wāw al-Kabīr	25°20' N,	016°43' E
Zalṭan (Zelten)	32°57' N,	011°52' E
Zlīṭan (Zliten)	32°28' N,	014°34' E
Zuwārah (Zuāra)	32°56' N,	012°06' E

LIECHTENSTEIN page 100

Balzers	47°04' N,	009°32' E
Eschen	47°13' N,	009°32' E
Mauren	47°13' N,	009°33' E
Schaan	47°10' N,	009°31' E
Triesen	47°07' N,	009°32' E
Vaduz	47°09' N,	009°31' E

LITHUANIA . . . . . . page 101

Alytus	54°24' N,	024°03' E
Anykščiai	55°32' N,	025°06' E
Birštonas	54°37' N,	024°02' E
Biržai	56°12' N,	024°45' E
Druskininkai	54°01' N,	023°58' E
Gargždai	55°43' N,	021°24' E
Ignalina	55°21' N,	026°10' E
Jonava	55°05' N,	024°17' E
Joniškis	56°14' N,	023°37' E
Jurbarkas	55°04' N,	022°46' E
Kaunas	54°54' N,	023°54' E
Kazly Rūda	54°46' N,	023°30' E
Kėdainiai	55°17' N,	023°58' E
Kelmė	55°38' N,	022°56' E
Klaipėda	55°43' N,	021°07' E
Kuršėnai	56°00' N,	022°56' E
Lazdijai	54°14' N,	023°31' E
Marijampolė (Kapsukas)	54°34' N,	023°21' E
Mažeikiai	56°19' N,	022°20' E
Naujoji Akmenė	56°19' N,	022°54' E
Neringa	55°22' N,	021°04' E
Pagėgiai	55°09' N,	021°54' E
Pakruojis	58°58' N,	023°52' E
Palanga	55°55' N,	021°03' E
Pandėlys	56°01' N,	025°13' E
Panevėžys	55°44' N,	024°21' E
Pasvalys	56°04' N,	024°24' E
Plungė	55°55' N,	021°51' E
Priekulė	55°33' N,	021°19' E
Radviliškis	55°49' N,	023°32' E
Ramygala	55°31' N,	024°18' E
Raseiniai	55°22' N,	023°07' E
Rokiškis	55°58' N,	025°35' E
Šalčininkai	54°18' N,	025°23' E
Šiauliai	55°56' N,	023°19' E
Šilalė	55°28' N,	022°12' E
Šilutė	55°21' N,	021°29' E
Širvintos	55°03' N,	024°57' E
Skuodas	56°16' N,	021°32' E
Tauragė	55°15' N,	022°17' E
Telšiai	55°59' N,	022°15' E

Trakai	54°38' N,	024°56' E
Utena	55°30' N,	025°36' E
Varėna	54°13' N,	024°34' E
Vilkaviškis	54°39' N,	023°02' E
Vilkija	55°03' N,	023°35' E
Vilnius	54°41' N,	025°19' E
Zarasai	55°44' N,	026°15' E

LUXEMBOURG . . . page 102

Bains (Modorf-les-Bains)	49°30' N,	006°17' E
Bettembourg	49°31' N,	006°06' E
Capellen	49°39' N,	005°59' E
Clervaux	50°03' N,	006°02' E
Diekirch	49°52' N,	006°10' E
Differdange	49°31' N,	005°53' E
Dudelange	49°28' N,	006°06' E
Echternach	49°49' N,	006°25' E
Esch-sur-Alzette	49°30' N,	005°59' E
Ettlebruck	49°51' N,	006°07' E
Grevenmacher	49°41' N,	006°27' E
Hesperange	49°34' N,	006°09' E
Junglinster	49°43' N,	006°15' E
Lorentzweiler	49°42' N,	006°09' E
Luxembourg	49°36' N,	006°08' E
Mamer	49°38' N,	006°02' E
Mersch	49°45' N,	006°06' E
Niederanven	49°39' N,	006°16' E
Pétange	49°33' N,	005°53' E
Rambrouch	49°50' N,	005°51' E
Redange	49°46' N,	005°53' E
Remich	49°32' N,	006°22' E
Sanem	49°33' N,	005°56' E
Schifflange	49°30' N,	006°01' E
Vianden	49°56' N,	006°13' E
Walfedange	49°39' N,	006°08' E
Wiltz	49°58' N,	005°56' E
Wincrange	50°03' N,	005°55' E
Wormeldange	49°37' N,	006°25' E

MACEDONIA . . . . page 103

Bitola	41°02' N,	021°20' E
Gostivar	41°48' N,	020°54' E
Kavadarci	41°26' N,	022°00' E
Kičevo	41°31' N,	020°57' E
Kočani	41°55' N,	022°25' E
Kruševo	41°22' N,	021°15' E
Kumanovo	42°08' N,	021°43' E
Ohrid	41°07' N,	020°48' E
Prilep	41°21' N,	021°34' E
Skopje (Skoplje)	42°00' N,	021°29' E
Štip	41°44' N,	022°12' E
Strumica	41°26' N,	022°39' E
Tetovo	42°01' N,	020°59' E
Tito Veles	41°42' N,	021°48' E

MADAGASCAR . . . page 104

Ambanja	13°41' S,	048°27' E
Ambatondrazaka	17°50' S,	048°25' E
Andapa	14°39' S,	049°39' E
Ankarana (Sosumav)	13°05' S,	048°55' E
Antalaha	14°53' S,	050°17' E
Antananarivo (Tananarive)	18°55' S,	047°31' E
Antsirabe	19°51' S,	047°02' E
Antsirañana (Diégo-Suarez)	12°16' S,	049°17' E
Antsohihy	14°52' S,	047°59' E
Fianarantsoa	21°26' S,	047°05' E
Ihosy	22°24' S,	046°07' E
Maevatanana	16°57' S,	046°50' E
Mahabo	20°23' S,	044°40' E
Mahajanga (Majunga)	15°43' S,	046°19' E
Mahanoro	19°54' S,	048°48' E
Mananjary	21°13' S,	048°20' E
Maroantsetra	15°26' S,	049°44' E
Marovoay	16°06' S,	046°38' E
Morombe	21°44' S,	043°21' E
Morondava	20°17' S,	044°17' E
Port-Bergé (Boriziny)	15°33' S,	047°40' E
Toamasina (Tamatave)	18°10' S,	049°23' E
Tôlañaro (Faradofay, Fort-Dauphin or Taolanaro)	25°02' S,	047°00' E
Toliara (Toliary or Tulear)	23°21' S,	043°40' E
Vangaindrano	23°21' S,	047°36' E
Vatomandry	19°20' S,	048°59' E

MALAWI . . . . page 105

Balaka	14°59' S,	034°57' E
Blantyre	15°47' S,	035°00' E
Chikwawa	16°03' S,	034°48' E
Cholo (Thyolo)	16°04' S,	035°08' E
Dedza	14°22' S,	034°20' E
Dowa	13°39' S,	033°56' E
Karonga	09°56' S,	033°56' E
Kasungu	13°02' S,	033°29' E
Lilongwe	13°59' S,	033°47' E
Mangoche (Fort Johnson)	14°28' S,	035°16' E
Mchinji (Fort Manning)	13°48' S,	032°54' E
Monkey Bay	14°05' S,	034°55' E

Mzimba	11°54' S, 033°36' E
Mzuzu	11°27' S, 033°55' E
Nkhata Bay	11°36' S, 034°18' E
Nkhota Kota (Kota Kota)	12°55' S, 034°18' E
Nsanje (Port Herald)	16°55' S, 035°16' E
Salima	13°47' S, 034°26' E
Zomba	15°23' S, 035°20' E

MALAYSIA ...... page 106

Alor Setar	06°07' N, 100°22' E
Batu Pahat	01°51' N, 102°56' E
Bau	01°25' N, 110°09' E
Bentong	03°32' N, 101°55' E
Bintulu	03°10' N, 113°02' E
Butterworth	05°25' N, 100°24' E
George Town (Pinang)	05°25' N, 100°20' E
Ipoh	04°35' N, 101°05' E
Johor Baharu	01°28' N, 103°45' E
Kangar	06°26' N, 100°12' E
Kelang (Klang)	03°02' N, 101°27' E
Keluang	02°02' N, 103°19' E
Kota Baharu	06°08' N, 102°15' E
Kota Kinabalu (Jesselton)	05°59' N, 116°04' E
Kota Tinggi	01°44' N, 103°54' E
Kuala Dungun (Dungun)	04°47' N, 103°26' E
Kuala Lumpur	03°10' N, 101°42' E
Kuala Terengganu	05°20' N, 103°08' E
Kuantan	03°48' N, 103°20' E
Kuching	01°33' N, 110°20' E
Lundu	01°40' N, 109°51' E
Melaka (Malacca)	02°12' N, 102°15' E
Miri	04°23' N, 113°59' E
Muar (Bandar Maharani)	02°02' N, 102°34' E
Petaling Jaya	03°05' N, 101°39' E
Sandakan	05°50' N, 118°07' E
Sarikei	02°07' N, 111°31' E
Seremban	02°43' N, 101°56' E
Sibu	02°18' N, 111°49' E
Song	02°01' N, 112°33' E
Sri Aman (Simanggang)	01°15' N, 111°26' E
Taiping	04°51' N, 100°44' E
Tawau	04°15' N, 117°54' E
Teluk Intan (Telok Anson)	04°02' N, 101°01' E
Victoria (Labuan)	05°17' N, 115°15' E

MALDIVES ...... page 107

Male	04°10' N, 073°30' E

MALI .... page 108

Ansongo	15°40' N, 000°30' E
Bafoulabé	13°48' N, 010°50' W
Bamako	12°39' N, 008°00' W
Diamou	14°05' N, 011°16' W
Diré	16°16' N, 003°24' W
Gao	16°16' N, 000°03' W
Goundam	16°25' N, 003°40' W
Kalana	10°47' N, 008°12' W
Kangaba	11°56' N, 008°25' W
Kayes	14°27' N, 011°26' W
Kolokani	13°35' N, 008°02' W
Koro	14°04' N, 003°05' W
Labbezanga	14°57' N, 000°42' E
Ménaka	15°55' N, 002°24' E
Mopti	14°30' N, 004°12' W
Nara	15°10' N, 007°17' W
Niafounké	15°56' N, 004°00' W
Nioro Du Sahel	15°14' N, 009°35' W
San	13°18' N, 004°54' W
Ségou	13°27' N, 006°16' W
Sikasso	11°19' N, 005°40' W
Taoudenni	22°40' N, 003°59' W
Timbuktu	16°46' N, 003°01' W

MALTA .... page 109

Birkirkara	35°54' N, 014°28' E
Hamrun	35°53' N, 014°29' E
Mosta	35°55' N, 014°26' E
Rabat	35°53' N, 014°24' E
Valletta (Valetta)	35°54' N, 014°31' E
Żabbar	35°52' N, 014°32' E
Żebbug	35°52' N, 014°26' E
Żejtun	35°51' N, 014°32' E

MARSHALL ISLANDS .... page 110

Majuro	07°09' N, 171°12' E

MAURITANIA .... page 111

Akjoujt	19°45' N, 014°23' W
Aleg	17°03' N, 013°55' W
Atar	20°31' N, 013°03' W
Ayoûn el 'Atroûs	16°40' N, 009°37' W
Bir Mogrein	25°14' N, 011°35' W
Bogué (Boghé)	16°35' N, 014°16' W
Boutilimit	17°33' N, 014°42' W
Chinguetti	20°27' N, 012°22' W
Fdérik	22°41' N, 012°43' W

Guérou	16°48' N, 011°50' W
Kaédi	16°09' N, 013°30' W
Kiffa	16°37' N, 011°24' W
Maghama	15°31' N, 012°51' W
M'Bout	16°02' N, 012°35' W
Mederdra	16°55' N, 015°39' W
Néma	16°37' N, 007°15' W
Nouadhibou	20°54' N, 017°04' W
Nouakchott	18°06' N, 015°57' W
Rosso	16°30' N, 015°49' W
Sélibaby	15°10' N, 012°11' W
Tichit	18°28' N, 009°30' W
Tidjikdja	18°33' N, 011°25' W
Timbédra	16°15' N, 008°10' W
Zouirât	22°42' N, 012°30' W

MAURITIUS ..... page 112

Port Louis	20°10' S, 057°30' E

MEXICO......... page 113

Acapulco	16°51' N, 099°55' W
Aguascalientes	21°53' N, 102°18' W
Caborca	30°37' N, 112°06' W
Campeche	19°51' N, 090°32' W
Cananea	30°57' N, 110°18' W
Cancún	21°05' N, 086°46' W
Carmen	18°38' N, 091°50' W
Casas Grandes	30°22' N, 107°57' W
Chetumal	18°30' N, 088°18' W
Chihuahua	28°38' N, 106°05' W
Ciudad Acuña (Las Vacas)	29°18' N, 100°55' W
Ciudad Juárez	31°44' N, 106°29' W
Ciudad Obregón	27°29' N, 109°56' W
Ciudad Victoria	23°44' N, 099°08' W
Colima	19°14' N, 103°43' W
Culiacán	24°48' N, 107°24' W
Durango	24°02' N, 104°40' W
Guadalajara	20°40' N, 103°20' W
Guadalupe	25°41' N, 100°15' W
Guaymas	27°56' N, 110°54' W
Hermosillo	29°04' N, 110°58' W
Jiménez	27°08' N, 104°55' W
Juchitán	16°26' N, 095°01' W
La Paz	24°10' N, 110°18' W
León	21°07' N, 101°40' W
Matamoros	25°53' N, 097°30' W
Matehuala	23°39' N, 100°39' W
Mazatlán	23°13' N, 106°25' W
Mérida	20°58' N, 089°37' W
Mexicali	32°40' N, 115°29' W
Mexico City (Ciudad de Mexico)	19°24' N, 099°09' W
Minatitlán	17°59' N, 094°31' W
Monterrey	25°40' N, 100°19' W
Morelia	19°42' N, 101°07' W
Nuevo Laredo	27°30' N, 099°31' W
Oaxaca	17°03' N, 096°43' W
Poza Rica	20°33' N, 097°27' W
Puebla	19°03' N, 098°12' W
Saltillo	25°25' N, 101°00' W
San Felipe	31°00' N, 114°52' W
San Ignacio	27°27' N, 112°51' W
Tampico	22°13' N, 097°51' W
Tijuana	32°32' N, 117°01' W
Torreón	25°33' N, 103°26' W
Tuxtla	16°45' N, 093°07' W
Veracruz	19°12' N, 096°08' W
Villahermosa	17°59' N, 092°55' W
Zapopan	20°43' N, 103°24' W

MICRONESIA, FEDERATED STATES OF....... page 114

Colonia	09°31' N, 138°08' E
Kosrae	05°19' N, 162°59' E
Palikir	06°59' N, 158°08' E
Weno	07°26' N, 151°52' E

MOLDOVA ...... page 115

Bălţi	47°46' N, 027°56' E
Calaras	47°16' N, 028°19' E
Căuşeni	46°38' N, 029°25' E
Chişinău	47°00' N, 028°50' E
Ciadâr-Lunga	46°03' N, 028°50' E
Comrat (Komrat)	46°18' N, 028°39' E
Drochia	48°02' N, 027°48' E
Dubăsari	47°07' N, 029°10' E
Făleşti (Faleshty)	47°34' N, 027°42' E
Floreşti	47°53' N, 028°17' E
Hânceşti (Kotovsk)	46°50' N, 028°36' E
Kagul	45°54' N, 028°11' E
Leova (Leovo)	46°28' N, 028°15' E
Orhei (Orgeyev)	47°22' N, 028°49' E
Râbnita	47°45' N, 029°00' E
Rezina	47°45' N, 028°58' E
Soroca (Soroki)	48°09' N, 028°18' E
Tighina	46°49' N, 029°29' E
Tiraspol	46°50' N, 029°37' E
Ungheni	47°12' N, 027°48' E

MONACO .... page 116

Monaco	43°44' N, 007°25' E

MONGOLIA ...... page 117

Altay	46°20' N,	096°18' E
Arvayheer	46°15' N,	102°48' E
Baruun-Urt	46°42' N,	113°15' E
Bulgan	48°45' N,	103°34' E
Choybalsan (Bayan Tumen)	48°04' N,	114°30' E
Choyr	46°20' N,	108°20' E
Dalandzadgad	43°34' N,	104°25' E
Darhan	49°29' N,	105°55' E
Dariganga	45°18' N,	113°52' E
Dzüünharaa	48°52' N,	106°28' E
Erdenet	49°02' N,	104°05' E
Ereen	49°15' N,	112°29' E
Hanh	51°30' N,	100°40' E
Hatgal	50°26' N,	100°09' E
Hovd (Jirgalanta)	48°01' N,	091°38' E
Mörön	49°38' N,	100°10' E
Öndörhaan (Tsetsen Khan)	47°19' N,	110°39' E
Saynshand	44°52' N,	110°09' E
Sühbaatar	50°15' N,	106°12' E
Tes	49°41' N,	095°48' E
Tosontsengel	48°47' N,	098°15' E
Tsetserleg	47°30' N,	101°27' E
Tümentsogt	47°27' N,	112°15' E
Ulaanbaatar	47°55' N,	106°53' E
Uliastay	47°45' N,	096°49' E

MONTENEGRO .. page 118

Bar	42°05' N,	019°06' E
Nikšić	42°46' N,	018°58' E
Podgorica (Titograd)	42°26' N,	019°16' E

MOROCCO ...... page 119

Agadir	30°24' N,	009°36' W
Asilah (Arzila or Arcila)	35°28' N,	006°02' W
Beni Mellal	32°20' N,	006°21' W
Berkane	34°56' N,	002°20' W
Boudenib	31°57' N,	003°36' W
Boulemane	33°22' N,	004°45' W
Casablanca (Ad-Dār al-Bayḍā' or Dar el-Beida)	33°37' N,	007°35' W
El Jadida (Mazagan)	33°15' N,	008°30' W
El-Kelaa des Srarhna	32°03' N,	007°24' W
Er-Rachidia (Ksar es-Souk)	31°56' N,	004°26' W
Fès (Fez)	34°02' N,	004°59' W
Figuig	32°06' N,	001°14' W
Guelmim (Goulimine)	28°56' N,	010°04' W
Kenitra (Mina Hassan Tani or Port-Lyautey)	34°16' N,	006°36' W
Khouribga	32°53' N,	006°54' W
Larache (El-Araish)	35°12' N,	006°09' W
Marrakech	31°38' N,	008°00' W
Meknès	33°54' N,	005°33' W
Mohammedia (Fedala)	33°42' N,	007°24' W
Nador	35°11' N,	002°56' W
Ouarzazate	30°55' N,	006°55' W
Oued Zem	32°52' N,	006°34' W
Oujda	34°40' N,	001°54' W
Rabat (Ribat)	34°02' N,	006°50' W
Safi (Asfi)	32°18' N,	009°14' W
Salé (Sla)	34°04' N,	006°48' W
Settat	33°00' N,	007°37' W
Tangier (Tanger)	35°48' N,	005°48' W
Tan-Tan	28°26' N,	011°06' W
Taounate	34°33' N,	004°39' W
Tarfaya	27°57' N,	012°55' W
Tata	29°45' N,	007°59' W
Taza	34°13' N,	004°01' W
Tétouan (Tetuan)	35°34' N,	005°22' W
Zagora	30°19' N,	005°50' W

MOZAMBIQUE .. page 120

Angoche	16°15' S,	039°54' E
Beira	19°50' S,	034°52' E
Chimoio (Vila Pery)	19°08' S,	033°29' E
Chokwe	24°32' S,	032°59' E
Inhambane	23°52' S,	035°23' E
Lichinga	13°18' S,	035°14' E
Maputo (Lourenço Marques)	25°58' S,	032°34' E
Massinga	23°20' S,	035°22' E
Memba	14°12' S,	040°32' E
Moçambique (Mozambique)	15°03' S,	040°45' E
Mocubúri	14°39' S,	038°54' E
Mopeia Velha	17°59' S,	035°43' E
Morrumbene	23°39' S,	035°20' E
Nacala	14°33' S,	040°40' E
Namapa	13°43' S,	039°50' E
Nampula	15°09' S,	039°18' E
Panda	24°03' S,	034°43' E
Pemba	12°57' S,	040°30' E
Quelimane	17°51' S,	036°52' E
Quissico	24°43' S,	034°45' E
Tete	16°10' S,	033°36' E
Vila da Manhiça	25°24' S,	032°48' E

Vila da Mocimboa da Praia . . . . 11°20' S, 040°21' E
Vila do Chinde (Chinde) . . . . 18°34' S, 036°27' E
Xai Xai (Joaõ Belo) . . . . 25°04' S, 033°39' E

MYANMAR . . . . . page 121

Allanmyo . . . . 19°22' N, 095°13' E
Bassein (Pathein) . . . . 16°47' N, 094°44' E
Bhamo . . . . 24°16' N, 097°14' E
Chauk . . . . 20°53' N, 094°49' E
Henzada . . . . 17°38' N, 095°28' E
Homalin . . . . 24°52' N, 094°55' E
Kale . . . . 16°05' N, 097°54' E
Katha . . . . 24°11' N, 096°21' E
Kawthaung . . . . 09°59' N, 098°33' E
Kēng Tung . . . . 21°17' N, 099°36' E
Kyaikkami . . . . 16°04' N, 097°34' E
Kyaukpyu (Ramree) . . . . 19°05' N, 093°52' E
Labutta . . . . 16°09' N, 094°46' E
Loi-kaw . . . . 19°41' N, 097°13' E
Magwe (Magwa) . . . . 20°09' N, 094°55' E
Mandalay . . . . 22°00' N, 096°05' E
Mergui . . . . 12°26' N, 098°36' E
Minbu . . . . 20°11' N, 094°53' E
Monywa . . . . 22°07' N, 095°08' E
Moulmein (Mawlamyine) . . . . 16°30' N, 097°38' E
Myitkyina . . . . 25°23' N, 097°24' E
Naypyidaw . . . . 19°44' N, 096°07' E
Pegu (Bago) . . . . 17°20' N, 096°29' E
Prome (Pye) . . . . 18°49' N, 095°13' E
Putao . . . . 27°21' N, 097°24' E
Pyinmana . . . . 19°44' N, 096°13' E
Sagaing . . . . 21°52' N, 095°59' E
Shwebo . . . . 22°34' N, 095°42' E
Sittwe (Akyab) . . . . 20°09' N, 092°54' E
Syriam . . . . 16°46' N, 096°15' E
Taunggyi . . . . 20°47' N, 097°02' E
Tavoy (Dawei) . . . . 14°05' N, 098°12' E
Tenasserim . . . . 12°05' N, 099°01' E
Thaton . . . . 16°55' N, 097°22' E
Tonzang . . . . 23°36' N, 093°42' E
Toungoo . . . . 18°56' N, 096°26' E
Yangon (Rangoon) . . . . 16°47' N, 096°10' E

NAMIBIA . . . . page 122

Aranos . . . . 24°08' S, 019°07' E
Bagani . . . . 18°07' S, 021°38' E
Gobabis . . . . 22°27' S, 018°58' E
Grootfontein . . . . 19°34' S, 018°07' E
Karasburg . . . . 28°01' S, 018°45' E
Karibib . . . . 21°56' S, 015°50' E
Keetmanshoop . . . . 26°35' S, 018°08' E
Khorixas . . . . 20°22' S, 014°58' E
Lüderitz . . . . 26°38' S, 015°09' E
Maltahöhe . . . . 24°50' S, 016°59' E
Mariental . . . . 24°38' S, 017°58' E
Okahandja . . . . 21°59' S, 016°55' E
Omaruru . . . . 21°26' S, 015°56' E
Ondangwa (Ondangua) . . 17°55' S, 015°57' E
Opuwo . . . . 18°04' S, 013°51' E
Oranjemund . . . . 28°33' S, 016°26' E
Oshakati . . . . 17°47' S, 015°41' E
Otjimbingwe . . . . 22°21' S, 016°08' E
Otjiwarongo . . . . 20°27' S, 016°39' E
Outjo . . . . 20°07' S, 016°09' E
Rehoboth . . . . 23°19' S, 017°05' E
Rundu . . . . 17°56' S, 019°46' E
Swakopmund . . . . 22°41' S, 014°32' E
Tsumeb . . . . 19°14' S, 017°43' E
Usakos . . . . 22°00' S, 015°36' E
Walvis Bay . . . . 22°57' S, 014°30' E
Warmbad . . . . 28°27' S, 018°44' E
Windhoek . . . . 22°35' S, 017°05' E

NAURU . . . . page 123

Yaren . . . . 00°32' S, 166°55' E

NEPAL . . . . page 124

Bāglūṅg . . . . 28°16' N, 083°36' E
Banepa . . . . 27°38' N, 085°31' E
Bhairahawā . . . . 27°30' N, 083°27' E
Bhaktapur (Bhadgaon) . . . 27°41' N, 085°25' E
Bhojpūr . . . . 27°10' N, 087°03' E
Biratnagar . . . . 26°29' N, 087°17' E
Birendranagar . . . . 28°46' N, 081°38' E
Birganj . . . . 27°00' N, 084°52' E
Dailekh . . . . 28°50' N, 081°44' E
Dandeldhūrā . . . . 29°18' N, 080°35' E
Ilām . . . . 26°54' N, 087°56' E
Jājarkot . . . . 28°42' N, 082°12' E
Jalésvar . . . . 26°38' N, 085°48' E
Jomosom . . . . 28°47' N, 083°44' E
Jumlā . . . . 29°17' N, 082°10' E
Kathmandu . . . . 27°43' N, 085°19' E
Lahān . . . . 26°43' N, 086°29' E
Lalitpur (Patan) . . . . 27°40' N, 085°20' E
Lumbini (Rummin-dei) . . . 27°29' N, 083°17' E
Mahendranagar . . . . 28°55' N, 080°20' E
Mustāng . . . . 29°11' N, 083°58' E
Nepālganj . . . . 28°03' N, 081°37' E
Pokharā . . . . 28°14' N, 083°59' E
Sallyān . . . . 28°22' N, 082°10' E
Simikot . . . . 29°58' N, 081°50' E
Taplejūṅg . . . . 27°21' N, 087°40' E

NETHERLANDS .. page 125

Alkmaar	52°38' N,	004°45' E
Almelo	52°21' N,	006°40' E
Amersfoort	52°09' N,	005°23' E
Amstelveen	52°18' N,	004°52' E
Amsterdam	52°21' N,	004°55' E
Apeldoorn	52°13' N,	005°58' E
Arnhem	51°59' N,	005°55' E
Assen	53°00' N,	006°33' E
Bergen op Zoom	51°30' N,	004°18' E
Breda	51°34' N,	004°48' E
Delft	52°00' N,	004°22' E
Den Helder	52°58' N,	004°46' E
Deventer	52°15' N,	006°12' E
Dordrecht (Dort or Dordt)	51°48' N,	004°40' E
Drachten	53°06' N,	006°06' E
Ede	52°02' N,	005°40' E
Eindhoven	51°27' N,	005°28' E
Emmen	52°47' N,	006°54' E
Enschede	52°13' N,	006°54' E
Geleen	50°58' N,	005°50' E
Gendringen	51°52' N,	006°23' E
Groningen	53°13' N,	006°33' E
Haarlem	52°22' N,	004°39' E
Heerenveen	52°57' N,	005°56' E
Heerlen	50°54' N,	005°59' E
Helmond	51°29' N,	005°40' E
Hengelo	52°16' N,	006°48' E
Hilversum	52°14' N,	005°11' E
Hoofddorp (Haarlemmermeer)	52°18' N,	004°42' E
Hoorn	52°39' N,	005°04' E
IJmuiden	52°28' N,	004°36' E
Langedijk	52°42' N,	004°49' E
Leeuwarden (Ljouwert)	53°12' N,	005°47' E
Leiden (Leyden)	52°09' N,	004°30' E
Lelystad	52°31' N,	005°29' E
Maastricht	50°51' N,	005°41' E
Meppel	52°42' N,	006°12' E
Middelburg	51°30' N,	003°37' E
Nieuwegein	52°02' N,	005°06' E
Nijmegen (Nimwegen)	51°50' N,	005°52' E
Ommen	52°31' N,	006°26' E
Oostburg	51°20' N,	003°30' E
Oss	51°46' N,	005°32' E
Purmerend	52°31' N,	004°57' E
Ridderkerk	51°52' N,	004°36' E
Roermond	51°12' N,	006°00' E
Roosendaal	51°32' N,	004°28' E
Rosmalen	51°43' N,	005°22' E
Rotterdam	51°55' N,	004°30' E
Schiedam	51°55' N,	004°24' E
's-Hertogenbosch (Den Bosch or Bois-le-Duc)	51°42' N,	005°19' E
Sneek (Snits)	53°02' N,	005°40' E
Soest	52°11' N,	005°18' E
Steenwijk	52°47' N,	006°07' E
Stein	50°58' N,	005°46' E
Terneuzen	51°20' N,	003°50' E
The Hague ('s-Gravenhage, Den Haag, or La Haye)	52°05' N,	004°18' E
Tholen	51°32' N,	004°13' E
Tilburg	51°33' N,	005°07' E
Utrecht	52°05' N,	005°08' E
Veenendaal	52°02' N,	005°33' E
Venlo	51°22' N,	006°10' E
Vlaardingen	51°55' N,	004°21' E
Vlissingen (Flushing)	51°27' N,	003°35' E
Zaanstad	52°27' N,	004°50' E
Zoetermeer	52°03' N,	004°30' E
Zwolle	52°30' N,	006°05' E

NEW ZEALAND .. page 126

Auckland	36°52' S,	174°46' E
Blenheim	41°31' S,	173°57' E
Cheviot	42°49' S,	173°16' E
Christchurch	43°32' S,	172°39' E
Dunedin	45°53' S,	170°29' E
East Coast Bays	36°45' S,	174°45' E
Gisborne	38°39' S,	178°01' E
Greymouth	42°27' S,	171°12' E
Hamilton	37°47' S,	175°16' E
Hastings	39°39' S,	176°50' E
Invercargill	46°25' S,	168°22' E
Lower Hutt	41°13' S,	174°56' E
Manukau	36°57' S,	174°56' E
Milford Sound	44°41' S,	167°55' E
Napier	39°31' S,	176°54' E
Nelson	41°17' S,	173°17' E
New Plymouth	39°04' S,	174°04' E
Oamaru	45°06' S,	170°58' E
Paeroa	37°23' S,	175°40' E
Palmerston North	40°21' S,	175°37' E
Porirua	41°08' S,	174°51' E
Rotorua	38°10' S,	176°14' E
Takapuna	36°47' S,	174°45' E
Tauranga	37°42' S,	176°08' E
Timaru	44°24' S,	171°14' E
Upper Hutt	41°08' S,	175°03' E
Waihi	37°24' S,	175°56' E
Wanganui	39°56' S,	175°02' E
Wellington	41°18' S,	174°47' E
Westport	41°45' S,	171°36' E
Whangarei	35°43' S,	174°20' E

NICARAGUA . . . . . page 127

Bluefields	12°00' N,	083°45' W
Chinandega	12°37' N,	087°09' W
Esquipulas	12°40' N,	085°47' W
Estelí	13°05' N,	086°21' W
Granada	11°56' N,	085°57' W
Juigalpa	12°05' N,	085°24' W
León	12°26' N,	086°53' W
Managua	12°09' N,	086°17' W
Masaya	11°58' N,	086°06' W
Matagalpa	12°55' N,	085°55' W
Nandaime	11°45' N,	086°03' W
Ocotal	13°38' N,	086°29' W
Puerto Cabezas	14°02' N,	083°23' W
San Carlos	11°07' N,	084°47' W
San Juan del Norte (Greytown)	10°55' N,	083°42' W
San Juan del Sur	11°15' N,	085°52' W
Somoto	13°29' N,	086°35' W
Waspam	14°44' N,	083°58' W

NIGER . . . . page 128

Agadez	16°58' N,	007°59' E
Ayorou	14°44' N,	000°55' E
Bilma	18°41' N,	012°56' E
Dakoro	14°31' N,	006°46' E
Diffa	13°19' N,	012°37' E
Dogondoutchi	13°38' N,	004°02' E
Dosso	13°03' N,	003°12' E
Filingué	14°21' N,	003°19' E
Gaya	11°53' N,	003°27' E
Gouré	13°58' N,	010°18' E
I-n-Gall	16°47' N,	006°56' E
Keïta	14°46' N,	005°46' E
Kolo	13°19' N,	002°20' E
Madaoua	14°06' N,	006°26' E
Magaria	13°00' N,	008°54' E
Maradi	13°29' N,	007°06' E
Mayahi	13°58' N,	007°40' E
Nguigmi	14°15' N,	013°07' E
Niamey	13°31' N,	002°07' E
Tahoua	14°54' N,	005°16' E
Tânout	14°58' N,	008°53' E
Zinder	13°48' N,	008°59' E

NIGERIA . . . . page 129

Aba	05°07' N,	007°22' E
Abuja	09°15' N,	006°56' E
Ado-Ekiti	07°38' N,	005°13' E
Asari	10°31' N,	012°18' E
Awka	06°13' N,	007°05' E
Azare	11°41' N,	010°12' E
Bauchi	10°19' N,	009°50' E
Benin City	06°20' N,	005°38' E
Bida	09°05' N,	006°01' E
Birnin Kebbi	12°28' N,	004°12' E
Biu	10°37' N,	012°12' E
Calabar	04°57' N,	008°19' E
Deba Habe	10°13' N,	011°23' E
Dikwa	12°02' N,	013°55' E
Dukku	10°49' N,	010°46' E
Ede	07°44' N,	004°26' E
Enugu	06°26' N,	007°29' E
Funtua	11°32' N,	007°19' E
Garko	11°39' N,	008°48' E
Gashua	12°52' N,	011°03' E
Gboko	07°19' N,	009°00' E
Gombe	10°17' N,	011°10' E
Gumel	12°38' N,	009°23' E
Gusau	12°10' N,	006°40' E
Ibadan	07°23' N,	003°54' E
Ibi	08°11' N,	009°45' E
Idah	07°06' N,	006°44' E
Ife	07°28' N,	004°34' E
Ifon	06°55' N,	005°46' E
Ikerre	07°30' N,	005°14' E
Ila	08°01' N,	004°54' E
Ilorin	08°30' N,	004°33' E
Iwo	07°38' N,	004°11' E
Jega	12°13' N,	004°23' E
Jimeta	09°17' N,	012°28' E
Jos	09°55' N,	008°54' E
Kaduna	10°31' N,	007°26' E
Kano	12°00' N,	008°31' E
Katsina	13°00' N,	007°36' E
Kaura Namoda	12°36' N,	006°35' E
Keffi	08°51' N,	007°52' E
Kishi	09°05' N,	003°51' E
Kumo	10°03' N,	011°13' E
Lafia	08°29' N,	008°31' E
Lafiagi	08°52' N,	005°25' E
Lagos	06°27' N,	003°23' E
Lere	09°43' N,	009°21' E
Mada	12°09' N,	006°56' E
Maiduguri	11°51' N,	013°09' E
Makurdi	07°44' N,	008°32' E
Minna	09°37' N,	006°33' E
Mubi	10°16' N,	013°16' E
Mushin	06°32' N,	003°22' E
Ngurtuwa	13°05' N,	013°34' E
Nguru	12°53' N,	010°28' E
Nsukka	06°52' N,	007°23' E
Ogbomosho	08°08' N,	004°16' E
Omoko	05°21' N,	006°39' E
Onitsha	06°10' N,	006°47' E
Opobo Town	04°31' N,	007°32' E
Oron	04°50' N,	008°14' E
Oshogbo	07°46' N,	004°34' E

Oyo	07°51' N,	003°56' E
Pindiga	09°59' N,	010°54' E
Port Harcourt	04°46' N,	007°01' E
Potiskum	11°43' N,	011°04' E
Sapele	05°55' N,	005°42' E
Shaki	08°40' N,	003°23' E
Sokoto	13°04' N,	005°15' E
Ugep	05°48' N,	008°05' E
Umuahia	05°32' N,	007°29' E
Uyo	05°03' N,	007°56' E
Warri	05°31' N,	005°45' E
Wukari	07°51' N,	009°47' E
Zaria	11°04' N,	007°42' E

NORTH KOREA . . page 130

Anju	39°36' N,	125°40' E
Ch'ŏngjin	41°46' N,	129°49' E
Cho'san	40°50' N,	125°48' E
Haeju	38°02' N,	125°42' E
Hamhŭng	39°54' N,	127°32' E
Hŭich'ŏn	40°10' N,	126°17' E
Hyangsan	40°03' N,	126°10' E
Hyesan	41°24' N,	128°10' E
Ich'ŏn	38°29' N,	126°53' E
Kaesŏng	37°58' N,	126°33' E
Kanggye	40°58' N,	126°36' E
Kimch'aek (Songjin)	40°41' N,	129°12' E
Kŭmch'ŏn	38°09' N,	126°29' E
Kusŏng	39°59' N,	125°15' E
Kyŏngwŏn	42°49' N,	130°09' E
Manp'o	41°09' N,	126°17' E
Myŏngch'ŏn	41°04' N,	129°26' E
Najin	42°15' N,	130°18' E
Namp'o	38°44' N,	125°24' E
P'anmunjŏm	37°57' N,	126°40' E
Puryŏng	42°04' N,	129°43' E
P'yŏngsŏng	39°15' N,	125°52' E
Pyŏngyang	39°01' N,	125°45' E
Sariwŏn	38°30' N,	125°45' E
Sinp'o	40°02' N,	128°12' E
Sinŭiju	40°06' N,	124°24' E
Songnim	38°44' N,	125°38' E
Taegwan	40°13' N,	125°12' E
Tanch'ŏn	40°28' N,	128°55' E
Tŏkch'ŏn	39°45' N,	126°18' E
T'ongch'ŏn	38°57' N,	127°52' E
Unggi	42°20' N,	130°24' E
Wŏnsan	39°10' N,	127°26' E

NORWAY . . . . page 131

Ålesund	62°28' N,	006°09' E
Alta	69°58' N,	023°15' E
Båtsfjord	70°38' N,	029°44' E
Bergen	60°23' N,	005°20' E
Bodø	67°17' N,	014°23' E
Brønnøysund	65°28' N,	012°13' E
Drammen	59°44' N,	010°15' E
Elverum	60°53' N,	011°34' E
Evje	58°36' N,	007°51' E
Fauske	67°15' N,	015°24' E
Finnsnes	69°14' N,	017°59' E
Flekkefjord	58°17' N,	006°41' E
Hamar	60°48' N,	011°06' E
Hammerfest	70°40' N,	023°42' E
Hareid	62°22' N,	006°02' E
Harstad	68°47' N,	016°33' E
Haugesund	59°25' N,	005°18' E
Hermansverk	61°11' N,	006°51' E
Karasjok	69°27' N,	025°30' E
Kautokeino	68°59' N,	023°08' E
Kolsås	59°55' N,	010°31' E
Kongsvinger	60°12' N,	012°00' E
Kristiansund	63°07' N,	007°45' E
Lillehammer	61°08' N,	010°30' E
Måløy	61°56' N,	005°07' E
Mandal	58°02' N,	007°27' E
Molde	62°44' N,	007°11' E
Mosjøen	65°50' N,	013°12' E
Narvik	68°26' N,	017°25' E
Nordfold	67°46' N,	015°12' E
Oslo (Christiania, Kristiania)	59°55' N,	010°45' E
Sandnessjøen	66°01' N,	012°38' E
Sarpsborg	59°17' N,	011°07' E
Skien	59°12' N,	009°36' E
Skjervøy	70°02' N,	020°59' E
Stavanger	58°58' N,	005°45' E
Steinkjer	64°01' N,	011°30' E
Svolvær	68°14' N,	014°34' E
Tønsberg	59°17' N,	010°25' E
Tromsø	69°40' N,	018°58' E
Trondheim	63°25' N,	010°25' E
Vadsø	70°05' N,	029°46' E
Vardø	70°22' N,	031°06' E

OMAN . . . . page 132

Al-Maṣna'ah	23°47' N,	057°38' E
Ar-Rustaq	23°24' N,	057°26' E
Bahlā' (Bahlah)	22°58' N,	057°18' E
Barkā'	23°43' N,	057°53' E
Ḍank	23°33' N,	056°16' E
Duqm	19°39' N,	057°42' E
Haymā'	19°56' N,	056°19' E
Ibrā'	22°43' N,	058°32' E
Khabura	23°59' N,	057°08' E
Khaṣab	26°12' N,	056°15' E

Khawr Rawrī (Khor Rori)	17°02' N,	054°27' E
Maṭraḥ	23°37' N,	058°34' E
Mirbāṭ	17°00' N,	054°41' E
Muscat (Masqat)	23°37' N,	058°35' E
Nizwā (Nazwah)	22°56' N,	057°32' E
Qurayyāt	23°15' N,	058°54' E
Rakhyūt	16°44' N,	053°20' E
Ṣalalah	17°00' N,	054°06' E
Shināṣ	24°46' N,	056°28' E
Ṣuḥār	24°22' N,	056°45' E
Ṣūr	22°34' N,	059°32' E
Tāqah	17°02' N,	054°24' E
Thamarīt	17°39' N,	054°02' E

PAKISTAN .... page 133

Badīn	24°39' N,	068°50' E
Bahāwalnagar	29°59' N,	073°16' E
Bannu	32°59' N,	070°36' E
Chitrāl	35°51' N,	071°47' E
Dādu	26°44' N,	067°47' E
Dera Ghazi Khan	30°03' N,	070°38' E
Dera Ismail Khan	31°50' N,	070°54' E
Faisalabad (Lyallpur)	31°25' N,	073°05' E
Gujranwala	32°09' N,	074°11' E
Gwadar	25°07' N,	062°19' E
Hyderabad	25°22' N,	068°22' E
Islamabad	33°42' N,	073°10' E
Karachi	24°52' N,	067°03' E
Khuzdār	27°48' N,	066°37' E
Kotri	25°22' N,	068°18' E
Larkana	27°33' N,	068°13' E
Las Bela	26°14' N,	066°19' E
Loralai	30°22' N,	068°36' E
Mardan	34°12' N,	072°02' E
Mianwali	32°35' N,	071°33' E
Mīrpur Khās	25°32' N,	069°00' E
Multan	30°11' N,	071°29' E
Nawabshah	26°15' N,	068°25' E
Panjgūr	26°58' N,	064°06' E
Peshawar	34°01' N,	071°33' E
Pishīn	30°35' N,	067°00' E
Quetta	30°12' N,	067°00' E
Rahīmyār Khān	28°25' N,	070°18' E
Rawalpindi	33°36' N,	073°04' E
Sahiwal (Montgomery)	30°40' N,	073°06' E
Sargodha	32°05' N,	072°40' E
Sūi	28°37' N,	069°19' E
Sukkur	27°42' N,	068°52' E
Thatta	24°45' N,	067°55' E
Turbat	25°59' N,	063°04' E
Wāh	33°48' N,	072°42' E
Zhob (Fort Sandeman)	31°20' N,	069°27' E

PALAU .... page 134

Airai	07°22' N,	134°33' E
Klouklubed	07°02' N,	134°15' E
Koror	07°20' N,	134°29' E
Melekeok	07°29' N,	134°38' E
Meyungs	07°20' N,	134°27' E
Ngardmau	07°37' N,	134°36' E

PANAMA......... page 135

Aguadulce	08°15' N,	080°33' W
Almirante	09°18' N,	082°24' W
Antón	08°24' N,	080°16' W
Boquete	08°47' N,	082°26' W
Cañazas	09°06' N,	078°10' W
Capira	08°45' N,	079°53' W
Changuinola	09°26' N,	082°31' W
Chepo	09°10' N,	079°06' W
Chitré	07°58' N,	080°26' W
Colón	09°22' N,	079°54' W
David	08°26' N,	082°26' W
Guararé	07°49' N,	080°17' W
La Chorrera	08°53' N,	079°47' W
La Concepción	08°31' N,	082°37' W
La Palma	08°25' N,	078°09' W
Las Cumbres	09°05' N,	079°32' W
Las Lajas	08°15' N,	081°52' W
Las Tablas	07°46' N,	080°17' W
Ocú	07°57' N,	080°47' W
Panama City (Panama)	08°58' N,	079°32' W
Pedregal	09°04' N,	079°26' W
Penonomé	08°31' N,	080°22' W
Portobelo (Puerto Bello)	09°33' N,	079°39' W
Puerto Armuelles	08°17' N,	082°52' W
San Miguelito	09°02' N,	079°30' E
Santiago	08°06' N,	080°59' W
Soná	08°01' N,	081°19' W
Yaviza (Yavisa)	08°11' N,	077°41' W

PAPUA NEW GUINEA .... page 136

Aitape	03°08' S,	142°21' E
Alotau	10°20' S,	150°25' E
Ambunti	04°14' S,	142°50' E
Arawa	06°13' S,	155°33' E
Baimuru	07°30' S,	144°49' E
Balimo	08°03' S,	142°57' E
Bogia	04°16' S,	144°54' E
Buin	06°50' S,	155°44' E
Bulolo	07°12' S,	146°39' E
Bwagaoia	10°42' S,	152°50' E
Daru	09°05' S,	143°12' E

Finschhafen	06°36' S, 147°51' E
Goroka	06°05' S, 145°23' E
Kandrian	06°13' S, 149°33' E
Kavieng	02°34' S, 150°48' E
Kerema	07°58' S, 145°46' E
Kikori	07°25' S, 144°15' E
Kimbe	05°33' S, 150°09' E
Kiunga	06°07' S, 141°18' E
Kupiano	10°05' S, 148°11' E
Lae	06°44' S, 147°00' E
Lorengau	02°01' S, 147°16' E
Losuia	08°32' S, 151°04' E
Madang	05°13' S, 145°48' E
Mt. Hagen	05°52' S, 144°13' E
Namatanai	03°40' S, 152°27' E
Popondetta	08°46' S, 148°14' E
Port Moresby	09°29' S, 147°11' E
Rabaul	04°12' S, 152°11' E
Saidor	05°38' S, 146°28' E
Samarai	10°37' S, 150°40' E
Tari	05°42' S, 142°57' E
Vanimo	02°41' S, 141°18' E
Wewak	03°33' S, 143°38' E

PARAGUAY ..... page 137

Asunción	25°16' S, 057°40' W
Caacupé	25°23' S, 057°09' W
Caaguazú	25°26' S, 056°02' W
Caazapá	26°09' S, 056°24' W
Capitán Pablo Lagerenza	19°55' S, 060°47' W
Ciudad del Este (Puerto Presidente Stroessner)	25°31' S, 054°37' W
Concepción	23°25' S, 057°17' W
Encarnación	27°20' S, 055°54' W
Filadelfia	22°21' S, 060°02' W
Fuerto Olimpo	21°02' S, 057°54' W
General Eugenio A. Garay	20°31' S, 062°08' W
Luque	25°16' S, 057°34' W
Mariscal Estigarribia	22°02' S, 060°38' W
Paraguari	25°38' S, 057°09' W
Pedro Juan Caballero	22°34' S, 055°37' W
Pilar	26°52' S, 058°23' W
Pozo Colorado	23°26' S, 058°58' W
Salto del Guairá	24°05' S, 054°20' W
San Juan Bautista	26°38' S, 057°10' W
San Lázaro	22°10' S, 057°58' W
Villarica	25°45' S, 056°26' W

PERU .... page 138

Abancay	13°35' S, 072°55' W
Acomayo	13°55' S, 071°41' W
Arequipa	16°24' S, 071°33' W
Ayabaca	04°38' S, 079°43' W
Ayacucho	13°07' S, 074°13' W
Ayaviri	14°52' S, 070°35' W
Bagua	05°40' S, 078°31' W
Barranca	10°45' S, 077°46' W
Cajamarca	07°10' S, 078°31' W
Callao	12°04' S, 077°09' W
Castilla	05°12' S, 080°38' W
Cerro de Pasco	10°41' S, 076°16' W
Chiclayo	06°46' S, 079°51' W
Chimbote	09°05' S, 078°36' W
Contamana	07°15' S, 074°54' W
Cuzco	13°31' S, 071°59' W
Espinar	14°47' S, 071°29' W
Huacho	11°07' S, 077°37' W
Huancayo	12°04' S, 075°14' W
Huánuco	09°55' S, 076°14' W
Huaraz	09°32' S, 077°32' W
Huarmey	10°04' S, 078°10' W
Ica	14°04' S, 075°42' W
Iñapari	10°57' S, 069°35' W
Iquitos	03°46' S, 073°15' W
Juliaca	15°30' S, 070°08' W
Lagunas	05°14' S, 075°38' W
Lima	12°03' S, 077°03' W
Macusani	14°05' S, 070°26' W
Miraflores	12°07' S, 077°02' W
Moquegua	17°12' S, 070°56' W
Moyobamba	06°03' S, 076°58' W
Nauta	04°32' S, 073°33' W
Pampas	12°24' S, 074°54' W
Pisco	13°42' S, 076°13' W
Piura	05°12' S, 080°38' W
Pucallpa	08°23' S, 074°32' W
Puerto Maldonado	12°36' S, 069°11' W
Puno	15°50' S, 070°02' W
Requena	04°58' S, 073°50' W
San Juan	15°21' S, 075°10' W
Tacna	18°01' S, 070°15' W
Tarapoto	06°30' S, 076°25' W
Trujillo	08°07' S, 079°02' W
Tumbes	03°34' S, 080°28' W

PHILIPPINES .... page 139

Angeles	15°09' N, 120°35' E
Aparri	18°22' N, 121°39' E
Bacolod	10°40' N, 122°56' E
Balabac	07°59' N, 117°04' E
Batangas	13°45' N, 121°03' E
Bayombong	16°29' N, 121°09' E
Borongan	11°37' N, 125°26' E
Butuan	08°54' N, 125°35' E
Cagayan de Oro	08°29' N, 124°39' E
Caloocan	14°39' N, 120°58' E
Cavite	14°29' N, 120°55' E

Cebu	10°18' N,	123°54' E
Daet	14°05' N,	122°55' E
Dagupan	16°03' N,	120°20' E
Dipolog	08°35' N,	123°20' E
Dumaguete	09°18' N,	123°18' E
General Santos	06°07' N,	125°10' E
Iligan	08°14' N,	124°14' E
Iloilo City	10°42' N,	122°33' E
Isabela	06°42' N,	121°58' E
Jolo	06°03' N,	121°00' E
Laoag	12°34' N,	125°00' E
Lucena	13°56' N,	121°37' E
Manila	14°35' N,	121°00' E
Masbate	12°22' N,	123°36' E
Mati	06°57' N,	126°13' E
Naga (Nueva Caceres)	13°37' N,	123°11' E
Ormoc	11°00' N,	124°37' E
Ozamiz	08°08' N,	123°50' E
Pandan	14°03' N,	124°10' E
Puerto Princesa	09°44' N,	118°44' E
Quezon City	14°38' N,	121°00' E
Romblon	12°35' N,	122°15' E
Roxas (Capiz)	11°35' N,	122°45' E
Surigao	09°45' N,	125°30' E
Tagbilaran	09°39' N,	123°51' E
Tuguegarao	17°37' N,	121°44' E
Zamboanga	06°54' N,	122°04' E

POLAND .... page 140

Biała Podlaska	52°02' N,	023°08' E
Białystok	53°08' N,	023°09' E
Bielsko-Biała	49°49' N,	019°02' E
Bydgoszcz	53°09' N,	018°00' E
Ciechanów	52°53' N,	020°37' E
Częstochowa	50°48' N,	019°07' E
Dąbrova Górnicza	50°20' N,	019°12' E
Elbląg	54°10' N,	019°23' E
Gdańsk (Danzig)	54°21' N,	018°40' E
Gdynia	54°30' N,	018°33' E
Gorzów Wielkopolski	52°44' N,	015°14' E
Grudziądz	53°29' N,	018°46' E
Iława	53°36' N,	019°34' E
Inowrocław	52°48' N,	018°16' E
Kalisz	51°45' N,	018°05' E
Katowice	50°16' N,	019°01' E
Kielce	50°50' N,	020°40' E
Konin	52°13' N,	018°16' E
Koszalin	54°12' N,	016°11' E
Kraków	50°05' N,	019°55' E
Krosno	49°41' N,	021°47' E
Legnica	51°12' N,	016°12' E
Leszno	51°51' N,	016°35' E
Łódź	51°45' N,	019°28' E
Łomża	53°11' N,	022°05' E
Lublin	51°15' N,	022°34' E
Malbork	54°02' N,	019°03' E
Mogilno	52°40' N,	017°58' E
Nidzica	53°22' N,	020°26' E
Nowy Sącz	49°38' N,	020°43' E
Olsztyn	53°47' N,	020°29' E
Opole	50°40' N,	017°57' E
Ostrołęka	53°05' N,	021°34' E
Piła	53°09' N,	016°45' E
Pińczów	50°32' N,	020°32' E
Piotrków Trybunalski	51°24' N,	019°41' E
Pisz	53°38' N,	021°48' E
Poznań	52°25' N,	016°58' E
Radom	51°25' N,	021°09' E
Rybnik	50°07' N,	018°32' E
Rzeszów	50°03' N,	022°00' E
Siedlce	52°10' N,	022°18' E
Słupsk	54°27' N,	017°02' E
Suwałki	54°06' N,	022°56' E
Szczecin (Stettin)	53°25' N,	014°35' E
Tarnobrzeg	50°35' N,	021°41' E
Tarnów	50°01' N,	020°59' E
Tczew	54°06' N,	018°48' E
Tomaszów Mazowiecki	51°32' N,	020°01' E
Toruń	53°02' N,	018°36' E
Tuchola	53°35' N,	017°51' E
Tychy	50°08' N,	018°59' E
Wałbrzych	50°46' N,	016°17' E
Warsaw (Warszawa)	52°15' N,	021°00' E
Włocławek	52°39' N,	019°05' E
Wrocław (Breslau)	51°06' N,	017°02' E
Zabrze	50°19' N,	018°47' E
Zamość	50°43' N,	023°15' E
Zielona Góra	51°56' N,	015°30' E

PORTUGAL ..... page 141

Alcobaça	39°33' N,	008°59' W
Almada	38°41' N,	009°09' W
Amadora	38°45' N,	009°14' W
Aveiro	40°38' N,	008°39' W
Barreiro	38°40' N,	009°04' W
Batalha	39°39' N,	008°50' W
Beja	38°01' N,	007°52' W
Braga	41°33' N,	008°26' W
Bragança	41°49' N,	006°45' W
Castelo Branco	39°49' N,	007°30' W
Chaves	41°44' N,	007°28' W
Coimbra	40°12' N,	008°25' W
Elvas	38°53' N,	007°10' W
Évora	38°34' N,	007°54' W
Faro	37°01' N,	007°56' W
Fátima	39°37' N,	008°39' W
Figueira da Foz	40°09' N,	008°52' W
Guarda	40°32' N,	007°16' W
Guimarães	41°27' N,	008°18' W
Leiria	39°45' N,	008°48' W

Lisbon (Lisboa)	38°43' N,	009°08' W
Nazaré	39°36' N,	009°04' W
Odivelas	38°47' N,	009°11' W
Oeiras	38°41' N,	009°19' W
Portalegre	39°17' N,	007°26' W
Portimão (Vila Nova de Portimão)	37°08' N,	008°32' W
Porto (Oporto)	41°09' N,	008°37' W
Póvoa de Varzim	41°23' N,	008°46' W
Queluz	38°45' N,	009°15' W
Santarém	39°14' N,	008°41' W
Setúbal	38°32' N,	008°54' W
Sines	37°57' N,	008°52' W
Tomar	39°36' N,	008°25' W
Torres Vedras	39°06' N,	009°16' W
Urgeiriça	40°30' N,	007°53' W
Viana do Castelo	41°42' N,	008°50' W
Vila do Conde	41°21' N,	008°45' W
Vila Franca de Xira	38°57' N,	008°59' W
Vila Nova de Gaia	41°08' N,	008°37' W
Vila Real	41°18' N,	007°45' W
Viseu	40°39' N,	007°55' W

QATAR . . . . page 142

Al-Wakrah	25°10' N,	051°36' E
Al -Rayyān	25°18' N,	051°27' E
Ar-Ruways	26°08' N,	051°13' E
Doha (ad-Dawhah)	25°17' N,	051°32' E
Dukhān	25°25' N,	050°47' E
Musay'id	25°00' N,	051°33' E
Umm Bāb	25°09' N,	050°50' E

ROMANIA . . . . page 143

Alba Iulia (Gyulafehérvár)	46°04' N,	023°35' E
Alexandria	43°59' N,	025°20' E
Arad	46°11' N,	021°19' E
Bacău	46°34' N,	026°54' E
Baia Mare	47°40' N,	023°35' E
Bârlad	46°14' N,	027°40' E
Bistriţa	47°08' N,	024°29' E
Botoşani	47°45' N,	026°40' E
Brăila	45°16' N,	027°59' E
Braşov (Oraşul Stalin)	45°38' N,	025°35' E
Bucharest	44°26' N,	026°06' E
Buzău	45°09' N,	026°50' E
Calafat	43°59' N,	022°56' E
Călăraşi	44°12' N,	027°20' E
Cluj-Napoca	46°46' N,	023°36' E
Constanţa	44°11' N,	028°39' E
Craiova	44°19' N,	023°48' E
Dej	47°09' N,	023°52' E
Deva	45°53' N,	022°54' E
Drobeta-Turnu Severin	44°38' N,	022°40' E
Focşani	45°42' N,	027°11' E
Galaţi (Galatz)	45°27' N,	028°03' E
Giurgiu	43°53' N,	025°58' E
Hunedoara	45°45' N,	022°54' E
Iaşi (Jassy)	47°10' N,	027°36' E
Lugoj	45°41' N,	021°55' E
Mangalia	43°48' N,	028°35' E
Medgidia	44°15' N,	028°17' E
Mediaş	46°10' N,	024°21' E
Mizil	45°01' N,	026°27' E
Oneşti (Gheorghe Gheorghiu Dej)	46°15' N,	026°45' E
Oradea (Nagyvarad)	47°04' N,	021°56' E
Petroşani	45°25' N,	023°22' E
Piatra-Neamţ	46°55' N,	026°20' E
Piteşti	44°51' N,	024°52' E
Ploieşti (Ploeşti)	44°57' N,	026°01' E
Reşiţa	45°18' N,	021°55' E
Roman	46°55' N,	026°55' E
Satu Mare	47°48' N,	022°53' E
Sebeş	45°58' N,	023°34' E
Slatina	44°26' N,	024°22' E
Suceava	47°38' N,	026°15' E
Ţăndărei	44°39' N,	027°40' E
Târgovişte	44°56' N,	025°27' E
Targu Jiu	45°03' N,	023°17' E
Târgu Mureş	46°33' N,	024°34' E
Tecuci	45°52' N,	027°25' E
Timişoara	45°45' N,	021°13' E
Tulcea	45°10' N,	028°48' E
Turda	46°34' N,	023°47' E
Vaslui	46°38' N,	027°44' E
Zalau	47°12' N,	023°03' E

RUSSIA . . . . page 144–5

Abakan	53°43' N,	091°26' E
Aginskoye	51°06' N,	114°32' E
Anadyr (Novo-Mariinsk)	64°45' N,	177°29' E
Angarsk	52°34' N,	103°54' E
Birobidzhan	48°48' N,	132°57' E
Biysk (Biisk)	52°34' N,	085°15' E
Cheboksary	56°09' N,	047°15' E
Chelyabinsk	55°10' N,	061°24' E
Cherepovets	59°08' N,	037°54' E
Chita	52°03' N,	113°30' E
Dudinka	69°25' N,	086°15' E
Gorno-Altaysk (Ulala, or Oyrot-Tura)	51°58' N,	085°58' E
Grozny	43°20' N,	045°42' E

Izhevsk (Ustinov)	56°51' N,	053°14' E
Kaluga	54°31' N,	036°16' E
Kazan	55°45' N,	049°08' E
Khanty-Mansiysk (Ostyako-Vogulsk)	61°00' N,	069°06' E
Kirovsk	67°37' N,	033°40' E
Komsomol'sk-na-Amure	50°35' N,	137°02' E
Krasnoyarsk	56°01' N,	092°50' E
Kudymkar	59°01' N,	054°39' E
Kurgan	55°26' N,	065°18' E
Kyzyl (Khem-Beldyr)	51°42' N,	094°27' E
Magadan	59°34' N,	150°48' E
Makhachkala	42°58' N,	047°30' E
Maykop (Maikop)	44°35' N,	040°10' E
Moscow (Moskva)	55°45' N,	037°35' E
Murmansk	68°58' N,	033°05' E
Nal'chik	43°29' N,	043°37' E
Nar'yan-Mar	67°39' N,	053°00' E
Nizhnekamsk	55°36' N,	051°47' E
Nizhny Novgorod (Gorky)	56°20' N,	044°00' E
Novgorod	58°31' N,	031°17' E
Novokuznetsk (Kuznetsk, or Stalinsk)	53°45' N,	087°06' E
Novosibirsk	55°02' N,	082°55' E
Omsk	55°00' N,	073°24' E
Orenburg (Chkalov)	51°45' N,	055°06' E
Orsk	51°12' N,	058°34' E
Palana	59°07' N,	159°58' E
Penza	53°13' N,	045°00' E
Perm' (Molotov)	58°00' N,	056°15' E
Petropavlovsk-Kamchatsky	53°01' N,	158°39' E
Petrozavodsk	61°49' N,	034°20' E
Rostov-na-Donu (Rostov-on-Don)	47°14' N,	039°42' E
St. Petersburg (Leningrad, or Sankt Peterburg)	59°55' N,	030°15' E
Salavat	53°21' N,	055°55' E
Salekhard	66°33' N,	066°40' E
Samara (Kuybyshev)	53°12' N,	050°09' E
Saransk	54°11' N,	045°11' E
Saratov	51°34' N,	046°02' E
Smolensk	54°47' N,	032°03' E
Syktyvkar	61°40' N,	050°48' E
Tomsk	56°30' N,	084°58' E
Tver' (Kalinin)	56°52' N,	035°55' E
Tyumen'	57°09' N,	065°26' E
Ufa	55°45' N,	055°56' E
Ulan-Ude	51°50' N,	107°37' E
Ussuriysk	43°48' N,	131°59' E
Ust'-Ordinsky	52°48' N,	104°45' E
Vladimir	56°10' N,	040°25' E
Vladivostok	43°08' N,	131°54' E
Volgograd (Stalingrad, or Tsaritsyn)	48°45' N,	044°25' E
Vologda	59°13' N,	039°54' E
Voronezh	51°38' N,	039°12' E
Yakutsk	62°00' N,	129°40' E
Yaroslavl	57°37' N,	039°52' E
Yekaterinburg (Sverdlovsk)	56°51' N,	060°36' E
Yuzhno-Sakhalinsk	46°57' N,	142°44' E

RWANDA . . . . . . page 146

Butare	02°36' S,	029°44' E
Gisenyi	01°42' S,	029°15' E
Kigali	01°57' S,	030°04' E
Ruhengeri	01°30' S,	029°38' E

SAINT KITTS AND NEVIS . . . . . page 147

Basseterre	17°18' N,	062°43' W
Brown Hill	17°08' N,	062°33' W
Cayon	17°22' N,	062°43' W
Challengers	17°18' N,	062°47' W
Charlestown	17°08' N,	062°37' W
Cotton Ground	17°11' N,	062°36' W
Half Way Tree	17°20' N,	062°49' W
Mansion	17°22' N,	062°46' W
Monkey Hill Village	17°19' N,	062°43' W
Newcastle	17°13' N,	062°34' W
New River	17°09' N,	062°32' W
Newton Ground	17°23' N,	062°51' W
Old Road Town	17°19' N,	062°48' W
Sadlers	17°24' N,	062°49' W
Saint Paul's	17°24' N,	062°49' W
Sandy Point Town	17°22' N,	062°50' W
Verchild's	17°20' N,	062°48' W
Zetlands	17°08' N,	062°34' W

SAINT LUCIA . . . . page 148

Anse La Raye	13°57' N,	061°03' W
Canaries	13°55' N,	061°04' W
Castries	14°01' N,	061°00' W
Dauphin	14°03' N,	060°55' W
Dennery	13°55' N,	060°54' W
Grande Anse	14°01' N,	061°45' W
Gros Islet	14°05' N,	060°58' W
Laborie	13°45' N,	061°00' W
Micoud	13°50' N,	060°54' W
Praslin	13°53' N,	060°54' W
Sans Soucis	13°59' N,	061°01' W
Soufrière	13°52' N,	061°04' W

SAINT VINCENT AND THE GRENADINES .... page 149

Ashton	12°36' N, 061°27' W
Barrouallie	13°14' N, 061°17' W
Calliaqua	13°08' N, 061°12' W
Chateaubelaír	13°17' N, 061°15' W
Georgetown	13°16' N, 061°08' W
Kingstown	13°09' N, 061°14' W

SAMOA .... page 150

Apia	13°50' S, 171°44' W
Fažaala	13°45' S, 172°16' W
Faleasižu	13°48' S, 171°54' W
Ležauvažu	13°45' S, 171°51' W
Lotofaga	13°59' S, 171°50' W
Matavai (Asau)	13°28' S, 172°35' W
Safotu	13°27' S, 172°24' W
Sagone	13°39' S, 172°35' W
Samatau	13°54' S, 172°02' W
Sili	13°43' S, 172°21' W
Sižumu	14°01' S, 171°47' W
Solosolo	13°51' S, 171°36' W

SAN MARINO .... page 151

San Marino	43°56' N, 012°25' E

SÃO TOMÉ AND PRÍNCIPE .. page 152

Infante Don Henrique	01°34' N, 007°25' E
Neves	00°22' N, 006°33' E
Porto Alegre	00°02' N, 006°32' E
Santana	00°16' N, 006°45' E
Santo Amaro	00°22' N, 006°42' E
Santo António	01°39' N, 007°25' E
São Tomé	00°20' N, 006°44' E
Trindade	00°15' N, 006°40' E

SAUDI ARABIA .. page 153

Abhā	18°13' N, 042°30' E
Abqaiq (Buqayq)	25°56' N, 049°40' E
ʿAfif	23°55' N, 042°56' E
Al-Bāhah	20°01' N, 041°28' E
Al-Badīʿ	22°02' N, 046°34' E
Al-Bātin Hafar	28°27' N, 045°58' E
Al-Bi'ār	22°39' N, 039°40' E
Al-Dammām	26°26' N, 050°07' E
Al-Hā'ir	24°23' N, 046°50' E
Al-Hufūf	25°22' N, 049°34' E
Al-Ju'aydah	19°40' N, 041°34' E
Al-Jubayl	27°01' N, 049°40' E
Al-Khubar	26°17' N, 050°12' E
Al-Mish'āb	28°12' N, 048°36' E
Al-Mubarraz	25°25' N, 049°35' E
Al-Qaṭīf	26°33' N, 050°00' E
Al-Qunfudhah	19°08' N, 041°05' E
Al-Sulayyil	20°27' N, 045°34' E
Al-Ta'if	21°16' N, 040°25' E
Al-Ulā	26°38' N, 037°55' E
Ar'ar	30°59' N, 041°02' E
As-Ṣafrā'	24°02' N, 038°56' E
Az-Zilfī	26°18' N, 044°48' E
Badanah	30°59' N, 040°58' E
Birkah	23°48' N, 038°50' E
Buraydah	26°20' N, 043°59' E
Buraykah	22°21' N, 039°20' E
Hā'il	27°33' N, 041°42' E
Halabān	23°29' N, 044°23' E
Harajah	17°56' N, 043°21' E
Jidda (Jiddah)	21°29' N, 039°12' E
Jizān (Qizān)	16°54' N, 042°32' E
Khamīs Mushayṭ	18°18' N, 042°44' E
Khawsh	18°59' N, 041°53' E
Laylā	22°17' N, 046°45' E
Madā'in Sālih	26°48' N, 037°57' E
Mecca (Makkah)	21°27' N, 039°49' E
Medina (al-Madinah; Yathrib)	24°28' N, 039°36' E
Miskah	24°49' N, 042°56' E
Muṣābih	18°42' N, 042°01' E
Na'jān	24°05' N, 047°10' E
Najrān	17°26' N, 044°15' E
Qanā	27°47' N, 041°25' E
Rābigh	22°48' N, 039°02' E
Rafhā'	29°38' N, 043°30' E
Ras Tanura	26°42' N, 050°06' E
Riyadh (ar-Riyad)	24°38' N, 046°43' E
Sahwah	19°19' N, 042°06' E
Sakākah	29°59' N, 040°12' E
Shidād	21°19' N, 040°03' E
Tabūk	28°23' N, 036°35' E
Taymā'	27°38' N, 038°29' E
Turayf	31°41' N, 038°39' E
ʿUsfan	21°55' N, 039°22' E
Yanbuʿ	24°05' N, 038°03' E
Zahrān	17°40' N, 043°30' E
Zalim	22°43' N, 042°10' E

SENEGAL .... page 154

Bakel	14°54' N, 012°27' W
Bignona	12°49' N, 016°14' W

Dagana	16°31' N, 015°30' W
Dakar	14°40' N, 017°26' W
Diourbel	14°40' N, 016°15' W
Fatick	14°20' N, 016°25' W
Joal	14°10' N, 016°51' W
Kaffrine	14°06' N, 015°33' W
Kaolack	14°09' N, 016°04' W
Kédougou	12°33' N, 012°11' W
Kolda	12°53' N, 014°57' W
Koungheul	13°59' N, 014°48' W
Linguère	15°24' N, 015°07' W
Louga	15°37' N, 016°13' W
Mbacké	14°48' N, 015°55' W
Mbour	14°24' N, 016°58' W
Mékhé	15°07' N, 016°38' W
Podor	16°40' N, 014°57' W
Richard-Toll	16°28' N, 015°41' W
Saint Louis	16°02' N, 016°30' W
Sédhiou	12°44' N, 015°33' W
Tambacounda	13°47' N, 013°40' W
Thiès	14°48' N, 016°56' W
Tivaouane	14°57' N, 016°49' W
Vélingara	13°09' N, 014°07' W
Ziguinchor	12°35' N, 016°16' W

SERBIA .... page 155

Belgrade	44°50' N, 020°30' E
Bor	44°06' N, 022°06' E
Cacak	43°54' N, 020°21' E
Gornji Milanovac	44°02' N, 020°27' E
Kikinda	45°50' N, 020°29' E
Knjaževac	43°34' N, 022°15' E
Kragujevac	44°01' N, 020°55' E
Kraljevo	43°44' N, 020°43' E
Kruševac	43°35' N, 021°20' E
Leskovac	42°59' N, 021°57' E
Majdanpek	44°25' N, 021°56' E
Nis	43°19' N, 021°54' E
Novi Beograd	44°49' N, 020°27' E
Novi Pazar	43°08' N, 020°31' E
Novi Sad	45°15' N, 019°50' E
Pancevo	44°52' N, 020°39' E
Pirot	43°09' N, 022°36' E
Priboj	43°35' N, 019°32' E
Sabac	44°45' N, 019°43' E
Smederevo	44°39' N, 020°56' E
Sombor	45°46' N, 019°07' E
Sremski Karlovci	45°12' N, 019°56' E
Subotica	46°06' N, 019°40' E
Titovo Užice (Užice)	43°52' N, 019°51' E
Valjevo	44°16' N, 019°53' E
Vranje	42°33' N, 021°54' E
Zrenjanin	45°23' N, 020°23' E

SEYCHELLES .... page 156

Victoria	04°37' S, 055°27' E

SIERRA LEONE .. page 157

Bo	07°58' N, 011°45' W
Bonthe	07°32' N, 012°30' W
Freetown	08°30' N, 013°15' W
Kabala	09°35' N, 011°33' W
Kailahun	08°17' N, 010°34' W
Kambia	09°07' N, 012°55' W
Kenema	07°52' N, 011°12' W
Koidu-New Sembehun	08°38' N, 010°59' W
Lunsar	08°41' N, 012°32' W
Magburaka	08°43' N, 011°57' W
Makeni	08°53' N, 012°03' W
Mongeri	08°19' N, 011°44' W
Moyamba	08°10' N, 012°26' W
Pepel	08°35' N, 013°03' W
Port Loko	08°46' N, 012°47' W
Pujehun	07°21' N, 011°42' W
Sulima	06°58' N, 011°35' W

SINGAPORE ..... page 158

Singapore	01°16' N, 103°50' E

SLOVAKIA .... page 159

Banská Bystrica	48°44' N, 019°09' E
Bardejov	49°17' N, 021°17' E
Bratislava	48°09' N, 017°07' E
Čadca	49°26' N, 018°47' E
Fil'akovo	48°16' N, 019°50' E
Humenné	48°56' N, 021°55' E
Komárno	47°46' N, 018°08' E
Košice	48°42' N, 021°15' E
Levice	48°13' N, 018°36' E
Liptovský Mikuláš	49°05' N, 019°37' E
Lučenec	48°20' N, 019°40' E
Martin	49°04' N, 018°56' E
Michalovce	48°45' N, 021°56' E
Nitra	48°19' N, 018°05' E
Nové Zámky	47°59' N, 018°10' E
Partizánske	48°38' N, 018°23' E
Piešt'any	48°36' N, 017°50' E
Poprad	49°03' N, 020°18' E
Považská Bystrica	49°07' N, 018°27' E
Prešov	49°00' N, 021°15' E
Prievidza	48°46' N, 018°38' E
Rimavská Sobota	48°23' N, 020°02' E
Rožňava	48°40' N, 020°32' E
Skalica	48°51' N, 017°14' E

Spišská Nová Ves	48°57' N,	020°34' E
Topoľčany	48°34' N,	018°11' E
Trebišov	48°38' N,	021°43' E
Trenčín	48°54' N,	018°02' E
Trnava	48°22' N,	017°36' E
Žilina	49°13' N,	018°44' E
Zvolen	48°35' N,	019°08' E

SLOVENIA . . . . . . page 160

Celje	46°14' N,	015°16' E
Hrastnik	46°09' N,	015°06' E
Idrija	46°00' N,	014°02' E
Javornik	46°14' N,	014°18' E
Jesenice	46°27' N,	014°04' E
Kočevje	45°39' N,	014°51' E
Koper	45°33' N,	013°44' E
Kranj	46°14' N,	014°22' E
Krško	45°58' N,	015°29' E
Ljubljana	46°02' N,	014°30' E
Maribor	46°33' N,	015°39' E
Murska Sobota	46°40' N,	016°10' E
Novo Mesto	45°48' N,	015°10' E
Postojna	45°47' N,	014°14' E
Ptuj	46°25' N,	015°52' E
Trbovlje	46°10' N,	015°03' E
Velenje	46°22' N,	015°07' E
Zagorje	46°08' N,	015°00' E

SOLOMON ISLANDS . . . . page 161

Buala	08°08' S,	159°35' E
Honiara	09°26' S,	159°57' E
Kirakira	10°27' S,	161°55' E
Lata	10°44' S,	165°54' E
Maravovo	09°17' S,	159°38' E
Munda	08°19' S,	157°15' E
Sahalu	09°44' S,	160°31' E
Sasamungga	07°02' S,	156°47' E
Takwa	08°22' S,	160°48' E

SOMALIA . . . . page 162

Baardheere (Bardera)	02°20' N,	042°17' E
Baraawe (Brava)	01°06' N,	044°03' E
Baydhabo (Baidoa)	03°07' N,	043°39' E
Beledweyne (Belet Uen)	04°45' N,	045°12' E
Berbera	10°25' N,	045°02' E
Boosaaso (Bender Cassim)	11°17' N,	049°11' E
Burao (Burco)	09°31' N,	045°32' E
Buulobarde (Bulo Burti)	03°51' N,	045°34' E
Eyl	07°59' N,	049°49' E
Hargeysa	09°35' N,	044°04' E
Hobyo (Obbia)	05°21' N,	048°32' E
Jamaame (Giamama or Jamame or Margherita)	00°04' N,	042°45' E
Jawhar (Giohar)	02°46' N,	045°31' E
Kismaayo (Chisimayu)	00°22' S,	042°32' E
Marka (Merca)	01°43' N,	044°53' E
Mogadishu (Mogadiscio or Mogadisho)	02°04' N,	045°22' E
Seylac (Zeila)	11°21' N,	043°29' E
Xaafun	10°25' N,	051°16' E

SOUTH AFRICA . . page 163

Bellville	33°54' S,	018°38' E
Bisho	32°53' S,	027°24' E
Bloemfontein	29°08' S,	026°10' E
Calvinia	31°28' S,	019°47' E
Cape Town (Kaapstad)	33°55' S,	018°25' E
Durban (Port Natal)	29°51' S,	031°01' E
East London	33°02' S,	027°55' E
George	33°58' S,	022°27' E
Germiston	26°13' S,	028°11' E
Hopefield	33°04' S,	018°21' E
Johannesburg	26°12' S,	028°05' E
Kimberley	28°45' S,	024°46' E
Klerksdorp	26°52' S,	026°40' E
Krugersdorp	26°06' S,	027°46' E
Kuruman	27°28' S,	023°26' E
Ladysmith	28°33' S,	029°47' E
Margate	30°51' S,	030°22' E
Newcastle	27°45' S,	029°56' E
Oudtshoorn	33°35' S,	022°12' E
Pietermaritzburg	29°37' S,	030°23' E
Port Elizabeth	33°58' S,	025°35' E
Port Nolloth	29°15' S,	016°52' E
Pretoria	25°45' S,	028°10' E
Queenstown	31°54' S,	026°53' E
Rustenburg	25°40' S,	027°15' E
Seshego	23°51' S,	029°23' E
Soweto	26°16' S,	027°52' E
Stellenbosch	33°56' S,	018°51' E
Uitenhage	33°46' S,	025°24' E
Upington	28°27' S,	021°15' E
Vanderbijlpark	26°42' S,	027°49' E
Welkom	27°59' S,	026°42' E
Worcester	33°39' S,	019°26' E

SOUTH KOREA . . page 164

Andong	36°34' N,	128°44' E
Anyang	37°23' N,	126°55' E

Ch'ang won	35°16' N,	128°37' E
Cheju	33°31' N,	126°32' E
Ch'ŏngju	36°38' N,	127°30' E
Chŏnju	35°49' N,	127°09' E
Ch'unch'ŏn	37°52' N,	127°44' E
Inch'ŏn	37°28' N,	126°38' E
Iri	35°56' N,	126°57' E
Kumi	36°08' N,	128°20' E
Kunsan	35°59' N,	126°43' E
Kwangju	35°10' N,	126°55' E
Kyŏngju	35°50' N,	129°13' E
Masan	35°11' N,	128°34' E
Mokp'o	34°47' N,	126°23' E
P'ohang	36°02' N,	129°22' E
Pusan	35°06' N,	129°03' E
Samch'ŏnp'o	34°55' N,	128°04' E
Seoul (Soul)	37°34' N,	127°00' E
Sŏsan	36°47' N,	126°27' E
Sunch'ŏn	34°57' N,	127°29' E
Suwŏn	37°16' N,	127°01' E
T'aebaek	37°10' N,	128°59' E
Taech'ŏn	36°21' N,	126°36' E
Taegu (Daegu or Taiku)	35°52' N,	128°36' E
Taejon	36°20' N,	127°26' E
Uijŏngbu	37°44' N,	127°02' E
Ulsan	35°33' N,	129°19' E
Wŏnju	37°21' N,	127°58' E

SOUTH SUDAN . . page 165

Bentiu	09°14' N,	029°50' E
Bor	06°12' N,	031°33' E
Juba	04°51' N,	031°37' E
Kakok (Kwajok)	08°19' N,	028°00' E
Malakāl	09°31' N,	031°39' E
Nagichot	04°16' N,	033°34' E
Nāṣir	08°36' N,	033°04' E
Rumbek	06°48' N,	029°41' E
Torit	04°24' N,	032°34' E
Aweil (Uwayl)	08°46' N,	027°24' E
Wāw (Wau)	07°42' N,	028°00' E
Yambio	04°34' N,	028°23' E

SPAIN . . . . page 166

A Coruña (La Coruña)	43°22' N,	008°23' W
Albacete	38°59' N,	001°51' W
Alcalá de Henares	40°29' N,	003°22' W
Algeciras	36°08' N,	005°30' W
Alicante (Alacant)	38°21' N,	000°29' W
Avilés	43°33' N,	005°55' W
Badajoz	38°53' N,	006°58' W
Barcelona	41°23' N,	002°11' E
Bilbao	43°15' N,	002°58' W
Burgos	42°21' N,	003°42' W
Cáceres	39°29' N,	006°22' W
Cádiz (Cadiz)	36°32' N,	006°18' W
Cartagena	37°36' N,	000°59' W
Castellón de la Plana	39°59' N,	000°02' W
Ciudad Real	38°59' N,	003°56' W
Cordova (Córdoba)	37°53' N,	004°46' W
Cuenca	40°04' N,	002°08' W
Elche (Elx)	38°15' N,	000°42' W
Ferrol (El Ferrol del Caudillo)	43°29' N,	008°14' W
Gernika-Lumo (Guernica y Luno)	43°19' N,	002°41' W
Getafe	40°18' N,	003°43' W
Gijón	43°32' N,	005°40' W
Granada	37°11' N,	003°36' W
Huelva	37°16' N,	006°57' W
Jaén	37°46' N,	003°47' W
León	42°36' N,	005°34' W
Lérida (Lleida)	41°37' N,	000°37' E
L'Hospitalet de Llobregat	41°22' N,	002°08' E
Logroño	42°28' N,	002°27' W
Lugo	43°00' N,	007°34' W
Madrid	40°24' N,	003°41' W
Málaga	36°43' N,	004°25' W
Mérida	38°55' N,	006°20' W
Murcia	37°59' N,	001°07' W
Palencia	42°01' N,	004°32' W
Pamplona (Iruña)	42°49' N,	001°38' W
Salamanca	40°58' N,	005°39' W
San Fernando	36°28' N,	006°12' W
Santander	43°28' N,	003°48' W
Santiago de Compostela	42°53' N,	008°33' W
Saragossa (Zaragoza)	41°38' N,	000°53' W
Segovia	40°57' N,	004°07' W
Seville (Sevilla)	37°23' N,	005°59' W
Soria	41°46' N,	002°28' W
Tarragona	41°07' N,	001°15' E
Terrassa (Tarrasa)	41°34' N,	002°01' E
Teruel	40°21' N,	001°06' W
Toledo	39°52' N,	004°01' W
Valencia	39°28' N,	000°22' W
Valladolid	41°39' N,	004°43' W
Vigo	42°14' N,	008°43' W
Vitoria (Gasteiz)	42°51' N,	002°40' W

SRI LANKA . . . . . page 167

Ambalangoda	06°14' N,	080°03' E
Anuradhapura	08°21' N,	080°23' E
Badulla	06°59' N,	081°03' E
Batticaloa	07°43' N,	081°42' E
Beruwala	06°29' N,	079°59' E
Chavakachcheri	09°39' N,	080°09' E
Colombo	06°56' N,	079°51' E

Dehiwala-Mount Lavinia	06°51' N,	079°52' E
Eravur	07°46' N,	081°36' E
Galle	06°02' N,	080°13' E
Gampola	07°10' N,	080°34' E
Hambantota	06°07' N,	081°07' E
Jaffna	09°40' N,	080°00' E
Kalutara	06°35' N,	079°58' E
Kandy	07°18' N,	080°38' E
Kankesanturai	09°49' N,	080°02' E
Kegalla	07°15' N,	080°21' E
Kilinochchi	09°24' N,	080°24' E
Kotte	06°54' N,	079°54' E
Kurunegala	07°29' N,	080°22' E
Madampe	07°30' N,	079°50' E
Mannar	08°59' N,	079°54' E
Moratuwa	06°46' N,	079°53' E
Mullaittivu	09°16' N,	080°49' E
Mutur	08°27' N,	081°16' E
Negombo	07°13' N,	079°50' E
Nuwara Eliya	06°58' N,	080°46' E
Point Pedro	09°50' N,	080°14' E
Polonnaruwa	07°56' N,	081°00' E
Puttalam	08°02' N,	079°49' E
Ratnapura	06°41' N,	080°24' E
Tangalla	06°01' N,	080°48' E
Trincomalee	08°34' N,	081°14' E
Vavuniya	08°45' N,	080°30' E
Watugedara	06°15' N,	080°03' E
Weligama	05°58' N,	080°25' E
Yala	06°22' N,	081°31' E

SUDAN . . . . page 168

Al-Damāzīn (Ed–Damazīn)	11°49' N,	034°23' E
Al-Dāmir	17°35' N,	033°58' E
Al-Duwaym	14°00' N,	032°19' E
Al-Fashir (El Fasher)	13°38' N,	025°21' E
Al-Fūlah	11°48' N,	028°24' E
Al-Junaynah (Geneina)	13°27' N,	022°27' E
Al-Mijlad	11°02' N,	027°44' E
Al-Qadārif (Gedaref)	14°02' N,	035°24' E
Al-Ubbayid (El-Obeid)	13°11' N,	030°13' E
An-Nuhūd	12°42' N,	028°26' E
'Aṭbarah	17°42' N,	033°59' E
Dongola (Dunqulah)	19°10' N,	030°29' E
Kāduqlī	11°01' N,	029°43' E
Kas	12°30' N,	024°17' E
Kassalā	15°28' N,	036°24' E
Khartoum	15°36' N,	032°32' E
Khartoum North	15°38' N,	032°33' E
Kūstī	13°10' N,	032°40' E
Marawi	18°29' N,	031°49' E
Musmār (Mismār)	18°13' N,	035°38' E
Nyala	12°03' N,	024°53' E
Omdurman	15°38' N,	032°30' E
Port Sudan	19°37' N,	037°14' E
Rashad	11°51' N,	031°04' E
Sannār	13°33' N,	033°38' E
Sawākin	19°07' N,	037°20' E
Shandi (Shendi)	16°42' N,	033°26' E
Wadi Halfa	21°48' N,	031°21' E
Wad Madanī	14°24' N,	033°32' E

SURINAME . . . . . . page 169

Albina	05°30' N,	054°03' W
Benzdorp	03°41' N,	054°05' W
Bitagron	05°10' N,	056°06' W
Brokopondo	05°04' N,	054°58' W
Brownsweg	05°01' N,	055°10' W
Goddo	04°01' N,	055°28' W
Groningen	05°48' N,	055°28' W
Meerzorg	05°49' N,	055°09' W
Nieuw Amsterdam	05°53' N,	055°05' W
Nieuw Nickerie	05°57' N,	056°59' W
Onverwacht	05°36' N,	055°12' W
Paramaribo	05°50' N,	055°10' W
Totness	05°53' N,	056°19' W
Zanderij	05°27' N,	055°12' W

SWAZILAND . . . . . page 170

Hlatikulu	26°58' S,	031°19' E
Kadake	26°13' S,	031°02' E
Manzini (Bremersdorp)	26°29' S,	031°22' E
Mbabane	26°19' S,	031°08' E
Nhlangono	27°07' S,	031°12' E
Piggs Peak	25°58' S,	031°15' E
Siteki (Stegi)	26°27' S,	031°57' E

SWEDEN . . . . page 171

Älvsbyn	65°40' N,	021°00' E
Falun	60°36' N,	015°38' E
Gävle	60°40' N,	017°10' E
Göteborg	57°43' N,	011°58' E
Halmstad	56°39' N,	012°50' E
Haparanda	65°50' N,	024°10' E
Hudiksvall	61°44' N,	017°07' E
Jönköping	57°47' N,	014°11' E
Karlskrona	56°10' N,	015°35' E
Karlstad	59°22' N,	013°30' E
Kiruna	67°51' N,	020°13' E
Kristianstad	56°02' N,	014°08' E
Linköping	58°25' N,	015°37' E
Luleå	65°34' N,	022°10' E
Lycksele	64°36' N,	018°40' E
Malmberget	67°10' N,	020°40' E
Malmö	55°36' N,	013°00' E
Mariestad	58°43' N,	013°51' E
Mora	61°00' N,	014°33' E

Örebro	59°17' N,	015°13' E
Örnsköldsvik	63°18' N,	018°43' E
Östersund	63°11' N,	014°39' E
Piteå	65°20' N,	021°30' E
Skellefteå	64°46' N,	020°57' E
Söderhamn	61°18' N,	017°03' E
Stockholm	59°20' N,	018°03' E
Strömsund	63°51' N,	015°35' E
Sundsvall	62°23' N,	017°18' E
Umea	63°50' N,	020°15' E
Uppsala	59°52' N,	017°38' E
Vänersborg	58°22' N,	012°19' E
Västerås	59°37' N,	016°33' E
Växjö	56°53' N,	014°49' E
Vetalnda	57°26' N,	015°04' E
Visby	57°38' N,	018°18' E
Ystad	55°25' N,	013°49' E

SWITZERLAND .. page 172

Aarau	47°23' N,	008°03' E
Altdorf	46°53' N,	008°39' E
Arbon	47°31' N,	009°26' E
Appenzell	47°20' N,	009°24' E
Arosa	46°47' N,	009°40' E
Baden	47°28' N,	008°18' E
Basel	47°35' N,	007°32' E
Bellinzona	46°12' N,	009°01' E
Bern	46°55' N,	007°28' E
Biel (Bienne)	47°10' N,	007°15' E
Chur (Coire)	46°51' N,	009°30' E
Davos	46°49' N,	009°50' E
Delémont	47°22' N,	007°20' E
Frauenfeld	47°33' N,	008°54' E
Fribourg (Freiburg)	46°48' N,	007°09' E
Geneva	46°12' N,	006°10' E
Glarus	47°02' N,	009°04' E
Grindelwald	46°37' N,	008°03' E
Gstaad	46°28' N,	007°17' E
Herisau	47°24' N,	009°16' E
Interlaken	46°41' N,	007°51' E
La Chaux-de-Fonds	47°08' N,	006°51' E
Lausanne	46°32' N,	006°40' E
Liestal	47°28' N,	007°44' E
Locarno (Luggarus)	46°10' N,	008°48' E
Lucerne (Luzern)	47°05' N,	008°16' E
Lugano (Lauis)	46°00' N,	008°58' E
Montreux	46°26' N,	006°55' E
Neuchatel (Neuenburg)	47°00' N,	006°58' E
Saint Gall (Sankt Gallen)	47°28' N,	009°24' E
Saint Moritz (San Murezzan, Saint-Moritz, or Sankt Moritz)	46°30' N,	009°50' E
Sarnen	46°54' N,	008°14' E
Schaffhausen	47°42' N,	008°38' E
Sion (Sitten)	46°14' N,	007°21' E
Solothurn (Soleure)	47°14' N,	007°31' E
Stans	46°58' N,	008°21' E
Thun (Thoune)	46°45' N,	007°37' E
Vevey	46°27' N,	006°51' E
Winterthur	47°30' N,	008°45' E
Zermatt	46°01' N,	007°45' E
Zug	47°10' N,	008°31' E
Zürich	47°22' N,	008°33' E

SYRIA .... page 173

Al-Bāb	36°22' N,	037°31' E
Al-Hasakah	36°29' N,	040°45' E
Al-Mayādin	35°01' N,	040°27' E
Al-Qāmishli (Al-Kamishly)	37°02' N,	041°14' E
Al-Raqqah (Rakka)	35°57' N,	039°01' E
Al-Safirah	36°04' N,	037°22' E
Al-Suwaydā'	32°42' N,	036°34' E
Aleppo (Ḥalab)	36°12' N,	037°10' E
A'zāz (I'zaz)	36°35' N,	037°03' E
Damascus	33°30' N,	036°18' E
Dar'ā	32°37' N,	036°06' E
Dayr azl-Zawr	35°20' N,	040°09' E
Dūmā (Douma)	33°35' N,	036°24' E
Hamāh (Hama)	35°08' N,	036°45' E
Ḥimṣ (Homs)	34°44' N,	036°43' E
Idlib	35°55' N,	036°38' E
Jablah (Jableh)	35°21' N,	035°55' E
Jarābulus	36°49' N,	038°01' E
Latakia (Al-Lādhiqīyah)	35°31' N,	035°47' E
Ma'arrat al-Nu'mān	35°38' N,	036°40' E
Ma'lūlā	33°50' N,	036°33' E
Manbij (Manbej)	36°31' N,	037°57' E
Mukharram al-Fawqāni	34°49' N,	037°05' E
Ra's al-'Ayn	36°51' N,	040°04' E
Salamīyah	35°01' N,	037°03' E
Tadmur	34°33' N,	038°17' E
Ṭarṭūs	34°53' N,	035°53' E

TAIWAN .... page 174

Chang-hua	24°05' N,	120°32' E
Ch'ao-chou	22°33' N,	120°32' E
Ch'e-ch'eng	22°05' N,	120°42' E
Chia-i	23°29' N,	120°27' E
Ch'ih-shang	23°07' N,	121°12' E
Chi-lung	25°08' N,	121°44' E
Chung-hsing Hsin-ts'un	23°57' N,	120°41' E
Chu-tung	24°44' N,	121°05' E
Erh-lin	23°54' N,	120°22' E

Feng-lin	23°45' N,	121°26' E
Feng-shan	22°38' N,	120°21' E
Feng-yüan	24°15' N,	120°43' E
Hsin-chu	24°48' N,	120°58' E
Hsin-ying	23°18' N,	120°19' E
Hua-lien	23°59' N,	121°36' E
I-lan	24°46' N,	121°45' E
Kang-shan	22°48' N,	120°17' E
Kao-hsiung	22°38' N,	120°17' E
Lan-yü	22°02' N,	121°33' E
Lo-tung	24°41' N,	121°46' E
Lu-kang	24°03' N,	120°25' E
Lü-tao	22°40' N,	121°28' E
Miao-li	24°34' N,	120°49' E
Nan-t'ou	23°55' N,	120°41' E
Pan-ch'iao	25°01' N,	121°27' E
P'ing-tung	22°40' N,	120°29' E
San-ch'ung	25°04' N,	121°30' E
Su-ao	24°36' N,	121°51' E
T'ai-chung	24°09' N,	120°41' E
T'ai-nan	23°00' N,	120°12' E
Taipei (T'ai-pei)	25°03' N,	121°30' E
T'ai-tung	22°45' N,	121°09' E
T'ao-yüan	25°00' N,	121°18' E
Tung-ho	22°58' N,	121°18' E
Yüan-lin	23°58' N,	120°34' E
Yung-k'ang	23°02' N,	120°15' E

TAJIKISTAN .... page 175

Dushanbe	38°33' N,	068°48' E
Kalininobod	37°52' N,	068°55' E
Khorugh	37°30' N,	071°36' E
Khujand (Leninabad, or Khojand)	40°17' N,	069°37' E
Kofarniqon (Ordzhonikidzeäbad)	38°34' N,	069°01' E
Külob	37°55' N,	069°46' E
Norak	38°23' N,	069°21' E
Qayroqqum	40°16' N,	069°49' E
Qŭrghonteppa	37°50' N,	068°47' E
Uroteppa	39°55' N,	069°01' E

TANZANIA ...... page 176

Arusha	03°22' S,	036°41' E
Bagamoyo	06°26' S,	038°54' E
Bukoba	01°20' S,	031°49' E
Chake Chake	05°15' S,	039°46' E
Dar es Salaam	06°48' S,	039°17' E
Dodoma	06°11' S,	035°45' E
Ifakara	08°08' S,	036°41' E
Iringa	07°46' S,	035°42' E
Kigoma	04°52' S,	029°38' E
Korogwe	05°09' S,	038°29' E
Lindi	10°00' S,	039°43' E
Mbeya	08°54' S,	033°27' E
Mkoani	05°22' S,	039°39' E
Morogoro	06°49' S,	037°40' E
Moshi	03°21' S,	037°20' E
Mpwapwa	06°21' S,	036°29' E
Mtwara	10°16' S,	040°11' E
Musoma	01°30' S,	033°48' E
Mwanza	02°31' S,	032°54' E
Newala	10°56' S,	039°18' E
Pangani	09°32' S,	035°31' E
Shinyanga	03°40' S,	033°26' E
Singida	04°49' S,	034°45' E
Songea	10°41' S,	035°39' E
Sumbawanga	07°58' S,	031°37' E
Tabora	05°01' S,	032°48' E
Tanga	05°04' S,	039°06' E
Tunduru	11°07' S,	037°21' E
Wete	05°04' S,	039°43' E
Zanzibar	06°10' S,	039°11' E

THAILAND ...... page 177

Bangkok (Krung Thep)	13°45' N,	100°31' E
Chanthaburi (Chantabun)	12°36' N,	102°09' E
Chiang Mai (Chiengmai)	18°47' N,	098°59' E
Chon Buri	13°22' N,	100°59' E
Hat Yai (Haad Yai)	07°01' N,	100°28' E
Khon Kaen	16°26' N,	102°50' E
Mae Sot	16°43' N,	098°34' E
Nakhhon Phanom	17°24' N,	104°47' E
Nakhon Ratchasima (Khorat)	14°58' N,	102°07' E
Nakhon Sawan	15°41' N,	100°07' E
Nakhon Si Thammarat	08°26' N,	099°58' E
Nan	18°47' N,	100°47' E
Nong Khai	17°52' N,	102°44' E
Nonthaburi	13°50' N,	100°29' E
Pathum Thani	14°01' N,	100°32' E
Pattaya	12°54' N,	100°51' E
Phichit	16°26' N,	100°22' E
Phitsanulok	16°50' N,	100°15' E
Phra Nakhon Si Ayutthaya (Ayutthaya)	14°21' N,	100°33' E
Phuket	07°53' N,	098°24' E
Roi Et	16°03' N,	103°40' E
Sakon Nakhon	17°10' N,	104°09' E
Samut Prakan	13°36' N,	100°36' E
Samut Sakhon (Samut Sakorn)	13°32' N,	100°17' E
Sara Buri	14°32' N,	100°55' E
Trang	07°33' N,	099°36' E
Trat	12°14' N,	102°30' E
Ubon Ratchathani	15°14' N,	104°54' E

Udon Thani	17°26' N,	102°46' E
Uthai Thani	15°22' N,	100°03' E
Yala	06°33' N,	101°18' E

TOGO .... page 178

Aného	06°14' N,	001°36' E
Atakpamé	07°32' N,	001°08' E
Bassar	09°15' N,	000°47' E
Blitta	08°19' N,	000°59' E
Dapaong	10°52' N,	000°12' E
Kara (Lama Kara)	09°33' N,	001°12' E
Lomé	06°08' N,	001°13' E
Palimé	09°21' N,	002°37' E
Sokodé	08°59' N,	001°08' E
Tsévié	06°25' N,	001°13' E

TONGA .... page 179

Nuku'alofa	21°08' N,	175°12' E

TRINIDAD AND TOBAGO .... page 180

Arima	10°38' N,	061°17' W
Arouca	10°38' N,	061°20' W
Chaguanas	10°31' N,	061°25' W
Charlotteville	11°19' N,	060°33' W
Couva	10°25' N,	061°27' W
Point Fortin	10°11' N,	061°41' W
Port of Spain	10°39' N,	061°31' W
Princes Town	10°16' N,	061°23' W
Rio Claro	10°18' N,	061°11' W
Roxborough	11°15' N,	060°35' W
San Fernando	10°17' N,	061°28' W
Sangre Grande	10°35' N,	061°07' W
Scarborough	11°11' N,	060°44' W
Siparia	10°08' N,	061°30' W
Tunapuna	10°38' N,	061°23' W

TUNISIA .... page 181

Al-Ḥammāmāt (Hammamet)	36°24' N,	010°37' E
Al-Mahdīyah (Mahdia)	35°30' N,	011°04' E
Al-Metlaoui	34°20' N,	008°24' E
Al-Muknīn (Moknine)	35°38' N,	010°54' E
Al-Munastīr (Monastir or Ruspina)	35°47' N,	010°50' E
Al-Qaṣrayn (Kasserine)	35°11' N,	008°48' E
Al-Qayrawān (Kairouan or Qairouan)	35°41' N,	010°07' E
Bājah (Béja)	36°44' N,	009°11' E
Banzart (Bizerte)	37°17' N,	009°52' E
Ḥammām al-Anf (Hammam-lif)	36°44' N,	010°20' E
Jarjīs (Zarzis)	33°30' N,	011°07' E
Madanīn (Medenine)	33°21' N,	010°30' E
Makthar	35°51' N,	009°12' E
Manzil Bū Ruqaybah (Ferryville or Menzel-Bourguiba)	37°10' N,	009°48' E
Nābul (Nabeul or Neapolis)	36°27' N,	010°44' E
Nafṭah (Nefta)	33°52' N,	007°53' E
Qābis (Gabes or Tacape)	33°53' N,	010°07' E
Qafṣah (Gafsa)	34°25' N,	008°48' E
Qibilī (Kebili)	33°42' N,	008°58' E
Safāqis (Sfax)	34°44' N,	010°46' E
Sūsah (Sousa or Sousse)	35°49' N,	010°38' E
Tawzar (Tozeur)	33°55' N,	008°08' E
Tunis (Tunis)	36°48' N,	010°11' E
Zaghwān (Zaghouan)	36°24' N,	010°09' E

TURKEY .... page 182

Adana	37°01' N,	035°18' E
Afyon	38°45' N,	030°33' E
Amasya	40°39' N,	035°51' E
Ankara (Angora)	39°56' N,	032°52' E
Antakya (Antioch)	36°14' N,	036°07' E
Antalya (Attalia or Hatay)	36°53' N,	030°42' E
Artvin	41°11' N,	041°49' E
Aydın	37°51' N,	027°51' E
Balıkesir	39°39' N,	027°53' E
Bandırma (Panderma)	40°20' N,	027°58' E
Batman	37°52' N,	041°07' E
Bursa (Brusa)	40°11' N,	029°04' E
Çorum	40°33' N,	034°58' E
Denizli	37°46' N,	029°06' E
Diyarbakır (Amida)	37°55' N,	040°14' E
Elâziğ	38°41' N,	039°14' E
Erzincan	39°44' N,	039°29' E
Erzurum	39°55' N,	041°17' E
Eskisehir	39°46' N,	030°32' E
Gaziantep	37°05' N,	037°22' E
Iğdir	39°56' N,	044°02' E
İskenderun (Alexandretta)	36°35' N,	036°10' E
Isparta (Hamid-Abad)	37°46' N,	030°33' E
Istanbul (Constantinople)	41°01' N,	028°58' E
İzmir (Smyrna)	38°25' N,	027°09' E
İzmit	40°46' N,	029°55' E
Kahramanmaraş (Maraş)	37°36' N,	036°55' E

Karabük	41°12' N, 032°37' E
Karaman	37°11' N, 033°14' E
Kars	40°37' N, 043°05' E
Kayseri (Caesarea)	38°43' N, 035°30' E
Kırıkkale	39°50' N, 033°31' E
Konya (Iconium)	37°52' N, 032°31' E
Kütahya	39°25' N, 029°59' E
Manisa	38°36' N, 027°26' E
Mardin	37°18' N, 040°44' E
Mersin	36°48' N, 034°38' E
Muğla	37°12' N, 028°22' E
Nevşehir	38°38' N, 034°43' E
Niğde	37°59' N, 034°42' E
Ordu	41°00' N, 037°53' E
Samsun (Amisus)	41°17' N, 036°20' E
Sinop	42°01' N, 035°09' E
Sivas (Sebastia)	39°45' N, 037°02' E
Trabzon (Trapezus or Trebizond)	41°00' N, 039°43' E
Urfa	37°08' N, 038°46' E
Uşak (Ushak)	38°41' N, 029°25' E
Van	38°30' N, 043°23' E
Yalova	40°39' N, 029°15' E
Yozgat	39°50' N, 034°48' E
Zonguldak	41°27' N, 031°49' E

TURKMENISTAN .. page 183

Ashgabat (Ashkhabad)	37°57' N, 058°23' E
Bayramaly	37°37' N, 062°10' E
Büzmeyin	38°05' N, 058°12' E
Chärjew	39°06' N, 063°34' E
Cheleken	39°26' N, 053°07' E
Chirchiq	41°29' N, 069°35' E
Dashhowuz	41°50' N, 059°58' E
Gowurdak	37°50' N, 066°04' E
Kerki	37°50' N, 065°12' E
Mary (Merv)	37°36' N, 061°50' E
Nebitdag	39°30' N, 054°22' E
Türkmenbashy (Krasnovodsk)	40°00' N, 053°00' E
Yolöten	37°18' N, 062°21' E

TUVALU .... page 184

Fongafale	08°31' S, 179°13' E

UGANDA .... page 185

Entebbe	00°04' N, 032°28' E
Gulu	02°47' N, 032°18' E
Jinja	00°26' N, 033°12' E
Kabarole	00°39' N, 030°16' E
Kampala	00°19' N, 032°35' E
Masaka	00°20' S, 031°44' E
Mbale	01°05' N, 034°10' E
Soroti	01°43' N, 033°37' E
Tororo	00°42' N, 034°11' E

UKRAINE .... page 186

Alchevsk	48°30' N, 038°47' E
Berdyansk	46°45' N, 036°47' E
Berdychiv	49°54' N, 028°35' E
Bila Tserkva	49°47' N, 030°07' E
Cherkasy	49°26' N, 032°04' E
Chernihiv	51°30' N, 031°18' E
Chernivtsi	48°18' N, 025°56' E
Chornobyl (Chernobyl)	51°16' N, 030°14' E
Dnipropetrovs'k	48°27' N, 034°59' E
Donetsk	48°00' N, 037°48' E
Kerch	45°21' N, 036°28' E
Kharkiv	50°00' N, 036°15' E
Khmelnytskyy	49°25' N, 027°00' E
Kiev (Kyyiv)	50°26' N, 030°31' E
Korosten	50°57' N, 028°39' E
Kovel	51°13' N, 024°43' E
Krasny Luch	48°08' N, 038°56' E
Kryvyy Rih	47°55' N, 033°21' E
Luhansk	48°34' N, 039°20' E
Lutsk	50°45' N, 025°20' E
Lviv	49°50' N, 024°00' E
Makiyivka	48°02' N, 037°58' E
Marhanets	47°38' N, 034°38' E
Mariupol	47°06' N, 037°33' E
Melitopol	46°50' N, 035°22' E
Mykolayiv	46°58' N, 032°00' E
Myrhorod	49°58' N, 033°36' E
Novhorod-Siverskyy	52°00' N, 033°16' E
Odessa	46°28' N, 030°44' E
Pavlograd	48°31' N, 035°52' E
Poltava	49°35' N, 034°34' E
Pryluky	50°36' N, 032°24' E
Rivne	50°37' N, 026°15' E
Rubizhne	49°01' N, 038°23' E
Sevastopol	44°36' N, 033°32' E
Shostka	51°52' N, 033°29' E
Simferopol	44°57' N, 034°06' E
Sumy	50°54' N, 034°48' E
Syeverodonets'k	48°58' N, 038°26' E
Uzhhorod	48°37' N, 022°18' E
Vinnytsya	49°14' N, 028°29' E
Voznesensk	47°33' N, 031°20' E
Yevpatoriya	45°12' N, 033°22' E
Zaporizhzhya	47°49' N, 035°11' E
Zhytomyr	50°15' N, 028°40' E

UNITED ARAB EMIRATES .... page 187

Abu Dhabi	24°28' N,	054°22' E
'Ajmān	25°25' N,	055°27' E
Al-'Ayn	24°13' N,	055°46' E
Al-Fujayrah	25°08' N,	056°21' E
Al-Khīs	23°00' N,	054°12' E
Al-Māriyah	23°08' N,	053°44' E
'Arādah	22°59' N,	053°26' E
Ash-Shāriqah	25°22' N,	055°23' E
Diqdāqah	25°40' N,	055°58' E
Dubai	25°16' N,	055°18' E
Kalbā	25°05' N,	056°22' E
Khawr Fakkān	25°21' N,	056°22' E
Ra's Al-Khaymah	25°47' N,	055°57' E
Tarīf	24°03' N,	053°46' E
Umm Al-Qaywayn	25°35' N,	055°34' E
Wadhīl	23°03' N,	054°08' E

UNITED KINGDOM.... page 188–189

Aberdeen	57°09' N,	002°08' W
Belfast	54°35' N,	005°56' W
Birmingham	52°29' N,	001°51' W
Bradford	53°47' N,	001°45' W
Bristol	51°26' N,	002°35' W
Cambridge	52°12' N,	000°09' E
Cardiff	51°29' N,	003°11' W
Carlisle	54°53' N,	002°57' W
Cheltenham	51°54' N,	002°05' W
Colchester	51°54' N,	000°54' E
Coventry	52°24' N,	001°31' W
Darlington	54°32' N,	001°34' W
Dartford	51°26' N,	000°12' W
Derby	52°55' N,	001°28' W
Derry (Londonderry)	55°00' N,	007°20' W
Dundee	56°29' N,	003°02' W
Edinburgh	55°57' N,	003°10' W
Exeter	50°43' N,	003°31' W
Glasgow	55°52' N,	004°15' W
Hastings	50°52' N,	000°35' E
High Wycombe	51°38' N,	000°45' W
Hove	50°50' N,	000°11' W
Ipswich	52°03' N,	001°09' E
King's Lynn	52°45' N,	000°24' E
Kingston upon Hull	53°45' N,	000°20' W
Leeds	53°48' N,	001°32' W
Leicester	52°38' N,	001°08' W
Lincoln	53°14' N,	000°32' W
Liverpool	53°25' N,	002°57' W
London	51°30' N,	000°07' W
Maidstone	51°16' N,	000°32' E
Manchester	53°29' N,	002°15' W
Margate	51°23' N,	001°23' E
Newcastle upon Tyne	54°58' N,	001°36' W
Newtownabbey	54°40' N,	005°57' W
Norwich	52°38' N,	001°18' E
Nottingham	52°58' N,	001°10' W
Peterborough	52°35' N,	000°14' W
Plymouth	50°23' N,	004°09' W
Poole	50°43' N,	001°59' W
Portsmouth	50°49' N,	001°04' W
Rhondda	51°39' N,	003°29' W
Sheffield	53°23' N,	001°28' W
Southampton	50°55' N,	001°24' W
Stoke-on-Trent	53°01' N,	002°11' W
Swansea	51°38' N,	003°58' W
Walsall	52°35' N,	001°59' W
Warrington	53°24' N,	002°36' W
York	53°57' N,	001°06' W

UNITED STATES .... page 190–191

Aberdeen, S.D.	45°28' N,	098°29' W
Aberdeen, Wash.	46°59' N,	123°50' W
Abilene, Kan.	38°55' N,	097°13' W
Abilene, Tex.	32°28' N,	099°43' W
Ada, Okla.	34°46' N,	096°41' W
Akron, Ohio	41°05' N,	081°31' W
Alamogordo, N.M.	32°54' N,	105°57' W
Alamosa, Colo.	37°28' N,	105°52' W
Albany, Ga.	31°35' N,	084°10' W
Albany, N.Y.	42°39' N,	073°45' W
Albuquerque, N.M.	35°05' N,	106°39' W
Alexandria, La.	31°18' N,	092°27' W
Alexandria, Va.	38°48' N,	077°03' W
Alliance, Neb.	42°06' N,	102°52' W
Alpena, Mich.	45°04' N,	083°27' W
Alton, Ill.	38°53' N,	090°11' W
Alturas, Calif.	41°29' N,	120°32' W
Altus, Okla.	34°38' N,	099°20' W
Amarillo, Tex.	35°13' N,	101°50' W
Americus, Ga.	32°04' N,	084°14' W
Anaconda, Mont.	46°08' N,	112°57' W
Anchorage, Alaska	61°13' N,	149°54' W
Andalusia, Ala.	31°18' N,	086°29' W
Ann Arbor, Mich.	42°17' N,	083°45' W
Annapolis, Md.	38°59' N,	076°30' W
Appleton, Wis.	44°16' N,	088°25' W
Arcata, Calif.	40°52' N,	124°05' W
Arlington, Tex.	32°44' N,	097°07' W
Arlington, Va.	38°53' N,	077°07' W
Asheville, N.C.	35°36' N,	082°33' W
Ashland, Ky.	38°28' N,	082°38' W
Ashland, Wis.	46°35' N,	090°53' W
Aspen, Colo.	39°11' N,	106°49' W

Astoria, Ore.	46°11' N,	123°50' W
Athens, Ga.	33°57' N,	083°23' W
Atlanta, Ga.	33°45' N,	084°23' W
Atlantic City, N.J.	39°21' N,	074°27' W
Augusta, Ga.	33°28' N,	081°58' W
Augusta, Me.	44°19' N,	069°47' W
Aurora, Colo.	39°43' N,	104°49' W
Austin, Minn.	43°40' N,	092°58' W
Austin, Tex.	30°17' N,	097°45' W
Baker, Mont.	46°22' N,	104°17' W
Baker, Ore.	44°47' N,	117°50' W
Bakersfield, Calif.	35°23' N,	119°01' W
Baltimore, Md.	39°17' N,	076°37' W
Bangor, Me.	44°48' N,	068°46' W
Bar Harbor, Me.	44°23' N,	068°13' W
Barrow, Alaska	71°18' N,	156°47' W
Bartlesville, Okla.	36°45' N,	095°59' W
Baton Rouge, La.	30°27' N,	091°11' W
Bay City, Mich.	43°36' N,	083°54' W
Beaumont, Tex.	30°05' N,	094°06' W
Bellingham, Wash.	48°46' N,	122°29' W
Beloit, Wis.	42°31' N,	089°01' W
Bemidji, Minn.	47°28' N,	094°52' W
Bend, Ore.	44°04' N,	121°19' W
Berlin, N.H.	44°28' N,	071°11' W
Bethel, Alaska	60°48' N,	161°45' W
Beulah, N.D.	47°15' N,	101°46' W
Billings, Mont.	45°47' N,	108°30' W
Biloxi, Miss.	30°24' N,	088°53' W
Birmingham, Ala.	33°31' N,	086°48' W
Bismarck, N.D.	46°48' N,	100°47' W
Bloomington, Ind.	39°10' N,	086°32' W
Blythe, Calif.	33°37' N,	114°36' W
Boca Raton, Fla.	26°21' N,	080°05' W
Bogalusa, La.	30°47' N,	089°52' W
Boise, Idaho	43°37' N,	116°13' W
Boston, Mass.	42°22' N,	071°04' W
Boulder, Colo.	40°01' N,	105°17' W
Bowling Green, Ky.	36°59' N,	086°27' W
Bozeman, Mont.	45°41' N,	111°02' W
Bradenton, Fla.	27°30' N,	082°34' W
Brady, Tex.	31°09' N,	099°20' W
Brainerd, Minn.	46°22' N,	094°12' W
Bremerton, Wash.	47°34' N,	122°38' W
Brigham City, Utah	41°31' N,	112°01' W
Brookings, S.D.	44°19' N,	096°48' W
Brownsville, Tex.	25°54' N,	097°30' W
Brunswick, Ga.	31°10' N,	081°30' W
Bryan, Tex.	30°40' N,	096°22' W
Buffalo, N.Y.	42°53' N,	078°53' W
Buffalo, Tex.	31°28' N,	096°04' W
Burlington, Ia.	40°48' N,	091°06' W
Burlington, Vt.	44°29' N,	073°12' W
Burns, Ore.	43°35' N,	119°03' W
Butte, Mont.	46°00' N,	112°32' W
Cairo, Ill.	37°00' N,	089°11' W
Caldwell, Idaho	43°40' N,	116°41' W
Canton, Ohio	40°48' N,	081°23' W
Cape Girardeau, Mo.	37°19' N,	089°32' W
Carbondale, Ill.	37°44' N,	089°13' W
Carlsbad, N.M.	32°25' N,	104°14' W
Carson City, Nev.	39°10' N,	119°46' W
Casa Grande, Ariz.	32°53' N,	111°45' W
Casper, Wyo.	42°51' N,	106°19' W
Cedar City, Utah	37°41' N,	113°04' W
Cedar Rapids, Ia.	41°59' N,	091°40' W
Chadron, Neb.	42°50' N,	103°00' W
Champaign, Ill.	40°07' N,	088°15' W
Charleston, S.C.	32°46' N,	079°56' W
Charleston, W.Va.	38°21' N,	081°39' W
Charlotte, N.C.	35°13' N,	080°51' W
Chattanooga, Tenn.	35°03' N,	085°19' W
Chesapeake, Va.	36°50' N,	076°17' W
Cheyenne, Wyo.	41°08' N,	104°49' W
Chicago, Ill.	41°53' N,	087°38' W
Chico, Calif.	39°44' N,	121°50' W
Chula Vista, Calif.	32°38' N,	117°05' W
Cincinnati, Ohio	39°06' N,	084°31' W
Clarksdale, Miss.	34°12' N,	090°35' W
Clayton, N.M.	36°27' N,	103°11' W
Clearwater, Fla.	27°58' N,	082°48' W
Cleveland, Ohio	41°30' N,	081°42' W
Clinton, Okla.	35°31' N,	098°58' W
Clovis, N.M.	34°24' N,	103°12' W
Cody, Wyo.	44°32' N,	109°03' W
Coeur d'Alene, Idaho	47°41' N,	116°46' W
College Station, Tex.	30°37' N,	096°21' W
Colorado Springs, Colo.	38°50' N,	104°49' W
Columbia, S.C.	34°00' N,	081°03' W
Columbus, Ga.	32°29' N,	084°59' W
Columbus, Miss.	33°30' N,	088°25' W
Columbus, Ohio	39°58' N,	083°00' W
Concord, N.H.	43°12' N,	071°32' W
Coos Bay, Ore.	43°22' N,	124°12' W
Coral Gables, Fla.	25°45' N,	080°16' W
Cordele, Ga.	31°58' N,	083°47' W
Cordova, Alaska	60°33' N,	145°45' W
Corinth, Miss.	34°56' N,	088°31' W
Corpus Christi, Tex.	27°47' N,	097°24' W
Corsicana, Tex.	32°06' N,	096°28' W
Corvallis, Ore.	44°34' N,	123°16' W
Council Bluffs, Ia.	41°16' N,	095°52' W
Covington, Ky.	39°05' N,	084°31' W
Crescent City, Calif.	41°45' N,	124°12' W
Crystal City, Tex.	28°41' N,	099°50' W
Dalhart, Tex.	36°04' N,	102°31' W
Dallas, Tex.	32°47' N,	096°49' W
Dalton, Ga.	34°46' N,	084°58' W
Danville, Va.	36°36' N,	079°23' W
Davenport, Ia.	41°32' N,	090°35' W
Davis, Calif.	38°33' N,	121°44' W
Dayton, Ohio	39°45' N,	084°12' W
Daytona Beach, Fla.	29°13' N,	081°01' W
Decorah, Ia.	43°18' N,	091°48' W

Denver, Colo.	39°44' N,	104°59' W
Des Moines, Ia.	41°35' N,	093°37' W
Detroit, Mich.	42°20' N,	083°03' W
Dickinson, N.D.	46°53' N,	102°47' W
Dillingham, Alaska	59°03' N,	158°28' W
Dillon, Mont.	45°13' N,	112°38' W
Dodge City, Kan.	37°45' N,	100°00' W
Dothan, Ala.	31°13' N,	085°24' W
Dover, Del.	39°10' N,	075°32' W
Dover, N.H.	43°12' N,	070°53' W
Dubuque, Ia.	42°30' N,	090°41' W
Duluth, Minn.	46°47' N,	092°07' W
Duncan, Okla.	34°30' N,	097°57' W
Durango, Colo.	37°17' N,	107°53' W
Durham, N.C.	36°00' N,	078°54' W
Dutch Harbor, Alaska	53°53' N,	166°32' W
East St. Louis, Ill.	38°37' N,	090°09' W
Eau Claire, Wis.	44°49' N,	091°30' W
El Cajon, Calif.	32°48' N,	116°58' W
El Dorado, Ark.	33°12' N,	092°40' W
El Paso, Tex.	31°45' N,	106°29' W
Elko, Nev.	40°50' N,	115°46' W
Ely, Minn.	47°55' N,	091°51' W
Ely, Nev.	39°15' N,	114°54' W
Emporia, Kan.	38°25' N,	096°11' W
Enid, Okla.	36°24' N,	097°53' W
Erie, Pa.	42°08' N,	080°05' W
Escanaba, Mich.	45°45' N,	087°04' W
Escondido, Calif.	33°07' N,	117°05' W
Eugene, Ore.	44°05' N,	123°04' W
Eunice, La.	30°30' N,	092°25' W
Eureka, Calif.	40°47' N,	124°09' W
Eustis, Fla.	28°51' N,	081°41' W
Evanston, Wyo.	41°16' N,	110°58' W
Everett, Wash.	47°59' N,	122°12' W
Fairbanks, Alaska,	64°51' N,	147°45' W
Falls City, Neb.	40°03' N,	095°36' W
Fargo, N.D.	46°53' N,	096°48' W
Farmington, N.M.	36°44' N,	108°12' W
Fayetteville, Ark.	36°03' N,	094°09' W
Fayetteville, N.C.	35°03' N,	078°53' W
Fergus Falls, Minn.	46°17' N,	096°04' W
Flagstaff, Ariz.	35°12' N,	111°39' W
Flint, Mich.	43°01' N,	083°41' W
Florence, S.C.	34°12' N,	079°46' W
Fort Bragg, Calif.	39°26' N,	123°48' W
Fort Collins, Colo.	40°35' N,	105°05' W
Fort Dodge, Ia.	42°30' N,	094°11' W
Fort Lauderdale, Fla.	26°07' N,	080°08' W
Fort Madison, Ia.	40°38' N,	091°27' W
Fort Myers, Fla.	26°39' N,	081°53' W
Fort Pierce, Fla.	27°26' N,	080°19' W
Fort Smith, Ark.	35°23' N,	094°25' W
Fort Wayne, Ind.	41°04' N,	085°09' W
Fort Worth, Tex.	32°45' N,	097°18' W
Frankfort, Ky.	38°12' N,	084°52' W
Freeport, Ill.	42°17' N,	089°36' W
Freeport, Tex.	28°57' N,	095°21' W
Fremont, Neb.	41°26' N,	096°30' W
Fresno, Calif.	36°44' N,	119°47' W
Gadsden, Ala.	34°01' N,	086°01' W
Gainesville, Fla.	29°40' N,	082°20' W
Gainesville, Ga.	34°17' N,	083°49' W
Galena, Alaska	64°44' N,	156°56' W
Gallup, N.M.	35°31' N,	108°45' W
Galveston, Tex.	29°18' N,	094°48' W
Garden City, Kan.	37°58' N,	100°52' W
Garland, Tex.	32°54' N,	096°38' W
Gary, Ind.	41°36' N,	087°20' W
Georgetown, S.C.	33°23' N,	079°17' W
Gillette, Wyo.	44°18' N,	105°30' W
Glasgow, Ky.	37°00' N,	085°55' W
Glasgow, Mont.	48°12' N,	106°38' W
Glendive, Mont.	47°07' N,	104°43' W
Glenwood Springs, Colo.	39°33' N,	107°19' W
Goliad, Tex.	28°40' N,	097°23' W
Goodland, Kan.	39°21' N,	101°43' W
Grand Forks, N.D.	47°55' N,	097°03' W
Grand Island, Neb.	40°55' N,	098°21' W
Grand Junction, Colo.	39°04' N,	108°33' W
Grand Rapids, Mich.	42°58' N,	085°40' W
Granite Falls, Minn.	44°49' N,	095°33' W
Great Falls, Mont.	47°30' N,	111°17' W
Greeley, Colo.	40°25' N,	104°42' W
Green Bay, Wis.	44°31' N,	088°00' W
Greensboro, N.C.	36°04' N,	079°48' W
Greenville, Ala.	31°50' N,	086°38' W
Greenville, Miss.	33°24' N,	091°04' W
Greenwood, S.C.	34°12' N,	082°10' W
Griffin, Ga.	33°15' N,	084°16' W
Gulfport, Miss.	30°22' N,	089°06' W
Guymon, Okla.	36°41' N,	101°29' W
Hampton, Va.	37°02' N,	076°21' W
Hannibal, Mo.	39°42' N,	091°22' W
Harlingen, Tex.	26°12' N,	097°42' W
Harrisburg, Pa.	40°16' N,	076°53' W
Hartford, Conn.	41°46' N,	072°41' W
Hattiesburg, Miss.	31°20' N,	089°17' W
Helena, Mont.	46°36' N,	112°02' W
Henderson, Nev.	36°02' N,	114°59' W
Hialeah, Fla.	25°51' N,	080°16' W
Hilo, Hawaii	19°44' N,	155°05' W
Hobbs, N.M.	32°42' N,	103°08' W
Hollywood, Fla.	26°01' N,	080°09' W
Honokaa, Hawaii	20°05' N,	155°28' W
Honolulu, Hawaii	21°19' N,	157°52' W
Hope, Ark.	33°40' N,	093°36' W
Hot Springs, Ark.	34°31' N,	093°03' W
Houghton, Mich.	47°07' N,	088°34' W
Houston, Tex.	29°46' N,	095°22' W
Hugo, Okla.	34°01' N,	095°31' W
Huntsville, Ala.	34°44' N,	086°35' W

Hutchinson, Kan.	38°05' N,	097°56' W
Idaho Falls, Idaho	43°30' N,	112°02' W
Independence, Mo.	39°05' N,	094°24' W
Indianapolis, Ind.	39°46' N,	086°09' W
International Falls, Minn.	48°36' N,	093°25' W
Iron Mountain, Mich.	45°49' N,	088°04' W
Ironwood, Mich.	46°27' N,	090°09' W
Ithaca, N.Y.	42°26' N,	076°30' W
Jackson, Miss.	32°18' N,	090°12' W
Jackson, Tenn.	35°37' N,	088°49' W
Jacksonville, Fla.	30°20' N,	081°39' W
Jacksonville, N.C.	34°45' N,	077°26' W
Jamestown, N.Y.	42°06' N,	079°14' W
Jefferson City, Mo.	38°34' N,	092°10' W
Jersey City, N.J.	40°44' N,	074°04' W
Joliet, Ill.	41°32' N,	088°05' W
Jonesboro, Ark.	35°50' N,	090°42' W
Jonesboro, Ga.	33°31' N,	084°22' W
Juneau, Alaska	58°20' N,	134°27' W
Kaktovik, Alaska	70°08' N,	143°38' W
Kalamazoo, Mich.	42°17' N,	085°35' W
Kalispell, Mont.	48°12' N,	114°19' W
Kansas City, Kan.	39°07' N,	094°38' W
Kansas City, Mo.	39°06' N,	094°35' W
Kapaa, Hawaii	22°05' N,	159°19' W
Kearney, Neb.	40°42' N,	099°05' W
Kenai, Alaska	60°33' N,	151°16' W
Ketchikan, Alaska	55°21' N,	131°39' W
Key Largo, Fla.	25°06' N,	080°27' W
Key West, Fla.	24°33' N,	081°49' W
King City, Calif.	36°13' N,	121°08' W
Kingman, Ariz.	35°12' N,	114°04' W
Kingsville, Tex.	27°31' N,	097°52' W
Kirksville, Mo.	40°12' N,	092°35' W
Klamath Falls, Ore.	42°12' N,	121°46' W
Knoxville, Tenn.	35°58' N,	083°55' W
Kodiak, Alaska	57°47' N,	152°24' W
Kokomo, Ind.	40°30' N,	086°08' W
La Crosse, Wis.	43°48' N,	091°15' W
Lafayette, La.	30°14' N,	092°01' W
La Junta, Colo.	37°59' N,	103°33' W
Lake Charles, La.	30°14' N,	093°13' W
Lake Havasu City, Ariz.	34°29' N,	114°19' W
Lakeland, Fla.	28°03' N,	081°57' W
Lansing, Mich.	42°44' N,	084°33' W
Laramie, Wyo.	41°19' N,	105°35' W
Laredo, Tex.	27°30' N,	099°30' W
Las Cruces, N.M.	32°19' N,	106°47' W
Las Vegas, Nev.	36°01' N,	115°09' W
Las Vegas, N.M.	35°36' N,	105°13' W
Laurel, Miss.	31°41' N,	089°08' W
Lawton, Okla.	34°37' N,	098°25' W
Lebanon, N.H.	43°39' N,	072°15' W
Lewiston, Idaho	46°25' N,	117°01' W
Lewiston, Me.	44°06' N,	070°13' W
Lewiston, Mont.	47°03' N,	109°25' W
Lexington, Ky.	38°01' N,	084°30' W
Liberal, Kan.	37°02' N,	100°55' W
Lihue, Hawaii	21°59' N,	159°23' W
Lima, Ohio	40°44' N,	084°06' W
Lincoln, Me.	45°22' N,	068°30' W
Lincoln, Neb.	40°50' N,	096°41' W
Little Rock, Ark.	34°45' N,	092°17' W
Logan, Utah	41°44' N,	111°50' W
Long Beach, Calif.	33°47' N,	118°11' W
Los Alamos, N.M.	35°53' N,	106°19' W
Los Angeles, Calif.	34°04' N,	118°15' W
Louisville, Ky.	38°15' N,	085°46' W
Lowell, Mass.	42°38' N,	071°19' W
Lubbock, Tex.	33°35' N,	101°51' W
Lynchburg, Va.	37°25' N,	079°09' W
Macomb, Ill.	40°27' N,	090°40' W
Macon, Ga.	32°51' N,	083°38' W
Madison, Wis.	43°04' N,	089°24' W
Manchester, N.H.	43°00' N,	071°28' W
Mandan, N.D.	46°50' N,	100°54' W
Mankato, Minn.	44°10' N,	094°00' W
Marietta, Ohio	39°25' N,	081°27' W
Marinette, Wis.	45°06' N,	087°38' W
Marion, Ind.	40°32' N,	085°40' W
Marquette, Mich.	46°33' N,	087°24' W
Massillon, Ohio	40°48' N,	081°32' W
McAllen, Tex.	26°12' N,	098°14' W
McCall, Idaho	44°55' N,	116°06' W
McCook, Neb.	40°12' N,	100°38' W
Medford, Ore.	42°19' N,	122°52' W
Meeker, Colo.	40°02' N,	107°55' W
Melbourne, Fla.	28°05' N,	080°37' W
Memphis, Tenn.	35°08' N,	090°03' W
Meridian, Miss.	32°22' N,	088°42' W
Mesa, Ariz.	33°25' N,	111°49' W
Miami, Fla.	25°47' N,	080°11' W
Midland, Mich.	43°36' N,	084°14' W
Midland, Tex.	32°00' N,	102°05' W
Miles City, Mont.	46°25' N,	105°51' W
Milledgeville, Ga.	33°05' N,	083°14' W
Milwaukee, Wis.	43°02' N,	087°55' W
Minneapolis, Minn.	44°59' N,	093°16' W
Minot, N.D.	48°14' N,	101°18' W
Missoula, Mont.	46°52' N,	114°01' W
Mitchell, S.D.	43°43' N,	098°02' W
Moab, Utah	38°35' N,	109°33' W
Mobile, Ala.	30°41' N,	088°03' W
Moline, Ill.	41°30' N,	090°31' W
Monterey, Calif.	36°37' N,	121°55' W
Montgomery, Ala.	32°23' N,	086°19' W
Montpelier, Vt.	44°16' N,	072°35' W
Montrose, Colo.	38°29' N,	107°53' W
Morehead City, N.C.	34°43' N,	076°43' W
Morgan City, La.	29°42' N,	091°12' W
Morgantown, W.Va.	39°38' N,	079°57' W
Moscow, Idaho	46°44' N,	117°00' W

Mount Vernon, Ill.	38°19' N,	088°55' W
Murfreesboro, Ark.	34°04' N,	093°41' W
Murfreesboro, Tenn.	35°50' N,	086°23' W
Muskogee, Okla.	35°45' N,	095°22' W
Myrtle Beach, S.C.	33°42' N,	078°53' W
Naples, Fla.	26°08' N,	081°48' W
Nashville, Tenn.	36°10' N,	086°47' W
Natchez, Miss.	31°34' N,	091°24' W
Needles, Calif.	34°51' N,	114°37' W
Nevada, Mo.	37°51' N,	094°22' W
New Albany, Ind.	38°18' N,	085°49' W
Newark, N.J.	40°44' N,	074°10' W
New Bedford, Mass.	41°38' N,	070°56' W
New Bern, N.C.	35°07' N,	077°03' W
Newcastle, Wyo.	43°50' N,	104°11' W
New Haven, Conn.	41°18' N,	072°55' W
New Madrid, Mo.	36°36' N,	089°32' W
New Orleans, La.	29°58' N,	090°04' W
Newport, Ore.	44°39' N,	124°03' W
Newport, R.I.	41°29' N,	071°18' W
Newport News, Va.	36°59' N,	076°25' W
New York City, N.Y.	40°43' N,	074°00' W
Niagara Falls, N.Y.	43°06' N,	079°03' W
Nogales, Ariz.	31°20' N,	110°56' W
Nome, Alaska	64°30' N,	165°25' W
Norfolk, Va.	36°51' N,	076°17' W
Norman, Okla.	35°13' N,	097°26' W
North Augusta, S.C.	33°30' N,	081°59' W
North Platte, Neb.	41°08' N,	100°46' W
Oakland, Calif.	37°49' N,	122°16' W
Ocala, Fla.	29°11' N,	082°08' W
Oceanside, Calif.	33°12' N,	117°23' W
Odessa, Tex.	31°52' N,	102°23' W
Ogallala, Neb.	41°08' N,	101°43' W
Ogden, Utah	41°13' N,	111°58' W
Oklahoma City, Okla.	35°30' N,	097°30' W
Olympia, Wash.	47°03' N,	122°53' W
Omaha, Neb.	41°17' N,	096°01' W
O'Neill, Neb.	42°27' N,	098°39' W
Orem, Utah	40°18' N,	111°42' W
Orlando, Fla.	28°33' N,	081°23' W
Oshkosh, Wis.	44°01' N,	088°33' W
Ottawa, Ill.	41°20' N,	088°50' W
Ottumwa, Ia.	41°01' N,	092°25' W
Overton, Nev.	36°33' N,	114°27' W
Owensboro, Ky.	37°46' N,	087°07' W
Paducah, Ky.	37°05' N,	088°37' W
Pahala, Hawaii	19°12' N,	155°29' W
Palm Springs, Calif.	33°50' N,	116°33' W
Palo Alto, Calif.	37°27' N,	122°10' W
Panama City, Fla.	30°10' N,	085°40' W
Paris, Tex.	33°40' N,	095°33' W
Parsons, Kan.	37°20' N,	095°16' W
Pasadena, Calif.	34°09' N,	118°09' W
Pasadena, Tex.	29°43' N,	095°13' W
Pascagoula, Miss.	30°21' N,	088°33' W
Paterson, N.J.	40°55' N,	074°11' W
Pecos, Tex.	31°26' N,	103°30' W
Pendleton, Ore.	45°40' N,	118°47' W
Pensacola, Fla.	30°25' N,	087°13' W
Peoria, Ill.	40°42' N,	089°36' W
Petoskey, Mich.	45°22' N,	084°57' W
Philadelphia, Pa.	39°57' N,	075°10' W
Phoenix, Ariz.	33°27' N,	112°04' W
Pierre, S.D.	44°22' N,	100°21' W
Pine Bluff, Ark.	34°13' N,	092°01' W
Pittsburgh, Pa.	40°26' N,	080°01' W
Plano, Tex.	33°01' N,	096°41' W
Plattsburgh, N.Y.	44°42' N,	073°27' W
Pocatello, Idaho	42°52' N,	112°27' W
Point Hope, Alaska	68°21' N,	166°41' W
Port Gibson, Miss.	31°58' N,	090°59' W
Port Lavaca, Tex.	28°37' N,	096°38' W
Port Royal, S.C.	32°23' N,	080°42' W
Portland, Me.	43°39' N,	070°16' W
Portland, Ore.	45°32' N,	122°37' W
Prescott, Ariz.	34°33' N,	112°28' W
Presque Isle, Me.	46°41' N,	068°01' W
Providence, R.I.	41°49' N,	071°24' W
Provo, Utah	40°14' N,	111°39' W
Pueblo, Colo.	38°15' N,	104°36' W
Pullman, Wash.	46°44' N,	117°10' W
Racine, Wis.	42°44' N,	087°48' W
Raleigh, N.C.	35°46' N,	078°38' W
Rapid City, S.D.	44°05' N,	103°14' W
Red Bluff, Calif.	40°11' N,	122°15' W
Redding, Calif.	40°35' N,	122°24' W
Redfield, S.D.	44°53' N,	098°31' W
Reno, Nev.	39°31' N,	119°48' W
Rice Lake, Wis.	45°30' N,	091°44' W
Richfield, Utah	38°46' N,	112°05' W
Richmond, Ind.	39°50' N,	084°54' W
Richmond, Va.	37°33' N,	077°27' W
Riverside, Calif.	33°59' N,	117°22' W
Riverton, Wyo.	43°02' N,	108°23' W
Roanoke, Va.	37°16' N,	079°56' W
Rochester, Minn.	44°01' N,	092°28' W
Rochester, N.Y.	43°10' N,	077°37' W
Rock Hill, S.C.	34°56' N,	081°01' W
Rock Island, Ill.	41°30' N,	090°34' W
Rock Springs, Wyo.	41°35' N,	109°12' W
Rockford, Ill.	42°16' N,	089°06' W
Rolla, Mo.	37°57' N,	091°46' W
Rome, Ga.	34°15' N,	085°09' W
Roseburg, Ore.	43°13' N,	123°20' W
Roswell, N.M.	33°24' N,	104°32' W
Sacramento, Calif.	38°35' N,	121°29' W
Saginaw, Mich.	43°26' N,	083°56' W
Salem, Ore.	44°56' N,	123°02' W
Salina, Kan.	38°50' N,	097°37' W
Salinas, Calif.	36°40' N,	121°39' W
Salmon, Idaho	45°11' N,	113°54' W

Salt Lake City, Utah	40°45' N, 111°53' W
San Angelo, Tex.	31°28' N, 100°26' W
San Antonio, Tex.	29°25' N, 098°30' W
San Bernardino, Calif.	34°07' N, 117°19' W
San Diego, Calif.	32°43' N, 117°09' W
San Francisco, Calif.	37°47' N, 122°25' W
San Jose, Calif.	37°20' N, 121°53' W
San Luis Obispo, Calif.	35°17' N, 120°40' W
Sanderson, Tex.	30°09' N, 102°24' W
Santa Ana, Calif.	33°46' N, 117°52' W
Santa Barbara, Calif.	34°25' N, 119°42' W
Santa Fe, N.M.	35°41' N, 105°57' W
Santa Maria, Calif.	34°57' N, 120°26' W
Sarasota, Fla.	27°20' N, 082°32' W
Sault Ste. Marie, Mich.	46°30' N, 084°21' W
Savannah, Ga.	32°05' N, 081°06' W
Scott City, Kan.	38°29' N, 100°54' W
Scottsbluff, Neb.	41°52' N, 103°40' W
Scottsdale, Ariz.	33°29' N, 111°56' W
Searcy, Ark.	35°15' N, 091°44' W
Seattle, Wash.	47°36' N, 122°20' W
Sebring, Fla.	27°30' N, 081°27' W
Seguin, Tex.	29°34' N, 097°58' W
Selawik, Alaska	66°36' N, 160°00' W
Seldovia, Alaska	59°26' N, 151°43' W
Selma, Ala.	32°25' N, 087°01' W
Sharpsburg, Md.	39°28' N, 077°45' W
Sheboygan, Wis.	43°45' N, 087°42' W
Sheridan, Wyo.	44°48' N, 106°58' W
Show Low, Ariz.	34°15' N, 110°02' W
Shreveport, La.	32°31' N, 093°45' W
Sierra Vista, Ariz.	31°33' N, 110°18' W
Silver City, N.M.	32°46' N, 108°17' W
Sioux City, Ia.	42°30' N, 096°24' W
Sioux Falls, S.D.	43°33' N, 096°44' W
Skagway, Alaska	59°28' N, 135°19' W
Snyder, Tex.	32°44' N, 100°55' W
Socorro, N.M.	34°04' N, 106°54' W
Somerset, Ky.	37°05' N, 084°36' W
South Bend, Ind.	41°41' N, 086°15' W
Sparks, Nev.	39°32' N, 119°45' W
Spencer, Ia.	43°09' N, 095°10' W
Spokane, Wash.	47°40' N, 117°24' W
Springfield, Ill.	39°48' N, 089°38' W
Springfield, Mo.	37°13' N, 093°17' W
St. Augustine, Fla.	29°54' N, 081°19' W
St. Cloud, Minn.	45°34' N, 094°10' W
St. George, Utah	37°06' N, 113°35' W
St. Joseph, Mo.	39°46' N, 094°50' W
St. Louis, Mo.	38°37' N, 090°11' W
St. Maries, Idaho	47°19' N, 116°35' W
St. Paul, Minn.	44°57' N, 093°06' W
St. Petersburg, Fla.	27°46' N, 082°39' W
State College, Pa.	40°48' N, 077°52' W
Ste. Genevieve, Mo.	37°59' N, 090°03' W
Steamboat Springs, Colo.	40°29' N, 106°50' W
Stillwater, Minn.	45°03' N, 092°49' W
Sumter, S.C.	33°55' N, 080°21' W
Sun Valley, Idaho	43°42' N, 114°21' W
Superior, Wis.	46°44' N, 092°06' W
Syracuse, N.Y.	43°03' N, 076°09' W
Tacoma, Wash.	47°14' N, 122°26' W
Tallahassee, Fla.	30°27' N, 084°17' W
Tampa, Fla.	27°57' N, 082°27' W
Tempe, Ariz.	33°25' N, 111°56' W
Temple, Tex.	31°06' N, 097°21' W
Terre Haute, Ind.	39°28' N, 087°25' W
Texarkana, Ark.	33°26' N, 094°03' W
Thief River Falls, Minn.	48°07' N, 096°10' W
Tifton, Ga.	31°27' N, 083°31' W
Titusville, Fla.	28°37' N, 080°49' W
Toledo, Ohio	41°39' N, 083°33' W
Tonopah, Nev.	38°04' N, 117°14' W
Topeka, Kan.	39°03' N, 095°40' W
Traverse City, Mich.	44°46' N, 085°38' W
Trenton, N.J.	40°14' N, 074°46' W
Trinidad, Colo.	37°10' N, 104°31' W
Troy, Ala.	31°48' N, 085°58' W
Troy, N.Y.	42°44' N, 073°41' W
Tucson, Ariz.	32°13' N, 110°58' W
Tulsa, Okla.	36°10' N, 095°55' W
Tupelo, Miss.	34°16' N, 088°43' W
Tuscaloosa, Ala.	33°12' N, 087°34' W
Twin Falls, Idaho	42°34' N, 114°28' W
Tyler, Tex.	32°21' N, 095°18' W
Ukiah, Calif.	39°09' N, 123°12' W
Utica, N.Y.	43°06' N, 075°14' W
Uvalde, Tex.	29°13' N, 099°47' W
Valdez, Alaska	61°07' N, 146°16' W
Valdosta, Ga.	30°50' N, 083°17' W
Valentine, Neb.	42°52' N, 100°33' W
Vero Beach, Fla.	27°38' N, 080°24' W
Vicksburg, Miss.	32°21' N, 090°53' W
Victoria, Tex.	28°48' N, 097°00' W
Vincennes, Ind.	38°41' N, 087°32' W
Virginia Beach, Va.	36°51' N, 075°59' W
Waco, Tex.	31°33' N, 097°09' W
Wahpeton, N.D.	46°15' N, 096°36' W
Wailuku, Hawaii	20°53' N, 156°30' W
Walla Walla, Wash.	46°04' N, 118°20' W
Warren, Pa.	41°51' N, 079°08' W
Washington, D.C.	38°54' N, 077°02' W
Waterloo, Ia.	42°30' N, 092°21' W
Watertown, N.Y.	43°59' N, 075°55' W
Waycross, Ga.	31°13' N, 082°21' W
Wayne, Neb.	42°14' N, 097°01' W
Weiser, Idaho	44°45' N, 116°58' W
West Palm Beach, Fla.	26°43' N, 080°03' W
Wheeling, W.Va.	40°04' N, 080°43' W
Wichita, Kan.	37°42' N, 097°20' W
Wichita Falls, Tex.	33°54' N, 098°30' W
Williamsport, Pa.	41°15' N, 077°00' W

Wilmington, N.C.	34°14' N,	077°55' W
Winfield, Kan.	37°15' N,	096°59' W
Winnemucca, Nev.	40°58' N,	117°44' W
Winslow, Ariz.	35°02' N,	110°42' W
Winston-Salem, N.C.	36°06' N,	080°14' W
Worcester, Mass.	42°16' N,	071°48' W
Worthington, Minn.	43°37' N,	095°36' W
Wrangell, Alaska	56°28' N,	132°23' W
Yakima, Wash.	46°36' N,	120°31' W
Yankton, S.D.	42°53' N,	097°23' W
Yazoo City, Miss.	32°51' N,	090°25' W
Youngstown, Ohio	41°06' N,	080°39' W
Yuba City, Calif.	39°08' N,	121°37' W
Yuma, Ariz.	32°43' N,	114°37' W
Zanesville, Ohio	39°56' N,	082°01' W

URUGUAY....... page 192

Aiguá	34°12' S,	054°45' W
Artigas	30°24' S,	056°28' W
Belén	30°47' S,	057°47' W
Bella Unión	30°15' S,	057°35' W
Carmelo	34°00' S,	058°17' W
Castillos	34°12' S,	053°50' W
Casupá	34°07' S,	055°39' W
Chuy	33°41' S,	053°27' W
Colonia	34°28' S,	057°51' W
Constitución	31°05' S,	057°50' W
Dolores	33°33' S,	058°13' W
Durazno	33°22' S,	056°31' W
Florida	34°06' S,	056°13' W
Lascano	33°40' S,	054°12'W
Las Piedras	34°44' S,	056°13' W
Maldonado	34°54' S,	054°57' W
Melo	32°22' S,	054°11' W
Mercedes	33°16' S,	058°01' W
Minas	34°23' S,	055°14' W
Montevideo	34°53' S,	056°11' W
Nuevo Berlín	32°59' S,	058°03' W
Pando	34°43' S,	055°57' W
Paysandú	32°19' S,	058°05' W
Rio Branco	32°34' S,	053°25' W
Rivera	30°54' S,	055°31' W
Rocha	34°29' S,	054°20' W
Salto	31°23' S,	057°58' W
San Carlos	34°48' S,	054°55' W
San Gregorio	32°37' S,	055°40' W
San José	34°20' S,	056°42' W
Santa Clara	32°55' S,	054°58' W
Suárez (Tarariras)	34°17' S,	057°37' W
Tacuarembó (San Fructuoso)	31°44' S,	055°59' W
Tranqueras	31°12' S,	055°45' W
Treinta y Tres	33°14' S,	054°23' W
Trinidad	33°32' S,	056°54' W
Vergara	32°56' S,	053°57' W
Young	32°41' S,	057°38' W

UZBEKISTAN.... page 193

Andijon	40°45' N,	072°22' E
Angren	41°01' N,	070°12' E
Bekobod	40°13' N,	069°14' E
Beruniy (Biruni)	41°42' N,	060°44' E
Bukhara (Bokhoro)	39°48' N,	064°25' E
Chirchiq	41°29' N,	069°35' E
Denow	38°16' N,	067°54' E
Fergana (Farghona)	40°23' N,	071°46' E
Guliston	40°29' N,	068°46' E
Jizzakh	40°06' N,	067°50' E
Kattaqürghon	39°55' N,	066°15' E
Khiva (Khiwa)	41°24' N,	060°22' E
Khonqa	41°28' N,	060°47' E
Kogon	39°43' N,	064°33' E
Marghilon	40°27' N,	071°42' E
Namangan	41°00' N,	071°40' E
Nawoiy	40°09' N,	065°22' E
Nukus	42°29' N,	059°38' E
Olmaliq	40°50' N,	069°35' E
Qarshi	38°53' N,	065°48' E
Qŭqon	40°30' N,	070°57' E
Samarkand	39°40' N,	066°58' E
Tashkent (Toshkent)	41°20' N,	069°18' E
Termiz	37°14' N,	067°16' E
Urganch	41°33' N,	060°38' E
Zarafshon	41°31' N,	064°15' E

VANUATU....... page 194

Ipayato	15°38' S,	166°52' E
Isangel	19°33' S,	169°16' E
Lakatoro	16°07' S,	167°25' E
Lalinda	16°21' S,	168°03' E
Laol	16°41' S,	168°16' E
Loltong	15°33' S,	168°09' E
Luganville	15°32' S,	167°10' E
Lumbukuti	16°55' S,	168°32' E
Natapao	17°37' S,	168°13' E
Norsup	16°04' S,	167°23' E
Port Olry	15°03' S,	167°04' E
Port-Vila (Vila)	17°44' S,	168°18' E
Unpongkor	18°49' S,	169°01' E
Veutumboso	13°54' S,	167°27' E

VENEZUELA..... page 195

Barcelona	10°08' N,	064°42' W
Barinas	08°38' N,	070°12' W
Barquisimeto	10°04' N,	069°19' W
Cabimas	10°23' N,	071°28' W

Caicara (Caicara de Orinoco)	07°37' N,	066°10' W
Caicara	09°49' N,	063°36' W
Caracas	10°30' N,	066°55' W
Ciudad Bolívar	08°08' N,	063°33' W
Ciudad Guayana (San Felix)	08°23' N,	062°40' W
Coro	11°25' N,	069°41' W
Cumaná	10°28' N,	064°10' W
Guasdualito	07°15' N,	070°44' W
La Asunción	11°02' N,	063°53' W
Maracaibo	10°40' N,	071°37' W
Maracay	10°15' N,	067°36' W
Maturín	09°45' N,	063°11' W
Mérida	08°36' N,	071°08' W
Pariaguán	08°51' N,	064°43' W
Petare	10°29' N,	066°49' W
Puerto Ayacucho	05°40' N,	067°35' W
Punto Fijo	11°42' N,	070°13' W
San Carlos de Río Negro	01°55' N,	067°04' W
San Cristóbal	07°46' N,	072°14' W
San Fernando de Apure	07°54' N,	067°28' W
San Fernando de Atabapo	04°03' N,	067°42' W
Santa Elena	04°37' N,	061°08' W
Tucupita	09°04' N,	062°03' W
Upata	08°01' N,	062°24' W
Valencia	10°11' N,	068°00' W
Valera	09°19' N,	070°37' W

VIETNAM .... page 196

Bac Can	22°08' N,	105°50' E
Bac Giang	21°16' N,	106°12' E
Bac Lieu	09°17' N,	105°43' E
Bien Hoa	10°57' N,	106°49' E
Buon Me Thuot (Lac Giao)	12°40' N,	108°03' E
Ca Mau	09°11' N,	105°08' E
Cam Pha	21°01' N,	107°19' E
Cam Ranh	11°54' N,	109°13' E
Can Tho	10°02' N,	105°47' E
Chau Doc	10°42' N,	105°07' E
Da Lat	11°56' N,	108°25' E
Da Nang (Tourane)	16°04' N,	108°13' E
Dong Ha	16°49' N,	107°08' E
Dong Hoi	17°29' N,	106°36' E
Go Cong	10°22' N,	106°40' E
Ha Giang	22°50' N,	104°59' E
Hai Duong	20°56' N,	106°19' E
Haiphong (Hai Phong)	20°52' N,	106°41' E
Hanoi (Ha Noi)	21°02' N,	105°51' E
Ha Tinh	18°20' N,	105°54' E
Hoa Binh	20°50' N,	105°20' E
Ho Chi Minh City (Saigon)	10°45' N,	106°40' E
Hoi An	15°52' N,	108°19' E
Hong Gai (Hon Gai)	20°57' N,	107°05' E
Hue	16°28' N,	107°36' E
Kon Tum (Cong Tum or Kontun)	14°21' N,	108°00' E
Lai Chau	22°04' N,	103°10' E
Lao Caí	22°30' N,	103°58' E
Long Xuyen	10°23' N,	105°25' E
Minh Hoa	17°47' N,	106°01' E
My Tho	10°21' N,	106°21' E
Nam Dinh	20°25' N,	106°10' E
Nha Trang	12°15' N,	109°11' E
Phan Rang	11°34' N,	108°59' E
Phan Thiet	10°56' N,	108°06' E
Pleiku (Play Cu)	13°59' N,	108°00' E
Quan Long	09°11' N,	105°08' E
Quang Ngai	15°07' N,	108°48' E
Qui Nhon	13°46' N,	109°14' E
Rach Gia	10°01' N,	105°05' E
Sa Dec	10°18' N,	105°46' E
Soc Trang	09°36' N,	105°58' E
Son La	21°19' N,	103°54' E
Tam Ky	15°34' N,	108°29' E
Tan An	10°32' N,	106°25' E
Thai Binh	20°27' N,	106°20' E
Thai Nguyen	21°36' N,	105°50' E
Thanh Hoa	19°48' N,	105°46' E
Tuy Hoa	13°05' N,	109°18' E
Viet Tri	21°18' N,	105°26' E
Vinh	18°40' N,	105°40' E
Vung Tau	10°21' N,	107°04' E
Yen Bai	21°42' N,	104°52' E

YEMEN .... page 197

Aden ('Adan)	12°46' N,	045°02' E
Aḥwar	13°31' N,	046°42' E
Al-Bayḍā'	13°58' N,	045°35' E
Al-Ghayḍah	16°13' N,	052°11' E
Al-Ḥudaydah	14°48' N,	042°57' E
Al-Luḥayyah	15°43' N,	042°42' E
Al-Mukallā	14°32' N,	049°08' E
Balḥāf	13°58' N,	048°11' E
Dhamār	14°33' N,	044°24' E
Ibb	13°58' N,	044°11' E
Laḥij	13°04' N,	044°53' E
Madīnat al-Sha'b	12°50' N,	044°56' E
Ma'rib	15°25' N,	045°21' E
Min'ar	16°43' N,	051°18' E
Mocha (al-Mukha)	13°19' N,	043°15' E
Niṣāb	14°31' N,	046°30' E
Raydah	15°50' N,	044°03' E

Sa'dah	16°57' N,	043°46' E
Ṣalīf	15°18' N,	042°41' E
Sanaa	15°21' N,	044°12' E
Sayḥūt	15°12' N,	051°14' E
Saywūn (Say'un)	15°56' N,	048°47' E
Shabwah	15°22' N,	047°01' E
Shahārah	16°11' N,	043°42' E
Ta'izz	13°34' N,	044°02' E
Tarīm	16°03' N,	049°00' E
Zabīd	14°12' N,	043°19' E
Zinjibār	13°08' N,	045°23' E

ZAMBIA . . . . page 198

Chililabombwe (Bancroft)	12°22' S,	027°50' E
Chingola	12°32' S,	027°52' E
Chipata (Fort Jameson)	13°39' S,	032°40' E
Isoka	10°08' S,	032°38' E
Kabwe (Broken Hill)	14°27' S,	028°27' E
Kalabo	14°58' S,	022°41' E
Kalulushi	12°50' S,	028°05' E
Kasama	10°13' S,	031°12' E
Kawambwa	09°47' S,	029°05' E
Kitwe	12°49' S,	028°13' E
Livingstone (Maramba)	17°51' S,	025°52' E
Luanshya	13°08' S,	028°25' E
Lusaka	15°25' S,	028°17' E
Mansa (Fort Rosebery)	11°12' S,	028°53' E
Mazabuka	15°51' S,	027°46' E
Mongu	15°17' S,	023°08' E
Monze	16°16' S,	027°29' E
Mpika	11°50' S,	031°27' E
Mumbwa	14°59' S,	027°04' E
Mwamfuli (Samfya)	11°21' S,	029°33' E
Nchelenge	09°21' S,	029°44' E
Ndola	12°58' S,	028°38' E
Senanga	16°07' S,	023°16' E
Serenje	13°14' S,	030°14' E
Zambezi	13°33' S,	023°07' E

ZIMBABWE . . . . . . page 199

Beitbridge	22°13' S,	030°00' E
Bulawayo	20°09' S,	028°35' E
Chimanimani (Mandidzudzure, or Melsetter)	19°48' S,	032°52' E
Chinhoyi (Sinoia)	17°22' S,	030°12' E
Chipinge	20°12' S,	032°37' E
Chiredzi	21°03' S,	031°40' E
Chitungwiza	18°47' S,	032°37' E
Empress Mine Township	18°27' S,	029°27' E
Gweru (Gwelo)	19°27' S,	029°49' E
Harare (Salisbury)	17°50' S,	031°03' E
Hwange (Wankie)	18°22' S,	026°29' E
Inyanga	18°13' S,	032°45' E
Kadoma (Gatooma)	18°21' S,	029°55' E
Kariba	16°31' S,	028°48' E
Karoi	16°49' S,	029°41' E
Kwekwe (Que Que)	18°55' S,	029°49' E
Marondera (Marandellas)	18°11' S,	031°33' E
Mashava	20°03' S,	030°29' E
Masvingo (Fort Victoria, or Nyanda)	20°05' S,	030°50' E
Mhangura	16°54' S,	030°09' E
Mount Darwin	16°47' S,	031°35' E
Mvuma	19°17' S,	030°32' E
Mutare (Umtali)	18°58' S,	032°40' E
Norton	17°53' S,	030°42' E
Redcliff	19°02' S,	029°47' E
Shamva	17°19' S,	031°34' E
Shurugwi (Selukwe)	19°40' S,	030°00' E
Triangle	21°02' S,	031°27' E
Tuli	21°55' S,	029°12' E
Victoria Falls	17°56' S,	025°50' E

World's Largest Lakes

Name and location	Area (square miles)
WORLD	
Caspian Sea, *Turkmenistan–Kazakstan–Russia–Azerbaijan-Iran*	149,200
Superior, *Canada–United States*	31,700
Victoria, *Kenya–Tanzania–Uganda*	26,828
Huron, *Canada–United States*	23,000
Michigan, *United States*	22,300
Aral Sea, *Kazakstan–Uzbekistan*	13,000
Tanganyika, *Burundi–Tanzania–Dem. Rep. Congo–Zambia*	12,700
Baikal, *Russia*	12,200
AFRICA	
Victoria, *Kenya-Tanzania–Uganda*	26,828
Tanganyika, *Burundi–Tanzania-Dem. Rep. Congo–Zambia*	12,700
Nyasa (Malawi), *Malawi–Mozambique–Tanzania*	11,430
Chad, *Cameroon–Chad–Niger–Nigeria*	6,875
Bangweulu, *Zambia*	3,800
AMERICA, NORTH	
Superior, *Canada–United States*	31,700
Huron, *Canada–United States*	23,000
Michigan, *United States*	22,300
Great Bear, *Northwest Territories, Canada*	12,028
Great Slave, *Northwest Territories, Canada*	11,031
AMERICA, SOUTH	
Maracaibo, *Venezuela*	5,150
Titicaca, *Peru–Bolivia*	3,200
Poopó, *Bolivia*	1,000
Buenos Aires (General Carrera), *Chile–Argentina*	865
Chiquita, *Argentina*	714
ASIA	
Caspian Sea, *Turkmenistan–Kazakstan–Russia–Azerbaijan-Iran*	149,200
Aral Sea, *Kazakstan–Uzbekistan*	13,000
Baikal, *Russia*	12,200
Balkhash, *Kazakstan*	6,650
Tonle Sap, *Cambodia*	2,525
EUROPE	
Ladoga, *Russia*	6,826
Onega, *Russia*	3,753
Vänern, *Sweden*	2,156
Saimaa, *Finland*	1,690
Peipus, *Estonia–Russia*	1,373
OCEANIA	
Eyre, *South Australia*	3,600
Torrens, *South Australia*	2,230
Gairdner, *South Australia*	1,845
Frome, *South Australia*	900

World's Longest Rivers

Name	Outflow	Length (miles)
WORLD		
Nile	Mediterranean Sea	4,132
Amazon–Ucayali–Apurimac	South Alantic Ocean	4,000
Chang (Yangtze)	East China Sea	3,915
Mississippi–Missouri–Red Rock	Gulf of Mexico	3,710
Yenisey–Baikal–Selenga	Kara Sea	3,442
Huang (Yellow)	Bo Hai (Gulf of Chihli)	3,395
Ob–Irtysh	Gulf of Ob	3,362
Paraná	Río de la Plata	3,032
AFRICA		
Nile	Mediterranean Sea	4,132
Congo	South Alantic Ocean	2,900
Niger	Bight of Biafra	2,600
Zambezi	Mozambique Channel	2,200
Kasai	Congo River	1,338
AMERICA, NORTH		
Mississippi–Missouri–Red Rock	Gulf of Mexico	3,710
Mackenzie–Slave–Peace	Beaufort Sea	2,635
Missouri–Red Rock	Mississippi River	2,540
St. Lawrence–Great Lakes	Gulf of St. Lawrence	2,500
Mississippi	Gulf of Mexico	2,340
AMERICA, SOUTH		
Amazon–Ucayali–Apurimac	South Alantic Ocean	4,000
Paraná	Río de la Plata	3,032
Madeira–Mamoré–Guaporé	Amazon River	2.082
Jurua	Amazon River	2,040
Purus	Amazon River	1,995
ASIA		
Chang (Yangtze)	East China Sea	3,915
Yenisey–Baikal–Selenga	Kara Sea	3,442
Huang (Yellow)	Bo Hai (Gulf of Chihli)	3,395
Ob–Irtysh	Gulf of Ob	3,362
Amur–Argun	Sea of Okhotsk	2,761
EUROPE		
Volga	Caspian Sea	2,193
Danube	Black Sea	1,770
Ural	Caspian Sea	1,509
Dnieper	Black Sea	1,367
Don	Sea of Azov	1,162
OCEANIA		
Darling	Murray River	1,702
Murray	Great Australian Bight	1,609
Murrumbidgee	Murray River	981
Lachlan	Murrumbidgee River	992

World's Tallest Mountains

Name and location	Height (feet)
AFRICA	
Kilimanjaro (Kibo Peak), *Tanzania*	19,340
Mt. Kenya (Batian Peak), *Kenya*	17,058
Margherita, Ruwenzori Range, *Dem. Rep. Congo–Uganda*	16,795
Ras Dashen, Simyen Mts., *Ethiopia*	15,157
AMERICA, NORTH	
McKinley, Alaska Range, *Alaska, U.S.*	20,320
Logan, St. Elias Mts., *Yukon, Canada*	19,551
Citlaltépetl (Orizaba), Cordillera Neo-Volcánica, *Mexico*	18,406
St. Elias, St Elias Mts., *Alaska, U.S.–Canada*	18,009
AMERICA, SOUTH	
Aconcagua, Andes, *Argentina–Chile*	22,831
Ojos del Salado, Andes, *Argentina–Chile*	22,615
Bonete, Andes, *Argentina*	22,546
Tupungato, Andes, *Argentina–Chile*	22,310
Pissis, Andes, *Argentina*	22,241
ANTARCTICA	
Vinson Massif, Sentinel Range, Ellsworth Mts.	16,066
Tyree, Sentinel Range, Ellsworth Mts.	15,919
Shinn, Sentinel Range, Ellsworth Mts.	15,751
Kirkpatrick, Queen Alexandra Range	14,856
ASIA	
Everest (Chomolungma), Himalayas, *Nepal–Tibet, China*	29,035
K2 (Godwin Austen), Karakoram Range, *Pakistan–Xinjiang, China*	28,251
Kānchenjunga I, Himalayas, *Nepal–India*	28,169
Lhotse I, Himalayas, *Nepal–Tibet, China*	27,940
EUROPE	
Mont Blanc, Alps, *France–Italy*	15,771
Dufourspitze (Monte Rosa), Alps, *Switzerland–Italy*	15,203
Dom (Mischabel), Alps, *Switzerland*	14,911
Weisshorn, Alps, *Switzerland*	14,780
OCEANIA	
Jaya (Sukarno, Carstensz), Sudirman Range, *Indonesia*	16,500
Pilimsit (Idenburg), Sudirman Range, *Indonesia*	15,750
Trikora (Wilhelmina), Jayawijaya Mts., *Indonesia*	15,580
Mandala (Juliana), Jayawijaya Mts., *Indonesia*	15,420
CAUCASUS	
Elbrus, Caucasus, *Russia*	18,510
Dyhk-Tau, Caucasus, *Russia*	17,073
Koshtan-Tau, Caucasus, *Russia*	16,900
Shkhara, Caucasus, *Russia–Georgia*	16,627